Rebuilding Community in America

Housing for Ecological Living,
Personal Empowerment,
and the New Extended Family

by Ken Norwood, AICP and Kathleen Smith

Foreword by Ernest Callenbach
Editing Assistance from Jean Hohl and Hank Obermayer

Shared Living Resource Center
Berkeley, California

ISBN #: 0-9641346-2-4
Library of Congress Catalog Card Number: 94-92061
Norwood, Ken and Smith, Kathleen
Rebuilding Community in America
Includes Bibliography, Glossary, Index
1 2 3 4 5 6 7 8 9 10

Categories by publisher:
1. Community life— Human settlements — United States, Africa, Europe.. 2. Environmental, degradation, protection — United States.   3. Architecture — Environmental aspects — United States, Africa, Europe. 4. Housing — Cooperative — Shared Housing — United States.

The Shared Living Resource Center is a nonprofit (501-c-3) organization dedicated to the promotion and development of affordable and ecologically sustainable communities.

Printed in the United States of America by the University of California Printing Services.
Printed on recycled paper with soybean inks.
  Text: International Paper's Springhill Incentive 100 Offset (100% recycled including 50% post-consumer waste and acid free).
  Cover: Sav-a-Tree Recycled 10 pt. C1S (50% recycled including 50% post-consumer waste).

Cover design by pollock/silk   Back cover photo by Bryan F. Peterson   Book design by Kathleen Smith and Ken Norwood
Front cover photo by Steve Evan   Cover illustration by Shared Living Resource Center

Order form on page 384

Grateful acknowledgment is given for permission to reprint the following material:

"EARTH'S TEN COMMANDMENTS," by Ernest Callenbach. Copyright © 1990 by Ernest Callenbach. A four-color poster by David Lance Goines incorporating the poem "Earth's Ten Commandments" that appears on pp. xxiv-xxv is available from Celestial Arts Publishing, PO Box 7327, Berkeley, CA 94710, (510) 524-1801.

Excerpts from *Earth in the Balance* by Al Gore. Copyright © 1992 by Senator Al Gore. Reprinted by permission of Houghton Mifflin Company. All rights reserved.

Excerpts from *Entropy* by Jeremy Rifkin with Ted Howard. Copyright © 1980 by Foundation on Economic Trends. Used by permission of Viking Penguin, a division of Penguin Books USA Inc.

Excerpts from *Environmental Design Primer* by Tom Bender. Copyright © 1973 by Tom Bender. Used by permission of Random House, Inc.

Illustration by Ernest H. Shepard appears on p. 271, reprinted with permission of Charles Scribner's Sons, an imprint of Macmillan Publishing Company from *The Wind in the Willows* by Kenneth Grahame, illustrated by Ernest H. Shepard. Copyright 1933 Charles Scribner's Sons; copyright renewed © 1961 Ernest H. Shepard.

Excerpts reprinted by permission of The Putnam Publishing Group/Jeremy P. Tarcher, Inc. from *Creating Community Anywhere* by Carolyn R. Shaffer and Kristin Anundsen. Copyright © 1993 by Carolyn R. Shaffer and Kristin Anundsen.

*To the
visionaries, creators, and builders
who are courageously taking steps,
whether small or large,
to rebuild healthy, harmonious, and
ecologically sound communities
in America and the world,
and to the hope that
you and others with you will be inspired
to create ecologically sustainable community.*

TABLE OF CONTENTS

ACKNOWLEDGEMENTS

I wish to express my deep appreciation for the array of synchronous events and the wondrous crossings of life paths that have led me as a planner/architect to explore community alternatives and found the Shared Living Resource Center. To all of you who have made it possible to produce this book and who have given encouragement and financial assistance — the Board of Directors, volunteers, apprentices, intern, staff, my family, and all the friends of SLRC — thank you.

Ken E. Norwood

With deep respect and love, I wish to thank my Mum and Dad, my family, my rich community of friends and teachers, and especially Chris, my husband, my dearest friend and lover, my soulmate and teacher. You have all taught me something about harmony and community, about life and love, about faith in the future and myself. A part of each of you is in this book — your insights, dreams, and hopes fill these pages as they fill my life.

K Smith

Book Project Staff

It has been a long road with many ups and downs, twists and turns, and a few big potholes, but here we are with a book we can actually hold. We sincerely thank you for your skills, insights, talents and perseverance in getting the job done and for sharing your hope and your dedication to socially and environmentally meaningful ways of living and housing ourselves. You have helped bring a vision to reality and for this we and all who benefit from this book, thank you.

Carolyn Adams	Jean Hohl	Rachele Rosi
Craig Burke	Shirley Lancaster	Adriana Sarramea
Brett Clavio	Hank Obermayer	Andrew Schmidt
Jennifer Cooper	Felipe Romero	Doris Smith
David Hawkins	Timothy Rood	Marjorie Smith

Volunteers/Interns/Apprentices

To all of you who swept in here with such energy and enthusiasm and gave of your resources and time, we thank you. In recognition of your quest for a livelihood and lifestyle that goes beyond the status quo and incorporates precepts of ecology, sustainability, and community, we offer best wishes for futures full of richness, harmony, and healthy community.

Carl Andrews	Jennifer Dieges	Jill Kruse
Dan Bandini	Loren Davidson	Fernando Marti
Cathy Barbour	Kaye Griffin	Chris Meland
Rhea Bouman	Daniel Hale	Maria Moscato
Roumel M. Butiong	Heidi Hirvonen	Russell Pechman
Edison Cardenas	Polly Horn	Kathryn Pilgrim
Michael Caruso	Tom Howlett	Ellie Schafer
Teresa Clarke	Laura Jerrard	Vincent Segal
Robert Collins	Megan Keelaghan	Tanya Sparnicht

SLRC Board of Directors

We wish to express profound gratitude to both past and present board members for sound advice, steadfast enthusiasm, and commitment to the mission and goals of SLRC and the book project.

David Gibson	Bonnie R. Mardis	John Steere
William F. Klein	Nick Peterson	William Welch
Kenneth Mahaffey	Lucy Radcliff	James D. Wilson, Jr.

Editing Advisory Committee

We received new insights, critiques, alternative wording, and much praise, thanks to the editing committee. For reading, reading, and being there for more, we are profoundly grateful.

Connie Dean	Christopher Gutsche	Bonnie R. Mardis
David Gibson	Willaim F. Klein	James D. Wilson, Jr.
Kaye Griffin		

Donors and Financial Supporters

To all those who have provided generous financial support throughout this project, we offer our sincere and heartfelt thanks. This book would not have been possible without your understanding, trust, and commitment to the Shared Living Community precepts that we are all working toward.

Ann Baier	Irwin Feinberg	Reiko & Takeo Koshikawa	Dorothy J. Norwood	Phyl Smith
Paula Ann Balch	Ruth Garbus	Marvin T. Levin	Sue Pierson	Dwight Steele
Duane Bay	David Gibson &	Dianne Liebert	Gertrude Lischner	John Steere
Ed Begley, Jr.	Betty Hood Gibson	Linda Maio	Christopher Ratcliff	Peggy L. Stull &
Kara Black	Grace Goldberg	Bonnie R. Mardis	Rosso/Fornoff	Michael Hoffman
Denise Blondo	Marigay Grana	Scott & Margaret Martin	Jane Sanford	Elizabeth Telfer
Judy Bradford	Jessie Gretzinger	Denis Martynowych &	Jack Sawyer	Kay & Floyd Tift
David Bruns	Daniel Grobani	Diane Hertick	Heidi Ann Schleicher	Mary Tsalis
Nate Brown	Alice & David Gutsche	Gail McConnell	Marie Schloss	Alice C. Turner
Craig Burke &	Christopher Gutsche	April McMahon	Larry Schlusser, Sun	Kenneth &
Molly Lazarus	Ron Hall	Mary Louise Metz	Frost	Nora Van Doren
Jean & Don Clark	Tom Howlett	B.J. Miller	Robert A. Schmugge	James Vann
Paul Corcoran	Human Investment Project	Claudia Miller	Ken Schwartz	Jack Lionel Warner
Dr. Lee DuMont	Judy Hunt	Frederick A. &	Rosemary Shearburn	William A. Whipple
Norman Emerson	Jacques Kaswan	Kathleen A.C. Morse	Miriam Simos	Delbert & Marj Wiens
Enterprises Inc.	William F. Klein	Nestor M. Noe, AFM	Phil & Eleanor Smith	

Advisors and Other Resources

We would like to acknowledge and thank some of the many wonderful people who have provided encouragement, guidance, and service along the way.

Tom Atlee
Baha'uddin Alpine &
Paul LeVine Mellion, "Common Ground"
Chaz Bufe
Claudia Cleaver
Lottie Cohen
Peter B. DuMont, Universal Star Alliance

Lois Arkin, Cooperative Resources and Services Project
Janet Geis & Bart Brodsky, "Open Exchange"
Janet Guastavino
Jaques Kaswan
Denis & Diane Martynowych
Carl Moodispaugh & Sandi Brockway, "Macrocosm USA"
Ruby and K.K. Chan, The Repro Express

Foundation Grants

The SLRC book project was assisted several times during the three years of production by grants from the Tides Foundation and the Foundation for Deep Ecology. Their support of the sustainable community movement is a major contribution to the well-being of us all.

Communities

We especially thank those of you who have been living your belief in community, for the stories you have shared with us and your time and patience for answering our questions, and the cooperation of those who showed us around. You provide inspiration and hope to us all. (To contact these and other communities presented in the book, see the resource guide at the back.)

Alpha Farm, Oregon
Ananda Village, Nevada City and Palo Alto, Calfornia
BJM House, Lafayette, Calfornia
Black Cat House, San Francisco, Calfornia
Eco-Village, Ithaca, New York
Emeryville CoHousing Community, Emeryville, Calfornia
Ganas Community, Staten Island, New York

Muir Commons Cohousing Commuity, Davis, Calfornia
N Street Cohousing Community, Davis, Calfornia
Nyland Community, Lafayette, Colorado
On-Going Concerns, Portland, Oregon
Raphael House, San Francisco, Calfornia
Sacramento CoHousing, Sacramento, Calfornia
Winslow Community, Bainbridge Island, Washington

Foreword

By Ernest Callenbach

A large and growing number of Americans have the distinct feeling that we are not living right — that we have somehow lost our way. Some blame greed, some blame corrupt politicians, some blame the globalization of the economy, some blame the decline of the family. There is, I think, some justice in all these charges, but they are too abstract and general to do much about personally. In practical terms, we live in the present; we live in the real physical and social landscape of our cities and towns; and we live in the actual structures of our built environment. These factors condition the possibilities open to us and we must start thinking about them in new ways.

If we are seeking concrete, specific causes of our malaise, the analysis offered in this book will point us in a productive direction. It demonstrates that the things that are wrong with the way we personally live, day by day and moment by moment, can be understood and fixed. We can have community instead of competitive loneliness. We can have structures that actually fit the way we want to live. And thus we can achieve a fit habitat for our species.

When we look at the physical desolation of American suburban sprawl and the emotional desolation of the isolated American individual or couple trying to survive while sustaining relationships dissolve around them, it's easy, even for Americans, to grow pessimistic. Cultures die, we may say glumly, when they get stuck in overwhelming contradictions. They become addicted to institutions (like multinational corporations) and technologies (like the private automobile) that cannot be sustained over the long run. The end is near. Read the handwriting on the wall, and weep.

But some cultures have managed to transform themselves and be reborn. When we look at the relatively vibrant and civilized countries of western Europe, it's easy to forget that they have gone through not only the devastation of World War II but much more ancient trials — revolutions, inquisitions, the Dark Ages — and somehow learned to thrive again. Surveying the whole historical record, including its many passages of folly and despair, we must recognize that human communities manifestly possess the power to recover from misfortune and their own worst mistakes, and to begin anew.

This is a book about renewal on the most fundamental level, "how we live now." It proposes that we do not have to accept social pathology merely because it is profitable to real estate developers, or injected into us by television and magazine ads, or foisted on us by the automobile-oil-highway lobby. We can devise better ways of living — ways more suited to our species, learning from our actual history, and perhaps prehistory — and then find ways to put them into practice.

In another epoch, Marx exhorted the workers to revolt because all they had to lose were their chains — and they had a new world to win. We like to think that we live in relatively privileged times, and revolt is (temporarily, I suspect) out of fashion. But, despite our apparent wealth, stop and consider how little *we* have to lose by making changes. Vast suburban masses could escape killing mortgages on houses whose location forces them to spend long hours in a car, and then more long hours working to pay for that car. Fathers who now spend, on average, ten waking minutes a day with their children, and mothers who have in effect two jobs, at work and at home, could experience the relief of having many adults around to share childcare and household maintenance. Changing the residential arrangements (and transit system sparsity) that lead middle-class parents to spend many hours each week serving as chauffeurs for their children could enable us to live much more compact, sociable, and satisfying lives. Reversing land-use decisions that give citizens only the private premises of the shopping mall to meet each other could lead to a rebirth of vibrant community life on our streets.

Like fish who always swim in water and therefore remain unaware of it, we live in a toxic fog of frustrating living situations. They do not nurture us, they do not encourage our natural cooperative sides, they are not even fun on a day-by-day basis, and they keep us from the awareness that it isn't necessary to live this way. All they do is keep up our standing as credit-card-carrying consumer-zombies. But life is more than working and buying, and we need a built environment that will encourage more than commercial interactions among us.

It is not news that many Americans have gotten fed up with the craziness of American living. But, instead of rethinking their situation where they are, those who can afford to have moved out — first to the suburbs, but now that the suburbs are urbanizing too, to small towns even farther out. The arrival of a lot of refugees, of course, soon ruins the small

towns, and tends to bankrupt the suburban cities; it is not a long-term solution. What is needed is to re-create the virtues we crave in small towns — their personal intimacy, their sense of mutual support (and forbearance), their slower personal pace, their feeling of a shared community destiny — but do it everywhere, in cities and urban suburbs where most of us in fact live.

The message of this practical yet visionary book is that we can do this — that we can, in fact, rebuild America as a decent habitat for its citizens. The process involved is not only architecture, not only planning, not only social organizing, not only individual soul-searching, but a holistic combination of all these. If we look at history carefully, we find that lasting, grand, revolutionary changes come in very small increments. Throughout this book, you will find useful suggestions about small — and not so small — things you and your friends and neighbors can do which will make a difference. You will also read about many people who have taken their lives in their own hands, and changed them for the better. We all begin where we are. What is important is to get going, and this thoughtful book offers you the tools you need.

Introduction

By Ken Norwood

While driving along Sherman Way in the San Fernando Valley recently, I had the feeling of déjà vu: "Didn't I just pass that McDonald's?" Then I realized that it was a different McDonald's, but it looked just like the last one. The car lots, signs, store fronts, apartments, and tract houses all looked the same as well. I felt suddenly disoriented.. I didn't know where I was. If it weren't for the sign announcing "Welcome to Reseda," I would have continued to feel like I was in a surrealist movie.

I remember, as a boy, visiting aunts, uncles, and cousins in towns throughout the San Fernando Valley during our yearly trips from Fresno to Los Angeles. Bumping along in my grandfather's big Willis Knight, watching hillsides turn to orchards, and seeing the landmarks that told me we were arriving at the City of San Fernando, I bacame aware that what was called "our town" was quite distinguishable from the "our town" of other members of our family. There were discernible differences in the relationship of each town to the hills, open space, and the farmlands that lay between them. And, there was always the entry sign, the one-story houses, and the compact business districts, each with a distinctive bank, theater, office, or market building that said this is Van Nuys, or North Hollywood, or Burbank. There was a sense of place, recognition, and belonging — a distinct feeling that each town had definable edges.

As I grew older, the Valley towns gradually merged into one sprawling urban conglomerate of identical single-family houses interrupted by identical McDonalds and superstores. Gone was the feeling of excitement when arriving and leaving that I had as a child. No downtown, no identity, no sense of community or place remained. Over time, I have come to realize how this environmental degradation has aggravated, if not spawned, the social alienation of our time. Being connected with people we know and love provides assurance, the basis for social interaction within an identifiable and mutually shared physical environment.

The unfolding of my architectural orientation towards the social and environmental concerns that I present in this book came about slowly through a combination of relatively ordinary and "peak" experiences. It took time, but I began to understand the conditioned imagery impressed upon me by my family and peers and the social, cultural, educational, and economic systems in which I grew up. These revelations enabled me to explore innovative concepts for housing and community design that would serve the needs of both people and the environment.

Born in 1924, I have had the fortune of experiencing first hand "the Great Depression" of the 1930's, World War II (WW II), and the post-war era. I say "fortune," because these events represent significant watersheds of change that underlie the socioeconomic and ecological calamities we face today. Growing up during the Depression, I enjoyed what today we call an "old fashioned" extended family of grandparents, parents, aunts, uncles, cousins, and hired hands. We all shared chores directed by my grandmother, who led the family out of the depths of financial ruin with her one and one-half acre, self-sufficient farm and chicken business. Thus began my appreciation of the difference between the hierarchical, male-dominated social order of that time and the nurturing atmosphere that emanated when women were in charge.

Experience with group gatherings continued at the Boy Scout and YMCA summer camps I attended. I enjoyed the group interaction when it was my cabin's turn to serve meals, clean up, and do other camp chores. I can see that through these experiences of extended family, group cooperation, and shared responsibilities, I had begun to learn the foundation for a sustainable community culture.

While with the U.S. Air Force during WW II, training with my B-24 bomber crew and flying combat missions out of England, I gained deeper insight into the social dynamics of belonging, male bonding, and close team work. These experiences were intensified during the year I spent as a Nazi POW, "kriegsgefangenen," sharing a room and meager rations with other American and British fliers. Each compound had 10 barracks of 10 rooms, designed for 10 men, but holding 16. The POW camp served as a human laboratory as we organized ourselves into village-like social structures. By creating our own democratic decision-making process, bartering system, rituals, shared responsibilities, and a mutual support system we survived and thrived. The exchange of cigarettes for chocolate and other items created a built-in economic system. That harrowing experience gave me insights into human interaction and behavior under conditions of stress and deprivation. I learned that Americans, with our individualistic bent, can

establish a nurturing community and democratic processes for mutual survival. In retrospect, I sense that the formation of a village or gang in the inner city can be based on similiar feelings of camaraderie, loyalty, common purpose, and a shared threat.

Having lived in both, I recognize the sharp differences between the relatively slow-paced life and feeling of community of the pre-war era and the fast-paced, changing world of the post-war era. To understand the nature of our present condition is to envision the neccessity of social and environmental harmony in community for ourselves and the planet. In this, I have become very much a part of the transformative era that began with other visionary thinkers during the 1950's and is now maturing into the 21st century.

I entered the University of Southern California (USC) School of Architecture in 1947 already married, like most of my war veteran classmates. We survived with the "GI Bill" and the help of our working wives. Together we all enjoyed the extraordinary security of extended family-like bonding and a strong sense of purpose reinforced by the seriousness of a generation of men and women who grew up on both sides of WW II. All of these early experiences, whether with family, buddies or classmates, stand as points of reference relative to the social and familial disintegration that has occurred since the 1950s. These earlier extended family and group-learning experiences are rarely enjoyed by younger generations today. The mass entertainment media have become a behavioral model and a substitute family for the many who have become alienated due to the impersonalization caused by dependency upon the automobile and the isolation of the single-family house. My observations of the social alienation and family deterioration trend that has been happening tol peoples among all income, class, age, and ethnic groups has added to my fervor to find a way for Americans to rebuild community.

In 1952 I graduated as an architect-planner from USC , and Dorothy and I began to raise a wonderful family of "Baby Boomers." I was imbued with an unquenchable desire to change the world. The glorious post-war future for America vividly imagined on long winter nights with my POW buddies, and later with my fellow design students, met its first test in development-oriented planning and architecture. I juggled commuting daily from the suburbs, supporting a young family, passing the licensing examination, learning the ropes of the profession, and combating the constraints of the established system. I rose to the rank of Project Planner in two of the few socially progressive and idealistic planning and architectural firms of that time. My hopes for finding fulfillment in my work faded as I often became the "agent" for land developers, designing "planned residential developments," shopping malls, and industrial parks on oak-studded rolling hills, tidal estuaries, and farmland.

In the mid-1960s, disturbed by the social and environmental implications of prior work and the others in the profession and hoping for breakthrough opportunities, I opened my own architectural and planning practice and became increasingly involved with the rising fair housing, human relations, Black power, and the environmental and energy conservation movements. In between regular planning and architectural works I did volunteer and sliding scale fee work for low-income people in the Watts community and in several barrios of Los Angeles. I closed my office in 1970 due to a building recession.

In the next year, I was named as the Director of the Venice Community Design Center in Venice, California. This was a "storefront," "on the street" advocacy planning program funded through UCLA by a federal Health, Education, and Welfare (HEW) grant. The Center's purpose was to assist the beach front, multicultural, mixed-income population to prepare their own community plan. In 1973, however, President Nixon abolished HEW and most antipoverty and community training programs. Many programs just beginning to be successful were branded as "creeping socialism" by conservatives, and destroyed. Nevertheless, in just two years the people inVenice of the early 1970s established a new sense of empowerment. They beat down a freeway and down-zoned a proposed highrise condo/hotel strip along Oceanfront Walk.

This initial social activism work furthered my awareness of the basic flaws in how land is used and urban environments are shaped. After all, I had seen the beloved San Fernando Valley become a continuous, low-density, smog-shrouded, sprawling urban mess, its satellite rural towns once connected to downtown Los Angeles by a high-speed rail system now hopelessly dependent upon the car. In the 1950's the famous Pacific Electric inter-urban rail system was dismantled by a consortium of car interest corporations such as the National City Lines and land speculators. This consortium had bought and dismantled passenger rail systems throughout the entire country, replacing them with busses, which in turn drove people to depend increasingly upon the automobile. Without rail transit I saw the root cause of urban sprawl — cars.

For many years the economic base for Southern California has been land speculation, subdivisions, and house building. I saw clearly that Los Angeles and most recent urban developments were not laid out with people, community, and the "public benefit" in mind. The *only* real goal was to profit from converting farmland to subdivisions and selling houses as a commodity.

Were continued urban sprawl, social alienation, and environmental destruction inevitable? I began to ask myself: 1) What would move the real estate, lending, building, design, and planning processes to create socially and environmentally responsible community development? 2) What economic incentives, lifestyle benefits, and community design concepts would motivate Americans to move from their consumptive, car-dependent, and stressfully competitive lifestyles towards more socially and environmentally harmonious ways of living? I deeply wanted to develop processes that I could propose as an architect and planner to advance these objectives. I also realized that if I were to become a designer and advocate for ecological communities, I would need to live in them myself.

Beginning in 1973, I worked as a carpenter-architect, and lived in and visited various types of communities in the San Francisco Bay Area and California's Sierra Nevada mountains, including the Ananda spiritual community. Over the years, Ananda has remained one of the more successful models of intentional community and has demonstrated the importance of a spiritual focus in sustaining a community. I assisted them in early planning and housing studies and was the architect for their "Expanding Light" retreat center and community building.

Through the summer and fall of 1979, I visited extended family group houses, intentional communities, and new towns in England, Scotland, Norway, Denmark, Holland, and France, sharing in the family-style meals, gardening, and carpentry responsibilities. Except for the differences in our languages it was clear that, within intentionally organized communities, food preparation, meal times, the roles of men, women, and children, and the sharing of responsibilities and resources were virtually identical from one country to the next, affirming my belief in the universality of community. By the early 1980's, I had conceived the basic prototypes of social-environmental designs for community oriented housing that I believe can best serve today's needs.

I have continued to live very well in Shared Living Communities, from group houses to spiritual and intentional communities. I am now living in a limited equity cooperative of 24 units in Berkeley, California. Through all of these experiences, I have observed that personal and group empowerment and environmental harmony flow from mutual decision-making regarding the cooperative sharing of responsibilities and resources.

To further develop and promote this work, I founded the Shared Living Resource Center (SLRC) in Berkeley in 1987. Its goal is to help people of all incomes, ethnic origins, and family compositions to find a Shared Living Community option that better serves their needs than does conventional single-family housing. Educational programs, workshops, and networking have reached thousands of interested people, also providing me with new learning experiences about the community process. Interest in the new community movement has accelerated with the publication of *CoHousing: A Contemporary Approach to Housing Ourselves* (1989), by Kathryn McCamant and Charles Durrett, introducing the Danish cluster model to the United States. The success of the CoHousing communities is testimony that a redefinition of the American Dream is occuring, suited to peoples' changing needs and desires for supportive social enclaves.

On the street, however, the view is more dire, resembling Bertrand Russell's prediction: that economic dependence on succeeding layers of technologic advances, which in turn become obsolete, would cause the breakdown of our society. As a student I listened to his lectures on BBC. Now we are living them. There is also no doubt that we, as a society, are on the leading edge of a transformative era, called "the crunch" by Margaret Mead and "the transformation" by others, where old age and new age cultures grind apart — a dying of the post-WW II housing/fossil fuels/freeway boom era, and a birthing of a new world view that will rebuild community.

Russell's and Mead's warnings are being amplified by more recent prophets such as Ernest Callenbach, author of *Ecotopia;* Marge Percy, author of *Woman on the Edge of Time;* Fritjof Capra, author of *Turning Point;* Jeremy Rifkin, author of *Entropy;* Jerry Mander, author of *In the Absence of the Sacred;* E.F. Schumacher, author of *Small is Beautiful;* Robert Bellah, author of *Habits of the Heart;* and Albert Gore, author of *Earth in the Balance.* Many others write prophetically about the unprecedented and immediate changes we must make to recover from the accelerated social and environmental degradation spiraling out of control in this country and the world.

The collapse of communism is another specter of change that is buffeting the United States. The rise of the "military-industrial complex" was a concern to some of us returning Air Force POW's who correctly anticipated that our high defense budget could become an economic dependency. It has been obvious to me since the mid-1970's that either the continuation of the Cold War, or its ending, would prove financially devastating to both sides, and that the systems of communism and capitalism would both be compelled to change. Worldwide, these changes are appearing in the form of an international economy, and in the U.S., as economic decline and increased unemployment and poverty. Survival pressures will force us away from treating housing, health care, jobs, and education as commodities in a market-based system and towards more people participation in a localized, community based, and resource-efficient bio-regional economy.

Obsolete and wasteful single-family house and lot planning, lending, and building practices perpetuate a lifestyle that is the largest contributor to atmospheric pollution and ozone depletion due to the mass consumption of products made from toxic chemicals and fossil fuels. I am disappointed that the environmental movement has not yet advocated alternatives such as the Village Cluster and CoHousing models, that could significantly reduce the "lifestyle" factor in pollution and promote stewardship of the land.

In the 1970's, I first perceived the need to introduce an integrated social, environmental, and architectural expression of habitat that would seriously address the growing social, economic, and environmental concerns. In the early 1980's, I knew it would soon be timely to publish a major book on how the Shared Living Community concepts could assist Americans to achieve social and economic justice, a high quality of living, meaningful livelihood for all, and a drastic decrease in energy consumption and pollution.

The increase of singles, single parents, and small families, the changing roles of men and women in relationships, the struggle for the rights of minorities and the poor, the aging of America, and other socioeconomic and environmental influences are all adding impetus to the community movement. From studying indigenous peoples and their villages, both historic and present, it is clear to me that the tribe, clan, extended family, village, family farm, church, and town/neighborhood served instinctual survival needs and provided for the growth and sustainability of cultures. I envision society readopting the historic patterns of human settlement and creating modern day villages, extended family households, and family compounds. It is from this thinking that the basic archetype for the "Village Cluster" emerged.

I am appalled that despite social and environmental advances in other fields, the planning and housing related professions are still based upon premises popular 50 years ago. The "tools" that I as a fledgling planner and architect acquired from the "experts" during the post-WW II development boom now contribute heavily to environmental despoliation. I speak of the simplistic conventional zoning, subdivision, and house design and building practices that have become an entrenched part of the system.

The Western heritage of mechanistic thinking processes accredited to Descartes, Locke, Newton, and others has little to do with understanding complex and whole issues. It provides a means by which parts of the whole can be separately dissected and then more easily understood. I have come to see "mechanistic thinking" as an adaptive reaction to an increasingly complex and busy world. The immensity of information overload has outrun the ability of the average person to assimilate it, creating a psychic numbing and encouraging an eagerness for simplistic answers. There is a loss of closeness and, in spite of the many marketplace diversions there is a pervasive hunger for bonding together in supportive groups. To regain our humanness, we need to see the interconnectedness of all things and to relearn communication at the daily face-to-face level of community.

I have come to respectfully believe that the age-old cycle of birthing, maturation, dying, and rebirthing is at work in all life forms and in all of our institutions. Thus, I am optimistic that "community" will be accepted as an integral part of an ecological and sustainable socioeconomic system that will rise out of the passing of outmoded ways of thinking. I also have faith in the inner architect in all of us, that intuitive power and awareness which can visualize, sense, create, and move us to strive for a harmonious and sustainable community. This aspect of our being calls upon us to fulfill our need for family, habitat, livelihood, and an expression of spirituality as we create community.

Introduction

By Kathleen Smith

As I look around, I see a world with so much life, and so much potential and beauty, in crisis — a crisis which threatens the integrity of the natural world and the human spirit. On my walk to work each day, a short two blocks, I pass a gas station, a large parking lot, a car dealership, and two vacant lots, one with a sign on the fence which reads "No Trespassing - Hazardous Wastes." I also pass homeless families, a bus shelter defaced by vandalism, and the spot where a friend of mine was robbed at knife point.

Things aren't all bad though. Often, I see lovers walking hand in hand, birds flying overhead, and familiar faces of people who smile to greet me. Sometimes I meet friends on the sidewalk and we stop to chat for a few minutes. Other times I see a group of school children laughing and holding hands as they walk with their teachers to visit some new and exciting place. This always makes me happy, but sometimes I can't help but wonder which children will grow up to be drug dealers, which will die young at the hands of crime or circumstance, which will end up on the streets, and which will be the lucky ones — the ones who have a home, a family, a chance to be happy, to help others, and to make choices.

I am one of the lucky ones. I grew up in basic middle class luxury. I had enough clothes and food, a nice roof over my head, even a car when I turned sixteen. Don't get me wrong, we weren't rich. The car was a 1960 Studebaker that cost $300. But it was mine. Basically, what I have had is the opportunity to choose what I want in my life. I'm not talking about the choice between eating lunch or dinner because you don't have the money to buy both. I'm talking about being in a position to make choices about how and where I live my life and to make changes when necessary. To me, it is this choice which marks true freedom.

Growing up the way I have, I've also had the chance to travel in Europe, Canada, Mexico, and Japan. I've had the opportunity to learn firsthand about other cultures and other ways of living and relating to each other and the land. In our society, we often forget that there are other ways of doing things — we forget that we have choices. If something isn't working right or fulfilling our basic needs, we do have the ability to change it. More than this, I believe, we have the responsibility to change it.

Crises of a social, economic, environmental, and political nature, too numerous to name, plague our world. These problems are often attributed to overpopulation. But that is only part of the equation. Consumerism is, perhaps, an even bigger player. We, in the U.S.A., comprise roughly 5% of the world's population, but consume nearly 25% of its resources. We criticize the indigenous peoples of Brazil and other countries for destroying their forests and overgrazing their lands, but who is buying the wood, meat, and other products they are producing? We are.

To make matters worse, this lifestyle of over-consumption is coming to be how virtually everyone, everywhere, seeks to live. Capitalism and the single-family house are being marketed throughout the world and children in areas as remote as the high mountainous region of Ladakh in Northern India are playing with Barbie dolls and watching Rambo movies. The poor and disenfranchised of our country and the world often do not have the choice to challenge mainstream values or to work for change. They are struggling simply to survive.

This is why I am interested in community. It is an alternative that empowers people, all people, to make choices — to nurture each other and grow. I chose the field of architecture because I wanted to work for change by helping to create environments which are healthy, sustainable, and enriching to the soul — to create choices in how we live. I am concerned with the impact of buildings and cities on the vitality of the natural world and the physical health of the people who inhabit them. I am equally concerned with the social, emotional, and spiritual implications of architecture and how to create environments which consider human needs, yearnings, and limitations. I have pursued a career in community design and education specifically because I want to help people see the choices they have. These choices may not be easy, but they are essential to our future.

Our lifestyle and attitude have changed so much from the days of Beaver Cleaver and poodle skirts. Dramatic demographic and economic changes have taken place in our society in the last 40 years, but for the most part our housing has remained the same. Conventional housing leaves a large number of us ill-housed and isolated. At the same time, an increasingly mobile society has distanced many of us from our extended families and the social and emotional support they provide. I grew up in a very supportive and loving family. Unfortunately, most of my extended family, including my two sisters, lived thousands of miles away in Canada. I saw my grandparents every Christmas and my cousins, aunts, and uncles even less. I was jealous of the few friends I had with large families near by. Their houses were always bustling with activity and laughter. I still yearn for this kind of connection.

The great malady of the 20th Century, implicated in all of our problems and affecting us individually and socially, is the loss of community. When our need for community is neglected, it doesn't just go away. It appears in the form of violence, loss of meaning, isolation, and a myriad of other symptoms. We try to isolate these symptoms, to eradicate them one by one, but the root problem, our loss of connection to others and the natural world, remains. The common complaints of our time — loneliness, loss of values and meaning, lack of personal fulfillment, emptiness, disillusionment, powerlessness, and fear — are all symptoms that reflect our loss of community.

We yearn for a sense of connection and belonging, but we do not necessarily identify it with community. We search, almost frantically, trying one church after another or one therapy after another, hoping to satisfy our unnamed hunger. We think we can satisfy our needs if we find the right job, relationship, church, or club, but without community *in our daily lives*, whatever we find will be unsatisfying.

Clubs, support groups, gyms, and churches, all offer some sense of community, social contact, and support. But they fall short of providing the intimacy, sense of belonging, diversity, and support we crave in our daily lives. What we really need is a daily living environment that satisfies our needs and desires and allows us to live more fully and more true to our nature as people and as members of our local ecosystem and the global community.

In the modern world, we tend to separate the various aspects of our lives — work, play, family, and friends. Community seeks to heal these separations and bring together the various aspects of ourselves. A strong sense of family and community provides the foundation that children and adults need to learn and grow. It provides a framework for passing along values and giving and receiving support. Community provides a sense of safety and security in knowing and relying on others in our lives. A close relationship with friends, neighbors, and the land around us can enrich our lives beyond any comparison with material wealth and technologic advance. Instead of narrowing our vision or making us insular, an intimate connection with others can expand our understanding of our relationships to others and ourselves. Ultimately, it is in relationships — to other people, other species, and the processes of nature — that we find meaning and direction.

Relationships are really what life is all about — the essence of our humanity. It is hard to imagine life without them. Everyone and everything has a relationship with someone or something else. The question is how healthy and fulfilling are these relationships. Divorce, rape, deforestation, species

extinction, and drug abuse are all evidence of how few healthy relationships we have today, even with ourselves. We are fragmented and isolated. An atom alone is interesting, but what is fascinating is what happens when atoms combine to form things, people, trees, water, and whole ecosystems. And what is inspiring and magical is what happens when people come together to form communities.

It is essential to the healthy functioning of all living things and all living systems to have a place in the larger environment, to see their connection to others and their role in the cycles of life. Community helps bring us closer to a richer understanding of these connections and our vital role. We gain security, self-esteem, satisfaction, and pride from knowing how we fit into the larger community and how we affect others and they affect us. It is in relationships that we define ourselves, create boundaries and overlaps, and gain an understanding of who we really are. For too long, we have denied our basic needs to see and touch others in a deep way, to feel the sun on our shoulders and the soil beneath our feet, to see the connections and impacts of our actions on a human scale, and to be part of something larger than ourselves or our immediate families. Community, more than any other way of life, can satisfy these needs.

We, as individuals and as a society, tend to want to pass the responsibility for change on to someone else. We place blame and develop a we/they dichotomy that doesn't really exist. The world is not black or white, good or bad, we or they. There is spirit in everything and soul in everything. We are connected to each other and to everything around us. What we do affects the health of ourselves, our society, and the planet. Understanding this unity may make the task of working for change and solving our problems seem overwhelming. But finding the points where the problems converge can make our attempts to solve them more effective. Then we just need to find the right threads to pull to affect the entire fabric. Only by acknowledging our interrelatedness can we move as a society beyond our present crises into community. Alone, we may feel powerless to affect any change, but working together in community we have the diversity of skills, experience and knowledge, and the time and energy to make effective change — to create the life we really want.

We can't just sit back and wait for community to happen. We need to make it happen, by going out into the world and talking and listening to people. By opening ourselves to others, we can start to experience our interconnectedness and what it means to truly belong. We can begin to see ourselves as connected to others and the natural world. And, as we begin to build with nature, live in community, and show concern for all living things, we will begin to heal.

This book takes you step-by-step through the process of forming a community. There are songs, stories, photos, drawings, case studies of existing communities, visions of new ones, techniques for working with people, and technical information about financing and building. We draw on past and present community examples from various cultures for guidance in restoring community to our lives today. This book isn't just about the idea of community, but concrete ways to foster it. What this book presents is hope — hope for a more

humane society and way of life, hope for respect and equality between all peoples, hope for a future free of hatred, stress, pollution, loneliness, and abuse, and hope that you will find the community you are looking for. Community is not the norm for how we live, but it can be.

I am thankful to have had the opportunity to work on this book, to share my experiences and the stories of so many successful communities. I find inspiring the work that is being done by ordinary people to improve their quality of life and that of those around them. These are people just like you and me who face the same daily struggles of work, family, housing, commutes, and crime. But they have said, "Enough is enough. This isn't how I want to live or how I want my children to live." They have banded together with others near them to create a different way of life, a better way of life, and they are succeeding.

In the past few years, there has been increasing talk about my generation, Generation X, as being caught in a "mood of darkness and inevitability." I admit that I'm a bit cynical and lack a basic trust in the system, as do most of my friends of any age, but I do not lack trust in the human spirit or the spirit of the earth.

I believe deeply in the power of little steps to make big changes. So, despite the obstacles, burdens, and challenges, go out there and make community. As you read this book it might be helpful to put aside any ideas you have about how things should be or how things are, and simple imagine how things could be — what your life could be like in community. Try not to say "no way, it can't happen," because right now thousands of people in the United States and millions of people throughout the world are living in some form of community. It is not only possible, it is a reality. You can start small. Say hi to a neighbor or gather a group to plant some trees, make jam, or discuss community. I know you've heard it before, but now let's do it – together.

I read recently that to be happy, a person needs three things:

> something to hope for
> something to do
> someone to love and be kind to.

In community, we can find all three.

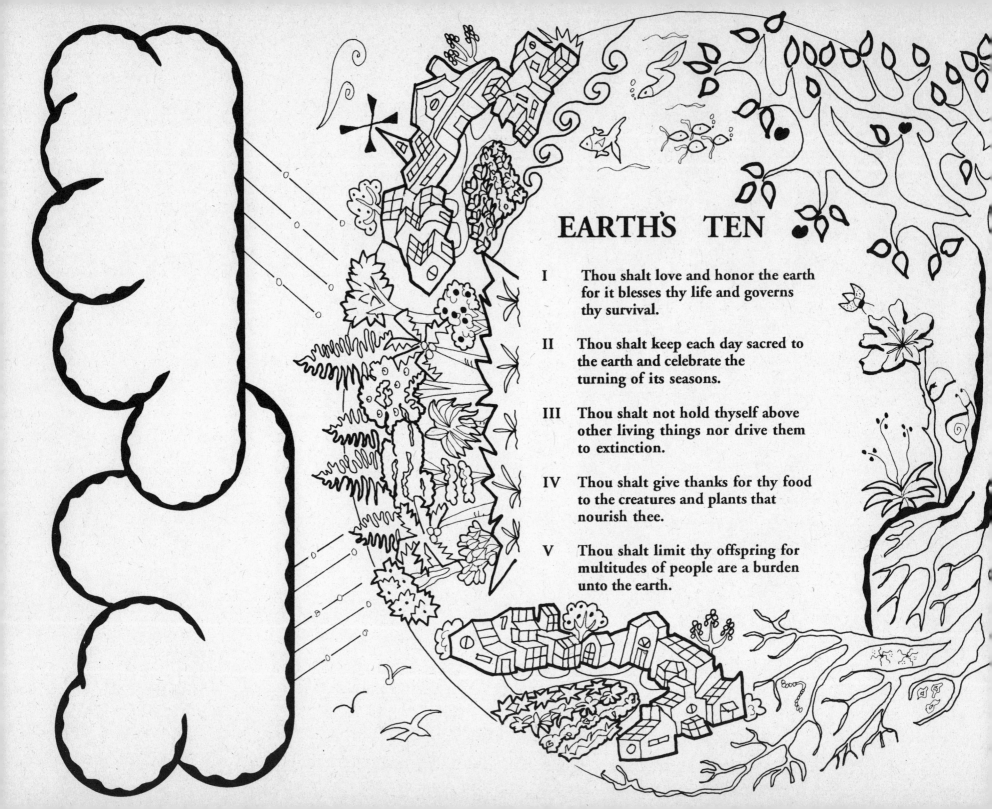

EARTH'S TEN

I   Thou shalt love and honor the earth for it blesses thy life and governs thy survival.

II   Thou shalt keep each day sacred to the earth and celebrate the turning of its seasons.

III   Thou shalt not hold thyself above other living things nor drive them to extinction.

IV   Thou shalt give thanks for thy food to the creatures and plants that nourish thee.

V   Thou shalt limit thy offspring for multitudes of people are a burden unto the earth.

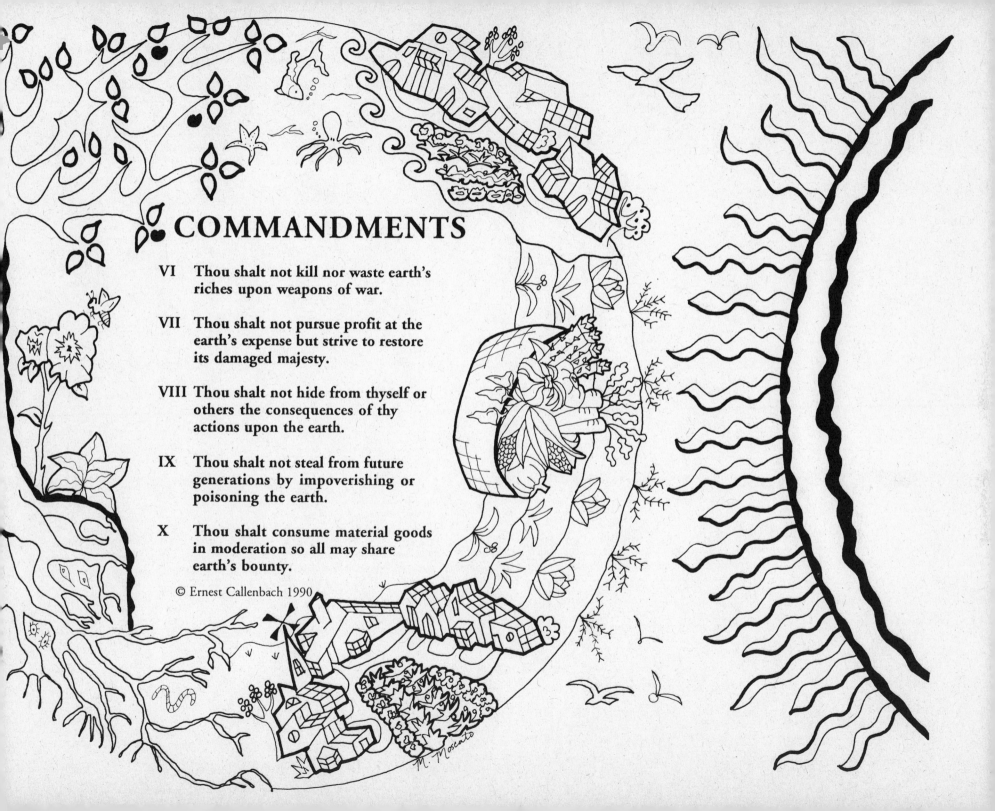

COMMANDMENTS

VI   Thou shalt not kill nor waste earth's riches upon weapons of war.

VII   Thou shalt not pursue profit at the earth's expense but strive to restore its damaged majesty.

VIII Thou shalt not hide from thyself or others the consequences of thy actions upon the earth.

IX   Thou shalt not steal from future generations by impoverishing or poisoning the earth.

X   Thou shalt consume material goods in moderation so all may share earth's bounty.

© Ernest Callenbach 1990

M. Moscato

VILLAGE ACRE COMMUNITY
Visiting the New American Dream

The Outdoor Social Court
This is the social beehive of the community. The physical form and location of the court, created by the arrangement of buildings, vegetation, pathways, and materials, invites spontaneous interaction and community gathering, aiding the growth of a sustainable community social fabric.

SLRC

CHAPTER ONE

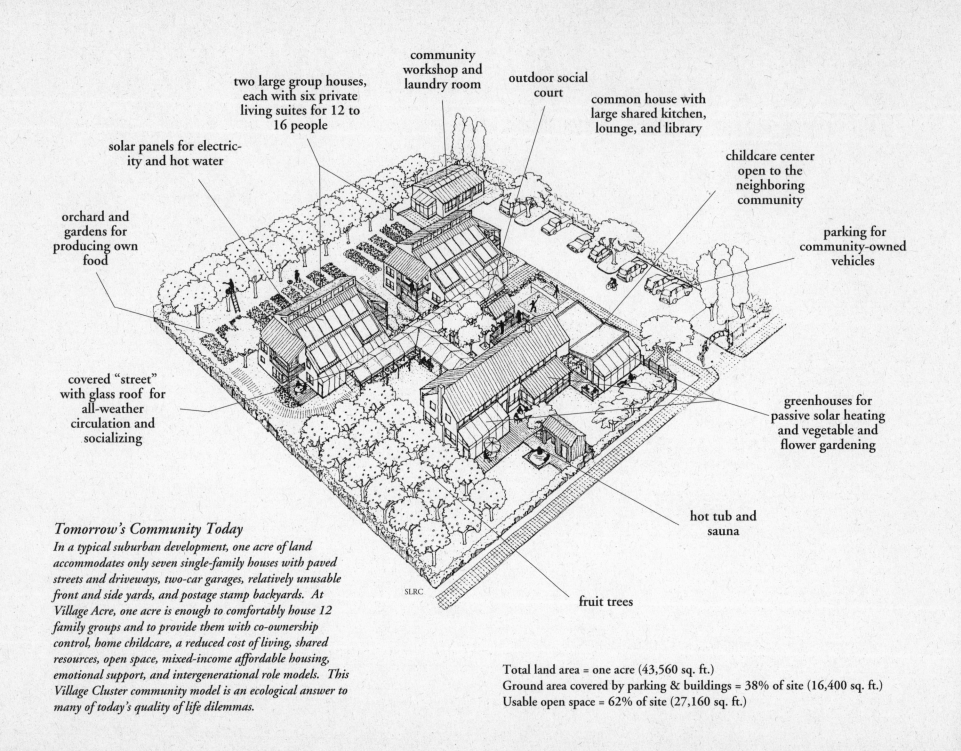

two large group houses, each with six private living suites for 12 to 16 people

community workshop and laundry room

outdoor social court

common house with large shared kitchen, lounge, and library

childcare center open to the neighboring community

solar panels for electricity and hot water

parking for community-owned vehicles

orchard and gardens for producing own food

covered "street" with glass roof for all-weather circulation and socializing

greenhouses for passive solar heating and vegetable and flower gardening

hot tub and sauna

fruit trees

SLRC

Tomorrow's Community Today

In a typical suburban development, one acre of land accommodates only seven single-family houses with paved streets and driveways, two-car garages, relatively unusable front and side yards, and postage stamp backyards. At Village Acre, one acre is enough to comfortably house 12 family groups and to provide them with co-ownership control, home childcare, a reduced cost of living, shared resources, open space, mixed-income affordable housing, emotional support, and intergenerational role models. This Village Cluster community model is an ecological answer to many of today's quality of life dilemmas.

Total land area = one acre (43,560 sq. ft.)
Ground area covered by parking & buildings = 38% of site (16,400 sq. ft.)
Usable open space = 62% of site (27,160 sq. ft.)

This is the story of Village Acre Community. The community is an ecological departure from ordinary single-family houses, apartments, and condominiums. It is an intergenerational, mixed-income "Village Cluster" that meets the daily and long-term living needs of its members.

The members of Village Acre Community represent real-life persons whom we have met, either through our work with Shared Living Resource Center (SLRC), sponsoring workshops, consultation sessions, and providing design services, or through our personal experiences of living in and visiting communities and shared living households. Many of these people have related to us their frustrations and unmet needs concerning the high costs, social isolation, and environmental inadequacy of conventional housing. They have also shared their wondrous visions about the companionship, affordability, and ecological benefits they see in Shared Living Communities.

You may feel that this community example is too idealistic, that ordinary people could not co-own land and buildings without conflict. For a society that has lost touch with its humanity, the story of Village Acre may seem too good to be true. Yes, conflicts may arise, but our premise is that integrating the physical and social structure of Village Acre would revive the lost art of person-to-person communication. Differences could then be resolved before they became conflicts.

We invite you to share the visions presented in this book, to challenge the status quo, examine your lifestyle, and create your own dream of a brighter and more sustainable future. See if you identify with any of the people and scenes of Village Acre Community, and then explore the other innovative community models in this book for the one that could best serve your needs and dreams.

Ken E. Norwood

Living as if Ecology Mattered

Imagine this community of 32 people, living on one acre of infill land on the edge of a typical American city. Each family or individual has a comfortable suite of rooms or a private room, and the whole community comes together in the large common house for evening meals, celebrations, meetings, and for relaxing and talking with each other. The children always have playmates nearby, elders have the contact they want with younger people, and adults have others around with whom to share household tasks and expenses, explore common interests, and share emotional support.

The buildings are ecologically designed to make direct use of solar energy for water and space heating and electricity. Members grow some of their own food, buy other food and supplies in bulk, and cook their dinners in the common house. Through cooperative agreements, they co-own the land, buildings, common vehicles, bicycles, appliances, tools, and garden equipment. The physical and social design makes it easy to recycle and conserve resources — to "live lightly on the land." This significantly reduces the number of car trips, the energy consumption, their cost of living, and consequently the overall environmental impact of their community! This is not a return to peasant villages or the communes of the 1960's. It is a way

The People of Village Acre Community

Mike	29 yrs.	computer programmer		Osvaldo	32 yrs.	carpenter in the community workshop
Yoichi	37	repairman for community		Rhonda	35	bank teller
Naomi	36	court reporter		Yvonne	5	
Roger	59	clothing store manager		Eleanor	48	office manager
Sangeetha	57	counselor		Ronald	67	retired farmer/community garden manager
Phil	27	telephone lineman				
Cathy	28	librarian/common house manager		David	31	building inspector
Tina	6 mos.			Melissa	33	firefighter/community construction manager
Javier	44	pharmacist				
Gabriella	42	nurse		Bruce	42	electrician in the community workshop
Rosalinda	16					
Jose	13			Joel	17	
Pablo	9					
Marion	28	insurance investigator		Clifford	61	woodworker in the community workshop
Rose	63	retired teacher/community childcare coordinator		Yung-Ho	29	freelance writer/community childcare aide
Pamela	37	secretary/artist in the community workshop		Libby	34	travel agent
				George	33	sanitation worker
Susan	11			Angela	2	
Adam	4					

Variety is the Spice of Life

The people of Village Acre represent the diversity of age, ethnicity, income, and avocation that exists within today's society but is often hidden by neighborhoods which are segregated by income, class, and race. In communities like Village Acre, everyone has the opportunity to experience the richness and benefits of diversity.

to live ecologically in a distressed world and at the same time rediscover a cultural heritage that has been lost in the name of progress.

The People of Village Acre

The people of Village Acre Community come from diverse backgrounds. Included are single, married, childless, and elderly people; couples, parents, and children of all ages; and people with disabilities. There is a mix of incomes as well. Some members were homeless or near homeless before they joined the community. Some brought equity from previous homes and paid more down at the start. Others with little capital to begin with make larger monthly payments. Some earn their livelihood through the childcare, gardening, bookkeeping, carpentry, or general repair they do for the community. Some work at outside jobs, some are retired or on fixed incomes, and others operate professional, trade, and craft enterprises out of the community workshop and office.

These adults all badly needed an affordable home, more free time, safe food sources, and a sense of belonging, and their children lacked nearby playmates, a safe and stimulating environment, time with their parents, and an extended family experience. Out of frustration each adult began to wonder: *"Aren't there any alternatives? Is this how life was meant to be?"* And then, reaching out, they asked others, *"Why don't we join together and create a cluster community that will truly fulfill our needs?"*

The story of Village Acre Community and its people demonstrates what may be the beginning of the end of poverty, homelessness, loneliness, and environmental destruction in this country and the world. What the members of Village Acre desire, like hundreds of thousands of people in this country, is the opportunity to gain more stability and security in their lives by working and sharing with others.

People contact us every day at the Shared Living Resource Center asking about shared living situations and how to gain a sense of community. To these people, community means more than just sharing a mortgage or using the same washing machine. It means sharing their joys, sorrows, needs, hopes, and dreams with their new extended family. In many cases, this is their only family, because their blood relatives are too far away or out of touch. The people of Village Acre Community come from diverse backgrounds, but they are now linked through the bonding that comes from sharing common purposes, responsibilities, and experiences.

Designing as if People Mattered

The community design process involves more than the physical design of housing. It is about the fullest expression of architecture to integrate the lives of people and their sense of well-being with their environment. This community was designed by the founding core group, whose members first spent an intensive weekend defining individual and common goals and needs, and visualizing their new living environment. They worked with an architect specializing in the facilitation of the group design process, who helped them translate their visions into reality through numerous follow-up sessions.

The layout of the community was designed to encourage interaction and cooperation while ensur-

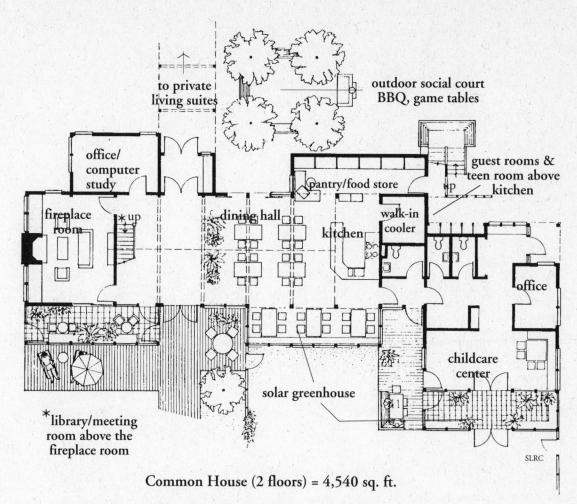

Common House (2 floors) = 4,540 sq. ft.

A Place to Be Together
The common house is the hub of the community. It is where the residents cook and share evening meals, work, relax, and play. The extensive shared amenities (such as the fireplace social room, office/computer room, library/meeting room, and guest rooms) provide space and opportunity for the community members to explore their interests and satisfy their social and practical needs. The childcare center connects Village Acre with the larger community by providing cooperative childcare and an informal after-school play space for the children of members and neighbors.

ing individual and family privacy. It follows layout relationships found in many traditional villages, in which private living spaces lead to semi-private patios and rooms, which then lead to semi-common courts and activity areas, finally opening into the common buildings and outdoor gathering areas. Humankind has lived for many thousands of years passing down this village heritage of hierarchical spatial relationships. "There is nothing new under the sun."

While the common places, such as the kitchen, dining room, and library, reflect the needs and desires of the entire group, the private living spaces respond directly to the needs of each community member. Each family and individual designed and completed their own interiors, which saved them money and gave them a strong sense of pride and belonging. Flexibility was built into the design by the use of soundproof, modular, movable wall units that are independent of the free-span structure. As

new members join the community and the families change in size, the building form can change with them. For example, a two-bedroom living suite could become two one-bedroom living suites sharing a compartmentalized bathroom; or a four-bedroom suite with two bathrooms could be formed out of two or three smaller suites; or a large studio could be formed out of two one-bedroom suites.

The financial support for Village Acre came from a combination of sources — the incomes of the people, equity from selling houses and condominiums, pre-development grants, and a Community Housing Trust Fund loan, which was financed through a combination of nonprofit lenders, banks, businesses, and government sources. The buildings and common amenities were built in stages. A low-interest, phased-development loan enabled members to do sweat-equity in finishing interiors, landscaping, and building other amenities. Chapter Nine proposes innovative funding programs and changes

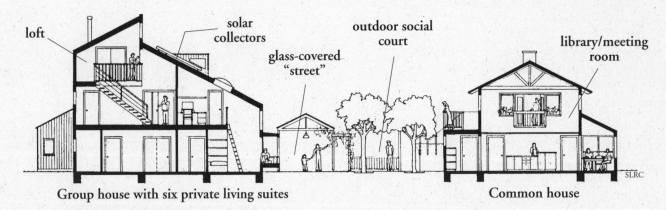

loft | solar collectors | glass-covered "street" | outdoor social court | library/meeting room

Group house with six private living suites — Common house

Privacy and Community
From the sanctity and calm of the private living suites to the festiveness and camaraderie of the common house, Village Acre offers its members a variety of experiences and opportunities for interaction.

needed in present lending and development practices to make the creation of communities like Village Acre more feasible.

A Visit to Village Acre Community

Pamela and Sandy had been friends for many years, meeting for the first time as next door neighbors in a suburban tract development. Since then, they had drifted in and out of touch with each other, through moves, divorces, unemployment, and child-raising.

The first time she came to visit her friend at Village Acre, Sandy was not ready to believe all that Pamela had told her. The picture she painted for Sandy seemed almost too perfect. Pamela's young son Adam was cared for in the community childcare center, and Susan, her older daughter, played and worked on projects after school with other children in the workshop. Pamela cooked dinner once a month, when she and a partner would plan a menu and cook for the whole community. The rest of the time she simply came home from work, picked up Adam, checked in on Susan, chatted with her neighbors, and relaxed until dinner was served in the common house. For more intimate meals, she prepared food in her group house kitchenette and ate in her own private suite or on her deck with a friend.

Pamela's job hours had been cut back recently. Instead of looking for another job and enduring two jobs and two commutes, she found she was saving enough money by living cooperatively that she could use the extra free time to pursue her talent as an artist.

Sandy found Pamela in the community workshop, paint spattered on her smock and a radiant

SLRC

smile on her face.

"Hi, Sandy!" Pam cried, throwing her arms around her friend, who noticed how happy and relaxed she looked. *"It's good to see you!"*

"This is some set-up you've got here," Sandy remarked. The skylights illuminated work tables, individual alcoves, storage bins, and shelves full of arts and crafts supplies. Other people were working too, but the room didn't seem crowded.

"Wait'll you see the common dining room," Pamela said. *"Everybody liked one of my paintings so much the community bought it from me so we could all enjoy it! C'mon, I'll show you around."*

They walked through the common kitchen and into the dining hall. Two people in their 60's were setting up for a party. Pamela stopped to introduce Sandy to Clifford and Rose.

"Welcome to Village Acre, Sandy," said Clifford.

Community Enterprises: Workplace of the 21st Century
Community members pooled their resources to build this strawbale workshop, which has facilities for art, pottery, woodworking, drafting, electrical work, and sewing. As the interests of members change, the workshop can be rearranged for different activities. Ecological practices are maintained through the use of non-toxic and non-polluting materials and processes, and the hand-craftsmanship and simple living of the users. This home workplace represents a trend away from the centralized, corporate-controlled work environment towards a community-based bioregional economy with more direct marketing of goods and services.

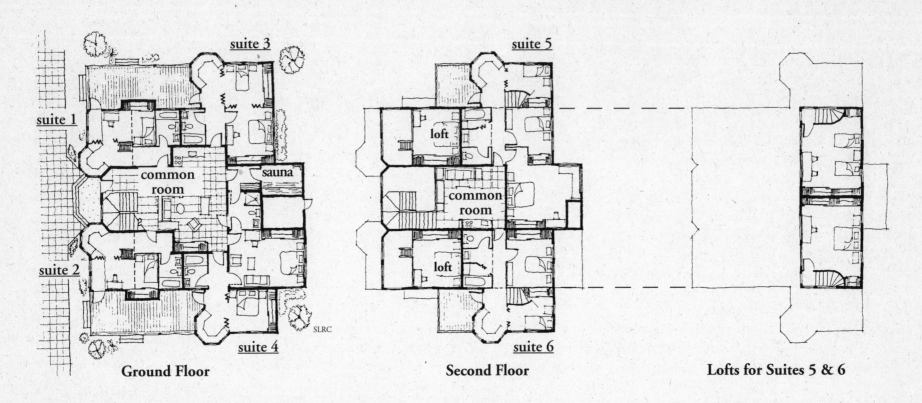

suite 3

suite 5

suite 1

common
room

sauna

suite 2

loft

common
room

loft

SLRC

suite 4

suite 6

Ground Floor

Second Floor

Lofts for Suites 5 & 6

Private Living Suites: Space to Call Your Own
The two large group houses are hybrids of an apartment building and a conventional single-family house. Each has six private living suites for up to 16 persons. These suites range in size from a studio with a loft to a four-bedroom suite. Members have adequate space for privacy and personal fulfillment. On each floor the suites open into a Common Room with a kitchenette for breakfast, lunch, snacks, and casual gatherings with guests and housemates. This shared space brings the members of each floor together as an extended family and saves valuable space for living suites where each person or family can maintain privacy. The main floor of each house has a sauna for health and relaxation.

AREAS OF TYPICAL GROUP HOUSE

Common Rooms	=	610 sq. ft.
<u>Six Private Suites</u>	=	<u>2,890 sq. ft.</u>
Total Area	=	3,500 sq. ft.
Average Area of Group		
House Living Suites	=	583 sq. ft.
(from 280 sq. ft. to 880 sq. ft.)		

SLRC

"I hope you can stick around for our community celebration tonight. It should be a lot of fun."

"What's the celebration for?" Sandy asked.

"Oh, it's our twentieth birthday," Pamela replied. *"The community's, I mean. Clifford's really excited about it. He and Rose are our newest members. They feel really lucky to have found us. Their apartment building burned down last year, and both of them stayed in shelters for six months."*

They walked on into the gardens. Fruit trees rose above the corn, beans, tomatoes, and squash.

"Everybody helps out in the gardens," she said, waving to an older man who was picking tomatoes with the help of a small child. *"But Ronald is in charge. He was a farmer for 40 years. Now he works for the community, managing the gardens."*

They paused at the edge of the orchard, where Pamela picked a pea and proudly remarked, *"Susan planted these."*

Sandy looked back at Village Acre, struck by its beauty and calm. The buildings, rich with individual embellishments, seemed to embrace the courtyards and gardens. *"Home?"* mused Sandy.

"Home," asserted Pamela, *"all mine,"* she teased.

Sandy took a deep breath, remembering her small apartment, her children coming home to

The Sweet Smell of the Earth

Sandy's nostrils tingled from the rich scent of the freshly turned soil. "I hadn't realized until I came here and started gardening again how therapeutic and relaxing it can be to have your hands in dirt – digging, planting seeds, picking vegetables…"

"Never doubt that a small group of thoughtful, committed citizens can change the world. Indeed, it's the only thing that ever has."
— *Margaret Mead*

empty rooms and a television set, the few quiet moments she had to herself each night before she went to bed, only to wake up, get the children ready for school and into the car, and then endure the long drive to work. How could Pamela's life here be so different? *"Pam,"* she said, *"can I move to Village Acre? Is there a waiting list?"*

****

The ideas advanced here may appear to be new or impossibly utopian, but they are as old as humanity itself. Working together to feed and house ourselves, sharing wisdom among generations, and living in balance with nature have been basic experiences of human society since its beginning. Only in the last 50 years with increasing social alienation, economic decline, and environmental degradation have these basics come to seem like unobtainable ideals. We can view the hardships and ominous changes of present times as unavoidable, or we can view them as inducements for change — a call for us to challenge present institutions and take personal responsibility for conserving natural and human resources and creating a better American way of life. It is an awesome challenge, but an exciting one, and we invite you, the reader, to put aside your preconceptions about "community," "alternatives," and "changes," and project yourself into the prototype designs and the actual working examples of Shared Living Communities.

WAKING UP
from the American Dream

Top Grads Face Grim Job Market

WASHINGTON — The richest

Society appears to be slowly but surely disintegrating before our eyes.

Poor get poorer: Half of income goes to housing

America wakes up from its Dream

For many of us, tomorrow may not bring a better day

By Jim Nesbitt
NEWHOUSE NEWS SERVICE

54-mile commute each way. He ha an executive-level job with a b corporation, but no promise that won't disappear in the next rou of layoffs.

Bauer, 42, weighs the good w the bad and feels satisfied with piece of the American Dream. I he sees no way to fulfill what m come to view a — the pron his children, a better

Problem is acute in S.F., Oakland,

Even affluent East Bay areas feel the pinch

War Between The Generations: A War Against the People

Woman, 91, Mending After Icy Ordeal

U.N.'s Dire Environmental Diagnosis

Part-Time Job Doesn't Pay Rent

21-year-old mother goes to school full time, wants to be a nurse
runs wire for an electrician.
Neither of his sons went to col-

The Middle Class Feels Betrayed,

Recession

SIERRA from the $130,000's

SIENA from the $120,000's

LEFT ON CAL

SIERRA from the $130,000's

U.N. Report Says World Faces Ecologic, Economic Disaster

Largest-Ever Number Of Families on Welfare

'Incredible' surge of laid-off workers

Knowing the Feeling Of America in Decline

35.7 million Americans fall behind

Class of '92 faces worst job market in 30 years

IBM to Eliminate 25,000 Jobs, Close Factories

Poorer and poorer

Longer Commutes Force Parents To Make Hard Child-Care Choices

Freeways: A recipe for sprawl

New Signs of Har From Ozone Loss

Is Financial Doom Stalking U.S.?

Under the surface, the world economy is in sad shape

Rise in ultraviolet rays detected in C

Drug Use Down — Except for Baby Boomers

Poverty rate climbs for older Americans

Top execs, new immigrants — they're all scrambling for jobs

Troubling Future as U.S. Grows Old

"America is undergoing a profound social crisis, and the nation has more or less decided to pretend it isn't happening." [1]

— *John Leo*
"Numbing Ourselves to the Growing Crises"

Gap between rich, poor widens

Income disparity

SLRC

CHAPTER TWO

EVERGREEN, EVERBLUE

Chorus: Evergreen, everblue
         As it was in the beginning
         We've got to see it through
         Evergreen, everblue
         At this point in time
         It's up to me, it's up to you

Amazon is calling "help this planet earth"
With voices from the jungle "help this planet earth"
Hear the tree that's falling "help this planet earth"
Rainforests are crying help this planet earth to stay

Ocean's wave is rumbling "help this planet earth"
With voices from the seaway "help this planet earth"
Water's for drinking "help this planet earth"
Beluga whales are singing help this planet earth to stay

   Right now is when we're needed
   We can all do something
   The young the old together
   The more we help this planet earth

So come all united nations "help this planet earth"
Children of one mother "help this planet earth"
With love for one another "help this planet earth"
For our sons and daughters' future help this planet earth
   to stay
                           — Raffi

A Chronicle of Our Times

Despite critics' claims of a "controlled press," most newspapers and magazines are an honest chronicle of our society, depicting day by day the story of economic collapse, environmental deterioration, depletion of natural resources, and the gradual disintegration of the family, social, and cultural institutions of our society — all effects of the relentless pursuit, by each successive generation, of a "higher quality of living" synonymous with the American Dream.

Taken one at a time, the stories range from informative to disturbing. Taken together, they reveal the unfolding of a vast and profound social disaster.

The ending of the Cold War and the lack of an "enemy" to justify huge defense expenditures, along with the thinning of the ozone layer, the introduction of AIDS, and the breakdown of cohesive community, are imposing an avalanche of social, economic, and environmental calamities that we seem to have no control over. Yet many people feel that somehow "we won the Cold War."

Pope John Paul II, on the other hand, viewed both capitalism and communism as losers. In his third social encyclical, "Centesimus Annus," he spoke of the demise of communism and how it is unacceptable to have capitalism as the only economic model. The Pope proposed "a society of free work, of enterprise and participation." He says that how one serves the common good must be the basis for judging economic systems, and that capitalism

has serious, sometimes disastrous shortcomings.[2] This sentiment is mirrored by Vice President Albert Gore, who writes, ". . . the partial blindness of our current economic system is the single most powerful force behind what seem to be irrational decisions about the global environment."[3]

The words of these two prominent leaders indicate that it is unreasonable to think we can sustain ourselves without making continual changes in our economic and political structure. We will be compelled to change the way we make a living, design and build houses, transport ourselves, and use energy if we want a society more in tune with human needs and desires. According to Jeremy Rifkin, this change is already underway:

> …the world economy is in the early stages of an historic transition from an extractive energy base of fossil fuels and rare metals to a solar age with renewable resources as the primary energy source…. The overriding principle is to balance our economic budget with nature. In other words, an effort is made not to consume faster than nature can produce. Emphasis is placed on decentralized institutions, labor intensive skills, greater diversity and regional self-sufficiency along with frugal and equitable use of nature's resources.[4]

Working models already exist that show us a way to this future.

Paramahansa Yogananda, a spiritual master from India who heralds the role of "community" as a positive change for society, founded the Self Realization Fellowship in Los Angeles in 1925. One of his disciples is Swami Kriyananda (Donald Walters). In *The Road Ahead*, Kriyananda predicts

"I don't see an American Dream, I see an American Nightmare."
— *Malcolm X*

"It may seem a big jump to be talking of global conflicts in the same breath as how we design our homes. But the two are intimately linked through our consumption patterns — and it is only by changing our own lives and homes that we can begin to save the environment."[5]

— *David Pearson*

"I believe that our civilization is, in effect, addicted to the consumption of the earth itself." [6]

— *Al Gore*
Earth in the Balance

"…the new machines actually do what they promise to do, which leaves us feeling pleased and impressed. It is not until much later, after a technology has been around for a while — bringing with it other compatible technologies, altering economic arrangements and family and community life, affecting culture, and having unpredictable impact on the land — that societies both familiar and unfamiliar with the machine begin to realize that a Faustian bargain has been made." [7]

— *Jerry Mander,*
In The Absence of The Sacred

massive worldwide depression and human suffering caused by recurring and progressively worsening cycles of indebtedness, devaluation of currency, inflation, and social upheaval.[8]

Kriyananda's insights are based upon the prophetic teachings of Yogananda, who warned his audiences, "There will be great upheavals and unemployment in America…. The time is growing short. You have no idea of the suffering that awaits mankind! A terrible depression is coming, far worse than the last one."[9] Kriyananda writes that "Yogananda repeatedly urged his listeners to band together in cooperative spiritual communities, to buy land together in the country and there to live simply, close to nature and to God, guided by the two-fold principle of 'plain living and high thinking.' Such communities would serve as models for the new age, when countless similar, self-sustaining communities will popularize voluntary cooperation over competition as the true key to lasting prosperity and inner fulfillment."[10] In 1968, Kriyananda founded Ananda Village, a spiritual cooperative community in the lower Sierra Nevada Mountains of California. This community is a model for how cooperation and cooperative living can bring about a transcendence of our current practices which exploit human and natural resources.

Meanwhile, corporations gain power and profits in the short term by buying and selling other corporations rather than by making and selling products. Manufacturers move overseas in search of cheaper labor and less rigorous environmental regulations, leaving low-paying service-sector jobs — fast-food careers — for the youth and unskilled working class of America. Telecommunications and computer technologies enable corporations to make

major cuts in highly skilled, white collar, and management jobs. Government and business mismanagement of the economy, such as the savings and loan scandal and bail-out, effectively reward greedy speculators for unwise investments, sending taxpayers the bill. The average real income and purchasing power per person steadily declined during the 12 years of the Reagan-Bush era, forcing many families to depend on two incomes, although massive layoffs make this difficult. The result of these trends is a multi-faceted economic, social, environmental, and energy crisis — evidence that the old system is no longer working for many people.

By continuing blithely along on the course that communism and capitalism have collectively trod, we ensure that our lifestyles will continue to diminish. By, instead, emphasizing the models for change that already exist and by inventing new ones — ones that balance the international economy with a strong bioregional economy — we will move towards a more joyous and fulfilling lifestyle that will serve our needs with a wider range of options.

Isolation, Fragmentation, and Cultural Decline — *the price we pay*

The loss of a strong personal identification with a common place shared with others is an underlying cause of social fragmentation for most people in this society, regardless of income, education, and ethnic background. The social isolation of the single-family house, apartment, and condo; the physical separation by ownership rights and fences; the many hours we spend closed off from each other in our cars; and the fewer opportunities for amiable dialogue with other people have all contributed to the breakdown of social cohesion and of our capacity to solve shared problems. It is considered "good business" to encourage the breakdown of society into smaller and smaller parts, because it creates more individual buying units, thus more profits. Yet, this is the "Achilles heel" of our present system, and ultimately cannot last.

The social, economic, and environmental difficulties we now face are all interconnected. "Individuality" is the ideal of our society, and new forms of families and lifestyles are emerging that represent a break from the nuclear family and "norms" of society. New names to describe them are also emerging: singles, single parents, mingles, childless couples, housemates, voluntary families, empty nesters, and gay/lesbian couples. Although many of the changes are the positive results of liberation movements and increased individual

freedom, alienation and loneliness are often the byproducts. As Corinne McLaughlin and Gordon Davidson write:

> Until recently a true sense of neighborhood existed in most places in this country, as people helped each other in work projects like barn raising and in times of crisis. They shared meals and childcare. Only as our society has become more technological, with increased wealth and urban growth and transient patterns, have people lost touch with a strong community consciousness. They have greater individual freedom, but the cost has been social isolation.[11]

In addition to the isolation, there is a growing "permanent" underclass, as well as a precipitous rise in homelessness; chemical dependency; dysfunctionality; mental illness; spousal, elder, and child

"One of the greatest sources of violence on the planet is unwanted, uncared for, unloved children. Such children as they grow older are not only typically angry and prone to violence, but are potential time-bombs that can capriciously explode and destroy whatever is around them." [12]

— *Diana Alstad &*
Joel Kramer,
The Guru Papers

Mothers' fears for kids: Education costs, violence

Study Finds Rural Children Poorer Than City Children

Shocking Find — 19 Children in Filthy Flat

U.S. Children Going Hungry, Study Says

Is Day Care Bad for Infants?
Penn State professor points to 'disquieting' find

Troubled kids leaving marks on the suburbs

Mothers who work have few options

Kids or Prisons?

Poor kids often home alone

Oakland Expands Plan To Help Latch-Key Kids

Children At Risk In the City

San Francisco Chronicle
THE VOICE OF THE WEST
We have the worst child welfare record in the state

Media Is Stealing Children's Innocence

Portraits of Childhood Emotion

WHAT ARE WE GOING TO DO ABOUT DAY CARE?

Art therapists help draw out the

S.F. FIRM CASHES IN ON CHILD-CARE DILEMMA

Day-Care Crisis Must Be Resolved

"Children truly cared for and cared about seldom commit crimes; thus, anything done to improve child care will help reduce crime." [13]

— *Gene Stephens,*
The 1990's and Beyond

The Mainstreaming Of Single Motherhood

25% of all children are now born out of wedlock

'Feminization of Poverty' Derided by Economist

More Divorced Women Risk Falling Into Poverty

ASSOCIATED PRESS

Growing numbers of women are at risk of retiring in poverty, according to a pair of new studies that blame no-fault divorce laws and antiquated pens...

Single Dads Lead More Families

Changes in society, laws brought major shift in '8(

By Judy Miller and Tim Schreiner Chronicle Staff Writers

Bad Times Seen For Singled Housewives

WASHINGTON POST

A new report warns of the worsening of the nation's 15.8 million...

OMS: Single Mothers Still Feel Under Attack

or Single Parents, Love Comes Last

BEYOND 'MURPHY BROWN' **Single Parents Struggle With Poverty**

By Jonathan Marshall Chronicle Economics Editor

The Nuclear Family Goes Boom! Big Increase in Number of Single Fathers

Deadbeat Dads

Kids Feel Mom's Stress

S.F. FIRM CASHES IN ON CHILD-CARE DILEMMA

SLRC

abuse; financial inequities; racism; sexism and economic exploitation. These ailments and the accompanying fragmentation deeply affect all of us, but especially our children. The time and energy spent by a single parent or two employed parents on commuting and earning money in a failing economy, can rob children of sufficient love and attention. We are all familiar with the syndrome of "latchkey children," but now there is also the emotional trauma of car key children — children spending hours in cars being driven from here to there with little opportunity to play, learn, or interact with others.

The single parent, usually female, finds it difficult, if not impossible, to serve the dual role of a mother/father and expose children to a wide range of interests, views, and alternative gender roles.

Most single parents are highly motivated people, but as "super moms" or dads they can become over-stressed in trying to fulfill their children's basic needs. Time, energy, and opportunities run out for everyone.

In the 1992 Presidential campaign rhetoric about family values, Dan Quayle brought the issue of single parenting to the surface. He was right in his statement that single parenting is on the rise. The problem with Quayle's remarks is that single parenting was addressed as a moral issue rather than as a broader socioeconomic and cultural one.

More and more of our children suffer from the loss of other adult role models, of shared family meals, of contact with elders and men, of shared responsibilities, and of a sense of community that the extended family and village once provided.

"What kids need most is a dad," proclaims an article in the February '92 issue of *Readers Digest:*

> Somehow men have got to find a place for themselves in the family. We're only beginning to see some of the consequences of fatherlessness, especially where boys are concerned…a society of children who don't understand men produces men who don't understand themselves. [16]

We need to reaffirm and elevate the importance of supportive and multiple adult role models, the presence of men and fathers with women and mothers in caring relationships, and the new extended family and "community" as criteria for a strengthened person and society.

The heritage of village life and the extended family, common among our Latino, Asian, and Afro-American populations, has stabilized their communities in the face of racial prejudices and economic adversity. These populations benefit culturally, socially, and economically from extended family relationships, often missing for White single-parent families.

However, Latino, Asian, and Afro-American ethnic groups are apt to forsake their cultures as they try to follow the consumptive and over-rated individualistic lifestyle of White, middle-income society. Illusions about the "American Dream" have influenced some within these ethnic groups to mimic the fragmented social and family patterns of the White, Euro-American population. More and more minority people are seeking to improve their lot by moving to single-family houses. This increases the number of small social units each living separately, using energy and resources separately,

and bringing separate cars up to the kitchen door. These practices are physically and socially alienating and environmentally damaging, regardless of a person's race, age, gender, or income.

Due to the declining economy and to automation, fewer industrial, service, and corporate jobs will be available to these ethnic minority groups. And due to the environmental necessity to conserve resources and energy, these groups will be even less able to upgrade their status individually, let alone attain the "American Dream." They and White people must share the responsibility for creating an ecologically sustainable community structure in which cooperation becomes the key for a higher quality of living.

We do not advocate a simple return to the conventional extended family of the past, with a patriarchal family head and secondary and oppressed roles for women and children. Instead, we advocate a new type of voluntary extended family that supports the needs of all people and family types for gender equality, personal growth, self-expression, mutual responsibility, and respect for individuality. Together we must learn to sustain the diversity and richness of our multi-cultural heritage.

"By the year 2000, one out of every three Americans will be a member of a minority group. At present, one out of every four American children is born into poverty, and the rate is increasing. While it was once possible for people to succeed in this society if they were simply willing to work hard, it is increasingly difficult for the poorly educated to find jobs." [17]

— Task Force on Teaching as a Profession

"In the end, our individual presence rests forever in the collective soul of the unfolding process itself. To conserve as best we can the fixed endowment that was left to us, and to respect as best we can the natural rhythm that governs the becoming process, is to express our ultimate love for all life that preceded us and all life that will follow. To be aware of this dual responsibility is the first step towards our transformation from a colonizing to a climatic mode. We are the stewards of the world." [18]

— Jeremy Rifkin

"Of course, wealthier Americans have been withdrawing into their own neighborhoods and clubs for generations. But the new secession is more dramatic because the highest earners now inhabit a different economy from other Americans. The new elite is linked by jet, modem, fax, satellite and fiber-optic cable to the great commercial and recreational centers of the world, but it is not particularly connected to the rest of the nation." [19]

*— Robert B. Reich,
in Creating Community Anywhere*

The Ecological Imperative — *saving the family and the planet by creating community*

This society, meaning all of us, has set the world-wide example for consumptive behavior. This behavior is epitomized by our ways of using land and resources to build and maintain urban sprawl, which produces serious consequences for the environment, community and family structure, our physical and emotional health, and our quality of living in general. It is imperative that we each assume responsibility and come together to establish ecological communities that can save ourselves and the planet from social and environmental disaster.

In the traditional extended family that existed, if only in a limited sense, until very recently in America, childcare, cooking, housekeeping and maintenance, care of animals, and gardening were shared by the entire family and others. Even in towns and cities, extended families lived together in large houses, in the same tenement building, or close by in the neighborhood.

It is understandable that so many of today's working parents feel taxed beyond their limits. We are asking them to do by themselves what mothers, fathers, grandparents, aunts, uncles, cousins, and hired hands used to do together.

The separation of workplace from the home environment, the long commutes, fixed working hours, computerized assembly-line production and specialization of labor, and the dependence on food and goods from distant sources all came about very recently in human history and translate into heavy energy use and isolation. Before the Industrial Revolution, many of the separatist practices we now take for granted would have been unthinkable, especially the harsh distinction between the work and home environment and the all-day absence of both men and women from the home.

Our dependence upon the car and its cohort, the single-family house in the suburbs, has seriously contributed to the fragmentation of the extended family and a lower quality of living for more and more people. We can get up in the morning, get in our car, and drive to work without encountering any other person face to face. *Is this the American Dream?* The way our neighborhoods are laid out and our housing is financed ensures that residential areas are segregated by economic class, age, and race. *Is this the American Dream?* It is obvious that the housing industry has not been a social/family/ community oriented process, but merely a way of doing business and making a profit, as if a house were like any other product sold over the counter. *Is this the only American Dream?*

Communication and Community

The common root of the words "community" and "communicate" is the Latin "communes," meaning common.[26] In this book we use "communicate" to mean: to share, impart, or partake of, and to participate in the process of passing ideas, services, or goods on to others in words, writing, and other forms of conveyance. To this definition, we add that human communication at its best implies both a speaker and listener, a sender and receiver, in an actual face-to-face experience.

It is necessary to differentiate between the socially and culturally sustainable person-to-person communication and what the marketplace calls "communication." We have satellites, fax machines, high speed/quality copiers, computers and modems,

TV's and VCR's, interactive video, voice mail, car-phones, beepers, answering machines, video-phones, and various other combinations. Yes, more people throughout the world can contact each other, exchange information faster, and travel and learn about other cultures and ways of living. And yes, very busy family members, friends, and co-workers can be in touch via these devices and share information that they might otherwise miss out on in their hectic lives. But the increased tempo, the rat-race, and the technology also interfere with communication.

Real person-to-person communication includes body language, eye contact, the ambience of the setting, and the feelings you share — the romance of the moment. Talking to someone on the phone or via a fax machine often spells the loss of this romance and of the subsequent intimacy and sense of community. How often do you hang up after talking to a dear friend and still yearn to see or touch them?

Tragically, communication technology, instead of bringing us together or educating us, encourages alienation, segregation, and misinformation. The growing number of low-income people who have already been cut off, culturally and economically, from the benefits of the system are further isolated by their inability to purchase and use new communication devices. Older generations of people are likewise affected. Unwilling or unable to keep up with new technologies, they are often alienated from the outside world.

Youths and children, as well as adults, are getting a distorted view of life from the most prevalent communication device — TV. "Hollywood" news and entertainment are overwhelmingly nega-tive and sensationalistic, most often emphasizing sex, violence, and the exploitation of women. The topics of guns, rape, psychotics, revenge, lawlessness, and all manner of negative behavior are being exploited primarily to make a profit. The pander-

"Why Can't I Cope?"

Reprinted with permission from
the Child Care Resource Center, Inc.

"To an increasing extent in today's workplace, computers are delegated the role of supervising; human beings have been assigned roles that involve working faster and faster while engaging in less social conversation — and all this in the name of a system called 'communications,' but one that drastically limits people's ability to communicate in a human sense."[20]
— *Langdon Winner,
"Artifact/Ideas and Human Culture"*

"The froth and frenzy of industrial civilization mask our deep loneliness for the communion with the world that can lift our spirits and fill our senses with the richness and immediacy of life itself."[21]
— *Al Gore*

"In the final analysis, the smartest way to save energy and promote a healthy and wise planet is to unplug the television set completely."[22]
— *Gar Smith,
Earth Island Institute*

"In the West we pride ourselves on our individualism, but sometimes individualism is a euphemism for isolation." [23]
— *Helena Norberg-Hodge*

"Aside from transmitting facts and figures the new media tools, like the pulpit in Gutenberg's times, can powerfully affect people's attitudes and behavior, good and bad. They can build consensus and they can confuse and popularize people.... we live in times of profound transformations, requiring enormous educational efforts. Will the grabbag loosely called 'multi-media' contribute towards that end? Gutenberg would certainly be intrigued." [24]
— *Hartmut Gerdes, "Multimedia — Good Bye Herr Gutenberg!?"*

ing by commercial interests to this lowest common denominator has replaced community with mistrust and fear.

There should no longer be any doubt that heavy exposure to television and film violence is one of the causes of aggressive behavior, crime, and violence in society... we have learned a lot about the dimensions of this effect since it was first reported in the 1960's. We know that television and film violence can affect youngsters of all ages, of both genders, at all socioeconomic levels and all levels of intelligence. The effect is not limited to children who are already disposed to being aggressive... young children imitate what they see others do — particularly if the other is a desirable hero with whom the youngster can identify. [25]

These phenomena have led to communication barriers between "you" and "me." In today's society, it takes tremendous will and planned circumstances to seek closeness, ask for help, or to help someone else.

The lack of regular communication at home between elders, parents, youths, and children not only contributes to our alienation and isolation but is unhealthy as well. Living and communicating with others carries with it the bonus of better health, as discovered by numerous medical studies. Dr. Redford Williams at the Duke University Medical Center in North Carolina followed up 1,368 patients nine years after they were tested for heart disease. Those living alone were three times more apt to die in five years than patients living in a family setting. In another study, Dr. Maurizo

Trevian at the University of Buffalo established that blood pressure was lowest in men from larger living groups. Women did better, even those living alone, because of the tendency for women to stay in closer touch with their kin and friends.

Communication also helps relieve pressures associated with a change in family composition or relationships, such as the arrival of a first baby. As Jerry Caroll wrote in "How the First Baby Tests a Marriage,"

Younger couples who don't have a long period of kinship to fall back on have a tougher time of (raising their first child). Research indicates a majority of new-parent couples experience "moderate or severe crisis..." In 12.5% of the marriages studied, couples were divorced by the time the child was a year and a half old.... Husbands and wives who got together in groups to talk about what was happening to them with the new baby were less apt to separate or divorce than those who tried to muddle through on their own. [26]

New mothers alone at home are especially vulnerable to the stress of trying to cope with the new responsibilities. According to Dr. Marianne Neifert, a clinical associate professor of pediatrics at the University of Colorado School of Medicine in Denver, "Many of the mothers who work right up to delivery enter labor already exhausted and never do catch up. They don't take a honeymoon with their baby because they are too busy trying to do tasks that they placed on themselves." [27]

Deep, personal communication, which includes sharing of feelings, values, experiences, and knowledge, is rare because the common physical setting and social context that encourage such a level of verbal exchange are missing. In earlier times, these person-to-person practices were the common social and civil experiences between groups of people in extended family, village, and larger community groups, and were the way that people personalized and civilized their methods of self-governance. In various village societies, people shared land in common, a practice that facilitated their survival through their ability to communicate. The most meaningful communication occurred in a common physical setting, often times in a specially designed place for sharing with others, such as a village square, town hall, and convention centers. It is the presence of warm human bodies, the expressions on faces, the fine nuances of voice tone and inflection, face and eye gestures, and the body language that mark the most memorable storytelling and human communication experiences.

Garrison Keillor, on one of his recent Lake Wobegone programs, notes that the person-to-person story is at the essence of a sustainable culture. "I change your story some as I tell it again and you change my story some as you pass it on, and our stories waft out into the world, personalized and enriched with human idioms. Changed stories are more fun and probably travel further. Somehow the story makes the world better, it doesn't suffer for the changing of it. The world only suffers when there is no story."[28]

The world now is suffering from too few stories, the kind told during coffee breaks, at meal times, within families, to children, between friends, at the end of the day and the end of lives. But where in a city of loners, singles, couples, and small families does storytelling get started and where can it go?

Modern life and media technology do not provide the communication opportunities that increased frequency of shared meal times in an appropriately designed common dining place could — this is where communication becomes community.

Women, Men, and Community

Women are experiencing a growing desire to move away from hierarchical, male-dominated relationships and to seek safer and more caring personal and family relationships. This represents a general shift away from male-dominated leadership and authority in religion, education, the workplace, government, and the military.

Women's new roles are precipitating much-needed major changes in social, family, political, and economic institutions that were formed over many centuries. As more opportunities for women become available and acceptable, men have had to reevaluate their assumed roles in society and in the family. Some of the initial results of this cultural transformation have been an increase in divorce, single-parent families, women choosing to put off childbearing indefinitely, a new acceptance of non-monogamous relationships, more gay and lesbian domestic partnerships, people of all ages choosing to remain single, and smaller nuclear families with mostly two employed parents.

These changes could rightfully be called the most epic cultural revolution since the change from agrarian to industrial society. This transformation in demographics and values, although liberating for women and men in many ways, has created the opposite of what most people desire, which is a supportive and secure place to live. The trend towards more single people and single parents,

"…before the Industrial Revolution, the quality of an institution that guaranteed its permanence was stability, now the desirable quality is flexibility, adaptability. Consequently institutions that were strong under the old order are found to be weak, unable to survive, under the new. One institution for which this is particularly true is the patriarchal family. Its magnificent, rock-like strength and inflexibility become under the new conditions, the very cause of its doom. Resistant to change, it proves, in an era when all is changing, incapable of survival."[29]
— *David & Vera Mace, Marriage: East and West*

"…there is often a big difference in the living standards of divorced fathers and divorced mothers with children. After divorce the average annual income of mothers and children is $13,500 for whites and $9,000 for nonwhites, as compared with $25,000 for white nonresident fathers and $13,600 for nonwhite nonresident fathers… Half the single mothers in the United States live below the poverty line."[30]
— *Barbara Dafoe Whitehead, Atlantic Monthly*

comprising 39% of the population, has been translated by developers into a "demand" for more small, single-family units. This assumption leads to devastating environmental consequences — car-dependent, single-family houses spreading out, cancer-like, to consume farmland and open space. Many single and divorced women trying to be responsibly independent cannot afford this new commuter housing. Income restraints compel many of them to rent or buy smaller or older places in the city, sometimes in unsafe neighborhoods. Given the economic disparities between men and women, discrimination in the workplace, and the lack of affordable and quality childcare, women are virtually guaranteed to experience a poorer quality of living.

Women typically earn 70% of what men earn for the same jobs, and the number of single-parent families is on the rise. The result is the feminization of poverty, with 50% of all single women and single mothers living below the poverty line and many more teetering on the edge.

What most women want from "liberation" is to be free of domination and gender constraints, which does not have to mean living alone in isolation and economic vulnerability. Of all those who attend SLRC workshops and complete the profile exercises, it is women who most seek community as an end to the loneliness of being single or trying to be a breadwinner, spouse, parent, and expressive individual all at once. It is not surprising that women have been and will continue to be catalysts in the Shared Living Community movement, because it is they who most often feel the brunt of society's ills. Social problems such as domestic violence, a lack of safety for women living alone, and double standards for men and women all contribute to women's desire to form community where they can determine new roles in a setting more responsive to their needs.

Men at SLRC workshops say that they also do not want to live alone without women around. They see community as a way of becoming liberated from the traditional roles of being the leader, the

BELOW THE POVERTY LINE[34]

These figures represent the increase in the percentage of people below the poverty line from 1970 to 1990.

	White	Black	Latino	Overall	(no data on Asians)
Male/Female	10.7%	31.9%	28.1%	13.5%	
Children	15.1%	44.2%	39.7%	19.9%	
Single mothers	12.8%	60.1%	24.2%	21.9%*	

*(with children under the age of 6)

The poverty level in 1990 was $7,829 for a two-person family, $10,419 for a three-person family, and $13,359 for a four-person family. These figures are national averages and do not take into account differences in the cost of living from region to region. This means that a four-person family living in San Francisco and earning $14,000 a year fares worse than a four-person family living in Des Moines and earning $13,000, even though the family in San Francisco earns more and is, statistically speaking, above the poverty line.

sole wage earner, the only "responsible" head of household, and numerous other labels that society assigns to them as men.

The favorable atmosphere that community creates for women and men is exemplified by the Intentional Community movement which began over 50 years ago in this country and Europe. These communities differ markedly from the anti-authority "communes" of the 1960's, and practice various models of democratic and participatory management and gender-equal interactions.

In most of these communities, you will find rotating responsibilities between men, women, and children for almost every function: food growing and processing, meal preparation, childcare, management, decision making, and livelihood through cottage industry and outside jobs and businesses. Women and men have opportunities for mutual respect as equal partners to find new ways of relating in trusting relationships. As Keenan, a member of Twin Oaks community, explains:

> Women at Twin Oaks (a community in Louisa, Virginia) don't have to sacrifice careers in order to have children or maintain a home. Women don't have to quit their jobs because of husbands who get more lucrative work in another part of the country. There is no cultural norm that sneers at women who wish to pursue professional careers…. At Twin Oaks there are constant opportunities for women to take on responsibility and gain skills they had little exposure to in mainstream society, like business management, construction, auto mechanics…in fact, women and men occupy positions of responsibility equal

to their numbers in the community.

There are exceptions, as in communities with hierarchical male leaders or spiritual gurus in which traditional gender roles prevail. Within some of these spiritual communities women have a strong voice in participative decision-making councils, but are still barred from leadership roles. In contrast, "we find that communities with the consensus method of decision-making have the most gender-equal power structure," says Caroline Estes, one of the founding members of Alpha Farm Community in Deadwood, Oregon. She is an example of a strong woman who contributes generously to her community, giving workshops on facilitation of meetings using consensus, and serving as a conference coordinator.

The Aging of America
— a change we cannot change

A whole society aging at once? This is an unprecedented phenomenon that will add more strain to the sustainability of the American society. Not only are we aging as a society, with the number of persons over 65 expected to more than double by 2050, but we are aging differently than ever before. We have more people growing older actively, living longer, healthier lives, and working long past the so-called retirement age. They are no longer primary consumers or raising families, and their interests have changed to travel, gardening, cultural and educational pursuits, volunteering, and enjoying their grandchildren. Many are working full or part-time to supplement their fixed incomes.

Many older people are barely making it, though,

"Communal life demands the ability to communicate and cooperate. These skills help people move out of their gender roles, men by the need to listen better and women by the need to assert more. Once these skills are developed both men and women find they can communicate better with friends and lovers as well. It is vital to the long term existence of an egalitarian community that each member believe they are equal to every other member."[35]
— *Keenan, "Equality and Sexism at Twin Oaks"*

"The oldest baby boomers are now but 23 years away from reaching current age of retirement. The longer today's generations fail to reduce the deficits, increase savings and invest in the future of the next generation, the more likely it is that the American future will consist of depression and a war between the young and the old…"[36]
— *Philip Longman, "Age War"*

"More than 54 percent of those over age 85 are living independently, yet health and mobility often decline with age. Disabilities, which affect 46 percent of people over 85, include mobility, hearing, and vision impairments. Other difficulties stem from older people's reduced incomes, often a half to a third less in retirement than during the wage-earning years. Old people must also cope with the loss of family and friends, seeking other sources of companionship, support, or assistance." [37]
— *Valerie Parker, Sherry Edmonds & Virginia Robinson, "A Change for the Better"*

"[There is a] rise of dramatically different 'cultures' in America — the culture of the old and the culture of the young. The old, self-indulgent in their withdrawal into protected enclaves, invite the contempt of the young. The young, by their heedless pursuit of self-fulfillment, self-realization, [and] self-expression… deepen their alienation from the old…" [38]
— *Page Smith, "Why Young and Old Need Each Other"*

according to U.S. Census data. Gene Stephens, writing in *The 1990's and Beyond* says that, "As the percentage of the population in the elderly ranks increases, the number of elderly living in poverty or just above the poverty line increases. Studies show some elderly steal (usually shoplift) out of need, while others pay for the necessities of life and steal the luxuries they can no longer afford." [39]

Can the generation war be avoided?

The aging of America is and will continue to aggravate economic decline. As the number of elderly in poverty and lower incomes increases, they will buy less, thus reducing the total demand for goods. This will likely cause the remaining population of younger working people to pay more per product sold due to the decreased volume of production. Due to the decreased demand for goods combined with the increased use of automation and computers in the workplace, there will likely be fewer jobs for younger workers, decreasing the market even more. Elders will continue to work because their pensions, investments, and/or social security will not be enough to sustain them and

According to *Sixty-five Plus in America*, the number of people over 65 will more than double by the year 2050. While Whites make up the highest number, note that percentile increase pales in comparison with aging Black and Latino populations. [40]

People Over 65

	1992	2050	Percent of increase (SLRC)
White	28.0 million	53.9 million	193%
Black	2.5 m	9.6 m	374
Latino	1.1 m	7.9 m	718
Other	0.6 m	5.0 m	833

because their skills and experience are valuable and inexpensively obtained. The average take-home pay will probably be less per household than it is today, as it is already smaller than a generation ago. Also, taxes may be higher for the younger generations, while the larger number of elderly will be paying less taxes per person. However, older peoples' demands for public services will not be reduced.

The "generation war," the social/financial crisis postulated by the above dichotomy between future younger workers and seniors, will happen if this country continues in its socially alienated, resource wasteful, and separatist ways. Instead of treating people, workers, and housing as commodities to be discarded when their wealth or productivity wanes, we should encourage extended family communities that can bring older and younger people together. There is no better time than now for rebuilding community in America. We have the reasons and most of the tools. We need to change financing policies and rebuild our communities into supportive mixed-age family living environments, thereby enabling youth and seniors to help one another.

Housing our aging society

The housing needs of older Americans are not being met in an imaginative and sensitive way. Subsidized senior apartments, old age homes, and nursing homes for the frail and those requiring total care are often bleak institutions which have no other purpose than to store the vegetating elderly. "Retirement communities" are typically very expensive, and more and more seniors do not like them because there are no younger people around, they feel out of touch with the real world, and they get bored doing the same managed activities all the time. And

---

Median household income/year for people 65 years and older[41]

(in $1,000's)

$100+	$80-100	$60-80	$40-60	$20-40	$10-20	under $10
2.1%	1.7%	3.3%	8.4%	26.9%	29.6%	28.0%

The poverty level for people 65 and over is lower than that for younger people. For a single person over 65, it is $5,767; for a two-person family it is $7,273. Based on these figures, over 25% of senior households are at or near the poverty level, which isn't to say the other 75% are living in affluence. The poverty level is an average figure determined by the federal government and does not necessarily take into account what is really required to survive and thrive.

---

as Patrick Hare comments:

> The typical single family home was designed for people who would never lose physical abilities. It is not a good home for someone who can't drive, use stairs, do at least simple home maintenance, or who cannot live alone without getting depressed.[42]

Senior house sharing, where an older person shares their large house with helpers/renters, with other seniors, or with younger people and single parents who together form a voluntary family, has increased dramatically in recent times and provides a partial answer to the senior housing problem. There are currently over 500 senior house-share organizations run by nonprofits and local government in the U.S. There is a need for more shared households where the seniors manage and cook for themselves, or hire a cook/housekeeper. The greater need is to prevent isolation of older people and integrate them into a community.

As Baby Boomers and other younger generations age, this trend is likely to increase. As one participant in an SLRC consultation session explains, "I am concerned about the long-term future,

and I don't want to spend my final days in a sterile 'rest-home' full of old people sitting around a television watching soap operas. I want to be part of a multi-generational community for my entire life."

The wisdom of elders

With the increase in the numbers of active, longer-lived older people comes opportunity for the cultural sustainability of our society. There is such a phenomenon as "wisdom of the elders." The development and sustainability of a culture has traditionally depended upon the stories and interchange between elders and youths, as was common in tribal, village, and extended family societies. We now have the opportunity to draw upon this tradition for strength and guidance. As Napolean Kruger, a Native American elder, says:

> You don't have to be a highly educated person to understand the simple truths that our Elders are speaking about. For there is much wisdom in the few words that each of our Elders speak…. Many of these things that are happening today were predicted by the Elders

"Until retirement was invented (very recently, incidentally), people did not regard the old as mentally deficient. Much more commonly the citizenry in general regarded the old as 'wise'… In a technological society, which lives by innovation, wisdom is replaced by knowledge — and yesterday's knowledge is useless."[43]

— *Page Smith*

Shared Housing =
Medicaid Savings

Shared Housing offers an alternative for people who cannot or choose not to live alone but do not need residential or nursing home care. It saves on health care expenditures because it does not cost as much to operate as licensed care homes, and because people who choose to live with others naturally help one another.[44]

— *Shared Housing News*

Photo by Greenbelt Alliance

"The Governmental Accounting Office has calculated that if present trends continue, traffic congestion in the United States will triple in only 15 years, even if we increase road capacity by 20 percent, a goal that is unlikely to be achieved." [45]
— *Union of Concerned Scientists*

a long time ago. And our living Elders are now repeating the prophecies of those Elders who have passed on to the Spirit World…. If all people, world-wide, will look up, listen to, and respect their Elders then many wonderful things and natural healings will start to happen once again. [46]

More Car Trips and There Go Our Lungs, the Ozone Layer, Our Skin
— and our sanity!

The Federal Environmental Protection Agency (EPA) that is responsible for monitoring air emissions and other concerns has been slow to measure the impact of rampant urban sprawl and freeway building on air quality. They try to regulate car exhaust and industrial smoke stack emissions, but

their mandate appears to be limited to measuring the symptoms. It does not extend to the broader socioeconomic and environmental effects in both urban and rural regions, caused by housing and job related development, building construction, and transportation practices. These are considerations that must be added to EPA equations for a healthy environment. Such a policy would serve as a catalyst for major positive changes in planning and housing policies.

Home buyers have few choices in transportation. They are only guaranteed long car trips, ozone depletion, and a house they may never be able to sell because of the oversupply of remote location tracts that are too far from services. In many of this country's urban regions, commutes of 60 or more miles each way are not uncommon. Americans drove one trillion more miles in 1990 than they did in 1973, and since 1982, gas consumption has gone up 10%. [47] Improved fuel consumption and cleaner fuels will not be enough, because increased emissions from car trips generated by faulty land use policy will soon exceed the emission levels previously set. According to Andrew Kleit, an expert at the Federal Trade Commission, if higher fuel standards for car manufacturers induce people "to get higher-mileage cars, they will drive more because the cost per mile is less. It will be cheaper to drive than to take the bus." [48] It is also worth noting that fuel standards for new cars have little to no effect on cars already in existence: "New cars could run 100 miles on a single drop of gasoline, without making much of an immediate dent in total fuel consumption simply because each years' autoproduction represents only about 7 percent of cars on the road." [49]

Electric cars will eventually reduce some need for petroleum based fuel, but recharging batteries will increase fuel consumption and pollution by power plants, transferring car pollution "upstream". This critique is not to discourage a reduction in the use of fossil fuels and an appropriate increase in the use of electric cars. This is a reminder that we need comprehensive ecologically sustainable energy and resource management policies, such as requiring a comprehensive Environmental Impact Report regarding electric cars. The California Environmental Quality Act (CEQA) is an example of an environmental policy that is not living up to its intention. Michael T. Henn, assistant planning director for the city of Lafayette, California (APA newsletter), criticizes the act as being too lenient in defining environmentally friendly development, allowing local politics and whims rather than objective analysis to determine the direction of development.

We must be willing to question the whole concept of single-occupancy vehicle usage as well as every aspect of our car-intensive lifestyle. During the 1980's, California's population increased by 26%, roadways grew by 1.9%, and traffic increased by 55%.[50] Even if we paved over the whole country, we could hardly build freeways fast enough to keep up with car use. Californians spend an average of 84 hours a year sitting in traffic jams — that's 10-1/2 work days, or a two-week vacation. And let's not forget the time it takes to run local errands. Think of what could be done with this time if it were available for our own and our families' productive efforts. And think about the emotional and cultural development of a child who is shuttled back and forth daily in a car with only one or two other people. They could learn more about life and

Photo by Greenbelt Alliance

The Root Source of the "Car Problem"
Planting single-family houses in outlying farmland or open space areas is directly responsible for the drastic increase of car trips generated per family. As a result, we have more air pollution, run-away freeway and street building, longer commutes, the fragmentation of family and community, and less personal time for self. The solution to these ills of "modern living" is not an improved-upon car with electric batteries and electronic highways; that will only invite more suburban sprawl like in the photo above. The answer lies in alternative designs for housing, land use, and transportation systems that drastically reduce the need for cars, such as Shared Living Communities.

"Half of all trips we take, and four-fifths of all commutes, are made by a single person alone in a car. To accommodate this habit, we now own enough cars to put every American in one — and no one would have to sit in the back seat."[51]
— Union of Concerned Scientists

"Large stretches of land have been given over to the automobile and its infrastructure. Parking a car at home, the office, and the shopping mall requires on average 4,000 square feet of asphalt. Over 60,000 square miles of land in the United States have been paved over: That works out to about 2 percent of the total surface area, and to 10 percent of the arable land. World-wide, at least a third of an average city's land is devoted to roads, parking lots, and other elements of a car infrastructure. In American cities, close to half of all the urban space goes to accommodate the automobile; in Los Angeles, the figure reaches two-thirds." [52]
— *Michael Remmer*
"Rethinking the Role of the Automobile"

"A growing number of commuters also have children in child-care. That poses a dilemma their parents never faced: Should they leave their children behind with care-givers in that nice suburban neighborhood where they moved to raise a family? Or should they commute with them to a child-care center close to work so that they can rush to them for lunch or emergencies?" [53]
— *Sue Shellenbarger*

people if they spent that car time playing with their peers and helping adults in an extended family village.

The president of California's largest single-family home building company, Bruce Karatz of Kaufman and Broad, says longer commutes are inevitable. "Driving further and further out to work is a cycle that's been going on long before you or I were born."[54] To blithely dismiss the never-ending spiral of longer and longer commutes as part of some cosmic cycle over which we humans have no control is

Bradley Inman

a pretty terrifying attitude. Just as with the shrinking Dream House, one is tempted to ask, "Where does it end?" Can we really expect people to drive 100 miles to work, just to live in a house they can afford? How about 150 miles? 200?

If Mr. Karatz, the homebuilder, is correct, and "driving further and further out to work" is an inevitable cycle, what will happen to our rural and wilderness areas? In California and elsewhere, the answer is clear: Except for a few protected areas, the whole state is up for grabs. His firm alone plans to build 20,000 homes by the year 2000 in such remote areas as Kern, Stanislaus, Merced, northern Stockton, San Bernardino and Riverside counties, and the northern tip of Los Angeles County, 84 miles from downtown Los Angeles, spreading urban sprawl over farmland, open space, deserts, and forest.[55]

How we use land and cars and provide housing are the first places to make fundamental changes in public policy. Builders claim, and financially strapped city governments willingly believe, for tax purposes, that building conventional suburban-style, single-family houses on virgin land is the only way to create "affordable" housing. The social, health, and ecological costs of the sprawl, the car dependency, and the mega-commutes are not figured into the costs of housing or government. Further, local government's dependence on tax revenues generated by a single kind of usage such as sales taxes from retail sales encourages land-use planning to maximize tax revenues rather than sustainability. While this leap-frogging of housing tracts into the country continues, the older suburbs and inner cities are left with an underutilized infrastructure of utilities, streets, transit systems, schools, hospitals, and employment centers. This resource waste should be a subject for state and federal legislative investigation hearings — let's get serious about ecology and sustainability.

Developer and lending interests need guidance. They need to re-think their dependency on subdividing sensitive urban fringe lands into separate lots, as if that were the only possible way to serve housing needs and stay in business. Ultimately, either through self-interest (when they realize the single-family house is obsolete) or citizen advocacy, developers and lenders will be forced to change their ways. The issue is multi-faceted and so deeply ingrained in the fabric of our society that all people, including every department of every government agency, and all private businesses, must be involved. The leadership required must be backed up by the kind of cooperative human spirit that permeated such group achievements as the community barn raising and the harvest, which were the initial strengths of our society.

We come now to the most significant "bottom line" challenge of all—we have the power to drastically reduce the number of car trips generated each day per family by making it possible for more people to design and build cooperatively owned and self-managed cluster housing communities. We need to specifically demand pedestrian and transit-fed neighborhoods that support ecologically sustainable daily lifestyles. We are capable of achieving this goal, but the responsibility lies very heavily on each of us. We must learn to cooperate with others in a community effort in order to change our consumptive lifestyles and "get people out of their cars." This approach can empower people to rebuild community from the local to the national

levels, unifying our interests and energies and saving costs, for today and tomorrow.

The Myth of Home Ownership

The prospect of everyone owning their own home evokes a nightmare image of endless single-family houses, apartment buildings, and condos sprawling over hill and dale, destroying farmland and forests, leading to increased car dependency, further fragmentation, excessive energy and resource consumption, and continued ecological damage. Neither the market nor the environment can support everyone in fulfilling this "American Dream."

Most White Americans are descendents of immigrants who came here seeking freedom and the chance to own land. Few opportunities existed in the Industrial Age factory towns and cities of the East, so settlers migrated westward. Government policies, such as the Homestead Act of 1862, allowed thousands of settlers to claim "unoccupied" land in the West (much of the land was actually the homeland or hunting ground of Native American tribes).

Mass home ownership came later through the mass-produced and financed single-family, "factory worker" tract house. Americans flocked to this model of housing in the late 1930's, when it was popularized by President Franklin D. Roosevelt's "New Deal" and the Federal Housing Administration's (FHA) home mortgage guarantee program which over the years has enabled about two-thirds of all Americans to own their own homes.

The economic reality of today however is that real estate speculation has steadily fueled rising prices while fewer Americans, especially women, single parents, younger people, new immigrants, and all

"Poor people, namely the inner cities, are subsidizing this society's love affair with the automobile. Poor communities pay a horrendous price through freeway blight in their communities and damaged health from living in high concentrations of auto emissions and smog. They also spend a higher percentage of income on basic energy and transportation needs than do middle class and wealthy households." [56]

— Henry Holmes
"Transportation, Social Justice and Sustainibility"

"The home, once a place where family members lived a close, self-contained life together, anchored to the land that provided for their needs, now became the place to which they returned periodically, from pursuing their separate individual enterprises, for food, rest and sleep." [57]

— David & Vera Mace

those of lower income, are able to afford the "American Dream." Real estate advertisements extol ways to "beat the system" in order to gain home ownership, but this involves: two incomes, large payments, long commutes, poor neighborhoods, smaller houses, or expensive "fixer-uppers."

62 S. E. GROSS, CHICAGO.

THE WORKING MAN'S REWARD.

WHERE ALL WAS DARKNESS, NOW IS LIGHT.

A HOME AT $10.00 A MONTH

S.E. GROSS'

ASHLAND AVE AND 47TH STREET SUBDIVISION

BRANCH OFFICE COR. ASHLAND AVE & 47TH ST.

South-east corner Dearborn and Randolph Sts.

"The Working Man's Reward"
This was the era of large extended families, "full employment," and streetcars.

"Chicago Historical Society Library"
From the Tenth annual illustrated catalogue of S. E. Gross famous city subdivisions and suburban towns, 1891, p. 62

The median price of existing houses in the U.S. has gone from $23,000 to $100,300 since 1970, while the median price of new houses has gone from $23,400 to $120,000. These increases have caused more than a 5% decrease, over the past 10 years, in the number of people between the ages of 35 and 44 who own homes.[60] This statistic is significant because it represents the first time there has ever been a drop. As Leonard Shane, U.S. League of Savings Institutions Chairman points out, "That downturn is not a statistic. That downturn represents a potential change in the American lifestyle."

In high-priced markets like the San Francisco Bay area, buying a house has become nearly impossible except for people with higher incomes. In 1989, only 12% of Bay Area households had the $77,000 annual income required to qualify for a mortgage on a $260,000 house — the median price in the area. Even a $40,000 a year income was hardly enough to finance buying a house; two incomes are often required to make the monthly payments of $2,000 or more. If one partner loses a job, they will probably lose the house. In other parts of the country, housing costs are much less, but so are salaries. As a result, more singles and small families of lower, moderate, and middle income are locked out of ownership. Young families need a secure home the most in their child-raising years. The increasing difficulty in owning a home at this time in their lives is an American tragedy.

The result is more renters, but for many even renting is a hardship now. In Los Angeles, 95% of lower income families pay more than 30% of their income for housing, with the lowest income families spending as much as 77% of their income for housing, leaving little left over for food, clothing, utilities, and fun. New affordable rental housing is not being built, because of zoning restrictions on higher densities in existing low-density urban areas and smaller cities and towns, and because builders and lenders prefer single-family lots and houses, few multi-family rental units are being built anywhere. Many of these people are just one paycheck away from homelessness. An unexpected illness or job layoff could put them on the street. As a result, many live in overcrowded conditions with friends or relatives in older housing neighborhoods that lack security, social stability, or conveniences, and where the absentee owners perform few physical repairs.

The American ideal of "owning" a home and lot represents more than just "buying a house." It is a reflection of our basic instinct and desire for a secure human habitat, to "feather our nest" and provide a place for our families and children. We equate owning a home with settling down, stability, being responsible, and a secure investment "in the future."

People are led to believe that the house they pay for during most of their working days will be a sound investment and a security blanket for their children's college education, vacation trips, retirement, medical emergencies, house repairs and renovations, or starting a new business. Yet many have found this to be a myth because the unstable real estate market and declining economy have given them little, if any, mortgage refinancing capability. As a result, this is the only "developed" country with so much personal insecurity concerning property in the midst of so much emphasis on individual ownership — a dubious claim to fame. The myth of home ownership as a "sound invest-

ment" is further debunked by Jaques Kaswan, Ph.D., a specialist on cooperative housing financing. He points out in a study, "Buying a House as an Investment: A Cautionary Tale," that there are several circumstances where renting or buying into a Limited Equity Housing Cooperative (LEHC) can be financially more advantageous than being committed to a mortgage, with high monthly costs, no liquidity unless by selling or refinancing, and

SLRC

Own Your Home by Yourself and Pay All the Costs by Yourself
Real estate ads have changed little since the 1890s but the family structure has changed drastically, and the single family house for small families has become an economic travesty and an ecological liability.

HOMELESS

HAVE A HOME, CAN'T PAY MORTGAGE

RENTER WITH STAGNANT INCOME

OWN A BUILDING COMPLEX, GETTING KILLED BY HIGH INTEREST RATES AND GENERAL ECONOMIC DOWNTURN...

©1991 NORMAN DOG

Downward Ownership Trend

provides a way for more people to enjoy the sense of ownership and resident control, with the bonus of a supportive community and other amenities not afforded by individual households.

The homeless and at-risk populations

Homelessness is not just a housing or health care issue; it is also a symptom of a massive breakdown of the social, economic, and cultural order. When the cracks in the system open wider and more people fall through, it is due to more than the decline in the economy, loss of jobs, ineptness of government housing, mental health care and welfare policies. The telltale sign of a complex and dysfunctional socioeconomic system is a deteriorating process that feeds upon itself and is amplified by the social isolation, family fragmentation, and lack of support that occurs when everyone tries to make it by themselves.

It is well documented that humans function best in social groupings. The extended family and village ways of life that still prevail in most parts of the world serve as models for how our society can become a village community. One of the contradictions, however, is that poverty is built into the system. Some legislators, homeless nonprofit, and social service agencies depend upon short-term "band-aid" solutions such as shelters and transition housing. These services are supposed to help people get on their feet and return to the mainstream — to compete for the too few jobs and the "affordable" housing. When they do start earning money, they are often booted out and left to fend for themselves. A large percentage of these people fall back into poverty and homelessness, due to the lack of continued financial and social support.

"The 'homeless' are not just those who we call homeless. Many of us even though there is a roof over our heads, don't have a real home, a physical place or territory controlled by a group with some psychological and emotional investment." [62]
— *Chandler Washburne from a paper written for SLRC*

"Homeless parents were predominantly women, and homeless individuals were predominantly men." [63]
— *Stanford Center for the Study of Families, Children, and Youth*

uncertainty regarding the vagaries of the real estate market. The alternative he proposes is to either rent or buy into an LEHC and invest the yearly savings in tax exempt bonds or such.[61]

Housing needs to be removed as a market commodity and looked at as an investment in a stable lifestyle and a place to build a long-term community. The establishment of many thousands of Shared Living Communities that are organized, financed, and committed to permanent affordability would do much to solve the country's housing woes and other socioeconomic problems.

The Shared Living Community concept does not question the desire for ownership. Instead, it

Underlying the syndrome of homelessness is the reality that our political system is based on market economics, and you as an individual do not count if you cannot afford the market price that returns the highest profit. There is no room for long-term affordability, economic security, family support, and community building in a housing supply system that treats housing as a commodity in the open market.

Our Housing is Socially, Economically, and Environmentally Obsolete

The housing industry — how and where it builds — creates massive environmental damage. Stick-frame construction is a high consumer of non-renewable resources and lumber. Other methods, which will be presented in Chapter Nine, such as rammed earth, straw bale, and adobe have existed for thousands of years. They are workable technologies that use renewable, readily available and, often, local resources. They are easy to work with and have inherent energy-conserving properties. Yet the building industry shuns them, grasping tightly to stick-frame construction even though lumber sources are dwindling and lumber prices are rising.

New housing is most often built in urban fringe and rural areas, causing further environmental degradation. As agricultural fields, wetlands, or open space, the land is inexpensive and too easily rezoned to be sold at higher urban land prices. This increases car emissions in direct proportion to the increased mileage generated by commuting trips and the high number of local errands each house-

This is More Than an Environmental Disaster
Photo by Greenbelt Alliance
"The Working Man's Reward" is now a social, cultural, and economic calamity, and a cause for more cars.

hold runs. The least considered consequences of the urban fringe approach to affordable housing are the environmental, financial, and emotional costs to the families moving out to these new suburbs.

In the guise of affordability are the "first-time home buyer" financing programs. The loophole here is the "three year rule" which allows previous home owners (who have not owned a home in the previous three years) to qualify as first-time home buyers. The implication is that these housing units are supposed to help low-income and young families — a dubious gift to the house-hungry public. Unfortunately, market-rate builders construct many of these units in rural areas, and then market them, with the help of realtors and lenders, to the middle and upper-middle income "first timers," because that is where the profits are.

Nonprofit and for-profit housing sponsors get

"Helping the poor by helping the rich is not only wasteful, but it forces the low-income housing community to court rich investors and it doesn't guarantee long term affordability." [64]

— Chester Hartman, Shelterforce

Higher Costs of Single-family Houses[65]

	Single-family detached home	Five or more unit building
energy use (mil BTU's)	115	64
space heating cost	$390	$206

All figures average per household per year.

SLRC

Stucco, Asphalt, and "Wheels"
The recipe for urban sprawl, mix well with two working parents and long commutes for an American nightmare.

on the financing bandwagon too, with the Federal Low Income Tax Credit program which allows a healthy income tax credit for investments made in "affordable" housing development. It adds "units" to their track record, and the developers' fees and land profits that they receive keep them in business. This investor "incentive" is costly to administrate, often making the real cost per square foot of this subsidized housing more expensive than market rate developments. Who it does favor are the investors, lenders, consultants, and builders who benefit from the tax credit plum. The extra costs of this expensive-to-produce "affordability" end up coming out of the hands of the taxpayers, creating an albatross around the neck of so-called affordable housing.

Bradley Inman, a real estate columnist, reports that Kaufman and Broad, California's number one builder, "...assumes that development in California will continue into the next century more or less as it has for the last 30 years."[66] According to this builder and others like them, there is no limit to development; the West is still the "new frontier." Apparently builders also expect that families will continue to be fully employed, have two wage-earners, and "move up" in five years or so.

Even with two wage-earners, today's smaller families are spending more money for less house, while others who are more affluent buy more house than they really need.

Some developers are promoting smaller houses and lots in the guise of traditional "New Town" developments. These are supposedly an innovative response to the demographic shift towards more single people, smaller families, declining income, and an "ecological" approach to creating a sense of community. But what are they really? What is

"new" about them? They have the same number of people, cars, and appliances per housing unit as other developments. They are built in rural areas. They are still just single-family house products catering to individual buyers, and they do not create any resident co-owned or managed common areas or shared resource facilities which could reduce the everyday strain and costs for the residents. They are basically conventional suburban tract developments with "village" type design features and catchy descriptions such as "ecological," "pedestrian scale," "new town," and "affordable community." They present all the same ecological, social, and economic problems as their large house counterparts. The worst aspect of these open space rape developments is that they are trying to cater to the "Urban Flight" market, and will serve few if any lower income people, unless mandated by law.

Compare the two diagrams on the next page and you will see that it actually takes more materials, energy, time, and land to build four 800 sq. ft. single-family houses each with a 300 sq. ft. studio over the garage, than it does to build one 4,400 sq. ft. house. In the single-family houses, walls, plumbing, appliances, fixtures, materials, infrastructure, and car trips are duplicated. The larger house can comfortably house a large extended family and contain more personal space and shared amenities per person without duplicating resources.

Experience has shown that people quickly grow out of small housing units that are marketed as "starter houses" for singles and young couples. Bought or rented as a short-term housing solution, such housing can later become high-turnover rentals that require higher maintenance and ultimately become less cared for as repair budgets are cut.

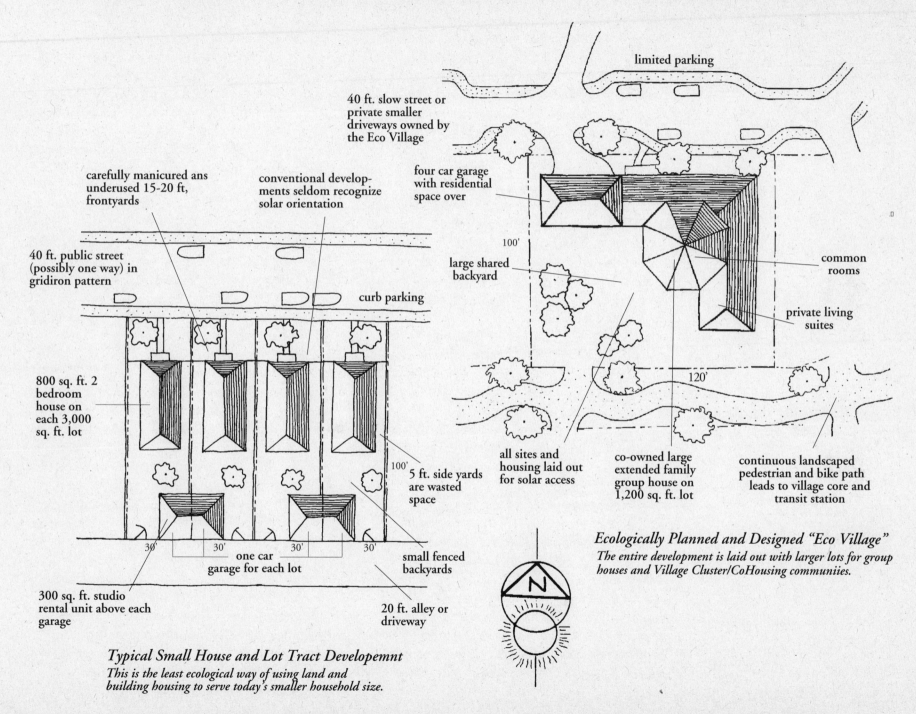

limited parking

40 ft. slow street or private smaller driveways owned by the Eco Village

carefully manicured ans underused 15-20 ft, frontyards

conventional develop-ments seldom recognize solar orientation

four car garage with residential space over

40 ft. public street (possibly one way) in gridiron pattern

large shared backyard

common rooms

curb parking

800 sq. ft. 2 bedroom house on each 3,000 sq. ft. lot

private living suites

100'

5 ft. side yards are wasted space

all sites and housing laid out for solar access

co-owned large extended family group house on 1,200 sq. ft. lot

continuous landscaped pedestrian and bike path leads to village core and transit station

30'   30'   30'   30'

one car garage for each lot

small fenced backyards

120'

Ecologically Planned and Designed "Eco Village"
The entire development is laid out with larger lots for group houses and Village Cluster/CoHousing communiies.

300 sq. ft. studio rental unit above each garage

20 ft. alley or driveway

N

Typical Small House and Lot Tract Developemnt
This is the least ecological way of using land and building housing to serve today's smaller household size.

"I'm looking for a sense of extended family — the emotional and spiritual support that can be shared there. I want to save energy by sharing with others, and share foods that can be bought in bulk. I also want to share personal gifts with others and have each other as resources and support in personal and spiritual growth."
— Member of SLRC profile session core group

"That poverty and homelessness exist to such a great extent in America says something about our society, it says indifference to the lives of people at the bottom, disbelief that life can be good for those for whom it has been bad. It says an unwillingness to pay the cost of making life work for all people."[67]
— James Rouse

Overcrowding often follows as absentee owners attempt to maximize profits and prevent vacancies by being more lenient in their tenant selection process. Cities and counties should be wary of the small lot "new town," and instead look to community oriented housing clusters located on larger parcels that meet established criteria for ecologically sustainable housing.

We have individuality but lack choices. Suburbs are designed for profits, not for the whole-life community needs of people or the environment. The real estate industry uses market surveys to develop advertising campaigns. These surveys seldom do not address home seekers as real people with values, concerns, desires, and needs, but as loan applicants, with the presumption made that they already want the product the builder will be offering. We need family living and community motivational surveys that reveal what people really want.

Let's face the facts. This society has changed; the economy has changed; the ecological balance on the planet has changed; everything has changed except how we think about our housing. We continue to build and to live in a form of housing that does not meet our needs as individuals or as a society.

Many bankers and developers do not recognize that fewer single women and men, young couples, small families, and older people need or want a conventional single-family house and the lifestyle it implies. Many of these people simply want affordability, supportive social relationships, and an attractive living environment where they can feel safe. What they are being offered is the classic developer's "Dream House" designed for a 1940's and 1950's nuclear family with an employed father, a stay-at-home mother, and 3+ children. Reality, however, is more complex: only about 20% of American households fit this typical description. Can you imagine the shoe industry designing all our shoes in only one single "typical" size? America is a diverse nation and we need diverse housing options.

According to the U.S. Census, the average family size in 1960 was 3.67; in 1991 it was 3.18, in the year 2000 it is expected to be even less.[68] Nevertheless, the square footage and number of rooms in the average American house increased rapidly in the post-WW II boom years, peaking in the early 1980's. Builders keep on cranking out acres of American Dream houses — one entrance for everybody, a "master" suite for Mom and Dad, smaller bedrooms with a shared bath for Johnny and Susie, a living room for entertaining, a kitchen for Mom, and a den for Dad.

But many Americans want an alternative to the single-family house, because they realize the current housing system does not work socially or economically for them, nor ecologically for the planet. They want the best of two worlds: economic security and the nurturing support of an extended family, shared amenities, and the option of privacy, either alone or with loved ones.

The combining of these ideals into one housing package is difficult to achieve through conventional housing and building systems. Fortunately, innovative forms of design, co-ownership, and resident control are providing the possibility of ecologically sustainable communities. Setting up these new communities will require people wanting it, direct participation in achieving it, and a new level of leadership and cooperation in the design, lending, and building professions, as well as in legislatures and the White House. It will take all of us working together as a community.

Change: by Choice or Necessity

The origins of resistance to positive changes in the political and economic system lie in our own fear of change, and from this the personal tendency to deny the root causes behind the dangers to society and ourselves. Our great need today is to clearly see that there are serious structural flaws in our system. What do we get from supporting the status quo, and how can we benefit by beginning to explore, talk about, and experience community in our lives?

It is a Buddhist precept that our pain ceases through understanding the origin of that pain. To make the necessary changes in order to solve the problems we face today, we must look at the origins of the problems and understand them from the perspective of history, our system and institutions, our values, and our own emotional baggage, addictions, and biases. Then we can make decisions from an awareness that moves us beyond the original problem and symptoms. We can then move towards a new definition of life and = relationships, and discover the new American Dream.

Although many people have felt powerless with little control over society's problems, it is time to turn the process around by demonstrating that the tools are available for making positive change. As the 20th century comes to a close, we need to honestly look at our own daily living practices and the "system." There we can see how the origins of the housing, socioeconomic, and environmental

problems around us are often obscured by our daily efforts to make our lives work, keep up with our obligations, pursue a livelihood, and feel good about ourselves. Within that array of demands, needs, and obstacles, one must also find, keep, and maintain housing. Change can be involuntary and oppressive, or it can be consciously initiated by us as we awaken to an intentional exploration of new directions.

Much of the time, worldly changes appear to lie outside the scope of our personal lives, seeming too remote and inconsequential to be recognized as events that may have a significant impact upon us, but they do. Becoming aware of this could represent a path to true personal empowerment. Working alone as individuals will not take us far enough along the road to responsible ecological living and the rebuilding of community in America. Efforts to this end are often thwarted because we lack the collective power of commitment to a common purpose. Such a change requires personal empowerment through a social support base, whether it be an extended family or a larger community of people.

We are creatures of habit, we have addictions, and we become used to our own special ways of acting and thinking. As you read about Shared Living Community, *you* may be thinking, "Naah! People aren't going to go for that, their minds are fixed." But remember when people were thinking, or not thinking about, and were saying, or were afraid to say, the following:

• Nuclear power is here to stay and will replace fossil fuel power plants.

• Solar power is just too expensive, and besides, the oil companies will kill it off.

• Trains and light rail systems are dead and could

"…what seemed like isolated events in distant places a few years ago, are now reaching across our very doorsteps… The tendency is to see these areas as separate and as being too large for us to cope with, and almost always as being for others to deal with. But the truth is that these problems are interlinked and often have the same roots in our daily lives. And they are too big for individuals or separate (local) governments to solve alone. The only way is for all of us to tackle them together." [69]
— David Pearson

"Given the enormous infrastructure and social patterning in place, it has so far been easier for people to keep living in the same old unsustainable ways than to pioneer sustainable communities." [70]
— Robert Gilman,
"The Eco-Village Challenge"

never be a viable option again.
• Nuclear war can happen at any time, the Cold War could end for everybodsy by either side pushing the button.
• Smokers will never give it up, and you can't ban cigarette ads, the tobacco companies would sue.
• Women will never choose to have babies by themselves, without a man; besides, it's not moral.
• Gays and lesbians won't come out of the closet, and will always be denied service in the government and military.
• The mentally ill and dysfunctional unemployables will always be cared for by institutions.
• Organic food and vegetarian eating is only a fad, the mainstream won't buy it.

The list goes on. You are invited to make your own list of changes that you thought couldn't happen, but are now realities. Recall the huge changes that this society has already experienced at an accelerated rate in the decades since World War II. Then look at the positive changes being proposed in this book. Perhaps you will see that changing to a more ecological way of living may be relatively easy.

However, there will be some who will say, "Oh, I'll never share cooking and meals in a common house kitchen and dining hall in a Village Cluster community." You may wonder how you could give up being individually responsible for your own food shopping and your own or your family's meals. What of the special habits that are uniquely yours? Remember the ego thrill you got as a child from being sent to buy groceries at the "big store," and when you had your own money burning a hole in your pocket? Do you still feel, or yearn to receive, that personal reward from your family or your

partner when you bring home the goodies and serve up a special dish?

Shopping and cooking have provided nurturing support for many of us, and the praise from our family or friends becomes a self-esteem boost. But family, housing, and social changes over the generations since World War II have caused many people to lose the opportunity to nurture or be nurtured. Shared Living Communities will bring many more people those much needed nurturing experiences, like those depicted in the *Village Acre* community in Chapter One. Nurturing will come just from cooking for others on a particular day, teaching a child how to plant seeds, watering someone else's tomato plants, or helping a teen with a computer question.

We hope that this discussion enables you to see community as a source of personal empowerment, and motivates you to attend a community core group workshop to find out for yourself what the options are. The tendency will be to think that you must make all the decisions regarding actual changes by yourself, and becuase that is percieved to be scary or time consuming it is postponed. That is an act of change in itself, a change from stepping into a sustainble community future to perpetuating the unsustainable status-quo of the present. The most effective change is an interactive group effort, but you must be there in full participation Real change starts in each individuals mind and heart, supported by others who also sense the same needs. The other sparkplug for change is the recognition that you have unmet needs and that you will need help. The forum for creating community change is the core-group, begun in a workshop where community facilitators can share their visions with you…

Our Heritage Leads Us Back into Community

— back to the warmth of the fold

Now let's look at what others have done in the past and are doing now to create community and sustain culture. As we wake up from our illusive American Dream and make the difficult changes toward a sustainable future, we need to understand and appreciate the value of our family-community heritage. Despite the many problems facing us, we should celebrate the fact that the concepts, resources, and opportunities for making positive changes are available.

We know that many people are seeking alternatives to the single-family house and environmentally damaging urban sprawl. By drawing upon selected historic and contemporary examples of village/community living and design, we can "rebuild America" in a manner that is appropriate for meeting the tough challenges of the 21st century. Classical literature, anthropology, and social-architectural history show that humans have always lived in groups. Even today, throughout the Third World and to a varying extent in Europe and Asia, extended families and village groups live together in physically defined communities. The rich, ethnic heritage in America is full of examples, as well, of how native and immigrant peoples have sought supportive social enclaves, providing us with workable models for modern day ecological village communities. Fundemental throughout all ages and in all regions of the world is the heritage of building settlements where work, food preparation, and family are supported by the nature of the design and layout of the structures — there is an intention.

Monasteries, convents, and guilds of the Middle Ages

Historically, monasteries were a worldwide example of places where groups of people joined to confront the harsh conditions and decaying values of their day, and developed their own standards for livelihood and community. A common desire to create a better life led the monks of various spiritual and religious paths to develop new spiritual, economic, and social systems, where trade guilds were introduced, and technological advances made that are still used today. The earliest of such settlements began in pre-Christian times in Asia, as Buddhism spread from India through Tibet, China, and into Japan. Christian monasteries spread through the Mediterranean and European world and were bastions of civilized order. Theodor Roszak writes,

> [The monks] had created a network of independent domestic economies that were the most stable, orderly, and productive in their society, with more than enough surplus to provide charitable care for the needy, the aged, the indigent. They became the best farmers

"Our Lady of the Fountains" Abbey of Yorkshire, England, circa 1143 AD.
This monastery, like others built by religious and spiritual groups, was highly self-reliant, a complete community, including workshops that made most goods, food growing and storage areas, libraries, schools, central kitchens and dining halls, chapels, market places, and housing. It became the focus for economic and social sustainability for large surrounding areas.

Taos Pueblo

Located along the Rio Gande River (near Santa Fe, New Mexico), and begun in the 1440's, Taos has the longest continous history of any pre-Hispanic Native American settlement. Even in the wide open spaces of the desert the ecological logic for compact village composition was recognized by the early Native Americans. Here is a community model that integrats the social, spiritual, cultural, and ecological spects of living in a way that has surely been an impotant to the sustainability of the Taos people.

Photo by John Hiller, Courtesy of Museum of New Mexico

and craftsmen of their age, the inventors and disseminators of many new technologies. They traded goods, kept schools, distributed alms, transmitted the culture… many of the most hostile wilderness areas of Europe were pioneered by the monks; many of the Western world's most basic techniques and machines were either invented or perfected in the monasteries. The economic style of the monastic communities assumes that, with sufficient ingenuity and hard work, one can reach a point of balance with the land and the life upon it."[71]

Native American communities

Native Americans inhabited this land and lived in highly organized villages and communities long before the arrival of Europeans. Tribes varied greatly in size, cultural systems, languages, symbolism, housing, and rituals. But all tribes shared certain values, beliefs, practices, and ways of relating to and understanding the natural world that are still manifest in their culture today.

Native Americans believed everything, including societies, were alive, not supernaturally but naturally alive. Societies were seen as creators of personality and sources of power and values for their members. They believed that to live in a consciously living and growing community was to be fulfilled as a person. They lived, therefore, in extended family villages tightly clustered together. Their homes reflected the geography and the climate of the region, and ranged from clay huts to rock masonry buildings to teepees. Each family had their own space, but they did not live as individuals. They were members of a community that shared resources, rules, rituals, religion, and the land around them. These communities produced artisans, evolved sophisticated economic systems, and with only a few exceptions functioned democratically.

Modern societies are based on the idea that competition is the basis of life and defines all relationships. Native Americans recognize competition and its importance in the world, but do not elevate it to the prime cause of life and action. Instead they believe that, in a world in which everything is alive and has a place, it is not competition between things, but rather their interconnectedness that governs the functioning of the world. This is the essence for creating sustainable commuities. Lucy

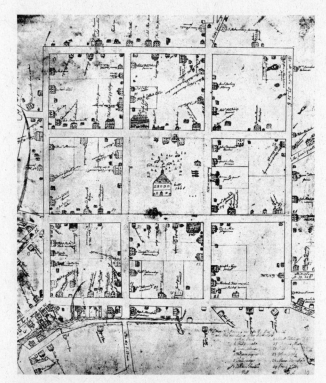

Permission by Beinecke Rare Books and Manuscript Library, Yale University: Reproduced from American Architecture and Urbanism by Vincent Scully

***New Haven, Connecticut** (Wadsworth Map of 1748, showing original plan of 1641)*

Smith, a Dry Creek Pomo, explains:

> We had many relatives and … we all had to live together; so we'd better learn how to get along with each other. She [my mother] said it wasn't too hard to do. It was just like taking care of your younger brother or sister. You got to know them, find out what they like and what made them cry, so you'd know what to do. If you took good care of them you didn't have to work so hard. Sounds like it's not true, but it is. When that baby gets to be a man or a woman they're going to help you out.[72]

American colonial communities

European colonial settlements in America are excellent examples of community. Settlers founded their own towns for mutual protection and livelihood, and sometimes because of shared religious or moral beliefs. They worked through problems together, came to a consensus on how to solve them, built self-governing systems, celebrated harvests and religious holidays, and organized schools. In a harsh and utterly alien environment these settlers worked together, sharing their skills and resources as they built a new life.

John Hostetler, *Amish Society*

Amish Barn Raising — A Spiritual and Practical Event

41

"It would have been inconceivable to these first settlers to strive for the good life in America by building model houses rather than working for a model community."[73]
— *Dolores Hayden*

Even though they usually tended their own fields, these settlers lived close together in villages and towns. In the process, they created special spaces, like the town common or village square with a church or meeting hall, where they gathered to discuss their common heritage and goals. The goal was not everyone for himself, but rather that each worked to build a community for all to share.

Utopian communities

In the 19th century, several hundred communities, some originating in Europe, were formed in a wave of reformist and spiritual ideology known as the "Utopian" movement. Though early Utopian communities were based on religious beliefs, many later ones adopted a socialist system in response to the injustices and inhumanities of the new industrial era. Some of the best known communities are the Shakers (New York, Indiana, Ohio, and Kentucky, 1787-mid 20th century), Oneida (upstate New York, 1848-1881), Amana (Iowa, 1843-1933), and the Harmony Society (Pennsylvania and Indiana, 1804-1904).

These Utopian communities made some lasting contributions to society. For example, the New Harmony community in Indiana pioneered kindergarten and infant schools, free public schools, trade schools, geological surveys, and public libraries. The Shaker communities show us how a workable social and economic community order can be achieved through commitment of the members to a larger ideal and sharing of resources for the common good.

The Amish and Mennonite communities, still in existence today, are self-sufficient enclaves whose members understand the limits and potential of their land and of the resources of the region, and have created a highly sustainable way of life. Their villages and towns exhibit a variety of ways of clustering and sharing common spaces, buildings, and resources.

Domestic reformers, socialist cooperatives, and the cooperative movement

Reformers like Frances Willard and Melusina Fay Peirce in the 1870's, and Jane Addams of the Chicago Settlement House movement of the 1880's, proposed alternatives to the role of the wife

Jane Addams at Hull-House, Chicago, Illinois

The University of Illinois at Chicago

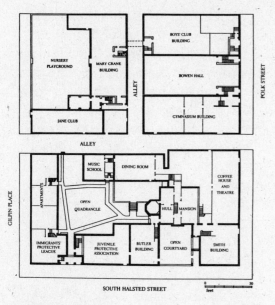

Hull-House Plan   The University of Illinois at Chicago

planning conference in 1909. They also wrote *Hull-House Maps and Papers,* "a survey of the physical and economic conditions of the slums of Chicago published in 1895… a major American research effort on the need for urban physical planning and social services."[75] These women gained a popular audience and influenced consideration of how innovative housing solutions could improve the lives of women and families, but because of the status-quo politicians, planners, ministers, and social workers in the leadership roles of that time, this social reform movement was not sustained. The planning process today is still missing a strong social innovation orientation.

However, valuable precedents were established by the beginning of the urban and land use planning movement in the early 1900's. We have since seen a great rise of nonprofit social service and housing organizations, many founded, directed, and staffed by women. This new generation of social change makers has begun to recognize the need and value of the extended family and the group house in which meals are shared. The extended family setting is an essential healing process for the women, children, men, and families they serve, and is critical to the process of rebuilding community in America for everyone.

Pioneers of Our Own Time

Ecologically sustainable community movements of today are being spawned by peoples' practical responses to the socioeconomic and environmental circumstances they are facing, not by an emotional attachment to any one ideological belief system or an attempt to revive the past. As we state repeatedly

"As a homelike public place in the heart of the slums, Jane Addam's Hull-House inspired over a hundred similar settlement house projects… At Hull-House groups of city gardeners cultivated vacant lots; the residents built the first urban playground in Chicago; they created a child care center for children of employed mothers. They ran education classes on all kinds of subjects for children and adults, cultural and practical, from symphonies to shoemaking."[76]
— Dolores Hayden

as a mere cook, maid, and nanny. Women's rights advocates, working with social scientists and other environmental reformers, came up with complete visions of ways of living that would not force a division between public life for men and domestic life for women. They "envisaged an ideal American city where landscape architecture, housing, and urban physical and social planning were intertwined."[74] Cooperative residential neighborhoods, municipal housekeeping programs, and shared cooking, meals, and childcare were all proposed and tried as ways to free women from the domestic drudgery that prevented them from taking part in public life as equal members of society.

Realizing that the social and physical set-up of the home had a profound influence on family life, Florence Kelley and Mary Simkovitch, members of Hull-House, called for the first national urban

Photo by Albert Bates, The Farm

*Intentional Community
in Scandanavia*
*Circle dancing during a gathering at
the Fjordvang Ecovillage Community,
Skumvej, Denmark. This beginning
community is among the hundreds of
communities in Europe founded on
the precepts of ecological living, self-
reliance, and stewardship of the land
that is the theme of most intentional
communities.in this international
movement.*

in this book, these movements arise from the
human heritage of extended family and village and
the instinctual human desire for a common social
and physical environment within which to communicate wants, needs, and feelings. Since WW II we
have witnessed compelling reasons to make major
changes in our lifestyles — to accommodate an
overpopulated world, correct for the physical abuses
to the ecosystem, and find alternatives to economic
exploitation. The formation of community is a
natural response.

The Intentional Community movement

There are over 350 Intentional Communities in
America, with others in Europe, India, Canada,
Australia, and Israel. In addition, there are thousands of cooperative, extended family, and voluntary family group houses in rural and urban areas.
Intentional Communities have formed around a
combination of agrarian, ecological, spiritual,
religious, and political orientations. Most are rural
and have a high degree of economic self-sufficiency,
with many members engaged in cottage industry
and organic farming within the community, and
some members operating businesses in the broader
community. Some are organized as nonprofit
cooperative enterprises, and follow the Rochdale
Principles (see Chapter Nine) for the operation of a
cooperative. There are also numerous housing
cooperatives that own their buildings, but the
degree to which these cooperatives are a "community" in the sense described in this book varies
considerably.

Intentional Communities begun in the early

Photo by KenNorwood

View of Common Green From Front Porch of Community Store, Ananda Village

part of the century and still in existence today provide testimony to their sustainability. Some include: Celo, North Carolina, founded (1939); Gould Farm, Massachusetts (1913); Koinonia Partners, Georgia (1942); Krotona, California (1924); Shiloh Community, Arkansas (1942); and Vivekananda Society, Illinois (1930). The movement continues to grow with strong communities like Shannon Farm, Virginia (1974); Sirius, Massachusetts (1978); Twin Oaks, Virginia (1967); Sandhill Farm, Missouri (1974); Alpha Farm, Oregon (1972); Ananda Village, California (1968); and many others, with new communities being formed all the time. The *Communities Directory* is a rich source of information on the location, history, features, and composition of many communities.

It is not possible to make one definition for Intentional Community, as each community is unique to the characteristics of the member residents. However, there are a number of characteristics that commonly prevail. Many of these communities practice a high level of group process, gender equality, and democratic self-management, and make use of consensus, conflict resolution, and personal growth techniques. The members tend to be of mixed age and income, come from mostly White, middle class backgrounds, and are well educated. Instead of retreating from society, many see themselves as building a new and better society, while making the best use of conventional institutions. Many have called themselves "New Age," or speak of "planetary consciousness," or of being "stewards of the earth."

There is a distinction between the earlier socialist cooperatives and the spiritual and political Utopian communities, and the present day Intentional Communities. The former were the result of dedicated, highly resolved individual leaders and their followers rallying around a fixed doctrine, theory, or belief, whereas the present Intentional Communities seem to arise more from the need of individuals to create an alternative to a stressful and impersonal society. Although some may have begun with one founder, most now follow an egalitarian and participatory social structure that respects an individual's needs while maintaining the unity of the group. Intentional Community happens when people personally choose to cooperate with others in mutual responsibility and for common social, livelihood, and environmental objectives.

"Hippie commune" was a largely negative epithet bestowed by the media upon the wide variety of voluntary or extended family, spiritual, and Intentional Communities of the 1960's and 1970's. What became "news" and attracted public attention was the lurid and rebellious behavior and the anti-establishment rhetoric of some highly visible communes. At the same time, however, serious "living lightly on the land" Intentional Communities were being formed. The members of both may have appeared the same — blue jeans, tie-dye shirts, and a VW bug or pick-up — but their lifestyle and attitudes were significantly different and the Intentional Communities lasted.

Even though the "commune movement" has passed, some newspaper editors even today cast aspersions on groups that share meals, own land together, have common values and objectives, and are doing an admirable and responsible job of ecological living. More recently, there is a media shift towards positive representation of the Inten-

"I live on Shannon Farm, an intentional community of 75 adults and children on the eastern slope of the Virginia Blue Ridge Mountains. I have watched Shannon grow for fifteen years and continue to marvel at how well it works. Our community grows richer, more beautiful, and generally more harmonious while turnover is negligible. Much of our success can be credited to many extraordinary members: creative, patient, and fair-minded people. But I firmly believe that the way we structure our community is also essential." [77]

— Peter Robinson, Shannon Farm: A Model for Community that Works

"To us, the new intentional communities are one of the mapmakers for humanity's journey into the future. They function as research and development centers for society, experimenting with new approaches to problems of inflation, pollution, energy shortages, job alienation, unemployment and rising health care costs. Many ideas and techniques being developed in communities are directly applicable to urban and suburban life, like reducing living costs while enhancing the quality of life and the sense of being surrounded by friendship and support."[78]
— *Corinne McLaughlin &*
Gordon Davidson
Builders of the Dawn

tional Community movement as a maturation and a contradiction to the alleged anti-authority "anything goes" hippie communes. Julie Mazo says:

> Articles on cooperative lifestyles have appeared in the *Boston Globe, Denver Post, Los Angeles Times,* and *St. Louis Post-Dispatch,* among other major publications. Even the *Wall Street Journal* found it relevant to report on the evolution of the people and places once called hippies and communes, as gray hair grows more plentiful among the Woodstock generation…. What [many present day communities] have in common is the offering of a viable opportunity for a lifestyle of one's choice, from a home with as many or few "middle-class" accouterments as one may desire to a primitive cabin in the woods. [79]

Shared Living Communities

Today a new, but parallel, community movement is growing from the pragmatic needs of mainstream people for economic survival, affordable housing, childcare, emotional support, companionship, family strengthening, relief of stress, safe food sources, and environmental protection. The movement generally represents an attempt to maintain and improve the quality of life in the face of a declining economy and difficult times.

To meet society's rapidly changing needs, an array of innovative lifestyle and co-ownership housing opportunities has been evolving. This is demonstrated by the wealth of descriptive terms and models: shared housing, group living, extended family, voluntary family, intergenerational housing, cooperative ownership, land trusts, ecological

village, and most recently and noteworthy, the Village Cluster and CoHousing. This is not a faddish trend, nor a recycling of the commune movement, but a direct adaptation and extension of our American and worldwide heritage of extended family, villages, and community, and good old-fashioned grassroots ingenuity.

"Shared Living Communities" is an umbrella term created by Ken Norwood to include those forms of ecologically sustainable housing communities that would appeal to a broad range of people in the United States. Some of the specific models include the "Village Cluster," the "Urban Cooperative Block," the "Octagonal Family House," CoHousing, and other variations. The term also includes Intentional Communities and the cooperative housing movement. Inspiration for the Shared Living Community precepts has come from personal experience, study, travel, and networking regarding all the forms of group shared housing and communities, including European examples of new towns and cooperative housing built since WW II.

These contemporary community concepts represent another historically significant break with the "lord of the manor" ethic of solitary control with each person or family owning his or her "castle." We support the precept that these models of community, when appropriately organized and designed, are synonymous with ecologically sustainability, and through co-ownership and cooperative management will provide people the opportunity for ecological living, personal empowerment, and the new extended family. With this approach families can be freed of the "consumer buying unit" role, and sensitively choose their housing design and how they use resources.

The New Road Ahead

We have reviewed how various community movements evolved to help people overcome the problems of their times. Founders created a vision, and community members imbued it with common goals, values, and aspirations, remaining committed to that vision. People today seek to create a more secure place for their families to live within a larger, imperfect world. It often takes a calamity to wake us up to possible alternatives. Ours is not the first society to experience massive social, economic, and environmental problems. For us, the important thing is how we will act in facing these problems, and whether we will choose to enact positive new directions in our lives or continue to view housing as an "over the counter" consumer product. The socioeconomic and environmental solutions to our present crisis do not lie in each person trying harder than before as lone individuals or isolated nuclear families. They lie in our working more effectively with each other in a system of cooperative enterprise by sharing property, resources, responsibilities, and purposes — that is the essence of ecological living and the way toward a sustainable society.

As the old American Dream collapses, we can continue to be lone individuals, compromising our dreams, our lives, and our environment, or we can make a bold declaration of what happiness, family life, good neighborhoods, and a healthy planet and world society really mean to us. To meet those desires, we must learn how to rebuild America with community as a sustainable foundation.

The process of creating Shared Living Communities will involve making changes in land use and development policies and practices, and in how people perceive their housing options. Unfortunately, the old practices and perceptions are strongly entrenched. We will need to change zoning ordinances, financing and ownership methods, and housing and neighborhood design, in order to acknowledge the new family/village configurations. Altering old patterns will require a major display of vision and personal commitment, as well as coordinated policy and support at federal, state, and local levels.

At present, housing development in the U.S. reflects the intertwined interests of lenders, developers, realtors, builders, and design professionals, with little or no involvement of the residents who are to be the ultimate users. We who will be the users must speak out to make our needs for Shared Living Community known. Change will be encouraged by people who are fed up with the brick walls of non-affordability and the accompanying social and environmental problems. We need to empower ourselves as a people and a nation to initiate policies and practices locally and globally to prevent the misuse of land, the destruction of resources, over-population, and the loss of our protective atmosphere. The ultimate possibility is for all people to live in socially and environmentally harmonious community on this planet.

"Pushing the Wrong Housing Buttons....
In America, houses are designed to sell, not to live in.... In no other country has housing become so dominated by concerns of the market place; in America, a house is first a consumer product."[80]
— *Witold Rybcznski,*
San Francsco Chronicle

Notes

Books listed only by name in the endnotes are highlighted in the resource guide at the end of the book, complete with author/publisher information and description.

1. John Leo, "Numbing Ourselves to the Growing Crisis," Feb. 2, 1993, *Seattle Times,* p. A8.
2. "As the Pope sees it, communism, capitalism, are both losers," *In These Times*, Vol. 15, No. 24, p. 14.
3. Earth in the Balance, p. 183.
4. Entropy, p. 258.
5. Natural House Book, pp. 8-9.
6. Earth in the Balance, p. 220.
7. In the Absence of the Sacred, pg. 35.
8. Paramahansa Yogananda, quoted by Swami Kriyananda, The Road Ahead, Ananda Publications, Nevada City, 1967, pp. 18-36.
9. *Ibid.*, pp. 35-36.
10. *Ibid.*, pp. 79-80.
11. Builders of the Dawn, p. 11.
12. Diana Alstad and Joel Kramer, The Guru Papers, North Atlantic Books, Berkeley, 1993, p. 373.
13. Gene Stephens, "Crime and Punishment: Forces Shaping the Future," The 1990's and Beyond, p. 102.
14. Barbara Dafoe Whitehead, *op. cit.*, p. 65.
15. Sue Shellenbarger, "Longer Commutes Force Parents to Make Tough Choices on Where to Leave the Kids," *Wall Street Journal*, August 18, 1993, p. B1.
16. Ralph Kinney Bennett, "What kids need most in a Dad," *Readers Digest,* Feb. 1992, pp. 93-96.
17. Task Force on Teaching as a Profession, "A Nation Prepared: Teachers for the 21st Century," *The Carnegie Forum on Education and the Economy*, May 1986, p. 14.
18. Entropy, p. 256.
19. Creating Community Anywhere, p. 92.
20. Langdon Winner, "Artifact/Ideas and Political Culture," *Whole Earth*, No. 73, Winter 1991, p. 20.
21. Earth in the Balance, pp. 220-221.
22. quoted by Gar Smith of Earth Island Institute, *ADPSR Update, the Newsletter for the Northern CA Chapter of Architects, Designers & Planners for Social Responsibility*, Nov/Dec 1991, p. 3.
23. Ancient Futures, p. 187.
24. Hartmut Gerdes, "Multimedia — Good Bye, Herr Gutenberg!?," *Northern News*, July/August 1993, p. 3.
25. Testimony of L. Rowell Huesmann, Ph.D., Professor of Psychology and Communication, University of Michigan, from the proceedings of the hearings of the U.S. House of Representatives Subcommittee on Telecommunications and Finance, Violence and the Media, May 12, 1993.
26. Jerry Carroll, "How the First Baby Tests a Marriage," *San Francisco Chronicle*, June 9, 1993, p. B5.
27. *Ibid.*, p. B3.
28. Based upon storytelling by Garrison Keillor, American Radio Theater, *KQED Radio*, Dec. 1992.
29. Marriage: East and West, p. 54.
30. Barbara Dafoe Whitehead, "Dan Quayle was Right," *The Atlantic Monthly*, April 1993, p. 62.
31. Discrimination by Design: A Feminist Critique of the Man-Made Environment, p.119 or p. 73. UNSURE????.
33. Keenan, "Equality and Sexism at Twin Oaks: What have we accomplished?," *Leaves of Twin Oaks,* April 1993, p. 12.
34. U.S. Census Reports, 1970 and 1990.
35. Keenan, "Equality and Sexism at Twin Oaks: What have we accomplished?," *Leaves of Twin Oaks,* April, 1993, p. 12.
36. Philip Longman, "Age War: The Coming Battle Between Young and Old," The 1990's and Beyond, p. 34.
37. Valerie Parker, Sherry Edmonds, and Virginia Robinson, "A Change For The Better: How to Make Communities More Responsive to Older Residents," American Association of Retired Persons, 1991, p. 3.
38. Page Smith, "Why Young and Old Need Each Other," *This World Magazine, San Francisco Chronicle*, March 12, 1989, p. 4.
39. Gene Stephens, *op. cit.*, p. 103.
40. "Sixty-five Plus in America," Bureau of the Census, 1992.
41. U.S. Census Report, 1992.
42. Patrick H. Hare, "The Frailty Boom," *Shared Housing News: A Newsletter of the National Shared Housing Resource Center*, July 1991, p. 3.
43. Page Smith, "The Aging of the Intellect," *This World Magazine, San Francisco Chronicle*, June 9, 1991, p. 6.
44. "Shared Housing = Medicaid Savings," *Shared Housing News: A Newsletter of the National Shared Housing Resource Center*, Spring 1993, p. 1.
45. "Energy on the Road: Transportation and the Environment," a brochure put out by the Union of Concerned Scientists, December, 1990.
46. Karie Garnier, Our Elders Speak: A Tribute to Native Elders, K. Garnier, White Rock, BC, 1990, pp. 7-8.

47 *"Briefing Paper: Motor-Vehicle Fuel Efficiency and Global Warming,"* a brochure put out by the Union of Concerned Scientists, May, 1991.

48 Jonathan Marshall, "How Higher Fuel Efficiency May Backfire," *San Francisco Chronicle*, July 23, 1991, p. A4.

49 *Ibid.*

50 From *BART TALK,* a publication of the San Francisco Bay Area Rapid Transit District.

51 "Energy on the Road…," *op. cit.*

52 Michael Remmer, "Rethinking the Role of the Automobile," *Worldwatch Paper 84,* June 1988, p. 46.

53 Sue Shellenbarger, "Longer Commutes Force Parents to Make Tough Choices on Where to Leave the Kids," *Wall Street Journal,* August 18, 1993, p. B1.

54 Bradley Inman, *op. cit.*, p. F8.

55 Bradley Inman, *op. cit.*, p. F8.

56 Henry Holmes, "Transportation, Social Justice, and Sustainability," *The Urban Ecologist,* Summer 1993, p. 6.

57 David and Vera Mace, Marriage: East and West, Dolphin Books/ Doubleday & Co., Inc., Garden City, 1960, p. 57.

58 Associated Press, "Many Prefer a Home to Retirement," *San Francisco Chronicle*, June 1, 1992.

59 Daniel Lazare, "Economics for a Small Planet," *E Magazine,* September/October, 1991, pp. 52-53.

60 U.S. Census Report, 1990.

61 Jaques Kaswan, Ph.D., "Buying a House as an Investment: A Cautionary Tale," The Alternatives Center, Berkeley, California.

62 Chandler Washburne, Ph.D. CSUF, from a paper written for SLRC, May 18, 1992, p. 6.

63 "The Stanford Studies of Homeless Families, Children and Youth," a report written and published by The Stanford Center for the Study of Families, Children and Youth, Nov 18, 1991, p. 11.

64 Chester Hartman, "Feeding the Sparrows by Feeding the Horses," *Shelterforce,* Jan./Feb. 92, p. 12.

65 U.S. Census Bureau, *Residential Energy Consumption Survey,* Jan/ Dec 1987.

66 Bradley Inman, "K&B is conquering the West: Strategy gives rise to growth debate," *San Francisco Examiner*, June 30, 1991, p. F1.

67 quoted by Claire Carter, "Whatever Ought To Be, Can Be," *Parade Magazine, San Francisco Examiner*, May 12, 1991, p. 4.

68 U.S. Census Report, 1991.

69 Natural House Book, p. 8.

70 Robert Gilman, "The Eco-Village Challenge," *In Context*, No. 29, p. 12.

71 Theodore Roszak, Person-Planet: The Creative Disintegration of Industrial Society, Anchor Press/Doubleday, Garden City, 1978, pp. 286-294.

72 Edited with commentary by Malcolm Margolin, The Way We Lived, Heyday Books and California Historical Society, Berkeley, 1993, p. 95.

73 Redesigning the American Dream, p. 19.

74 *Ibid.*, p. 28.

75 *Ibid.*, p. 31. Refers to Florence Kelley, ed., *Hull-House Maps and Papers*, 1895, New York, Arno, 1975.

76 Ibid., p. 31.

77 Peter Robinson, with help from Bernie and Clay, "Shannon Farm: A model for Community that Works," *Green Revolution,* Vol. 46 No.4, Winter 1989-90, School of Living, Cochranville, PA.

78 Builders of the Dawn, p. 2.

79 Julie Mazo, "Communities for the Mainstream," Directory of Intentional Communities, p. 25.

80 Witold Rybcynski, *New York Times,* "Pushing the Wrong Housing Buttons," *Hone section, San Francisco Chronicle,* September,18, 1991

STARTING A COMMUNITY
the People, the Motivation, and the Process

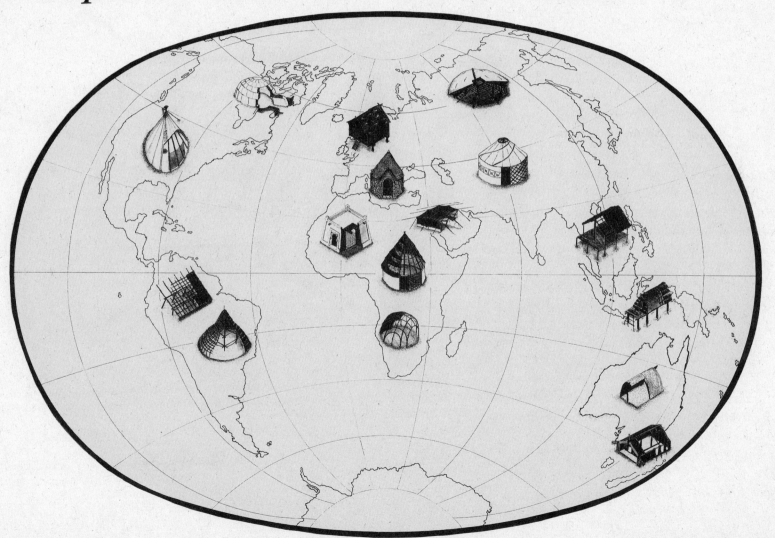

CHAPTER THREE

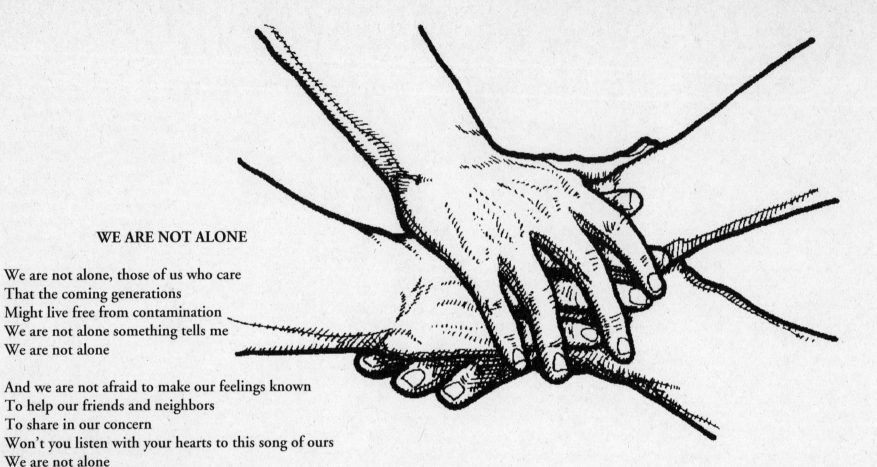

WE ARE NOT ALONE

We are not alone, those of us who care
That the coming generations
Might live free from contamination
We are not alone something tells me
We are not alone

And we are not afraid to make our feelings known
To help our friends and neighbors
To share in our concern
Won't you listen with your hearts to this song of ours
We are not alone

For the sake of our children let us come to our senses
In the name of love let us come to our senses
In the threat to life nobody profits
There is no moment to lose
While we still have the chance to choose
Where our future goes
— Raffi

Moving Toward Community

We are not alone in our assertions about the social and environmental problems facing our society today. There are many books, newsletters, experts, and organizations dedicated to studying these problems. Too often, however, they simply cite statistics documenting our impending doom and offer narrow solutions based on status quo techniques or technology. As Mary King, writer for the Association for Humanistic Psychology, muses, "There must come a point when people don't need any more information. They already know the statistics and crises you're going to recite to them. There's more need for motivation than information."[1]

Beyond motivation, there is also a need for practical alternatives to the way we live now — alternatives which better serve our needs and fulfill our longings. Based on our experience, we believe that there are many people looking for change — looking for community. Unfortunately, there are not enough communities in existence to meet this growing demand — a situation this book seeks to change.

What is it that motivates people to form community? Part of this motivation comes from realizing the tremendous benefits of living in a community: family support, co-ownership, resident control, more personal and family time, companionship, co-parenting, childcare and after-school activities, environmental protection, energy savings, gardening and food processing, access to urban culture and conveniences, and reduced use of the car.

But more than that, people yearn for a deeper human connection to others in a common place where they can say, "We belong."

In this chapter, we explore this yearning, describe existing models of community, present profiles of different types of people who would benefit from living in community, and describe methods for coming together as a core group to create a community.

The process for forming a Shared Living Community can be intense and lengthy. It may involve many meetings, design sessions, and consultations with lawyers, planners, developers, and bankers, and probably some conflicts. But it is also rich and rewarding, resulting in the creation of a new extended family of people with common concerns, values, and aspirations.

Guidelines and structures created by the community members govern how the community is designed, financed, owned, and managed, but it is commitment to each other and the sense of family that make it a community.

Defining an Ecologically Sustainable Community

Considering the loose use of "green" terminology today, we feel it is important to clarify, in the beginning, what we mean when we use the terms "ecological," "sustainable," and "community." We do not mean to dwell on semantics, but rather offer clarity to definitions that mean different things to different people.

"Ecology" refers to the system of interactions

"Today we are well versed in how to pursue technological knowledge but virtually untutored when it comes to pursuing empathetic knowledge. Technological knowledge gives us foresight so that we can better appreciate the life around us. Empathetic knowledge gives us foresight so that we can better cooperate with the community of life. With technological foresight, security comes in exercising power over nature. With empathetic foresight, security comes from belonging to a community.... To end our long, self-imposed exile [from nature]; to rejoin the community of life. This is the task before us."[2]

— Jeremy Rifkin,
Algeny

"The words ecology and economics share a common root (eco) which means 'house' in Greek (oikos). Ecology refers, then, to "nature's science of housekeeping," and economics to "house management." Our planing for the future needs to view these two terms as interdependent."[3]

— Dr. Bill Roley

between organisms and their environment. An ecosystem is made up of organisms and the environment functioning as one interdependent entity. In context with human community, "ecological living" refers to a balanced interaction with the environment in ways that provide for the replenishment and healthy vitality of the larger whole. This means more than just moving to the country and "living lightly on the land," but living fully with other people, working cooperatively, and sharing resources and responsibilities to create a lifestyle that is balanced and sustainable. People are part of an ecosystem as much as plants, animals, and soil are. For our ecosystem to be healthy and vital, we must recognize that we play a powerful role in it. This means we must take into account our interdependence with others and with the land.

The word "sustainable" is often used in conjunction with terms such as agriculture, economy, culture, society, and family. It comes from the word "sustain," which means to maintain and to supply with necessities. We call something sustainable when it provides for the self-renewal and self-replenishing of a whole system and maintains the continued vitality and health of that system. In our terms this includes supporting and strengthening the human spirit to flourish and rejoice.

As defined in the previous chapter, the term "community" derives its meaning from the common circumstances in which people effectively communicate on a daily basis in both a social and physical context.

Today, however, community is often used to refer to everyone who lives or works in the same general area (a part of a city or even the entire city) but have little or no shared social structure or

values. It is also used to refer to those who share a certain ethnic or cultural heritage, and/or social activities, interests, and beliefs, as found in church groups, employee associations and unions, kids' clubs, sports teams, or gangs. These situations provide a shared social structure and experience, but often lack a permanent shared place. These various types of community provide a myriad of economic, social, and cultural benefits, but fall short of being ecologically sustainable.

For community to exist in the way we describe, there must be a physical domain — a turf, village, town, or cluster of some kind — under the control and management of a secure social structure you can belong to, such as an extended family, a council, association, committee, or some other group.

With these definitions in mind, an "ecologically sustainable community" occurs only when all parts and processes of a system — the physical location, natural environment, social and economic structure, physical and emotional health of the inhabitants, factors promoting spiritual, cultural, and personal growth, and resource and energy use — are all sensitively integrated and functioning with each other in a way that provides for the deep harmony, well-being, and perpetuity of each part of the whole system and the system itself. With this kind of harmonious process at work, a stable and cohesive community can take form.

In the search for a harmonious and ecologically sustainable way of life, the asset we most need to cultivate is the lost art of cooperation or operating together for a common goal. Unfortunately, the cooperation skills necessary for living in ecologically sustainable communities are not taught in our schools. Even in the increasing numbers of workshops and publications about ecological farming, pedestrian neighborhoods, healthy building materials, and Eco Villages, there is little mention of people cooperatively sharing land, resources, and daily responsibilities as a way to achieve an ecologically sustainable lifestyle. In this book we describe some of the cooperative skills we feel are necessary for the fullest expression of human community.

Models for Shared Living Communities

In the previous chapter, we reviewed past and present community models from monasteries and villages of the 1200's to the present day communities. Today, a truly ecological approach to community design will take many different forms. But whatever form a Shared Living Community takes, the underlying precepts will likely reflect the traditional patterns of human settlement in which people voluntarily and cooperatively share land, housing, energy, and resources. Here we introduce the designs and benefits of a variety of community options. These models are explored in more detail in succeeding chapters of this book.

"Voluntary Family" house sharing

There are many examples of successful co-owned or co-rented long-term, socially supportive, and affordable voluntary extended family households. It has become a rapidly growing trend in this country for singles, seniors, students, single parents, couples, and young families to use conventional single-family houses, flats, and apartments for shared housing. Some people share housing solely for the economic benefits of shared rent, utilities, and kitchen appliances, while others desire the added companionship

---

The Goose Story
by Dr. Roger Fritz

Next Fall, when you see geese heading south for the winter, flying along in "V" formation, you might consider what science has discovered about why they fly that way.

As each bird flaps its wings, it creates an uplift for the bird immediately following.

By flying in a "V" formation, the whole flock adds at least 71% more flying range than possible if each bird flew on its own.

People who share a common direction and sense of community can get where they are going more quickly and easily because they are traveling on the thrust of one another.

When a goose falls out of formation, it suddenly feels the drag and resistance of trying to go it alone and quickly gets back into formation to take advantage of the lifting power of the bird in front.

If we have as much sense as a goose, we will stay in formation with those who are headed the same way.

When the head goose gets tired, it rotates back in the wing and another moves ahead to fly point.

It is sensible to take turns doing demanding jobs, whether with people or with geese flying south.

Geese honk from behind to encourage those up front to keep up their speed.

What do we say when we honk from behind? Get out of my way!

Finally — when a goose gets sick or is wounded by gunshot and falls out of formation, two other geese fall out with that goose and follow it down to lend help and protection. They stay with the fallen goose until it is able to fly or until it dies. Only then do they launch out on their own or with another formation to catch up with their group.

If we have the sense of a goose, we will stand by each other like that.[6]

---

and emotional support that is possible in an organized shared household. We want to be clear that group house sharing is not the same as living together in overcrowded conditions with more than one person or couple in each bedroom.

"Home Share" programs are one type of voluntary shared housing that benefits the elderly. In this program, an older person with a large and nearly empty house shares it with one or two others who

"The idea that man is a small-community animal is supported by the science of anthropology. For the most part early man was a small-village dweller, and the villages in which he lived were not just accumulations of dwellings, but had well-developed social organization. In fact, the community may be older than mankind, for some of man's nearer relatives among the apes and monkeys also live in organized communities which have [a] definite range of size, characteristic of the species."[7]
— Arthur E. Morgan, "Homo Sapiens: The Community Animal"

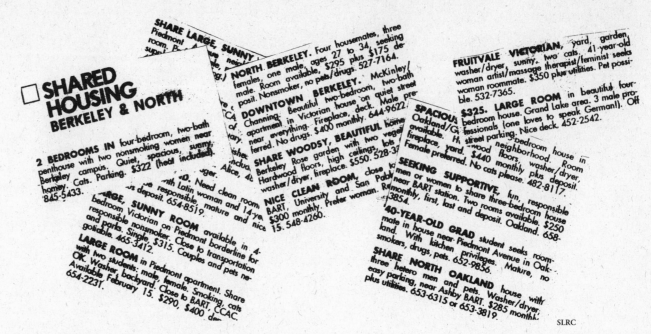

Ads for People Seeking Shared Living Opportunities - A Daily Feature in Most American Newspapers

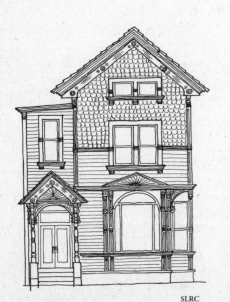

SLRC

provide companionship, assistance with daily tasks, and extra income. These programs have expanded rapidly, and some now serve single-parent families as well as intergenerational households.

The redesigned group house

The problem that arises with the attempt to form voluntary family group houses is the scarcity of appropriately designed houses. Many conventional houses and apartments do not have the right distribution, size, and layout of private rooms and common spaces to meet the long-term needs of the new extended family. Therefore, some extended family groups work together to redesign and remodel existing houses or units in apartment/condo buildings into one larger shared living household.

The key criteria in the redesign is to create a balance between private places and common spaces. However, without creative financing programs that will lend to groups of "unrelated" individuals or extended families, it is difficult to acquire and appropriately redesign existing houses for group living.

The Octagonal Cluster House

This prototype design by Ken Norwood is a 1990's version of the large, extended family house popular in the 1890's, specially redesigned to meet the economic, social, and physical needs of the new extended family. This model is designed from the ground up by the founding core group of future residents, and follows the same precepts for private and common spaces as the redesigned group house

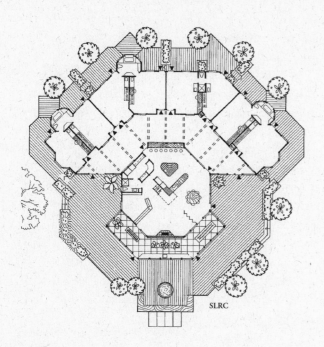

The Village Cluster and CoHousing

The most popular models of community in the United States today are the Village Cluster and CoHousing. The basic layout of these communities consists of approximately 20 to 30 (or more) private units of various sizes clustered around village-like courts or streets, and a common house with a central kitchen, dining and social areas, work studios, childcare facilities, and other amenities.

"A problem with the small size of the nuclear family is that it is not seen as a group, but merely as a relationship not requiring rules. What often happens is that the most powerful gets their way in the absence of rules. The larger enduring household of the extended family has a chance to develop and perfect a wonderful living situation." [8]
— *Chandler Washburne, Ph.D.*

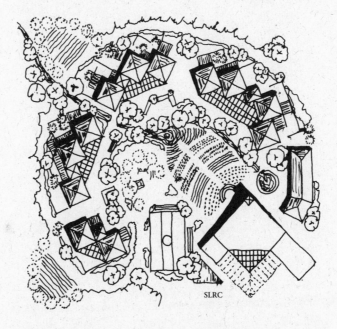

mentioned previously. The basic plan consists of a series of private living suites clustered around common kitchen, dining, and living spaces, and a passive solar court. This is a way for a small group of people or several families to co-design, finance, and build a new, large house which none of them could afford as individuals. This concept offers the advan-tages common to all Shared Living Communities, but with minimal land area requirements, because everything is built under one roof. In Chapter Seven, we present prototype models and actual examples of group houses showing ways that conventional single-family houses and apartment buildings can be redesigned into socially supportive and ecologically sustainable Shared Living Communities, and also the social living processes involved.

Extensive shared gardens and orchards, recreation areas, and open space are common features as well. These communities are co-owned, co-organized, and co-designed, and can be developed by the community itself and/or by a nonprofit or for-profit housing developer. Chapter Four describes fully the social structure and environmental design criteria of the Village Cluster/CoHousing community concept, and presents prototype and actual examples.

57

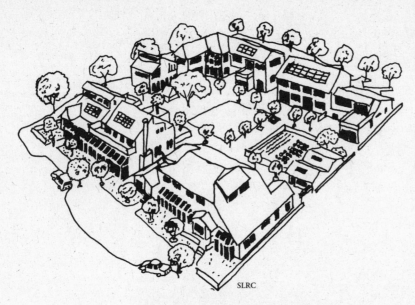

SLRC

The Urban Cooperative Block
This model offers the most socially and environmentally responsible way to transform existing urban and suburban housing into vital, affordable, safe, socially stable, family-supportive, and pedestrian-oriented intentional neighborhoods. It consists of joining together existing adjacent single-family lots and houses through voluntary partnership (agreeing to share the use of adjacent backyards, for example), various forms of co-ownership, or sponsorship from a for-profit or nonprofit housing organization.

Small units and additional bedrooms can be added to convert existing houses into larger group houses. Shared open space, gardens, and recreation areas can be created in joined and redesigned backyards. A central house can be created from one of the original houses or built to create a shared kitchen, dining room, childcare room, activity rooms for older children, teens, and adults, and other amenities.

Another method for creating shared living in the city consists of redesigning existing multi-family buildings and apartment complexes by combining several smaller units into larger extended family units or a series of private living suites with shared areas. Even high-rise multiple-unit buildings can be adapted, with an entire floor or several floors becoming a larger group living residence.

These urban re-use and infill solutions offer affordability, reduced car use, an improved living environment, and a resident-managed community atmosphere. When enough of these community variations are incorporated within walking distance of transit stations and commercial corridors, a truly ecological city will emerge. Chapter Six further discusses the Urban Cooperative Block and other mixed-use examples of Village Cluster/CoHousing in the city.

Intentional Communities
Another successful form of community in the United States and other parts of the world is the Intentional Community. It is composed of a group of people who are more likely to hold a common set of philosophical or religious beliefs that guide their everyday lives. Some also have a strong commitment to promoting the precept of ecological and cooperative community to the rest of the world. Most Intentional Communities are rural and located on farming or forested land, but more are being organized in urban settings in large group houses, converted buildings, or existing urban neighborhood blocks. People in these communities are apt to redesign or build their own dwellings as a group effort, sometimes in phases, and without commercial lending sources. Natural energy, food

self-reliance, and economic independence through community-based enterprises are other common characteristics of Intentional Communities that are not yet prominent in other community models. This model is further explained in Chapters 5 & 6.

Eco Villages
This could be the ultimate in ecologically sustainable and affordable community planning and design, because it links residential Village Clusters with a mixed-use, pedestrian-oriented town core with retail, office, community service, cultural, recreational, and educational facilities. Creating an Eco Village around a station stop on a local light rail and/or interurban high-speed rail line would provide a tremendous opportunity for social revitalization, economic stabilization, and environmental protection of America's inner cities and suburbs. Be aware, however, that many of the "Eco Villages" that are proposed today are just pretty, planned subdivisions with dressed-up streets and front yards, and conventional single-family houses and condos. They are not served by a network of integrated rail and bus systems, and therefore lack one of the most essential ingredients for ecological sustainability.

To qualify as a valid Eco Village there must be numerous pedestrian-oriented Shared Living Community type developments nestled around the community core and transit station. The same principles of resident participation, co-ownership, and designing for cooperation and ecological living as proposed for the other examples presented above is a essential criteria. The criteria for creating workable and sustainable Eco Villages is presented more fully in Chapters Six, Nine, and Ten.

Despite the differences between these various models, they all tend to share a common commitment to democratic self-management and cooperative sharing of land, resources, and responsibilities. It is no accident that people in these types of communities are apt to be environmentally concerned, family and children centered, attuned to humanistic values and gender-equal roles, and committed to some or all shared meals, safe food sources and healthy eating practices.

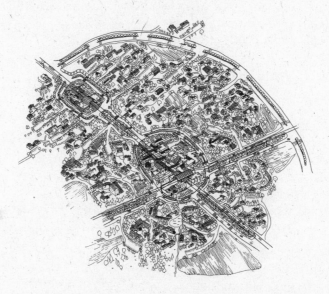

SLRC

The successful formation, growth, and sustainability of Eco Villages, whether planned for new construction or rebuilding existing neighborhoods around a transit station, will be based upon the integrated functioning of the social, economic, and environmental aspects of peoples' lives in a community setting. When peoples' family, social, habitat, and livelihood needs and wants are provided for in a mutually responsible setting, harmonious human dynamics can result.

"I realize that the part of "Intentional Community" which I have long misconstrued is, "intentional." I thought that Intentional Community had to do with the intention to acquire land and develop it in unison with others. But that was just the intention to create something material and was only partially satisfying.... After three years of community planning it occurred to me that even though no land had been purchased or physical plans finalized, the process had already created a community."[9]

— Craig Elevitch,
The Basics of Unintentional Community

"Community may be hard to define, but people know it when they see it, and increasingly those who don't have it are trying to create it. This trend can be seen on all levels of community involvement, from the proliferation of neighborhood salons and discussion groups ... to the astonishing growth of interest in CoHousing and other forms of cooperative community." [10]
— Lynn Murray Willeford, *"Creating Community"*

"We believe that community is something families — whatever their form — hunger for. Families used to find community in churches and synagogues and in extended families. Since these don't work for many of us, we are searching for new forms. Group living is part of that search." [11]
— *The Boston Women's Health Book Collective, Inc.*

More on Terminology — *distinguishing between Village Cluster and CoHousing*

What are the distinctions between the popularly used terms Village Cluster, and CoHousing? In the media and in recent books about community, these terms are intermingled and the meaning of each has become obscured. The term "CoHousing" has come to be been used for almost any housing variation, from a shared or modified single-family house or condo to a large house cut up into separate units. Even co-purchased country acreage on which separate houses are scattered has been called "cohousing" or anIntentional Community.

What is accurately called "CoHousing" in this country originated in Denmark approximately 20 years ago with architect Jan Gudmand-Høyer. It was successfully introduced to this country in 1988 by Charles Durrett and Kathryn McCamant, co-authors of the book *CoHousing*. The "Village Cluster" model was conceived in the early 1980's by Ken Norwood and Claudia Cleaver as they searched for housing alternatives to better satisfy the changing needs and values of the U.S. population. Both of these community types are resident-initiated, co-designed, and self-managed communities with individual household units clustered village style around a common house and other shared facilities.

It has been a basic precept of CoHousing thus far for each home or unit to include a complete, though sometimes smaller, kitchen. In contrast, the Village Cluster model offers the option of having private living suites of several rooms and a bathroom. Instead of private kitchens, several living suites share an adjoining kitchenette and social and eating area (See Village Acre in Chapter One).

These differences, however, are not fundamental. They arise out of individual circumstances and applications. Conceptually, the Village Cluster and CoHousing models are the same. Therefore, in this book we use the combined term of Village Cluster/CoHousing.

Who Wants Community and Why?

These ecologically sustainable community designs are not for everyone. There are many people who will continue, out of both habit and desire, to pursue and place trust in the illusive "American Dream," believing that a car, a mortgage, access to every new product on the market, a 40 (or 50 to 60) hour per week job, and two-plus children are the keys to happiness. These people will abandon the dream only if severe economic and social conditions leave them no choice.

There are many others whose needs, values, and lifestyles are not being accommodated by the American Dream. In the city, the underpaid and non-paid seek redress while housing deteriorates and violence worsens. In the country, pollution grows with every single-family housing development that replaces farmland and open space. People living in both places feel isolated, powerless, and deeply disturbed by the economic, social, and environmental calamities they see around them.

The profiles and stories in the boxes scattered throughout this section represent a cross-section of the types of people — individuals, couples, and families — we have encountered in our work who have expressed a need for or have actually joined some form of Shared Living Community. These stories are composite sketches of real people.

WHY PEOPLE JOIN COMMUNITY

Everyone, regardless of age, income, ethnicity, and family situation, enjoys benefits from living in a community. Some of the benefits are universal, like affordability, shared meals, a sense of belonging, companionship, and more amenities for less cost. Some benefits, however, may be more specific to certain population groups. The following list highlights the key benefits to each population group. Find yourself on the list. Would you like to enjoy some of these benefits? If so, community living may be for you.

Children
- Safe place to play
- More time with parents, elders, and other role models
- Playmates nearby
- Stimulating environment and people/lots to do besides watch TV
- Exposure to new ways of doing things

Low Income/Homeless
- Security/acceptance/respect
- Stability/not moving from place to place or shelter to shelter
- Self-esteem and empowerment from helping others and self
- Power to create own environment and own future
- Responsibility and commitment

Singles
- Chance to co-own in a community
- Companionship
- Extended family environment
- Independence
- Contact with kids and elders
- Learn new skills

Elderly
- Contact with people of all ages
- Independence in own living unit
- Help with household chores when needed
- Security of friends close by
- Responsibility/sense of being needed
- Physical activity and stimulation
- Companionship and social interaction
- Nutritious, varied meals with a supportive group

Teens
- Exposure to multiple role models
- Chance to be a role model for younger children
- Opportunity to learn new skills, hobbies, and ways of living
- Self-esteem from working in community and making decisions with the community
- Leadership and responsibility opportunities
- Peer group/friends nearby
- Special places for play, study, and personal expression

Single Parents
- Help with childcare and household chores
- More free time to pursue interests
- Strong social network/interaction and companionship
- Secure environment
- More role models for kids/don't have to be everything to kids
- Childcare and social needs met on site

Disabled Persons
- Opportunity to design environment and home to be free of any physical barriers
- Interaction and support
- Companionship
- Accepting and safe environment
- Opportunity to be a role model
- Enhanced self-esteem from playing active role in community

Couples
- Privacy with companionship
- Exposure to new ideas
- Interaction with children (not necessarily their own)
- More free time

"Most groups begin when someone holds up a flag to see who salutes. Somebody feels a need to get something done, but realizes they need help. So they begin talking to others, usually friends and associates." [12]
— *Claude Whitmyer*

Although our society still holds the nuclear family as the ideal household type for everyone, increasingly more people are finding that the Shared Living Community concept offers exactly what they need for a fulfilling and supportive social environment in a new kind of extended family.

The people who can benefit from Shared Living Communities are a diverse group, covering a wide range of circumstances and ages, from children to centenarians. These people may be singles or couples, older persons, "empty-nesters," remarried step-families, those recovering from addiction or abuse or struggling with poverty, homelessness, or just plain loneliness, or someone else. Many of these people now rent houses and apartments with

no hope of ever owning, or they have houses that are too large for their needs, and do not know how to best use them. All seek a sense of family in a supportive, affordable, and safe environment.

Singles, single parents, and elders, partly because they make up such a large percentage of our population and partly because they are often the most isolated and alienated groups, can benefit immensely from community and can contribute most to making change for a positive future. Imagine what would happen if large numbers of single people and single-parent families lived in supportive, affordable, and ecologically sustainable communities. The burdens, pain, and isolation of modern living would be lightened or eliminated. Time and energy to pursue personal interests and social change would be abundant.

All these people are looking for ways to use energy responsibly, have safe, fresh, and natural food, and enjoy the diverse and expansive architectural amenities and material possessions made more affordable through shared, rather than individual, ownership. Although immediate physical, economic, and emotional personal needs are often the motivating factors in searching for and creating community, many people are also expressing a desire to work for social and environmental change, and see community as an appropriate vehicle. Despite widespread denial, the connection our lifestyle has to species extinction, ozone depletion, violence, and a host of other serious problems facing our society is becoming obvious. Living in a community and cooperating with others is a way to enjoy a full range of ecological, social, financial, physical, and spiritual benefits, while making a positive contribution to society and the natural

---

• Dave, age 36, the single-parent father of Tommy, 11, and Hillary, 6. He wants:
　　Right livelihood
　　Help with childcare
　　Adult role models for his children
　　Connection with other adults

SLRC

Dave lives with his son and takes care of his daughter part-time. *"I want to live where there are people to watch my children while I'm working. I want the security of knowing my children are safe and well cared for and not watching TV or playing in the streets."*
In a Village Cluster community, Dave is secure in knowing that Tommy and Hillary are well cared for in the common house after-school programs. Dave is committed to working toward ecological solutions to today's problems through his livelihood. By sharing resources and responsibilities in the community, Dave has gained the financial stability to establish a business in his home and provide services to people on a sliding scale. He feels that every business venture he's involved with *should in some way be part of the solution, environmentally and socially.*

• Bob and Doris, ages 60 and 64, retired, on a fixed income.
  They want:
      Active adults around them
      Access to the countryside
      Affordable housing
      A supportive social group

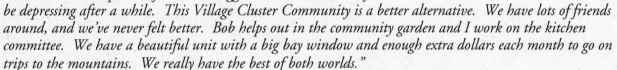

This is how Bob and Doris describe their situation: *"We have one Social Security check now, another in two years, and a few thousand dollars in savings. We were considering buying a small piece of land up north and building our own home, but even there land is too expensive for our nest egg, and the isolation may be depressing after a while. This Village Cluster Community is a better alternative. We have lots of friends around, and we've never felt better. Bob helps out in the community garden and I work on the kitchen committee. We have a beautiful unit with a big bay window and enough extra dollars each month to go on trips to the mountains. We really have the best of both worlds."*

environment. Positive change follows naturally from the formation of community.

When people find that something no longer works for their individual survival, they will very often reluctantly conform anyway, or if well moptivated and financialy able, seek innovative changes, or resort to antisocial and ultimately criminal behavior. Without positive working models, attempts to change established institutions often repeat the same old cycles, making conformity, suppression, and/or rebellion inevitable. Shared Living Communities offer a workable alternative for a positive and fulfilling future in uncertain times. Fortunately, the elements for positive change already exist in the form of innovative social models, examples of ecological community design, and a variety of inventive alternatives that can inspire and move us toward socially and environmentally harmonious community.

New Forms of Family

New social and cultural relationships and environmental living methods are evolving, partly in response to old hierarchical institutions of male domination and suppression and subordination of women. There is no reason to believe that these new relationship models will mirror the old forms called marriage, monogamy, and the nuclear family. We are now seeing the possibility of more diversity, gay and lesbian couples and families, women not having children, having children later or having fewer children, unmarried single mothers, single-parent fathers, the new extended family, and more interest in and information about polyfidelitous families (nonmonogamous group marriages). Despite the fact that some of these new sub-groupings may not be socially and culturally acceptable for all, the movement toward exploration of family alternatives shows significant evidence that a self-

"Older people need to pare down the responsibility of maintaining a larger home on a fixed income. But retirement communities [are not the answer. They] are isolated from the real world. We like the mix of ages and families that CoHousing communities attract." [13]
— *A Member of the Winslow CoHousing Group*

"If physical violence is the foundation upon which the oppression of women by men is built, then shattering that fear must precede any effective attempts at equality…. Being free of any physical intimidation, being able to stand on a level playing field economically, gives women and men the freedom to begin cleansing themselves of their accumulated sexist attitudes and internalized oppression…. It is vital to the long term existence of an egalitarian community that each member believe they are equal to every other member. Living communally seems to have one common positive effect: boosting confidence." [14]
— *Keenan, Twin Oaks Community*

• Heather and Tobi, ages 26 and 29, nurse and law student/poet, parents of Alex, age 3. They want:

    An open-minded community
    Male role models they can trust
    Help with childcare
    Affordable housing

As a lesbian couple, Heather and Tobi need support and acceptance for their lifestyle, and male role models for their son. Because they joined a core group for an Urban Cooperative Block community, they were able to get to know the community members before they moved in, giving them assurance that the community would be supportive and safe for their son and themselves. The community also built a childcare center next to the common house. Now, Alex can be cared for right in the community by people he knows.

• Amy, age 22, a student and single. She wants:

    A place of her own
    Companionship
    Independence
    A well-equipped kitchen
    Affordable housing
    Access to shared tools

Amy longed for a place away from her domineering parents, but didn't have the money to set up her own household with the amenities and tools she was used to having. In her Shared Living Community group house, she is able to afford the monthly rent for a small suite of her own, which gives her the privacy and independence she wants. Amy also enjoys her turn to cook using the well-equipped group kitchen. Best of all, she has the companionship of her fellow community members instead of the isolation of living alone.

renewing and self-correcting social process is arising out of the social upheaval we are now witnessing.

The Baby Boomers — *why so many changes from one generation?*

Fairly recently in our history another movement toward social and cultural change took place, a movement that really consisted of several movements. These movements began with the Black liberation movement and continued with the women's rights movement, and a myriad of others. Baby boomers were an integral part of this process. When we say Baby Boomers (BB's) we mean primarily the early BB's, those born between 1946 and 1954, although the later BB's, and every generation since, have been making significant changes.

Now, as the movement toward ecologically sustainable community takes hold, we see BB's again at the forefront. Approximately 80% of the people who have been involved in SLRC workshops and profile sessions have been BB's. Intentional Communities and CoHousing communities are also heavily populated with BB's.

When we look at why so many socially progressive activists have arisen from this one generation, we see an unprecedented social-political phenomenon. Their role today is in part due to their large numbers and in part due to their financial status and ability to make choices in how they want to live. But that is not the only answer.

BB's have been socially, culturally, and politically preconditioned in ways that most generations before or since were not. The BB parents brought to their children personal stories of the gore and glories of "defending America against tyranny" in

WW II, of growing up in the Depression of the 1930's, and of having Franklin D. Roosevelt as President during most of that time, and of the opportunities, especially for education because of the GI Education Bill that existed in America after the war. BB's grew up in an atmosphere of post-war euphoria, a mind-numbing fear of nuclear holocaust, and the trauma of the Vietnam War.

This induced many of them, on both sides of the political fence, to become protesters, activists, and survivalists. They reached for higher levels of self-expression and self-actualization, and they reached beyond status quo patterns of behavior. They overtly dismissed organized religion in search of alternative belief systems and ideals that better dealt with the dissatisfactions and frustrations of the 1960's. Women began to question hierarchical male domination and a few men began to question their conditioning and role as sole provider. Not-withstanding, it is also true that the BB generation and their parents have had the most serious impact upon the environment due to their high level of material consumption.

Among the reasons why subgroups of BB's are showing interest in creating new extended family and community-oriented living arrangements today is that they were more apt to grow up in larger nuclear families with or near their intergenerational extended family. They were in closer touch with their elders than are recent generations growing up in the smaller and more fragmented family structure of today. BB's are therefore more apt to have experience with sharing responsibilities in family and community from stories passed down from elders and being a part of larger extended families. This not so long ago heritage must be restored.

The Social-Economic Changes are Being Matched by a Multitude of Solutions

As the large numbers of BB's become senior citizens, we may see even more spectacular changes in American lifestyles and housing options. Solving the health care, declining income, housing, and finally the elder-care needs of this group could be the catalyst for major advancements in the Shared Living Community movement, especially regarding intergenerational housing objectives. It is naive to think that the generation that spawned the flower children will be content with the insulation and isolation of "seniors only" housing.

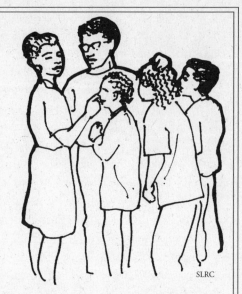

- Roberta and Franklin, ages 45 and 46, physical therapist and computer repair specialist, parents of Tamika, 15, Jamaal, 10, and Oman, 7. They want:

    A safe neighborhood in the city

    A large natural area for play

    A diverse group of people to interact with

    Proximity to schools

    Convenient transit access to jobs

    Affordable housing

"Raising three kids anywhere is difficult, but especially in the city. We feel it's important for our kids and us to participate in a nearby school. But in the city, decent housing near schools and transit was too costly even for our two paychecks. But the alternative — moving to the suburbs — meant a two-hour drive to work. Besides, the suburbs are so White. We want our kids to grow up in a place where there are more Black people like us, and they can get to know other cultures as well. We don't like them watching TV all day and seeing so much violence. We want them to live in a place where there is lots to do and see, where they may even forget about TV. We want to provide them with the best life we can without putting ourselves in debt." In an Urban Cooperative Block, Roberta and Franklin are able to enjoy the best qualities of the city — social diversity, access to school and cultural centers — as well as the security of community and lots of protected yard space for their kids to play in. They even created live-work places in their home, allowing them more time with their kids while still working full-time.

SLRC

Expanding Community Building Resources to Lower Income Populations

Thus far, the opportunities to work intensely with lower income groups to create participatory community have been few. Poverty and low-income programs have tended to provide only immediate emergency services and conventional rental housing. Some nonprofit developers, government housing agencies, and nonprofit and for-profit financial institutions have treated low-income housing like a market-rate commodity in which resident control, a cooperative social structure, and environmental design amenities are not given sufficient priority.

The Habitat for Humanity program is one example of a growing trend to involve low-income people as participants in meeting their own housing needs. Their work to date, however, has mostly involved conventionally designed and owned single-family houses. Their expertise, however, in organizing for self-help building remains a model that could be readily adapted to the cooperative community building process and design prototypes presented in this book. In fact, the San Francisco Bay

Area Chapter of Habitat for Humanity is working with a CoHousing community core group in Pacifica, California on a mixed low- and moderate-income housing cluster. This may be a valuable precedent for obtaining more funds to organize and train lower income groups for community self-building and management. This use of housing funds has often been denied by conventional lenders and some governmental funding sources. As a result, most of the constituency of past Shared Living Community workshops and profile sessions, as well as CoHousing workshops, has been moderate to middle income white people.

The important, although limited, work that has been done with poverty level and low-income people in organizing for Shared Living Communities demonstrates that, when given the opportunity and organizing tools, these people eagerly seek self-

• Janine, formerly homeless and on welfare, single mother of twins, Rachel and Rabine, 4. She wants:
    Affordable housing
    A safe place to raise children
    Childcare so she can work
    Support from other adults

"Since I had my children, I've had a hard time getting good housing. I couldn't work because I couldn't afford childcare. Welfare paid my bills, but it was barely enough to pay for food and health care, let alone housing. With twins it's especially difficult because it's twice the cost of one kid and rents go up faster than welfare benefits. The most home my children ever knew was life in the shelter. Now we can start our new lives. As a single parent, this intergenerational group house gives me a new start. It's affordable, has built-in childcare, and provides mutual support from everyone for everyone — it's great for single moms."

SLRC

• Raj and Kathy, ages 29 and 32, architecture student and counselor. They want:
    To own their own home
    Contact with a larger community
    Wheelchair accessibility for Kathy
    Affordable monthly payments

Since Kathy uses a wheelchair, they found that their housing options were limited. Modifying an apartment for wheelchair access was too expensive, especially since they might live there for only a few years. They attended a slide presentation sponsored by a Shared Living Community core group in their area that was planning an Octagonal Cluster House. Kathy and Raj worked with the group to make the whole community barrier-free so that Kathy and other wheelchair users could have full access to community life. This meant that as the members aged and their ambulatory abilities changed, they could remain in the community instead of being forced into an elder-care home.

SLRC

"If you are a Boomer approaching elder status, you are likely to be more receptive than your forebears to sharing schemes that encourage community. As Jerry Gerber and his coauthors point out in Lifetrends, 'Given their experiences with communal living while young, [boomers] should have fewer inhibitions about sharing housing than have any previous generation of elders.'"[17]
    — *Carolyn R. Shaffer & Kristin Anundsen*

- How do the children feel?
Toshiro, Brianna, Jordan, and Abraham, ages 10, 11, 8, and 10, friends in an Urban Cooperative Block community:

Toshiro: *"I never had any kids to play with at our apartment. Just Mom and me. I watched lots of TV then. Now I hardly watch any cause there's so many kids here to play with."*

Abraham: *"With all the kids here I feel like I've got lots of brothers and sisters. And our neighbor Bob showed me how to make a crane out of a piece of paper. It's so great."*

Jordan: *"I like best the pottery shop, gardening, and the big jungle gym in the common courtyard. We could never have anything like this when we lived in our apartment, we didn't even have a yard."*

Brianna: *"I like having more time with Mom and Dad. Since there are other people to help with chores, that gives them more time to play with me."*

"Mother Nature didn't intend for all of us to be parents…. Parenting isn't the only reason for an adult to relate to children. Kids also make excellent friends. I relate to an ever-increasing number of families as a sort of extended member … children's energy is necessary to adults. An adult who pays respectful attention to kids will get a lot of food for thought." [18]
— Margie Menzel, Utne Reader

sufficiency, co-ownership, and community responsibilities. Low and moderate to middle income working people must have equal access to socially supportive extended family and participatory community. They represent a large and growing segment of our population not served by the lenders and developers of market-rate housing. Competition for the limited supply of moderate to lower-cost housing pushes the middle income people against low-income people, who, in turn, push poverty-level people through the cracks into overcrowded housing or homelessness. The Shared Living Community concepts presented in this book are part of the rising "Third Sector," housing

movement which consists of community, co-ownership, self-management, and permanent affordability for all people.

Responsible change will not come from the outside through some omnipotent power. We must look to ourselves for the resources and motivation needed to make positive changes. We have seen from the example of the BB's, and from minority and other protest groups since the 1960's that many significant changes can be effectively initiated with a relatively small handful of people — 15% to 25%. Remember that the civil rights movement began with one woman, Rosa Parks, refusing to give up her seat to a younger White man. It was just 30 years ago that abortion was illegal and Blacks went to separate schools. In a short period of time with a few dedicated people working together, we can greatly increase the acceptance of ecologically sustainable communities in our society.

- Sara, age 61, retired widow. She wants:
Companionship
Contact with children
A smaller home that she can maintain by herself
A lower cost of living

"I was all alone in the house I owned. I have no interest in a retirement community, and living with my children was not an option. I want to have the stimulation of children and people of all ages. Here in our Village Cluster I have all I wanted."

Children and the Family in Community — Avenues for Growth and Maturity

In Chapter Two we addressed some of the issues facing families and children today — less time together, isolation, latchkey child syndrome, difficult or costly childcare choices, high costs of living, boredom, and lack of security. Despite changes in demographics, the nuclear family is still viewed as the traditional family form, and although, in many ways, it offers support, stability, and continuity to its members, it can also be ingrown and insulated from other people and experiences. It can protect, but it can also limit the life experiences and opportunities of its members by narrowly defining gender roles and patterns of behavior, and by not offering the family or the individual opportunities for growth or change.

Shared Living Communities offer the best of both worlds — a small intimate family group that provides privacy and continuity, as well as a larger extended family group that provides diversity, expanded opportunities, and social interaction. For children this balance is especially important. The insular world of the nuclear family and overexposure to violence, bigotry, and sexism through the entertainment and news media give children a narrow vision of the world and few avenues for exploring their talents, skills, and dreams. In the context of a community, children can learn new skills, new definitions of self, and new ways of doing things.

To begin, communities are often child-friendly places with abundant areas for play. Because members co-design the community, they can consider the full range of children's needs and design accordingly. Members can avoid use of space conflicts by creating specially designed areas to accommodate different activities for both children and adults. This is a benefit rarely enjoyed by families in tract houses. Involving children in the design process is a fun way to give them a sense of ownership and belonging.

Placing cars on the periphery and creating centrally located play/social areas creates a safe and secure environment in which children, even young ones, can play and roam freely. Parents know that the area is safe and that community members — friends — are watching out for their children. Outside baby-sitters are rarely, if ever, needed because there are so many "aunts," "uncles," and "grandparents" in the community who the children feel comfortable with and the parents trust. Often when children get to be eight or nine, parents in communities don't even bother arranging formal baby-sitting — they just leave their children at home, knowing that people will be near by if they need help. From this experience, children gain a sense of confidence and responsibility at a young age — a sense of independence that is wholly different from that which comes from being left alone in front of the TV all day while parents are out working.

Children in communities are not dependent on their parents to meet all of their emotional, physical, and social needs. They have ready-made playmates and friends right next door. These friends are not always just children. Communities provide children with unique opportunities to develop meaningful, secure, and legitimate friendships with adult men and women other than their parents. What this means for children is a broader support base and more people in their daily lives who care for and are interested in them. What this means for parents is freedom from the burden and stress of being the only role model in their child's life.

If a child has only one or two adult role models (i.e. parents) what happens when that person(s) is tired, irritable, or angry? The child has no other person to turn to, and therefore must suffer the consequences of that adult's quite normal inability to provide appropriate care all of the time. Existing communities have proven that children freed from exclusive dependence on one or two adults for love, support, and guidance tend to be healthier, more emotionally balanced, and more mature. Parents in community tend to be more relaxed and open, with more time to relate to their child's unique characteristics.

This broader support system is especially critical for teenagers who in community have other adults to connect with and seek help from when they are in the process of individuating from their parents. Teens also have the opportunity to gain responsibility, experience, confidence, and self-esteem by becoming role models and friends to the younger children in their community. They can develop caretaker skills, especially important for boys to learn, and they are encouraged to question their own sense of who they are as they help guide someone younger in becoming who they are. This is also true for adults acting as mentors who may feel they understand themselves and the world, but in relating to children or teens discover new questions and aspects of themselves to explore.

It is important for children (and adults) to see life from many points of view. Maturity, cultural development, and understanding come from participating in a variety of activities and interacting with people with varying backgrounds, interests, lifestyles, and standards of behavior. Children in community can see that different adults respond to similar events in different ways. In seeing this variety and diversity, children can learn that nothing is set in stone — that there are different ways of doing things, of seeing, of thinking, and of being. They can learn to relate to people as individuals and to make decisions for themselves about how they think or feel or want to respond to a situation.

Children in community also have more opportunity to witness adult men and women in healthy, respectful relationships — to see how they make decisions and resolve conflicts. The world is not a homogeneous place, with standardized ideals and practices. Living in a community can demonstrate that people with varying backgrounds and beliefs can live together successfully. This does not mean that there will not be problems. But by learning to resolve them in an atmosphere of love, support, and continuity, children can build greater self-esteem and competence, a willingness to take chances, an ability to stick up for themselves, a sense of respect for others, and a sense of responsibility.

Multiple role models also means children can learn more skills as they develop relationships with adults who share their interests. Children can learn to paint, garden, or work with wood even if their parents don't know how. They can develop their own skills, not based on whether they are a boy or a girl, but based on their talents, dreams, and desires. When they see Bob and John making bread and Jennifer fixing the leaky faucet, their definitions of themselves and the possibilities for their future are expanded.

Some parents may feel threatened by their children developing strong friendships with other adults. But you are not less of a parent if you can't teach your child yoga and the person next door can. In fact, being a good parent may mean that you allow your children to develop and explore their own interests and relationships, giving them the security and love to do so with confidence. Parents can't possibly be everything to their children. For example, a single mom just can't be a "dad" to her child. A balance between male and female modeling is critical to the healthy development and maturation of a child. Far too many children are growing up with no male role models or father figures in their lives. Often, all they know of men is what they see on TV and these images are often of violent and sexist men. In communities, children get to see men in multiple roles — as cooks, carpenters, meeting facilitators, fathers, husbands, and friends.

Children also develop a strong sense of identity as they participate in the workings and decision making of the community. Everyone needs to feel a sense of belonging, control, and participation. In community, kids have this. They are seen, heard, appreciated, and respected for their role and contribution to the group. From participating in meetings, workgroups, and activities, children can learn to work cooperatively with others and effectively articulate their ideas and feelings. Most communities work hard to develop effective meeting facilitation, conflict resolution, and other group process techniques. Children learn these, as well as the value of working things out in a respectful way. They take these skills with them into their schools and their adult lives.

Adults, especially those without children of their own, benefit from having relationships with children. The unconditional love they receive, the connection to the renewing and magical world of childhood, and the perspective children offer through fresh eyes is something to be cherished. As Shoshana Alexander, author of "In Praise of Single Parents" states,

> To relate to a child is to recognize what it is to be an adult. To take on responsibility for a child is an avenue to genuine maturity....When adults give time to children, they are preparing those children to do the same when they mature.[45]

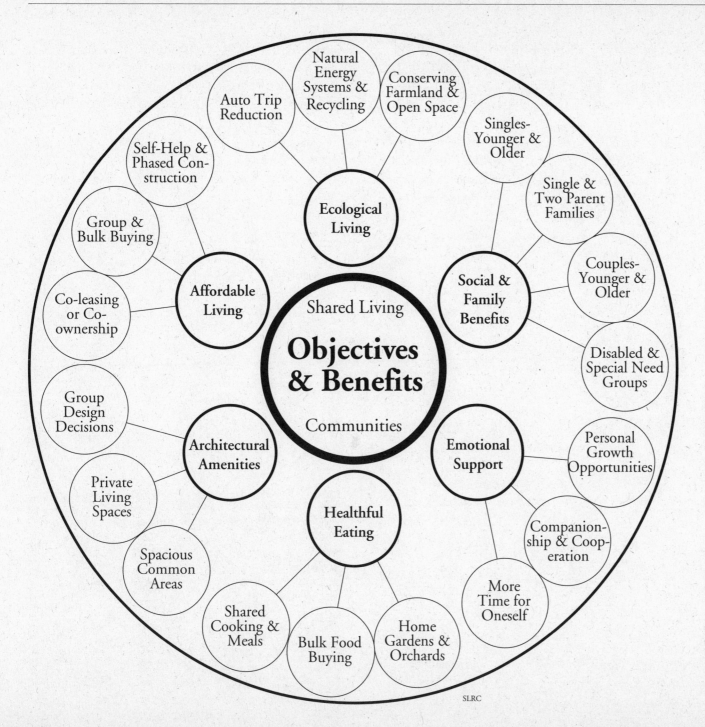

Natural Energy Systems & Recycling

Conserving Farmland & Open Space

Auto Trip Reduction

Self-Help & Phased Construction

Singles- Younger & Older

Group & Bulk Buying

Single & Two Parent Families

Ecological Living

Co-leasing or Co-ownership

Affordable Living

Social & Family Benefits

Couples- Younger & Older

Group Design Decisions

Shared Living

Objectives & Benefits

Communities

Disabled & Special Need Groups

Private Living Spaces

Architectural Amenities

Emotional Support

Personal Growth Opportunities

Spacious Common Areas

Healthful Eating

Companion- ship & Coop- eration

Shared Cooking & Meals

Bulk Food Buying

Home Gardens & Orchards

More Time for Oneself

SLRC

This diagram represents all the components of a fully developed Shared Living Community. These are the topics that a community core group will need to become familiar with during the formation of the community. The workshop process described in this chapter goes into these topics in detail.

These objectives and benefits can apply equally to a small group, a new extended family and the larger of human gatherings — the entire neighborhood, city, region, or the entire society of humankind on this planet. This is an universal model for sustainability.

Objectives and Benefits

All humans share fundamental needs and desires that stem from and ultimately surpass the basic instincts to survive and perpetuate the species. In our culture, these range from the need for economic security to the desire for personal/spiritual development that often appears when basic needs are met. The *Objectives and Benefits Diagram* identifies six areas of our lives in which Shared Living Communities can offer a higher quality, more ecologically sustainable way of life.

Social and family benefits

Because of its design and participatory organizational structure, a Shared Living Community encourages diversity in social interaction, gender equality, communication and sharing between generations, and family support more than conventional housing does.

"Community gives me a greater sense of friendship on a spontaneous basis which allows me to be supported in life issues. My family has more time to spend together in the evenings before dinner without working to prepare food. My children have outlets to play with their peers rather than hanging on us as they did in our old single family home."
— *Participant in SLRC Workshop*

Photo by Tim Hinz, Courtesy of Country Almanac

Shared House Residents
Human Investment Project, San Mateo, California sponsors senior and single patent shared houisng.

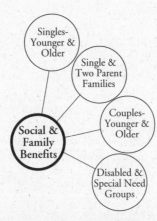

• **Single people, younger and older**, have the opportunity to interact with others and feel a sense of family while maintaining the privacy they want

and need. The mix of people and experiences enhances communication, the cultivating and sustaining force of culture and heritage.

• **Single- and two-parent families** can share the responsibility of caring for their children. Community-based childcare and after-school activities make the task of parenting easier. Childrencan have playmates inthe community, a variety of male and female role models, and opportunities to gain self-esteem and confidence.

• **Couples, younger and older**, can have private time, individually and together, while still enjoying interaction with others. Because community members share responsibilities, working parents have more time for their children, themselves, and each other. Couples can choose to be child-free and have children in their lives. Communities founded on gender-equal principles offer a supportive and safe environment for women and men.

• **Disabled and older persons,** as well as members of other special-needs groups, can live independently knowing that others are nearby. They have the opportunity to interact with

Father and Son   Photo by William A. Porter people of all ages and abilities, learn new skills, participate in the responsibilities and decision-making of the community, and share their "wisdom of experience" with younger people. This interaction helps to restore the intergenerational communication that modern society has lost.

Emotional Support
Our personal needs for companionship, nurturing, and self-esteem are seldom mentioned as housing concerns or criteria, yet there is no better place than where we live for fulfilling these needs. Designing community-oriented housing with resident cooperation and interaction from the beginning opens the way for serving the fullest range of human needs.

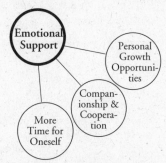

• **Personal growth opportunities** are provided through day-to-day social interactions and the use of specific conflict resolution exercises to work out differences in a caring and supportive atmosphere. Shared responsibilities offer the chance for individuals to contribute to the well-being of others and gain self-esteem and confidence for themselves. In this way abusive relationships will be discouraged.
• **Companionship and cooperation** are inherent in the self-managed, self-sufficient structure of Shared Living Communities. With open sharing, people of different cultural backgrounds, income levels, and

ages can come to know and support one another, contributing to the sense of community and pride in self that used to come from the extended family.
• **More time for oneself** comes from distributing the responsibility for community chores such as cooking, childcare, and gardening within the larger group. This should be particularly beneficial for women, who would be relieved of the weight of domestic chores which many "modern" men still do not perform.

Healthful eating
There is a fast-moving national movement towards healthy and safe food. More people are exploring community as a way to take control of their own food production. Considering both declining incomes and the desire for ecological living, the community approach to sharing food becomes a win-win solution.

• **Home gardens and orchards** can provide an abundance of tasty, pesticide-free food and a relaxing and fulfilling way for community members to spend time working together. Community members could also profit from the livelihood and income produced by bartering or selling extra crops.
• **Bulk food buying** reduces packaging waste, cuts down on the number of car trips for day-to-day

"When Beatrice asked her daughter what she thought she would think later about having lived in this community, her daughter replied, 'Think about? Think about! I'll still be here.'"[19]
— *The Boston Women's Health Book Collective, Inc.*

"For American women terrified of being mothers, communal life removes the threat of exclusive responsibility for children."[20]
— *Kathrin Perutz, Liberated Marriage*

"When we act collectively to meet our needs we are more free to share resources and to do the political and community work needed for social change. The very process of experimenting with living and work communities gives us tools to build a cooperative society. Examples of intergenerational cooperation can help shape our children's and our own sense of the possible. Our community can be the testing ground for our wider vision."
— *Participant in an SLRC Consultation Session*

shopping, makes it easy to eat nutritious food for less, and provides big savings in time, money, and resource consumption.

• **Shared cooking and meals** can become the sustaining experience that will bond members and build community. The opportunity to socialize at common meals can enhance the lives of adults and children alike, providing each with the opportunity to learn, share, and grow.

Architectural amenities

The uniqueness of the Shared Living Community approach to designing and developing housing stems from community members' participation in the process from beginning to end. In this system, the members become an essential part of the developer, lender, builder, and architect loop.

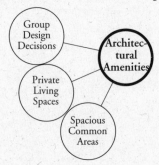

• **Group design decisions** enable all to participate in planning for the immediate and long-term needs of the group, as well as the special needs of the individual members. Special care is given to adequately distinguish between private and common areas.

• **Private living spaces,** whether individual rooms, living suites, apartments, or houses, are essential for every person and family. Each living space can have a separate entrance, loft, balcony, deck, court, and/

or movable partitions to meet varying space needs as family size, needs, and reource capabilities change over time.

• **Spacious common areas** can include a common kitchen, dining and living areas, a childcare room, teen room, elder-care facilities, library/study, offices, workshops, darkroom, music room, exercise and meditation spaces, hot tubs, saunas, and other special features. These amenities become affordable when people work cooperatively and pool their resources.

Affordable living

In a co-owned community, the members can more equitably share the full costs of mortgages, taxes, insurance, and maintenance. They can also cooperatively reduce other costs of living such as food and energy expenses, all of which add to increased affordability.

• **Self-help** is more practical on the larger scale of a Shared Living Community than on the small scale of a single-family house. Individual living units or suites can be finished by each resident and enlarged or redesigned to meet changing needs, and common amenities added with a phased-development plan. This reduces costs, allows personalization of each unit, and builds a sense of personal and group empowerment.

• **Group buying and sharing** of household and community supplies, appliances, health and car insurance, and even cars can significantly reduce the costs of living, packaging waste, and consumption of resources.

• **Co-leasing or co-ownership**, with taxes, insurance, maintenance, and management fees shared by all, leads to significant cost savings. Mixed-use and mixed-income developments that incorporate some rental units allow those people without enough cash or equity to buy in and still share in the benefits of a Shared Living Community.

Ecological living

The ultimate success of ecologically sustainable communities will come when we move away from the production of car-dependent, low-density, detached housing on separate lots and adopt the new directions offered by Shared Living Communities in which people can cooperatively use land, resources, and energy — a very significant message about ecological living is sent to every-one.

• **Conserving Farmland and open space** would be furthered by the compact clustering of units in already urbanized and developed areas. Cluster housing commuities could be built in rural/mountain areas, but only with close and careful planning

to prevent open-ended sprawl and increased demand for local governemtal services.

• **Natural energy systems, recycling,** and the conservation of resources are facilitated by the large scale of a Shared Living Community. Alternative energy sources like wind and solar power are not economical on the scale of today's single-family units. The cooperative economic and social structure and community desig make such long-term investments practical and less time-consuming..

• **Car trip reduction** is one of the most important ecological benefits of the Shared Living Community housing and urban planning model. Sharing responsibilities reduces the need for many daily trips

"I own a shared house (formerly a duplex) in Sacramento. I don't know very many things for sure, but I know that people are healthier and happier in groups. I believe suburbs are marketing devices to get people to be consumers. The more separate houses, the more appliances and floor covering and cars and "stuff" people will need to buy."
— Participant in an SLRC Workshop

Car Sharing: Getting More People Into Fewer Cars

Many people in SLRC workshops and profile sessions indicate a willingness for more than car pooling. They say they would co-own cars, trucks, and vans with members of their community. The cost savings of shared ownership can be tremendous, since the fixed costs of owning a car (payments, interest, maintenance, insurance) are much higher than the per-mile costs (gas, oil, tires). Recent studies by the American Automobile Association also show that the costs in both categories are rising every year. For example, average total insurance costs, including collision, comprehensive, and property damage/liability, increased from $645 in 1989 to $744 in 1993. Average tax, license, and registration costs rose from $144 in 1989 to $178 in 1993. Depreciation has risen as well, from an average of $2,018 in 1989 to $2,830 in 1993.

Aside from these costs, which visibly affect the owner's wallet, there are the hidden costs — to human health, to the land, air, and water, and to society "Getting people out of their cars" cannot happen in a vacuum — there must be a socioeconomic structure, an environmental design structure, and a public transit system, that serve all people equally. This is where Shared Living Communities and Eco Cities come in. As people share responsibilities and have daily interactions during shared meals and activities in common places, we are building towards a time when people will not only co-own cars but also use cars less.

"Ironically, skyrocketing per capita consumption has largely failed to make the people of consumer societies much happier. Repeated opinion surveys show, for example, that the share of Americans reporting they are 'very happy' has stayed around one third since 1957, despite a doubling of personal consumption expenditures.... Worse, adopting the consumer lifestyle may have eroded what psychologists recognize as two key sources of fulfillment in life — social relations and leisure time. Informal visits between neighbors, family conversations, and family meals have all diminished in the U.S. since 1950." [21]

— Alan Durning,
Worldwatch Institute

Down With Mini-Condos, Up With Co-Owning a Whole Village

"I've found it, the perfect house for us. It's got everything!" Janice dropped the groceries on the counter of the mini-kitchen of the mini-condo she and Jim had bought six months earlier. She moved into and out of a quick hug as her words and hands joyfully expressed the new find. *"Can you imagine — for less than we're paying for this cubby hole, we could share a large wood-beamed living room, a fabulous fully equipped kitchen, a food processing pantry, and a hot tub, decks, garden space in a huge yard, and we would have our own master suite with two rooms, bathroom, and a loft."* She danced circles around the astonished Jim until his outstretched arms caught her.

"Where? What is it? How much?" he pleaded, grinning. *"Wow, you're really hyped up."*

As they stocked the mini-refrigerator and the mini-cupboards, Janice filled in the details. *"It's the Lorimer Cluster Community across town near the light rail station. There are 24 group houses around a huge common house on 3-1/2 acres, but there's plenty of open space. Some of the houses have two, some have three master suites. They all share the common house which has a kitchen, a dining room, childcare facilities, a store, library, and more — it was too much for me to see on the first round."*

Jim couldn't help but respond to Janice's excitement. He recalled how they had so enthusiastically jumped at the idea of buying the mini-condo. It had seemed so right at the time to invest in their own place instead of paying rent for years. He'd been having second thoughts for some time. Her new find sounded good. He listened eagerly.

"It's a cooperative ownership cluster, and they have it well organized. Core group workshops are part of the package with long-term, co-owner mortgages, and the private suites are really well designed with skylights, decks, and a large wood stove...." She laughed. *"I wouldn't be surprised if you didn't believe me."*

"Believe you?" Jim retorted as he crammed a can of soup onto the eight inch wide shelf and slammed the door. *"I'd believe anything to get out of this — this mini-hovel! Remember how the real-estate ads called this 'getting your start at the American Dream?' Ugh! We're living the American nightmare!"*

They hugged each other, and Janice admitted, *"Good! I've already signed us up for the next core group workshop."*

The above scene represents the real-life dilemma of people trying to find decent, affordable housing that they can call home. Cooperative ownership of a community is an option that many Americans who have given up on the "Dream House" are beginning to explore.

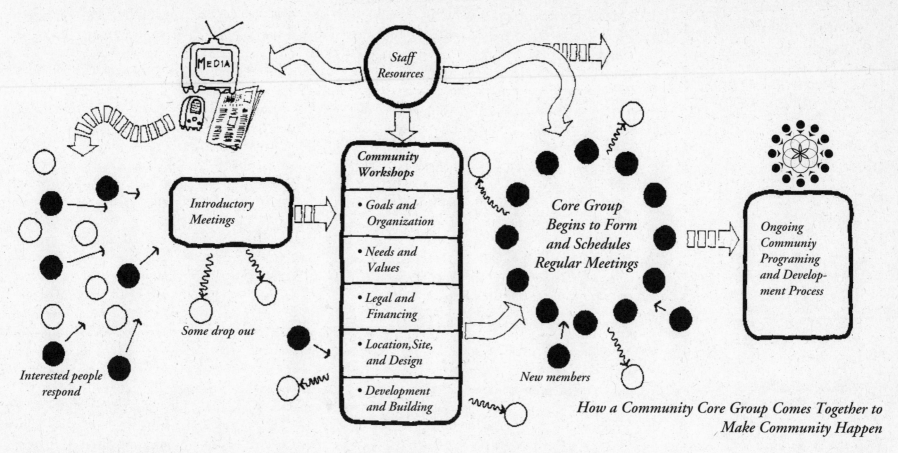

How a Community Core Group Comes Together to Make Community Happen

and allows for car pooling, van pooling, community owned or leased vehicles, and an increase in the use of public transit systems.

Having a safe, secure, and attractive co-owned living environment with the amenities just described can provide us with a quality of life and sense of cooperative responsibility that we may never have realized was missing By making changes in our lifestyles to join with others in these ecological goals, a fascinating group interaction experience can occur that opens us to new ways of learning about human nurturing. The remainder of this

chapter describes techniques for organizing a core group and starting a community. Profile and workshop methods will be described, as well as meeting facilitation and conflict resolution techniques.

How Shared Living Communities Form

A founding core group may consist of low to moderate income residents of a public subsidized housing complex, tenants in an absentee-owned apartment building who want more control of their living environment and a stronger sense of belonging, or renters or home owners who feel isolated in

"Mankind, the Ecotopians assumed, was not meant for production, as the 19th and 20th centuries had believed. Instead, humans were meant to take their modest place in a seamless, stable-state web of living organisms, disturbing that web as little as possible." [22]
— *Ernest Callenbach, Ecotopia*

the "American Dream" and want to form some variation of a co-owned Shared Living Community.

It is in the formation stages that successful communication, mutual agreement and decision-making process, and a sense of commitment begin to form. The process requires working as a group for a common goal — not a skill that many Americans are experienced in. Forming an ecological community around cooperative principles is a new and unique experience. Outside resources familiar with Shared Living Community may thus be a necessary part of the process.

Finding compatible people

The process for selecting prospective community core group members who are compatible yet also diverse was well demonstrated at an introductory workshop in 1992. The workshop was sponsored by Geoph Kozeny of the Community Catalyst Project, and Ken Norwood, for a group of about 30 people. It began with a slide presentation on alternative community design possibilities, including group houses, cooperative apartment buildings, Village Cluster/CoHousing, and an array of Intentional Communities, in rural and urban locations. Following the slides everyone shared priorities, personal values, needs, objectives, and interests. This led to a spirited discussion of the process of selecting members for compatibility while allowing for diversity within the group. A concern that was raised was that unless major differences are discovered and addressed at the beginning of the process, major conflicts would likely arise later on. This does not mean that everyone must agree on everything, but that differences must be understood and conflicts dealt with up front, insofar as possible.

A myriad of basic values and lifestyle practices can divide a room of people enthusiastic about "community." The initial group will need to determine through further meetings whether differences are resolvable or if they should break into several smaller core groups. Some groups have failed to form a community because they mistakenly felt that they "should" try to "stay together." If properly handled by a skilled facilitator, the process of breaking into several groups can be a healthy one.

The 30 people mentioned above explored many issues in that one-day workshop, including: rotational cooking of daily meals, vegetarian or meat eating diets; keeping animals for food; kinds of pets; an ecological urban community or ecological rural/mountain community; a spiritual basis around one teaching or a community open to all; co-parenting and shared childcare versus no children, or nuclear families only; economic and livelihood independence of members, or community economics and enterprises, or a mix of both; relationship/gender preferences, intimate family formation options, or strictly monogamous relations; and egalitarian or patri/matriarchal community governance. Once these and other personal choices were shared, basic values and belief systems came to the surface.

Here are some generalized types of community around which groups may coalesce:
- Urban/suburban community, meat/dairy
- Urban/suburban community, vegetarian
- Urban/suburban spiritual community, vegetarian
- Rural/mountain ecological community, meat/dairy
- Rural/mountain ecological community, vegetarian
- Rural/mountain ecological and spiritual community, but not strict vegetarian

By including "ecology" and "sustainability" as criteria when deciding on location, the founding core group is compelled to consider lifestyle responsibilities critical to our future as a species. The people who only want "community" to escape from the city (and become commuters) will hopefully have their motivations and values challenged.

Issues of location, diet, ecological living, control, responsibility, and lifestyle tend to be the most critical for many founding groups. Others, such as childcare, relationships, finances, and designing for privacy and common amenities, can be negotiated, and/or left to individual discretion, to allow for diversity without jeopardizing the cohesion of the group. Having a tight, well-organized group and vision that attracts compatibleg partners may be desirable, but be careful that a group does not become too closed. Compassionate understanding and respect for differences in everyday interactions can be a personal growth and spiritual experience.

Obviously, one community type is not going to be for everyone. Do not fear a loss of diversity — but do not clone the core group. Learn what affinities will work for harmony, and what differences can enrich the group. In the workshops you can spot bigoted and dysfunctional behavior and see the virtues of compassion and understanding.

The core group formation process

The core group process together with the profile exercises and the workshop(s) can be an intense and emotionally rewarding experience. It is intended to focus values and visions, identify necessary steps, and empower the group to meet the many forthcoming challenges. The following core group outline, although not necessarily in the right order

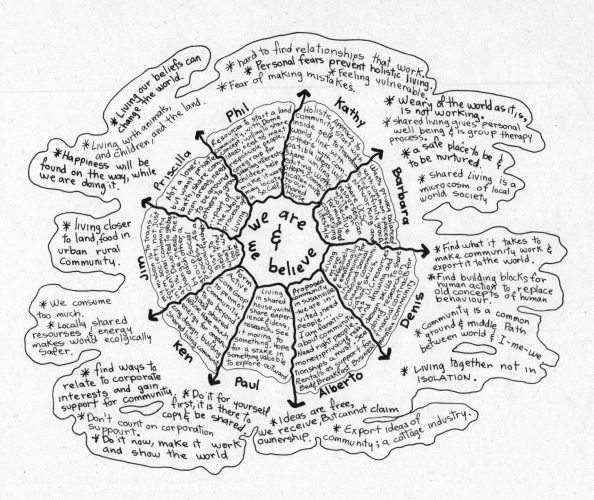

A Mandala of Lives Seeking Community
Participants at a workshop created this mandala on a large sheet of butcher paper while sitting around a table. The comments around the outer edges came from the follow up discussion after the mandala was created. It is by communicating openly and in a non-threatening atmosphere that the beginning of bonding and commitment can begin to happen.

"Whether single, married, raising a family, or nearing retirement, many men and women in today's fragmented world long for community. Even if they have plenty of friends and opportunities to socialize, they want something deeper. And, although they feel competent at getting what they want or need in most situations, developing community baffles them. We often hear the refrain, 'Of course, I want more community in my life. I just don't know how to get started.' This is not surprising given our fears about community, the hectic nature of our lives, and the number of options available. It is easy to become confused, to hesitate, to put off taking the first step." [23]

— *Carolyn R. Shaffer &
Kristin Anundsen*

"Start communities. Start one in your church. Start one in your school. Start one in your neighborhood. Don't worry for the moment about what to do beyond that…. [Worthwhile activities and projects] are not likely to succeed unless they are grounded, one way or another, in community. Form a community first." [24]

— *M. Scott Peck*

for every group, can serve as a guideline for bringing people together in community.

• **Attracting "lots of people to choose from"** to introductory meetings or to join an already successful starter group can be accomplished through ads in newsletters, articles, flyers, and posters. Advertise with organizations you are interested in and post notices in places you spend time — work, churches, childcare centers, and family gatherings. Seek out places where you feel people with mutual needs and social/environmental concerns and interests would gather: natural food stores, bookstores, other places of work, other churches, health gyms, senior centers, ecology centers, and nonprofit organizations. (The Resource Guide at the end of the book lists organizations that help people network to form community.) Invite several friends over to dinner to discuss how to cope with today's housing, economic, and social concerns. Ask people to attend an introductory slideshow & talk or a workshop on the new community movement. Discuss community with co-workers at lunch time. They may discover they share common concerns.

• **Hiring a trained community facilitator** should be considered at the first organizing meetings. There are often tendencies to try for consensus before the group is ready for that intimate process, or to hold together in order "not to lose anyone" when actually there may be two or three (or more) separate core groups in the one group. People can easily burn out from long meetings with many strangers. Some may drop out, discouraged by the inevitable divisions that occur. A skilled facilitator can be very helpful in alleviating these circumstances, serving as a moderator, mediator, or mentor. They can serve as a third-party monitor,

identifying those who are not ready to join the core group, advising those who should split off and form another group, and helping new groups mature into ongoing committed core groups.

• **A small core group of three to seven** persons who know each other well may be a good way to start. This core group could enter into a research and study phase, read up on the community movement and ecological living precepts, and develop exploratory site and design criteria and a tentative program. Then, as a committed group, they can design promotional outreach materials that announce their community vision, goals, and membership process. Newsletters and community education seminars and retreats are great ways to interest potential members. There are advantages and disadvantages to a small core group. One advantage is having a tight and well-organized group and vision that attracts compatible working partners. A disadvantage is the group may become too closed, self-serving, and protective, thereby discouraging the diversity of members necessary to build a sustainable community.

• **Determining the size of the community** is integrally connected with creating family and group cohesiveness, face-to-face rapport between members, a self-management structure, and the financial and people-resources needed to support the community purposes. The number that can sit around a table or gather together in the available common areas is a good yardstick. In general, odd numbers of people, especially in smaller groups of three, five, or seven, are the most stable. Two to three people can comfortably share a small house or apartment; five to 12 are workable for an appropriately redesigned group house; and 13 to 25 would work well in a newly designed cluster . Fifty to 150 people (or 20 to 50 families) could share a larger redesigned cooperative building, an Urban Cooperative Block, or a Village Cluster/CoHousing community. Ideally, larger numbers of people than this could group in several cluster villages that together could form a complete Eco Village or Eco City with a mixed-use central core served by rail systems.

• **Deciding between urban, suburban, or rural locations** depends on the group's ecological, livelihood, and lifestyle needs and values. Inevitably almost half the participants in workshops indicate that they want a rural site for their community, yet they also say they want easy access to city jobs, culture, and entertainment. Prospective community members with "back to the land" ideas need to honestly evaluate if in fact they are really acting out of "Urban Flight," which we discuss in Chapter Five. They will need to examine the environmental implications and the personal time, cost, and stress of commuting to city jobs. Locating the community in an already urbanized or suburban area, near public transportation, can allow easy access to city jobs, culture, and shopping while keeping agricultural and natural open space areas from being destroyed. Many times, after really evaluating the alternatives, people realize that existing urban or even suburban locations better meet their needs by giving them access to urban conveniences while not contributing to more urban sprawl. Chapters Five and Six explore the very important socioeconomic and environmental implications of rural or urban locations for communities.

• **The community social/organizational structure** really begins to form at the first meetings. These are the times to share visions, values, and personal and spiritual growth aspirations; identify practical needs and goals; and develop trusting relationships. Meetings are usually held once a month to make major decisions, discuss common issues, and resolve ongoing problems. Agreements are needed on meeting facilitation, decision-making and conflict resolution methods, shared responsibilities, committee formation, and scheduling of specific steps. Smaller subcommittees dealing with these specific issues may meet more often. But with time, in most communities, these meetings will become less frequent and less structured, because the organizational systems have already become established as a part of community life. The ownership and management structure must also be addressed early in the process. Assign a committee to explore operating rules, bylaws, partnership agreements, elections, and possible incorporation as a nonprofit, a land trust, or some other legal entity.

• **An outreach and promotion committee** to interest more members can be formed to write news articles and ads to announce your group's overall visions and objectives. You may need a community information program including a newsletter, position papers, and public talks to develop the support you may later need from the neighborhood you wish to live in and from government officials and lenders. It is good to have a clear vision and process in mind before trying to attract new members or obtain approvals and assistance from the institutions of our society.

• **The philosophic values, social ideals,** economics, ethnicity, ecological precepts, and spiritual practices of the group will influence the form of the community and how it relates to the broader society. For example, some groups will want to

"The community does not need to be big. It is enough to have ten or fifteen permanent residents who emanate freshness and peace, the fruits of living in awareness. When we go there, they care for us, console and support us, and help us heal our wounds." [25]

— Thich Nhat Hanh, "Awareness: The Consciousness of Community"

"Making community is a process that requires dedication. It is simply not enough to be inspired by or feel passion for the idea of community. Except for the very small, ad hoc groups you might join from time to time, almost every other community experience will involve long hours and hard work. Even in a small, short-term community experience (a political campaign, a support group, or even the line at the grocery store), the basic tools for getting along, communicating, reaching compromise, and seeing to it that everyone's needs are met, are the same." [26]

— *Claude Whitmyer*

design a larger common house and individual living suites without separate kitchens, dining rooms, and living rooms. Other groups might want the option of full kitchens and dining and living rooms in each individual unit, but still be clustered around the common house. Spiritual, religious and ethnic communities may need special places for meditation, prayer, ceremonies or celebrations together. Live-work units may also be desired. Whatever the group's special needs, the most important thing is that the physical design and the social and organizational structure of the community reflect the purposes, ideals, and needs of the whole group.

• **Creating a diversified socioeconomic composition** is an especially important objective so that new Village Cluster communities and Urban Cooperative Block neighborhoods do not become ghettoes composed of a single income, age, or class group. Most urban housing projects, suburban developments, and even some Intentional Communities, CoHousing, and shared living households of today are segregated in these ways. Community groups have the choice of seeking a mix of generations, ethnic groups, and incomes. This healthy social and economic diversity can empower everyone involved by providing a stronger base of experiences, abilities, and resources to draw upon in carrying out community co-ownership and mutual self-help endeavors. Such diversity also contributes to community. longivity and sustainability.

• **The economic and livelihood needs** of members and/or the community also require early attention, including consideration of individual and group income from home businesses, cottage industries, live-work spaces, community-owned businesses, and/or jobs in the city in the case of rural communities. The source of future income will be a major factor in choosing a location. The building size, design, and costs for supporting various kinds of livelihood must be factored into the master planning and ecological living processes in the early stages of development. This is also the time for a finance committee to consider a mutual savings account, a mixed income economic structure, financial planning and sharing agreements, and a plan for cost savings from energy and resource sharing and group purchases.

• **The community design** process is an important decision-making time for the core group. This is the time to crystalize the overall ecological design and specific energy-saving features of the community. Exploratory design criteria should be developed during the earlier meetings when needs and values are first shared, and will continue to evolve as the core group progresses. Final design workshops should be organized for those people who have shown a financial commitment to the group. Before beginning this intensive process, which may involve financial obligations with an architect, developer, or builder, allow time for people to drop out and new members to come in. The design criteria and process for new or redesigned community sites and buildings are presented more thoroughly in Chapters Four through Seven.

• **Co-ownership, financing, property acquisition, and development** processes including how members deposit their share of the required funds and approve the legal papers need to be finalized by the core group. This is a process that requires a dedicated committee of qualified people and/or professional resources to consider forms of ownership, permanent affordability, resale restrictions, and other legal matters. This process should begin even before the core group has made decisions about the possible site or building(s). See Chapter Nine for more on this process.

• **Becoming a community** is a humanizing process whether in Village Cluster/CoHousing, Urban Cooperative Block, Octagonal Cluster House, redesigned group house, or a cooperative in an existing building. It occurs when there is a group identification with a physical place and when all members have a common interest, frequent social interaction, respect for each other's needs, and a willingness to attend meetings and accept responsibility. Just as important as the design of the environment is the creation of a social process. Community does not just appear like magic with common walkways, front porches, and clustered housing. Community must be cultivated and nurtured by sharing life directions and desires, familial ties, and a sense of common destiny. As Craig Elevitch, describing his experience in trying to form a Permaculture community in Hawaii, explains,

"…Community does not begin when the land is purchased and people begin to live on it. It begins the moment people think and talk about it: Community is happening right now, in this moment, and not off in some future time and place…community arises out of shared work and play. [It] is the accumulation of experience of group interaction."

This is why it is so important to make the core group meetings times of sharing and fun, as well as work. Combining meetings with pot-luck suppers or desserts is a good way to start. In addition, schedule other social events such as birthday parties, picnics, and field trips. These gatherings will allow core group business to be discussed as people get to know each other. These frequent and nurturing interactions often ensure that fewer conflicts will arise when the decision-making process becomes more intense. The essence of community living is building communication. It is never too soon or too late to start — face to face talking can be magic.

The Profile Consultation Process

To facilitate the community core-group and workshop process, SLRC has developed profile consultation exercises that seek to stimulate an awareness of basic assumptions, needs, lifestyle characteristics, resources, and concerns relative to forming a community. The objective is to create a basis for questioning your own "status quo" and for making decisions about personal life direction with regard to forming or joining some type of co-owned/co-rented Shared Living Community. This profile process includes surveys and worksheets concerning:
• Attitudes and values about socioeconomic and ecological issues.
• Personal needs, housing options, income an financial resources, and time schedules.
• Basic priorities — one exercise looks at visions, life direction, and personal needs; the other at fears, aspirations, and special needs regarding living in community.
• What personal belongings and practices one must keep, is willing to give up, and is willing to share with community mates.
• Family circumstances and experiences from childhood to now, both positive and negative.

"If living in community is so difficult, why do so many people yearn to live together? Intuitively, we sense that living together for our mutual benefit is more fulfilling than the highly individualistic lifestyle that exists in our society. We know that people from various cultures benefited from living together harmoniously for centuries. It seems like a natural way to live, we just have to relearn the process. We also know that community provides a vehicle for immense personal growth, while providing a solution to many of American society's problems. It's profoundly satisfying to nurture supportive, trusting friendships in a turbulent and transient society." [27]
— *Duma Community, Eugene, OR*

"I want privacy within a community, but not isolation, in a natural setting, with low maintenance, both separate and group meals, an intergenerational group, and a communal gathering place."
— *Statement from a Profile Prioritizing Exercise*

- Projection of desired criteria for the future community: size, social composition, amenities, and other design, economic, and environmental features.

"I feel ready to make some big lifestyle changes. Out of isolation and into community."
— *Statement from a Profile Feelings and Attitudes Exercise*

From hundreds of profile exercises conducted with individuals and groups both small and large, the characteristics of those interested in community living have become apparent. The responses clearly demonstrates that there are many disillusioned and concerned middle to moderate income people who have been facing declining incomes and other socioeconomic problems and want to try something different. These exercises can be used with all population subgroups, but selected changes may be needed to reflect diversity in cultures, lifestyles, and income. The profile consultation process is best used in a workshop process and core group.

The Workshop Process

The following workshop process was designed to motivate people to see beyond the old industrial American paradigm of the single-family house and lot and car, to the new paradigm for ecological living expressed in the various forms of Shared Living Community. Although the format and focus vary depending on the particular group, there are two basic workshop models. The first is designed primarily as an introductory session for the general public newly exploring the idea of community. The second model is appropriate for a founding core group who has already been meeting on their own and wishes to use a community facilitator to guide them in the serious work of organizing and implementing their Shared Living Community. Although we present here the model used by SLRC, many other similar workshop models are used by other organizations and facilitators.

It is important that each workshop program address the cultural, ideological, and spiritual aspirations of the participants while also respecting their existing lifestyle conditioning. This is best achieved when participants complete the series of profile exercise worksheets previously described prior to the workshop. These can then be reviewed by the workshop facilitator before the workshop begins, giving him or her a familiarity with the individuals and the group from which to guide the workshop.

SLRC

A Workshop in Process — Alcyone, SLRC 1992
This is the time and place for people who want community in their live to set into motion events that will change the rest of their lives, and by so doing change the lives of many others as well. This workshop was held in the passive solar common house designed by workshop co-leader Lawrence Schechter of Alcyone.

The profile process also gives the participants a deeper understanding of their own needs and feelings, which enables them to participate more fully in the workshop process.

The workshops are designed to create the ambiance of community and the spirit of community through discussions, group exercises, stories, songs, games, a party on Saturday night, and other celebrations. Workshops can also include an early morning meditation time, circle dancing, swimming, or hiking.

Ideally, the workshop is located in a peaceful urban or rural environment. Private homes can also provide an appropriately soft atmosphere, but the event may take on more significance when held in a memorable place removed from the bustle of daily life. Having food preparation and dining facilities available is ideal so that shared meal preparation, eating, and clean-up in a cooperative atmosphere can be experienced.

Keep in mind that the following workshop format can be adapted to meet the particular interests, needs, and cultural, ethnic, or social characteristics of any group. Be sensitive to the possible need for bilingual interpreters. An introductory workshop for a group of architects, planners, HUD officials, White House staff, or real estate developers interested in learning about Shared Living Communities would take different forms altogether.

The following workshop outline takes you step by step through a two and one-half day workshop that starts on Friday evening, goes all day Saturday, and closes Sunday afternoon. It is directed to those people who are exploring extended family communities for the first time and want to learn the first steps to form a community core group.

Friday Afternoon and Evening

• **People start arriving** in the late afternoon. After registration is completed, workshop materials are handed out, sleeping accommodations are verified, and meal cooking, cleanup, and childcare duties are assigned. Try giving out name tags (a recyclable material is recommended) in four to six colors for later use in rotating assignments.

• **The evening meal** opens the workshop and is the first shared experience. A silent meditation is suggested so everyone can wind down from the fast pace of getting to the workshop. After eating, the group could remain at the tables for the evening discussion and socializing, or move to another room or outside.

• **Everyone introduces themselves** and states their goals and visions: why they are there and what they expect from the workshop.

• **The workshop leader,** the host, and volunteers are introduced and tell why they became involved in the community movement. A brief preview of what the facilitator(s) plans for the workshop is presented.

• **The "Badge of Ecological Courage,"** a self-awareness survey for examining one's lifestyle in ecological terms, is passed out to be completed before Saturday's meeting.

• **Discoveries from individual profile exercises** completed earlier are voluntarily shared. This can lead into the sharing of readings, poetry, and music that participants were asked to bring to express themselves.

Saturday Morning

• **An early morning greeting to the sun,** or other exercises and rituals are shared, subject to the

"When the banner of community is unfurled as a realization of necessity, then life will become winged in each day's action: as long as it is thought that the community is an experiment, so long will the community be found in the alchemist's jar. Only a firm realization of historic necessity will bring community to life." [28]
— *Agni Yoga Society*

Can You Wear a *BADGE OF ECOLOGICAL COURAGE*?

How ecologically do you live? Do this exercise and compare your present lifestyle with the lifestyle necessary to earn the Badge of Ecological Courage.

Add up your scores: (a=3, b=2, c=1, d=0)

24-30:
EXCELLENT—Wear your BADGE OF ECO-LOGICAL COURAGE with pride, and tell everybody!

16-23:
GOOD—But there are more things you can do for the Earth and yourself.

8-15:
FAIR—You're doing some things right, but you have a way to go. Don't do it alone; get friends to help.

0-7:
POOR—Think about the effects of your lifestyle on the planet. What can you do to make a difference?

Ecological Transportation

• I walk, bike or use public transportation to get places:
_____ a) almost always
_____ b) usually
_____ c) sometimes
_____ d) never

• I:
_____ a) don't own a car
_____ b) own a car, but car/van pool often
_____ c) share a car
_____ d) use a car a lot

Ecological Housing

• My home is within walking or biking distance of:
_____ a) shopping, work, and public transit
_____ b) two of the above
_____ c) one of the above
_____ d) none of the above

• I live in a household of:
_____ a) 3 or more adults in a group or extended family that cooperatively shares resources and responsibilities
_____ b) 3 or more adults that partially shares resources and responsibilities all the time
_____ c) a household of 3 or more adults living conventionally
_____ d) a household of 1 or 2 adults living conventionally

Ecological Energy Use

• I rely on gas or electric for space and water heating:
_____ a) not at all, e.g., active/passive solar system, etc.
_____ b) partially, e.g., as a backup to solar heating system, or south facing house that is well insulated
_____ c) quite a bit, e.g., for water heating and some space heating; house gets some solar gain and is partially insulated
_____ d) always

• My electrical system is:
_____ a) off the grid; use of solar, wind, or hydro power, or no use of electricity
_____ b) some solar, wind or hydro power and (c)
_____ c) conventional electricity, but use energy-saving appliances, good natural lighting and all fluorescent fixtures
_____ d) conventional lighting and electricity when needed

Ecological Lifestyle

• I buy unpackaged bulk food and other products:
_____ a) almost always
_____ b) usually
_____ c) sometimes
_____ d) never

• I buy or grow organic foods and use nontoxic products:
_____ a) almost always
_____ b) usually
_____ c) sometimes
_____ d) never

• Of my household waste, I recycle, compost or re-use:
_____ a) virtually all cans, bottles, paper, cardboard, and organic materials
_____ b) more than half
_____ c) less than half
_____ d) none

• I co-own or share with others my laundry appliances, power tools, and other equipment and possessions:
_____ a) almost all
_____ b) more than half
_____ c) less than half
_____ d) virtually none

ethnic, cultural, or spiritual backgrounds that are represented in the group. Be sure people feel comfortable and not coerced into participating.
• **Breakfast** can be a getting-acquainted time by setting up four- to six-person tables. Seating at other meals can be different. Try eight to ten person tables or even one large table.
• **Open the discussion** with an inspirational reading, meditative silence, or poem, inviting participation by everyone present who agrees to join in.
• **The "Musical Card Game,"** a popular and fun exercise, can "jump-start" the group sharing process in a way that encourages everyone to express ideas and feelings equally — it works wonderfully. Experience has shown that everyone apears to enjoy the opportunity to share equally.
• **A slide presentation** includes a review of current social and environmental problems in contrast with the benefits offered in community. Prototype designs and real examples of successful community from around the world are also shown, including shared houses, Intentional Communities, CoHousing, and prototype designs of Village Clusters, Urban Cooperative Blocks, the Octagonal Cluster House, and Eco Village/Eco City concepts.
• **The "Objectives and Benefits"** diagram (shown on pg. 71) is presented and brainstormed in the group, including how "ecological," "sustainable," "community," and other terms are defined.
• **The "Badge of Ecological Courage"** survey results are shared by the facilitators. This is when the philosophy, criteria, and values for ecological community living begin to be examined.
• **Community location criteria** are discussed relative to lifestyle, livelihood, cost of living, and environmental issues. The pros and cons of urban,

suburban, urban-rural fringe, and rural locations are reviewed and possible locations are considered. This is a very important decision, and is often the most difficult for a founding core group to agree on.
• **Small groups form** according to various community types and location choices. Each group brainstorms visions, benefits, criteria, and design ideas for an ecologically sustainable community. Each person uses their own profile exercise as a basis for organizing their thoughts about designing their community.
• **The large group reconvenes** and each small group shares their initial community formation and design criteria. This serves as a prelude to the afternoon community design sessions within the small groups. At this point, people can change to another small group if it better meets their needs regarding location, values, resources, etc.
• **At lunch the small groups stay together** and continue to develop criteria and visions for their community design.

Saturday Afternoon
• **The "Musical Card Game"** is played again, dealing specifically with questions about design criteria and costs.
• **A brainstorming session about cost savings** in community is held in the large group, revealing the many ways that a group of people can collectively and individually save money, energy, resources, time, and emotional strain by sharing responsibilities through planning, coordination, cooperation, and sharing. This session leads into a quick review of land, construction, operation, living costs for different kinds of communities based on size, location, materials, and methods of construction.

Comments made at SLRC workshops

A single man, age 43, a route salesman.
"I want a social community, affordability, cost of living savings, and environmental and energy conservation. I'd like being a part of building a community of cluster houses on shared land with common buildings such as workshops, meeting rooms, and a kitchen for common meals."

A couple, ages 28 and 27.
"We want to live in the city near transit so we don't have to drive so much. But we want the self-reliance of country living where we can process a lot of our own food, have enough land for a lot of trees and an orchard. Getting a whole block together and taking down the backyard fences and creating a community in our own backyard is our ideal."

The "Musical Card Game" Expresses People's Feelings About Community

Participants are each given a 3x5 index card and asked to divide it into four sections. In each section, they write their response to one of a list of questions or statements about community goals, fears, etc. that has been passed out or posted on a wall sheet. Then the cards are passed around rapidly while people make some kind of musical sound. Someone calls out "stop the music." Then everyone in turn reads from the card they are holding. This continues around the circle. Everyone is assured of equal participation and because the cards are anonymous, thoughts that some people might feel are too personal to share are more easily expressed. This game is repeated at various times throughout the workshop.

We have selected, from several workshops, some of the musical card game opening statements and participants responses

My greatest personal desire that "community" living might fulfill is:
— *"Comradeship and loving relationships with an extended family."*
— *"An extended family situation — people nearby on a long-term basis with whom to form friendships, gain inspiration and knowledge from, and share tasks and projects with."*
— *"Closeness of family and not having to be fully responsible for everything — a way of being taken care of while taking care of others too."*
— *"The creation of a working model of a peaceful and nurturing live/work community that people everywhere can follow."*

My worst fear about cooperative living is:
— *"My privacy won't be protected."*
— *"That it won't be cooperative."*
— *"People will always be wanting me to help with something."*
— *"That I won't be able to sell my unit for what I put into it."*

The amenity (extra goodie) that I want in a Shared Living Community is:
— *"Sharing of high cost equipment and tools, sharing of services such as childcare and expensive toys; i.e., pools, sauna, hot tub."*
— *"Meals prepared by others so I've more time to myself; energy for a large garden that is shared for lots of healthy food; shared transportation so less energy is used for travel and a car."*
— *"Shared care of animals such as chickens; shared food purchases; shared ownership of my car with other housemates."*

The best personal trait I have to offer community living is:
— *"A design sense for creating physical buildings and energy systems that have identity and integrity."*
— *"Love and openness of heart for all types of people because it adds vitality to the community through acceptance. A good sense of myself."*

— *"I usually try to do more than my share and don't expect things to always be fair."*
— *"Willing to listen to people with attention and no judgment."*

I would like my community mates to have the following characteristics:
— *"Spirit of cooperation; imaginative, inventive, tenacious — stick at it, get it done! Non-attachment to expectations."*
— *"Open and sharing of feelings; all ages; conscious about personal growth and planetary awareness; creative in some areas; willing to communicate and try/risk new ways."*
— *"Peaceful, sense of humor, forgiveness, love of gardening, willingness to dance, spiritual orientation, positive energy, passion for living."*

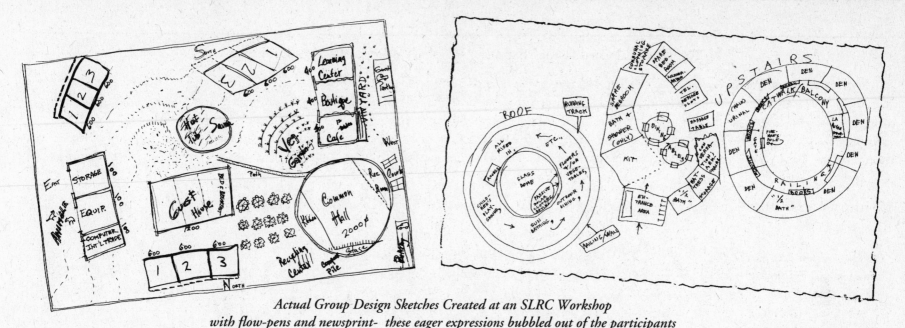

Actual Group Design Sketches Created at an SLRC Workshop
with flow-pens and newsprint- these eager expressions bubbled out of the participants

• **The design session** is the focus of the small groups for the entire afternoon and evening. Drawing materials and maps of hypothetical sites (or an actual site map, if the group has already identified property) are distributed. This is a design "charette" for co-designing the community, using bubble diagram techniques, wooden blocks, and paper cut-outs to explore the site layout and schematic relationships of private places and common spaces. The workshop facilitator(s) help the participants translate their previously created design criteria into an actual physical form.

Saturday Evening
• **The small groups stay together for dinner.**
They continue to brainstorm to complete their plans and decide who will present them to the larger group. By this time everyone whats to share their ideas and the many alternatives that flooded out.

• **Each group shares their design presentations** with the others following dinner. This is done with lots of fanfare and camaraderie as many imaginative, original, and extremely thoughtful concepts are shared — "So, you didn't know you were an architect?" Architects and builders in the group are guickly up-staged by those who have newly rediscovered design skills they were nmot aware of. The evening could continue with a group sing-along, or other group activities — maybe a decadent chocolate mousse or a simple peach cobbler with ice cream. It is time to celebrate.

Sunday Morning
• **Ownership, financing, and self-governing methods** used for various types of communities are presented and discussed. Participants can form small groups and, guided by the facilitator, brainstorm their own ideas and resources for developing

"I want to live in a community where there is emotional intimacy, support, caring, and respect. It must be environmentally sound and energy efficient — a living solution to the world's environmental problems. I want a private unit with shared facilities, such as a dining hall, work and play space, massage room, meditation space, and lots of land … with horses maybe."
— *Participant in an SLRC Workshop*

"I want to work with others committed to transforming the present climate of 'privacy' and 'individualism' and 'resignation' into one of shared commitment to possibility and workability."
— *Participant at an SLRC/Alcyone Workshop*

A Group Design Workshop in Full Swing
Everyone has the chance to share ideas about private places and common spaces.

methods appropriate to their needs. Issues discussed often include:

— Alternative lifestyles and sources of income.
— Social organization/participatory management.
— Partnerships, legal agreements, and co-ownership methods.
— Financing methods — conventional and innovative.
— Resource sharing, internal economics, and cost of living savings.
— Limitations and constraints to be encountered.

• The "Musical Card Game" is played again to bring out peoples' concerns and perceived limitations about implementing their group's visions.

• **Decision-making, conflicts, and resolutions** are introduced as healthy human processes for large numbers of people or a small family. Various techniques for facilitating meetings, making decisions, reaching consensus, and resolving conflicts are presented. A mock conflict resolution session can be play-acted with volunteers. Sometimes a real conflict arises during the workshop that the persons involved are willing to work on within the group.

• **The core group process** for forming and developing a successful community is presented in a series of small group and large group exercises. This includes how to attract new members, clarify needs and goals, translate community criteria into an action program, work with professionals, and share responsibilities, democratic management, and scheduling of project development.

• **Plan the last workshop lunch as a festive gathering**, perhaps as a picnic and field trip, with all the participants encouraged to share stories, poetry, songs, artwork, or anything else that they wish to with the group. This is also the time for the

The Inner Architect

The process of forming a Shared Living Community is based on the premise that within each of us has an "inner architect," an instinctive facility that enables us to visualize, sense, create, and strive for harmonious living environments. People all over the world have used this sense, consciously and unconsciously, to create monasteries, villages, churches, craft guilds, family farms, and all the enjoyable and productive collective living environments developed over the ages. It can be a spiritual and spontaneously instinctual process, whereas trying to "think it out" may cause creative blocks.

Although most modern day Americans have lost touch with the ancient heritage of the inner architect, nearly anyone can find and utilize this natural ability when given access to the right tools and resources. The participatory process of forming a Shared Living Community encourages the architect within, enabling people to get in touch with their intuitive thoughts and feelings, structure them into tangible images, and translate them into an architectural solution uniquely suited to their needs and aspirations.

Abby has a Vision at the Design Workshop

She closed her eyes to the workshop room, but opened her mind's eye to see the sunlight on the textured wall next to her loft bed. She saw herself reach for the hand-rail of the ladder. Then she opened her eyes and wrote in her notebook, "hand-carved madrone for the rail." More ideas floated to the surface: a wash basin close to the ladder; a sun deck for morning exercises. Sometime later, she finished writing down all of her ideas, amazed at their quality and volume.

"A living community develops its own rituals, to celebrate life passages and ease times of transition, to connect us with the round of the changing seasons and the moon's flux, to anchor us in time. When we attempt to create community, ritual is one of our most powerful tools."[29]
— *Starhawk,
"Celebration: The Spirit
of Community"*

facilitator to introduce the subject of commitment, possibly reading and/or handing out the poem "Commitment," by W. H. Murray. (See pg. 98)

Sunday Afternoon

• Why are you here, anyhow? This is a valuable opportunity to review visions, goals, and criteria. Use the Musical Card Game to bring out personal aspirations leading to a commitment to form or join a community.

• **A declaration of commitment** is written by each person pertaining to their personal goal of Shared Living Community. Sharing these expressions of

commitment can be an exultant and emotionally rewarding way to cap off the workshop.

• **Wrap-up** is a time for announcements, parting comments, and networking. Participants are reminded that the workshop is not the end of their work on forming a community, but actually the start of the ongoing core group process and the real beginning of community.

• **The end of the workshop** can be a variety of shared celebrations: a group sing-along, music and dancing, chanting, and/or a silent meditation circle. If it is a multicultural group, someone from each ethnic group could lead the others in a song or ritual native to their own background.

A Dialogue During a Group Design Process

This dialogue depicts a core group design committee of four women and three men in a meeting to discuss the design of their proposed new group house patterned after the Octagonal Cluster House. This is one of a series of group design sessions being held by the core group.

Jack, the meeting facilitator, pointed to a sheet of newsprint on the wall. The composition of multi-colored circles, arrows, and notes signified the relationships of areas for living, eating, food preparation, and special activities. *"This is where we're at,"* he said. *"We've got the common room design down to a bubble diagram. Does everyone have their design sheets? We need to work on the kitchen-entry area next."*

For a while there was silence except for the sound of pen strokes.

Toni, a small, dark-haired woman in her early

Photo by Albert Bates, The Farm

Closing Ceremony at the Celebration of Community Conference, August, 1993
There were approximately 800 people representing 13 countries at the conference held at Evergreen State College, Olympia, WA. In these gatherings members of communities and people interested in and seeking community share their experience, hopes, and future plans about how to create and live in sustainable communities — and enjoy the warmth and camaraderie of people celebrating the growing community movement on this planet.

thirties, was the last to complete her design sheet. She handed it to Jack with an exaggerated sigh. *"This is a waste of time,"* she said. *"We can't afford to make the entry into a multi-purpose room. I agree that the entry belongs near the kitchen-pantry area, but a separate room…?"*

"Okay, Toni, I understand your concern, but actually at this point in the design we're not talking about specific rooms and sizes, but functions and relationships. We won't forget about the costs that come next."

Ollie raised his hand. *"I see the entry like a workroom, with boots, rain gear, a place for mops and brooms, and maybe a source of heat and a place for wood storage. But let's not put bulletin boards there, it's too busy a spot. Why not near the kitchen, where people hang out and where the action is?"*

Leslie's hand shot up, and she blurted out, *"No bulletin boards in the kitchen, please. When I cook, I want the whole space. I can't work in crowds. I move fast."*

"Yeah, I've seen you." Dave responded. Then, to the group: *"But look, you'll find that the new kitchen is a lot different, with more room at the central counter and more efficient storage in the wall pantry. Leslie, you'll have to accept people being around the kitchen. It'll be one of our main gathering spots."*

Leslie shook her head. *"Look what happens now. People hang out reading newspapers at the table, they use the phone and look at the bulletin board. It's always cross-trafficked confusion. I want solitude when I cook. But if we can design it both ways, great!"*

Helen spoke without raising her hand. *"Leslie, that's right, it doesn't work in this old house we're in now. But now we have the chance to design something better, like hanging the main poster boards in a wider*

entry and putting a telephone near it. Or how about a semi-private telephone niche, with the kitchen work desk out of the way, but near the telephone too. We can put all the bulletin boards there." She frowned. *"Oops, we need to know what kinds of posting to do. Let's see now, we've got a chore list, and a work schedule, and…"*

"Keep it coming," said Leslie. Armed with a blue flow pen, she walked over to the wall sheet. *"Let's have all the bulletin boards we can get."* She drew a blue line down the middle of the newsprint sheet. *"Let's make two columns, for kinds of poster boards and places we want to put them."*

Leslie made notes, as the other members called out ideas. At the first pause, she stepped back to examine the list. *"Hey, we're really making progress. There are lots of good ideas here. Any more?"*

The above dialogue illustrates how group decision-making can work. It is also essential to address points of difference in a timely manner and with an agreed upon conflict resolution process

Bulletin Board Ideas	Location Possibilities
• Environ. & political activities	Common house near entry
• Cooking schedules	Mailbox board and on refrig. door
• Shopping schedule & list	On refrigerator door
• Chore list for house & yard	On business board near entry
• Work schedule for garden, cars, childcare, & meals	On business board near entry
• Billing for dinners, phone, etc	On business board near entry
• Community financial reports	Common house office
• Telephone Messages	Common house telephone booth
• Personal messages	Common house near telephone
• Emergency phone # list	At each phone
• Common house activities/events	Common house near entry

Meetings, Decisions, and Conflicts
— *successful ways of being human*

"Just as trying to control and manipulate the environment for one's own needs and purposes is an innate human trait, attempting to control others is also part of being human. This occurs whether for self-protection or to get one's way, for less-than-benign purposes, or out of the presumption that one actually knows what is best. Since control is inevitable between people, especially in intimacy, the question then becomes, what to do with it?" [30]
— Diana Alstad & Joel Kramer,
The Guru Papers

"Aesthetic and value-based decisions (solar panels vs. outside power, overhead electric lines vs. underground, raising animals for meat, using chemical fertilizers, shooting woodchucks and deer, allowing mobile homes, etc.) can be decided by the entire community. The necessity and difficulty of making these and many other decisions provide the forge and anvil on which the spirit of the community is refined." [31]
— Peter Robinson,
Green Revolution

As we rebuild community in America, we need to learn ways of meeting together that are enjoyable, time saving, and facilitate taking care of business and making decisions that represent the feelings and needs of all the members. The inevitable conflicts that arise from being human should be welcomed as a sign that some healing is needed The more that everyday face-to-face communication occurs, the less likely it is for tensions to boil over, and the easier it becomes to resolve any differences that are likely to arise. The Ladakhi people of Northern India provide an excellent example of this.

The Ladakhis live together in close-knit villages of a few hundred people. They are mostly farmers and largely independent. They have developed a "formal" structure for making decisions and settling disputes which involves *chutsos*, or groups of ten households, a village council, and a *goba*, or village head. The chutsos meet to discuss issues affecting the group, and to share responsibilities. This group operates much like a large extended family. Each chutsos has a representative on the village council which meets periodically throughout the year to make village-wide decisions. The council is presided over by the goba, who is appointed for a short period, usually a year.

Although the structure exists, most decisions are made and most conflicts are resolved by the individuals involved and not by the village council or goba. Because villages are relatively small, people directly experience their connection and interdependence with others. They understand the networks and relationships of which they are a part, and they see the effects of their actions; thus they feel a sense of responsibility and compassion. When problems arise they are settled on a grass roots level, through discussion. Their closeness and intimacy with each other helps them make fair and sound decisions based on the demands of the particular situation. They have no need for rigid laws. Instead, each situation brings forth a new response. "We must live together" is their attitude toward life, and they follow it. They cooperate to maintain a balance and a peace, knowing that the good of another is the good of oneself is the good of the community.

This attitude and this method of resolving conflicts and making decisions locally is not entirely unique to the Ladakhis. Intentional Communities, Kibbutzim, cooperatives, and other village communities throughout the world practice similar methods. We could learn a lot from studying and adapting these methods. Imagine what would happen if all economic, political, and social interactions were carried out face to face. Carelessness, deceit, corruption, and abuse of power would be almost nonexistent. Who wants to hurt or take advantage of someone they eat dinner with every night? Through the creation of small scale, modern day village communities, we can learn how to carry on our daily lives, make decisions, and resolve conflicts in ways that are easier and more indigenous to the physical and social environment we have created for ourselves — ways that are more positive and saner than the methods of violence, revenge, and alienation that are often depicted by the media about our society. Throughout the process of creating sustainable communities lies the primary precept this book is based on — design for socially interactive community and you will get it.

The facilitation method — for meetings you want to enjoy

Today's society has generated alienated and fragmented ways of relating that make meetings and decision-making chores to avoid. Forming and sustaining a community requires meetings, lots of them at first. People living in a community will have conflicts — it is part of the human investment required in order to claim the rewards of community. A close, small group may be able to stay informal, but if a core group has people coming and going, the meetings may need facilitation. The following meeting techniques will help with personal and group empowerment in this new realm of participatory self-management.

• **Plan the meeting ahead** with agenda suggestions and committee reports already roughed out on a newsprint sheet. Possibly prepare a printed handout for each of the participants as well.

• **Arrange the chairs in a circle** or a half-circle. Avoid a formal lectern stand setting unless the group is very large and has many presenters.

• **A sharing circle** is an ice-breaking way to begin meetings and meals and get to know each other better. The purpose is to let the others know the good or not-so-good news in your life, not to bring up agenda items or engage in general socializing. You can, however, let someone know that you need to resolve a difference with them after the meeting.

• **Choose a facilitator, recorder, and time keeper** for each meeting, giving members an opportunity to rotate responsibilities. This also provides core group leaders, committee chairpersons, and board members with a way to make presentations without being encumbered by facilitation duties. Another role is that of a process observer, who reminds the others of the operating rules and takes notes regarding possible improvements in the meeting process.

• **Present the agenda for additions or deletions**, assign time for each item, and decide if some items should be deferred until the next meeting. Start on time and stay with the agenda schedule (when necessary, agree on shifting the order of items).

• **Review the decision-making process** to determine when decisions are to be made by a full consensus and when a voting system is to be used. Remind members of how the consensus process works.

• **Decide on recognition of speakers** by using the raised hand "stacking" method (the facilitator only recognizes raised hands and calls them in order), or possibly try the "musical card game" technique to give everyone an opportunity to express themselves.

Consensus made easy with consensus agreements

The often recommended and not so well understood consensus method of making decisions is flying under new colors through an idea accredited to the Dominican Sisters in San Rafael, California. This is a color card technique that is being used to make the valuable consensus process easier to work with, especially for a large group. First is a review of the consensus principle.

Basically, consensus means that no action is taken until either full agreement is reached or there is no recorded opposition, meaning that objectors have either changed their position or decided not to block passage. The point is, if everyone agrees, then everyone will work toward the goal, and if no one disagrees, no one will work against it. Reaching that objective, however, requires an experienced facilitator, advanced preparation with printed

"We are born with the desire to be together, but the skills that really make community must be learned. Unfortunately, we don't learn these skills in school or in our families. We are given some rough guidelines for how to get along with others, and, in generations past, we were even taught the value of following the rules that promote social harmony. But more and more of us are escaping from our childhood education without a sufficient sense of social responsibility and the social skills that make it possible for us to come together for mutual support and the good of the community." [32]
— *Claude Whitmyer, In the Company of Others*

"Communal life demands the ability to communicate and cooperate. These skills help people move out of their gender roles, men by the need to listen better and women by the need to assert more. Once those skills are developed both men and women find that they can communicate better with their friends and lovers as well." [33]
— *Keenan, "Equality and Sexism at Twin Oaks"*

THE DECLARATION FOR UNIVERSAL ALLIANCE —
EVERYONE'S COMMITMENT TO OUR HIGHEST COMMON IDEALS
By Peter DuMont
Universal Star Alliance Foundation
Peter DuMont and Ernest Siravo, Co-founders, San Francisco Bay Area, California

When it comes to actually achieving the practical community-oriented planning, housing, land-use, transportation, and social and economic recommendations in this book, an enormous amount of communication and cooperation is going to be required. This will be needed at all levels of society — among individual citizens, groups, businesses, churches, government agencies and the media — and it will have to be sustained over months, years, and decades.

What can we do to make the processes of communication and cooperation easier, more effective, and more pleasurable? As we form and enrich our communities, how can we encourage win-win outcomes for ourselves and others? How can we minimize at every step divisive tendencies and social conflicts, breakdowns and alienation?

At the Universal Star Alliance Foundation we emphasize the importance of everyone helping to harmonize the value systems in the world by commiting to *key common goals and values*. In a kind of cosmic or all-inclusive sense, this business of life is all about how we grow and evolve as individuals, families, communities, and nations. Maintaining mutual and universal respect, goodwill, and integrity, while continuing to communicate through conflicts — so that mutual understanding, resolution, and cooperation can be gained — is one of life's trickiest and yet most rewarding lessons. Too often we have been culturally and personally habituated to lapsing into ill will at the very first sign of conflict. Yet even when present in a subtle sense, this ill will can be the primary handicap to resolving conflicts — especially if we "cherish" our ill will. To help resolve this and other dilemmas we have created the *Declaration for Universal Alliance*. The "highest common ideals" we present for discussion and commitment include: "Self, mutual and universal consciousness, integrity, goodwill, respect, appreciation, responsibility and support; maximum alertness and pro-active communication for unity of understanding and encouragement; conflict prevention, forgiveness and transformation; dynamic cooperation for personal, social, and economic achievements, in fairness and freedom without harm to self or others; optimal health in clean, beautiful, highly supportive environments; and continually growing knowledge, friendships, and advancements towards ever-expanding peace and happiness for all."

(For the condensed (8" x 11") or complete (11" x 17") Declaration, call 1-800-DECLARE.)

factual information, a clear vision of one's support or opposition to a proposal, the possible use of multiple wall sheets and recorders, the exercise of understanding and compassion by all parties, and the willingness of everyone to try to see the big, long-range picture.

The discussion should be guided towards looking at all of the possibilities and contributing factors, and avoiding confrontation regarding narrow issues that the various sides may have attached themselves to. Consensus creates a personal dialogue and exchange of ideas that parliamentary or majority rule systems do not. Consensus requires personal reflection and communication skills in a deeper level of involvement and understanding — this is what community builds on.

The colored card technique uses five 3x5 inch colored cards that are handed out to each person and collected at the close of the meeting. The cards are green, blue, yellow, orange, and red, and when held up signify the following:

- Green   In agreement with the proposal. If all cards are green, the whole group is in agreement.
- Blue   Holding a neutral position or with slight reservation.
- Yellow   Has a question which needs answering before deciding.
- Orange   Serious reservation but is not going to block decision.
- Red   Completely against the proposal.

Some consensus groups use a variety of back-up methods to assure expeditious resolution of certain critical issues, which if unresolved could jeopardize individuals or the community group, such as safety issues, financial payment deadlines, etc. One method is to allow passage of a contested item with an agreed upon percentage of votes at that or subsequent meetings.

It is important for members to recognize that only those conflicts that are acknowledged and discussed can be resolved. Personal "hidden agendas" can fester and cause problems; they need to be brought into conscious awareness and responded to honestly. Fantasies and fears that act as barriers to open interaction will ultimately not stand up to the scrutiny and inquiry of a sensitive group. However, members must agree to wield the truth gently so each person will feel comfortable expressing feelings. They must also be willing to listen and to discuss their wants and needs, and what attachments they are willing to give up in order to live cooperatively with each other. Here are some basic techniques for coming to resolution of differences:

• **Speak directly with each othe**r, at a time when they can thoroughly discuss the problem. (See the Diad and Triad section following.) Others should try not to take sides in the process, but should be present at the discussion and assist by remembering everything they can about the situation.

• **Plan ahead of time** what to say about the problem, and give information about their own feelings without interpreting the other.

• **Listen carefully**, try to put themselves in the other's position, and confirm what they have heard by asking questions about what they didn't understand and summarizing what the other person said.

• **Talk about all their concerns,** not leaving anything out that seems too difficult or too trivial.

• **Work on a concrete solution** to the problem that they and the group can agree to live with, and

follow through by checking with each other at specific times to see that progress is being made and agreements are kept. [34]

The Diad and Triad — *a way for two to settle a feud*

The diad technique has proven especially helpful in conflict resolution. The two people in conflict sit facing each other, in silence at first while they cool off and let go of the resentment and anger they feel towards the other person. If three or more people are involved in a conflict, they should still do the exercise in pairs. By agreement, one person speaks for a predetermined period of time (three to five minutes works well), stating his or her feelings without making accusations. When the time has elapsed, the other person is given the same opportunity to speak, expressing their feelings rather than defending themselves against the first person's statements. The silent person is to practice meditative listening, being there to hear the other without judgment. The guidelines for conflict resolution presented above can be used in this exercise.

Selct a physical environment for this experience that is nuetral and mutually agreeable, that is quiet and out of the way of the main flow of activity, and that has an ambience of peacefulness and solitude. The space should not be confining or too elaborate.

The diad is repeated several times and ends with a statement from each person as to the progress they feel was made and what they learned from the experience. The people in the diad often end up hugging and forgiving each other after just one or two exchanges. Another variation is the triad, in which a third person acts as observer, timer, and referee in case of misunderstandings.

"...very few people have experience creating durable relationships with people who are very different from themselves. Communication and conflict resolution skills are extremely important in creating community. Without these skills, people who engage in conflict often leave the community and those remaining frequently don't represent a diversity of viewpoints and backgrounds. Unfortunately neither businesses, schools, nor parents teach these skills, so most of us have to make the decision to consciously learn these skills as adults."[35]
— *Duma Community*

"Individuals exist only in the context of the larger whole, embedded in and defined by a nurturing web of relationship. The stronger and healthier the community, the stronger and healthier is the individual, and vice versa. You do not need to decide whether you are an individual first and in community second, or whether the rights of the community come first and your individual rights second. Both are essential to the system."[36]
— *Carolyn R. Schaffer & Kristin Anundsen*

Coming to Commitment and Community

There are many reasons for wanting to create community. Connections around shared hopes, values, beliefs, and needs, and cooperatively working together are the glue that binds a group together and stimulates a sense of commitment.

Many communities in the past have formed around a strong religious or philosophic figurehead. This is no longer a necessary or popular requirement, but we do need personal inspiration and commitment to make a group functional and to realize a dream. Spiritual beliefs and practices, political leanings, similarities in lifestyles, personal growth, economic security, and emotional support are all considerations when forming compatible relationships. Belief in ecologically sustainable community living, a strong extended family, a good place to raise children, organic food growing, and cooperative ownership and management methods may be a strong bond for some groups.

Members must commit to openness in their dealings with each other. The success of the group will be directly dependent on the ability of each person to communicate, to be clear and open with feelings and needs, and to be aware of others' needs and feelings. The process of getting to know each other and reaching commitment in community involves letting down defensive barriers and letting go of expectations. It should be entered slowly and carefully with honesty and compassion, so that trust between members can form. The musical card game, consensus, and the diad experience provide some of the tools to help this happen. Making a conscious declaration of common ideals and then agreeing on practical goals for realization is a way for building commitment.

A deep core of commitment should not be expected at the initial meetings. The movement towards commitment takes time, and talking is only part of the process. Each person must arrive at commitment from their own sense of empowerment, not from group pressure. At some point the combined feelings about the community goal will rise to empower the group. There are messages in the eyes, a knowing receptive look, the wanting to smile flickering around the mouth, and then it happens. A new connection is made, and group members are no longer simply individuals with an idea. A group consensus comes — a community.

"We don't think commitment is something you go off and do by yourself, just two of you. It has to have a structure, social surroundings you can rely on. Human beings are tribal animals, you know. They need lots of contact."[37]
— *Ernest Callenbach,*
Ecotopia

"The individual fares best when he is a member of a group faring best. All human beings, in young childhood at least, are members of groups. The group is the tree and they are the fruit it bears. At least up to a certain age-level, the individual reft from his group is hurt or destroyed. The ruin inflicted on Red Indians through the white man's denial of their grouphood, and his leading them to deny their own grouphood is only a special case of something that is universal. It may be that contemporary white life is being injured nearly as much by the submergence of its primary social groupings as the denial of Indian grouphood injured Indian life."[38]

— *John Collier,*
"Ancient Community in America"

Coming to Commitment

An inspiration, a spark of recognition, a fleck of insight in individual minds and souls, a sense of knowing in each person. A recall of things known before but now openly remembered. It's all there, already inside each of us. Individuals learning new ways, teaching themselves how to function as a group. Learning about each other, letting down barriers, releasing tension, sharing conflicts, experiencing social and personal familiarity and seeing the individual in each person. A testing time for personalities. Grouping, learning, and feedback — what each causes to happen. Reactions. Sharing resources and learning skills. Discovering what roles each may play. Do they work for the group? Are there hidden agendas? What does each person really want and need? What will each give up or give to obtain their dream, to reach agreement? The vision will blur, spin out, and come back together, tightening, focusing, moving towards commitment, an electric wave of enchantment and an undercurrent of commonality. Us here, on the planet — the possibility of love.

Ken Norwood 1993

Notes

Books listed only by name in the endnotes are highlighted in the resource guide at the end of the book, complete with author/publisher information and description.

1   Mary King, "A Psychology is Born - an Interview with Theodore Roszak," *AHP Perspective* (a newsletter from the Association for Humanistic Psychology) May/June 1993, p.11.

2   Jeremy Rifkin in collaboration with Nicanor Perlas, Algeny - A New World, Penguin Books, New York, 1984, pp. 251-252.

3   Dr. Bill Roley, "Sprout Acres: Experimental Field Station," pamphlet, Laguna Beach, California.

4   Creating Community Anywhere, p. 24.

5   Arthur E. Morgan, The Heritage of Community, Community Service, Inc., Yellow Springs, Ohio, 1956, pp. 4-5.

6   Dr. Roger Fritz, "The Goose Story," *ARC News,* Vol. 7, No. 1, Jan.1992.

7   In the Company of Others, p. 17.

8   Chandler Washburne, *Op. Cit.*, p. 9.

9   Craig Elevitch. "The Basics of Unintentional Community," *The Permaculture Activist*, No. 29, p. 30.

10 Lynn Murray Willeford, "Creating Community," *New Age Journal,* May/June 1993, p. 70.

11 The Boston Women's Health Book Collective, Inc., Ourselves and Our Children: A Book by and for Parents, Random House, New York, 1978, p. 185.

12 In the Company of Others, p. 34.

13 A member of Winslow CoHousing quoted by Joan DeClaire in "Coming Together," *Pacific Northwest,* Aug/Sept 1991, p. 16.

14 Keenan, "Equality and Sexism at Twin Oaks: What have we accomplished?," *Leaves of Twin Oaks*, April, 1993, p.12.

15 David and Vera Mace, Marriage: East and West , Dolphin Books, Garden City, New York, 1960, p.58.

16 Alice Kahn, "The New Generation Gap," *San Francisco Chronicle*, 2/18/92. p. C3.

17 Creating Community Anywhere, p. 173.

18 Margie Menzel, "Parent Aid: A single friend helps out," *Utne Reader*, March/April 1990, pp. 83-84, (article first appeared in Spectrum, Summer 1986).

19 The Boston Women's Health Book Collective, Inc., *Op. Cit.*, p. 183.

20 Kathrin Perutz, Liberated Marriage, Pyramid Books, New York, 1973, pp. 158-159.

21 Alan Durning, How Much Is Enough? The Consumer Society and the Future of the Earth, W.W. Norton & Company, New York, 1992.

22 Ecotopia, p. 47.

23 Creating Community Anywhere, pg. 36.

24 The Different Drum, p. 326

25 In the Company of Others, p. 101.

26 *Ibid.*, p. 34.

27 Alan Hancock, "The Reality of Living in Community," *Newsletter of the Northwest Intentional Communities Association*, Summer 1993, p. 5.

28 Builders of the Dawn, p. 25, quoting Agni Yoga Society.

29 In the Company of Others, p. 93.

30 Diana Alstad & Joel Kramer, The Guru Papers, North Atlantic Books, Berkeley, 1992, p. 283.

31 Peter Robinson, "Shannon Farm: A Model for Community that Works," *Green Revolution,* Vol. 46 No. 4, School of Living, Cochranville, Pennsylvania.

32 In the Company of Others, p. 33.

33 Keenan, "Equality and Sexism at Twin Oaks: What Have we Accomplished?," *Leaves of Twin Oaks*, p.12.

34 These guidelines are based on "How to Resolve Conflicts" by Community Boards, "Seven Practices of Reconciliation" by Thich Nhat Hanh, and "Listening Exercises" by Harriet Whitman Lee of the Berkeley Dispute Resolution Service.

35 Alan Hancock, *Op. Cit.*

36 Creating Community Anywhere, p. 31.

37 Ecotopia, p. 36.

38 John Collier, "Ancient Community in America," The Heritage of Community, Community Services Inc., Yellow Springs, Ohio, 1956, p. 33.

THE VILLAGE CLUSTER
A New Approach to an Old Idea

Santorini, also called Thira, is one of the southernmost islands of Greece. It enjoys a long history of advanced civilization and is the object of much speculation and wonder, identified by many as the lost continent of Atlantis. This painting offers a powerful and romantic vision of a thriving village on the island: whitewashed houses perched atop plunging cliffs with clear blue waters below, flourishing gardens and trees, and narrow, winding, cobbled streets densely lined with craft shops and houses.

Painting by Sally Bookman

CHAPTER FOUR

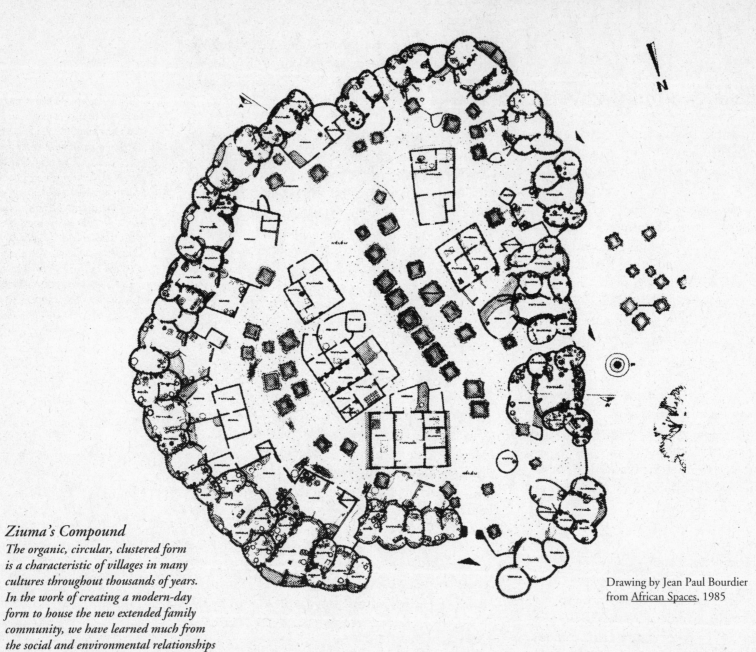

N

Ziuma's Compound

The organic, circular, clustered form is a characteristic of villages in many cultures throughout thousands of years. In the work of creating a modern-day form to house the new extended family community, we have learned much from the social and environmental relationships within Ziuma's compound.

Drawing by Jean Paul Bourdier
from <u>African Spaces</u>, 1985

Villages Around the World

Throughout most of human history, community has been the normal pattern, with people living in large extended families and tribal networks. Even today, much of the world still lives in these kinds of villages. Santorini is just one example. There are countless others — Neve Shalom/Wahat al-Salam, Breuberg, Kamikuri, and the list goes on.

The Village Cluster and other Shared Living Community models are derived from years of investigation into humankind's rich collective history of village and community culture.

Both authors have visited and researched historic and present day villages of cultures throughout the world in order to better understand the relationships between physical environment, social organization, and community. Here we will look at two examples: Ziuma's compound, an extended family village which is part of the larger village of Poa in Burkina Faso, and the historic Native American village of Pueblo Bonito located in what is now northwest New Mexico.

Ziuma's compound

Because of its remote location, Poa is one of the few villages of the Lela people that shows little Western urban influence. Ziuma's extended family compound is one of 10 that make up Zyilliwèlè, a quarter of Poa.[1] The compounds, each surrounded by cultivated farmland, are 150 to 300 meters apart and 30 to 200 meters from the main village path. The surrounding farmland, an obscured entrance path, the senior man's shelter, and the solid, undulating walls and heavy wooden gate of the compound all work to create a distinct transition and protective zone between the compound and the larger community.

Once through the compound gate, a visitor enters the main common court or kéléu which houses a maze of adobe granaries, a well, several living units, and large open areas. This space serves simultaneously as a circulation, transition, and gathering space. The kéléu is encircled by a ring of private living suites inhabited by either an individual or a family group. These private living areas vary in size from three to seven rooms and consist of the kono, a packed earth court; the nachobo, a bathing enclosure; the tutuiñi, the indoor living area; the zoñi and djena or cooking areas; and the djipu, a locked storage area. The kono has one entrance and is the focus of most community life. It is the place where daily chores and rituals are performed, cooking is done, children play, and families talk into the night. The kono, like all spaces except the indoor cooking areas, facilitates a variety of activities depending on the season, the time of day, and the mood of the resident. For example, during the hot season, the kono is also used for sleeping.

Each living unit is private, and is arranged and occupied in a definite order that spatially reflects the social organization and values of the extended family. The senior men and women, for example, are given prominent positions facing the main compound gate. Each unit, including those belonging to the latter, is integrally connected to the others through form and function. From each kono one can see into the kéléu, offering all a sense of cohe-

"We modern Westerners have much to learn about community. How did the ancients weave their intricate and time-tested webs of inclusion? What do the salons of pre-Revolutionary France have to teach us about the community's need for conversation, and especially for listening and speaking from the heart? What do tribal people know about ritual, place and the invisible world that can help us in our efforts to rebuild community for ourselves and our children?"[2]

— Eric Utne

Drawing by Jean Paul Bourdier from *African Spaces,* 1985

Private Dwelling in Adono's Compound [3]
This drawing of the senior women's private dwelling in Adono's compound offers a clear picture of the forms, relationships, and uses of the spaces that, when clustered together, make up an extended family village compound. Make particular note of the personalized motifs and how the low walls and private court help create a sense of privacy and transition between spaces.

sion and safety. Because some tools such as grinding stones and special cooking pots are shared by adjacent dwellings, a small adobe platform is built that interrupts the surrounding walls and allows access from one private court to the next. In this way, "The architecture reveals at the same time the inhabitants' close dependence and self-sufficiency."[3]

Both men and women take part in building and maintaining the compound. Women carry water and earth which the men knead into clay balls with their feet. The balls are then stacked and molded to form circular walls which intersect with surrounding walls to form a rigid honeycomb structure that effectively dilutes external forces. The women then coat the walls with a locust-bean pod varnish and an adobe-cow dung mixture on which patterns and designs are imprinted. This process serves a dual purpose. It allows individuals to personalize and identify their space, and it waterproofs the dwellings by creating channels in the adobe which break up the flow of rain and allow the adobe to dry more quickly, adding to its strength and durability. This integration of structure, form, and function reflects the intimate unity and interrelationship of the inhabitants to each other and their environment.

Pueblo Bonito [4]
Pueblo Bonito, the apparent capital of Chaco Canyon (a region of the Anasazi people), offers another example of how the built environment can both reflect the values of the people and support their social structure and way of life.

Between 1100 and 1300 AD, when their culture was at its height, the Anasazi populated vast areas of what is now northwest New Mexico. Pueblo Bonito is regarded as the "signature masterpiece" of

Pueblo Bonito
Without question the most elaborate native architecture in North America was produced by the Anasazi. Originally the Anasazi lived in semi-subterranean structures, but around 700 AD they began living above ground, eventually inventing an original stone architecture and evolving a complex community structure. This reconstruction drawing of Pueblo Bonito by William H. Jackson shows the relationship between the surrounding environment and the human community.

their culture. It is the largest "Great House," a single building which is really more like a city or village, covering nearly three acres and containing 800 rooms, 37 small kivas (circular structures used for gathering), numerous towers, terraces, and a large divided plaza with two great kivas.

The Anasazi seemed to have mysteriously vanished or migrated to some unknown place around 1300 AD. Therefore, we cannot know them from their language, literature, or customs, only from the architecture that remains. We can tell a lot from examining the design, location, and

materials used in Pueblo Bonito. We can tell, for example, that they were a resilient and adaptive people with a highly organized community support structure. They must have been to have flourished in such a dry and desolate area, if that was actually the climate during their existance The layout of this Great House, as a compact village, along with the complex systems of dams, irrigation canals, roads, and communication relays (fire beacons) that linked the more than 400 sites in the area provide further evidence of the sophistication of their large-scale cooperation and social interaction.

"Throughout most of human history, community was the normal pattern.... There is something in the human condition that eternally yearns for a greater sense of connectedness, yearns to reach out and deeply touch others, throwing off the pain and loneliness of separation to experience unity with others. In all times and all places people have consciously reached out to feel their connectedness with a larger whole. This is the experience of community."[5]
— *Corinne McLaughlin & Gordon Davidson*

The design of Pueblo Bonito also shows a deep understanding, connection, and celebration of nature and their place in it. The Anasazi used materials native to the area — stone and earth — to create thick walls which soaked up solar heat during the day and radiated it into the rooms at night. The whole complex is oriented to the south, opening to the sun. The high stone wall and cliff to the north provide shelter from the wind and create a solar backdrop during the winter. Abundant roof terraces and plazas, as well as cooking artifacts found there, suggest that they worked communally and socialized outside during the warmer months and inside during the cooler months. The cooler, darker innermost rooms were used for storing and processing corn, squash, and other produce. Complex and varied patterns in the rock and adobe plaster walls suggest both a high level of craftsmanship and a personalization of space.

The circular structures are kivas, which were used for sacred and social occasions. Some believe the kivas represented the existence of a clan form of social organization, with larger kin groups or neighborhoods sharing suites of rooms each with their own kiva or meeting room. The great kivas in the main plaza were thought to be the central gathering places for the whole community.

All we really know about these people is what the architecture tells us — that they were a vibrant people, with a deep understanding of natural cycles, place, order, and community. In Pueblo Bonito, as in Ziuma's compound, the organization of the private dwellings, kivas, and open spaces in an interconnected, hierarchical pattern reflects the inhabitants' desire to balance privacy and community for a supportive and sustainable way of life.

Village Life Today

By studying examples from other cultures, we can gain insight into ways of living, interacting, and building that are more socially and environmentally responsible than the methods employed in our society today. We can incorporate into our own society elements from these cultures that seem appropriate to our culture, values, and aspirations. The models of Shared Living Communities presented throughout this book are all variations on the common theme of the village. Very few Americans live in villages today, yet villages still have a powerful pull on our collective imagination regarding "the good life."

What comes to mind when you think of a village? A compelling vision is offered by a visit to Woodstock, New York. A tall, white New England church spire directs you to the triangular-shaped town square, complete with benches, a statue, and a common green that is bustling with activity. The quaint gable-roofed shops and cafes that line both sides of the streets leading away from the village center are filled with local residents, tourists, and city dwellers visiting their country houses. People casually wander from shop to shop, buying groceries, tasting sample treats, and greeting friends and neighbors at every turn. The ambiance is festive. Even store clerks, tellers, and street cleaners find time to watch the children and dogs frolicking in the winter's first snow. Despite the tourist-supported economy and the hordes of cars crowding the streets, Woodstock, like Nevada City, California, Yellow Spring, Ohio, Savannah, Georgia, and other architecturally preserved villages, is as genuine a living village as can be found today in America..

Village communities were once an integral part of our American way of life. Numerous cities throughout the U.S. began as small villages, but as industry and commerce prospered, many were overwhelmed by growth and overrun by the car. Others have simply died out. Remnants of our village community heritage, such as town squares and meeting halls, still persist in some areas, but most of the socioeconomic, cultural, architectural, and environmental character of the original villages has been lost, along with interaction and cooperation between people.

Elsewhere in the world, and hidden away in the U.S., are villages that industrialism and modernization have passed by. In these, the basic elements of a sustainable system of village life continue. In other traditional villages, however, life is not so ideal. We do not want to romanticize all traditional village life. As Robert Gilman explains:

> While it is true that there is much to be learned from these [traditional] villages, …few people today — including most traditional villagers! — would describe these villages as either full-featured or supportive of healthy development. The work is hard, life expectancy is short, opportunities for personal development and education are few (almost non-existent for women), and the diversity of livelihoods is small. ... In addition, the harmony between these villages and the natural environment has often depended on low population densities — a luxury we no longer have.[6]

These problems are not due to the failure of the village way of life, but to overpopulation, oppressive

Photo by Mark Antman, The Image Works

Woodstock, New York

Woodstock was founded as an Arts and Crafts Colony in 1902 by Ralph Whitehead, a Utopian English philosopher. Today, Woodstock retains its small town village charm, in spite of being a thriving community with world renowned artists, writers, and dancers, and the site of several major corporate offices.

control, and the depletion of natural resources — byproducts of the industrial world, our world.

The Village Acre example presented in Chapter One and the other Shared Living Community models presented later in the book do not represent a return to the past or to arduous methods of production and living. Instead, these new community forms are modern-day villages that draw on the best of the village heritage of cooperation and social, cultural, and resource sustainability. Wood or coal fires for cooking, hand-carried or pumped water, cesspools, uninsulated walls, and other undesirable artifacts of low-tech lifestyles are fortunately gone. Today, we have the environmental design and the social skills and the natural energy technology to create comfortable, attractive, and ecologically sustainable community housing that can combine telecommunications, supportive interrelationships, and self-reliant simple living in one place. We must make the effort to create more of such housing. As Carla Cole, writing in *In Context,* explains:

> We all share a common destiny, and traditional villages have much to teach us — from their deeply rooted understanding of community to their tenacity in the face of adversity. By taking the best from what are now called the First and Third Worlds, we have the potential for developing a world in which these sad distinctions no longer apply."[8]

© Photo by Dave Carter, Writer /Photographer

The objective in examining, both historically and conceptually, the extended family village approach to community living is to observe, understand, and improve upon those forms of community organization and habitat design that enable groups of people to cooperatively live in ecologically responsible and socially enriching ways. The new community examples we present serve as valuable educational tools for helping Americans learn how to share long-term responsibilities and resources on a day-to-day level.

These new forms of housing have the potential to instill in people a new sense of what ecological living and personal empowerment can mean. It is useless to criticize single-family houses without providing attractive alternatives. We have to show people how they can satisfy their quality-of-life needs in a co-owned cluster community. The benefits must include an increased sense of privacy, security, belonging, and self-esteem, and cost savings — qualities that are needed to attract the fragmented income, ethnic, and cultural groups of our society.

Real Life Village Communities Today
— *a cultural metamorphosis*

The rising groundswell of interest in participatory community building that has recently re-emerged is telling evidence that many Americans are ready for a new approach to living. The "Village Cluster" model, like CoHousing, seeks to bring the social, ecological, and economic benefits of extended family village life to the largest possible number of people in the United States. The Danish-originated CoHousing model, although new in this country, is

"The new intentional communities…are a conscious response to societal problems and are working to restore a sense of community in our neighborhoods and towns…. [These] communities are demonstrating we can blend the best aspects of our tribal roots and the feeling of closeness to others with the technological advances of modern times that save labor and hardship."[7]
*— Corinne McLaughlin &
Gordon Davidson*

Nevada City, California
Nevada City provides another example of a small town that has survived in the modern era. It was developed as a gold mining town along the banks of Deer Creek in 1849. Early reports told of miners who pulled a pound of gold a day from the creek. By 1851 the town was the county seat and had a population of over 10,000. While many California gold rush towns have disappeared, Nevada City has retained its charm and authority as a small town and a living museum.

rapidly gaining acceptance and leading the way in an extended family "village renaissance." There are already seven completed CoHousing communities in California, Washington, Colorado, and New Mexico, with over 100 more being planned throughout the United States. In Denmark and other Scandinavian countries, 150 or more Village Clusters in addition to other cooperative communities exist today. Underlying this new community movement are the more than 350 successful and well-established Intentional Communities in this country, and the estimated several thousand housing cooperatives, Urban Cooperative Blocks, group households, nonprofit sponsored Group Homes, and other resident controlled rental housing — all people-participation based ways of living.

A combination of high housing prices, socioeconomic decline, people willing to experiment with new ideas, and the availability of for-profit developers, nonprofit sponsors, and community facilitation resources are making this form of housing increasingly popular and accessible. Below we review several CoHousing communities that have recently been completed, examining both their form and social composition, as well as their methods of development and management.

Muir Commons CoHousing, Davis, CA

Muir Commons was the first CoHousing community to be built entirely new in the United States. Its birth followed the popular reception of the book, *CoHousing,* by McCamant and Durrett. The community members moved in starting in August of 1991. Unlike the buyers of typical developer housing, most of the 45 adults (mostly in their 30's and 40's) and 25 children were not

strangers. For almost three years they had been learning about each other and community life at core group meetings in which they co-organized and co-designed the community.

The development process began in 1988 with a core group inspired by a slide show given by McCamant and Durrett. Also at this event was Virginia Thigpen, a developer with West Davis

"We are in the midst of a major era of change, as significant as any in our history. The contemporary melange of conspicuous poverty and affluence, of ecological awakening and technological advance, of spiritual renewal and political integration, is affecting every level of society. As in every past era intentional community will play a role." [9]

— *Allen Butcher,*
Directory of Intentional
Communities

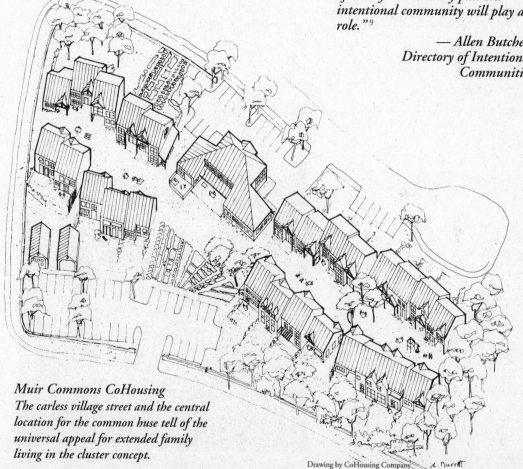

Muir Commons CoHousing
The carless village street and the central location for the common huse tell of the universal appeal for extended family living in the cluster concept.

Drawing by CoHousing Company A. Durrett

A Play Structure at Muir Commons

Most children really enjoy living in CoHousing because they have friends nearby and lots of open space to play in. As two parents at Muir Commons explain,"This is kid heaven... They're having a blast—you can hardly drag them in for dinner."

"They've never had this kind of mobility before — there was too much traffic where we used to live, and we couldn't let them play outside on their own like this."[11]

Associates who had previously visited several Village Clusters in Denmark. She met with the core group several times and eventually offered them a three-acre site in the Aspen housing development she was working on. For Virginia, this was a way to fulfill the City of Davis planning commission's affordable housing requirement and develop a form of housing she felt was needed in our society. For the core group, this meant they had the land, technical resources, and financial backing to turn their dream into reality. The only catch was, they did not have

Photo by Don Lindemann

independent control of the project. They nevertheless were able to work successfully with the developer and the developer's architect to design the community. The architect was open to the input and needs of the core group, but because he was not versed in the participatory community design process, there were some conflicts. To ameliorate some of the problems, the core group hired McCamant and Durrett to help them more specifically define what they wanted and needed in the design of the common house and the individual units. Having a clear and unified program, the core group could then better express their needs and negotiate with the developer and architect. After countless hours of meetings, negotiations, and problem solving, the group of single- and two-parent families and single adults had a new kind of home — a community.

Muir Commons follows the basic Village Cluster/CoHousing precepts described later in this chapter. The 26 housing units are smaller in floor area than in typical housing developments. They contain two to three bedrooms, one bathroom (usually), a small living space, and a small kitchen. The common house, a large and beautiful 3,670 sq. ft. structure, is embellished with a well-designed commercial kitchen and food pantry, large dining room, cozy sitting room with a fireplace, laundry room, teen room, children's room, craft room, exercise room, and guest room/study. Outside is a recycling and refuse storage area, a tot lot, a covered patio, and a bicycle parking area.

The common house was intended to be — and is — the heart of the community. Its frequent use has as much to do with the attractive amenities as with the members' commitment to shared evening meals five times per week. The cooking and clean-up teams operate on a rotating schedule, each working no more than half a day per month. In exchange, they enjoy, without lifting a finger, approximately 20 delicious and nutritious meals per month, each costing approximately $1.50.

From the beginning the group felt it was important to their sense of ownership and community that they, as a group, participate not only in the design, but the building of the community. Due to safety and liability issues, it was not possible for them to work on the construction of the units. Instead, they took responsibility for all the landscaping work. Because the group volunteered their labor, all of the $50,000 allocated for landscaping went to plants, tools, and other landscaping materials. The site looked rather bare and row-house like in the raw dirt days prior to completion. But now, vegetable gardens and a fruit orchard flourish and flower gardens, trees, and native plants, along with personalized front porches, sitting courts, and children's play areas, line the intimate pedestrian path that runs east-west through the middle of the clustered units. The feeling is friendly as children play and adults gather to talk and relax. Community members feel proud of their home, because they worked together to create it.

Recently the community has had another opportunity to strengthen their sense of ownership and personal and group empowerment by building a much needed 500 sq. ft. workshop (located on the west end of the north parking lot). The workshop is basically a glorified barn, housing a woodshop, a one-car repair shop, storage space, all the co-owned gardening and building tools, and two covered areas for bikes. The workshop was supposed to be built

The Sanctity of Village Spaces at Muir Commons

Photo by Don Lindemann

at the same time as the community. But in the last moments of the final development phase, the developer eliminated it due to financial constraints. In an ordinary single-family house or condo development that would have been the end of the story, but as a co-owned and self-managed community, the members were able to develop a capital fund and obtain a building permit for the workshop. They hired contractors to build the main structure, but did everything else themselves, including painting, wiring, and installing finishes and wall-board.

It is important to remember that what the people of Muir Commons have developed in the way of social bonding, a sense of belonging, coop-

"To get the most out of life, you need to see a lot of life going on — babies being born, people dying, seeing examples of good relationships to model and seeing bad relationships to know how to handle your own problems — to have support and not feel like you are the only person going through those life experiences!"

— A Member of Muir Commons CoHousing

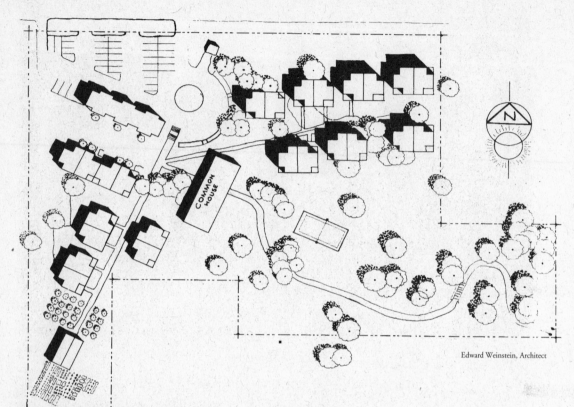

Edward Weinstein, Architect

Winslow CoHousing
This 30 unit community occupies five acres of land on Bainbridge Island and it is home to 75 people.

"...the desire for consensus brings so much energy and so much commitment."

— *A Member of Winslow CoHousing*

erative management, support for family and children, and ecological living has not been the result of any dramatic philosophic or ideological fervor. Rather, the core group came together around the simple realization that it was all right to express their need for alternatives to over-priced conventional housing, a rat-race competition for personal and family time, and the lack of meaning in modern life. Now, in their third year, the Muir Commons group has established new meanings for family, community, neighborhood, and sharing. Festive rituals such as monthly birthday parties in the common house are only the beginning.

Winslow CoHousing Group, Bainbridge Island, WA

The Winslow CoHousing group was initiated by Chris Hansen who read *CoHousing* in December 1988, started putting up flyers, and organized the first meeting in February 1989. The community is the second entirely new CoHousing project to be completed in the U.S., and the first to be designed and developed by the community members serving as their own developer developer. The process was intense and exhausting, with over two years of initial planning and designing, eight months of construction, 4,000+ hours of meetings, and about 140 different people involved at some point in the process. But in early 1992, when the first families began moving in, Winslow CoHousing became a reality. Now, 75 people ranging in age from 5 months to 70 years, with most in their late 30's to early 50's (Baby Boomers), live in the 30-unit community.

The community is located on a five-acre wooded site, half of which has been preserved as open space. Three landscaped pedestrian paths lined with living units radiate toward the centrally located common house. The 5,000 sq. ft. common house contains a dining room, commercial quality kitchen, meeting space, childcare and children's activity rooms, a teen space, recreation room, laundry room, and storage space. Outside, there is also a guest house, recycling center, bike shed, gardens, and a fruit tree orchard — the hallmarks of the new village community movement. A multi-purpose barn/workshop is being planned.

From the beginning, the group wanted to reduce car trips and car ownership. Therefore, they got a special waiver from the city to build a smaller than code parking lot. They also purposely chose a site on Bainbridge Island within walking distance of the Winslow ferry port for commuters to Seattle, and near neighborhood stores, a post office, library, and schools. Subsequently, some people have sold their cars and now share vehicles with their neighbors.

There are two types of private units: townhouses and flats. The 24 townhouse units range in size from one to four bedrooms. All are self-sufficient with a living room, dining room and kitchen downstairs, and bedrooms upstairs. A large building called the Carriage House contains six additional units — three upstairs and three downstairs. The three downstairs units are handicapped-accessible to accommodate disabled persons and other members as they age or their abilities change.

Some of the members, who are mostly business and professional people, previously lived in Intentional Communities or other group living situations. For others it is a radical but welcome change in lifestyle, for all members now enjoy the amenities of the community and the sense of empowerment and security that comes from co-owning and managing their own living environment. The community is organized as a market-rate cooperative corporation. Members buy shares in the cooperative and receive a proprietary lease for a specific unit. For many, this provides the financial clout needed to become a homeowner. As Linda Townsend, a single mother in the community, explained, "It was the first time in my life I felt empowered when it came to a financial institution."[12] She qualified for her home loan based not just on her own financial resources, but on those of the whole group.

Photo by Therese Kunzi-Clark

Village Environment at Winslow CoHousing
Three pedestrian walkways converge creating an environment that encourages interaction and the free expression of companionship The site design preserved the woodland around the community.

Opportunities for participation and empowerment continue with ongoing committees that handle the organization of meal preparation and children's activities, among other things. There are dinners in the common house Sunday through Thursday, as well as special meals on holidays.

One of the most exciting features of this community is the daycare center in the common house. The center is supported by six families. For each daycare shift that a parent works they earn two days of care for their children. This is a real benefit for hardworking parents in a society where only half as much childcare is available as is needed .

There is some owner turnover at Winslow, as has been the case in all the new CoHousing communities. Most is due to job relocation and economics, not fundamental problems with the community. This is not to say that problems don't exist, but as Kim Clark, a resident of Winslow explains, "...we have developed a shared sense of what it takes to get along together. We are all willing to be a little softer, to listen to people, and to reconsider what we want in light of what other people want."[13]

Nyland CoHousing Community, Lafayette, CO

The first CoHousing community in Colorado, Nyland, is the largest in the U.S., with 42 units on 43 acres. It was founded in 1988 by architect Ron Ricker, who discussed with several friends the possibilities for environmentally responsible communities and shortly thereafter read the book, *CoHousing*. An initial core group was formed which, operating as a partnership, acquired the property, completed a feasibility study, and wrote a land use plan. After 1-1/2 years, they contracted with a developer to take care of the zoning and financing approval, building permits, engineering, and construction of the project, while the growing core group worked on designing the community and developing an organizational structure. McCamant and Durrett provided community design workshop services to help develop the overall layout and design. A local facilitator was brought in later to help finalize the design and work out specific organizational details.

Families started moving in August of 1992. As of 1994, there are 120 people, including 35 children ranging in age from 18 months to 18 years. The site layout differs somewhat from other CoHousing models, because it has two separate clusters of units, with most of the parking in a common lot. The 6,500 sq. ft. common house is centrally located and contains a large commercial kitchen, dining room, licensed daycare space, and many other amenities. On site there are also a greenhouse, woodworking shop, recycling center, one-acre vegetable garden (in process), and outdoor recreation facilities including a sand volleyball court, basketball court, and soccer field. The group also plans to build a stable and barn. So far, common meals occur four nights a week. Most members hope to increase the frequency of these events, but at present are too busy with landscaping the site and finishing their own units.

The individual units vary in size and layout, reflecting the diversity within the community. There are two large detached custom houses, six houses with their own garages and driveways, and a mixture of duplexes and triplexes. The units have from two to five bedrooms, and some are set up as shared households. One design includes two master bedroom suites, one on each side of a shared kitchen, dining, and living area. All of the houses are market rate, but people from lower and moderate income levels were accommodated by including some smaller, lower priced units (starting at $80,000) and some rentals, actually suites of rooms in larger houses that the homeowners rent out to individuals or couples who cannot afford to buy. Methods of creative financing have also been arranged by the community to help some people with their down payments.

The community is located six miles outside of Boulder and enjoys stunning views of the Rocky Mountains. Because of its remoteness the community has taken several steps to reduce car trips. First, they pressured for and got local bus service extended past their front entrance and into adjacent communities. Second, they implemented a bus pass program that allows them to ride on any bus in the Denver/Metro area. The program was designed to create affordable transportation alternatives and encourage public transit use. Several car pools have also formed among those who commute to Denver to work. Other members have started a food cooperative to enable them to buy in bulk at a cheaper price, with less packaging waste and less time spent shopping. It is too soon in this young community's life to know if these provisions and the community structure as a whole can significantly reduce the number of car trips the community generates, but they are starting on the right track.

The most unique aspect of this community is the energy efficiency and environmental health program that the house owners participate in. This program is financed by $100,000 in grants from the

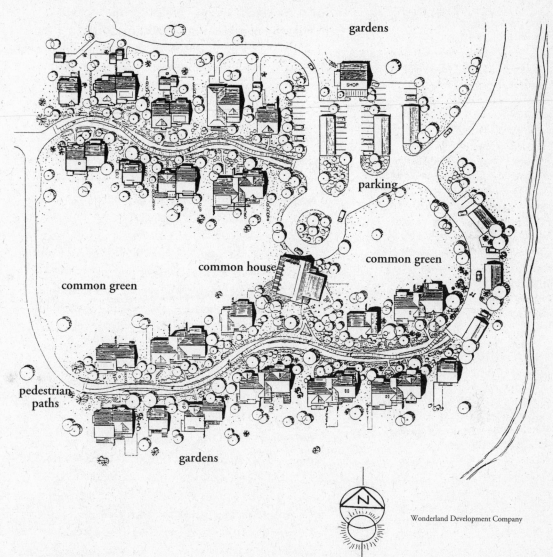

Wonderland Development Company

Nyland CoHousing
Clustering provides large open spaces for orchards, gardens and walkways between houses, athletic fields, and for replanting native plant life that provides the potential for a high level of self-reliance.

Colorado State Office of Energy Conservation and the Environmental Protection Agency. Much of the money so far has been spent on energy-efficient insulation and on testing the health safety of various materials. All of the houses were sited on an east-west axis for optimum solar access from the south, and a few have passive solar greenhouses and solar water heating systems. A key goal of the program is to demonstrate that "you don't need a lot of high-tech stuff to be extremely energy efficient."[14]

The 2-1/2 Acre Prototype Village Cluster Community

This prototype 2-1/2 acre Village Cluster community plan combines in one model all the precepts of village housing and community living. It is designed and organized to be ecologically sustainable by making the best use of both human and natural resources.

It is designed for an extended family of 16 to 25 people living on a suburban fringe or urban infill site, but could be modified for larger or smaller groups and other locations, urban or rural. We want to stress the importance of carefully considering the location when designing a Village Cluster/CoHousing community. As we cautioned in Chapter Three, there is a tendency among some core groups to want to locate in urban fringe or rural areas away from the perceived stress and violence of city life. In doing so, they will also be locating far from transit systems, cultural centers, jobs, and stores, thus increasing their car dependency.

The cooperative nature of the Village Cluster makes car pooling and errand sharing feasible, meaning fewer trips, less wear on cars and public roads, less fuel use, and less pollution. Unless a community is highly self-reliant the benefits of cluster housing alone will not outweigh the environmental consequences of increased energy and car usage from living in the country. The ecological alternative is to locate in the city or suburbs near a bus or rail line and create a social and environmental design that includes elements of country living.

Following is an outline of the basic elements which comprise the Village Cluster model, wherever the location is.

- **The common courtyard** has a multipurpose game court, a mini-amphitheater, vegetable and flower gardens, play areas, paths, benches, sitting areas, outdoor eating tables, a stream, a small pond, and other amenities that can be built or added in phases.

- **Gardens, orchards, and preserved natural areas** are located around the edges of the site and in the common courtyard. The gardens and orchards, provide food for the community and may even be a source of income and livelihood for some members.

- **All buildings are clustered** on the site to leave as much land as possible in its natural state and to create areas for gardens and recreation. Meadows, streams, ponds, native trees and wooded areas, and natural contours are preserved to be enjoyed by the members of the Village Cluster and the broader community. Village Clusters in suburban or even urban settings can appear more rural by providing attractive and natural outdoor areas. The goal is to create usable spaces while preserving the integrity and beauty of the natural world.

- **The passive solar-heated common house** is the focus of the community, and is designed for group

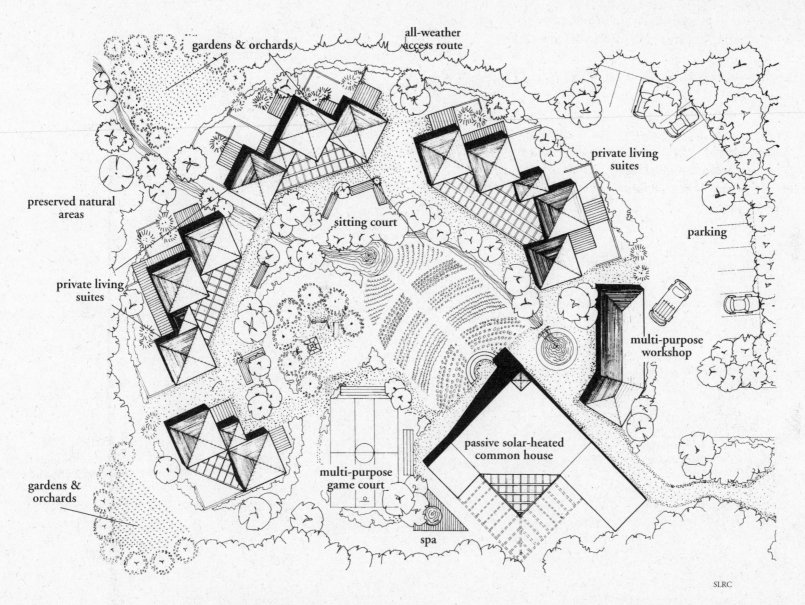

gardens & orchards

all-weather access route

private living suites

preserved natural areas

sitting court

parking

private living suites

multi-purpose workshop

multi-purpose game court

passive solar-heated common house

gardens & orchards

spa

SLRC

The 2 ½ Acre Village Cluster Community
This prototype design provides the features neded for a high level of self-reliance, natural energy production, low car dependency, a paradise for children, commuity-based livelihood, and a sense of belonging.

• **Private living suites** are clustered around the pedestrian courtyard in order to provide open space and easy access to common facilities. In this prototype all of the 12 units are small starter units, designed for later additions and/or a second story. Other Village Cluster designs can accomodate more units.

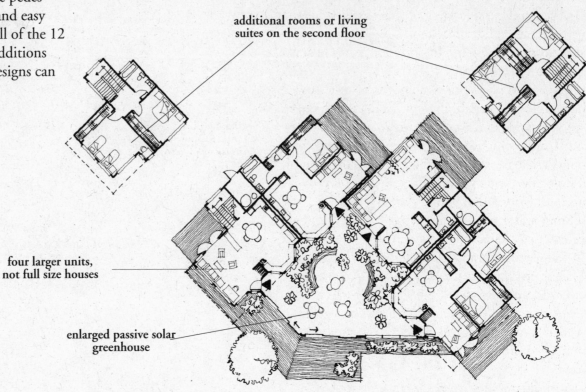

additional rooms or living suites on the second floor

four larger units, not full size houses

enlarged passive solar greenhouse

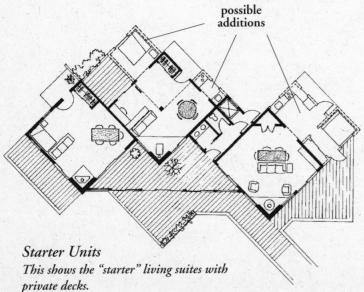

possible additions

Expanded Units

The private units shown in the 2-1/2 acre Village Cluster prototype design were envisioned as starter living suites, and were carefully sited to allow for room additions on two to three sides, as well as a second story. Expansion would be optional, occurring when children are expected or other family needs arise. The kitchen of a unit does not need to be full size as in a typical nuclear family tract house, and for some people could even be left out.

Starter Units

This shows the "starter" living suites with private decks.

cooking, shared meals, food processing, social activities, and guest lodging. It has shared amenities such as a sauna, hot tub, library, child care room, work office, computer/telecommunications center and laundry facilities.

• **Maximum solar gain** is achieved by orienting the building clusters to the south and designing for passive heating and cooling with greenhouses, sun courts, and skylights. Natural ventilation systems, roof overhangs, and vine arbors control the amount of heat gain inside the buildings, while still providing abundant natural light.

• **Solar water heating** and electric power systems are more cost-effective and efficient with a compact cluster of units around the common house.

• **The infrastructure needs** of the community are reduced by clustering the buildings, centralizing energy distribution systems, and restricting parking to an area near the street entrance. This reduces the number of driveways, roads, and power connections.

• **A multi-purpose workshop** with a tool room, art studios, a telecommunications/computer office, a childcare facility, and general storage is adjacent to the common house. This space serves members' home businesses and community-owned enterprises. The building is separate from the common house both for sound insulation and to allow expansion in phases using self-help construction techniques.

• **Sensitive planting of trees and vegetation** reduces the effects of weather extremes. Evergreen trees and dense foliage to the north of the site protect against cold winter winds. Deciduous trees and vine arbors to the south allow solar access during the winter and protect from excessive sun in

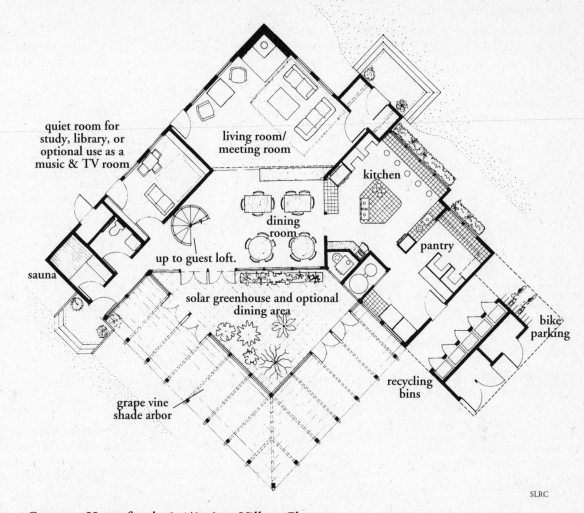

SLRC

Common House for the 2-1/2 Acre Village Cluster
The size of this prototype common house is only 2,100 sq. ft., but there are others being built in Intentional Communities and CoHousing Communities from 3,600 to 6,000 sq. ft.

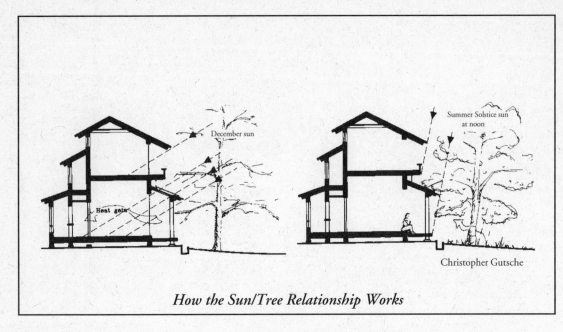

How the Sun/Tree Relationship Works

Christopher Gutsche

"The word "sustainable" development identifies a concept and attitude in development that looks at a site's natural land, water, and energy resources as integral aspects of the development design. Rather than changing the landscape to fit the development plan, a sustainable design uses the natural landscape whenever possible and provides means for maintaining, or 'sustaining' this landscape." [16]
— *Robin K. Vieira, Florida Solar Energy Center*

the summer. Trees and plants also help distinguish spaces, and define pathways, play areas, and gathering spots.

• **All-weather access routes** for delivering supplies to the common house and occasional large items to units are wide enough for trucks. Local codes may mandate, or you may want, emergency access to all the units.

• **Pathways are ramped** and made with a firm but permeable material, such as compacted, decomposed granite instead of asphalt or concrete. This allows easy travel with tote carts, wheeled toys, bicycles, and accessibility for wheelchairs, and allows water to be absorbed and tree roots to breathe. Many a stately oak tree has died from sheltering a paved picnic area or driveway. There are circumstances where impervious surfaces are necessary becuase of soil conditions or local regulations. Use brick or flat rocks when available.

What Makes a "Village Cluster" a Village?

The communities we have just reviewed — Ziuma's compound, Pueblo Bonito, and the various CoHousing developments — provide vivid and compelling images of an alternative way of life. But what is it about these communities that gives them that feeling of intimacy, unity, and calm that we associate with villages? With the 2-1/2 acre Village Cluster prototype, we presented specific elements and design features that define Village Cluster/ CoHousing, but it takes more than these to create a community.

There are several qualities or principles of physical design and social organization that are essential to create and sustain a modern day village community. These principles are universal in nature and can be adapted to serve the needs, values, and ideals of any group. We previously introduced some of the basic principles such as co-ownership, intergenerational extended family, participatory management, and integration of physical form and social structure. Now, we will examine other related principles necessary to successfully create modern-day, extended family and village communities.

Human scale/pedestrian oriented
A Village Cluster must be small in scale, not so small as to preclude a sense of diversity, space, and freedom, but small enough for all areas to be quickly accessible by foot and visually accessible from a few key areas. The layout should encourage face-to-face interaction, where people are able to know and be known by others in the community, and each person feels that he or she influences the

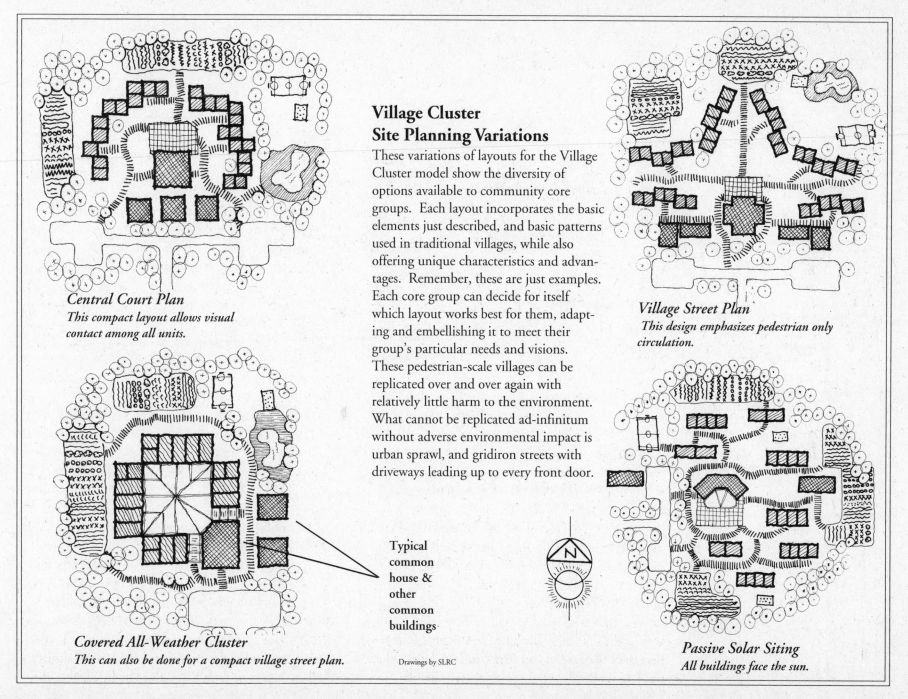

Central Court Plan
This compact layout allows visual contact among all units.

Village Cluster
Site Planning Variations

These variations of layouts for the Village Cluster model show the diversity of options available to community core groups. Each layout incorporates the basic elements just described, and basic patterns used in traditional villages, while also offering unique characteristics and advantages. Remember, these are just examples. Each core group can decide for itself which layout works best for them, adapting and embellishing it to meet their group's particular needs and visions. These pedestrian-scale villages can be replicated over and over again with relatively little harm to the environment. What cannot be replicated ad-infinitum without adverse environmental impact is urban sprawl, and gridiron streets with driveways leading up to every front door.

Village Street Plan
This design emphasizes pedestrian only circulation.

Covered All-Weather Cluster
This can also be done for a compact village street plan.

Typical common house & other common buildings

Drawings by SLRC

Passive Solar Siting
All buildings face the sun.

SLRC

*Sunday Morning
in a Village Cluster*
*This idyllic community scene is what
happens when people have a commonly
owned place, mutual responsibilities,
and shared goals.*

*"While they [new village communi-
ties] draw on lessons from all of
human experience, they are not a
return to any previous period or
way of life."[17]*
— *Robert Gilman,
In Context*

life of the community. Unlike today's cities and
suburbs with skyscrapers, seas of parking lots,
highways bisecting neighborhoods, and streets with
no sidewalks, the Village Cluster is designed for the
human, not the car. All components of the village
environment — buildings, paths, parks, and vegetation — are scaled to provide visual interest and
meaningful experiences for people walking, gathering, or working. Parking on the periphery of the
community protects indoor and outdoor living
spaces from car noise and visual intrusion. People
must walk from their cars through the community
to their living unit, instead of driving right into
their garage. This encourages personal communication on a daily basisand, reduces the amount of
paving, and removes the intrusion of the car.

Continuity, compatibility, and closeness
Compare the Village Cluster and CoHousing plans
to those of Ziuma's compound and Pueblo Bonito,
and note the similarity in the overall form and
layout. The scale is intimate and pedestrian-
oriented with a strong sense of closeness and continuity. The designs are compact and well-contained
within the site, creating a self-supporting and
physically coherent village community with a
distinct center, defined boundaries, smaller subcenters of activity, and open areas flowing around
the buildings. The line of sight from doorways of
living units gives a glimpse of the community.
    Clustering buildings is preferred when the goal
is to create a social atmosphere that encourages
diversity, growth, and sharing. In most housing

developments, the houses are spread out with no real connection to one another, alienating residents, especially the young, elderly, and handicapped. In a Village Cluster/CoHousing solution, houses are integrated in a coherent relationship, clustered around pedestrian paths and courts in a manner that provides a sense of enclosure without diminishing the qualities of open space. We have learned from studying historic villages that when the physical environment reflects and supports an interactive cultural and social structure, a sustainable society can be created. We look to the Muir Commons CoHousing in Davis, California as good model...

Even when a community is built in phases or grows over time, as with some Intentional Communities, a sense of overall continuity is maintained. Similar materials, forms, and building systems are used to tie the dwellings together even if each is personalized by the occupants. In Ziuma's compound, this is done by structurally connecting the units in a honeycomb pattern and then allowing each resident to embellish the walls of their unit with artistic designs. In Muir Commons, the units are designed as row houses with the same roof pitch, outside color, and basic window design, but each unit has front and back areas that the residents can personalize with plants, patios, benches, or artwork. By envisioning the community as a unified entity, people can express themselves, and a sense of security, interdependence, and belonging will likely emerge.

Co-built, co-owned, and co-managed

Throughout history, human habitats were not built by outsiders and then sold or rented to the resi-

Front Yard Sitting Court at Muir Commons

Photo by Kathleen Smith

dents. A primary objective in creating Village Cluster communities today is for members to be involved in all phases of development to the greatest extent possible, and for the members to co-own and co-manage the community after it is built.

Even if consultants, architects, lenders, developers, and/or builders are involved in the process, it is the members who are physically, financially, and emotionally invested in and committed to creating a secure and enriching place to live. Being responsible, members feel empowered and in control, leading to a strong sense of belonging and pride. This has been the experience of the Intentional Community, CoHousing, Urban Cooperative Block, and Habitat for Humanity movements. Problems and possibilities with involving developers

"I think [community] teaches children to respect others' rights to privacy and property, and teaches greater skills in community interaction and consensus building, all valuable skills in a true democracy. Economically we can each be richer by buying bulk foods, sharing newspaper subscriptions, and pooling our tools. By clustering houses we increase density but do not reduce open space since the land savings are accomplished by reducing paved driveways and unused side yards."
— An SLRC Profile Exercise Participant

125

"Some folks had never had their own space before and didn't know where to begin, but there are lots of people to help and advise, lots of expertise in the group from Botany to Carpentry. There are so many different levels of interaction, experience, and education. It was wonderful to see my friend Sharon, an MBA from Harvard, out laying bricks."

— *A Member of Muir Commons CoHousing*

"Shared Living Community housing is not just producing a relationship and communication between individuals, it is creating a group. It is hard for Americans to see the reality of groups. They see only a collection of individuals, and not a new entity. The term 'Shared Living' suggests a relationship between individuals, or several groups. But in actuality, a new entity is being created that takes on a life of its own.... Individuals may come and go, but the group as an organized entity remains."[18]

— *Chandler Washburne, Ph.D.*

Photo by Don Lindemann

Landscaping Work Party at Muir Commons
Self-help construction is increasingly becoming a common experience in the new community movement.

in the production of Village Cluster/CoHousing communities are further discussed in Chapter Nine.

Working with what is given

Traditional villages rarely use imported labor, materials, or resources to build or operate their community. They work with the materials, resources, and methods of construction that were native to their area and familiar to them and which tend to be more energy efficient, renewable, and ecologically sound, and easier to maintain than those that are imported. Historically, societies that use imported methods and materials tend to be less stable, because they depend on outside knowledge and sources to maintain their environments.

In the U.S. today, it will be difficult to be locally self-sufficient in a consistent manner, but it is imperative that communities be designed and built in a way that minimizes harmful impacts to the land and people, and that encourages the use of safe, locally grown or manufactured materials and native building techniques. In rural, suburban, and urban settings, this is an opportunity to build stronger relationships with surrounding neighbors and suppliers. In this way, each local community gains a sense of place and contributes to the economy and sustainability of the whole region.

Common spaces and private places

A village community provides a distinctive balance between common and private space, offering each person the opportunity to join in the benefits of community living and sharing or to retreat to the solitude and peace of their own private living suite or unit. In Ziuma's compound, the common space is the social and visual core of the community, incorporating cooking and eating functions. The private living spaces are close by, but are intentionally arranged for a high level of privacy. In the Village Cluster, this same balance is accomplished through a hierarchy of spaces — a gradation from private to semi-private to semi-common to common spaces. It is best to think of the common and private areas as a unified whole rather than divided into isolated public versus private realms as is done in conventional housing. Each space in the Village Cluster design helps define the boundaries, size, and functions of the others. A series of transitions such as walls, changes in elevation, materials, and porches help to define each space from the others.

In the Village Cluster approach, the practice is to intentionally design smaller private units, or as in the Village Acre community, individual living suites without kitchens. Because the common house has abundant shared facilities and amenities, nothing is lost by having a smaller house. The common house and the pedestrian street or court become an extension of each house — their living, family, dining, and play rooms — where daily meals, special activities, meetings, and celebrations take place.

A member of Muir Commons, commenting on why they don't like outside groups meeting in their common house, explained, "We think of the common house as our house. So when others meet there it feels strange." Careful thought must be given to the activities, conveniences, and amenities that are most important for common use and to those most important for individual private use. This forethought will translate into lower costs, less energy use, and more space for amenities such as hot tubs or saunas.

Commitment to sharing

A commitment to sharing and cooperation is a key precept universal to village communities. In Village Clusters and other Shared Living Communities, members voluntarily share resources, land, energy, and cars, and are co-responsible for the community. This sharing does not mean that each individual loses a sense of self in the group, but rather becomes empowered by the self-esteem that comes from being nurtured and in turn nurturing others.

Some people will view any shared living situation as a threat to their individual families, yet community life often strengthens family life by helping to meet each family's social and daily living needs — which otherwise would be met outside the home and away from family life. The goal for Village Cluster/CoHousing is to create a new definition of "home" to include the closeness, camaraderie, and caring that is shared among an extended family of neighbors, friends, and family. Today's small families will thrive when home is part of a larger community, connected to other people with whom they can share emotional support, joys, hardships and sorrows, responsibilities, and frustrations. Proof of this is found in the testimony of members of existing communities:

Seif, a 37-year-old owner of a direct-mail advertising company, had concluded [that] traditional single-family housing was all wrong for him: "I was driving down my empty street, past blocks of empty homes, to my empty house," he recalls. "Suddenly the isolation of typical suburban life just hit me…."[19]

"Finally, we were landowners, and it felt good. We had an identity. It was like getting married — the state and the banks now looked at us as a legitimate being. What would be our community now had a self of its own…."[20]

"I'm savoring the process of building our CoHousing community step by step, observing the alliances that are made, the deep, far reaching sense of unity that is growing…."[21]

"If we didn't have a history of working together and learning to compromise and building trust, we wouldn't be sitting here right now in the common house eating dinner together…."[24]

"The highest goal of community life is to overcome the fragmentation caused by society and to create whole people integrating mind/body/feelings/spirit so that all parts of the self function harmoniously. The greatest challenge of community life is to create a synthesis, embracing diversity in a unified whole, resolving differences with the healing spirit of love and dedication to the good of the whole." [22]
— *Corinne McLaughlin & Gordon Davidson*

"Their goal was a way of life that revolves around the community rather than the individual." [23]
— *Susan Diesenhouse, Commenting on Sirius Community*

"Living a sane and ecologically responsible life doesn't mean self-sacrifice and austerity; on the contrary, it should mean a richer, fuller, longer, and healthier life." [25]
— Ernest Callenbach

Photo by Therese Kunzi-Clark

Neighbors Visiting at Winslow CoHousing
Every American neighhborhood can be transfornd into a safe and beautiful place to live by sharing responsibilities for ownership, management, resources, and amenities.

Conclusion

As economic, social, and environmental problems continue, fundamental changes in our homes and lifestyles, our ways of doing business, and our land use and transportation planning become imperative. The Village Cluster approach presents an ecological answer through social interaction that encourages energy savings, resource sharing, and car trip reduction. In the Village Cluster/CoHousing models, physical design and socioeconomic structure are wed. This integration supports the well-being of the group and its individual members, thereby providing for its own sustainability as a living village.

These thoughts may seem idealistic. And making the transition from single-family house lifestyles to sharing meals in a common house will be a big leap for most mainstream Americans. It will also be a stretch to apply these Village Cluster principles broadly to urban, suburban, and rural locations. Each new community will have its own unique set of problems and processes. However, the socioeconomic and environmental calamities facing us suggest the shift to ecologically sustainable community must be made quickly.

Comprehensive urban planning, such as networks of Eco Villages and Eco Cities linked by high speed and light rail systems could bring about a permanent end to sprawling suburbia. In rural areas, Village Cluster communities can be separated by organic farmlands, thus forming a new rural society within an agricultural Green Belt. In cities, new community housing could take the form of infill, re-use, and mixed-use Urban Cooperative Blocks linked by light rail or bus lines. As density increases around transit stations, urban green strips would form over reclaimed public streets. This is what rebuilding community in America is all about. In the following chapters, we will focus in turn on rural, suburban, and urban communities, to see how these Village Cluster principles and design concepts can be applied.

Notes

Books listed only by name in the end notes are highlighted in the resource guide at the end of the book, complete with author/publisher information and description.

1 Jean-Paul Bourdier & Trinh T. Minh-ha, <u>African Spaces: Designs for Living in Upper Volta</u>, Africana Publishing Company, New York, 1985, pp. 32-48.
2 Eric Utne, <u>In the Company of Others</u>, p. x.
3 Jean-Paul Bourdier, *Op. Cit.,* p. 48.
4 Much of the writing in this section is based on information from the following two sources:
   •Peter Nabokov & Robert Easton, <u>Native American Architecture</u>, Oxford University Press, New York, 1989, pp. 356-363.
   •Jeffrey Cook, <u>Anasazi Places: The Photographic Vision of William Current</u>, University of Texas Press, Austin, 1992, pp. 3-24.
5 <u>Builders of the Dawn</u>, pp. 10-11.
6 Robert Gilman, "The Eco-Village Challenge," *In Context: A Quarterly of Humane Sustainable Culture* , No. 29, p. 11. (In Context Subscriptions $24/yr; Single Issues $6; PO Box 11470, Bainbridge Island, WA 98110)
7 <u>Builders of the Dawn</u>, p. 12.
8 Carla Cole, "What about Traditional Villages?," *In Context,* No. 29, p. 12.
9 <u>Directory of Intentional Communities</u>, p. 37.
10 Ellen Smith, "Residents Move into Muir Commons," *CoHousing,* Fall 1991, Vol. 4, No. 2, p. 1.
11 *Ibid.,* p. 4
12 Joan DeClaire, "Come Together," *Pacific Northwest,* August/September 1991, p. 15.
13 Various members of Winslow CoHousing, "Winslow CoHousing: A Self-Portrait," *In Context,* No. 35, p. 41.
14 Don Lindemann, "Site Development Underway in Colorado," *CoHousing,* Fall 1991, Vol. 4, No. 2, p. 6.
15 <u>New Households, New Housing</u>, p. 6.
16 Robin K. Vieira, "Designing Sustainable Environments," *Solar Today,* September/October.
17 Robert Gilman, *Op. Cit.,* p. 11.
18 Chandler Washburne, Ph.D., CSUF, from a paper written for SLRC, May 18, 1992, p. 10.
19 Claudia Morain, "CoHousing: A '90s Style Return to the Commune," *San Francisco Chronicle,* May 13, 1992, Home Section, p. 6.
20 Chris Hansen, "The Winslow Story: A Personal Recollection," *CoHousing,* Fall 1992, Vol. 5, No. 2, p. 15.
21 Jon Greer, "Hooked on a New Way of Living," *CoHousing,* Fall 1992, Vol. 5, No. 2, p. 16.
22 <u>Builders of the Dawn</u>, p. 54.
23 Susan Diesenhouse, "Communal Living, an Idea that is Gaining Ground," *New York Times,* November 11, 1990, Sec. 8, p. 1.
24 Ellen Smith, *Op. Cit.,* p. 4.
25 Ernest Callenbach, "The Green Triangle," *Solar Mind,* July/August, 1991, No. 6, p. 3.

RURAL COMMUNITIES
the Romance and the Reality

Amish Society Communities are Dedicated to a Sustainable Way of Living

Photo *Amish Society* by John A. Hostetler

CHAPTER FIVE

Let's walk under the oaks, splash in the stream, rest on the grass, sleep out under the stars, and court our love — get to know this valley. Then we can create our community in this valley with feeling and understanding.

Dear Valley

"It's too beautiful to cut up into single-family lots. We'll have to buy it somehow," said Carol, turning excitedly to her friends, all of whom were members of the Arch Street Group, a cooperative household in the San Francisco Bay Area.

John, who was squatting at the edge of the little hill, answered, *"Yes, so we can save it from the developers. I'm full of ideas already. I'd like to see a large duck pond, a canoe dock, a swimming hole at the creek, and a volleyball court."*

"We'll need more co-buyers, but if we can get $50,000 down, we can start — right?" Carol remarked, *"I'd sure like to settle down here. Let's start planning. I want my house down by those three oaks, and…"*

She was interrupted by Helene, who had been standing behind the other members of the group. She was also excited, but held back from the joyful chatter of the others who were already buying, planning, and building in the pleasant meadow. Finally she spoke up. *"Stop it! You're already raping the valley, using it up! You're talking like city folks rushing off for a country lark. What's happened to our values about ecologically sustainable living? You're right, Carol. It is beautiful. But for us to suddenly play God and plan it just for ourselves is wrong."*

Helene moved to stand next to John. For a long time they were silent, looking down into the valley which could be home to their dream community. Helene spoke again. *"Let's wait for the others before we start making plans for this virgin place.*

Then, slowly and sensitively, we can explore and understand its intricate beauty. Let's walk under the oaks, splash in the stream, rest on the grass, sleep out under the stars, and court our love — get to know this valley. Then we can create our community with feeling and understanding."

"Yes," John spoke softly, looking down at the valley with moist eyes. *"She is beautiful. We've got to show her we really care. We can begin by growing organic food in that rich loam. But first we've got to get the down payment together, or what we love will be used up for one-acre country estates."*

Carol responded, *"I agree! I'm sorry for sounding so 'my house' like. If we don't design our community and our lifestyles ecologically, we might really abuse this dear valley."*

****

In this dialogue, we are trying to portray the feelings and dreams of the many people who are searching for satisfying alternatives to the turmoil and strain of everyday life. What they are searching for is a better quality of life and the time and resources for personal interests, for family and children, and for building supportive community. The names we use are fictitious, but the feelings, needs, visions, and personalities of the people come from observations and experiences.

The socially and environmentally responsible planning, housing, farming, and financing programs proposed in this dialogue are conceptual, but based on ideas being reintroduced by many of today's brave pioneers and top innovators. We offer this community scenario as an inspirational model for encouraging sustainable living in Organic Farm Village Cluster communities throughout future

"There was a recent time when people moving to the country had some inchoate, improbably agrarian notion that guided their escape. Today, one senses that simple escape, uncomplicated by ideals of self sufficiency, is the primary motive of the latest pilgrims." [1]
— *Thomas H. Rawls, Small Places: In Search of a Vanishing America*

"I believe in beauty, I believe in stones and water, and soil, people and their future...."
— Ansel Adams

Green Belts surrounding American cities.

The community models we propose are attainable now, but introducing new programs, legislation, and attitudes will enable ecological sustainable communities to be built more quickly and in larger numbers. Keep these thoughts in mind as you read this chapter. And imagine how you, your family, and your friends can benefit by creating your own community. You don't have to be a political activist to live in a community, but it is important to understand the complexity of certain issues pertaining to rural communities.

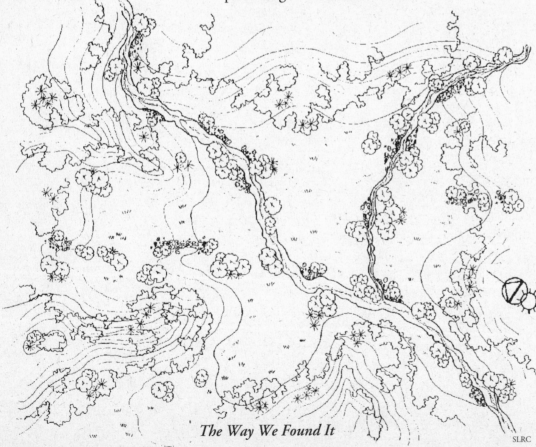

The Way We Found It

SLRC

The Dear Valley Development Options

The way we found it

"...natural, virgin, rolling hills." Helene's words were carefully and reverently pronounced, as she finished showing slides at the new member meeting for the proposed Dear Valley community. *"It's so beautiful. The creek sides are covered with plantain, ferns, lupines, and sage. The oaks and madrones are majestic, and there's plenty of open space around them to build our Village Cluster and grow crops. We want to reintroduce other native plants as well, and locate the community buildings in a way that protects wildlife corridors. We've seen quail, lizards, ground squirrels and deer — it's a complete ecosystem."*

"If we want to save this valley from the bulldozer's blade, we'll have to buy it. We can probably get help from the Green Belt Environmental Quality Commission in the form of sustainable agriculture start-up grants, deferred interest loans, and zoning for additional units, all because of our ecologically planned Organic Farm Village Cluster." She paused, looked thoughtfully around and added, *"You can help by joining and investing in the community. Remember, our success in this venture will be an example to encourage other community organic farms in the Green Belt. There'll be a good return for the environment, for you, and for us."*

The developer option

If a developer were to acquire this land, the natural beauty and the integrity of the ecosystem would be destroyed. Developers, typically, must follow certain rules to be successful — that is, to make a profit selling land and houses. Here are some typical rules and common practices:

- Maximize profit by re-zoning agricultural land for single-family or commercial development.
- Maximize the number of lots allowed by zoning.
- Minimize or eliminate government regulations.
- Clear the site of vegetation, and make flat pads for easy-to-build single-family houses by cutting off the hilltops and filling in the low areas.
- Provide wide, paved streets for direct car access to each two or three car garage.
- Where possible, omit public sidewalks and front entry walks from the street. Place a walkway from the driveway only.
- Build a marketable house as quickly and cheaply as possible, without consideration of siting for passive solar heating.
- Plant lawns and shrubbery in a formal manner to give the appearance of a high-end development.
- Reduce costs, maximize profits, and avoid risks in any way possible.
- Standardize the houses for a particular income market, usually the highest income range available in the general area.

The typical housing development process has become indifferent to social and environmental consequences. The attitude is, "People are buying these houses, so what's the problem?" Certainly, people are buying into and living in these houses, but only because there are no other options.

The Organic Farm Village Cluster option
The Arch Street Group knew that Dear Valley could be subdivided into one-acre lots, the most dense rural residential zoning allowed by the county. They knew that the rolling hills would then be cut down to create flat building sites. They

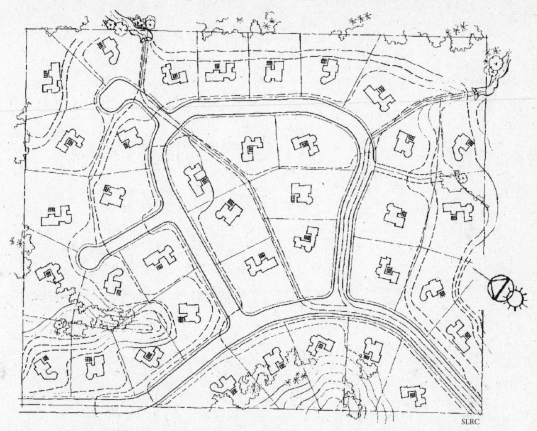

A Typical One Acre "Rural Estate" Subdivision — This Was the "Valley"

knew that much of the rich topsoil would be buried under earth fill and paved streets. They knew the creeks would be covered over, and that most of the oaks, madrones, and wildlife would disappear.

In response, the group organized a series of planning meetings at which they formulated their goals. They decided they wanted to build and operate an Organic Farm Village Cluster based on successful examples of rural Intentional Communities, small-scale organic farms, and cooperative farm businesses. With the help of nonprofit organiza-

"...a society can obtain a high quality lifestyle while consuming far less, per capita, of the world's resources than developed nations currently use. It is quite possible to capitalize the entire world while eliminating poverty and protecting the ecosystem and scarce resources." [2]

— J. W. Smith, World's Wasted Wealth 2

Give Me the Splendid Silent Sun
By Walt Whitman

*Give me the splendid silent sun
   with all his beams full
   dazzling,
Give me juicy autumnal fruit ripe
   and red from the orchard,
Give me a field where the
   unmow'd grass grows,
Give me an arbor, give me
   trellis'd grapes,
Give me fresh corn and wheat,
   give me serene-moving
   animals teaching content,
Give me nights perfectly quiet as
   on high plateaus west of the
   Mississippi, and I looking
   up at the stars,
Give me odorous at sunrise a
   garden of beautiful flowers
   where I can walk
   undisturb'd.* [3]

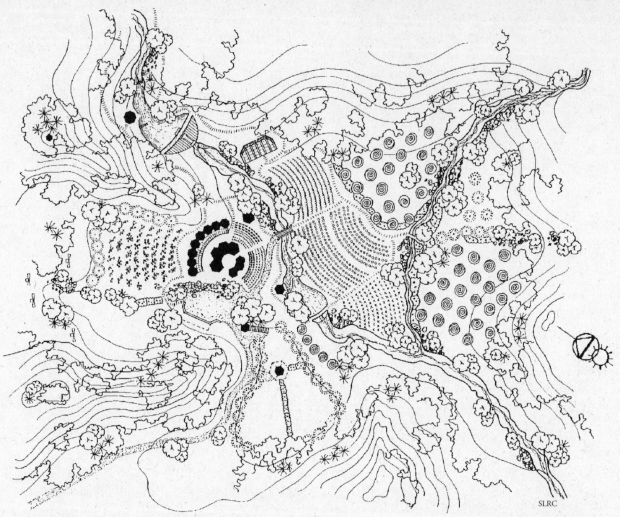

Site Plan of a 40 Acre Organic Farm in "Dear Valley," Designed for Ecological Sustainability

tions that specialize in ecological community design, organic farming, Permaculture, and sustainable agriculture, they studied information on sustainable agricultural practices, alternative construction methods, use of natural materials, and living in Shared Living Communities. From this work, they came to see the entire 40 acres as an integration of both natural forces and human endeavors.

The Dear Valley core group followed the design principles presented in Chapter Four for co-designing a compact Village Cluster of 12 private units around pedestrian-only courtyards and a common house. The courtyards have patios, meandering walkways, benches, small play areas, shade canopies, and herb and flower gardens. Permaculture-inspired organic vegetable gardens, vineyards, and fruit orchards blend with the native plant life that surrounds the cluster. Further out they would use 25 acres for cultivated fields, equipment and storage compounds, and animal enclosures.

The common house has a large kitchen, dining/social areas, food processing areas, and other amenities, such as childcare and teen rooms, a library, art/craft/work studios, and a telecommunications and computer room.

All of this happened several years ago. Dear Valley is now an intergenerational and multicultural community of 22 adults, six children, and two teens. It has become a Community Land Trust and operates with a participatory management structure. The organic farm offers full-time livelihood to most of the members, although some now operate small businesses (herbs and teas, newsletters, and graphic design). Others work for the community, doing accounting, teaching, childcare, and maintenance.

One of Dear Valley's greatest ecological achievements has been breaking free from their car dependency. They bought, traded, and sold their vehicles, resulting in co-ownership of only three cars, a pickup, a van-bus used for car pooling and errands, and a fleet of mountain bicycles and tote carts . A flat-bed truck is shared with a nearby organic farm for marketing trips to the city.

This scenario is intended to present an ideal ecological community example to illustrate how people can move to the country and have a low impact on the rural environment, by creating a permanent Green Belt around urban centers. In reality, however, many people have illusions about rural living and small towns. Let's look now at the underlying motivations and consequences of fleeing the city for "country living."

"Let's Move to the Country"

The romance of country living

At one time or another, most of us have imagined ourselves living on a classic country farm. Unless you grew up on a farm and have your own memories of country life, you probably imagine a lively, colorful place — a nostalgic storybook farm. The air is fresh. The blue sky is dotted with puffy clouds. Rain falls only at appropriate times. The sun shines most of the time, radiating life into the growing crops — wheat, rice, potatoes, and other fruits and vegetables too numerous to mention. The corn sways in the late summer breeze, ready to be picked for the evening meal. A rustic red barn houses the animals, and of course, there is a chicken yard. A dog or two keep the cows in line, while a family of cats make short work of the mice.

Back at the farmhouse, Mom and Grandma are preparing a supper of fresh tomatoes and corn, sourdough bread with home-churned butter, and trout caught just hours before in the stream next to the yard. Mom steps out into the backyard to pick peaches for dessert — fresh cobbler. Meanwhile, Grandpa completes the evening milking while Dad takes a few last turns on the tractor before heading home for the day. The kids are walking up the road, returning from school.

This may seem like the ecological ideal — living simply on the land, enjoying good food, family life, and a supportive livelihood. But, it is also a product of our ignorance about a way of life most of us never knew.

"Evidence that the rural counties are becoming bedroom communities of Charlottesville can be seen by the increasing number of residents commuting to work and shopping in the city. In fact, three out of five counties in the region export more workers to the city than they retain....Realtors are finding that residents with moderate incomes who want to own their own homes are increasingly ending up in the rural counties. Moreover, low income residents can more easily attain homeownership in rural counties through Farmer's Home Administration. This is unfortunate because these persons have less time and higher costs due to commuting than city residents."[4]
— *"Economic Growth Within the Capacity of the Environment to Support it," The Thomas Jefferson Planning District Commission*

"Apparently with the rise of industry, we began to romanticize the wilderness — which is to say we began to institutionalize it within the concept of the 'scenic.' Because of railroads and improved highways, the wilderness was no longer an arduous passage for the traveler, but something to be looked at as grand or beautiful from the high vantage of the roadside."[5]
— *Wendell Berry, Recollected Essays, 1965-1980*

The country movement

This image, along with changing cultural, economic, and employment patterns, draws many people out of the city and into the suburbs, small towns, and country. At SLRC, we receive frequent inquiries from individuals, couples, families, and beginning core groups interested in forming a community in rural or mountain areas. Often their motivation is to get away from congestion, crime, noise, air pollution, high housing and land costs, and the lack of open space. They see no options for creating community in an urban setting. Many working or retired people of moderate to low income also express a desire to abandon city life for the imagined self-reliance and savings of country living. Creating "community" in the country sounds good, but is often just another form of "urban flight."

Most people moving to the country share the mistaken public attitude that moving out of the city and into the country will still their fears and solve their problems. Unfortunately, this attitude is reinforced by developers and other economic interests who use idyllic images of country living in real estate ads, in the hopes of making a profit by selling land and houses to disillusioned urbanites. People often believe that forming an "Intentional Community," "Village Cluster," or "CoHousing" community simply means co-buying rural land, splitting it into parcels, scattering out separate houses among the trees, and sharing a few common recreational and utilitarian amenities.

All too often, the country these people seek disappears within a few years of their arrival, replaced with the pollution, congestion, noise, housing sprawl, and crime they were trying to avoid.

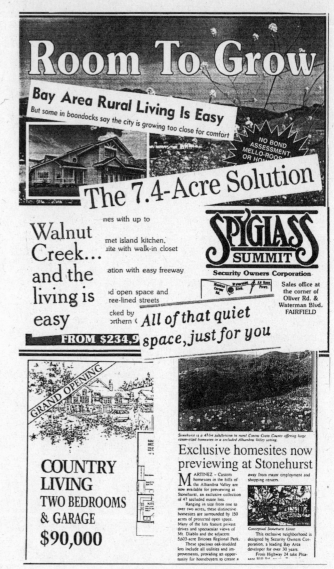

SLRC

Most people are not sufficiently aware of the environmental impact a commuter lifestyle has on the land, the air; and their own emotional well-being. Nor do they realize the social isolation that can come from living in the country, or the suburbia that inevitably follows. There can never be a permanent country environment unless tere is a public policy that a permanent rural society is desirable.

We would also like to dispel the myth that moving "back to the land" is easy. It can involve generating a livelihood, raising children, providing schooling, tending animals, and making the many long car trips needed for the myriad of errands any family has to run. More and more, there are dangers from crime and gangs, and an increasing number of accidents on narrow, dangerously overcrowded roads.

Some stalwart people have attempted a rural, simple-living and low-impact lifestyle, such as the Colfax family who homesteaded a piece of land in the backwoods of Mendocino County, California. As Silvia Rubin, a writer for the San Francisco Chronicle, explains:

> [They]…came up here to live like those on the prairie 100 years ago…. Today they may seem like every yuppie's dream, taking in the sun on the deck of the redwood house they built themselves. But they tell another story…. They went eleven years without electricity. Eight years without a telephone. Twelve years without hot running water. [9]

The truth is that only a few are suited to such wilderness survival, which is good. If too many people tried to replicate what the Colfax's did, the wilderness would be devastated. We are not saying that nobody should move to the country. We want to underscore the significant difference between ecologically sustainable rural living and urban commuters living on scattered lots or in condominium developments.

Gangs Trouble Sonoma County

Once-tranquil suburbs are trying to cope with a 'big-city' problem

By Glen Martin
Chronicle North Bay Bureau

No longer a phenomenon of the inner city, youth gangs and the "gangsta" culture have infiltrated the suburbs of Sonoma County.

Police and sheriff's deputies say gangs are active not only in Santa Rosa but also in the county's outlying hamlets. Most recently, the bedroom community of Rohnert Park has experienced a spate of gang-related incidents that have left residents apprehensive and city police over-extended.

Billed as "The Friendly City," Rohnert Park was founded 33 years ago as a fully planned community, one that would provide its middle-class residents with first-

class amenities, security and a sense of place.

But the town has grown in a sprawling fashion, undermining the original vision of Main Street America. No longer a wholly suburban enclave, it now has big-city problems, including youth crime.

"We've identified 75 confirmed gang members in Rohnert Park, and we suspect that 200 or more may live around here," said Lieutenant Robert Williams of the Rohnert Park Police Department, as he surveyed University Square, a shopping center across the street from Rancho Cotate High School.

The square has been the scene of increasing gang violence — and the most recent incident there has prompted officials at the high

school to stop some students from leaving campus during the school day.

At noon on February 7, about 60 gang members squared off at the shopping center and prepared to fight. Rohnert Park police officers and detectives literally stepped between the two factions to prevent them coming to blows.

"They were screaming and flashing each other gang hand signs," said Williams. "There's no doubt in my mind that things would've gotten very ugly if we hadn't been on hand."

The conflict was the result of a drive-by shooting, in which there were no casualties, the previous

GANGS: *Page A11 Col. 5*

San Francisco Chronicle

The Signs of Community Breakdown are Everywhere
Gangs are no longer just an urban phenomenon. Suburbs are now affected as well.

Fortunately, many community minded groups of people are expressing the desire to form rural cooperative communities and organic family farms, to practice sustainable agriculture and a truly self-reliant lifestyle. These ideals for resettling rural America have been described for decades by survivalists, futurists, organic farmers, and agricultural ecologists like Buckminster Fuller, Jeremy Rifkin, Ernest Callenbach, Wendell Berry, Wes Jackso, and others. The Organic Farm Village Cluster is one approach to creating a socially responsible and ecologically sustainable rural society.

"The domination of what is left of rural America by agribusiness corporations is not only accelerating the migration patterns of recent decades but raises the specter of a kind of twentieth century agricultural feudalism in the culture that remains." [10]

— Nick Kotz,
"The Poor People's Coops"

"…we lose an additional three billion tons of rich and irreplaceable topsoil each year through wind and water erosion! Believe it or not, there are years when our biggest 'farm export' is topsoil."[11]
— *Ralph Grossi, American Farmland Trust*

Photo by Greenbelt Alliance

"Please…make it possible for my people to buy their own land and to care for it with hands that are full of love for the soil. As a simple man I do not know how this can be done. But if it is, we will be able to build a life for ourselves that will make this country more fruitful and more aware that, unlike others, we have never resorted to violence to bring about change."[12]
— *Manuel Leon, "A Farmworker Speaks" (translated from Spanish)*

The Reality — *a rude awakening*

The family farm, a tradition that is truly American, has all but disappeared. Farming has largely been taken over by agribusiness corporations, and hundreds of thousands of acres of agricultural and open space land in the U.S. have been lost to rural sprawl and suburbanization. According to Ralph Grossi, President of the American Farmland Trust, "We lose nearly 2 million acres [nationally] of our most productive farmland each year to development — an area the size of New England in just 25 years."[13]

A staggering amount of evidence tells us that rural areas cannot tolerate an influx of commuting urbanites to so-called "New Towns," or the continuation of agribusiness practices, such as the use of pesticides, mechanized equipment, and mono-cropping. We will now examine more closely the factors that contribute to this devastation.

• **The decline of a stable and economically viable rural society** is in large part due to the decline of the small family farm. This disappearing piece of American society is no match for large agribusiness with its high investment capital and dependence upon low-paid and poorly housed farm workers. Nor can small farmers survive the higher land costs and taxes due to urban pressures. They fall prey to land speculators, who buy the land and rezone it .

• **Expensive and energy-intensive agricultural mechanization** tends to make the more labor–intensive and natural methods of small-scale organic farmers less competitive. The rationale behind such technology is that it facilitates a higher rate of crop production and harvesting at a lower cost to the producer, not necessarily the consumer. Social and environmental costs are not considered.

• **Loss of biodiversity** due to agribusiness use of chemical fertilizers, insecticides, and herbicides destroying the nutrients of the soil and the natural ecosystem is common. Insects, native plants, and birds are killed or forced to relocate, and human health is jeopardized.

Topsoil loss, from wind and water erosion, is hastened by mono-cropping, (the repetitive growing of one crop type), repetitive, mechanized tilling of agribusiness' large fields. Windbreaks and native vegetation that once existed on smaller family farms helped to maintain the topsoil as well as sustain biological diversity. Extensive animal grazing, which kills off the plant life ecology of grasslands, and invites erosion, is another damaging practice.

Why should the disappearance of a species of beetle or a bird concern us? After all, crops seem to be flourishing and food is getting to the stores and the dinner table. But every species of life, from microscopic organisms to humans, is interconnected in an intricate ecosystem on which we all depend. Time after time, creatures thought to be useless or harmful are found to play critical roles in natural systems, and their annihilation brings disaster.

• **Farmers, workers, their families,** and rural residents are all at risk from pesticides and herbicides, a poor standard of living, and the lack of adequate housing, education, and health services. The rate of cancer and birth defects is disproportionately high among farm workers. We in this society benefit from the cheaper food. We eat off the backs of these families. Yet we too are at risk as chemicals contaminate our soil, water, and food.

• **Exploitation of farmlands, open space, and wetlands** to build single-family developments destroys natural resources and ecosystems, and is detrimental to the economy and social and cultural stability of rural areas. Today's "new towns" are as much of an ecological threat to rural areas as land speculators were to the agricultural land and open space of the Southern California region a few decades ago. As J. Barry Cullingworth, the author of *The Political Culture of Planning*, explains:

> Speculation has never been frowned upon in the United States. In many countries, land is regarded as different from commodities. It is something to be preserved and husbanded. In the United States, the dominant ethic regards land as a commodity, no different than any other. [14]

This attitude has got to change. The effects of uncontained development on ecosystems, species, and human life is devastating. The very ability of the planet to sustain life is in jeopardy. It should be considered immoral to cover over fertile valley loam, which took thousands of years to be deposited, with sprawling developments. Careful planning policies must be implemented to preserve the most fertile soils for growing crops, and sensitive and diverse natural areas for wildlife.

• **The impact of growth upon small towns** has accelerated in the 1980's with the influx of commuters who were attracted to the country or mountains by lower-cost housing and the lure of country living. This growth increases the land value in small towns, causing local workers to move away to find affordable housing. The local economy suffers from a rise in prices, as workers demand more pay to offset the rising costs of living and commuting.

In addition, the cost of local government and taxes skyrockets due to increased infrastructure

A8 San Francisco Chronicle ★★★★★· WEDNESDAY, JUNE 23, 1993

All of Vermont in Peril, Preservationists Warn

Washington Post

Marlboro, Vt.

Judging by the Hogback Mountain Gift Shop along Route 9 in southern Vermont, this state remains a land of historical, rustic charm. The store offers maple syrup, local crafts and a chance to tour the museum of wildlife taxidermy. Outside, the steep green hills roll away south to the Holyoke Range in Massachusetts.

But looks can be deceiving, according to the National Trust for Historic Preservation. The trust believes that Vermont is in danger of succumbing to "Sprawl-Mart," the kind of development that has devoured large chunks of the American landscape.

To prevent this, the trust is taking the unprecedented step of designating an entire state No. 1 on its annual list of "endangered" historic places. Scheduled for official release today, the list of 11 places also includes Thomas Edison's invention factory in West Orange, N.J., downtown New Orleans and Brandy Station Battlefield in Culpeper County, Va., site of the Civil War's largest cavalry battle, in 1863.

Richard Moe, president of the National Trust — a congressionally chartered nonprofit group — said yesterday that the group believes the biggest threat to historic preservation this year is in Vermont.

Acknowledging that an entire state has never been listed before, Moe said, "We think it's justified in this case for two reasons: the unique nature of Vermont and the unique nature of the threat it faces through the intrusion of unplanned and uncontrolled development of large shopping malls, which threaten to suck the economic vitality of towns nearby."

All 50 States are Endangered
Damage to the landscape and the environment generated by car-fed "Sprawl-Marts" has become widespread.

demands (for roadways, water lines, etc.) necessary to support new housing developments. The industries and businesses that employ the incoming commuter populations are most often based in another city or county, and carry no financial responsibility.

Most small towns are either withering away from the lack of economic stimuli and from the loss of young people who leave for better opportunities, or they are being drowned by rapid growth.

"The way that a national economy preys on its internal colonies [of rural America] is by the destruction of community — that is, by the destruction of the principle of local self-sufficiency not only in the local economy but also in the local culture. ...having cast off the colonialism of England, we have proceeded to impose a domestic colonialism on our own land and people.... The washed-out farm and bankrupt farmer, the strip-mined mountain and the unemployed or diseased miner, the clear-cut forest and the depressed logging town — all are seen as the mere natural results of so-called free enterprise." [15]
— Wendell Berry,
Home Economics: Fourteen Essays

"It's becoming clearer to more and more farmers that pesticides are not panaceas. Despite the huge increase in insecticide use since World War II, crop losses from insect pests have increased from 7% to 13%. It's time to turn back the clock and take a close look at safer, non-chemical methods of growing, storing, and preserving crops...." [17]
— Anne Montgomery,
"America's Pesticide Permeated Food"

The loss of this aspect of American culture is aptly expressed in the following passage from the book *Small Places: In Search of a Vanishing America,* by Thomas H. Rawls:

> …it seems that in every small place, one of two things is happening: it is dying or it is being killed. The ones that are dying are out-of-the-way places that don't offer work…. The places that are being killed are an entirely different matter…. Many are resort towns, places blessed by a striking natural beauty…. Other doomed towns are those that once were beyond the urban fringe but soon will be no longer…. They are all seeing multitudes of new residents move in. The newcomers have money, and are using it to transform the rural town into a neo-suburb — better schools, paved roads, rising real estate values and property taxes to match. The next generation of natives can't afford to live in their home-towns. Then there is the 'Wal-Mart virus.' A chain of businesses sets up on the outskirts of town. …[L]ocal money flows to the national chain and away from the local merchants.[18]

To further illustrate how unplanned development is destroying our rural heritage, consider the plight of an organic farm near Clovis, California, leased and farmed by Tom and Denesse Willey since 1985. Sibella Kraus, staff writer for the San Francisco Chronicle, describes how the town of Clovis allows low-density suburban and commercial development on its rich farmland as it expands from a population of some 55,000 to more than 200,000 residents. The Willeys built soil fertility, trained a crew, and cultivated loyal customers for their superb organic and specialty crops, but are now being threatened with extinction. Kraus writes that:

> ...in the center of the farm, a stand of 60-foot cottonwoods, which provide summer shade for packing vegetables, are budding out. Families of quail dart from nests in the wild berry brambles, foraging in a two-acre garden of fruit trees and evergreens that surround the century-old farmhouse.... The new planting of potatoes, turnips, radishes, arugula, squash and peas are thriving as warm, sunny days alternate with drenching rains.... According to current plans, this fertile ground will soon be scrapped, flattened, its trees uprooted.[19]

The changes happening in Clovis are symptomatic of the cancerous growth of urban sprawl throughout the U.S. The devastation is total, from a rural economy and social structure, to a bedroom community that is 100% dependent on the car. Tom and Denesse are farmers — they will move further out. But Clovis, like many other small towns, will have lost much, if not all, of its rural heritage and culture.

• **A lack of comprehensive city and regional planning** policies and programs exist. Conventional growth management policies do not adequately encourage socially and environmentally positive action programs, such as clustered housing and agricultural preservation easements. Many rural towns and counties attempt to discourage growth, using the low-density "rural-estate" zoning practices, which allow only one house per parcel, with parcels ranging in size from one-half acre to as high as 160 acres. This low-density rural sprawl handicaps productive farming, discriminates against low-income people, inflates rural land values, creates

Photo by Greenbelt Alliance

"Rural Estates,," a Form of "Country Sprawl"
One, two, and three acre lots can eat up a lot of good agricultural land, generate the need for street widening, more car trips, and inflate the cost of land and housing.

enclaves for the "landed gentry," and provides avenues for future suburban housing development.

In response, some areas have enacted more strenuous growth management policies, which do not allow any housing development outside of the urban limit lines except for a farmer's own house. Housing for existing local farm workers and other low-income rural people is also excluded. Although farmland is protected, rural people of African-American, Asian, Native American and Latino descent are forced to live urban lifestyles, deprived

"For far too long, government at all levels sat back and watched population growth, poorly-planned development and unwise farming practices bring us to the brink of disaster. America has ignored the way cities and suburbs push our most productive farmland quite literally "off the map" in an onslaught of concrete, asphalt and postage-stamp sized lawns."[20]
— Ralph Grossi

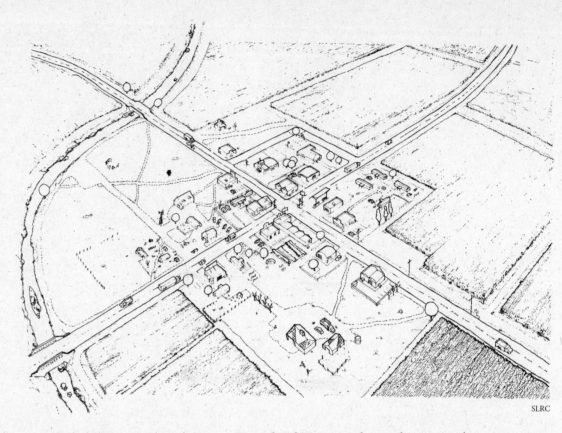

Small Rural Towns Are Vanishing

This once-upon-a-time rural hamlet is now only sparsely populated by seasonal farm workers, who are still needed despite the chemical weeding and mechanical planting, watering, and harvesting devices used by the large farm corporations. The original inhabitants, family farmers, have moved away, because they were pushed or bought out by multinational agribusiness investors. Like abandoned gold-rush towns, the houses have fallen down, leaving mostly vacant lots where some farm laborers live in old, overcrowded mobile homes, travel trailers, and camper shells. Water is obtained by running garden hoses or PVC pipes from the few remaining wells. Some derelict farmsteads are now used for storing farm implements. The remaining businesses are marginal and mostly serve the full-time farm managers and workers who pass through, and the seasonal farm laborers who hang out during picking seasons, hoping for work. The school is closed, and the church is barely attended. This drawing depicts a far too familiar scene — the passing of many culturally rich and economically viable rural communities in America.

SLRC

"With growth restrictions in the cities, with the cost of land and with the continued demand for entry-level housing, the industry is being forced further and further from urban job centers,' says Gary Hambly, president of the Building Industry Association of Northern California. Kaufman and Broad has 13 master-planned communities under construction or on the drawing boards, representing 27,000 units of new housing to be built-out over the next 10 years. All are located in far-off locations."[21]
— *Bradley Inman,*
Real Estate Columnist

of their cultural heritage and ability to make a living on the land. In essence, the result is cultural, social, and economic discrimination.

Growth issues are often viewed as independent phenomena. Consequently, farm preservation, housing, transportation, and air quality policies are administered separately, without an effective overall statewide vision or comprehensive regional planning policies for the creation of a Greenbelt. It is often the small town or rural county officials who invite "Wal-Mart virus" developers. Local officials too often erroneously believe it will bring new revenue to the area in the form of jobs and an increased tax base. As Elisabeth Scott Graham of the American

Farmland Trust explains, this is not the case:

Another misperception is that development increases the tax base. But studies show that [agricultural] land requires about 30 cents of services per dollar of tax revenue, compared to $1.30 to $1.89 cents of services per tax dollar for suburban development. The impact fees that developers pay are only a short-term fiscal fix for financially strapped cities.[22]

Socially and environmentally responsible community housing must be included as an essential element of comprehensive city and regional planning policies. Ultimately, the responsibility is on all of us to develop the vision and leadership to promote ecologically sustainable planning for both urban and rural areas. It is in this approach that Shared Living Communities and small-scale agricultural enterprises will have the greatest opportunity to become a widespread, desirable alternative.

New Towns — a threat or a promise

One particular housing model proposed for urban fringe and rural areas is the "New Town Development" (NTD), also known as the neo-traditional town. This requires careful examination; we express our concern because of the unique threat NTDs pose to the viability and sustainability of natural open space, farming areas, and small rural towns.

The NTD concept, as promoted by architects Peter Calthorpe and Andres Duany among others, is publicized as a breakthrough in ecological community design and an innovative response to today's demographic and economic changes. The designs use narrower grid streets and pedestrian-scale artifacts such as street trees, sitting areas and benches, ornamental street lights, and front porches to try to capture the charm of the 1800-1900's small towns built before the car in an era of large extended families and the "transit neighborhood." Although there are short-comings with the neo-traditionalists approach, they are contributing to the movement away from the conventional car dependent subdivision and are promoting valid ideas such as pedestriain designed mixed use town centers with residential over retail.

The premise, advanced by proponents of some NTDs, is that a light rail or bus lines will attract people away from their cars, and the retail "village"

Photo by Greenbelt Alliance

Housing Tracts Have an Insatiable Appetite for Fertile Farm Valleys
The tendency for many local governments to allow the continual eating away of farm lands and open space rises from the misuse of zoning as a tool for land speculation, and the failure of State and Federal levels to interfer in matters of local land economics, despite the adverse environmental damage.

"... most of what are known as 'growth problems' are the problems caused by sprawl, and sprawl requires dependence on the automobile. The automobile offered mobility, the ability to move from place to place. It eventually reduced drivers' accessibility (the ability to get to another place easily), and the lack of transportation alternatives virtually destroyed the mobility of those without, or unable to use, a car." [23]
— Sierra Club

"Chaes Wonder, AICP, the planning director of Bolingbrook, describes himself as an 'in-the-trenches planner.' "But sometimes I wonder if neotraditional planners aren't just nostalgic for a lifestyle that has gone away." Today's reality....is a Walmart; how can a mom-pop store compete..... "And in this climate .... I for one want my attached garage." [24]
— Ruth Knack,
"NeoTrad Meets the Midwest"

core will allow daily shopping trips to be done on foot or by bicycle. Yet each new house is sold as a separate unit and is designed for direct car access right up to the kitchen door. The truth is, most of these developments do not yet have transit stations and are not likely to in the future, because of their relatively low density and remote locations. Such developments must be a part of a comprehensive rail planning process where the transit lines are specifically planned for, budgeted for, and scheduled. Otherwise they are nothing more than romanticized sprawl, and add little incentive for people to form resource sharing communities, and to let go of their cars.

A mistaken assumption regarding NTDs is that the people who buy into them will actually be the ones who work in the shops, offices, or industrial parks that may be master-planned into the development. The retail shops, larger stores, and plants of these developments will probably be chains or franchises, and hire lower-paid workers who will not likely afford to live there unless a full range of affordable housing is intentionally planned. Workers will live outside the area and commute to the NTD. Those who can afford to buy homes in the NTD, usually families with two incomes, will have higher paying jobs elsewhere. Thus, two commuter populations are generated.

NTD's developments without rail transit services will tend to contribute to the increase of car trips around the perimeters of cities. Michael Renner of the Worldwatch Institute reports that:

Two-thirds of all jobs created in the United States from 1960 to 1980 were located in suburbs... while the number of trips between central cities and suburbs and from suburb to suburb doubled within the same period of time. When suburban communities are too scattered to be served efficiently, public mass transit... walking and biking are not serious options, because distances are mostly too great and sidewalks and bicycle lanes are relatively rare. The automobile has created more distance than it overcomes. [25]

The NTDs do not offer any real solution to this pattern. Whether the individual home owners or renters use transit or cars, the developments tend to become commuter villas and do not belong in rural areas or the Green Belt. They heat up demand for the surrounding rural land, and strip commercial quickly follows. "New Towns" are artfully promoted at public hearings, where developers lobby to rezone farmland and open space. Their nostalgic appearance and the talk of job centers, community, and ecological design often gains approval. But there is nothing inherent in the nostalgic design itself that creates social and economic diversity, housing affordability, community interaction, and the creation of an ecologically sustainable community culture There is the danger that marketing practices will cause such developments to become no more than racially and economically segregated suburban subdivisions, inducing more urban flight.

Sustainable Agriculture and Permaculture

The energy and resources consumed in the creation of urban sprawl would be better spent on actual production of healthy food products, and direct marketing of them to urban customers. Here we examine sustainable agriculture and Permaculture, two of the best known methods for growing food in harmony with natural cycles, and for creating a truly integrated and sustainable community.

The practice of "sustainable agriculture," as advocated by the Sustainable Agriculture Research and Education Program, at the University of California at Davis, and as defined in their paper, "What is Sustainable Agriculture,"[26] consists of a human-intensive and holistic natural process. Social concerns, lifestyle, emotional well-being, and the living environment of all people involved, both workers and farmer families, become integral parts of the agricultural process. This process operates in balance with and makes use of the natural cycles, recycles and restores natural nutrients to the soil, conserves water, and protects the soil from erosion and overuse. These sustainable agriculture methods are being advocated by many university agricultural departments, and ecological farming organizations and experts as well.

Another increasingly popular movement is "Permaculture" (**perma**nent agri**culture**). As conceived and advanced by Bill Mollison of Australia, author of *Permaculture: A Designer's Manual,* Permaculture is the conscious design and maintenance of agricultural ecosystems that have the diversity, stability, and resilience of natural ecosystems. It is also the harmonious integration of landscape and people that generates food, energy, shelter, and other needs in a sustainable way. In our ecologically sustainable rural community planning approach, we combine the meanings of sustainable agriculture and Permaculture. We include all the processes, policies, and practices that are lasting and renewable, and that meet the needs of today, without damaging our ability or the ability of future

generations to meet future needs. Thinking and acting in such an interconnected manner can best be accomplished in a cooperative commuity setting.

One precept of Permaculture is to do as little applied work or alteration to the natural system as possible, allowing the ecosystem to continue its natural processes. Ecological farming therefore embraces stewardship of both natural and human resources, including social and environmental, and health responsibilities, and consideration of:

• Compatibility of residential, agricultural, and related land uses.

• Land management to protect soil from misuse, enhance soil building, and reduce tillage.

• Animal/crop variety appropriate to the location, including crop rotation practices and intercropping (growing two or more crops simultaneously in the same field).

• Preservation and/or (re-)introduction of native plants, wildlife, and cover crops to promote an ecological balance that enriches the soil and controls

"A stable farm community includes the greatest possible variety of plant, animal and soil microbial life. It is the dynamic interaction of vegetables, flowers, herbs, grains, trees, livestock, reptiles, birds, insects, earthworms, microbes, and humans that guarantees stability. Uniformity of crops and varieties is a major factor inviting pest and disease problems." [27]
— *Ecology Action*
"Bio-intensive Mini-Farming - What Is It?"

"When picking a plant for Indian Medicine, first we give an offering and an apology. Then we take only as much as we need." [28]
— *Edna Bobb, a Stollo born in 1914, Chehalis, B.C.*

"…productivity must be based on wise husbandry of resources. Mechanized agriculture consumes 6-20 times the calories in energy as it delivers in food and it consumes as much as 300-1000 times more energy per calorie produced than successful Asian forms of biologically intensive agriculture. An effective agriculture should be energy efficient. This can be done manually without back breaking labor, if wisdom and skill are applied and rewarded."[29]
— *Ecology Action*

"The conservation and preservation of nature; the substitution of intelligence for resources in our economy; the substitution of quality for quantity in our personal lives; the development of community wealth, rather than just individual wealth; the pursuit not of wealth but of well being; these are just some of the conditions of sustainability."[30]
— *Guy Dauncy, "Sustainability: Using Less and Enjoying More"*

pests, with natural resistance methods such as Integrated Pest Management. (A technique which employs cultural and mechanical controls, pest-resistant plants, and release of beneficial organisms.)
• Avoidance of toxic and energy-intensive (fossil fuel based) soil additives through the use of on-farm, natural, renewable, and biodegradable compost materials.
• Minimal use of vehicles and non-renewable energy, through coordinated management of farm operation and marketing practices, efficient use of on-farm human labor, and cooperation between farm families in the area.
• Include hired farm workers as a permanent part of the culture and life of rural communities by diversifying crops and coordinating planting and harvesting to provide year-round work, and by providing equal access to stable employment, permanently affordable housing, community education and health services, and participation in community decisions.
• Re-establishment of rural villages and towns that are economically stable, supportive of family farms, and part of the Green Belt plan around cities.

Through these practices, as well as through cooperative interrelationships between food producers, consumers, and other businesses, a food supply system and rural society can be established that is healthy and sustainable. We believe, as does Bill Mollison, that "Without permanent agriculture there is no possibility of a stable social order."[31] The Organic Farm Village Cluster concept we present in this chapter incorporates all of the above practices and serves as a model for creating a way to revitalize the ecological integrity and social and cultural richness of rural America.

The Organic Family Farm Movement

The annual Ecological Farming Conference held every January at Asilomar, California, reveals a new breed of organic family farmers eager to share their experiences, enthusiasm, and concerns for the future of ecological farming. The increased number of organic family farms is a response to the increased demand by urban populations for fresh, organically grown food. Changing social, cultural, economic, and employment patterns in the U.S. will influence significantly more people to seek food-growing and related cottage industry lifestyles for their basic livelihoods. This trend can be the foundation for a revitalization of rural farming communities and the establishment of growth-limiting Green Belts around urban centers.

Despite this trend, however, the economic survival of small, family-run organic farms remains threatened due to competition from agribusiness' attempting large-scale organic food production. Some agribusiness growers and food processing plants are relocating to Mexico and other Third World countries, to avoid the higher standards of housing, health, environmental, and labor laws in the U.S. Such companies will likely undersell U.S. food producers who comply with regulations and environmental standards. The new American small farmers will need a supportive community approach to compete and to handle the demands of marketing, high land and property tax costs, family life, emotional stress, and dedication to sustainable agriculture/Permaculture methods. Our objective is to demonstrate ways for small farm families to enjoy emotional and social support with significant time, labor, and cost savings.

Community Elements

1 Storage and recycling yard
2 Auto, carpentry, and tool shop
3 Plant greenhouse and animal shed
4 Equipment, supplies, compost, etc.
5 Aqua-culture tanks, wind generators
6 Studios, meeting rooms, and guest rooms above food processing, kitchen and food storage
7 Bathing center, hot tub, sauna, laundry, solar water heater
8 Pond for swimming, fire fighting, rain catchment, fish, etc.
9 Animal/chicken yards (optional)
10 Photovoltaic collectors, water tank, and wind generators
11 Organic gardens
12 Two-family shared houses

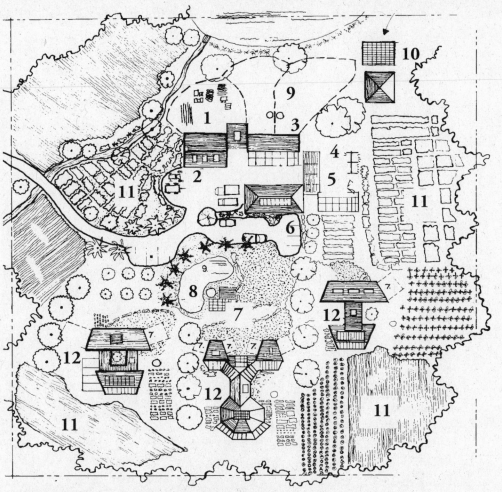

A Six–Family Organic Farm Village Cluster

This rural cluster community is sited on approximately four acres in the agricultural green belt or urban fringe infill land. The three houses are each designed for two families to share a common kitchen, dining room and activity rooms, and enjoy their own private suites. (These prototype group house designs are presented in Chapter Seven) They can achieve a high level of self-reliance from growing herbs, vegetables and orchards, natural composting methods for soil additives, and from active and passive solar heating and cooling, and solar and wind electric power. Their livelihood can come from organic food growing for direct marketing to armers markets, food stores, restaurants, and urban Shared Living Communities, and possibly from "you-pick" contracts with urban people.

Kazlowski Farms, in rural Forestville, California, a cottage industry in its second generation, provides a prime example of how this works. As Perry Kazlowski, who operates the farm with his two sisters, explains:

A lot of factors have gone into our success. But the biggest one was our willingness to work together. We all could have had other jobs and pursued other careers and earned better income the first five or ten years of our working lives. But we knew in the end, there was something here — for the family and for our kids.[33]

A group of family farmers can best maintain a successful farm enterprise within a protected agricultural Green Belt, and together form a socially, economically, and environmentally responsible enterprise. The Organic Farm Village Cluster and the surrounding farmland can be cooperatively shared/owned by the individuals and families, or long-term leased from a Land Trust or other non-profit sponsoring organization for the purpose of ecologically sustainable farming.

The farm cluster plan (on page149) depicts how this might be done on a co-owned farm plot combining cottage industries with intensive organic food production for self-reliance and for income from direct marketing, "U-pick," or "community-garden" contracts.

The Dear Valley story also speaks directly to our prime proposal that Organic Farm Village Cluster communities can be a successful way to enjoy the family experience, earn a good livelihood, and practice Permaculture and sustainable agriculture without burnout, breakdown, or break-up.

A Dessert Social with the Families of Dear Valley

The high, curved ceiling of the common house dining room overflowed with children's laughter and the background conversation of adults. All of Dear Valley was gathered for the spring equinox celebration, with the theme of birth and renewal resplendent in the calliope of colorful and crazy hats worn by most of the members.

Quiet settled over the room as Tim and Dolores Jones played their flutes for the beginning of the sharing. Sylvia, a white-haired and distinguished woman of 72, the elder of the community, caught everyone's attention by banging on a pie-tin with a wooden spoon.

"Hi, everyone! I'm happy to be your madam of ceremonies this evening. We're here to celebrate this bountifully pregnant spring, and our largest gathering yet at Dear Valley. Before we start our sharing circle, six of our children are going to perform a feat that the world has never before heard. They will read in unison their group-written poem about living here on the farm. It's called…well, I'll let them tell you."

Amy, the youngest, announced, *"We all composed a poem together. It's more like a song. We call it, 'Springing Along Together.'"*

The four girls and two boys fidgeted and giggled, as they looked at each other to get their cues, and then sang their poem in an attempt at unison.

*"Springing along together,
    planting trees and plants we go,
Springing along together,
    learning the ropes as we grow.*

We love all the people, the birds, and the flowers,
Food is yummy, gives us magical powers.

Springing along together,
　　　gathering grapes, beets, and peaches,
Springing along together,
　　　we love you all and what you teach us."

They hurried through two more verses, with increasing spells of laughter, until everyone was laughing with them.

When they finished, Sylvia tried several times to start the sharing circle. At the first lull, in the enthusiastic standing ovation, Sylvia invited the newest members, Rosalinda and Eduardo Valindez and Arnold and Betty Arney, a couple from South-Central Los Angeles, to share first. Both families are Permaculture apprentices at Dear Valley.

Betty spoke first. *"Thank you for the chance to get to know everyone better. I want to say what a blessing it has been to learn about community — we never thought we'd be environmentalists."* She laughed. *"We thought only white middle-class liberals did that. But what we're learning about here is ecological living and personal empowerment."*

Arnold continued excitedly. *"Yes, and we've gotten so hooked on organic farming and Permaculture that we've decided to start organic farming training communities, for inner-city teens and ex-cons, in Los Angeles."*

Betty grinned. *"Yes! We grew up there and want to go back to help rebuild L.A. with community, urban farms, and cottage businesses — so we'll be leaving early next year. But in the meantime, we're here to learn and to support this community."*

Rosalinda walked up front, being easier with crowds than her husband. *"As a farm worker, I never thought I'd get out of living in a truck camper, and almost starving in the winter time. Eduardo and I love working outdoors farming, but when he got sick from those chemical sprays the big fruit growers were using, we had to quit. Here we have a home and work. We are in charge of our lives. This is like the ejidos, the Mexican peasant collectives, that my grandmother told me about. We also have to tell you, we'll be leaving you soon too. Our farm worker friends came here to see Dear Valley for themselves. Now we're working with them to organize our own sustainable farm and village community. Thanks to your blessing and support, we're applying for Community Economic Development grants, tax credits, and loans. We agree, it is time for community in the U.S.A."*

A bit later John, Carol, and Helene, the Dear Valley founding group, reviewed the history and progress of the community. Helene led as usual.

"It certainly is time for celebration. We've come a long way since Carol, John, and I stood on that hill and looked down into the charms of this valley. Now we're one big family, and doing a three-crop-a-year business serving farmers' markets in the city."

John stood up with a big smile. *"I want to express my thanks to you all for the canning and drying work done last fall. What a pleasure it has been to enjoy the fruits of our labor and still have free time for family and fun. Joan and I tried to do an organic farm once ourselves, but we just burned out."*

"Speaking of burnout," said Sarah, age 16. *"I want to say that before we moved here, my grades were not so hot, but now with all you people helping me, I'm doing great."* She looked around at the faces. *"I really love being a farm kid. At first I didn't want to leave my friends in the suburbs, but now when they come to visit me, they don't want to leave."*

Photo by Greenbelt Alliance

This Land is Your Land
by Woody Guthrie

As I was walking that ribbon of highway,
I saw above me that endless skyway,
I saw below me that golden valley,
This land was made for you and me.

When the sun comes shining and I was strolling
and the wheat fields waving and the dust clouds rolling,
As the fog was lifting, a voice was chanting,
This land was made for you and me.

Nicole Turner, an African-American woman, stepped forward followed by Tony, her nine-year-old son. *"This has been great for me and Tony,"* she said. *"I was laid off from my job at the department store, when the shopping mall went bankrupt. I didn't know what to do until I saw your first core group ad. Then I took hope. I love being the school teacher and car-pool manager here. Now, I want to start working in the garden too. What a great life!"* She squeezed Tony's shoulder and his face became one big smile.

Rose Kim, one of several Dear Valley members who still commutes to the urban area for work, spoke up. *"These celebrations are so wonderful. I often don't hear all the news and views, being away a lot in the city. I'm sad to hear that Rosalinda and Eduardo and Arnold and Betty will be moving on, but I'm happy to hear of their great projects. This community is beginning to work out like America was meant to. Let's keep our arms open so we can maintain our cultural diversity. And I want to tell you that those of us who commute in the Melon [the green van-bus] share our own diversity on the way to the transit station — we sing a lot. Up until now, we've only sung to ourselves, but now we're going to sing to you."* She gestured with both arms to the others, and the 'Melon Chorus' rose to their feet and sang *This Land is Your Land.* As the music faded the smell of hot peach cobbler rose from the kitchen.

Existing and Prototype Sustainable Rural Communities

We present a cross-section of examples of sustainable rural communities, including a case study of an existing intentional rural community, and several previously proposed prototype rural communities.

Ananda Village, Nevada City, CA

The Ananda World Brotherhood Village, located in
the lower Sierra Nevada mountains, is an example
of a successful spiritual Intentional Community. It
was founded in 1968 by Sri Kriyananda (J. Donald
Walters). Starting with 67 acres, Ananda acquired
nearby ranches in the early 1970's, and now has
688acres of forest and meadow land. The community has an intergenerational resident population of
approximately 300, including singles, couples,
families, and approximately 100 children. The
spiritual path that members follow is based on
meditation and Yogananda's teachings of communion with God, service to one's fellow beings, and
formation of "world brotherhood colonies." In
response to this last directive, Ananda has spawned
sister communities in Sacramento, Palo Alto,
Seattle, and Italy. Their commitment to the spiritual path, community work parties, creative human
service outlets, and opportunities for individual
entrepreneurship create a strong bond and active
participation in community affairs.

The Ananda community created an extensive
master plan in the mid-1970's, which they follow
closely and update regularly. The plan includes
residential clusters separated by forest and meadow
preserves, a community building, retreat facilities,
a village center with stores and businesses, a work
center, a school, recreation facilities, several ponds,
and gardens. The fertile flat land of the original
farmstead is maintained as an open grassy commons
for recreation fields and small gardens. It is held in
reserve for future food growing, as part of the
community's long-term self-reliance and survival
plan. Most of the families live in traditional single-
family houses.

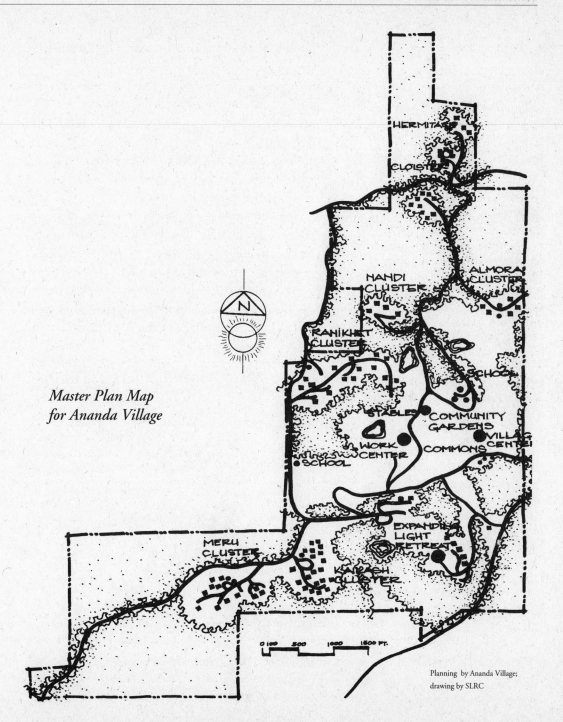

*Master Plan Map
for Ananda Village*

Planning by Ananda Village;
drawing by SLRC

"The harvest, although also seasonal, is somewhat easier to organize, for various reasons. Until recently, we used to buy a large portion of the vegetables that we preserved. Lately we have been growing most of the vegetables on the kibbutz, which increases our profits. Harvesting is done by sophisticated agricultural machines or, in the case of olives, by our school children. The important fact is that we avoid employing hired labor. I believe that this is one of the factors that keeps our sons from leaving the kibbutz. People feel more at home and more involved in our autonomous economy; they would feel completely different if they met strange workers in every corner of the kibbutz." [34]**

"The harvest, although also seasonal, is somewhat easier to organize, for various reasons. Until recently, we used to buy a large portion of the vegetables that we preserved. Lately we have been growing most of the vegetables on the kibbutz, which increases our profits. Harvesting is done by sophisticated agricultural machines or, in the case of olives, by our school children. The important fact is that we avoid employing hired labor. I believe that this is one of the factors that keeps our sons from leaving the kibbutz. People feel more at home and more involved in our autonomous economy; they would feel completely different if they met strange workers in every corner of the kibbutz." [34]

— Amia Lieblich,
"The Economics of a Kibbutz"

"The community might, in short, be similar in many ways to any village, with the basic distinction that it would be an intentional community. It would be based on cooperation, not competition, and on self-unfoldment rather than on self-aggrandizement at the expense of one's fellow beings." [35]

— J. Donald Waters,
Ananda Village

However, there are two shared living clusters, where bedrooms are grouped around a common kitchen and dining room. There are also several shared houses with individual family suites of 3 to 5 rooms located on each side of a common kitchen, dining/living room, meditation room, and an office or childcare space. (An example of this shared living model is presented in Chapter Seven.)

One five-house cluster is entirely "off the grid," deriving all electrical power from photovoltaic solar cells. Environmental design and the use of alternative technology, however, are individual choices, as there appears to be no requirement that solar energy be used throughout the community. The community learned that scattering the housing clusters and work locations throughout the site has generated a

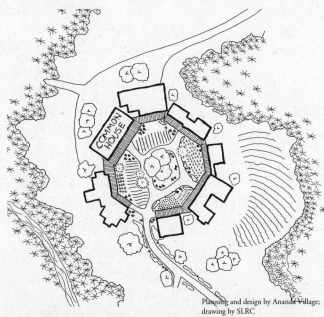

Planning and design by Ananda Village; drawing by SLRC

Shared Living Cluster at Ananda
The "Ayodhya" cluster has 14 living suites around a common kitchen and dining room and a beautiful flower garden.

lot of individual car trips within and out of the community. The new master plan which is underway is considering a more compact village core with residential buildings clustered around it.

The community has made a significant accomplishment in creating local and community-based jobs for its members. There are over 18 community-owned businesses located in both the community and nearby towns, and 20 private businesses owned by members and based in the community. Approximately 75% of Ananda members work within the community. This is an environmental and economic plus, since it decreases the car traffic out of the community. The resulting economic stability encourages face-to-face interaction which strengthens the sense of community. Numerous other Intentional Communities in the U.S., such as Alpha Farms in Oregon and Twin Oaks in Virginia, are also economically self-sufficient with a strong community spirit.

The Kibbutz — *a planned village community* [36]
The kibbutz, a Jewish invention more than 80 years old, is another example of humankind's rich heritage of extended family and village forms. The kibbutz experience has much to teach us, especially that community designs work best when there is a strong, underlying social and cultural purpose.

Each kibbutz expresses the uniqueness of its location and its individual members and member families. Each shares the common purpose of self-reliance, providing livelihood, mutual defense, and shared responsibilities for family support. Traditionally, kibbutzim have an agricultural base, commonly owned land, and other elements which have proven essential for the sustainability of community. Close proximity of housing to the common dining room, childcare services, schools, administrative offices, and recreation areas is one such element. Even the circulation routes through a kibbutz are carefully designed to preserve the pedestrian and communal nature of the community center. Agricultural fields, work centers, and heavy traffic routes have been placed on the periphery of the community to protect living areas from noise, pollution, dust, and foul odors.

The kibbutzim in Israel were government-supported, centrally planned, and architecturally designed to create a way of life to survive harsh physical conditions and an adverse political climate. The kibbutz has proved to be a successful answer, with its planning and development processes and the building and site designs changing over the decades to meet changing needs. We in the U.S. can create our own inventive socioeconomic and environmental means to solve our problems.

A prototype study for a rural, low-income Village Cluster, Watsonville, CA

This example in the agricultural Pajaro Valley of Santa Cruz County tells a story, of the conflict between strong urban growth control and agricultural preservation policies, and the plight of low-income rural people and farm workers. In 1989, the American Red Cross provided funding for SLRC to study replacement housing options for a group of Pajaro Valley Native Americans who lost their homes in the Loma Prieta earthquake. Represented by the Tierra Espiritual de Nuevo Aztlan (TENA) Council, their objective was (and still is) to own the land and build a modern Native American village with housing and self-sufficient gardens, and add a

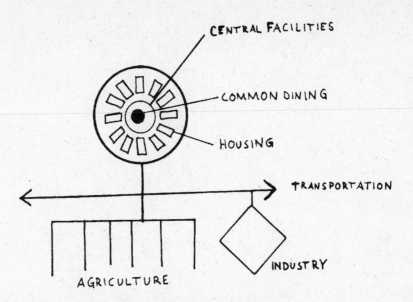

The Basic Elements for Planning a Kibbutz

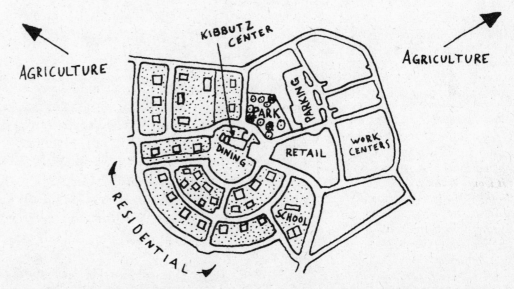

The Kibbutz Core Area Plan Represents Basic Precepts for Ecological Planning
This is an intentional neighborhood that is pedestrian oriented and focused on the Kibbutz center with it's family-oriented dining hall. Note how the pollution-causing uses, such as parking and work centers, are furthest away from the residential areas.

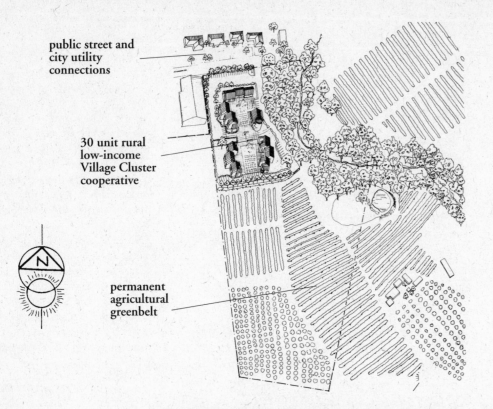

public street and
city utility
connections

30 unit rural
low-income
Village Cluster
cooperative

permanent
agricultural
greenbelt

acres of lower quality soil next to the city line. The planning strategy was to acquire the whole agricultural parcel, and then annex only the housing site to the City of Watsonville, in order to obtain the necessary utility hook-ups. Since the cost of the farmland in the county outside the Urban Limit line was much less than inside the city, the 30-unit project was financially feasible.

Support was gained from some key city and county officials for the zoning and annexation process on the condition that the remaining 11 acres of active agricultural land were to be preserved for organic farming and held as an agricultural land trust or a county Agricultural Conservation Easement. This would establish a permanent edge between the city and the agricultural lands. The basic strategy was to establish a precedent that could be applied wherever strong growth control regulations make it difficult to create low-income rural housing.

Problems with the project arose because housing advocates, county planners, farmers, and environmentalists held conflicting views regarding the strict growth management policies. These policies forbade any construction of housing on agriculturally zoned lands, even for the many low-income rural people and farmworkers, who were living in substandard conditions. Rural people are expected to move to higher-cost housing within the designated Urban Limit Lines of Watsonville and other cities. Instead they are often forced to live in country hovels and camper shells, or in miserably overcrowded conditions in the city. The consequence is that onprofit housing sponsors end up building fewer affordable units in the city due to the tripling of land costs.

nearby traditional village with a sweat lodge, ceremonial arbor, and other traditional structures. The proposed plan created by SLRC called for a Village Cluster to operate as a Limited Equity Housing Cooperative — permanently affordable and managed by the residents, but initially owned by a nonprofit housing developer. The intention was for it to eventually become a self-reliant rural community, co-owned by Native Americans and other low-income people.

A mixed-density 14-acre parcel of agriculturally zoned land, with access to city utilities, was found immediately adjacent to the city of Watsonville. A Village Cluster of 30 units, with a large common house and gardens, was to be located on the three

The TENA project ultimately failed due to the lack of funding for site acquisition. The Pajaro Valley Native Americans, and other rural people in the area, are still searching for adequate housing to meet their cultural and lifestyle needs.

The "Agrovillage" and our heritage of rural community experimentation [37]

To understand the possibilities for creating ecologically sustainable rural villages and towns that maintain permanent agricultural Green Belts around cities, we will examine historic and recent American attempts to revitalize rural America with colony settlements and planned cooperative communities. In a June 1977 report, David Thompson and Cherle Gossett, members of a UCLA School of Architecture and Urban Planning project team, described historic examples of cooperative rural enterprises founded by various groups in California's San Joaquin Valley, one of the world's largest and most productive food growing valleys. The agricultural "colony" was introduced in California in 1881 by George Chafee, who proposed the mutual water company concept, in which residents shared resources to survive in the arid climate. From that beginning in 1881, many more colony type settlements were generated by ethnic groups — Danes, Swedes, Japanese, and English. Utopian, religious, secular, and socialist colonies were also founded which experimented boldly with forms of leadership and communal ownership to realize their visions of community.

These early experiments were undoubtedly a factor in the founding in 1917 of two planned settlements under the auspices of the State of California. One was at Durham and one at Delhi, and they lasted from 1917 until 1931. A new era of farm community innovation began in 1935 under Roosevelt's Farm Security Administration (FSA). The policies they enacted emphasized ecology, decentralization, economic democracy, and cooperation. The FSA completed almost 100 community projects, eventually housing more than 5,000 families.

Another program started during this era established the "Greenbelt towns," based on the Garden City concept of Ebenezer Howard, and the Radburn Idea developed by Clarence S. Stein and Henry Wright. These called for ultimate town populations of 3,000 people each. Three towns were completed: Greenbelt, Maryland; Greenhills, Ohio; and Greendale, Wisconsin.

These pre-WW II attempts faded during wartime prosperity, were further obscured by the economic and political powers of the consumer-fed postwar boom, and are all but forgotten today. Now, the people, not the government, are the initiators as we again experience a critical need to rebuild society, and to create an economic system that will sustain both us and our environment. It is time again to explore and test innovations, but we do not have to reinvent the wheel.

Out of the UCLA study mentioned earlier came the "Agrovillage" concept for a planned agricultural cooperative community. Although the physical layout and housing design differ from the Organic Farm Village Cluster model, its overall intent and organizational and economic structure show major parallels. The Agrovillage proposal was an alternative land distribution and management system for the San Joaquin Valley Westlands Water District. Under the 1902 Reclamation Act, the land was

"Sixty percent of the adult kibbutz members work in the service divisions — education, administration, kitchen, laundry…. [Of the remaining] 40 percent, two-thirds are employed by industry and the remaining third by agriculture. Actually, very few people work in agriculture because we operate no branches that require any manual labor. With the aid of mechanical innovations, we've been able to increase production while using a smaller number of workers. We have excellent farmers here, I can assure you of that. It's incredible what we have been able to accomplish in such a short period of time…." [38]

— *Amia Lieblich*

"[Thomas Jefferson's] strong feelings that inequity in property ownership caused 'much misery to the bulk of mankind' led him to distinguish it as the central threat to democratic rights. Agrarian democracy was a clear attack upon landed aristocracy whose monopoly over property fundamentally undermined the basis of a democratic society." [39]

— *David Thompson & Cherie Gossett*

supposed to be reallocated into smaller acreage, resident-owned and managed farm parcels. It was proposed that a series of culturally diverse, self-governing communities of 10 to 30 households, or up to 100 persons, be distributed throughout the district. They could become community associations with private ownership of land, or cooperative communities in which members would own shares, or land trusts that would hold the land in common, in perpetuity, and lease rights of usage to the members. They were not developed, but serve as alternative models for revitalizing farming communities today.

Revitalization of Rural Communities and Small Towns

In a best-of-all-worlds scenario the interconnectedness of all things would be highly recognized in our daily lives. Citizens and their governing bodies would have risen to the responsibility to resolve the environmental, land use, housing, job, and transportation issues within their urban limit lines. Transportation corridors and transit nodes would be more densely populated, with pedestrian-oriented residential and mixed-use Eco Villages served by a network of local light rail and bus lines. These

The Image of a Rural Green Belt Village Society
However nostalgic and old-fashioned this may appear, we are reminded that whenever people gather in a cooperative spirit for the sharing of ecologically sustainable ways of living, there is likely to be seen the vestiges of humankind's village heritage — here is an universal expression of the "common ground."

From "Ananda Village Planning Brochure." Art by Carol Padget

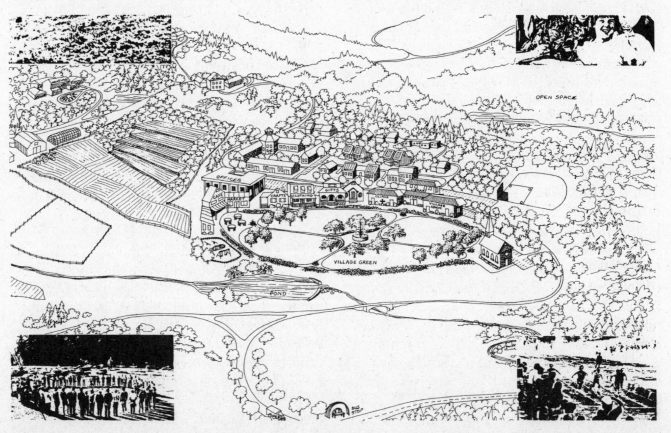

areas would be connected to regional and state centers by a high-speed train system. This would have all been comprehensively planned. The public would have demanded that federal, state, regional, and local governments sensibly plan for and manage urban growth relative to conservation of water and natural resources. Green Belts would have been established for wetlands, open space, and agricultural preservation.

If the above policies had been in place all along, urban fringe and rural areas would not have the growth problems they do today. Community empowerment programs and participation by the people would reduce race and class divisions and improve social, economic, housing, and environmental problems in the inner cities. Taxes would be lower, because of the savings due to the advanced planning and coordinated management of policies and programs. A permanent Green Belt would be in place, protecting farmlands and rural communities from the pressures of encroaching development and higher taxes. Affordable housing would not be an issue, since more people would be living in some kind of Shared Living Community where costs are reduced and personal time for alterantive livelihood and family enjoyment. Homelessness would be greatly reduced, because the processes of community would have closed the cracks in the system, with various cooperative, self-help, shared housing, and social benefit programs. The national economy would prosper with all kinds of new jobs created by urban rebuilding projects around rail terminals and transit stops in the urban centers. Feeding our cities from the surrounding Green Belt farms would have created many local jobs and created a new American rural society.

Energy and resource conservation

Below is a summary of ecological planning practices and criteria that would encourage the kinds of changes we are describing, and a summary of some of the benefits that would arise from implementing such policies.

• Water conservation would be encouraged through community designto share cooking, gardens, etc., and the use of central water circulation, grey water, drip irrigation lines, and rain collection systems.

• On a broader scale, the formation of a permanent Green Belt around cities would enable coordination of water, land, energy, and resource conservation and management practices and provide a basis for special incentives to rural communities for implementing such goals.

• Waste recycling, re-use of used goods, composting systems, energy-efficient construction, water and wind power generation, and passive and active solar energy systems for heating and cooling would be encouraged when buildings are clustered and the community is self-managed. (Alternative energy systems for communities are discussed in more detail in Chapter Nine.)

Car trip reduction

• Activities that generate a lot of traffic, such as large businesses, retail centers, public gathering halls, theaters, apartment buildings, and hospitals, must be kept within the urban limit lines, preferably in the core of already-developed areas. These high traffic generators should be limited in accordance with the local infrastructure capacities, the environmental impact, and Transportation Management Programs for the area.

"What we do to the Earth, we do to ourselves, because we are the Earth."
— *Chief Seattle*

"We are the population problem in the world, not the poor but numerous south. We have to try to achieve net-positive agriculture in the north. It may be unknown to you but we are basically eating oil. We are supporting the vast populations of the north by putting about three calories of oil energy into our farming for every one calorie of food we get out. This is net-negative energy agriculture we are practicing. [40]

— *Ernest Callenbach, "Our Sustainable Future,"*

"In the longer-term, more fundamental reductions in transportation energy use will require major lifestyle changes and altered land use patterns."[41]
— *California Energy Commission*

"[A recent proposal states that] cars should account for no more than 40 percent of all urban trips within the U.S. within 20 to 30 years. (Currently, automobiles are used for 82 percent of trips in the U.S., while 40 percent is the average for Western European Countries.)"[42]
— *Ronald J. Kilcoyne, The Urban Ecologist*

"Interestingly, the qualities that make housing affordable also make for environmentally sound development patterns, because they make efficient use of limited, and expensive resources — land, fuel (for transportation and home use), and materials. Sprawl is expensive and wasteful; it requires costly extension of sewers and transportation systems, water supply and utility networks, and new schools."[43]
— *Sierra Club*

• A TransportationManagement Program (TMP) should be required for all residential, business, and agricultural development in rural towns and surrounding areas. Residential developments could be allowed more units, less parking, more remote locations, or other allowances when the TMP proposes reductions in car trips by:
— Sharing activities like group meals, and buying food and other products in bulk as a group.
— Providing internal childcare, group projects, community gardens, and other resource-sharing and self-reliance practices.
— Car pooling and co-owning cars, van-buses, pick-ups, and bicycles.
• Businesses could gain points for the workability of a TMP that effectively reduces employee car trips, supports employee housing over and/or near the business, and encourages pedestrian access by patrons and employees.

Rural housing affordability and social and cultural equity

• The cost of living can be greatly reduced by sharing the costs of mortgages, taxes and insurance, group purchases, community gardens, the use of energy conservation, and car trip reduction.
• The inclusion of seniors, first-time home buyers, single-parent families, disabled people, and low-income rural people in Shared Living Communities is socially responsible, and adds cultural diversity. Such efforts may also qualify the community for housing assistance programs based on a density bonus or other incentive zoning points.
• Permanently affordable housing, co-owned or rented, could be initiated and supported through

the efforts and use of nonprofit/for-profit housing sponsorship, Community Land Trusts, Limited Equity Housing Cooperatives, Mutual Housing Associations, and community development corporations. (Discussed in Chapter Nine.)

Rural land-use and zoning

• A permanent Green Belt policy could be incorporated into the regional and local planning process. Special farmland preservation, land use, housing, and incentive zoning processes could place a priority on sustainable agriculture practices and Organic Farm Village Cluster communities.
• Special incentive residential zoning processes could encourage and give preference to Village Cluster/CoHousing, Urban Cooperative Blocks, new and redesigned group houses, and mixed-use residential above commercial, thereby encouraging existing rural small towns to create more compact pedestrian/human-scale villages.
• Larger lots with a higher density should be given preference, by permitting the merging of existing subdivided lots and record-of-survey map parcels into larger consolidated properties. This would encourage implementation of Shared Living Communities and preservation of open space, in lieu of scattered-site conventional housing development. For example: Assemble 20 lots of five acres each (one unit per lot = 20 houses) into a 100 acre parcel, and receive an incentive bonus allowing 25 housing units when clustered on only 2-1/2 acres, thus preserving 98.5% of the parcel as open space, gardens, agriculture land, and forest. Additional units may be offered as an incentive for incorporating other social and environmental amenities and benefits. The Village Acre, the 2-1/2 acre Village

Cluster, the three acre Muir Commons, and the five acre Winslow communities are examples of larger properties planned and developed as one co-owned community, without further subdividing into lots and public streets.

The ecologically sustainable elements of the New Rural Town

Imagine what a New Rural Town, rebuilt from a bypassed rural hamlet, like the one depicted earlier, could be like when hundreds of family farmers, workers, residents, and small businesses cooperatively come together for the intended purpose of rebuilding a rural society that supports ecological living, personal empowerment, the new extended family, and economic interdependence. Here are the elements of this New Rural Town:

• The town center contains mixed-use retail shops and offices, a medical clinic, a human and social services center, a library, schools, a telecommunications center, a meeting hall, restaurants, daily farm produce markets on the town plaza, live-work spaces and community workshops, art and craft studios, a recycling center, and a transportation management center.

• Ecologically designed housing of varied types and costs are clustered over the shops and around the town center. Most of the housing is designed and organized for extended family shared meals and a diversity of residents, workers, and travelers. The housing types are:

— Community hotels for single people and travelers, with residential suites located on the second and third floors over the kitchen, dining room, and social and game rooms. A restaurant and retail shops, offices, and live-

work units could also be located on the ground floors.

— A mixture of three to six bedroom shared living apartments for singles, couples, and short-term residents over the shops and community buildings.

— Large, specially designed and clustered six to ten bedroom group houses for voluntary extended families, located around the immediate town center and facing onto the inner "slow street" that loops the core area.

— Village Clusters with 12 to 20+ living suites or units and a common house on 1-1/2 to 2-1/2 acre co-owned sites located around the periphery of the town center, but inside the outer loop road. Each cluster includes common gardens, play lots, and recreation areas. Walkways, bikeways, and a series of courts connect the buildings and shared open space amenities to each other and to the town center.

• Individual cars are not encouraged and are allowed by permit only. Through the Community Land Trust (CLT) or other community management processes, the farm families, workers, and residents co-own a fleet of vehicles, van-buses, trucks, and bicycles, as well as farm vehicles and equipment. The transportation management center administers group vehicle insurance, scheduling, cost accounting, bus services, and a maintenance center.

• Satellite farm work centers, with food processing shops and equipment yards, are located at intervals in the farmlands surrounding the New Rural Town. Certain kinds of mechanized equipment can be shared, through producer cooperatives that agree to

"All communities need land: the bedrock upon which to build our hopes and dreams. Relationships change; loved ones die; children leave home; but the land is always there. I believe that the survival of any community and, ultimately of the entire earth, depends on our willingness to reinhabit and cherish our land." [44]

— Peter Robinson, "Shannon Farm: A Model for Community That Works"

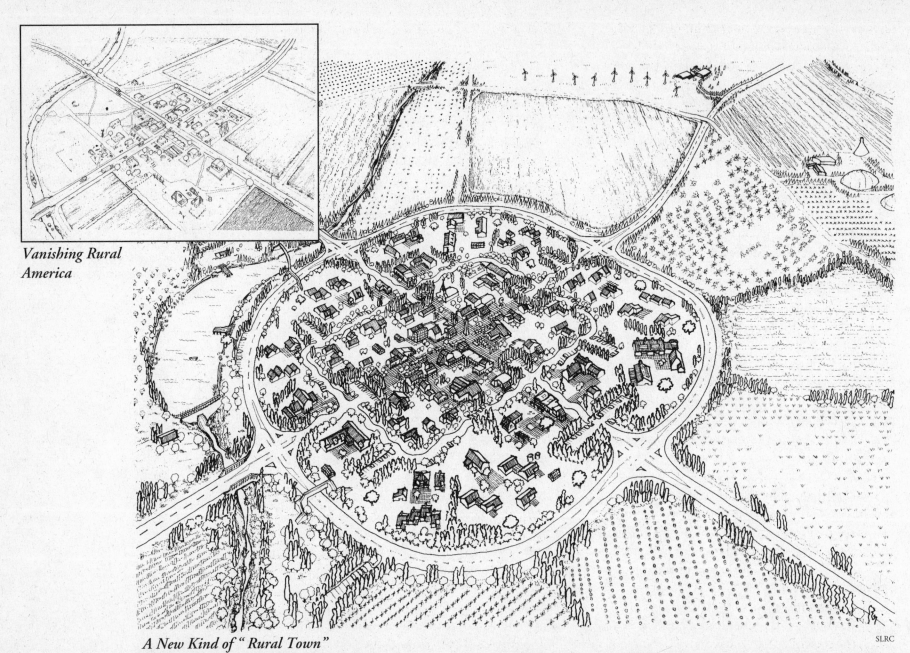

Vanishing Rural America

SLRC

A New Kind of "Rural Town"

The primary distinction here is that this New Rural Town is organized initially by the people who will be living there, just the way a Limited Equity Housing Cooperative, a Community Land Trust, an Intentional Community, or a Village Cluster/CoHousing community comes together.

labor saving devices when they can be effective, and socially and environmentally responsible.

• Organic farming, sustainable agriculture, and Permaculture methods are used throughout the community farming enterprises. This includes diversified and rotated crops, selected animal grazing, and the introduction of native plantings and edible landscaping in farming areas, residential clusters, and the town core.

• Community-supported health and social service programs are sponsored through the CLT and managed by the members. Included are full medical care, prenatal and maternal care, childcare, preventative health care, elder care facilities, and job retraining. Profits from these operations are re-invested into the community.

Conclusion — *a rural community ethic*

We propose the end of suburban sprawl through the creation of permanent Green Belts and a network of ecologically sustainable, agriculture-based rural communities, villages, and towns. These communities are not proposed as a place for commuters and urban escapees to buy individual lots and houses, nor as a way to make millions in real estate ventures. The purpose is to create a sustainable local rural economy to accommodate the increasing numbers of people seeking a self-sufficient lifestyle to compensate for the changing social, economic, cultural, and employment patterns due to the impact of a burgeoning international economy and a strong national economy. This would be accomplished through enterprises that are co-owned and managed by the farm families and workers. The task now is to influence planners, elected officials, and local community groups to advocate and enact land planning, environmental standards, and supportive programs that will simultaneously rebuild rural communities and existing urban centers.

Our recommendation to those aspiring to create a rural Village Cluster/CoHousing, or some other form of rural community, is this: "Move to the country only if you are able to create a truly self-reliant lifestyle." Think carefully whether your "community in the country" will revitalize rural areas and enhance the Green Belt, or whether it makes you merely another commuter, catching fleeting impressions of a vanishing country environment. If you care about ecological living and your own and your children's future well-being, look seriously at the Urban Cooperative Block in the next chapter, and at the group houses in Chapter Seven. Consider redesigning existing urban and suburban neighborhoods or using infill sites for building an ecologically sustainable community.

If you and your core group still want to move to the country, then explore the Organic Farm Village Cluster approach, and use the rich alluvial soil of valleys and meadows for what they are best suited — growing food. Let the wetlands, woods, farmlands, and natural rolling hills remain as a heritage we can pass on for seven generations. Plan your rural community and your livelihood, as a food-related enterprise, and use the land in a gentler way than just planting houses and depending on the car for everything. Whether for country or city living, assume the responsibility for looking at all of your group's interests, needs, resources, and options in terms of the social and environmental consequences of your community venture. The Shared Living Community approach is an introduction to the

"We must be committed to planning with social purposes and social consequences just as we have long recognized our commitment to physical planning with environmental purposes and consequences in mind.... we should be pleased to see a return to an integrated and comprehensive planning effort ... to find solutions for our communities so they are economically viable, environmentally sustainable and socially just, now and in the future." [45]

— *Janet M. Ruggiero, American Planning Association*

"...when you think of farms as the source of food for our children now and in the next century, I think you'll agree that farms are also a key to our future well-being.... The results [of our present practices are] grocery shelves stocked with foreign produce, often from countries with lax pesticide laws — higher food costs — and a greater reliance on pesticides and fertilizers — not to mention the loss of America's rural character and the working landscape so important to our sense of place." [46]

— *Ralph Grossi*

"In our every deliberation we must consider the impact of our decisions on the next seven generations."
— *Great Law of the Haudenosaunee Six Nation Iroquois Confederacy*

"Property belongs to a family of words that, if we can free them from the denigration that shallow politics and social fashion have imposed on them are the words, the ideas, that govern our connections with the world and with one another: property, proper, appropriate, propriety." [47]
— *Wendell Berry, "Whose Head is the Farmer Using"*

ecologically sustainable lifestyle that we must embrace as the 21st Century emerges and the remnants of the Industrial Revolution continue to fall away.   The transformation to a sustainable planet culture must begin with rebuilding community in America so that our children and their children's children will inherit a legacy of a safe, beautiful, and livable planet to grow up on

Photo by Greenbelt Alliance

Notes

Books listed only by name in the endnotes are highlighted in the resource guide at the end of the book, complete with author/publisher information and description.

1   Small Places, p. 244.
2   The World's Wasted Wealth 2, p. 493.
3   Walt Whitman, Leaves of Grass, Random House, New York, 1881, p. 249.
4   "Economic Growth Within the Capacity of the Environment to Support it"The Thomas Jefferson Planning District Commission, "The Thomas Jefferson Study to Preserve and Assess the Regional Environment: Economic Growth Within the Capacity of the Environment to Support it, A National Demonstration Project," Charlottesville, November 1993, p.15.
5   Wendell Berry, Recollected Essays 1965-1980, North Point Press, San Francisco, 1981, p. 272.
6   Gregory Bergman, "You Can't Talk to the Trees," Gray Panther Newsletter, March 1992, p. 5.
7   Ibid., p. 5.
8   Robert Gilman, "The Idea of Owning Land," Directory of Intentional Communities, p. 113.
9   Silvia Rubin, "A Back-to-the-Land Family that Never Lost the Faith," San Francisco Chronicle, July 21, 1992, p. D3.
10 Nick Kotz, "The Poor People's Co-ops," The Peoples Land: A Reader on Land Reform in the United States, edited by Peter Barnes for the National Coalition for Land Reform, Rodale Press Book Division, Emmaus, PA, 1975, p. 204.
11 Ralph Grossi, Letter, American Farmland Trust, Feb. 1994, p. 1.
12 Manuel Leon, translated from Spanish, "A Farmworker Speaks," The Peoples Land: A Reader on Land Reform in the United States, edited by Peter Barnes for the National Coalition for Land Reform, Rodale Press Book Division, Emmaus, PA, 1975, p. 236.
13 Ralph Grossi, Op. Cit., p. 1.
14 The Political Culture of Planning, pp. 220-221.
15 Wendell Berry, Home Economics: Fourteen Essays, North Point Press, San Francisco, 1987, pp. 185-186.
16 Policy Before Planning, Sierra Club, p. 8.
17 Anne Montgomery, "America's Pesticide Permeated Food," Nutrition Action Healthletter, June 1987.
18 Small Places, pp. 6-7.
19 Sibella Kraus, "Farm in Peril, Fresno Family Farm Threatened by Suburban Development," San Francisco Chronicle, April 21, 1993, p. Food-1.
20 Grossi, Op. Cit., p. 1.

21 Bradley Inman, "K&B conquering the West," San Francisco Examiner, June 30, 1991, p. F-1.

22 Kraus (quoting Elizabeth Scott Graham), Op. Cit., p. Food-10.

23 Policy Before Planning, p. 2.

24 Ruth Eckdish Knack, "Neotrad meets the Midwest," *Planning*, April 1993, Vol. 59, no. 4, p. 31

25 Michael Renner, Worldwatch Paper 84: Rethinking the Role of the Automobile, Worldwatch Institute, Washington D.C., 1988, p. 47.

26 "What is Sustainable Agriculture," by the Sustainable Agriculture Research and Education Program, at the University of California, Davis, California, 1991.

27 "Biointensive Mini-Farming — What is it?," *The Endeavor*, Feb. 1993, p. 5. (For more information contact: Ecology Action, 5798 Ridgewood Road, Willits, CA 95490)

28 Karie Garnier, Our Elders Speak: A Tribute to Native Elders, K. Garnier, White Rock, BC, 1990, p. 52.

29 "Biointensive Mini-Farming — What Is It?", Op. Cit., p. 5.

30 Guy Dauncy, "Sustainability: Using Less, Enjoying More," *The Permaculture Activist*, Feb. 1993, Vol. IX, No. 1, p. 12.

31 Permaculture: A Designer's Manual, p. ix.

32 Terry Mollner, "Grow-Power for Land Trust," In Context: A Quarterly of Humane Sustainable Culture, Winter 1984, No. 8, p. 12. (In Context Subscriptions $24/yr; Single Issues $6; PO Box 11470, Bainbridge Island, WA 98110)

33 Carla Marinucci, "Cottage Industries," San Francisco Examiner, April 19, 1992, p. E-1.

34 In the Company of Others, pp. 73-74.

35 J. Donald Waters, Intentional Communities: How to Start them and Why, Crystal Clarity Publishers, Nevada City, CA, 1990, pp. 31-32.

36 Much of the information in this section is based on information from: Freddy Kahana, "The Kibbutz as an Urban Alternative," Kibbutz Bet Haemek, Israel, Sept. 1991.

37 Much of the writing in this section is based on information from: David Thompson & Cherie Gossett, "Agrovillage," Communities:Journal of Cooperative Living, No. 34, pp. 35-41.

38 In the Company of Others, p. 74

39 "Agrovillage," Communities: Journal of Cooperative Living, No. 34, p. 38.

40 Earnest Callenbach, "Our Sustainable Future," *Northern California, ADPSR Bulletin,* January/February, 1994, Vol. 2, No. 1, p. 2.

41 California Energy Commission, Biennial Report, 1989.

42 Ronald J. Kilcoyne, "A Sustainable Transportation Policy," *The Urban Ecologist,* Fall 1992 (Northern Hemisphere), p. 5.

43 Policy Before Planning, p. 6.

44 Peter Robinson with help from Bernie and Clay, "Shannon Farm: A Model for Community that Works," Green Revolution, Winter 89-90, Vol. 46, Nol. 4, p. 1.

45 Janet M. Ruggiero, "Agenda for American Communities," *California Planner,* March/April 1993, p. 5.

46 Grossi, *Op. Cit.*, p. 1.

47 Wendell Berry, "Whose Head is The Farmer Using?," Meeting the Expectations of the Land: Essays in Sustainable Agriculture and Stewardship, Edited by Wes Jackson, Wendell Berry, and Bruce Colman, North Point Press, San Francisco, 1984, p. 30.

COMMUNITIES IN THE CITY
Models for Ecological Living

San Francisco

San Francisco

Santa Cruz

London

Dynamic New Eco Villages

San Francisco

CHAPTER SIX

"El Greco's Toledo;" © 1992 Gerdsa S. Mathan

Magnificent Cities Surrounded by Bountiful Green Belts
— a magic formula for sustainability

Let us be romantic, see our cities as a proud display of the heritage of humankind living in balance with nature. Here we can have a source for nourishing the human spirit with the interchange of knowledge, creative expression, spiritual growth, and social support. The source for nourishing the body is also close by. Every week the farmers market their goods in the town plaza — there is no better way to sustain the roots of culture than to be surrounded by the nurturing goodness of life supporting resources.

Where to Locate Your Community
— in the city or country?

When most people hear about Intentional Communities, Village Clusters, CoHousing, or other types of Shared Living Communities, they tend to imagine them in the urban fringe near small towns or in rural or mountain settings. You may have even thought this book was primarily a "how to" guide for leaving the city and forming a community in the country. We are actually proposing the opposite. The most ecologically sustainable way to equitably serve the most people with the highest quality of living and to preserve the natural environment is to create community in existing cities and suburbs.

In this chapter, we look at several prototype and existing models for urban Shared Living Communities on small and large scales to see how ordinary people can make use of what the city has to offer. We introduce a broader vision of revitalized urban centers — Eco Villages and Eco Cities linked by comprehensive rail transit systems. First, however, let's review the status of cities today, how they came to be the way they are, what works and what does not, why people want to leave them, and what everybody gains from creating community in our own backyards in the city.

City Living — *the possibilities and promises*

People have always looked to cities as places to fulfill dreams, improve themselves, find jobs and a

more satisfying life, and to escape both economic and physical constraints and hardships of earning a living off the land. The population shift away from agrarian life to the artisan, craft, and mercantile life of the commercial trade centers of medieval Europe is viewed in historical perspective as progress, but for many people, it meant going from rural poverty to urban poverty. The Industrial Revolution aggravated the urban environment, especially in coal-burning industrial cities. Nevertheless, cities became centers for education, prosperity, culture, and sophistication.

In the past, food was grown in the surrounding countryside and transported to the city markets, creating a rural and urban socioeconomic balancing process that, to some degree, persists today. Freed from the chores of rural life, urbanites were able to devote their energies to trades, commerce, and personal development. Cities grew into dense,

"Respect the rural country side — we will lose it if we use it. And respect the city — we will lose it if we do not use it."

— Ken Norwood

Photo by Ken Norwood

Farmers Markets in our Cities — Gathering Places for Sustaining Humankind

compact, and, in some places, congested and unhealthy neighborhoods. The introduction of railroads in Europe allowed for some spreading out

Photo by William Porter

Gathering Places are for Everybody

of congested urban areas and the growth of new smaller, yet still relatively dense, cities. The historical dependence on the agricultural Green Belt and the scarcity of land also helped contain the spread of European cities, thus sustaining their economic and social vitality. Finally, the invention of modern water supply, sewer, and waste disposal systems, rail transit, and the rise of the municipal management professions made cities more livable and stable.

The older pre-car American cities developed in a way similar to their European counterparts. They continued to thrive in a relatively compact and pedestrian-oriented manner through the 1800's and into the early 1900's, served by intercity railroads and local transit lines. In the 1920's, the increased use of cars and the gradual elimination of rail lines hastened the spread of low-density urban growth. Although some pre-car cities, like Toronto, New York, Boston, and San Francisco, have retained strong central areas supported by adjacent, high-

density pedestrian neighborhoods by maintaining strong public transit systems, most newer cities became sprawling car-fed suburbias. After WW II, the trend continued. The intentional dismantling of rail transit systems by a conspiracy of car interests, and the mass financing of single-family tract houses gave rise to endless urban sprawl, concurrent with economic and social decline of central city areas.

Despite the socially and environmentally debilitating influence of urban sprawl, the function of cities as human gathering places endures. People are still attracted to cities for the romance and excitement they offer, the varied food and entertainment, the many people to share interests and creative talents with, and the diversity of products, services, and lifestyles. In such cities, there is something to do anywhere you turn, often for little cost. In San Francisco, for example, Chinatown, Japantown, the Mission District, North Beach, and the Italian District all offer a variety of smells, sensations, and adventures with people, ideas, and customs from around the world. In one afternoon you can visit an Asian art museum, watch a Brazilian folk group perform in a park, go rollerblading, and eat Burmese food. These opportunities do not exist on the farm, in small towns, or in suburbs. An unmistakable efficiency, vitality, and even nurturing exists in cities, arising from the co-existence of diverse human resources, ethnic groups, and cultures, and economic and educational opportunities.

An April 5, 1992 feature article in the Oakland Tribune titled, "Why City Living? Reasons: No Commute, Cultural Diversity, Night Life,"[3] expresses why many people are attracted to urban centers. The author interviews urban residents, like

David Hanson, a Berkeley-Oakland resident for 12 years. Hanson grew up in the rural town of Davis, California, and says he could only be happy in an urban environment. His family always had to leave Davis to find things to do, either in San Francisco or the mountains. In the Bay Area, "You can instantly get away to the nearby regional parks, you can windsurf during the day, and then you can go have Thai or Ethiopian food."

Not having a long commute is another often-cited reason for living in the city. Businesses and industries often locate in cities for many of the same reasons that people do — for easy access to both physical and human resources. Regional planning agencies across the country are trying to encourage developers to build housing close to job centers so that people won't have to commute far to work. Compact, stable, and well-planned cities with pedestrian access and good public transportation means avoiding the difficulties, frustrations, and costs of owning a car. This is necessary for people who can't drive or cannot afford a car.

Additionally, cultural opportunities and the sense of neighborhood is a reason many people live in the city. In older cities with compact neighborhood centers, especially those with a streetcar-era heritage, there are bustling sidewalks with shops flanking both sides, and apartments above. Social services to assist disadvantaged people are more easily provided in the city because of a large tax base and economy of centralization.

Laura Hager, a back-to-the-land survivor, wrote an article, "Aargh, Wilderness — In Which Two City Slickers Lose Their Money and Their Minds in Search of Rural Paradise," describing her disappointments on moving to the country and her own

surprise upon returning to the city. "We missed the city…. We didn't miss the big things that people always say they'll miss about the city when they contemplate moving to the country. We didn't miss the museums, the opera, the ballet, or the theater. What we missed was not being able to go to Peet's [a coffeehouse in Berkeley] on the spur of the moment when we ran out of coffee. What we missed was movie theaters with a choice of first-run movies and restaurants." [4]

What is Not Working in American Cities

What about the violence, homelessness, pollution, anti-social behavior, noise, and general social alienation in the city? Are people really going to want to stay in the city, or come back to stay? Are we even asking the right questions?

The bottom-line question is whether these problems are inherent to cities, or whether they indicate structural flaws in our socioeconomic system. America is becoming internationally known as the most violent society in the world. In our system, both the officials and the general public see the "criminal" as the cause, and cling simplistically to the illusion that punishment and prisons alone are a means of control. Very few people are willing to examine more deeply the role our culture may play in these problems. Most prefer to hide behind locked doors or run away to the suburbs in search of less crime. Many of us are too befuddled and fearful for our own well-being to see the larger picture. The knee-jerk reaction to these problems is urban flight.

Chapter Two introduced critical issues that contribute to urban flight such as the often ignored

"Put a man among large masses of men and he will begin to gather a few of them together to build a small community. Such efforts take the forms of college fraternities, clubs, secret orders, church congregations, luncheon clubs, study clubs, and numberless other associations of limited numbers. We have here evidence of one of the most fundamental and universal of human traits — a craving of human nature which cannot safely be ignored." [5]
— *Arthur E. Morgan, In the Company of Others*

Photo by William Porter
Cars, Cars, Cars
But where are the gathering places?

"But gates and guardhouses are also popping up in established neighborhoods —poor one as well as rich. In Los Angeles, walls and gates have been erected around two public housing projects to keep out gangs and drug dealers. 'We want the same protection as white folks,' a resident of Mar Vista Gardens told a Los Angeles Times reporter in March 1992.... These walls and gates are leading to more segregation and more isolation, and the outcome is going to be tragic for all of us," warns Norman Krumhol, AICP, professor of urban planning at Cleveland State University. 'We're all Americans together, and have to learn to live in a culturally diverse place.'"[6]

— *David Dillion,*
"Fortress America"

"Of course, making cities more humane requires far more than just a redesign of urban spaces. Deep social alienation and the decline of central cities result from the formidable forces of racial and class discrimination and income disparities."[7]

— *Marcia D. Lowe,*
"Reclaiming Cities For People"

influence of "Hollywood" and the so-called information and entertainment media. It is no mere coincidence that the rise of violence, sexual assaults and exploitation of women, and the proliferation of guns has increased in proportion to the violent content of TV and film media. As Dr. Brandon Centerwall explains,

...following the introduction of television in the 1950's, United States homicide rates doubled over the next 10-15 years as the children exposed to violence on television on a regular basis grew to maturity.... in the 10-15 years following the introduction of television in Canada, exactly the same thing happened there: the homicide rate nearly doubled.[8]

The media, news, advertisements, and entertainment, has done more to destabilize American

Increase in homicide rate following the introduction of TV[9]		
	1945	1974
U.S.	3.0 per 100,000	5.8 per 100,000
Canada	1.3 per 100,000	2.5 per 100,000

society with a climate of fear and destructive, desensitized and aberrant behavior, than any terrorists could have. There are other interrelated causes of the increasing social alienation, family fragmentation, and community breakdown. Decades of living in housing designed for maximum "individuality" and "privacy," and travelling on hostile highways, usually alone, has led to a nation of people afraid to make contact. We have been on an endless tread-

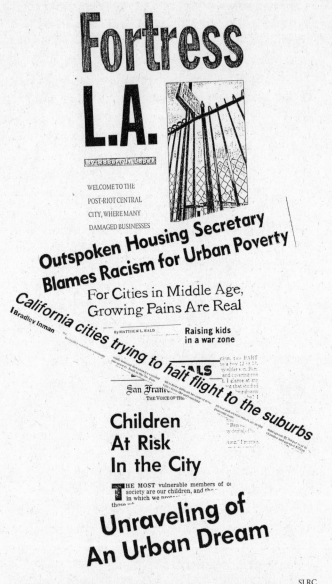

Let's End the Deterioration of American Society
The rebuilding of American Cities with many Eco Villages could be the antidote to the deadly malaise that pervades our aging inner cities and suburbs, and threatens to destroy the fabric of democracy — alienation and fragmentation.

mill of consuming ever more houses, cars and products. This system has little to do with sustaining the extended family, community, socioeconomic justice, efficient transportation systems, or ecological living. It is simply about making a profit by selling products, without responsibilitiy for the social and environmental consequences. As people buy more, they must work more, and as they work more, they have less time for their family and friends. As people buy more things, they become less dependent on others for sharing. This contributes to insulation and isolation.

Cosequently, a "fortress America" mentality has emerged in which "security" has become big business and more "gated communities" are being built, raising the question of whether this is the end of our democratic society. The magnitude of the problems leads us to the most frightening question of all: Can our cities be fixed, or are we (meaning those who can afford to) going to abandon the inner city to the poor and move out to "new towns" or to our own private rural community refuges? The latter kind of indifferent behavior aggravates class divisions, lack of opportunity, joblessness, poverty, emotional stress, drug use, gangs, transience and anti-social behavior, and eventually causes more violence and crime. But we must also realize that the breakdown of community is the fault of our own indifference, of our social, economic, and political institutions, and of the basic physical structure and layout of our cities. No part of the system can be ecologically sustainable without all other parts working toward the same end. Being an inividual, in terms of a high self esteem and sense of being a person, is not to be forsaken. The culprit in today's urban deterioration scene is the separate consumer buying unit.

Taking Responsibility for the Future of Our Cities

In order to make our urban centers socially, economically, and environmentally healthy, we must practice the highest skills of human relations, democratic governance, and economic justice within the new extended family and out to the neighborhood, the city, the urban region, the nation, and the world. Social alienation and the plight of our urban poor must be seen as more than a "city" problem; there is needed inspirational leadership based on a fundamental vision of profound responsibility for rebuilding community in America's cities. Informed leaders backed by informed people must now repudiate practices that permit greedy, vested interests to make huge profits by exploiting people and the environment.

It is obvious from the descriptions of city lovers that the people most satisfied with their urban housing are those that are affluent. City living for those of moderate to lower income should provide the same advantages, but it does not, at least not without exacting a higher percentage of their income for housing and transportation costs. Our responsibility now is to provide ways for working people to improve their housing opportunities in the city as a beneficial trade-off against the social/emotional and financial costs of the suburban commute. The Shared Living Community approach underscores the need for social, economic, and environmental justice in our urban policy processes. Our challenge is to create personal and group empowerment for all city dwellers through "community" sharing of resources and participatory resident control of permanently affordable housing.

"The co-operation of neighboring families also declined. They had little need of each other's help. In the impersonal life of the city people split up into special interest groups, and often scarcely knew their next-door neighbors. Increasing mobility of families…made for more and more superficial involvements with each other. Modern cities became places where a person might, in the midst of crowds, feel completely alone." [10]

— David and Vera Mace,
Marriage: East and West

"In many cities today, you do not see a lot of trees, because so many trees have been cut down. I imagine — and I believe it is very close to reality — a city which has only one tree left. (I don't know what kind of miracle helped preserve that one tree.) Many people in that city have become mentally ill because they are so alienated from nature, our mother. In the old time, we lived among trees and we sat in hammocks. Now we live in small boxes made of concrete. The air we breathe is not clean, and we get sick, not only in our bodies but in our souls." [11]

— Thich Nhat Hanh

"Two-thirds of all jobs created in the United States from 1960 to 1980 were located in suburbs… while the number of trips between central cities and suburbs and from suburb to suburb doubled within the same period of time." [12]
— *Michael Renner, Worldwatch Paper 84*

"In many urban areas, homes were razed, businesses displaced, and neighborhoods destroyed to build freeways. Streetcar companies went bankrupt in a single generation. Automobile interests made sure that the streetcars disappeared; more than 100 electric trolley systems were bought up and scrapped starting in the 1930s by National City Lines, a company owned by General Motors, Standard Oil, Phillips Petroleum, Firestone Tire and Rubber, Mack Truck and others." [13]
— *Michael Schafer & Stephen Wheeler, The Urban Ecologist*

We need to design our cities and neighborhoods to encourage more amiable and spontaneous cultural and social interaction and economic vitality. This can be done by providing an ecologically sustainable transit system that can provide easy pedestrian access to common places for people-to-people connections, where one can slow down long enough to become familiar with the passing scene, and strangers can begin to be part of the community activities and feel accepted.

There are many great cities throughout the world (and some in America) that testify to the importance of people-oriented transit cities in sustaining a vital urban culture. Michael Shaffer and Stephen Wheeler, writing in "The Urban Ecologist," tell of this worldwide trend:

Most European cities as well as older American cities (which many Americans love to visit) are compact and walkable. Many of these European cities are now moving aggressively towards giving even greater priority to pedestrians, bicycles, and public transit. The Netherlands has constructed more than 9,000 miles of bicycle paths. Cars are being progressively banned from central Amsterdam. Since the early 1980's, Florence, Naples, Bologna, Genoa, and Rome have all implemented partial or total automobile bans in downtown areas. By the year 2000, Bordeaux, France, plans to reserve half its streets for bikes and pedestrians. Elsewhere in the world as well, in cities such as Buenos Aires, Mexico City, Hong Kong, Singapore, Brisbane, Melbourne, and Curitiba, Brazil, innovative programs have been developed to reduce automobile use. [14]

The responsibility for revitalizing our urban environments, which then also protects the rural environment, does not lie just with planning officials and developers. It also lies with those who bought into urban neighborhoods years ago, or are wealthy enough today to acquire the better single-family houses or apartments in an area. Urban dwellers can no longer condone NIMBYism (Not In My BackYard), keeping other people from living in an area because the current residents feel that they or their housing would be threatened in some way. Everyone is responsible for bringing to the city a diversity of housing types and multicultural neighborhoods with a mix of incomes, ages, races and ethnicity. The allegations that affordable housing developments, an increase of density, or a cooperative community hurt nearby housing values have proven to be untrue numerous times. What does hurt the livability of a neighborhood is the number of car trips generated per day. Why not reduce cars in favor of people?

The introduction of frequent rail service will reduce traffic and "car-time," and increase our ability to create self-reliant cooperative communities in intentional transit neighborhoods or nodes. This would enable more people to afford to live close to jobs and transportation, enjoy more living amenities, and create more secure, sociable, and attractive urban living environments than in conventional neighborhoods.

Clearly, there is much that is right about cities today. Revitalizing cities in the way we describe in this book is possible. People are, in fact, doing it now. We will present prototype models and visit real communities located in Oregon, California, New York and elsewhere. First, let's visit Cornelia and find out this how this single, older woman was able to satisfy all her needs in the city and enjoy more amenities than people living in suburbia or the country. This story illustrates the benefits of forming and living in an ecologically sustainable community in the city. Though fictitious, it can be and is being done today.

Children in the Twin Oaks Community
The building of a sustainable society happens when children can grow up in a culturally enriched community in which they can interact with peers and adults in a safe environment.

Photo by Susan Graverly/Twin Oaks

A Story — *Cornelia Finds "Community" in the City*

Cornelia's bedroom windows open onto a large expanse of greenery, gardens, a small orchard, and lots of flowers. There is the serenity of a country farm, even though her group house faces onto upper Market Street in San Francisco. For Cornelia, being able to live in this kind of neighborhood is a dream come true. She had been close to homelessness several years before. Prices in the area had skyrocketed, and the rent on her former apartment, a small, poorly maintained studio, was more than half of her fixed income.

Cornelia is not married, and has no biological family in the area. But she has a wonderful extended family of six housemates: an older couple, a single mother with a young daughter, and two single men. She has her own living suite with two rooms and a bath in a large group house that they redesigned from two flats in a block of Victorian row houses. The house operates as a Limited Equity Housing Cooperative and is now part of a larger Urban Cooperative Block cluster of single-family houses, group houses, and apartments that they have named City Garden. All of them share a large common house with a kitchen and dining room, childcare facilities, and other activity rooms. There are also social courts, decks, gardens, and recreation areas in what used to be fenced backyards.

What Cornelia really likes about her new neighborhood is how convenient it is. There is a supermarket two blocks away, a small deli, and a mom and pop store around the corner. A coffee and pastry shop is on the ground floor of her building. Within blocks are a variety of restaurants,

"In modern America, the village, the neighborhood, the hamlet, or the city, often has become but an economic aggregation or only an incidental grouping, without the acquaintance, the personal relationships, and the common interests and activities, which are the essential characteristics of a community. Such aggregations do not fully satisfy the emotional cravings for fellowship, common interests, and unified planning and action." [15]
— Arthur E. Morgan

"Traditionally, the city is a collection of well organized sub-groups like families. It is not a collection of individuals. The modern American city, on the other hand, is not really a cohesive group and tends to be merely a collection of individuals." [16]
— Chandler Washburne, Ph.D.

David Spellman

The Transforamtion of American Cities to People Places is the Next Frontier

This "Eco-City Los Angeles" proposal unifies an existing inner city neighborhood with infill housing, social and cultural amenities, and transforms streets into pedestrian ways and courts. (See Cooperative Resources and Services Project in Resource Guide.)

a video rental store, a drugstore, and a bar with a pool table. It is a short walk to similar attractions on lower Haight and in the Castro District. Both neighborhoods have activities going on well into the night. The ethnic diversity is appealing. She is close to other African-American people, and Asian, Latino, Middle Eastern and white friends as well.

Getting around the city is easy without a car. She lives near three bus routes and two streetcar lines. On weekends she sometimes takes the street-car out to Golden Gate Park, one of the museums,

or to a matinee movie at one of San Francisco's repertory movie houses.

Cornelia enjoys an abundance of amenities at City Garden. She enjoys coming home to the delicious shared meals cooked most nights in the large, well-equipped common kitchen, and she enjoys taking her turn cooking. She finds it a pleasure to have others with whom to do household chores and projects, and just to talk and share her day. She likes sitting by the fireplace in the living room of her group house, using the sewing and crafts room in the common house, and tending to the community vegetable garden.

In City Garden, she enjoys the best of the city, a supportive extended family, and the privacy of her own living suite. Best of all, she feels safe. Since the community was formed, the ambiance of the entire neighborhood has changed. People are friendlier, more open and helpful, and there has been less crime and vandalism. Other cooperative communities have formed nearby, adding to the feeling of neighborhood for everyone.

The Urban Cooperative Block (UCB) concept illustrated by Cornelia's story represents a way to build a cooperative community in the city. The diversified range of people, energy, existing build-ings and a sense of place are bountiful resources in urban neighborhoods, and when combined can provide a sense of security, empowerment and a self-reliant neighborhood.

Tearing Down Fences in America

"Just saying no" to fences may be the easiest way to learn about cooperation and begin to recreate what is missing in urban society. A voluntary cooperative block community can begin when two or three families remove fences between their properties. The community will grow to include more members when other neighbors see its success. Once again, our challenge is to design for more people, not fewer, and to recognize and celebrate the instinctual gregariousness of the human species.

Consider the rewards of fenceless backyards. There are more possibilities for recreational and leisure time amenities, such as different kinds of play equipment for children, game courts, a pool and/or hot tubs, dining patios, larger garden plots, and more fruit trees — you can enjoy more for less. The following dialogue depicts how this process begins.

Listening in on a fence-removal party

I can't believe they're going through with it, Chuck Windsor thought to himself, shaking his head as he peered through a big hole in his fence. On the other side was Tom and Jill Hughes' backyard and a table with food and drinks. Where the neighbors, and the new back fence neighbors on the other side of the Hughes' were all gathered. The new neighbors had also approached Chuck and his wife Gladys about the idea of tearing down the fences between all of the backyards. Chuck had made it clear that he wanted no part of their crazy environmentalist scheme.

"Gladys!" Chuck called. *"Come over here and check this out!"*

Gladys came out of the kitchen and climbed onto a chair to look over the fence. *"Their peas and snap beans are coming along nicely,"* she commented, waving to her neighbors. Gladys was always more friendly to the neighbors than Chuck, who only spoke to Tom because they both liked fishing.

"Oh, sure," grumbled Chuck, *"but what's the point of having a backyard that you have to dig up and replant every spring? All I have to do is water, mow, and fertilize my lawn, and it's green the whole year."*

Tom came over to Chuck's knothole with a glass of iced tea. His good-natured response to Chuck's usual show of ambivalence was, *"You and Gladys come on over, Chuck. We're going to need some help tearing down our fence, too."*

"You?" Chuck replied incredulously. Tom and Jill Hughes had always seemed so normal. Was this craziness contagious?

"Well, yeah," said Tom. *"Our new neighbors, Doug, Kim, and Rosalinda, talked to us a couple of weeks ago about taking down the fences, and what they propose for our backyards makes a lot of sense. Jill and I have always wanted to do more gardening and have a hot tub, but we don't have the time, money, or the space for all of that. When we heard that they and the Cohens were going to tear down their fences and start a big garden, we decided to join. With all of us helping we can have a really big garden. We could plant fruit trees, build a greenhouse for seedlings, a grape arbor, and add a hot tub and volleyball court later. Isn't that great? How about joining in?"*

Gladys joined Tom and Chuck. *"They really have some lovely plans, Chuck,"* she said. *"It's sort of too bad that our fence is so high. It'll cut off the view of their new grape arbor from over here."* She paused significantly and raised an eyebrow at Chuck, who knew from long experience what this meant.

"All right," Chuck finally said. *"You and I can talk about this later. Right now I'm willing to meet the new neighbors. Hi Tom, got any more iced tea and cookies?"*

"...people gathered in concentrations of city size and density can be considered a positive good, in the faith that they are desirable because they are the source of immense vitality, and because they do represent, in small geographic compass, a great and exuberant richness of differences and possibilities, many of these differences unique and unpredictable and all the more valuable because they are. Given this point of view, it follows that the presence of great numbers of people gathered together in cities should not only be frankly accepted as a physical fact. It follows that they should also be enjoyed as an asset and their presence celebrated: by raising their concentrations where it is needful for flourishing city life, and beyond that by aiming for a visibly lively public street life and for accommodating and encouraging, economically and visually, as much variety as possible." [17]

— Jane Jacobs, *The Death and Life of Great American Cities*

Photo by Philip Thompson

Partial View of the N Street CoHousing Community's Shared Back Yards
The community built walkway connects private houses, gardens, common house, chicken pen, laundry facilities, patios, and play areas in a village-like environment.

The previous fictional dialogue is similar to what is really happening. In 1986, two neighbors in Davis, California decided to remove the fence between their yards. Other neighbors eventually joined them and a community was formed. Here are four examples from across America of how urban communities can be formed in similar ways.

N Street CoHousing, Davis, CA

This Urban Cooperative Block community of existing houses in central Davis follows the Village Cluster/CoHousing model, with a common house, shared meals, and numerous other shared amenities. It began in 1979, when two families on N Street came together to share interests in Permaculture. It was not until 1986 that they tore down their fences. Today, their community consists of 12 houses and one large backyard with play areas, outdoor dining patios, gardens, laundry lines, compost bins, and a chicken pen. One of the original houses was redesigned as the common house with a new large kitchen, dining room, and office. Upstairs are several rental rooms for single people.

The community grew as houses in the neighborhood came up for sale and they found buyers interested in their community goal. Absentee owners of adjacent rental houses were willing to master-lease to the N Street community, which then assumed responsibility for maintenance, paying taxes, and sub-leasing to new members. (This is also called a triple net lease.) Some absentee owners eventually sold their houses to community members.

The community is composed of single- and two-parent families, couples, and single people. In all, there are 33 adults and 14 children. They enjoy sharing meals and responsibilities on a daily basis, and share special celebrations throughout the year, like birthdays, births (three babies have been born into the community), weddings (two so far), Easter egg hunts, Thanksgiving dinners, and a recycled gift party at Christmas.

They use a participatory management structure and sign-up schedules for rotation of tasks and cooking. Through cooperative decisions they have endeavored to create an ecologically sustainable way of living. They use Permaculture techniques in the gardens and have solar collectors on several of the houses. The redesign and rehabilitation of existing houses and maintenance was done mostly with community labor and pay-as-you-go financing. Their most recent endeavor was the building of 550 linear feet of flagstone walkway to connect all the houses. The path was christened by a wedding procession soon afterwards. They present a working example of supportive extended family values, co-parenting, positive role modeling for children, healthy eating, child care and mutual responsibility.

Walkway Work Party at N Street   Photo by Steve Evans
This projectt took many weekends to complet and in the process further unified the community in spirit and place.

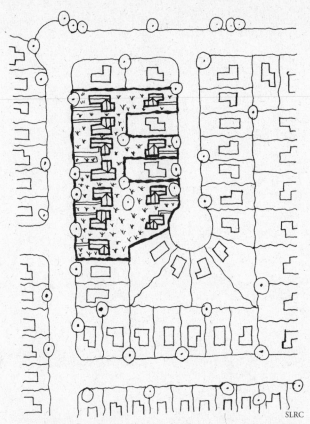

SLRC

An Urban Cooperative Block that Shows the Way
The N Street CoHousing Community in Davis, CA has put together 12 houses that share a back yard, gardens, and a common house with a large kitchen, dining room, and office. The esthetic and utilitarian amenities occur as both individual and organized group projects — it belongs to everyone.

This group has also demonstrated that moderate to low-income people can improve their quality of life without going into debt. They have also shown that an Urban Cooperative Block of existing houses can be created and maintained with less initial cash outlay and work than newly built CoHousing communities. So what happens when you start taking down fences? *You get community!*

"I hope our co-housing community develops in a similar way [referring to Permaculture] — a little chaotic, definitely diverse, yet in a wild and living harmony; a place of awe, of work, of belonging, of growth, of spirituality; a place in which to be born; a neighborhood in which to grow old and die; a community to know as home." [17]
— *A Founding Member of the N Street Community*

Photo by Kathleen Smith

Without Fences, Gatherings are Easy at the N Street Community

On Going Concerns
This is a cluster of seven existing houses with shared backyards and a common house.

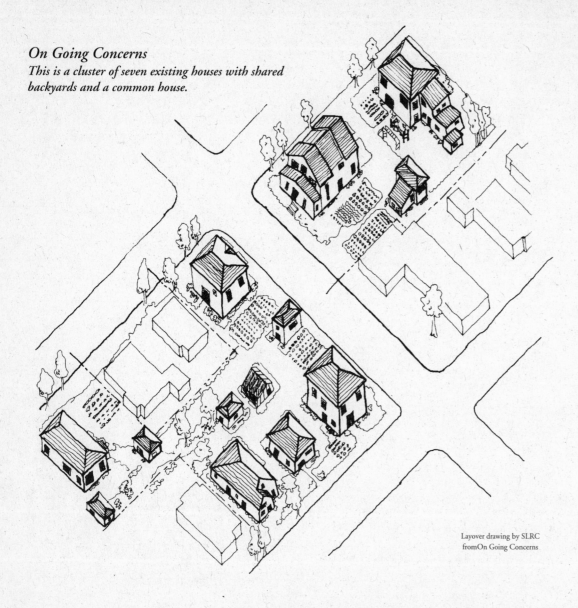

Layover drawing by SLRC
fromOn Going Concerns

On Going Concerns, Portland, OR
This is an example of a group of people that created a vibrant and supportive Urban Cooperative Block from seven existing houses on Going Street in the

inner city, mixed-race, low-income neighborhood of Sabin in Portland. The community of 11 adults and five teenagers, plus friends in the neighborhood, shares meals two times a week in a co-owned kitchen-dining-meeting room that was added to one of the houses. They also gather for meetings, work parties, holidays, birthdays, and other celebrations. Community members were able to buy, at a relatively low cost, the old and deteriorated houses that make up the community. All are in the process of being rehabilitated with community labor. Although each house is a private residence, common activity spaces, such as a ceramics studio, a common laundry, and sitting rooms, are being developed in various houses. Among the other shared amenities are a tool bank, a food-buying club, orchards, and gardens.

Their goal of ecological living is being accomplished through the use of upgraded insulation, double-pane windows, recycled building materials, summer shading grape arbors, rain barrel and greywater systems to irrigate the gardens, and solar water heating systems in three houses. This community proves that high quality living and affordable lifestyles can really happen without government subsidies.

On Going Concerns also serves as one of the catalysts in the community-strengthening process of the Sabin Community Development Corporation (SCDC) and the Ujima African-American women's drug and alcohol recovery transition house programs. The SCDC plans to be the sponsoring agency for other transition houses, and low-income/self-help housing projects organized by local African-American residents for permanent affordability and resident control. The goal in Sabin is to upgrade the old neighborhood by gradually buying, rehabilitating, and leasing houses, and creating neighborhood amenities. They plan to turn the holdings into a land trust in which the existing low-income and minority residents can co-manage their housing and have ownership opportunities. In this way, the neighborhood can resist outside investment/gentrification, and maintain its cultural integrity and racially mixed character.

Ganas Community, Staten Island, NY

Ganas is an Intentional Community that shows how the Urban Cooperative Block can be a stabilizing element in old, central-city neighborhoods. Started in 1980, Ganas is co-owned by a resident core group of three people, but is intentionally organized to provide democratic self-governing, social/family support, a shared income economy, and housing for approximately 60 people. The community consists of seven residential buildings (one with a large common kitchen and dining room) and five adjoining shared backyards with gardens, a playground, and a pool. Nearby, the community operates three cooperative stores called "Every Thing Goes" where they sell recycled and refurbished goods. They do a thriving business and employ a number of Ganas residents. Others work elsewhere in the city, but everyone participates in group decision-making, meals, and responsibilities.

Southside Park, Sacramento, CA

Southside Park CoHousing is a variation of the Urban Cooperative Block approach to revitalizing inner-city neighborhoods. This 1.3-acre site was close to downtown Sacramento in an area of old houses with a history of poverty and crime. There

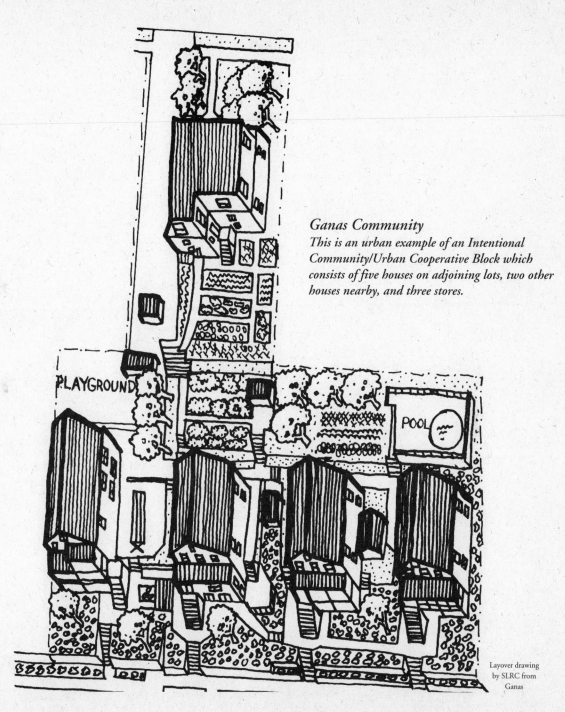

Ganas Community
This is an urban example of an Intentional Community/Urban Cooperative Block which consists of five houses on adjoining lots, two other houses nearby, and three stores.

Layover drawing by SLRC from Ganas

were four old houses on it, owned by the Sacramento Redevelopment Agency, which rehabilitated one two-story house, moved one to another block and rehabilitated it, and demolished the remaining derelict houses. This community was sparked by the groundswell of interest following the release of the book *CoHousing.* Several founding members of the Sacramento group saw an introductory slide show by McCamant and Durrett in Davis in 1988. In 1989, they formally organized and began a four-year process of creating their 25-unit CoHousing cluster.

Some members of the original core group wanted to locate in a Sacramento suburb. The remainder formed the Southside Park CoHousing Group with the objective of living in-town so members could walk, bike, or bus to their downtown jobs. In October of 1993 they began moving in. The members of this interracial, mixed-income community are mostly in their late 30's and 40's,

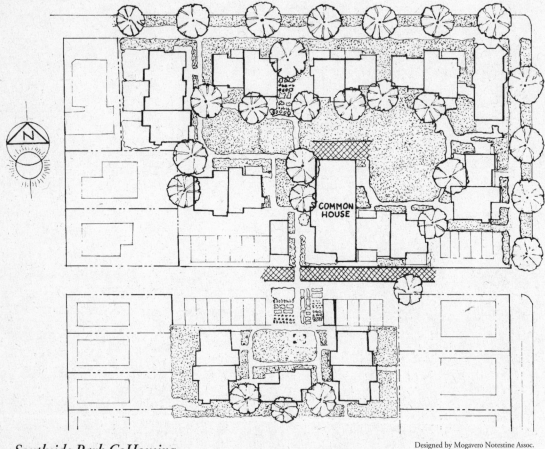

Designed by Mogavero Notestine Assoc.

Southside Park CoHousing
Here is an example of an inner-city infill community. There are 25 new townhouse units, including one rehabilitated existing house, with shared yards and a large 2,500 sq. ft. common house in a pedestrian environment.

Deck Builders at Southside Park Photo by Don Lindemann

with several retired people and empty nesters, some single-parent households, and some younger couples without children. There are 22 children from ages one to 15. This location could have been a problem for conventional financiers, but they purchased the site from the Redevelopment Agency by meeting the requirement of providing 11 units, or 40%, for low and moderate income buyers. This process added about a year to the time schedule, but ultimately made for a more successful project. Working with city departments was arduous, because the group had to continually explain the CoHousing concept to city officials. The initial financing to buy the site from the Redevelopment Agency came when the core group formed a partnership and raised money from their savings, equity from selling their homes, and loans and donations from other sources. The Southside Park experience provides the helpful lesson that creating Urban Cooperative Blocks in urban neighborhoods can be done working with a planning department and redevelopment agency to do the complex job of assembling properties and financing for mixed-income residents.

Organizing, Designing, and Rebuilding an Urban Cooperative Block Community

Here is a pragmatic, people-oriented approach to the "pedestrian neighborhood" concept that has eluded city planners, architects, nonprofit housing organizations, and sociologists for decades. Here is the opportunity to rebuild community in America and live ecologically. With the empowerment gained from the extended family, and groups of neighbors, you can have more amenities, more leisure time, a greater sense of fulfillment, and more

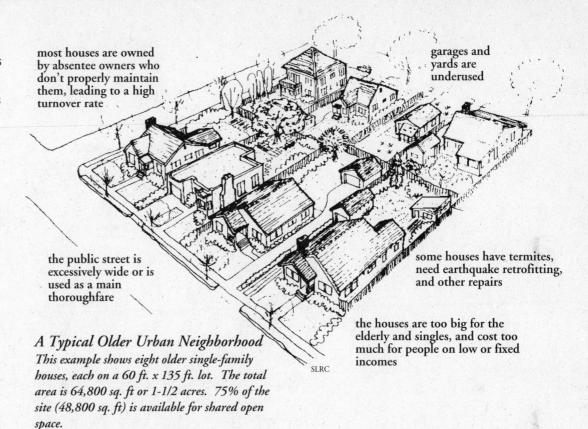

most houses are owned by absentee owners who don't properly maintain them, leading to a high turnover rate

garages and yards are underused

the public street is excessively wide or is used as a main thoroughfare

some houses have termites, need earthquake retrofitting, and other repairs

SLRC

the houses are too big for the elderly and singles, and cost too much for people on low or fixed incomes

A Typical Older Urban Neighborhood
This example shows eight older single-family houses, each on a 60 ft. x 135 ft. lot. The total area is 64,800 sq. ft or 1-1/2 acres. 75% of the site (48,800 sq. ft) is available for shared open space.

community support than ever before. The economic advantages of forming a UCB in an existing neighborhood come from the fact that much of the organizing and remodeling can be done with your own labor while you live there. The overall cost and environmental impact will be less than if you built a new CoHousing project or Cooperative Community on raw land.

Begin by creating a core group
If several neighbors are already in agreement, start your community by removing your fences and initiating voluntary mini-projects. Gradually attract the participation of other neighbors,

"The friendships that have blossomed during this project have been wonderful. I must confess that I would not have taken the time nor had the opportunity to get to know many of the people in our project if it had not been for the common dream that we shared and the willingness to put in the hard work to make it happen. I'm sure that these friendships will be long-lasting and [become] deeper as we live side by side." [19]

— A member of Southside Park CoHousing

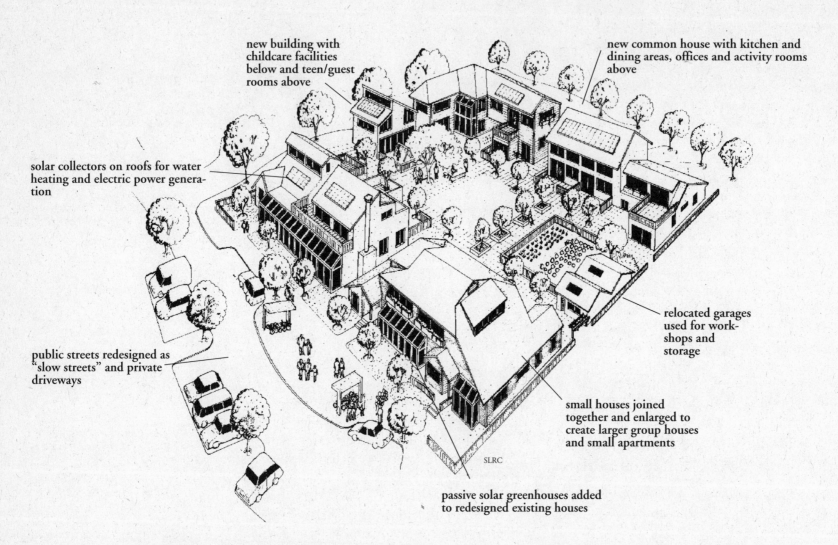

new building with
childcare facilities
below and teen/guest
rooms above

new common house with kitchen and
dining areas, offices and activity rooms
above

solar collectors on roofs for water
heating and electric power generation

relocated garages
used for work-
shops and
storage

public streets redesigned as
"slow streets" and private
driveways

small houses joined
together and enlarged to
create larger group houses
and small apartments

SLRC

passive solar greenhouses added
to redesigned existing houses

A Prototype Urban Cooperative Block
This is a future co-owned, medium-density community created out of an existing neighborhood. Backyard fences have been
removed, and existing houses remodeled and enlarged into four- to eight-bedroom group houses with some individual apartments.
The usually wasted space between houses has been used for adding new rooms.

perhaps with home childcare or an after-school supervised play time.

Invite other possible participants and nearby neighbors to share in these events. Hold potluck supper meetings, classes, and workshops on the concepts of self-sufficiency, urban clusters, cooperative communities, gardening, childcare, eldercare, and shared living skills. Begin a dialogue on subjects of common interest in order to create an understanding of potential benefits.

During the UCB community formation process, use the profile, meeting facilitation, and design workshop techniques introduced in Chapter Three. The profile exercises will help to bring out the personal aspirations, needs, values, lifestyles, and agreements about community goals and the interests of the individual members.

Finding and acquiring property

Selecting the general neighborhood for your community and bringing together contiguous lots and houses to form a UCB community will require commitment, resources, skills, and determination. It is advisable, given the myriad of possibilities and decisions, to use a trained community facilitator for guidance in the organizing and conceptual planning phases. If you already live in the block, try to interest present neighbors in joining and be aware of houses for rent or for sale by resident or absentee owners.

One strategy is for the core group to rent and buy existing available houses in a three to four block radius and gradually consolidate into the same block as houses become available so that a cluster begins to form. Some core group members can start by sharing a larger house until the time comes for

adding rooms or living suites, or buying or leasing another house for the cluster. The short-term result may be a neighborhood community composed of two houses on one block, three in the next, and four in another, such as Ganas in New York and On Going Concerns in Portland. During the intervening time, the community formation and planning process can take place. The more frequent the close daily contact and physical proximity is among group members, the more committed the group will become. The N Street community started rotating dinners at various houses or in their backyard patio several years before they actually converted one house into a common house with a large kitchen and dining room. They saved money, shared responsibilities, and built a cohesive community.

Inner-city and even older suburban neighborhoods will tend to have more absentee owners. This presents some difficulties, but also brings tremendous opportunities. Absentee owners may be eager to sell, or to grant a long-term master lease of their house(s) at a lower cost, if you agree to take over all landlord responsibilities as was done by the "N" Street community for several houses. Renting with an option to buy and offering the right of first refusal is another way to secure the beginning of a UCB cluster. Evictions of existing tenants must be avoided; including them in the UCB should be part of the community plan. However, when extensive rebuilding is required, tenants may have to be relocated temporarily into other houses. A nonprofit housing sponsor is another way a community core-group can obtain financing and technical assistance. They would be able to qualify for a wider array of low and moderate income housing financing and grant programs.

Cooperative ownership and leasing options

You may achieve a more financially stable and secure UCB community by co-owning all of the properties as a cooperative association or other entity. The entire property could be bought in partnership, or as a tenancy-in-common and converted to a condominium. Each unit would be separately owned, and all the common land and facilities owned by the community. This method is usually more expensive and does not provide for continued affordability or for building a cohesive community.

It is better to organize all the houses as a Limited Equity Housing Cooperative. This helps maintain the UCB as a community and guarantees permanent affordability because of the equity or resale limits imposed by these forms of ownership. A Mutual Housing Association, Community Land Trust, or a local Community Development Corporation could serve as the organizing support group, and acquire the entire block and form a cooperative. This would benefit both original and buy-in members of the UCB: renters would not be at the mercy of absentee owners or managers. Ownership costs would be reduced for everyone, and the future maintenance of their houses and neighborhood would be in their own hands. This provides personal empowerment through group empowerment. These and other methods of group ownership are presented further in Chapter Nine.

UCB management structure

Whether you start out small as in the story with Chuck and Gladys, or plan extensive shared amenities as in the dialogue with Cornelia, it is wise to activate a managing process such as a neighborhood council, or board of directors. These bodies, whether informal, elected, or incorporated, should create a process for determining goals and decision-making and recording of all actions regarding agreements, financial transactions, legal and zoning plans, master plan proposals, scheduling priorities, and actual development. Remember to have fun at your meetings, though. Share what is going on in your lives at potluck suppers or desserts. Try making peach cobbler or other foods together.

A master development plan

Making a master development plan is just as important in the city as it is in the country. The new common uses and amenities, landscaping, and building redesign and additions are decisions that will require participation by all the members. Using a community design facilitator is advised. Appoint a planning and design committee that involves the general membership in the process, coordinates with other committees, and keeps the community vision in focus. The master plan process should start with an accurate inventory of what exists on the properties, such as site drainage; the location, species, characteristics, and condition of trees and other plants; soil type and condition; and the location, use, and condition of buildings and other physical improvements such as gardens, paved areas, sprinkler systems, or electrical lines.

This is a time to use the personal profile and design workshop techniques detailed in Chapter Three to create a "wish list" of the members' personal needs and aspirations. Include social, economic, and environmental community goals, such as housing types and cost, energy efficiency, home livelihood or cottage industry, and a transportation

The Urban Cooperative Block on a Sunday Afternoon
Take eight (or more) single-family houses and lots, remove the backyard fences, add more people, redesign the houses and yards into an urban Intentional Community, and you can have the best of both worlds — urban conveniences and a rural-like self-reliance. In this picture, identify how many age groups and opportunities for interaction, sharing, and fulfillment there are. Could this be an answer for you and your family?

SLRC

management plan for reducing car trips.

From these lists, develop criteria based on what features are no longer necessary, what requires a redesign, and what new buildings and amenities you desire. Turn the master plan into an action plan by including cost and labor estimates, financial sources, prioritizing lists and time schedules. Do your

homework regarding zoning, planning laws and housing programs. Using a community facilitator is advised.

The common house and/or common rooms
As in Village Cluster/CoHousing communities, an appropriately sized and located existing house in the

Recycling Obsolete Garages
Because fewer cars are needed in a community, old garages can be easily relocated and converted to garden and tool sheds or workshops.

UCB cluster could be copurchased and redesigned as the common house, as in the "N" Street community, or a new kitchen and dining room wing can be added to an existing house as in the On Going Concerns community. Special common rooms for crafts, reading, exercise, childcare, and work can be incorporated into the main common house or in unused bedrooms, attics, basements, or garages of existing family houses in the cluster. The drawing of the prototype UCB shows how old garages can be relocated, redesigned, and added for a variety of shared uses.

Rehabilitating and redesigning houses
Survey the room types and sizes of all the existing houses and other buildings in the UCB, and match this with the personal interests and needs profiles of your members and the composition of the community as a whole. There are many options, such as dividing larger houses into smaller apartments or suites of several rooms and a bath, for a couple or small family, without a full kitchen, and redesigning smaller houses into larger houses with more bedrooms for large nuclear families or as an extended family group house. In the UCB, existing single-family houses can continue to be used for each family's own private living space.

When the UCB includes a common kitchen and dining area, households with children may wish to keep at least a minimal kitchen for children's meals, snacks, and off-schedule meals. The original kitchen could be redesigned as a work room including a kitchenette, with a variety of built-ins like a work desk and computer nook, book and magazine shelves, stereo and TV, and other conveniences. Here again, the basic needs and aspirations of

everyone in the group will need to be well understood to determine the importance of shared meals and other common house amenities relative to their daily household needs. Examples of group house redesigns are presented in Chapter Seven.

Gardens, chickens, and self-reliance
In the abundant space created by combining backyards, a community could plant vegetables, herbs, flowers, and fruit trees. During the master planning process, new trees and plantings can be chosen that better relate to the redesigned features and new

Photo by Ken Norwood

N Street Chicken Pen
Enjoy organic eggs, recycle your kitchen waste, and create ecological sustainability right in your own backyard.

desires of the members. This is the opportunity to introduce permaculture, organic growing, composting, and edible landscaping techniques. Trellises for growing berries and other vined fruits and vegetables could be added onto buildings, and smaller gardens could be planted in side and front yards. Before planting anything edible, especially in yards adjacent to streets, it is important to check the soil for lead deposited from car exhaust, and for pesticides and herbicides used by prior owners. Plan space for compost piles, a garden tool and potting shed, and a greenhouse for spring or winter starter plants. Greenhouses and sundecks could go on the roofs of relocated garages.

An Urban Cooperative Block could also have chickens and possibly goats, depending upon the characteristics of the surrounding neighborhood, zoning and health codes, and whether a suitable location lies sufficiently away from the neighbors or your own living spaces. Noise, odor, flies and the possibility of attracting rats are problems to consider. By creating your own combined backyard environment there may be no opposition. The animals and fowl help create a mini-ecosystem, eating kitchen scraps and providing manure for the yards and gardens. Determine what degree of self-reliance you desire, then evaluate your community's resources, and make decisions accordingly, remembering to review them in the context of the master plan.

Recreation amenities

A UCB's common yard can be a great source of low-cost pleasure. Here is where large and small common grass areas can be located for children, teens, and adults to romp and play. Many cozy

Photo by Kathleen Smith

Story Telling Time at the N Street Urban Cooperative Block
In the shared back yards there is the sanctity for spontaneous litle gatherings that everyone can enjoy.

corners of the commons can be claimed for story telling time. Together your neighbors and you can build a hot tub, game courts, play yards, a jungle gym, and relaxation and conversation nodes under shade arbors, pagodas, or whatever your group fancies. Don't duplicate facilities in the surrounding neighborhood. There may already be a park, sports courts, or a playground nearby, or other neighbors may already have recreation facilities they would share for common use. On a larger scale, the UCB could revitalize the broader neighborhood by exporting the UCB model to other blocks.

This is a great way of encouraging neighbors to get to know about each other and the benefits of sharing backyards. The security asset is provided by increasing the numbers of persons that can be observers and participants in the use of common amenities. A neighborhood watch group could expand its scope to include taking down the back-yard fences, sharing activities, converting the streets into "slow street" like driveways. They can exert direct control over the previous through streets with speeding cars and noisy trucks. Use them for parking only, or in rail transit nodes redesign them into green strips with walking and bicycle paths, community gardens, and pay areas. These green strip reclaimed spaces could serve as links between housing and recreation areas, schools, childcare centers, shops, bus stops, and transit stations.

The UCB neighborhoods can reduce car usage

The Urban Cooperative Block offers away for rebuilding community in city neighborhoods that can satisfy many social, economic, and environmental needs through the direct participation of the residents. You can organize the UCB neighborhood for car-pooling and car sharing for even more ecological living. Several neighborhoods could co-buy van buses or a larger tour type bus for commuting to transit stations, for special events, ski trips, and even group vacations. The breaking of car dependency can mean a more affordable and higher quality way of living. See Chapter Nine for ideas about use of zoning, financial, and other incentives to get people to share use of alternative transportation systems.

Water, sewer, gas, and electrical utilities

Creating a UCB community in an existing neighborhood, rather than in the country, can save time and money, because the utilities, a major infrastruc-ture investment, do not need to be installed. Solar energy can be used for water heating, electrical generation, and space heating. By using solar electrical power, you can be "off the grid" if you choose to invest in a shared solar power system. See Chapter Nine for more on alternatives for ecologically sustainable community design.

In this next fictional dialogue we explore how an Urban Cooperative Block community group can participate in making decisions about their own future using their own resources.

The Phoenix Urban Cooperative Block Planning and Finance Committees Meet

Members of the Phoenix community are in the common house for an after-dinner meeting of the master plan and finance committees.

Janice, in her late 60's, recently widowed, and one of the original house owners in the block, is facilitator for this meeting. She is discussing her favorite community master plan item. *"Remember the number of times last year we had to give away surplus produce because we couldn't can or freeze it?"*

"I agree," said Barbara, a single parent of a three-year-old. *"I'm willing to contract with James and Melinda to be the community garden and food processing team. We really had great meals last summer and I saved money, but we lost out during the winter from not having food stored away properly. We had too many tomatoes, which we should have bartered for corn, which we didn't have at all. We do need a food managing team."*

James, a recently unemployed computer programmer, nodded. *"Bartering with all the other community gardeners around the city is a good idea. I* believe that Melinda and I can make enough from the garden and fruit trees to keep us all in beans. We could build a passive solar greenhouse on the front of the common house. We'll get free heat this winter, and grow more veggies too."

Janice observed the colored consensus cards the members were holding up and found out that Sam Tompkins agreed on the contract with James and Melinda, but deferred on the greenhouse idea for later. With everyone agreeing on the original proposal, she declared, *"Consensus! We now have our first in-house urban farmers. Congratulations."*

Sam, a retired school teacher and a new member of Phoenix, signaled for the floor. *"I deferred on James' greenhouse idea because I want to combine that with the next item on the agenda, which is building an eldercare center right here in our own backyard. I'm going on 76, and although I'm really fit now, that may change. Ellen is 79, and Eve is 84 — they'll need more assistance soon. It's only a matter of time until the rest of us will need a planned eldercare wing here at Phoenix."*

Melinda, the mother of two small children and recently married to James, was recognized. *"Look, we have a master plan list of ideas, so let's slow down a bit and see how this eldercare suite can dove-tail with other ideas. The new national health care act also encourages home childcare improvements, and we all know that our childcare room lacks a state-approved toilet room and a work sink. So let's…"*

Barbara excitedly cut in. *"Yes, let's go for the package, let's put the elders on one side and the kids on the other with one plumbing stack in the middle, and…"*

Melinda bounced back with, *"…and we can pour a two-story foundation so we can add on a*

second-floor teen suite — soundproofed, of course — sometime in the future— a tri-generational building."

"Wow!" blurted Brennan, age 12. *"It's about time us teenagers — well, almost — got a place. Judy and Tim and me don't fit in anymore in the kids' play room. So what else can we do — watch TV?"* He looked mischievously around the room, noting the scowls that appeared at the mention of television.

Robert smiled enthusiastically. *"Okay, we've got a real project budding here. I've been thinking about our carpentry resources, and we can put quite a crew together. Brennan, you and your friends can form a crew too. We've got three members who are out of work, so this is good timing. We can get tax credits and grants for putting people to work on healthcare-related projects."* He turned to Cynthia, a recent architecture graduate. *"Are you ready for a job?"*

Cynthia stood up and patted Robert on the shoulder. *"You bet! I'd love to make use of my computer design and cost estimating software programs. But let's keep the idea of a greenhouse separate for now, I'll come up with some alternative proposals."*

Janice asked for and got consensus for the tri-generational proposal. She concluded with, *"Thank you all for a great meeting. Let's raid the kitchen — I smelled peach cobbler baking a while ago."*

New Life for Old Buildings

Shared Living Communities can be located in recycled existing buildings not normally considered as permanent housing, such as vacated motels, convalescent hospitals, mortuaries, restaurants, elementary schools, supermarkets, discount department stores, and even whole shopping centers and office parks. Most of these building types have

"Among the most admirable and enjoyable sights to be found along the sidewalks of big cities are the ingenious adaptations of old quarters to new uses. The town-house parlor that becomes a craftman's showroom, the stable that becomes a house, the basement that becomes an immigrants' club, the cobbler's that becomes a church with lovingly painted windows — the stained glass of the poor — the butcher shop that becomes a restaurant: these are the kind of minor changes forever occurring where city districts have vitality and are responsive to city needs."[20]
— Jane Jacobs

toilet rooms, showers, and kitchens that can be re-used for community purposes. They have large areas that can easily be divided into common rooms, leaving ample space for private rooms, and live-work spaces. If the community co-owns cars, carpools, or is close to a transit system, they could dig up the parking lots and uncover the bare soil of Mother Earth. There is an oversupply of buildings due to business failures and over investment encouraged by tax laws, and special-interest zoning decisions. Vast areas of inner cities and older suburbs are treated like second-hand goods and are bypassed as the next wave of speculation spreads outward.

These "white elephant" properties are being added to the tax burden of all of us when financiers are "bailed out."

A local Community Development Corporation (CDC) could sponsor an entrepreneurial cooperative community group to start using an old shopping center, or hospital, or restaurant almost as-is. Selected modifications could be done by the community members themselves. (The CDC model for local community ventures is further presented in Chapter Nine.)

Live-work communities and cottage industry

Combining living and working spaces is a village trait carried on by craftsman and trade guilds of medieval Europe and earlier industrial America. Today, faxes and computers are enabling more technicians and professionals to work at home. The problem is that working at home in a typical single-family house, condo, or apartment can be both lonely without coworkers and have an intrusive impact on other family members, especially in small units. Having a home office, studio, or workshop in a Shared Living Community, however, offers affordability and a companionable place for livelihood. At the Winslow community on Bainbridge Island in Washington, nearly one-third of its members work at home at least part time. Many find their productivity increases just by knowing that people are nearby. As one member says, "[I value] the increased contact with kids and adults that can be mine when I step out of the door. It makes my workdays so much less isolating." [21]

The recycling of old industrial and warehouse buildings into live-work cooperatives, offices, and mixed-use developments serving artists and

Tom Levy, Photographer; San Francisco Chronicle

Transformation of Parking Lot to a Garden in Berkeley
University Avenue Housing, Inc. received approval from the City to dig up a 30 x 30 foot area of asphalt behind renovated permanent low-cost housing. Ecocity Builders and UA Housing members

craftspeople is now commonplace. This trend fosters a return to localized economies and self-employment. Uncertain employment in industrial and electronic fields due to the shifting economy, trade pacts, the exportation of factories, and layoffs due to automation may encourage more decentralized, small-scale community enterprises and employee-owned cooperatives to appear.

If the community objective is to provide a place for some or all of its members to earn their livelihood through cottage industry, home businesses, or full-scale retail businesses, find a residential block with existing properties that are or can be zoned for commercial use. Floors above store buildings can be used for business and professional offices, rented for income, or used for live-work places, as when merchants lived above their stores on the traditional American Main Street. Numerous present day Intentional Communities include a live-work economic base, such as the Ganas Community, Ananda Village, Alpha Farms, and Twin Oaks.

Urban Cooperative Block communities can develop affordable live-work spaces in several ways. The cost to upgrade older buildings to meet fire and safety standards is often prohibitive for those who need and want live-work studios. By starting with a smaller-scale residential UCB, building in stages, and pooling community resources, live-work units could be created. The financing leverage of the community-owned properties can provide construction materials and business equipment when needed. Be aware that some trades and light manufacturing businesses use toxic materials and/or require hazardous materials storage and disposal. Take care that home businesses do not violate zoning or fire and building safety ordinances, exceed

Community Residents Working at Home

sound levels for the residents in the vicinity, or affect the residential character of the surrounding neighborhood.

The object of live-work oriented urban communities is to keep capital circulating locally rather than having it drained off by external investors. UCB live-work enterprises could be financed through individual efforts, nonprofit/for-profit groups, or as a joint venture with a local Community Development Corporation, possibly assisted by the Community Empowerment Zone Enterprise proposed by the Clinton Administration. Large-scale sponsorship of live-work Urban Cooperative Blocks throughout older central cities would provide housing, livelihoods, and community, making a significant contribution towards rebuilding today's deteriorating socioeconomic structure. Giving old buildings new life is one of the ways Shared Living Communities can revitalize our cities, our suburbs, and our lives.

Apartment complexes can become sustainable communities

Existing urban multiple-family apartment complexes and buildings can be converted to cooperative communities by residents or nonprofit housing organizations. Some people use tenancy-in-common, condominium, or cooperative ownership methods merely to cut mortgage costs. Although saving money is an important benefit, we are also interested in helping people to form extended

family and community structures that include shared meals, common amenities, energy-efficient design, and participatory co-owner management.

Cooperatively owned buildings can be both socially responsible and ecologically sustainable community enterprises, and neighborhood stabilizers once they are organized. (See Chapter Nine for innovative financing ideas.)

Apartment and condo buildings originally designed for maximum separation of people can be redesigned into an environment that encourages group interaction and shared living. Here is an example of how multiple-family buildings can be converted to urban Shared Living Communities, and have ecological community without the commute.

"Suburbanization cannot simply be reduced. But suburbs are the most vulnerable to any future oil shortages or restraints on auto use that may be taken to curb pollution. If these communities are to enhance their future viability, they need to become self-contained — that is, to evolve into subcenters that are less urban in character than traditional cities, but more compact than they currently are." [22]
— *Michael Renner*

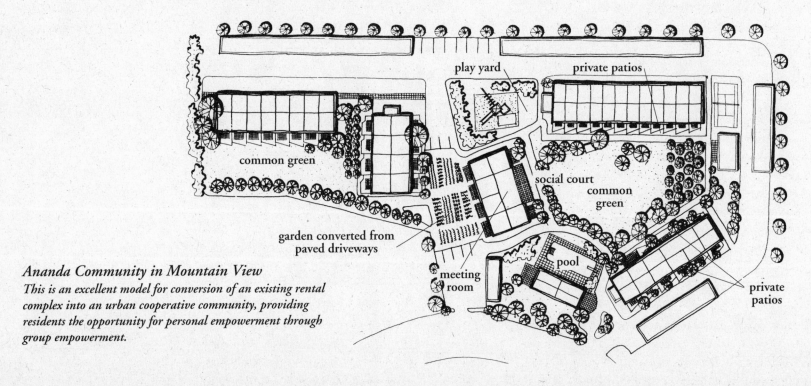

Ananda Community in Mountain View
This is an excellent model for conversion of an existing rental complex into an urban cooperative community, providing residents the opportunity for personal empowerment through group empowerment.

Ananda Village apartment communities

The parent Ananda Village community in California's lower Sierra Nevada Mountains has spawned several urban Intentional Communities in apartment complexes. In Mountain View, CA, Ananda converted what was a poorly maintained 1960's garden apartment complex of 72 units on $5 \frac{1}{2}$ acres to a successful spiritual cooperative community for their San Francisco Bay Area members. Ananda has sponsored similar urban communities in Seattle, WA with 32 units, and in Sacramento, CA with 48 units.

All were founded by Ananda members, and are owned by investment partnerships that include Ananda members. The partnership leases to each local Ananda community, which in turn leases to the community members. Original tenants were gradually replaced with Ananda members through attrition and an organized relocation program. Some member-investors also live there. Member participation and mutual help maximize affordability through reduced costs of operation.

This community is based on the cooperative community precepts taught by Donald Walters, the founder of the Ananda community. Five dinners per week are shared by approximately 30 adults. Though shared meals are optional, community members find them to be a "strong bonding force."

True to the principles of Shared Living Community, Ananda's social and spiritual practices are integrated with the physical design. Some ground-floor apartments have been converted to meeting and dining rooms, a meditation room, a childcare room, and an office. Bedrooms over these activity rooms are rented to single persons. Remodeling included adding small private front yard courts to

Mariel Hernandez, Ananda Community

Parking Lots to Gardens
At the Ananda Community, members agreed to abandon a section of paved roadway and give up some driving convenience for the benefit of having more garden space — a sign of the times.

most units which serve as a privacy buffer and a pleasing transition to the large common green. They have also built an outdoor dining court next to the dining room, and converted a long section of paved driveway into a lush and fertile community garden that provides produce for common use. Members are paid to take care of the commons, play yard, swimming pool, and gardens, although much work is also done as a contribution to the community.

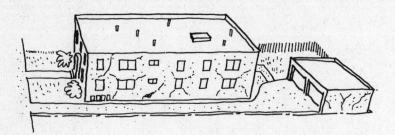

An Older Rental Apartment Building
A common feature of inner cities and older suburbs is rental properties that are absentee-owned and poorly maintained. The people who live in them often would love to have the opportunity to become co-owners and to work on improving their living environment.

Converting an Apartment Building into an Ecologically Sustainable Cooperative Community
Imagine that the moderate- to low-income tenants of this building of eight one-bedroom units have decided to co-buy it and create a Limited Equity Housing Cooperative, possibly under the legal and financial umbrella of a Mutual Housing Association or Community Land Trust. This building originally housed 10 adults and three children, with eight cars. As a community, they could have 18 adults, including six seniors, and eight children. They share a community-owned van/bus, three cars, and 20 bicycles. They redesigned the building to create one large two-story group house with 12 private suites, some shared and some private bathrooms, an enlarged common kitchen and dining/family room, a TV room, an exercise room, a children's play and crafts room, and a computer room and office. The roof has been raised to form loft spaces for the second-floor private suites. They added a roof deck with a shade trellis and hot tub. A passive solar greenhouse, added on to the south side of the building, will provide them with vegetables year-round. They also added a second story to the original garage to make space for workrooms and offices for home businesses. Everyone has access to the laundry room, workshop, and tool room located on one side of the garage. Thousands of resident groups could establish cooperative ecological communities like this with the support of enlightened nonprofit sponsors, lenders, and government agencies.

Doyle Street CoHousing, Emeryville, CA

Here is a perfect example of how old industrial buildings can be transformed into vital urban communities. From 1990 to 1992 an obsolete 7,700 sq. ft. industrial building was converted into a CoHousing community of 12 units (720 to 1,500 sq. ft. each) and 2,200 sq. ft. of common space. Like all other CoHousing communities, it began with a small core group several years before move-in time. A developer was brought in to acquire the property, arrange financing, and handle the development process. The CoHousing Company, the architect William Olin, and the dedicated but always evolving core group of city dwellers participated in the arduous project, making decisions by consensus — an involvement that most developers are not used to, and tend to avoid. Today there are families, single parents, and single people with a mix of ages and incomes living in this urban Intentional Community.

The building was gutted and redesigned with private units ranging in size from 780 to 1,600 sq. ft., with a 2,100 sq. ft. of common spaces: a large dining room, well-equipped kitchen, children's playroom, workshop, bicycle parking area, storage room, outside decks, patios, and hot tub. They share three to four evening meals together each week; members rotate cooking about once a month. Kathryn McCamant and Charles Durrett, the authors of *CoHousing,* also live in this community.

"As a warehouse conversion, the Doyle Street development adds to the diversity and life of the neighborhood. The location — in a transitional neighborhood of residences and light industry — provides round-the-clock activity which is a sure deterrent to crime. The intergenerational community benefits everyone. By directly speaking to the desires of its residents to create a community in which they feel secure, the Emeryville project faces the pressing question of how to create a comfortable and safe urban home for those who have most to fear in the city — women, children, and seniors." [23]

— Kathryn McCamant, Charles Durrett, & Ellen Hertzman

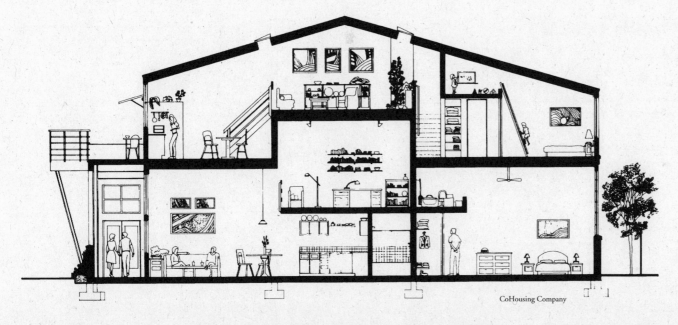

CoHousing Company

Cross Section through the Doyle Street CoHousing Project

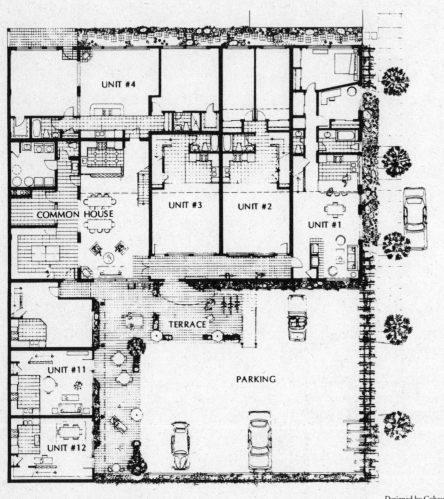

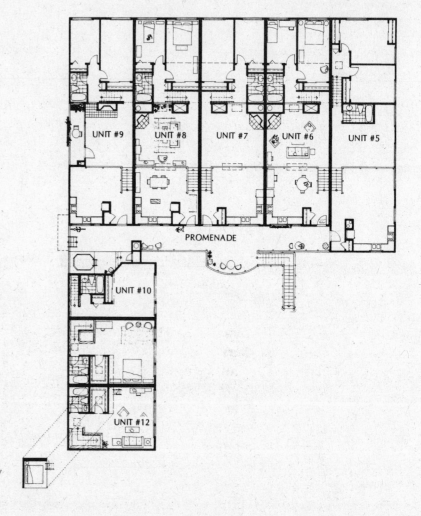

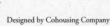
Designed by Cohousing Company

Floor Plans of Doyle Street CoHousing
Conversion of a 7700 sq. ft. industrial building into a two-story
residential community.

Here they describe an evening dinner in the common house:

> The meal is delicious, a Hungarian stew from a recipe of Joani's grandmother. At dinner, the upcoming local election is the primary topic of conversation. The common house telephone rings; it's Chris saying she'll be home late and could someone please save her something to eat.

By 9:30, dinner has been over for some time. Gary and Joani are finishing up the dishes. They won't have to cook and clean again for another month. A few people are still drinking coffee and chatting in the dining room. Judy is back at her magazine; she could take it home to read but she prefers the swirl of life in the common house. Chris dashes in to grab dinner, then heads home for a late night of desk work. The little ones have reluctantly been persuaded to leave the children's room and go home to bed. These individuals, who didn't know each other two years earlier, have become a community. [24]

The Transformation into CoHousing
This example expresses the benefits of community in the city. In the immediate area are numerous mixed-use, convenience, retail, and cultural facilities, including a park and community garden. There is also convenient access to the attractions of downtown Berkeley and San Francisco and the bicycle and running paths of the Emeryville Marina.

Photo by CoHousing Company.

The Industrial Building Before Conversion

Photo by CoHousing Company.

199

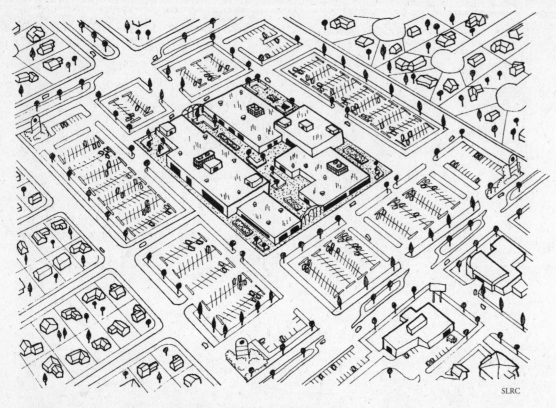

SLRC

Elements of a Typical Suburban Shopping Mall
Shopping malls are typically built on 40 to 100 acres, with most of the site used for paved parking lots. They are accessible only by car and sometimes by bus and have little or no pedestrian connections to surrounding businesses and residential neighborhoods. The merchandise is limited to the goods sold by large chain stores and costly franchised retail specialty shops and food outlets, with few to no competitors. Some include theaters and personal services, but there are virtually no offices and absolutely no residential space

Recycling Surplus Shopping Centers

A big surprise to many people today is that older, and even some recently built, regional shopping centers and smaller local centers across the country are becoming vacant and being torn down. Department stores are being replaced by chains of warehouse outlets, "shopping clubs," and TV shopping

channels. Some old centers are being converted to warehousing or industrial parks; others are being demolished in order to build single-family housing or apartment/condominium complexes. As car trip generators, malls were bad, but in most cases the reincarnations are not any better. How much healthier it would be to transform these centers into sustainable communities.

An attempt to create a new town from an old mall seems to be working at Mashpee Commons in Cape Cod, MA.[25] A 1960's shopping mall of 65,000 sq. ft. is being transformed into 150,000 sq. ft. town with small stores fronting on a classic downtown street, complete with curb parking, sidewalk benches, and street lights. The Fields Point Development Company added a church and a library to the development, and 24 senior apartments were built immediately adjacent to this new "downtown." Additional mixed-density housing, public greens, and residential units over retail shops are planned. Although the designers, Elizabeth Plater-Zyberg and Andres Duany, speak of serving this and other such redesigned centers with rail transit, the actual developments are most often designed with conventional streets, individual garages and driveways, and separate houses with their own large kitchens, all of which encourage car dependency.

Converting an old shopping center into an ecologically sustainable Eco Village is what we propose in the following prototype. We propose converting these old centers into co-owned, cooperatively managed, ecologically sustainable, mass-transit-fed Eco Villages that are virtually car-free. Failed shopping centers could become hubs of cooperatively owned community enterprises, drawing upon venture capital, tax credits, and loans from a Community Development Bank, possibly under the umbrella of a nonprofit Community Development Corporation. These new multipurpose Eco Village community centers could be locally and cooperatively owned and managed by an association composed of a residential council, live-work council, office and retail council, and a garden council, all made up of residents, co-owners, and business and trades people.

An example of a community-based multi-service center is the "Generations Center" pioneered by the Kentucky River Foothills Development Council in Clark County.[26] It provides services and facilities for seniors, Head Start, self-help home repair and weatherizing, job training, meals, and family and community social events. It was partially financed by Community Development Block Grant funds,

More Cities Abandon Old Shopping Centers

By John King

MALLS: Developers Eye Old Shopping Centers for Demolition

BLOWING THE LID OFF THE MALL

Before The New Seabury Shopping Ce... by the Fields Point development company.

SLRC

and other local and governmental funds. This is a model for a Community Empowerment Zone on a larger scale in which multiple social services can be incorporated into community centers, together with live-work and craft shops, performing arts theaters, entertainment, restaurants, local shops, farmers' markets, meeting halls, and business offices.

Conclusion

In these kinds of multipurpose Eco Village places human communication is fostered; many stories are passed around, and there are many people with whom to connect and share stories. Be aware that the culture and the stories wither and die when places for person-to-person communication disappear. This kind of exchange is not found on the freeway, at work, or in front of the TV. It is

---

The Trade
By Gary Snyder

I found myself inside a massive concrete shell lit by glass tubes, with air pumped in, with levels joined by moving stairs.

It was full of the things that were bought and made in the twentieth century. Laid out in trays or shelves

The throngs of people of that century, in their style, clinging garb made on machines,

Were trading all their precious time for things. [27]

"'But are shopping malls really so evil?' Mr. Storrs (Mashpee Commons developer) maintains that they are. 'Children are a pervasive force in the growth of our communities right now,' he said. 'And we don't want to see them going to the suburban mall and living within the four walls of a car. I think it's the responsibility of everyone to open the front door, get out in the yard, take a walk down the street and get involved.'" [28]

— *Barbara Flanagan,*
"A Massachusetts Mall Is Just Disappeared"

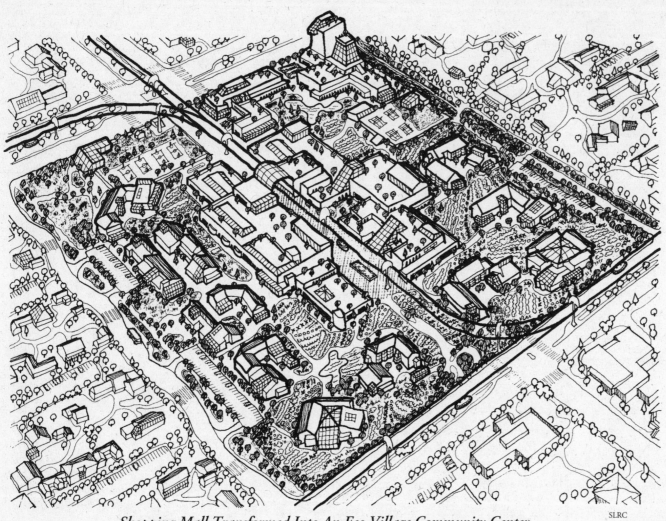

The transit system shown is based on the Suspended Light Rail Transit (SLRT) technology developed by The Transyt Canada Inc., founded by Lyman Richardson, Ontario, Canada.

SLRC

Shopping Mall Transformed Into An Eco Village Community Center

- *A Suspended Light Rail Transit (SLRT) system runs through the new, relatively car-free, community center. It rides over a pedestrian-only "main street" (the old mall) and connects with other centers, the city, the airports, and high-speed rail lines.*
- *Former department stores and retail spaces are converted into smaller, locally owned shops and services, live-work spaces, recreational facilities, theaters, galleries, and entertainment places.*

- *1,500 to 2,000 residents can live in Village Cluster/ CoHousing and group house communities on what were parking lots and roofs. There is a reduced need for parking because of the accessibility to the transit system, local live-work jobs, and shopping, and the self-reliant extended family/village housing.*
- *Office buildings in the upper middle corner provide pedestrian- and transit-accessible workplaces with very few parking spaces required.*

- *Excess parking lots are recycled into gardens, orchards, tree groves, recreation fields and courts, and meandering walking and bike paths.*
- *Such recycled shopping centers would mark the end of suburbia and become new Eco Villages. They would be lively places, with courts and decks for social, cultural, and community interaction for those who work and live there. These centers are sustainable due to local ownership and self management.*

SLRC

From a Car-fed Mall to a Transit-fed Community Common Court

What was once a magnet for consumers is turned into a mixed-use Eco Village transit node where several thousand people live, work, and play in a self-reliant, democratically managed community. Community-managed shops, cafés, social services, theaters, and restaurants cluster on the pedestrian-only common court around the transit stop — the old suburban cocoon is transformed into a new, ecologically sustainable urban form.

The lively heart of this Eco Village includes most of the essential components which will enable this new type of community center to become socially, economically, culturally, and ecologically integrated and therefore sustainable. In this sketch you will find some of these amenities and services:

- *Solar greenhouse flower shop*
- *Bicycle sales, rental, and repair shop*
- *Continuous farmers' market supplied by organic farmers on the Green Belt*
- *Restaurant, outdoor dining*
- *Suspended Light Rail Transit system, with frequently scheduled stops*

- *Live-work units added to roofs of existing buildings*
- *Rooftop community gardens and starter plant greenhouses*
- *Offices for small businesses, nonprofits, and special services*
- *Residential units over retail stores*
- *library*

not found in overpriced cafés and shopping malls, or during the mealtimes of single persons alone, or single parents and small nuclear families isolated from their elders and neighbors. By starting at the dinner tables and in the backyards of Shared Living Communities, we can create new extended families and Eco Villages and begin to rebuild our cities.

We have attempted to convey a serious message about today's social and environmental situation. No technology, no amount of capital expense, and no design concept alone can restore our loss of community. Direct, personal, face-to-face communication is needed, in common places that we know will always be there. Extended family meal times, shared backyards, work parties, and neighborhood childcare are sure means of raising communication to a level that can sustain community. Several more steps are taken when we create courts, plazas, walking and bike ways, and other shared facilities in the neighborhood and near the Eco Village transit station. The root source of a healthy urban culture lies in cooperation and communication, cultivated in the place where one stays. On a sufficiently large scale, these communities will enrich the marketplace and revitalize the city.

Notes
Books listed only by name in the endnotes are highlighted in the resource guide at the end of the book, complete with author/publisher information and description.

1 In the Company of Others, p. 252.
2 Professor Sherman Lewis, "The Evolution of Modern American Neighborhoods," *Neighborhood Systems: A Quarterly Journal of the Neighborhood Systems Association*, Vol. 1, No. 4, May 1987, p. 27.
3 Blake Hallanan, "White City Living? —Reasons: No Commute, Cultural Diversity, Night Life", *Oakland Tribune*, April 5, 1992, Section E.
4 Laura Hagar, "Aargh, Wilderness — In which two city slickers lose their money and their minds in search of rural paradise," *East Bay Express*, October 29, 1993, p. 9.
5 In the Company of Others, p. 17.
6 David Dillion, "Fortress America," reprinted with permission *Planning*, copyright, June 1994 by the American Planning Association, 1313 E. 60th St., Chicago, Ill. 60637, p. 8
7 Marcia D. Lowe, "Reclaiming Cities For People," *World Watch*, July/August 1992, Vol.6 No. 4, p. 20.
8 "Rise in Real-life Violence Follows TV Exposure: New Statistical Evidence," *Americans for Responsible Television Newsletter*, Spring 1991, p. 1.
9 *Ibid*.
10 David and Vera Mace, Marriage: East and West, Dophin Books, Garden City, NY, 1960, p. 56.
11 Reprinted from A JOYFUL PATH: Community, Transformation, and Peace, by Thich Nhat Hanh and friends (1994) with permission of Parallax Press, Berkeley, California.
12 Michael Renner, Worldwatch Paper 84: Rethinking the Role of the Automobile, Worldwatch Institute, Washington D.C., 1988, p. 6.
13 Michael Schafer and Stephen Wheeler, "Ecological Transportation," *The Urban Ecologist*, Summer 1993, p. 1.
14 Michael Schafer and Stephen Wheeler, "Ecological Transportation," *The Urban Ecologist*, Summer 1993, p. 1.
15 In the Company of Others, p. 17.
16 Chandler Washburne, Ph.D., CSUF, from an interview with Ken Norwood in 1991.
17 Jane Jacobs, The Death and Life of Great American Cities, Vintage Books, New York, 1961, pp. 220-221.
18 Kevin Wolf, "Suburban Permaculture," *Permaculture Activist*, November 1990, p. 31.

[19] Bob O'Brien, "Colorful Victorians Transform the Neighborhood," *CoHousing,* Fall 1993, Vol. 6, No. 3, p. 6.
[20] Jane Jacobs, *Op. Cit.*, pp. 194-195.

[21] <u>CoHousing</u>, p. 238.
[22] Michael Renner, *Op. Cit.*, p. 52.
[23] <u>CoHousing</u>.
[24] *Ibid.*
[25] Barbara Flanagan, "A Massachusetts Mall Is Just Disappeared,"
New York Times, March 14, 1991.
[26] "CDBG Funds Used to Construct 'Generations Center' in
Kentucky," *Targeting Times,* Fall 1993, Vol.4, No. 4, p. 7.
[27] Gary Snyder, <u>No Nature</u>, Pantheon Books, New York, 1992,
p. 191.
[28] Barbara Flanagan, *Op. Cit.*

DESIGNING for GROUP LIVING
Private Places and Common Spaces

*"When people work together for a common cause,
one man does not deprive the other of space;
rather he increases it for his colleague by giving
him support"* [1]

— *Yi-Fu Tuan,
Space and Place*

CHAPTER SEVEN

Sacred Places

Let us each have a place where we live that is free from the stormy and trivial forces of everyday life. Free from electricity, machines, media, symbolism, economics, and pride – free from the flux of comings and goings that fill our lives – free from the questions, empty words and concepts that make and fill our places and minds.

Let it grow sound, built of the materials of nature and by the hand of man. Let it speak of what we love and are. Let it become filled with the tranquility and serenity of a peaceful heart.

Let it become sacred to our lives to spend time there, free from the noise of culture and power, growing close again to our roots and the nourishment which bonds us to all else, able once again to hear the subtle and quiet voices that speak of deeper and forgotten things. Let that place be sacred, for it is so – a manifestation of those things that lie beneath and before the visible outwashings we call our world. [2]

— Tom Bender,
Environmental Design Primer

Co-own a Mansion
—and have more for less

There are many exciting ways to rebuild community in America. In Chapter Six we presented variations of the Village Cluster/CoHousing models, ranging from clusters of existing single-family houses, to redesigned apartment buildings and complexes, to live-work block communities of mixed-use retail and residential, to the conversion of regional shopping malls into multi-service Eco Village community centers. The common denominator among all these community forms is that the resident members are also the founders and participants throughout the development process, with the living environment designed by them for shared meals, social interaction, livelihood, and ecological living. The universality of values, purposes, needs, and ideals represented in the community movement reflects humankind's heritage of extended family and village living.

In this chapter, we show how group houses, the Group Home, and other variations of shared living households are becoming a popular and easy way to satisfy the growing numbers of people interested in the new extended family. We will examine the relationship of physical design to the personal issues of privacy, intimacy, and community in group living situations. The following dialogue introduces the first of several prototype models of new and/or redesigned group houses to be presented in this chapter.

We would like you to meet the Bay Street Community core group Paul, Barbara, Stephanie, James, Brennan, Alice, and Joan. This story imagines how a group of seven people could form an extended family group house near a new light rail transit station in an older, built-up neighborhood of a San Francisco Bay Area city.

The people
Paul, 42, Barbara, 39, and Stephanie, their 11-year-old daughter, moved to the Bay Area from a small city in Missouri. They had planned to live for only a few months in the apartment of James, their long-time friend. They quickly discovered that the equity from their house in Missouri would barely buy them a small two-bedroom condo in a remote suburb, and a long commute.

When Paul and Barbara realized that buying a house was going to take years, they and James co-rented a three-bedroom house on Bay Street with an option to buy. James was tired of living alone and could not afford large mortgage payments on his salary. Now he had house mates with whom to share stories, meals, and bills. However, the group soon found that they got on each others nerves. The house was not designed for community living, and they never seemed to have enough private space to themselves. They wanted to live together, but this was not working. They liked the large backyard, and the location was close to schools, shops, and the new transit station. They began to think about buying the house and redesigning it to make living together more workable.

Now let's meet the other participants. Brennan, age 28, a part-time carpenter, and Alice, age 26, a recent nursing school graduate, wanted to start a

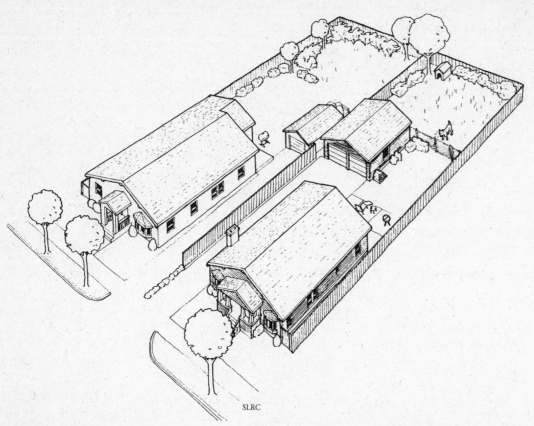

SLRC

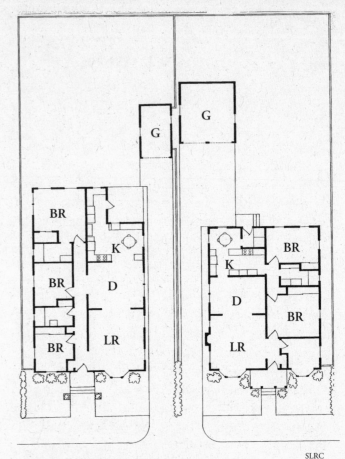

SLRC

Two Existing Older Houses
Many older neighborhoods include houses that often become rental properties. Low and moderate income people usually can not qualify for loans because of income limitations, or the redlining (discrimination in lending) of the area they want to buy into.

family in a few years. They were trying to save money for a downpayment on a house, and had begun looking for something that met their needs. With nursing school debts, they realized it would be years before they could afford a house in the city; even a fixer-upper was out of their reach.

Joan, age 67, a recently widowed artist, had met Brennan and Alice about two years before when her husband was one of Alice's teachers. They became good friends and often shared dinners at each other's homes. After her husband's death, Alice had only a small monthly income, but considerable equity in her hillside house. She felt lonely in her house, which was too big for just her. She thought

Floor Plans of Two Existing Houses
Many older houses like these are too expensive for today's small households, yet the houses are too small and not properly laid out for the larger new extended family.

of moving, but that still meant eating and living alone. She loved to garden and dreaded the thought of being cooped up in an apartment. She was not ready for, nor did she want to live in a board and care or retirement community, but she knew that later on she would require some assistance in her daily life.

How the Bay Street Community formed

When James said he had heard about Community Endeavors (CE), a multi-service nonprofit that helped people set up urban Shared Living Communities, Paul, Barbara, and Stephanie responded enthusiastically. The community facilitator from CE introduced them to the city's Ecological Incentive Planning District (a new idea discussed in Chapter Nine) that encourages mixed-density infill housing in transit station neighborhoods. This was what they had been looking for. With the help of the CE facilitator, they posted notices announcing an introductory slide show for those who wanted to start a community. Brennan and Alice saw a notice and invited their friend Joan to go with them. On the night of the presentation, Brennan, Alice and Joan met James, Paul, Barbara and Stephanie. The seven of them decided to do the Profile Consultation process (described in Chapter Three), and arranged to meet again.

Shortly after, they all committed to becoming a core group, and began to meet regularly. They learned that the house next door on Bay Street was going up for sale. Since the group liked the location, they decided to try to buy both houses and remodel them into one large group house. The strategy was for Joan to sell her house in the hills, and to co-purchase the adjacent house with Brennan and Alice, while James, Paul, and Barbara exercised their option to buy the house they were renting.

The CE facilitators provided training to the group on shared living, cooperative ownership and management, and how to form a Limited Equity Housing Cooperative (LEHC). Under the financing umbrella of a Community Land Trust, the

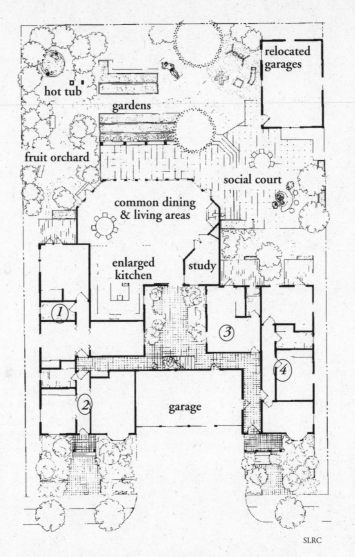

SLRC

group would be able to qualify for low-interest loans for the purchase and for the self-help construction. They were required to meet specific ecological incentive criteria including mixed-income, permanent affordability (a LEHC has resale price limits), increased density, intergenerational composition, energy conservation,

Two Existing Houses Converted into a Group House

The two existing one-story houses now consist of four living suites, each with its own bathroom. One kitchen is enlarged and redesigned, and an entirely new common room hass been added to the rear, for dining, social activities, and study.

The two backyards have been opened up and designed for various special-use areas including a quiet, secluded tree grove, a hot tub retreat corner, a lawn, a raised garden area, children's play yard and a social court.

The garages have been moved together and converted into a childrens play room and storage area. The living room of one house has been cut off and used for part of the four-car garage. The upstairs addition adds another three living suites, for a total of 23 rooms for the large new extended family who will live here.

Private living suites 1,2,3,4, on the ground floor and the three suites upstairs all have private bathrooms, separate entrances, and range in size from one to three rooms each.

Transformation into a Magnificent Group House
The front of the house retains the design features of the original two houses, with the second-floor addition carrying out the same architectural details for compatibility with the neighborhood character.

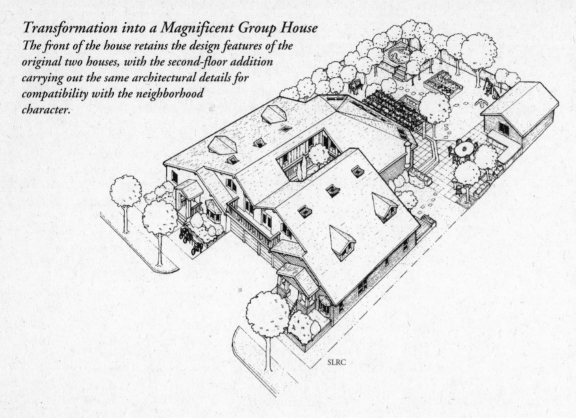

SLRC

Section Through the New Group House
The space between the original houses is filled by a two-story addition, with a new roof line and gable windows over the added loft spaces. Old foundations are underpoured to support the new second floor.

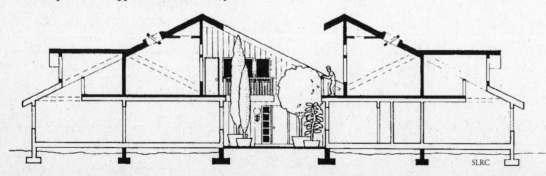

SLRC

and a Transportation Management Program to reduce car trips. (Innovative techniques for implementing both available and new ideas, programs, and processes, are presented in Chapter Nine.)

While they worked out the details of the financing and the plans to rebuild the two houses, Brennan, Alice, and Joan moved into the house next door. They worked with Melissa, the staff architect from CE who was familiar with extended family group house design and self-help construction processes. Melissa helped them clarify their goals and design criteria at a weekend design workshop. They planned abundant common spaces and shared amenities, and private living suites for each individual and family household.

An after-dinner conversation with the Bay Street group
A few weeks after Brennan, Alice, and Joan moved into the house next door, the group sat around the table after dinner, eating peach cobbler while discussing design ideas. Melissa, the architect from CE, had drawn up floor plans based on sketches the group made at the design workshop the weekend before.

"This new living room looks great," offered Paul, coffee cup in hand as he gestured over the plans. *"And this little room at the front of our living suite will make a great office for my counseling practice. We could even add another door from the porch, so my clients won't have to trip over Steph's roller-blades in the hallway."*

Barbara nodded. *"Also, Steph might want a bigger room farther away from us when she starts high school, so when we finish the upstairs, maybe Steph could have one of those rooms."*

Stephanie leaned forward to add her ideas. *"What I really want is a separate entrance, so when I'm older I can come home any time I want."*

Barbara, smiling at Steph, said, *"Thank you, dear. I appreciate your up-front input. Planning for private access to your room needs to go on the design agenda. I've been crunching these numbers, "* she continued, holding up some papers. *"I just received the financial feasibility study from CE, and it says that with only six of us as income earners, the payments are going to be high. So maybe we should plan to complete the second floor and then bring in additional members. We could finish it off as a self-help project. Let's start holding introductory potluck suppers now, so there'll be time to choose new members before we begin the construction process. It's important for everyone to be involved."*

Brennan nodded, *"I agree, we'll need new members. The remodeling will take a long time if we do the work ourselves, but it's worth it if we can really cut our monthly payments."* He looked around for reactions. *"C'mon, you guys! I've worked as a carpenter for 10 years, I can be the foreman and teach you all what to do."*

"He's right. We'll save a lot of money if we do the work ourselves," said James, more seriously. *"And I've always wanted to learn how to build."*

"I don't know how much help I'll be during construction," Joan said, looking doubtful, *"but I'll gladly take charge of calling in orders and paying material bills. Maybe Stephanie can help me."*

An enthusiastic nod and smile radiated from Stephanie, who replied, *"Yeah, but I want to do carpentry too."*

Barbara spoke. *"Joan's offer, and Stephanie's, are really important. We'll also save a lot of money on food*

bills by growing our own food, buying in bulk, and cooking our dinners together. But none of this can happen unless we get the special incentive loan for the rebuilding, which means we need to figure out our Transportation Management Plan. So, why don't we work on that for awhile?"

James spoke up. *"Okay, you-all, I've got some ideas for this TMP thing. We're projecting an ultimate group house of eight living suites, or about 10 to 14 people. We have six drivers in the house right now, and more to come. We're showing parking for only four cars in the new garage, plus the two spaces left at the curb, so we get credit for six cars total. That's the maximum we can have to qualify for the special ecological incentive loan. We've got to come up with transportation alternatives for the future number of people who'll be living here."* He paused to let that sink in, and then volunteered his personal solution. *"I can ride my bike or take the train most of the time, but I'll still need a car for client visits on Thursdays."*

"I can get picked up by the hospital shuttle most of the time," offered Alice. *"We could work out a deal to share our car with you, provided my White Knight over here will agree."* She nodded at Brennan, who was apparently absorbed in his peach cobbler. She cleared her throat loudly.

"Huh?" Brennan looked up. *"Oh yeah, sure thing. But if we're going to keep one car between us, why dont we keep James'? His convertible is so much zippier than our clunky little wagon."*

"I don't think the gas-gulping convertible or the little wagon are practical," Joan replied slowly. *"I'd like to sell my car. I only use it for grocery shopping anyway. Paul and Barbara also have a small car. Why don't we trade in two cars for a van-bus? It could double as our construction vehicle."*

Paul said, *"That's a great idea, Joan, but for now we can all get by with just our compact, and we'll all save on insurance costs. Let's see, Steph takes the school bus, and she can ride her bike to soccer practice. I can take the train to work at the agency. I'll be working at home more anyway with the computer system. Barbara, what about you?"*

"We chose this neighborhood because it was so close to everything— stores, the library, parks, and the transit station," Barbara reminded him. *"There's a transit station four blocks from my office in Berkeley. My company doesn't reimburse parking costs for part-time workers, so I can't afford to use a car anyhow."* She smiled. *"Since we'll be rotating our shopping, bulk food buying, and recycling trips, we've just gotten rid of two of our cars. That leaves two garage spaces for newcomers. Getting new members should be on the agenda for the next meeting."*

Joan broke in with a big smile. *"There's still one piece of peach cobbler in the kitchen."* Brennan, James, and Stephanie looked at each other and bolted for the kitchen. The meeting was over.

In the 2-1/2 years following that meeting the Bay Street Community completed remodeling, planted a flourishing vegetable garden, began work on a children's play area for Brennan and Alice's baby, Lisa, and welcomed five new housemates and only two cars into their community. The story of this fictional group exemplifies the possibilities for a typical new extended family, and how it can build a community around existing public transit stations.

This story and the proposed house design also raise critical issues familiar to communities and extended family groups of all kinds— the issues of privacy, community interaction, and personal space. These are especially important in American communities, since Americans have such strong feelings about privacy and personal space. To be successful, a community must address these issues intentionally. Two tribes in West Africa can serve as primary models for how to design for living cooperatively and intimately with others, while allowing for abundant personal space.

Hierarchy of Space in African Villages

In earlier chapters we have shown villages and communities from various cultures around the world. A closer look at the Igbo and Gurunsi tribes of West Africa yields important insights into the relationship of private living places to shared common areas and transition spaces or buffer zones.

The Igbo and Gurunsi tribes, among others, built their society around many principles, one of which was hierarchical spatial structure. In these village cultures, there is a discernible hierarchy of space from private to semi-private to semi-public to public, giving people the freedom to choose how and when they wish to be alone, to be intimate with another, to have contact with a small group, or to interact with the larger community.

The Igbo

The Igbo[3] people of eastern Nigeria manage to ensure personal privacy and identity while maintaining a strong sense of community and cohesion because their building form and layout directly reflect their social structure and values.

The Igbo first settled in the forest along the east bank of the Niger River in 3000 B.C. With time they became a settled, agricultural people. Village groups formed to share land, goods, and customs.

Rituals, title-making societies, and peer groups were established, as well as a local system of trade. Skilled artists and craftspeople emerged and, over time, villages evolved into cohesive bodies with sophisticated social, political, and cultural institutions that have been sustained to this day.

• The Igbo house

The importance of privacy is evident in the definition of space. The land each household occupies is held in common, but generally each adult has their own house. Most houses have a veranda for communal activities such as cooking and gathering. The interior space consists of one or two rooms and is completely private; sleep, private meetings, and personal reflection occur within this sanctuary. It is a sacred place to the individual, and the community respects this by entering a house only when invited.

• The family compound

Individual dwellings and communal structures such as granaries and animal pens are organized around a shared earthen court in which cooking, religious rituals, washing, and craftwork all take place.

• The nchi

Several family compounds organize to form a nchi or hamlet which shares a common market/meeting place. Within this larger context, each family is still an autonomous unit, but interacts socially and economically.

•The village and village group

From the nchi market place, a wide path leads to a larger gathering place shared by several nchis which form a village. From here, another path leads to a still larger gathering space which is the marketplace for a number of villages that form a village group. A central market is held every eight days, but the real importance of this space is its use as a public

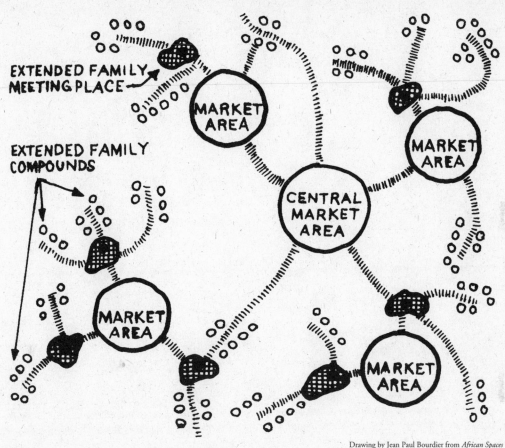

IGBO (IBO) VILLAGES

EXTENDED FAMILY MEETING PLACE

EXTENDED FAMILY COMPOUNDS

MARKET AREA

MARKET AREA

CENTRAL MARKET AREA

MARKET AREA

MARKET AREA

MARKET AREA

Drawing by Jean Paul Bourdier from *African Spaces*

Igbo Village Group
This plan identifies the major components of the Igbo village group:: the house, the family compound, the nchi, and the village and shows how these elements are connected to reflect the Igbo's concern for cooperation, community, and privacy.

square, playground, religious center, and meeting place. A village group has relations with other village groups, but is itself the largest cohesive entity. This heritage of village community is there available for us to use for the most sustainable pattern for modern day living — the Eco Village and Eco City.

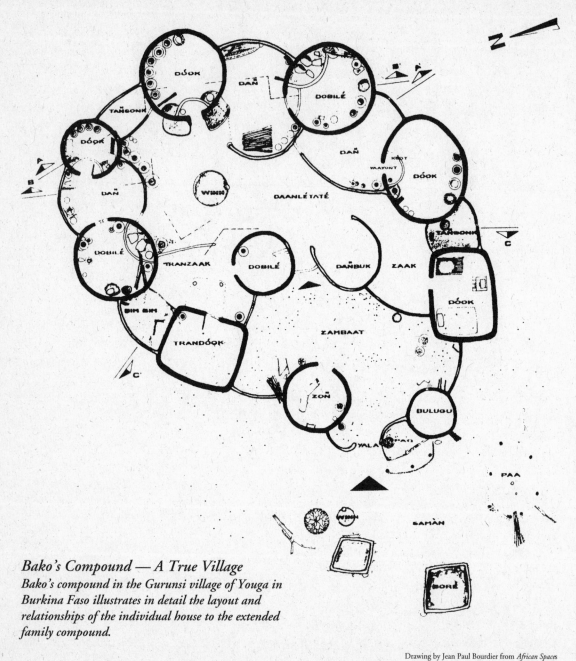

Bako's Compound — A True Village
Bako's compound in the Gurunsi village of Youga in Burkina Faso illustrates in detail the layout and relationships of the individual house to the extended family compound.

Drawing by Jean Paul Bourdier from *African Spaces*

The Gurunsi

The Gurunsi people of Burkina Faso, like the Igbo, place a value on privacy and community interaction. The structure of their extended family compounds makes the balance possible. The family compound is surrounded and protected by earthen wall, and one enters through an opening to the west. The first court, called the zambaat or cattle kraal, also contains a chicken house or bulugu, a sitting area, and the zo¨n or goat and sheep pen, and is an important transitional space where gatherings and rites of passage take place. From the Zambaat, one enters the daanlétaté or main family court where there is a shrine and outdoor cooking and gathering areas. The private dwellings consist of a sleeping and storage area, the dóok; an indoor cooking area, the dobilé; and an outdoor private court, the da¨n. These private areas are protected by front porches or low walls which one must pass through or climb over to enter. As Jean Paul Bourdier and Trinh T. Minh-ha write, "The customs that have evolved around the compound entrance and the zo¨n, and the significance given to doorways and transitional spaces brings into play, with every particular situation, the sacredness of the living realms,"[4] and provides evidence of the close interaction between dwellings and dwellers.

Much about the lives of these West African villagers parallels the village experiences of historical and contemporary people throughout the world, as well as in the United States. The universal connection is the extended family and sharing meals. We have this to learn from the past as we look forward to the exciting challenge of designing housing that expresses the principles of village, as we rebuild community in America.

The Octagonal Cluster House

The Octagonal Cluster House was designed to serve as the prime prototype design of a group house for the new extended family. This innovative house layout was directly influenced by the study of traditional villages and large family houses in turn-of-the-century America. It can easily accommodate from eight to 18 persons, subject to the design of the private living suites, on a 125 ft. by 135 ft. lot (1/3 acre), providing a low to moderate density development. This house is designed to meet today's criteria for an ecologically sustainable lifestyle and also provide abundant private and common amenities to all the residents.

The compact design combines under one roof the village concept of hierarchy of space and the Village Cluster principles described in Chapter Four. Eight private living suites, each with its own deck, loft, closets, sink and small counter, are grouped around the solar court that serves as the semi-private transition space to the octagonally shaped common area. This common area includes a large central kitchen, dining and social areas, a wood-burning stove, a library, a laundry/workroom, a bathroom, a guest loft above, and a solar greenhouse for heating and indoor gardening. There are spacious outdoor decks, a hot tub and gardens. The solar collectors provide hot water, and photovoltaic panels generate electricity. These features, the organic gardens and orchards surrounding the house, and the cooperative sharing of resources by the community members give them the potential to be very self-reliant and almost completely energy self-sufficient. The stylized wind turbine on top of the common house is only a symbol of energy

Octagonal Cluster House
This is a new generation of large houses for the era of ecological living and the new extended family. This design includes passive solar heating, solar collectors for water heating, and photovoltaic solar panels for electrical power.

independence. In windy locations, a real wind generator would be placed away from the buildings, because of noise and electromagnetic energy fields.

The Octagonal Cluster House can be applied to many locations and siting layouts. For example, several Octagonal Cluster Houses could be located together to form an Eco Village of group houses around a transit center with live/work spaces, shops, offices, and apartments above.

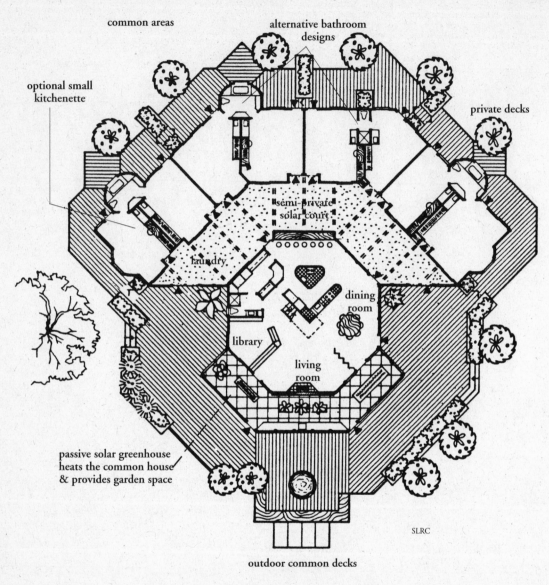

common areas

alternative bathroom
designs

optional small
kitchenette

private decks

semi-private
solar court

laundry

dining
room

library

living
room

passive solar greenhouse
heats the common house
& provides garden space

SLRC

outdoor common decks

A New Kind of House Plan

A commonly told tale of woe and a happy ending
Here are two contrasting scenarios that depict the differences between conventional and extended family lifestyles, and why the Octagonal Cluster House is ideal for the special needs of small families and singles who choose to form a community.

• Scenario one
Sarah, Ian, and Leonel are single persons living in separate apartments. David and Jen are single parents with one child each; they are also living alone. Joseph and Maria are married and are both employed. They have two children in day-care, and a large mortgage. All of these people commute an average of two hours a day, except Joseph and Maria, who have additional commutes to childcare. Every day these people return to their separate houses and apartments and put away the groceries, do the laundry, cooking, and housecleaning, and the parents try to find time for their children. They rarely pursue personal interests or socialize with friends, because by the time their errands and chores are finished, they are exhausted. This is not the American Dream that people are searching for — it is a familiar American reality.

One Place
There can be, will be, one place for home, family, and community, a place for dreams to come true, where hopes, needs, and desires can be fulfilled. A place for sharing lives, children, companionship, love, and the rituals that connect us to the land and each other. A special place created by cooperation, a family-village of interrelating beings, young and old, a safe place for children to grow. Call this place home as together we build a community.

Ken Norwood, 1991

SLRC

You Can Share a Mansion and Have More for Less.
This new kind of family room, with intimate conversation and play areas, also accommodates large gatherings. The passive solar greenhouse roof would be protected by insulated movable panels or rolling shades for both summer and winter conditions.

• Scenario two

These same women, men, and children are now living together in a new Octagonal Cluster House that they co-designed and built with the help of a nonprofit community facilitator/architect. Each individual and family has a comfortable private living suite, but for reasons of economy, every two suites share a large bathroom. They all share the common area and its many amenities, and enjoy a private deck outsde each suite that faces the common gardens and fruit trees. By sharing the costs and responsibilities of meals, chores, car pooling, and childcare, each person and family can enjoy abundant amenities, the luxury of their private

suite, and the joys and benefits of supportive friends. They will be able to greatly reduce use of energy, consume fewer products, and have more free time.

This moderate income group was able to accomplish their new group house by attending a series of community planning and cooperative living core group meetings. It was at one of these meetings that Ian proposed the concluding action plan: "Let's face it, this is going to be a tight squeeze. But wow! This Octagonal Cluster is so full of energy-saving designs, we could get tax credits and cost savings too. I propose we all move into one large house, rent our other houses until we get the

"Longer Commutes Force Parents to Make Tough Choices on Where to Leave the Kids, is an article from the Wall Street Journal which tells of a 70-mile commute/working parent/childcare saga: …her daily routine is a race against the clock. Ms. Bussey wakes up at 4 a.m. to get to Mrs. Robillard's house by 5:45 a.m. so she can get to work on time. Nicholas, now six, 'is still sleeping then, and I have to carry him in,' Ms. Bussey says, 'I have no back left from that.'"[5]
— Sue Shellenberger

219

"I need lots of private time and space. I love people and am very giving, but I suffer greatly if I don't balance that with time alone."
— From a letter to SLRC

"Homes should be built not to shut out reality, but to permit communication with reality on one's own terms. They could never seem homelike if they didn't grant the owners privacy as well."[6]
— J. Donald Walters, Ananda Community

common house built, and then move into that with temporary room partitions. Then we can co-build our private living suites, finish off our own interiors, and make our final move. At the same time, we'll save on living expenses, and be able to get rid of our extra cars. It'll be fun to get the hang of being a group, and we can still sponsor potluck suppers to attract other members."

"I Want My Privacy!"

Privacy is the issue raised most often by Americans who are considering some form of community. It is very important to understand the myths about privacy, where our feelings and attitudes come from, and what we do to "protect" our privacy. The issue of privacy can arise in a Shared Living Community even when the design for privacy has been carefully considered. For example, after a hard day, a community member may want to just come home and be alone, but could run into other members on the way to their own living space. In a group house or even in a Village Cluster, the perception of loss of privacy may be amplified. Therefore, very specific social and/or design methods must be exercised to assure that privacy and personal space are respected.

We all carry images in our heads of what privacy means. We create boundaries or limits between ourselves and other people, expanding and contracting them depending on whether we feel comfortable or threatened. What privacy means to any one person depends on many things, including childhood experiences, emotional maturity, cultural conditioning, and age. Young people, for example, often live together in a large house with lots of people around, because as they struggle to create

self-identity, they have a greater need to develop self-assurance and validation through their peers. As we age, we often tend to individualize more, losing the need for such close identification with peers, and preferring more private space. Communities that recognize this life change and are sensitive to different temperaments and needs tend to retain members more successfully.

Privacy for some means a separate bathroom, a suite of rooms, and a private entrance, while for others who see privacy as merely a closed door, sharing a bathroom may not be an issue. How to achieve ecological living and personal empowerment while maintaining agreed–upon levels of privacy, is a social organization and design challenge.

Boundaries related to cultural conditioning

People from various cultures use different behavioral patterns to create boundaries around themselves that are acknowledged by others. These signals regarding boundaries are formed by the individual and by the family or group through both verbal and non-verbal interaction, eventually becoming conditioned behavioral and cultural norms.

For example, Mexican people often stand much closer to each other and are more physically affectionate during conversations than Americans are, and Arab people do not think of spaces or rooms as being for just one person. They share spaces with all family members, seeking privacy not through spatial isolation like most Americans, but by being silent when they need time to themselves. Left alone, it is hard for an Arab to feel comfortable. According to an old Arab saying, "Paradise without people should not be entered because it is Hell."

Many Americans have come to feel that the only

way to ensure privacy in an increasingly invasive world is by living alone in separate, single-family units. This concept of defining privacy through physical isolation is a new one even for us. Until the 18th century, even upper-class European homes did not assign specific functions to rooms. Beds and tables were set up and taken down as the need arose. Strangers and family members alike moved freely through all the rooms, including those being used for sleeping —still true for much of the world.

When the practice of catering to the nuclear family as a consumer buying unit became dominant for the middle and upper class, the distinction of separate lots and separate houses divided into living and sleeping rooms and adult and childrens spaces divided society into private and public realms. Suburbs were laid out to codify these distinctions, and to create security and "individuality." Unfortunately isolation is also a result. When the front lawn is the only buffer between the private (the house) and the public (the street) realms, going outside puts people on display. The interaction is either all or nothing, leaving people feeling vulnerable and uncomfortable, which in turn forces them back inside. In the suburb, privacy means isolation, and community fades away like a forgotten dream.

Being with self is revitalizing

No matter the definition or the image, the need for privacy exists in all people. As Yi-Fu Tuan says in his book, *Space and Place,* "Privacy and solitude are necessary for sustained reflection and a hard look at self, and through the understanding of self to the full appreciation of other personalities."[7]

Without thoughtful social and spatial definitions, living, working, playing, and eating with the same people day after day can create "people-overload" and breed pettiness and frustration. In the book, *Community Group Homes: An Environmental Approach,* we are reminded that "people who have private places are more likely to interact frequently with others than are people without privacy," because the balance between private and communal spaces gives them an enhanced sense of self, control, and choice.[8] When there is assured privacy within a group, the sense of belonging is strengthened. What we have now in our society is privacy without group support, which translates into isolation or involuntary privacy and the breakdown of community.

The compulsion to follow a trend, a sales pitch, or a popularized practice, or to comply with a dominant belief system has led many people to a false sense of belonging. What people instinctively want is to be agreed with, to be validated, and to feel wanted. The consumption-oriented, media-based business systems of today understand how to appeal to people's need for self-esteem and their yearning to belong to a larger group through the satisfaction of possessing products. When advertisers cater to people in this way, people feel they are being included, and that they somehow belong to something. But this preoccupation with "things" has also led to disillusionment and community breakdown.

One of the main reasons people resist shared living arrangements is that they fear a loss of privacy, of power to make decisions for themselves, or a loss of refuge. In fact, as Charles Durrett and Kathryn McCamant explain in their book, *CoHousing,* many early CoHousing communities in Europe were reluctant to commit to large common

"Fears of groups also arise from a deeper source, the illusion that humans are separate by nature. Corollary to this is the belief that community is a social construct that people can choose or reject ... Newtonian physics, the description of reality that shaped European and American thinking for centuries, tells people that they, like all other particles of matter, are separate. Only in the last few decades have physicists, biologists, and systems thinkers discovered what mystics and ancient religious traditions have been telling people for millennia: everything is connected to and both influences and is influenced by everything else."[9]
— Carolyn R. Shaffer &
Kristin Anundsen

"It's been very important for us to take personal space when we need it — to nourish ourselves — otherwise we get burned out and we're of no use to anyone."[10]
— Linda Burnham, the Center of
the Light in Massachusetts

"A Randolph, Vermont resident eligible for Medicaid, had to choose between a nursing home or moving into a group shared residence. He was recovering from a fall, was confined to a wheelchair and was living alone. This man entered the shared residence and arranged for home health aides to attend to his personal needs. The annual cost for his home health services is $2,500 as compared to $30,730 in Medicaid costs for one year in a nursing home in Vermont. This is a direct savings of $28,230 in Medicaid dollars over one year."[11]
— Shared Housing News

Home is...

Home is where you go to warm your hands and feet, an escape to safety and security — a warm blanket on a cold night.

Home is eternal sunshine — energy recharging, spiritually renewing.

Home is stability, comfort, familiarity, and security. It is like a big sigh — a release of tension and grief, an inhaling of laughter and joy.

Home is sitting at the dining table with family or friends, and putting together a puzzle as a fire glows, giving warmth and light.

Home is cuddling up with a good friend and a warm cup of tea, sharing tales and laughter.

Home is more than a place. It is a feeling, an experience, a sense of community. Home is where you come after a hard day — smiles and hugs await you. You can drop your guard. You can say, do, feel anything, and be accepted for who you are. Everything flows and works together. You know your role, your responsibility, and your gift.

At home, things are exactly as they should be. The porch light on, the welcome mat out, the door unlocked ... we were waiting for you.

— Kathleen Smith

---

areas and common meals, especially at the expense of private living space and personal time. People generally felt that common meals would be nice once or twice a week, but not every day. Yet common meals have actually become the most popular part and the mainstay of most communities. With community experience, and time the common house has increased in size and importance, and in some CoHousing communities the private unit has shrunk to allow more extensive common facilities.[12] Having one's own space to gain a sense of self and control is as important as having the opportunity to share casual, unplanned contact with others. A well-designed Shared Living Community provides both.

Special issues for group houses and the new extended family

People tend to be attracted to the group house model of community because it presents a family structure and size that they can more easily relate to. It may arouse memories of an extended family environment from their childhood, or feelings about what is missing in their lives — a big family all under one roof, eating meals and lounging on the front porch together. Also, because of its family scale and adaptability, the group house model provides the easiest, quickest, and lowest-cost way to create a community. A group house can be built new as in the Octagonal Cluster House example, or redesigned from an existing house or houses as in the Bay Street group example. It can be built in the city or the country as a separate entity, arranged in a cluster with other units and group houses as in the Village Acre and Urban Cooperative Block examples, or created from units in a condo or apartment building. These models bring to the new extended family all the benefits and opportunities of ecological living and emotional support that are possible in any kind of Shared Living Community.

This new extended family model is a voluntary family that we create ourselves, and might not include blood relatives. This choice allows us to share in the experiences and joys of supportive extended family living and learn new social skills and patterns of interaction, offering a change from the hierarchical, male-dominated, and perhaps dysfunctional family traits that many of us grew up with. The objective is for a democratic and gender-equal management structure without male-dominated hierarchical rule. The exception may be seen, however, in the trend toward reuniting several generations of one family in one house or in a "family compound" of several houses. In these cases, a "mother" or "father" figure, or both, may prevail, although there are signs today of kin-related large families coming together in an attempt at non-hierarchical cooperative management.

It is fundamental that the physical design of a community both reflects and reinforces its social and organizational structure. It is not enough to simply sell separate units to a group of unrelated people and call it a community. As McCamant and Durrett explain, "Most single family houses are not designed for adults to live together equally."[13] Most housing has been developed for the conventional nuclear family, with a master bedroom suite for the parents. The larger new extended family requires housing with adequate and equal private spaces for all the adults, as well as for the children when they return home.

Like all Shared Living Communities, the extended family group house can accommodate different types of people, families, and lifestyles. We encourage the exploration of varied types of extended families, whether intergenerational, gay, bilingual, or any other combination. It is when members intentionally share resources and social, financial, and management commitments to each other that a fully cooperative group house emerges. Some group houses are cooperative and egalitarian for awhile, but then revert back to old hierarchical and patriarchal patterns. This can happen because members do not understand or practice shared living skills.

Issues around compatibility, choice, tolerance, exertion of power over others, and privacy arise in all types of communities, but especially in extended family group houses, because the demand on each member is usually greater and the responsibilities and chores are split between fewer people. If someone doesn't take out the trash or pay a bill, or temporarily needs more time away from community activities to pursue personal interests, the burden on everyone else and the possibility of conflict is proportionately greater than in a larger community.

"More problems may arise living cooperatively, but the avenues for resolving them exist. Ultimately, your life is more enriched."
— *A Member of Muir Commons CoHousing*

Therefore, it is important for the group house members to develop a clear understanding of each other's needs, and agree upon a process for settling differences. In a house that is not appropriately designed for group living, there will tend to be a perception of more interaction, a loss of intimacy, a disregard for individual responsibility, and increased friction. The smaller size and more intimate nature of the group house also has its positive side. It allows members to know each other in a more intimate way and to learn and refine shared living skills more quickly. For example, a closed door or a quick hello in passing may tell others to keep their distance, but it can also arise from fear, a brewing conflict, or simply a difference in culture. Because everyone has times that they want to be alone, these subtle methods of communication need to be explained and respected.

Creating the option for voluntary participation in community events makes growing together as a group easier, because it is not forced. Busy schedules, the need for private time, and timidity may make initiating sociable personal exchanges with others difficult or strained. Therefore, regular meetings are necessary. These meetings could include an opening sharing circle as a helpful way for each person to express their feelings and needs.

Nevertheless, not all members in a community or group house are going to be "best friends." Power struggles may arise around gender and generation gaps. A young person may react to an older person as an "authority figure," or a man may exercise "male dominance" toward women and children. A "super mom" may want to control the kitchen and household tasks, or a person with low self-esteem may try to play the "victim" role and assign a "victimizer" role onto others. These and other power issues will arise as group members adjust to each other. Member selection, conflict resolution, and other group process techniques presented in this book are designed specifically to help alleviate such issues. They must be used in a purposeful and timely manner.

The Building Blocks of Community

The success of a community depends on the residents' and/or designer's understanding of the key role that social and physical environments play in setting up boundaries and opportunities for privacy, intimacy, and communication. As Dolores Hayden, in describing 19th century communities, explains, "Some communities were skillful enough to design accommodations which combined some of the best features of both communal and private dwellings, but developing such designs usually required years of experience with communal living."[14]

We recommend working with a facilitator/architect versed in Shared Living Community design, since she or he will be able to offer examples, options, and insights that the members themselves might overlook. As you begin to visualize the possibilities for the design of private and common spaces, allow the design to evolve from a deep understanding of personal and community criteria. The best design solution often comes from an intuitive mix of feelings about the physical resources, space needs, cost factors, and visual and emotional responses.

The composition of each community is different and each design must be based on the needs, values, purposes, and personalities of the individual members and the collective purposes of the group. There are also real examples and common design patterns, elements, and spatial relationships that can help create a livable, workable, and inspirational community environment. These criteria are further influenced by the consideration of location, climatic, environmental, social, and economic factors. If patience, care, and understanding are employed, these elements and influences can work together.

Let's look at the specific design elements and spatial relationships — the building blocks of community — in more detail to better understand how they work together to create a spirit of empowerment and social harmony that supports the individuals and builds group cohesiveness. The design criteria and principles presented here can be applied to urban or rural Shared Living Communities, from the Village Cluster to the new or redesigned group house.

Common Areas in Community

The common areas are the heart of any Shared Living Community, whether in a common house or a group house. Whatever the physical form, when the key elements of a sustainable community are initiated, designed, and managed by its members, supportive social contact, shared responsibility, and simple enjoyment of a well-designed gathering place then become possible. Community members can share common rooms for cooking and dining, reading and studying, meditation, crafts and hobbies, indoor games and play, childcare, teen activities, guests, music, exercise, media/computer/office equipment, performances, dance and yoga, laundry,

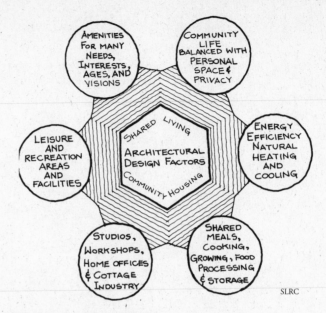

and storage. These amenities can be large or small, interconnected or separate depending upon the social composition, ages, daily schedules, aspirations, needs, interests, and economics of the community members, and the self-help capabilities of the group.

During a visit to Muir Commons CoHousing, the common house was a bustle of activity. Dinner had ended about a half-hour before. Some folks stayed on, talking and drinking coffee, while others tidied up and washed the dishes. Others began to rearrange tables for a committee meeting to be followed by a country dance, while some of the teenagers and their friends readied the exercise room for a small costume party.

A basic design premise for minimizing congestion and conflict in the community common areas is to provide several entry points and alternative circulation routes that converge at selected key locations. For example, upon arriving at the com-

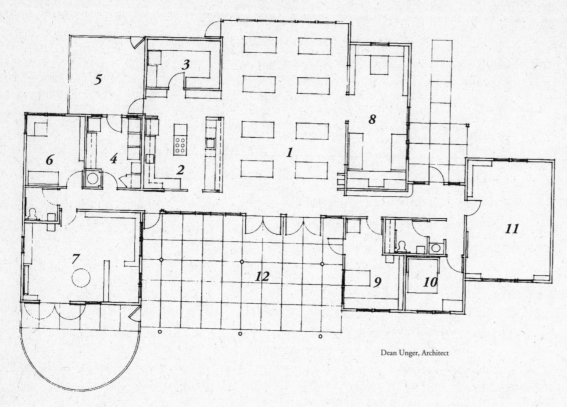

Dean Unger, Architect

The Common House at Muir Commons
The building is full of amenities for everyone. The kitchen and dining room are the focus for the sharing of responsibilities, socializing, meeting, celebration, and other special activities. The prime features of this 3,670 sq. ft. building are:

1 Dining and meeting room
2 Kitchen
3 Food pantry
4 Laundry
5 Storage/recycling
6 Teen room
7 Childcare/playroom
8 Family fireplace room
9 Office/crafts room
10 Guest room
11 Exercise room
12 Outdoor dining and
    social court

munity, members could have a choice of entering either into the common rooms or directly into their private unit. The circulation path should take them by a central point like the mail boxes, with some key posting boards located at or near the common entry. Despite initial concerns about ensuring sufficient privacy, Danish CoHousing communities have found that members almost always prefer to enter through, or at least pass by, the common house or spaces on the way to their homes, seeking out conversation and informal interaction with friends as they choose.

From morning to night and day to day, most common houses change from childcare centers and exercise rooms to dining halls and meeting rooms and back again. With time, the functions of the common house and other common buildings may change altogether. Members of Nonbo Hede, one of the oldest CoHousing communities in Denmark, for example, share meals in the common house only once a week as opposed to four or five times like in the past. The rest of the time the common house is used for frequent club meetings such as the Sheepherder's Club, and other social events. The common house is still the heart of the community, just beating to a different rhythm — one that now better suits the members.

We advise trying to build the common house, or at least the common kitchen and dining room, first, to provide a place for the community to gather together while the members work onthe living units. . As members of the Lama Community in New Mexico suggest, "Create the center first.... Keep that area very special.... Try to build a daily ritual into your lives so that you use the space to share special moments."[15]

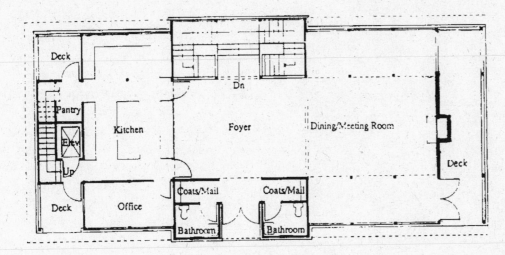

Upper Level

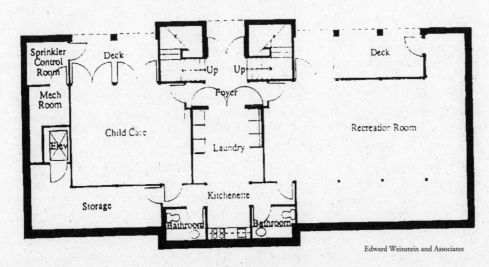

Edward Weinstein and Associates

Lower Level

The Common House, Winslow CoHousing
This 5,000 sq. ft., two-story common house was placed at the convergence point of the community's three village streets, illustrating the importance of its role in the community. The childcare room and the recreation room on the lower floor open out to large outdoor activity areas and the woods. On the main floor, the dining/meeting room opens to the central outdoor courtyard as well as to a deck on one side.

Decision-Making Time at Muir Commons
The Muir Commons' common house is used for meetings of all kinds, as well as for meals, parties, dances, weddings, and celebrations

Photo by Don Lindemann

The living room as a multi-purpose social space
There should be at least one common, quiet, social room adjacent to the dining room. This may be the location for a fireplace, or preferably a high-efficiency wood burning stove (check local codes and EPA regulations for what is permissible in your area). The kachelofen ceramic stove shown in the adjoining scene is presented in Chapter Nine.

Newspapers, magazines, and books that tend to accumulate in private living spaces can be gathered together in reading nooks or an entire reading room or library/study. If the building is large, there can be several kinds of small sitting/reading/activity rooms in addition to the central living/social room.

Common kitchen and dining room
Cooperative cooking and shared meals are a central theme of communities, so these spaces should be prominent and central in the circulation flow. This is the place where the members can casually come and go or hang out. The dining room should be well lit, have a good view of the community, and offer a relaxing environment. Since this room will be relatively large, it can accommodate many extended family functions and group activities, such as parties, bazaars, study meetings, and committee and neighborhood meetings. Nooks and alcoves designed around the edges can be great spaces for smaller gatherings and guest sleeping spaces.

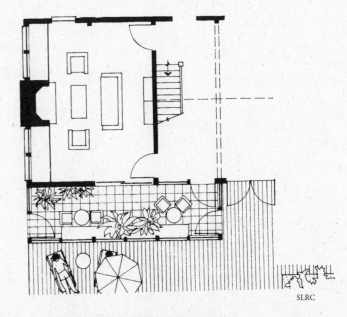

SLRC

Quiet Family/Adult Social Place

"What's the occasion?" asked Pamela as she and her daughter Susan entered the common house an hour before dinner. The living room was filled with happy faces. People were occupying nearly every space.

"Nothing special," answered Henry from the sofa. "People just drifted in. They must have been drawn by the sound of Bob's guitar."

"Oh, yeah!" Bob chuckled and strummed a chord. "There she is," he sang, "love-ly Paaam-me-la…"

"Hey, don't forget lovely Susan," added Yoichi, perched atop the tile Kachelofen stove that filled the room with its warmth. Susan giggled.

"Seriously, Pam," said Naomi, lying on the couch. "We were discussing whether we should expand the garden next year and grow more of our own food."

Pamela nodded. "I've been thinking about that, too. It'll be more work, but I bet we could almost double the amount of food we've been growing." She pulled an armchair closer to join the discussion. Susan ran to play with two-year-old Kim. There was plenty of time before dinner for Pamela to relax with her friends and contemplate next year's harvest

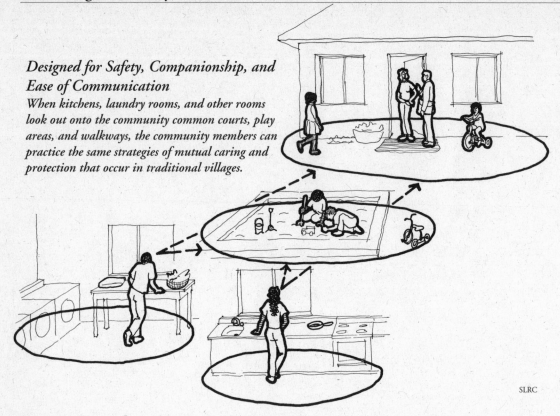

SLRC

Designed for Safety, Companionship, and Ease of Communication

When kitchens, laundry rooms, and other rooms look out onto the community common courts, play areas, and walkways, the community members can practice the same strategies of mutual caring and protection that occur in traditional villages.

"Watching out for each other can mean noticing the mail carrier trying to deliver a parcel to neighbors on vacation, a child perilously close to a busy street, a visitor having trouble finding an address, or a stranger acting suspiciously. Such casual responsibility sharing can be enhanced by the site layout, window placement, and building access. Care must be taken however that privacy is not violated."[16]
— *Clare Cooper Marcus & Wendy Sarkissan,*
Housing as if People Mattered

Laundry and work room

Parents of small children may need to wash clothes as often as every day, and may think they are better off with their own washing machines. But that phase of child raising passes quickly. Scheduling and cost sharing agreements between other parents and members can be arranged to make efficient use of a common laundry. This could be a complete workroom with high-performance washing machines, dryers, laundry sinks, folding tables, and both indoor and outdoor drying lines. This will save everyone time and money, conserve energy, and reduce the number of appliances and space required in each unit. If this room is located near

the dining room and common social areas, it could fulfill a function similar to the old village well. Furnishing it like a "family room" with game tables or a lounge area means it could double as a multi-purpose work, storage, and social room. Soundproofing the doors and the walls between the laundry room and other common rooms is advised, since washers and dryers can be noisy.

Play spaces for everyone

There should be a safe playroom and outdoor play area for small children, close to parents and other adults who might be conversing in the dining room or working in the kitchen or laundry room, but separate enough for a noise buffer. Children of all ages need places where they can be noisy and expressive, make messes if they want, and shape and decorate their space in their own way. They need a place they know is theirs to store their favorite toys, where they can build things, draw and paint, and have access to supplies. These facilities could be managed by paid or volunteer community members or by an outside childcare worker. With time, as kids grow older, the children's rooms can be used by teens or fulfill some other function which better meets the changing needs of the community.

There is also a need for spaces around the common areas where children of different ages can find nooks and crannies near the hub of adult activity where they can have their own sense of belonging. Some Intentional Communities and CoHousing communities have a separate room for teens and an exercise room for adults. Some of these functions could be combined in one room with an agreed upon time schedule to meet everyone's needs.

Hobby, craft, and home business workshops

Usually people only dream about having a specially designed music or audiovisual studio, a carpentry shop with a full set of tools, a pottery room, darkroom, telecommunications/computer/media center, or an art studio, but in a community these can all be a reality. Since high-tech telecommunication devices are becoming part of our daily lives, a community media room may serve a special function. In the future, fiber-optics will make even more advanced information processing systems available for home entertainment and businesses. A common media room as part of the community's live-work activities could allow the shared use of these developing technologies in a more resource-efficient and cost-effective manner.

Working at home increases the opportunity for social support and provides a more relaxed working environment. Men and women working at home create new adult models for children to learn from. The location of home/work places away from one's own living space may be desirable in order to separate work from home, but some may enjoy having their work nook right in their own living unit or suite.

Guest, teen, and extra rooms

Since individual houses, apartment/condo units, or living suites are often not big enough to allow for spare bedrooms, it saves money for everyone to provide extra rooms for visiting relatives or friends in the common house. These rooms can also serve as alternative private bedrooms, sick rooms, or rooms for frail elders.

Moving into community-oriented housing can strongly affect teenagers because of their need for their own space and territory. Some communities intentionally provide more remote hide-away rooms or dorms for teens who may need to feel independent but are not yet ready to move away from home. Teens can still eat in their parents' private unit or share in the common meals, while enjoying the privacy of their own space. Soundproofing of a teen music room can be an investment that will benefit everyone.

Planning for discretionary spaces for future community use in the master plan is recommended. This could include a large attic or, on sloping sites, an excavated but unfurnished underfloor space, or a basement.

Childcare and community schools

Reliable nursery, childcare, and educational facilities within the community can offer a sense of well-being for parents. The beneficial effect upon children in both urban and rural communities is already well known. Where else can children observe other peer and adult role models daily while in a safe and familiar atmosphere? Having children stay in the home atmosphere for childcare and even primary education brings stability and security into their lives, enhances personal development, and strengthens the community. The size and complexity of the childcare and local education services will depend on the lifestyles of the families, the number of children in the community by ages, and the number of new children entering the community.

Some Intentional Communities have established a certified school system within their own community. For example, Ananda Village, a spiritual cooperative community, has over 100 children from the community and the surrounding area in their

Childcare Spaces, Indoor and Outdoor
This example is located near the common kitchen and dining area. It can be adapted later on for older children and teens.

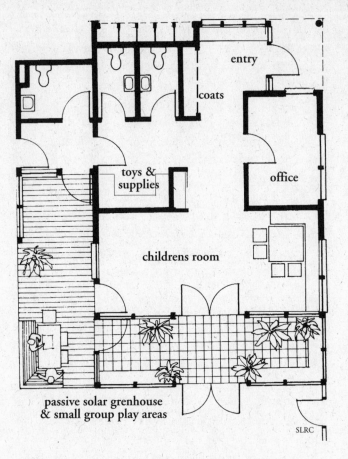

entry

coats

toys & supplies

office

childrens room

passive solar grenhouse & small group play areas

SLRC

"In a village-like community, child care and education are provided as in an extended family. Children learn cooperation and sharing. They observe and participate in adult work and recreation, and peer groups provide opportunities for children to learn together." [17]
— *Allen Butcher, "The Wonders of Communal Economics"*

own school system. Local and state laws covering operation of nonprofit cooperative childcare and education services must be examined.

Creating Private Living Places

Instead of full-size houses or apartment units, we advocate the design of private living suites which can range in size from a single room (with private or shared bathroom) for an individual to a suite of several rooms for a couple or small family. The group must work to satisfy the different lifestyles,

relationships, family compositions, needs, preferences, and building budgets of the individual members, as well as meet the overall needs and criteria of the group.

It is best to design the private living suites to meet the needs of the current members while being flexible enough to adapt to different living configurations in the future. A freespan roof design would allow for future adaptation, as described in Chapter One. Members can create a master plan with all the desired amenities, and then build in phases as time and money allow.

To ensure the emotional well-being of the individual as well as the family group, each adult and older child should have their own room within a private unit or living suite. Most couples will share a bedroom, but each should have some other space for him or herself. In almost all group houses and Intentional Communities, it is consistently acknowledged that tensions are minimized and cooperation heightened when each person has a sanctuary that they alone control and can retreat to. Although there is a basic need in our western culture to personalize one's own space and make it their own, other cultures may arrange private spaces according to their heritage. Individuals or family groups should be given the opportunity to design their own environment and do the finishing work, painting, or landscaping themselves. In the West African village examples previously presented and in most villages worldwide, house building is a community process, but personal decorations are up to the individual or family and are taken very seriously.

Large living, dining, and family rooms in private units are not necessary because of the central kitchen and dining room and the other abundant common amenities within the community. In the Village Cluster prototype designs and some existing CoHousing communities, the houses and apartment units have a smaller kitchen or only a kitchenette, since most evening meals are served in the common house. However, there is concern that developer-originated CoHousing-type developments may cater to buyers on the open market by building conventional single-family housing with full kitchens, formal dining rooms, etc. Such housing is usually designed for the "buying" market and not for creating "community." With full-scale conventionally designed units, people may become isolated and not interact with others, detracting from the cohe-

siveness of the community. This is less likely to happen when individual units do not have a full kitchen, dining, and living room, and the common house is creatively co-designed by the community members to reflect their needs and desires.

However, a small three to six foot long kitchenette or a convenience food counter may be desired by some people for their living suites, with a sink/wash basin, wall cabinet or under-counter refrigerator, and a microwave or hot plate. This simple convenience food counter is still prohibited by some old-paradigm zoning ordinances, but as housing designs continue to reflect demographic changes, the idea of what constitutes a unit or kitchen will

"Our goal should be to achieve that wonderful balance between the inner and outer person, between the need for privacy and the need for companionship and socialization." [18]

— *Dayna Ehlen, Innovative Housing*

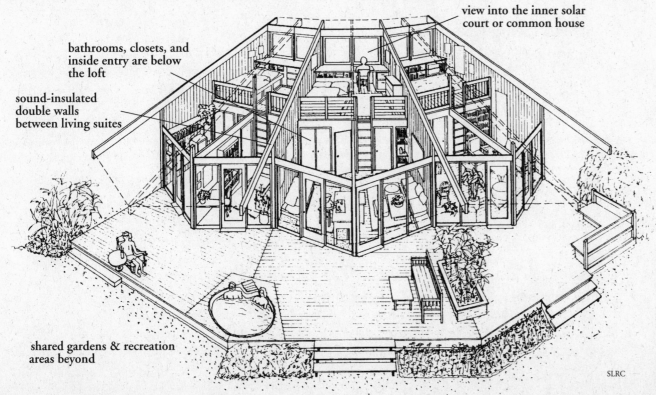

view into the inner solar court or common house

bathrooms, closets, and inside entry are below the loft

sound-insulated double walls between living suites

shared gardens & recreation areas beyond

SLRC

A Cluster of Private Living Suites for Couples and Singles
These 500 sq. ft. private living suites could be in a group house like the Octagonal Cluster House. This design shows three variations of how the spaces could be arranged. The common house is reached through the passageway under the loft that also connects to a bathroom for each suite.

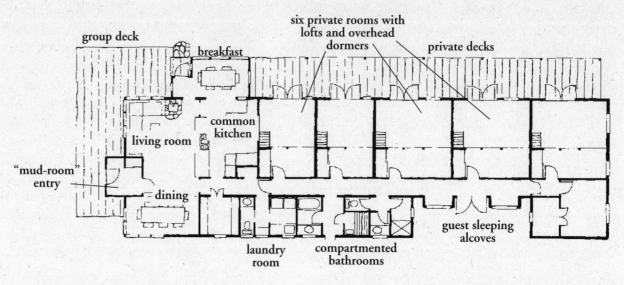

six private rooms with lofts and overhead dormers

private decks

group deck

breakfast

common kitchen

living room

"mud-room" entry

dining

laundry room

compartmented bathrooms

guest sleeping alcoves

Shared Living Houses at Ananda Village, California

Common House at the Meru Cluster

This complete common house, with five private rooms with lofts, serves a shared living cluster of five nearby sleeping cottages for single people. Other shared amenities include a meditation chapel, hot tub and deck, wood storage, water tank, and parking.

Extended Family Shared House

This is one of several Ananda Village houses designed with family living suites located on each side of a common area that includes a full kitchen, dining and social space, a meditation room, and laundry room.

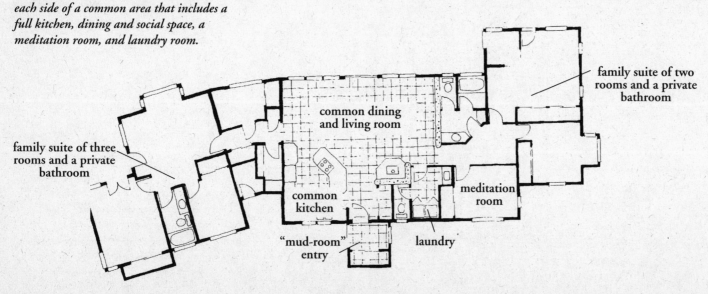

family suite of two rooms and a private bathroom

common dining and living room

family suite of three rooms and a private bathroom

common kitchen

meditation room

"mud-room" entry

laundry

Design by Ananda Village
Overlay drawings by SLRC

change as well. Planners, lenders, and developers need to anticipate these trends and respond positively to the "community" approach to housing design with all its social-environmental innovations and benefits. This is discussed further in Chapters Eight and Nine.

There are many creative possibilities for how the interior of a small house, apartment, living suite, or rooms in a group house can be designed for the specific needs of a single person, a couple, or a small family. To accommodate a future partner and/or children, you can use lofts, alcoves, movable dividers, and separate entrances. Suites can be one large room or divided into individual sleeping rooms or with alcoves on each side. A small work studio/social alcove, or two adjacent private studio/work areas con join the couple's shared leisure-time sleeping alcove or loft. Use personalized movable dividers, furniture arrangements, built-in or movable counters, closets, and work tables or desks as options for defining social, work, and sleeping spaces. An alternative to work space in the private unit or suite is to plan for sufficient work space in the common areas. These needs should be discussed in the core group design meeting for inclusion in the master plans and budget.

Children's sleeping rooms

Treating children as people, with individual rights and equal access to privileges and resources as adults, is a practice that nuclear families, extended families, and cooperative living groups have learned works to the benefit of all. There are two major schools of thought, however, concerning how to plan and design communities in order to enhance children's growth and learning processes.

Some community advocates believe that children need a strong sense of individuality and independence, gained by not sleeping immediately next to their parents' rooms. Until recently, children in most kibbutzim slept in nurseries and dormitories separated by age and gender. This is no longer done in most settlements in Israel, although some Intentional Communities, such as Twin Oaks in Virginia, continue this practice. We mention this as an option because it may meet the special needs of some community groups or special population groups in shelters or group homes. The same principles of privacy and private rooms that we described for adults and families are necessary for children of different ages and gender. For example, there could be a common sleeping area for children under five years of age. As the chil-

---

Space, Place, and the Child

By Yi-Fu Tuan, *Space and Place*

"A child's idea of place becomes more specific and geographical as he grows. To the question, where do you like to play? a two-year-old will probably say 'home' or 'outdoors.' An older child will answer 'in my room' or 'in the yard.' Locations become more precise. 'Here' and 'there' are augmented by 'right here' and 'right there.' Interest in distant places and awareness of relative distance increase. Thus a child three to four years old begins to use such expressions as 'far away' or 'way off.' To the question where do you live? a two-year-old will probably say 'home.'.... Except for nurseries and playgrounds few public places are made to the scale of young children. Do they feel a need to be in places that conform to their own size? Hints of such need exist." [19]

dren grow, split the dormitory space into sleeping alcoves, and then into individual rooms.

The children's spaces should not be isolated from the parents and the rest of the community. They should be integrated into the community cluster. The dorm model can also apply to teens in the process of individuating from their parents, and in situations when there are internal family conflicts. If your community chooses this type of model, it is important to have a strong and well-developed social structure for co-parenting that provides a loving and participatory atmosphere for children and teens, with positive adult models always around.

The second school of thought is that children need a sense of belonging to their blood-family group, and therefore should have their own rooms in their parents' unit or suite of rooms. Regardless of the sleeping room arrangements, an important aspect of community living is providing children with the means to participate in community responsibilities, and with activity spaces of their own. From the love and guidance of their parents' house to the attention and support of the community, children in communities can have the best possible environment for growing up.

Bathing Facilities
— private and communal

Shared Living Communities offer the opportunity to create a beautiful and spacious bathing area for water-related leisure and therapeutic activities. Community members may decide to economize by having shared bathroom facilities for two or three rooms or living suites, or satisfy the need for privacy by each having a small private bathroom. Several basic option are presented in the following diagrams.

A community bathing place — pools, hot tubs, and saunas

To save money and live more sustainable and socially, some groups may choose to build one central bathing facility and eliminate private showers or tubs in each unit. Such a central bathing center could be designed as a focus of the community plan, with the private living suites and common amenities

Freeform Community Bathing Center
This grand bathing center could be an option for a community group that has come to agreement regarding group bathing, respect for individuals' personal rights, and parameters of sexual behavior. Those who choose may put their resources into such a luxury.

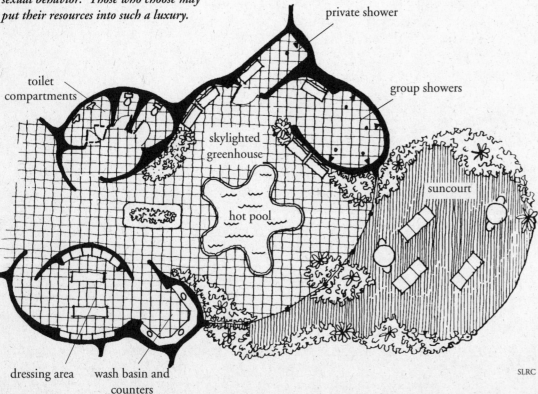

private shower

group showers

toilet compartments

skylighted greenhouse

suncourt

hot pool

dressing area

wash basin and counters

SLRC

Bathroom Design Options for Group Houses/Group Homes

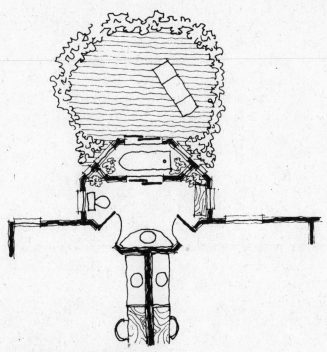

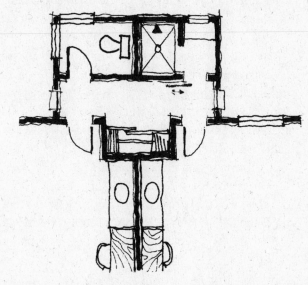

Compartmentalized Shared Bathroom
This option saves the cost of duplication of fixtures and water and waste lines, and provides privacy for the two adjoining rooms or living suites.

Full Shared Bathroom
This deluxe bathroom and suncourt can serve two adjoining bedrooms or living suites.

clustered around in a radiating pattern. The materials, plumbing, and energy savings from eliminating, say, 25 separate showers and bathtubs, would free up the resources for this much more luxurious amenity. Less costly options can be selected to create smaller bathing centers — a sauna and/or hot tub would be a luxury for most groups.

A hot pool, or hot tub, and a shower area could be built next to an outside suncourt or in a greenhouse where plants become part of the bathing environment. Maximum sun exposure and privacy can be provided by having the common bathing

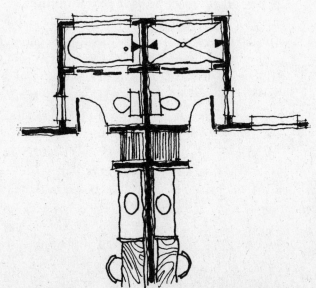

Individual Private Bathrooms
Each room or living suite has a private bathroom, with choice of a large shower or shower-tub, plus a sink and counter in each private living space.

Drawings by SLRC

facilities on the second floor with sliding doors opening onto a deck. A central bathing room and area could be designed as a visually sensual delight — a very open and free–flowing space with curved walls, colorful tiled surfaces, hanging plants, skylights, and sliding doors opening to the outdoors. Nooks and alcoves could accommodate a massage table, clothes racks, dressing nooks, and storage for towels and cleaning supplies. A standard bathtub nearby might be desired for the special needs of older people and small children. If more privacy is the group choice, provide separate shower stalls or a ceiling track for a curtain that can enclose just one or several shower heads. The concept of a common bathing center may seem too radical to many community groups. But it can be part of an ecologically sustainable lifestyle that provides a new sense of support, intimacy, security, and empowerment for community members.

Other bathroom options for communities

There are two basic wash basin options to consider in group design sessions. Having a wash basin and a small built-in counter in a closet or wall recess within each sleeping room or in each living suite is a popular request and quite workable. The lavatory counter can also be combined with a small food preparation counter as described earlier.

Private bathrooms may be eliminated altogether and replaced by compartmentalized ones, with wash basins placed in a hallway near the enclosed toilet rooms for accessibility. Another economical approach is a freestanding island or a counter in a central bathroom, with a number of basins so that several people can wash simultaneously. These may be desirable for groups with lots of children and/or

others who leave for school or work at the same time.

The toilet can be in a full bathroom or in a separate, small toilet room with its own door. You may want amenities such as plants, shelves, benches and skylights for the toilet room and the bathroom as described above. In group design workshops, some people have expressed a desire for a full private bathroom in their own unit or living suite, but others felt that in order to save resources and costs they would not mind sharing a nicely designed toilet room located between two or three rooms for only those several people to use, usually a maximum of three. The ratio of fixtures to occupants will vary with individual, community, and family choices, and according to building codes and possibly septic tank regulations, if applicable. A central compartmentalized bathroom can have privacy and variety designed into it, with separate door access to a small toilet room or partitioned stalls.

Alternative toilet design is another valuable investment for ecologically sustainable living. The conventional flush toilet sends valuable materials — nitrogen, minerals, and organic matter — on the last leg of a one-way trip that starts at farms, turns to food, gets eaten by people, and ends up in the ocean or septic systems. The composting toilet keeps human waste in a container mixed with organic materials that allow bacterial action to break it down so that it is ultimately usable as fertilizer. One person's yearly waste production will compost down to about one or two cubic feet of non-odorous finished product. The "Clivus Multrum," and similar systems can require attentive maintenance, and for that reason local health departments must be convinced that an installation will be cared for.

However the Sun-Mar Corporation in Buffalo, New York, manufactures four models of low maintenance manual and electric no- to very-low-water use composting toilets. This technology does not require a septic system, and it accelerates the composting process by mixing the waste with air and in some models, a small amount of water. Electric power can be provided by a small photovoltaic collector and short-term storage system. Although these toilets are used as specialty items in rural and remote locations and are approved in some rural counties, there is still a need for more education on their appropriate use and better acceptance by regulatory agencies.

Form, Structure, and Space

Shape, height, area, spatial volume, relationship, continuity, contrast and color, the cultural heritage of the group, and local resources are essential factors for designing the living environment, and are intuitively used by indigenous peoples. Americans tend to rely on a system of building influenced almost entirely by industrial and consumer economics, using imported, non-renewable and manufactured materials, and energy and cost intensive building methods. Most people get rectilinear spaces that look like hotel rooms, with square corners, flat ceilings, and windows positioned in the center of the end wall.

Group design processes, community self-help techniques, and alternative materials and structural methods provide opportunities for exposed beams, sloping ceilings, skylights, and angled and curved walls. You can even explore innovative circular, hexagonal, and splayed designs. Multi-sided rooms

with various configurations of sloping ceilings can create a pleasing visual focus, making the space seem larger than a square room of the same size. Chapter Nine reviews alternative construction techniques that are especially suited for creative building forms.

Transition of space in community from private to common

A well-designed Shared Living Community provides intentionally designed places for private activities, special semi-private spaces for social interaction with a few others, and very public places for being together as a large group. Having privacy means having a choice about interacting with others, and having control over your physical place. The design features that distinguish private from common spaces are not intended to keep people apart, but enable them to live closely together and interact more comfortably, by defining specific places for personal privacy and other kinds of spaces for varying degrees of social interaction with others.

The relationships between these spaces and places influence how the community functions and is perceived by its members. Depending on how the spaces are allocated and shared, they can either enhance or diminish the sense of group cohesion, privacy, and well-being. Density and overcrowding, for example, cannot be determined by simply dividing the number of people by the square footage of the buildings or rooms. And having a lot of space doesn't necessarily provide privacy. On the contrary, it can make one feel exposed, vulnerable, and isolated, because the only place to be is in the middle or on the edges. Without appropriate design and/or agreements on privacy, people may tend to feel crowded, resort to hierarchical or

Sun Mar Corporation

A Mid-Level Technology for Composting Toilets
The Sun-Mar Coporation mass-produces both mechanically and electrically operated toilets — if it is done in space, why not on earth?

In the Village Cluster Heritage

— *transitions from private space, tosemi-private, to semi-common, to common space*

These gradations of kinds of spaces and places are accomplished through the creation of a design language: structure, furnishings, materials, plantings, shapes, textures, colors, and patterns that form transition zones, such as courtyards, screens, arcades, or porches. Each space is intended to be distinct and original, with its own character, boundaries, and sense of place, yet comfortably unified into the larger composition through design and materials, including personal artifacts and furnishings that express the individual personalities of the residents.

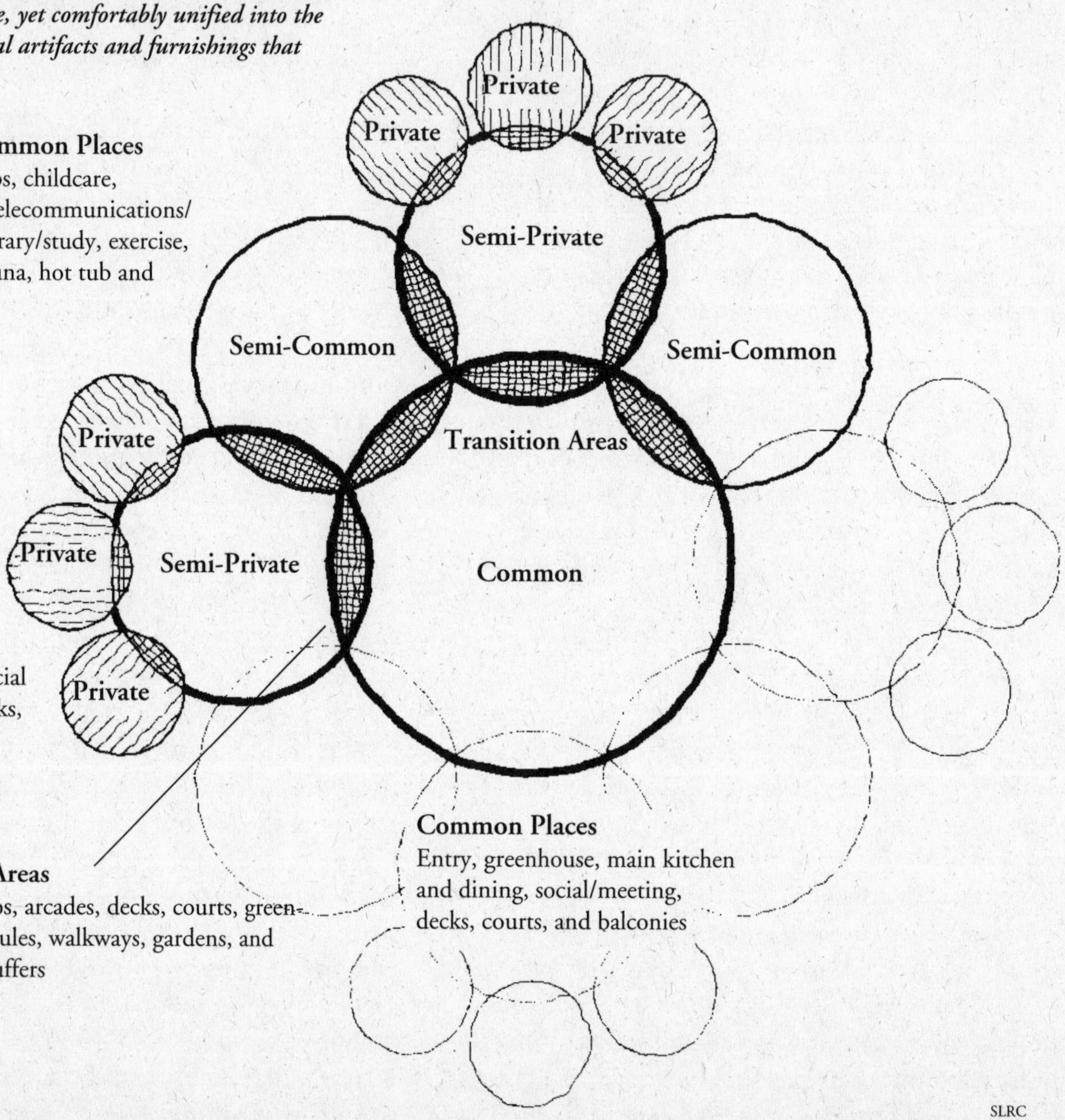

Semi-Common Places
Workshops, childcare, laundry, telecommunications/ media, library/study, exercise, games, sauna, hot tub and pool

Private Units or Living Suites
Sleeping rooms, social areas, work areas, bathrooms, private decks, courts, or balconies (optional small kitchenette and eating nook)

Semi-Private Places
Shared kitchenette and social lounge, quiet/reading nooks, alcoves, courts and green- houses

Transition Areas
Porches, patios, arcades, decks, courts, green- houses, vestibules, walkways, gardens, and landscaped buffers

Common Places
Entry, greenhouse, main kitchen and dining, social/meeting, decks, courts, and balconies

SLRC

240

authoritarian control of space, or withdraw and put up psychological barriers, feeling they have no other choice.

Breaking up a large space into several areas or nodes of activity creates the illusion of more space. Factors by which people perceive space have to do with whether doors, partitions, or walls can be moved to open up or close off a space. Other factors include the ceiling height; the openness to outdoor spaces; the acoustics or how sound is carried through a space, the size, shape, and arrangement of furniture, carpets, and lighting fixtures; and the physical and visual transitions between spaces that give people more choices and control over how and where they spend their time.

Designing for personal touches in community
Architectural details in a co-designed community can be more than decoration in the "House Beautiful" style. Personalized touches can create an intimate feeling within larger spaces, and make small spaces appear larger. You don't need to be completely alone or withdrawn to experience a sense of privacy within the common areas. Your group can develop a design language that contributes to the feeling of varied personalities for different areas: touches of color; a variety of wood trim around openings, at base boards and for picture moldings; varieties of plant forms; and differences in wall coverings. Allow the richness and diversity of your community group to show.

• **Entrances**
Ordinarily the typical tract house front porch, if it exists at all, is just a design appendage that juts out into the rawness of a car-dominated street. Similarly, apartment building entries are rarely used

except for passage. These spaces are not comfortable to be in because they do not create an adequate distinction between public and private. It is either all or nothing. There needs to be an intermediary space to act as a transition between what is personal and what is public.

The entry to the common house, a private living suite, or a group house should be clearly defined and welcoming. The layout of the building should allow each resident, in the case of a private living suite, and the group, in the case of the common house, to personalize the entry. A front porch, courtyard, or deck can act as a transition between the public and private realms, providing a place for residents to relax in semi-privacy while they watch people walking, gardening or playing.

• **Trellises and Arbors**
These structures can soften the hard, flat surfaces of buildings by providing a structure for vines and hanging plants to grow on. In addition to its aesthetic appeal, a vine-covered arbor or trellis can provide valuable sun shading, a visual definition of the transition of space to place, and a food source— grapes, peas, berries and tomatoes are just a few of the foods that grow well on vines.

• **Built-in wall storage systems**
Many items requiring short-term storage and convenient access can be kept in the common house. Built-in wall units can hold board games, books and magazines, work desks, computer-equipment, a telephone, sewing machine, extra clothes, or folding chairs and tables. These wall storage systems can be used as movable space dividers, with pullout, foldout, or removable features. In a community, the need for storage in the individual units lessens, because many items can be shared with the

Personalized Entrances
Entrances opening into semi-private common spaces that are co-owned in a community can be designed for privacy and socialbility.

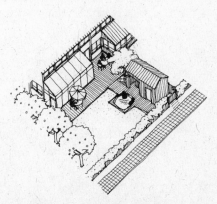

Special Areas for Adults
Design a quiet secluded place for adults to relax and socialize without children.

241

group, including gardening equipment, kitchen and eating ware, and exercise equipment. Nevertheless, the wall storage system can also be applied to individual living suites.

• **Lofts**

Lofts can add variety to the interplay of spaces and can be used for meditation, sleeping, a quiet and removed work space, a guest sleeping space, a children's play area, or storage. Lofts in couples' spaces can give one or both partners a work niche or alternate sleeping space. One person's work space could be in a loft above the other person's desk. Lofts are easily designed by careful positioning of higher peaked roofs and window dormers over rooms with low ceilings such as a corridor, closet, or bathroom. Similarly, in redesigning an older conventional house for group living, a usable loft can be formed when a room falls under a high ridge line, by removing the ceiling and

Photo by SLRC

A Hallway Sitting Nook
This also serves as an overnight guest sleeping place as well as livening up a long hallway in a large shared living house at the Ananda community.

Sunday Morning Looking Over the Community Commons
This couple enjoys the privacy of their 600 sq. ft. living suite, which includes a sleeping loft, social and eating areas, a small kitchenette, a bathroom, and closets. This private living suite is attractive, comfortable, and affordable. They share most of their meals in the common house, and have access to many special activity rooms and outdoor social decks, recreation facilities, and gardens and fruit trees.

SLRC

Seeing My Space, Knowing Place

Sending out, receiving —
Skin alive, eyes sensing, sounds, telling me my space.
Relationship to edges —
Cells, molecules, all one with cosmic vibrations.

To what do I relate?
Distances, height, reaching, feeling the rightness.
Walking the middle path —
Finding the form of my existence.

Spaces —
What happens to my being as the sides close in or recede?
Feeling good, natural in this space, this structure I call my place —
Minerals, fibers, chemicals all vibrating.

My environment —
How did I choose it? Can I create better — for my feelings? For others?
Sharing this space, what then? What do new vibrations do to it?
Who is using this space?

Encroachment, psychic space —
Vibrations with other bodies. Is it lost to me for my solitary use?
When are they too close, too many? How can I know, what tells me?
Comfort — with two, with five?

Sensing, skin alive —
Awareness of feedback, too tight, just right, overpowering,
People in my space vibrating, tuning in physically, day and night —
Irritation. Get away, leave me alone!

Privacy needed. Why?
Is it me, them, or the space? Tissues and cells vibrating. Me, he, she, them.
My environment. Do I pass through it or carry it with me?
Drums vibrating, defining the space.

What is it? A room?
Space, carved out of air, penetrated, crossed, and filled with denser space.
How learned are the reactions to shape, proportions, size?
Why a box? Is square and plumb sacred?

Who tells me the space of my being?
When silent, talking, preparing food, passing in the hallway. Why a hallway?
Memory, conditioned consciousness, adaptability of the species —
Cultural dictates, class, pride, attachments.

Fear, paranoia, locked doors —
Walls with holes, seeing into the closed out world.
Privacy, rest, intimacy, womb, common origins. Needs are ancient —
Castles, fortresses, temples, hogans, tipis, and huts.

Universal heritages —
Our space and place came from all the continents.
The Mayflower, slave ships, around the Horn, lost and rebuilt in 1906 —
People on the move.

Who tells you, me?
The shapes of our places to live — why not me, now, and you now —
And you and me, now.

— Ken Norwood, 1980

Quiet Reading and Conversation Alcoves
The common house or group house is made more sociable with hideaway alcoves located around the edges of the common activity ares. These spaces can also be used to accommodate overnight guests.

for dining or coffee/tea and conversation, located adjacent to the large common room, allowing users to watch the larger group while engaging in activities of their own.

Transitional edges for places and spaces
Some kind of edge is necessary to define and shape various site areas, functions, and building relationships, and to provide a transition from one place and space to another. A central green or courtyard lined with flower beds and a protective row of trees can identify the main gathering places of the community. A shade kiosk or pagoda, sculpture, and even play equipment can become a focal point for a common outdoor area. It is important to have a gradual transition between the private indoor living places and the more public places and spaces. A "soft edge" between private living places, yard areas, and the common green can be created with porches, stoops, plantings, or just a change in pavement materials or color. Common house walls facing the common green should be open, with double doors and/or operable windows to encourage interaction and impart an invitation for residents to participate. Flat, solid walls can be uninviting and discourage interaction, or can be purposely used as a backdrop for landscaping, for enclosure and privacy, and as sound buffers against street noise or intensive enthusiasm during the recreational games.

• Decks and patios
Decks and patios can be private, semi-private, or public depending upon their size and location, and can be used to define areas. A small balcony or roof deck attached to a private living suite located on the second floor may be an intimate spot for sunbathing and private dining. Conversely, a large tiled patio

adding new rafters to the roof. Skylights and dormers can provide critical headroom and light where needed.

• Nooks and alcoves
Nooks and alcoves not only serve as intimate places, but also provide variety and relief from a large expansive space and add breadth to a small one. The inglenook is a compact place next to a fireplace. Other possibilities are a reading nook, a game table area, and other semi-private alcoves that can be used

covered with a vine arbor adjacent to the common kitchen can be an outdoor eating area and a neighborhood "watering hole" on warm days.

• **Outdoor seating areas**

Benches, as well as low walls, ledges, and steps make great sitting, gathering, and people watching places. If seating areas are not built in, residents will probably want to bring tables and chairs out into the courts and patios between common and private areas.

• **Walls and fences**

Walls and fences can be used as overt physical barriers or as implied spatial divisions, defining areas without actually inhibiting communication. A waist-high fence will clearly mark the distinction between private and public spaces without alienating neighbors, whereas a six foot high wall will prevent all communication. Walls and fences can be made out of a variety of materials, including plants or earth berms as well as traditional materials such as wood, brick, or stone.

• **Greenhouses**

Solar greenhouses can also serve as activity focal points and for spatial definition for almost any south-facing building wall or rooftop. Or they can be built as freestanding structures on terraces and courtyards, and in gardens. They can be arranged to allow residents to enjoy small sitting and dining places, gardening, and other activities. A potting counter and sink is a neccessary amenity. The planting choices can include indigenous vegetation requiring minimal care, seedlings and starter plants, and fruit trees, vegetables, flowers, and herbs for year-round consumption. Communities can be more self-reliant and generate a cash-crop enterprise. (See Chapter Nine regarding passive solar.)

Prototype Designs for Group House Community Living

We will now present three alternative designs of prototype group houses to show how extended family groups can combine the privacy and comfort of a traditional single-family house with the supportive social environment of a Shared Living Community. Each family, couple, or individual has their own private living space and shares the common kitchen, dining, social, and activity areas with the rest of the group members. By sharing their food preparation, meals, transportation, recycling, household tasks and mutual responsibilities, the members of these new extended families can have a higher quality of life than even a millionaire could have alone, because not only do they share a mansion — they share their lives. These group houses foster the essence of an ecologically sustainable lifestyle.

The first prototype example is a large but compact group house designed for two extended family groups of 12 to 16 people. This plan can easily be adapted for multiple-floor buildings in moderate to high-density transportation node Eco Village and Eco City locations. Two individualized front entries (or stairways if on an upper floor) on opposite sides of the house open into cozy, semi-private social lounges. On either side of the shared social space are private living suites with three private rooms and a bathroom. Each of these suites could be shared by one family or a voluntary family composed of singles, couples, and single- or two-parent families. From the social lounge, family members and guests pass through a greenhouse or court where each family or person can plant their favorite vegetables and flowers, and on into a large common kitchen and dining area shared by the whole house. A library/computer room, game/TV room, sitting room, and two decks open off of this common social area, the heart and soul of this group house. The variety of spaces and transition areas creates the opportunity for a changing panorama of experiences. The group house would be surrounded by social decks or courts, play areas, game courts, and gardens. These outdoor amenities could be shared by other adjacent group houses within one Village Cluster or larger Eco Village.

The next two designs for ecological living, the "Suncourt" and the "SunWing" houses, are conceived as starter houses for a growing extended family group. Both houses could start with two individuals, couples, or small families, and grow into a larger extended family group. The houses have many features for energy self-reliance and ecological living. The Suncourt is the more compact design, with a protected solar court in the center of the house and a greenhouse on the south side to provide passive solar heating. The common kitchen, living/dining room, and activity rooms surround the suncourt and open onto a shared deck and garden. The "SunWing" house is so named because its winglike configuration exposes the maximum length of its perimeter walls to passive solar heat gain from morning to afternoon. The angled walls add variety and pleasing aesthetics, and offer a dramatic change from conventional building forms.

The common kitchen in both plans is located in the center of the circulation flow for social interaction reasons, leaving the living suite wings and the common dining and social wing as relatively secluded areas, allowing the choice for when and where to be sociable. Over the living/dining space and study an overhead guest loft is reached by a spiral staircase. The living suites each have their

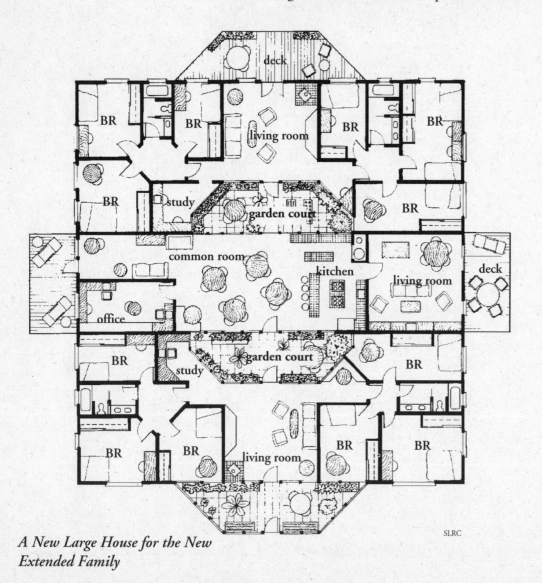

A New Large House for the New Extended Family

SLRC

own deck, sleeping or storage loft, sitting/work area, bathroom, and their own small kitchenette and side entrances, and can be relatively independent when desired. The dotted lines shown around the living suites show how they can be expanded with additional rooms or other living suites, both upstairs and/or to the sides, to accommodate children and/or additional community members. With the common facilities already in place, the initial

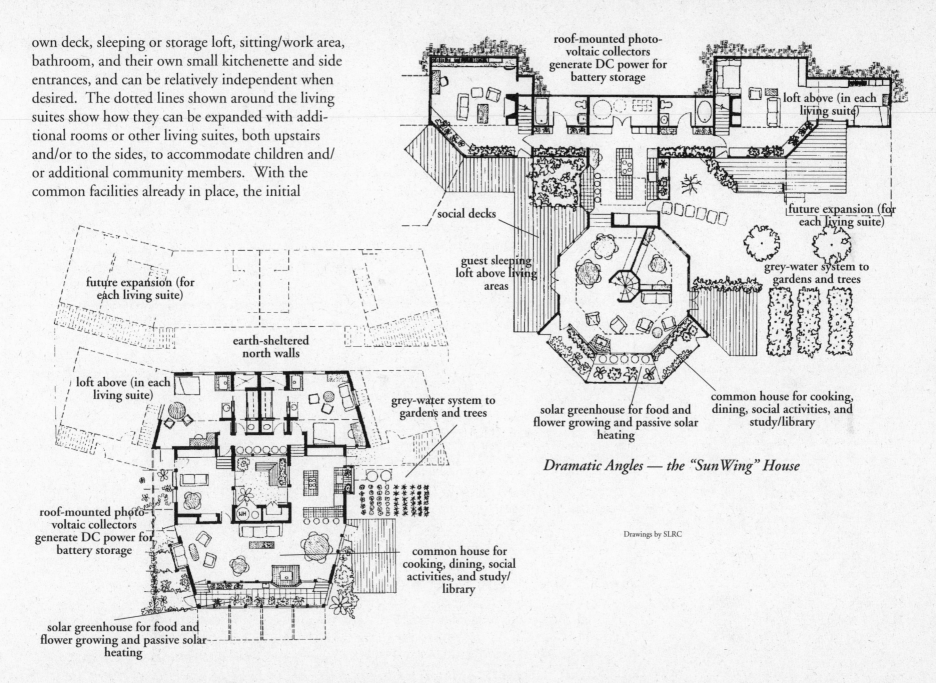

roof-mounted photo-voltaic collectors generate DC power for battery storage

loft above (in each living suite)

social decks

future expansion (for each living suite)

guest sleeping loft above living areas

grey-water system to gardens and trees

common house for cooking, dining, social activities, and study/library

solar greenhouse for food and flower growing and passive solar heating

Dramatic Angles — the "SunWing" House

Drawings by SLRC

future expansion (for each living suite)

earth-sheltered north walls

loft above (in each living suite)

grey-water system to gardens and trees

roof-mounted photo-voltaic collectors generate DC power for battery storage

common house for cooking, dining, social activities, and study/library

solar greenhouse for food and flower growing and passive solar heating

Letting the Sun Shine in — the "Suncourt" House

"Ken Norwood is a pioneer in designing for group living. He was the architect for the renovation of my own collective group house. His work shows the way to a practical basis for new styles that can take us into the 21st Century."
— Starhawk,
San Francisco, California1992

"Blackcat" Victorian Group House in San Francisco, CA ^{SLRC}

community members can live comfortably while additions are being built.

Both houses are designed for solar electricity subject to location, and solar water heating for domestic use and radiant heating. A grey-water system recycles household wastewater from sinks and showers to the gardens, and electric composting toilets generate garden fertilizer. Both houses could be adapted to various alternative materials and building systems, including factory-built components and modular sections. The north side walls of the living suites of each house are earth sheltered. (See Chapter Nine for more about alternative systems.)

Existing Examples of Extended Family Group Houses

Throughout the U.S. in large cities and in rural areas, many large existing houses have become voluntary group living places for new extended families. Some are rented, and last as long as the owner chooses to rent to the group or the group chooses to stay together. Some house owners choose to rent to cooperative living groups indefinitely, because there is no vacancy factor and little risk, and because house groups usually take excellent care of the house and yard. Other houses are co-owned by residents as a partnership or as tenants-in-common. Sometimes one or several of the residents are the owners, while the others have a lease or a buy-in share arrangement. It is the most cost-effective and sociable way to live in urban or rural areas. There are many cooperative group houses throughout the US. Lending and developer interests, however, continue to resist making loans to

groups made up of non-blood related members and especially to low and moderate income or minority groups even when they do have qualified buyers.

Increasing interest is being shown in remodeled and new cooperatively owned group houses. Here we highlight two of the several forms group houses can have.

The "Black Cat" House, San Francisco, CA

The photo to the left may look like any old, turn-of-the-century Victorian house with two apartments and a large attic. But it is not — instead of the original five bedrooms in two apartments, there are now eight bedrooms and five common rooms in this new remodeled group house that defines new physical and social relationships. The eight people living there form an intergenerational, extended family of low-to-middle income and mostly single persons. In 1989, SLRC provided the original group with profile, consultation, and design counseling sessions that defined their needs and the new group house design. SLRC went on to provide the final architectural drawings.

The adjacent diagrams show how the existing floor plans were subdivided and expanded to create additional private rooms and make use of the vacant attic space. The original smaller kitchen, dining room, and service porch on the second floor were opened up into one large kitchen/dining/family room. The old first-floor kitchen and porch is now a multi-purpose craft/laundry/work/storage room, and the dining and living rooms became bedrooms. The attic became the new third floor and contains two bedrooms, a shared bathroom, and a large living room that is often used for meetings. An adjacent third-floor deck was added. On the second floor there are now a separate TV room and an office. The group has lived together happily since 1990, with a very low turnover of members.

BJM Group House, Lafayette, CA

On the other side of the San Francisco Bay and lifestyle spectrum is a more upscale group house in Lafayette. BJM stands for the first names of the two women and one man, long-time friends who, in their late 30s to 40s, decided to build a house together rather than continue to socialize from three different cities in the Bay Area. They, like the Black Cat group, began the process with SLRC's profile/ consultation process. They continued with an extensive site-finding analysis and exploratory group design sessions, which led to finding a site with a spectacular view of Mount Diablo that was accessible to BART (Bay Area Rapid Transit). They proceeded with SLRC's group design process, followed by final working drawings and construction. The house was completed in mid-1989.

The BJM house has three private living suites, a guest suite, and a sleeping loft for visiting children. Each private suite has its own large living area, walk-in closet, personalized bathroom, and a private deck with views. What makes the decks private is a large landscaped earth berm, or mound, between each bedroom's deck and the several common

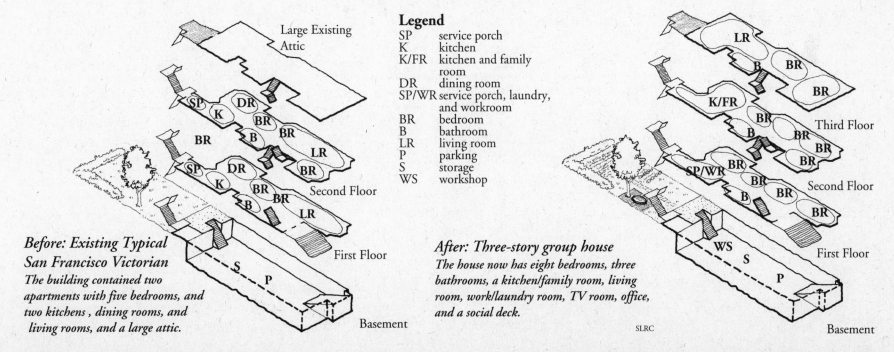

Legend

SP	service porch
K	kitchen
K/FR	kitchen and family room
DR	dining room
SP/WR	service porch, laundry, and workroom
BR	bedroom
B	bathroom
LR	living room
P	parking
S	storage
WS	workshop

Large Existing Attic

Second Floor

First Floor

Basement

Before: Existing Typical San Francisco Victorian
The building contained two apartments with five bedrooms, and two kitchens, dining rooms, and living rooms, and a large attic.

Third Floor

Second Floor

First Floor

Basement

After: Three-story group house
The house now has eight bedrooms, three bathrooms, a kitchen/family room, living room, work/laundry room, TV room, office, and a social deck.

SLRC

decks. The house also has a shared office and meeting/recreation room, common kitchen and dining room, a VCR/TV alcove, a wine cellar, and a swimming pool.

The house energy design includes the extensive south solar-gain openings, the eight foot high earth berm on the northeast side, and the active solar water and space heating system consisting of solar collectors and 500 gallon water storage tanks that feed a five-zone radiant heating system in the concrete slab. In addition, the swimming pool and hot tub are solar heated.

Nonprofit Sponsorship of Special Care Group Homes

The housing and social service needs of population sub-groups that need special care and services, such as single parents, frail elderly, disabled, battered women and children, homeless persons and families, people recovering from chemical addictions and mental health problems, and ex-inmates, are increasingly being met by shared living and Group Home programs that combine social services with extended family and community living. This is happening under the umbrella movement called "social housing," sponsored by nonprofit organizations that support the participation of the residents within permanently affordable housing. The new emphasis is to empower residents to improve their economic opportunities and their living environment, obtain healthcare services, and learn group living social skills. The shared meals and the co-responsibility atmosphere provided by this new direction for "social housing" is generating a marvelous healing energy and contributing to the rebuilding of community in America. Here are some of the successful Group Home programs that represent this emerging social responsibility trend in housing.

Senior shared housing — alternatives to board and care homes
One of the big "social housing" breakthroughs is the senior home-share programs that provide an alterna-

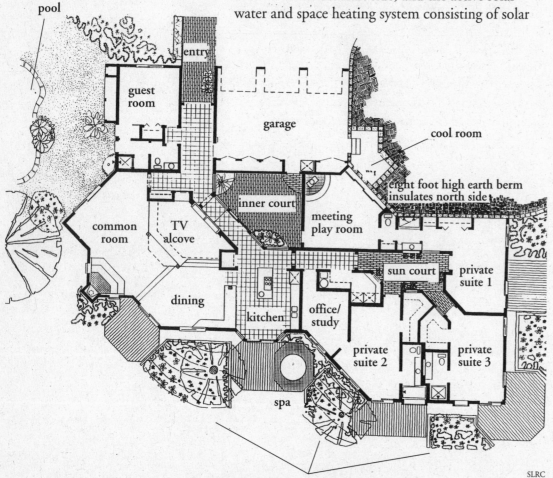

A New Design Group House with Three Private Living Suites
This 3,600 sq. ft. group house serves need for both privacy and mutual activities, including working at home.

SLRC

tive to the trauma of elderly people being forced into elder care institutions when they can no longer afford their homes or fully manage living alone. Though a few are well managed and regulated, board and care homes are often characterized by an institutional setting that no one resident or even a group of residents can have much control over. The management style in the "old people's home" is warehousing, and at best, people are often forced to share small rooms and are given no "territory" to personalize; thus they take no pride or responsibility in their surroundings. In this desensitized setting, the elderly are often pushed out into the common areas to interact because "it will be good for them," or they are forgotten about. This does not work, because the resultant situation of no personal choice or privacy causes people to withdraw emotionally. Having choices about when and how to interact is what nurtures independent living and most distinguishes community life from institutional life.

Senior shared housing programs have developed in answer to the above dilemma. The Shared

Dinner time, Senior Shared House   Harvest House

Housing Resource Center in Burlington, Vermont, founded by Maggie Kuhn, is a co-sponsor of three senior shared housing programs, and has identified over 500 of these successful programs in the United States. Originally, senior shared housing programs focused upon the substantial supply of unused bedrooms in existing houses of older people who need live-in assistance and/or companionship and help with living costs. These programs are rapidly changing to become more diversified, and now are beginning to include intergenerational or mixed-age, single-parent, and extended family shared living households. This represents a phenomenal recognition of the new extended family approach as a workable, successful, and socially, physically, and emotionally healing solution to the "welfare crisis." The "caretaker" model is transformed into a self-care process in which people gladly participate and share responsibility for their own future.

Innovative Housing, San Rafael, CA

Innovative Housing, Inc. (IH) is a pioneering nonprofit shared housing sponsoring organization. Founded in 1980 by Ann Howell and based in Marin County, California, it has organized hundreds of extended family houses of various types. The organization helps people form and maintain compatible living groups through self-selection workshops; locates and master leases or acquires houses for sharing (the residents pay rent to the organization); and assumes legal, financial, and maintenance responsibility for the houses. IH helps to fill vacancies, mediate problems, and foster resource sharing and support networks among the various households for services like childcare and household repairs, and for items like toys and

"Focusing on shelters to solve homelessness diverts people's attention from creating a solution that will work. A shelter, however well designed, is not a home." [20]
— *Barbara Cappa, Project Share, Inc.*

Two Friends Raking Leaves   Harvest House

Three Cooks Do Not Spoil the Soup   Harvest House

"Including Shared Housing in Health Care Reform"
From an Editorial in the Shared Housing News [21]

Health care reform may well be the single most important and complicated issue Americans are faced with today. It is an enormous task that we who work for shared housing must be involved in, because we know that our health begins with where we live. And we want to make sure that shared housing is included in health care planning on both state and national levels.

We must provide more housing options for the increasing number of people who find it difficult to live alone, but do not need all the services associated with living in nursing or intermediate care homes. It is important to recognize two issues that stand in the way of promoting the shared housing option. One is that our society so strongly emphasizes the notion of independence — which, for many, translates into living alone— that interdependence can seem undesirable. The other issue is that licensing and zoning regulations, which vary from state to state, are often barriers to developing shared housing.

Any discussion of health care must include housing. With a new administration in Washington that fully supports health care reform, shared housing programs across the country have the opportunity to contribute to new legislation. Current data on all shared housing programs and their clients will support the connection of health care and housing on state and national levels.

One of Marin's most stunning success stories in recent years has been a new kind of shared housing, available in attractive, affordable packages and in forms which accentuate the positive. The old stigma attached to "living with strangers" and "losing one's privacy" has been eliminated. Instead, for the right people, shared housing can mean losing practically nothing and gaining something of value — something available almost no place else in today's housing market." [22]
— Ecumenical Association for Housing, Inc.

recreation and gardening equipment.

IH has extended its shared housing services to low and very low income single parents, seniors, those in recovery from substance abuse and domestic violence, the disabled, and people with AIDS. Service-enriched shared housing for homeless families and individuals is also provided by IH in their uniqe transitional housing programs. IH has utilized the idea of the two-tier approach to graduate the homeless and special-need populations from the healing process in a transition house to the life-building process in long–term or permanent shared housing.

The extended family shared living experience provides a peer support group, sharing of resources, and a cost–of–living savings that enables people to live quite comfortably. IH's trained housing staff provides a sensitive understanding of the needs and circumstances of the individual applicants, and assists the residents to obtain other social services to help with their personal development. Several of the IH houses have been purchased and remodeled with added bedrooms and common space, thus making them more suitable for long-term use as shared houses. Some groups who become financially capable choose to stay together after the IH shared housing assistance has ended. They either assume the leases themselves or find other houses to share. The two-tier "enriched" transitional housing is now being used elsewhere in the U.S., and serves as an excellent model for how the extended family lifestyle can make use of our existing housing stock and greatly reduce the cost of housing, reduce social isolation, improve parenting skills, and provide access to critical services.

Fairfax "Vest Pocket" Community, Fairfax, CA
This IH sponsored shared living cluster community is an extension of their very successful supportive, shared housing rental programs. The Fairfax project is for single parents. Five houses have been specially designed for shared living and for compatibility with the existing neighborhood, with a sixth "house" designed as a community building. The project is on two adjacent sites with three houses on each site. There are a total of 19 bedrooms, with three to four bedrooms per house, plus the common kitchens, dining, living and other spaces in each house. The community building has mail boxes,

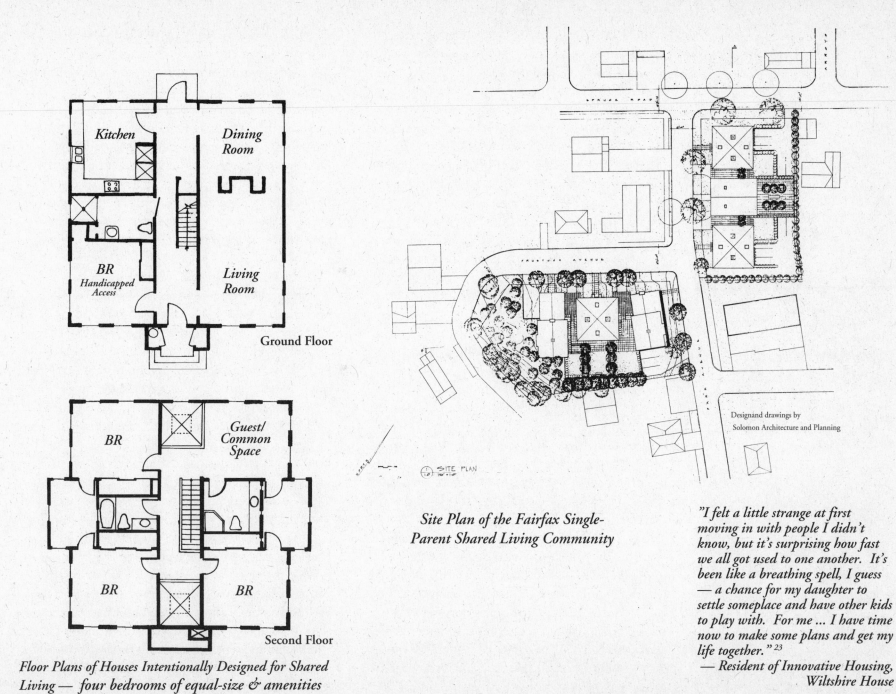

Kitchen

Dining Room

BR
Handicapped Access

Living Room

Ground Floor

BR

Guest/ Common Space

BR

BR

Second Floor

Floor Plans of Houses Intentionally Designed for Shared Living — four bedrooms of equal-size & amenities

Designand drawings by
Solomon Architecture and Planning

SITE PLAN

Site Plan of the Fairfax Single-Parent Shared Living Community

"I felt a little strange at first moving in with people I didn't know, but it's surprising how fast we all got used to one another. It's been like a breathing spell, I guess — a chance for my daughter to settle someplace and have other kids to play with. For me ... I have time now to make some plans and get my life together." 23
— *Resident of Innovative Housing, Wiltshire House*

253

"I really appreciate HIP's help in getting such a great tenant. I've never had a better housemate. Because I live on Social Security, I needed extra income and I can always count on Michael to pay his rent on time. He helps a lot around the house. He is one great guy!"[24]
— A senior homeowner in a Human Investment Project house.

Raphael House

4th of July Picnic on Roof of Raphael House
This downtown San Francisco extended family transition house demonstrates intensive use of a high density building for creating a geniune community.

laundry facilities, a kitchen and a community room for group meals and celebrations, and a living suite for an on-site resident manager. Although planning started in 1982, the project is just now ready for development due to planning and zoning delays, funding restraints, and neighborhood opposition. (Some neighbors have been opposed to the project "in their backyard" and have filed a lawsuit, despite the excellent design and the social benefits for single parents and the broader community.)
The ability of IH to blend the provision of this housing with community building and personal development is unique. Combined with the perseverance and sensitive architectural design of Daniel Soloman, IH has brought this project to national attention even before completion.

Single-Parent and Intergenerational Shared Housing, San Mateo County, CA

Two new single-parent family houses have been built in Redwood City by the Human Investment Project (HIP). HIP has pioneered Group Share residences for over 20 years, serving single parents, seniors, and persons with special needs. HIP now owns or leases nine extended family shared houses and manages an additional eight for the city of San Mateo. In all, HIP aided over 2,000 households in 1993. Their two newest shared houses are specially designed for single parents and seniors to share household responsibilities, childcare, and meals. The 3,200 sq. ft. Hilton House in Redwood City has six bedrooms and three bathrooms, with a common kitchen, dining room, and living space downstairs. They were able to build these two new houses with the aid of grants and loans from local governments, the State of California, and HUD.

HIP has furthered the intergenerational shared housing movement with an on-going, senior-housemate match program and the Home Equity Conversion Program, which assists senior homeowners to stay in their homes and find house mates. HIP provides a series of technical assistance workshops and a manual called "Homesharing — Successful Strategies," and has established the California Homesharing Association. They have proven that shared housing with built-in services creates a major cost-saving alternative to expensive government programs and revolving–door shelters.

The Raphael House, San Francisco, CA.

The Raphael House is not merely a shelter, but a warm haven for troubled families to regain a stable pattern of daily life, begin a healing process, learn parenting skills, and have access to individual and family counseling, financial planning, and assistance in obtaining housing and setting goals.

Raphael House was founded in 1978 with a decidedly Christian ethos by a brotherhood group of the Greek Orthodox Church. The emphasis, however, is on providing services and emotional support, not converting people to Christianity. They function as a full-scale Intentional Community, striving to be self-reliant without government subsidies. They have a dedicated staff that practices simple living, and many volunteers. They are funded through donations, grants, and the Brothers Junipers Restaurant and catering businesses at their San Francisco location. Their building is a transition home for 50 or so adults (18 to 20 families) and children, complete with private family bedrooms, a community dining room for family-style meals, activity rooms, a library, laundry and work

Raphael House

Thanksgiving at Raphael House
Volunteers help serve dinner in an atmosphere where
volunteers, resident families, and staff become one community.

rooms, a children's play space, and gardens on a rooftop deck.

A major contribution to ending homelessness and the poverty cycle is the Follow-Up Services program, which includes long-term case management, the Raphael House Extended Family Program, and the Family Support Network. They recently enlarged their family stabilizing program by obtaining the building next door for families to live in. The physical and spiritual healing nature of community is truly evident at Raphael House.

Dwight Way Shelter/Transitional House, Berkeley, CA

This project provides another testimony that sharing meals and family responsibilities creates an atmosphere for healing and recovery. The homeless shelter on the ground floor, and the transitional house for eight to 12 homeless women on the second floor demonstrate how two nonprofits can team up to provide social housing services. Resources for Community Development is a nonprofit affordable housing developer that recently acquired, restored, and seismically braced an 1880's Victorian commercial building on Dwight Way. with residential uses on the second floor. The Berkeley Emergency Food Project operates both the overnight shelter and the upstairs Transitional Home for women with various mental disabilities. The project is funded by HUD.

Whereas the shelter operates more typically as an emergency facility for men, women, and a few families, the transitional house residents and 24-hour staff persons strive to work as an extended family community where the women share chores, pool their food money, share shopping and cooking, and have weekly peer group meetings. The women are faced with the challenge of discovering and honoring their individuality, and developing social skills to contribute to community, while avoiding slipping into isolation because of socialization that is too abrupt or intense. These are the same kinds of learning experiences and skills relative to self and community that would benefit the entire American society.

The Dwight Way Transitional House is well located on major bus routes and within walking distance of downtown Berkeley, where the residents

"'Economic and social problems are more severe than they were fifteen, twenty years ago,' said Fr. David. 'We saw the need for a more formal follow-up program because families have a hard time after they move out — all their money has gone to the apartment they're getting, children have fallen behind in school and parents feel isolated and alone.'" [23]

— Raphael House newsletter

can participate in community life at the YMCA, public library, churches, and other places to further develop their independent living skills. The rationale for living in the city and having access to healing resources of a supportive community is just as important for the rest of society as it is for these women. During the tour of the Dwight Way Transitional House some important principles of group living design were observed. The kitchen needs to be open to the social areas and large enough for several people to work around a central counter so that the cooks can socialize with other housemates. A transition house should be approached no differently in layout and design than any group living house, and therefore needs more individual common rooms for art and other special activities separate from the main social room, and rooms for staff-client counseling. Opportunities for eating at small tables and informally around the social room are preferred. The nurturing warmth of the staff of Dwight Way Transition House is a wonderful testimony to the possibility that we can rebuild community in America for all people though the extended family model.

Conclusion

The new extended family shared house examples presented throughout this chapter are in direct response to the breakdown of family and community in our society in recent years. The response to SLRC and the indication from many sources is that people want to regain the lost sense of belonging to a stable and supportive group. To answer that need we recommend a major increase of specially designed extended family houses with five to ten bedrooms, two to four bathrooms, and a diversity of common areas. We need more choices for people wanting to live together in extended family houses as an alternative to one or several people living in little units. It is important that HUD, the banking and lending institutions, and nonprofit and for-profit developers recognize that the new extended family, shared living way of providing affordable housing is needed on a large scale as a permanent housing solution.

It is equally important that people participate in creating an ecologically healthy and sustainable place to live and work that is rewarding and obviously obtainable. We must make changes in the status-quo way of living in order to reverse the tremendous ecological damage already done, and to bring an ecologically sustainable way of living into the 21st century. The process of forming and co-designing socially and environmentally integrated living places will provide opportunities for developing skills necessary to deal with conflicts and adjustments inherent in human interactions. In such a community support system difficulties are balanced by the rewards of self-esteem, nurturing, and personal and group empowerment. American society is awakening to the possibility of new extended family and ecological village community as a way of life. Our society will hopefully be a magnificent example of success in self-healing and renewal as the facades of outmoded systems fall away.

Notes

Books listed only by name in the endnotes are highlighted in the resource guide at the end of the book, complete with author/publisher information and description.

1 Yi-Fu Tuan, <u>Space and Place</u>, The Perspective of Experience, University of Minnesota, 1977, p. 64.

2 Tom Bender, <u>Environmental Design Primer</u>, Shocken Books, 1976, p. 190.

3 Kathleen Smith, "Unity of Edifice, Ethics, and Environment: A Study of Social Organization and Building Form in Igboland," paper written at UC Berkeley, November 1990.

4 Jean-Paul Bourdier & Trinh T. Minh-ha, <u>African Spaces: Designs for Living in Upper Volta</u>, Africana Publishing Company, New York, 1985, p.196.

5 Sue Shellenbarger, "Longer Commutes Force Parents to Make Tough Choices on Where to Leave the Kids," *Wall Street Journal,* August 18. 1993. p. B1.

6 J. Donald Walters, <u>Cities of Light: What Communities Can Accomplish, and the Need for Them in Our Time</u>, Crystal Clarity, Publishers,1987, pg. 50.

7 <u>Space and Place</u>, p. 65.

8 Architecture, Research, Construction, Inc., <u>Community Group Homes: An Environmental Approach</u>, Van Nostrand Reinhold Company, New York, 1985, p. 73.

9 <u>Creating Community Anywhere</u>, pp. 30-31.

10 <u>Builders of the Dawn</u>, p. 67.

11 "Shared Housing=Medicaid Savings", *Shared Housing News,* Spring 1993, p.1.

12 <u>CoHousing</u> p.39.

13 <u>CoHousing</u>, p. 62.

14 Dolores Hayden, <u>Seven American Utopias: The Architecture of Communitarian Socialism 1790-1975</u>, MIT Press, Cambridge, 1976, p. 45.

15 Ram Dass, <u>Be Here Now</u>, Hanuman Foundation, Boulder, 1971, p. 105.

16 Clare Cooper Marcus & Wendy Sarkissan, <u>Housing as if People Mattered: Site Design Guidelines for Medium-Density Family Housing</u>, University of California Press, Berkeley, 1986, p. 82.

17 Allen Butcher, <u>Directory of Intentional Communities,</u> co-published by Fellowship for Intentional Community and Communities Publications Cooperative, 1991, p. 94.

18 <u>Prolonging the Good Years</u>, p. 79.

19 <u>Space and Place</u>, p. 30

20 Quoted in M.C. Daniels, <u>Alternatives to Compassionate Fatigue: Homelessness and the Charitable Heart</u>, 1990, p. 5. Spring/Summer, 1989.

21 Editorial, *Shared Housing News,* Fall 1992, pp. 5-6

22 *EAH Newsletter,* Ecumenical Association for Housing, Inc., Winter 1987.

23 *EAH Newsletter,* Eucumenical Association For Housing, Inc.,

24 *Ibid.*

25 *at Raphael House,* Vol. 4, Summer 1994.

THE CELEBRATION OF FOOD
Cooking and Dining as the Foundation of Community

Serving at Ananda Village

Ken Norwood

Dining at Doyle Street CoHousing

CoHousing Co.

Berkeley Farmers Market

Ken Norwood

Ananda Kitchen Team

Dining at Harvest House

Harvest House

"Eating should be a pleasure. It should be a celebration and communion with life." [1]
— *John Robbins, Diet for a New America*

C H A P T E R   E I G H T

Have you noticed that guests at a party or dinner often abandon comfortable living and dining rooms to congregate in the kitchen? The kitchen is like a magnet. Its warmth and familiarity reach out and draw you in like the outdoor cooking fires of our ancestors.

The kitchen of a Shared Living Community is no different. This timeless gathering place, where food is prepared and eaten, and the sense of family nurtured through closeness and communication, is the heart of the community and the source of a rebirth of culture. The culture of a community is not necessarily sustainable and cannot endure without continual exposure to the diversity and richness of human interactions.

The kitchen, dining, and social areas that comprise the common houses of these new communities become a sanctuary for all to come together and share daily experiences, problems, and joys. The evening meal provides a time to relax and wind down with loved ones after the rush of the day, a time for elders to share with youth their wealth of ideas and experiences from the past and insights on the present and future. It is a time for children to express themselves and for adults to enjoy sharing common tasks and exchanging their experiences of the day. This is a valuable, intergenerational activity which stimulates communication, personal growth, and the spirit of belonging to community.

Our Common Heritage

Gathering together to share meals has been a basic ritual of humanity from tribes, extended families, and villages to the communities of today. In the past, harsh conditions forced men and women to band together in the struggle to survive. In Consuming Passions: The Anthropology of Eating, Peter Farb and George Armelagos research the connection between eating, social structure, and community-building in cultures around the world. They write, "In all societies both simple and complex, eating is a primary way of initiating and maintaining human relationships." [2] The Bantu of southern Africa, for example, regard food sharing as the foundation of a temporary covenant between individuals and call it a 'clanship of porridge.' The Chinese regard the giving and sharing of food as the most basic social relationship, and eat alone only when living in abject poverty. The Javanese often celebrate 'slamentan,' a communal feast, to obtain protection from the spirits, promote social harmony and unity, and confer a feeling of "physical and mental equanimity during which everyone feels that nothing upsetting will happen." And in English, the word 'companion' comes from Latin and French words meaning 'one who eats bread with another.'[3]

Today in western societies, "progress," technology, and mobility have all but eliminated the experience of group food gathering and growing, although some rituals survive. At birthdays there is cake and ice cream to celebrate life. Church members take communion by sipping wine and eating bread to symbolize their union with God. At weddings the bride and groom cut cake and feed all in attendance as they begin their lives together. We go out to eat to celebrate a new job or victory at a softball game. At harvest time there are feasts and dances, potluck dinners, and picnics. And there are the business lunches, the conference banquets, and the wake-feast when a loved one dies. Eating together can celebrate union with each other and with higher forces. It marks beginnings and endings. There is something primal, sensual, and equalizing about eating together that goes beyond mere physical survival, to satisfy social and spiritual yearnings.

In the first part of this chapter, we show how the sharing of food-related activities in communities can strengthen the family structure and work to bring about social and cultural sustainability, cost and time savings, environmental regeneration, and other practical and personal daily living benefits. In the second part, we explore in-depth issues and ideas relating to the design of common cooking and dining areas.

Social and Cultural Sustainability

We humans are a gregarious species and can easily adapt to and enjoy community and shared mealtime activity when the physical and social environment is accommodating and compatible. Unfortunately, the reality today is just the opposite. Whereas technology, the automobile, and the single-family house, condo, and apartment were meant to bring us independence and convenience, they have instead brought us processed food, unhealthy eating habits, higher costs, isolation, and loneliness.

"Within the context of a strong spirit of community, even eating and its pleasures can be transformed. Whether it's at a Lutheran Church supper or a Jewish Sabbath dinner, at a block party or a family reunion, when we gather together to celebrate, when we linger in the moment, even the simplest fares can seem rich in our mouths and our memories…" [4]
— Jeremy Iggers, "Innocence Lost: Our complicated relationship with food"

"The overriding importance in human evolution of cooperative hunting and sharing … [dates] back to between two and three million years ago … When several families come together in one camp, they engage in endless exchange of information typical of human activity … the exchange and sharing of food means that the one who gives today can expect to receive tomorrow. And from that expectation stem reciprocal obligations, rules to enforce fair sharing, and marital ties between kin groups to make sharing permanent. The human family probably could not have arisen without those early and simple steps toward the sharing of food." [5]
— Peter Farb & George Armelagos

Television's Big Impact on Children

Other than family or peers, nothing has as much influence on a child's behavior as television. The average child today spends more time in front of a TV set than she does studying in school or talking...

FAMILIES TODAY

THE KITCHEN GARDENER

Organic Gardens Get Back to Basics

The key idea is that healthy soil produces healthy plants

the method, which are:

■ **Soil fertility** — Feed soil, and the soil will feed what they need, as they pr the forms they prefer it. Th fed actively decaying organic ma compost from a pile

San Francisco Chronicle

Consumerism blamed for much of damage to planet

Growing fixation on shopping malls ripped in study

No Time for Neighborliness

MISS MANNERS
Judith Martin

How 'Green Consumers' Are Changing the Marketplace

BY CONNIE KOENENN
Los Angeles Times

There is a new order of shopper in consumerland: men and women on a mission, customers with a moral tone.

Environmentally aware shoppers eschew phosphates and plastics.

OPEN FORUM / DOUGLAS MATTERN

Lifestyle Changes Needed To Save the Environment

Warning Signs of Ecological Decline

From Page 1

global environmental degradation, one already affecting the welfare of hundreds of millions.

All the principal changes in the earth's physical condition

able global economy, tree cutting and tree planting, soil erosion and soil formation, carbon and carbon

The Living Arts
The New York Times

Urban poor pay most for food, study says

Big gap between cities and suburbs

By Mark S.R. Suchecki
HEARST NEWS SERVICE

A Communal Type of Life With Dinner for All And Day Care, Too

BY JO GIESE

■ ENVIRONMENT

Need to Reduce Our Consumption

Too much wealth — and even too much poverty — can result in destruction to the planet

BY LESTER R. BROWN
Special to The Chronicle

BOOKS Patricia Holt

Society Must Admit Its Woes Before It Can Be Cured

The Green Lifestyle: It's Not Too Late — Yet

From Page B4

Cultivating Kids Into Gardeners

Budget travails can't stem growth of school gardens

BY SIBELLA KRAUS
Chronicle Staff Writer

All around the Bay Area, school gardens are sprouting up like mushrooms after rain.

Families that dine together eat better

CHILDREN WHO eat meals with the family have better nutritional habits. So says a registered dietitian for the California Dietetic Association (CDA).

"Children learn good eating habits by the examples set by adults," says dietitian Rose Mary

FOOD JOURNAL
Compiled by Jan Townsend

Oaks restaurant still hasn't escaped the effects

Sticks, Hazelnut Praline Cheesecake). The cheesecake is 193 calories per slice with 8 grams of fat.

To order the 45-minute video

"In community, food nurtures both stomach and soul."
— Kathleen Smith

SLRC

Increasingly, due to divorce, singlehood, single parenting, and two-income families, the ritual of sharing food has declined as a focus in daily life. Hectic days do not allow many of us to sit down with others and enjoy a meal. Even in families, it is rare to have everyone together at any meal, especially without the TV on. As we eat in these smaller and smaller groupings or alone, we lose opportunities for human nurturing, communication, the giving of ourselves, and growth. This can be especially damaging for children, who in today's technological world may communicate only during TV commercials and between video games.

It has also been established that single people, younger and older, rarely take the time to cook something elaborate or nutritious, and instead many tend to munch on junk food, microwave their dinner, or eat out in restaurants where they are near others but still alone. Cooking has become uninspiring — a chore to be finished quickly.

Is it any wonder, then, that some people in SLRC workshops are uneasy about cooking and eating with others in a community setting? Growing up in a modern culture has not prepared many of us for intimacy and sharing. Interacting with a larger group involves expressing desires, needs, and feelings to more people, causing correspondingly greater feelings of vulnerability and risk for the inexperienced or timid. Too often in our culture these fears are "resolved" by further isolating ourselves in private houses or hiding behind walkmans, TVs, burglar alarms, and windshields. This breakdown of face-to-face communication, especially around the dinner table, is perhaps the most significant factor that has contributed to the breakdown of community and the increase of urban alienation.

KEN'S STORY

From my own rich portfolio of experiences with extended family, group, and community shared responsibilities around food, I can attest to the sense of wonder, growth, nurturing, and empowerment that can come from mealtime convergence of human energies. Compared to the times of regular meals by myself or with the same one or two people, some of the larger group meals stand out as quantum leaps in terms of gaining self-esteem and fulfillment. I realize now that during many of these times, I felt more valued and complete as a person and less alone than I have at other times in my life.

In my childhood days during "the Great Depression," evening and weekend meals with the extended family of grandparents, parents, aunts, uncles, and cousins were exhilarating and reassuring. I could choose to bask in the center of attention by chattering and performing shenanigans, or withdraw to be a silent observer. The fun continued away from home, too. Meals in the dining halls of the Boy Scout and YMCA summer camps I attended were incredibly enjoyable. I will never forget the competitive camaraderie of cabin tables, the "sing-offs," the exchanges of worldly knowledge and nonsense, and the sense of group and personal empowerment that came when it was our cabin's turn to serve meals and clean up. But I realize now how easy it is for us to lose touch with the culture of family and community.

During WW II, I gained invaluable learning experience in the social dynamics of community and the differences between cultures concerning the sharing of resources. As a POW under the Nazis I shared a room and meager rations with 10 to 16 other war prisoners. We created our own democratic social order, bartering system, mealtime rituals, shared responsibilities, and mutual support system on every scale, from our prison compound to our barracks, and within each room. The food distribution and mealtime systems that emerged left me with valuable insights into how Americans are addicted to the cult of individualism.

We owed our survival to the International Red Cross food parcel which was meant to sustain one person for a week. Due to Allied air raids and pilfering, we usually got only one parcel for two POWs, so we would pair up with a chosen buddy to split the rations. We Americans each maintained our own food stash, waiting in rotation for access to the tiny stove top in each room to warm Spam or corned beef and German potatoes. Often we ate by ourselves or in pairs, sitting on the edges of our bunkbeds. The British, Canadian, and Australian POWs, however, most often pooled their rations, cooperatively cooked their meals, and ate in a circle around a small table. I envied the camaraderie of their mealtimes and the apparent abundance and quality of the meals their cooks concocted.

By the time I entered the USC School of Architecture in 1947 and joined the Alpha Rho Chi architectural fraternity, I was a confirmed group living junkie. I always enjoyed mealtimes with the "brothers," talking about design, world problems, and the Trojans' chances of winning next week's game.

The family of three children my wife and I raised (BBs) marked the end of the larger nuclear/extended family that prevailed until just following WW II. This book attempts to draw attention to restoring severed social ties and the ability as a society to harmoniously survive and thrive into the 21st century through creating an environment for sharing of food.

"While there are clearly exceptions, the extended family generally provides more space and flexibility and far less pressure on each individual, both emotionally and in terms of responsibility. It is particularly beneficial for the elderly and for women and children. Within the extended family, older people are appreciated for their wisdom and experience, and their slower pace does not prevent them from making an important contribution to the community."[6]
— Helena Norberg-Hodge
Ancient Futures

"At the common dinner, the TV is off and only people are left to stimulate, tantalize, and soothe."
— Kathleen Smith

In promoting Shared Living Communities, we hope to counteract societal disintegration by creating supportive environments in which barriers are removed and the symbolism, joyfulness, and fun of cooking and eating together are brought back into daily life. The group-designed common house for sharing cooking and meals creates a forum that encourages us to honestly express and explore our feelings, revel in the joy and love of human contact, and become fully rounded persons. As David Elkins explains, "All real living is in meeting. It is in the I–Thou experience and in the 'We' of community that personhood is born and nurtured. By conscious living and by holding tightly to the hands of others we become persons." [7]

It is important to remember that in most intentional and organized communities, no one is required to eat with the group, but almost everyone does. Because of the strong sense of family and support that is generated from sharing meals and lives, even the most timid can be enticed to come to the tables. However, the intentions of the founding group and those who join the community will determine the degree of participation in shared meals. The long-lasting strength of a community, and certainly the cost of living, is closely related to its observation of group meals and activities in common. Unless a group is committed to working and eating together, the effort and expense that go into designing a fully equipped kitchen and comfortably furnished dining hall and social area may be wasted.

The Village Cluster and other forms of Shared Living Communities provide the essential physical setting for shared evening meals to become a daily restorative and revitalizing ritual. The following sections describe in more detail the personal and group benefits of sharing meals.

Bringing the Wisdom of Elders to the Table

Elders living in an extended family or community and sharing meals provide companionship and enjoy an important arena for realizing themselves. Victoria Fitch, in "The Psychological Tasks of Old Age," [8] points out that because the elderly are old does not mean that they are no longer subject to change or development. In fact, she says a four-stage evolutionary process is experienced by the elderly: slowing, life review, transmission, and letting go.

Shared meals facilitate all these processes, but especially life review and transmission. According to Ms. Fitch, life review means sorting through the past, handling artifacts and memories, and telling stories. "Repetition of stories about one's life is part of the process of finally understanding one's identity." [9]

Transmission is "…the handing on to others the essence of their knowledge of the world around them; how to do things; how to think about things; how to simply be." [10] Forced into rest homes and isolated from contact with people of other generations, most elders are denied a chance to continue their natural evolution. In contrast, common community activities such as cooking, planning events, and eating together become a time when elders can offer advice and wisdom to those younger, and at the same time gain recognition and understanding of themselves and their lives. The gifts that older people bring to a community can play a vital role in the empowerment and cohesiveness of the group.

Many people from African, Asian, Latino, and other cultures, including some European ones, have a tradition of intense family and intergenerational interaction. The Native American culture, for example, has always recognized the important role of elders in a community. As Karie Garnier, author of Our Elders Speak, explains, "…they traditionally were — and still are — teachers of time-tested values that are rooted in reverence for nature. It is not only the words of the Elders that teach; it is also their non-verbal warmth and kindness and humour that touches, teaches and heals."[11] Today, Shared Living Communities can help give this vital role back to elders and contribute to a sustainable society for peoples of all races, ethnicities, and economic backgrounds.

Getting Mom Out of the Kitchen

The need to nurture and be nurtured is innate in all of us, yet the opportunity for this is lacking in conventional housing and social structures which isolate individuals and small families, placing all responsibility for caregiving and providing meals on the woman. In a Shared Living Community, everyone helps to cook and shares in nurturing the health of the "family."

Pax House, a student community in Berkeley where Kathleen lived for a semester, has sign-up sheets at the beginning of each semester. Each student signs up for one shift, cooking, washing dishes, washing pots, or shopping, to be done on the same night each week. The schedule suits the students' needs since they can easily plan their

classes, jobs, and social life around it.

At the Arch Street group house in Berkeley where Ken lived for six years, an evening meal was served four times a week. The kitchen and household tasks were equally shared by the eight men and women. They rotated shopping once a month with a partner, and cooking once every two

Parents Magazine, 1945, Reproduced from
Redesigning the American Dream by Delores Hayden

The Days of the "A Womans Place is in the Kitchen" Are Over — in Community

"Women all over the world work longer hours than men. Mothers work longer hours than anyone else because their family responsibilities to household and children are not equally shared by fathers — anywhere. In industrialized countries, whether in the Western or Eastern worlds, mothers do the majority of the shopping, house cleaning, cooking, laundry, and child care, in addition to their paid employment. Whereas fathers in these societies work an average of 50 hours per week in combined employment and household work, mothers work an average of 80 hours per week at the same tasks."[12]
— Sandra Scarr, Deborah Phillips, & Kathleen McCartney, "Working Mothers and Their Families"

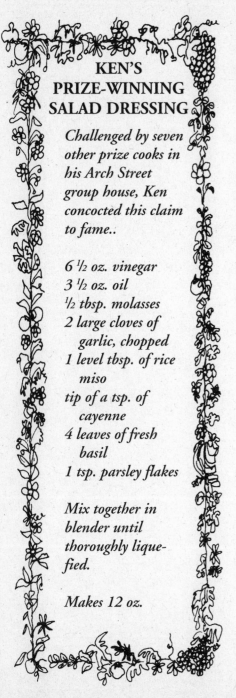

KEN'S PRIZE-WINNING SALAD DRESSING

Challenged by seven other prize cooks in his Arch Street group house, Ken concocted this claim to fame..

6 ½ oz. vinegar
3 ½ oz. oil
½ tbsp. molasses
2 large cloves of garlic, chopped
1 level tbsp. of rice miso
tip of a tsp. of cayenne
4 leaves of fresh basil
1 tsp. parsley flakes

Mix together in blender until thoroughly liquefied.

Makes 12 oz.

weeks. With this routine, the "mother" or "father" types were dissuaded from their conventional hierarchical roles. According to Ken, they ate so–o–o–o well for so–o–o–o little, they lived like Robin Hoods.

An added benefit of everybody sharing the food related responsibilities is that everybody can learn to cook. Since community members usually cook only once a week to once a month, they tend to really take pride in their cooking and take time to use fresh, nutritious ingredients to create healthy dishes rich in taste, color, and love. The delightful dishes relished in evening group house and community meals could equal those from any home or the finest restaurants. Good food makes people happy, and happy people make good food.

Having a larger variety of tasty and nutritious recipes tends to motivate people to experiment more in their culinary creations. Eric Raimy describes group living thus: "Before I lived communally, I could cook scrambled eggs and TV dinners. Now I can cook curry, quiche, frittata, shark steak, crepes, and tamales, to list a few specialties. Living with people who enjoy eating anything and everything is a broadening experience in more ways than one."[14]

Providing healthy, delicious food for an extended family household or a larger community is a way of cooking up pride and confidence for children and adults alike. Members will be happy to come home and find a delicious meal waiting for them, and will show this in appreciation for the

Photo by Kathleen Smith

Cooking for the Community at Muir Commons CoHousing

cook. For that day, the cook is the provider and the "mother," and the gourmet chef whom all love, appreciate, and admire. In the Native American tradition, ones who cook are part of the backbone that makes all things work together. The value of sharing in mealtime responsibility is especially important for children, for they are not "just kids." They should not be given "token" jobs, but rather included as important participants in the community.

Children growing up in single-parent and two-income nuclear families tend to be isolated from other adults and often suffer the "latchkey" syndrome of too much TV. In a community setting, children have the opportunity to observe, work, and talk with people other than their parents or siblings, resulting in more role models and experiences to learn from. Their cultural and personal development is enhanced proportionately. This may be the only antidote to TV's socially debilitating influence on younger generations.

Growing up on the 1-1/2 acre homestead of his maternal grandparents from Germany and Denmark, Ken remembers well how they grew and bartered for most of their food. His grandmother managed a remarkably egalitarian household for those Depression days of the 1930s. Everyone — uncles, aunts, and children — was taught every task and assigned whatever needed to be done. No one finished first, but rather joined to help others until everything was finished. In this mini-community, Ken and his brother and cousins learned at an early age to be helpers and to take over many household tasks normally relegated to adults and older children as "men's" or "women's" work. They gleaned from those experiences how group and individual empowerment bolster each other, and how self-esteem is cultivated and sustained by giving and receiving the gifts of sharing and responsibility.

"Laurel has always tended to be a relatively shy child. She rarely ventured out, particularly not to meet other adults…Now over time she and the other kids have [found] so many adults they feel comfortable relating to and learning from…"[14]
— *Evan, describing his daughter in community*

"In sharing meals, residents satisfy more than physical needs. They fulfill dreams, awaken talents, build a sense of self, and come together as a community."
— *Kathleen Smith*

— *I can't wait for dinner tonight. I saw little Chris and Betha in the garden today picking carrots and spinach.*
— *Oh, I hope Chris is going to make his carrot cake.*
— *Well, I know Betha is making spinach salad. Let's keep our fingers crossed for the cake. What time is it anyway?*
— *6:00.*
— *Hm, half an hour until dinner. Want to go for a walk to see how the new teen room addition is coming?*

Food Choices — the Gathering Point or the Dividing Line

What your mother put on your plate as a child probably established the food likes and dislikes you have now. Many of us heard varying degrees of persuasion: "Eat it and like it," or "Try it, you'll like it," or "Please, no more complaints, your mother worked hard cooking for you." Your food choices may also have been set by the predominant diet of your ethnic, cultural, religious, class, or regional influences. Ken's maternal grandparents operated a poultry business, selling dressed chickens for the traditional Sunday dinners for which many pre-WW II families religiously gathered. Even though he is now mostly a vegetarian and knows that the "factory" chickens of today are no match for the truly organic, yard varieties of those "pre-factory chicken" days, Ken still has a latent craving for Sunday chicken dinners.

In today's ecohealth-conscious and multicultural society, the process of forming new communities inevitably involves the question of diet. Although family-bred food dislikes — "I won't eat _____, or _____, or _____ " (fill in the blanks yourself) — are mostly negotiable and not necessarily fatal to group harmony, there can be serious schisms about food today, involving ethnic, spiritual/religious, ecological, health, and political beliefs. A random sample of a group may contain adherents to meat-eating, vegetarian, lacto-vegetarian, macrobiotic, animal-raising and killing for food, organic farming, fish and chicken only, no processed or fatty foods, and so on.

These issues are often based on known dangers associated with the use of chemicals. The lack of regulations or enforcement in food production and processing are rife. Commercial cattle-raising and slaughtering practices are being politically challenged for health and spiritual reasons, as well as for environmental reasons such as the excessive amount of land used for grazing and grain production to feed cattle. This issue and others are finely written about in *Beyond Beef,* by Jeremy Rifkin:

> There are currently 1.28 billion cattle populating the earth. They take up nearly 24 percent of the landmass of the planet and consume enough grain to feed hundreds of millions of people… Today, about one-third of the world's total grain harvest is fed to cattle and other livestock while as many as a billion people suffer from chronic hunger and malnutrition. In developing nations, millions of peasants are being forced off their ancestral lands to make room for the conversion of farmland from subsistence food grain production to commercial feed grain production… The devastating environmental, economic, and human toll of maintaining a worldwide cattle complex is little discussed in public policy circles… Yet, cattle production and beef consumption now rank among the gravest threats to the future well-being of the earth and its human population.[16]

Food, the source of harmony, can easily be a divisive issue for a community if not resolved early. The issue should be brought up at the very beginning of the community formation and member selection process. Unfortunately, it often comes up after you move in, make agreements, and assign responsibilities regarding food buying and meal

"It now takes the equivalent of a gallon of gasoline to produce a pound of grain-fed beef in the United States. To sustain the yearly beef requirements of an average family of four people requires the consumption of over 260 gallons of fossil fuel. When that fuel is burned it releases 2.5 tons of additional carbon dioxide into the atmosphere — as much CO_2 as the average car emits in six months of normal operation."[15]
— *Jeremy Rifkin, Beyond Beef: The Rise and Fall of the Cattle Culture*

sharing. A rural community that is successfully dealing with the issues of what is moral, natural, healthy, and fulfilling for them, is discussed below.

The Windward example

The Windward Community in Washington state is located on 80 acres of second-growth forest land. They attempt to be mostly self-sufficient and live a truly ecological and sustainable lifestyle, partaking of goat, chicken, turkey, and sometimes pork and veal. They consider this organic living because they produce and eat their food in tune with natural cycles, and have a loving and caring relationship with the plants and animals that they eat. They believe that all aspects of existence are present at every moment and that by a humble understanding of this universal truth, we can all exist harmoniously for the purposes the universe has provided to each living thing. This credo is exemplified by the dozens of goats, geese, chickens, and other creatures that roam free on the land with the humans who lovingly tend to them.

This is the "Windwardian" contribution to a sustainable, ecological lifestyle in which the animals, plants, and humans are integral in the cycles of life. The animals give loving companionship, milk, cheese, wool, skins, eggs, fertilizer, feathers, meat, and livelihood. For this they are cared for and loved, and when they die or their population needs to be thinned down, their lives and their deaths are blessed with thankfulness. In the wholeness of the Windward lifestyle, every person and thing has a place and function, with recycling, composting, reuse, selling, and bartering all part of the process. This community may not be a reproducible model for many people to follow, but it illustrates the spectrum of choices available in community food practices.

Empowered to make it work

For many people, especially insulated, isolated, and individualistic urban dwellers, organic vegetarian eating may be the only way they know to obtain safe food from commercial food sources. In a well-organized community, with its common dining area and kitchen, and centralized food buying, home growing and processing, food safety is within the members' control. In this situation, being organic becomes more important than being vegetarian. Communities that integrate animal-raising and eating in tune with organic methods and natural cycles may then become the true ecologists.

Most of us do *not* want to cause harm to other beings or experience our standard of living at the expense of the well-being and health of others. Most of us *do* want to live in a way that is sustainable. It is a powerful act, therefore, to take these concerns seriously and ask how our food choices reflect our values and affect the ecosystem. Even with the usually lean meat from home-raised animals, the amount of land and resources used for raising meat must be considered, as well as the moral and spiritual implications of killing animals for food. A more appropriate question is whether or not we could all survive quite well without domesticated herd animals being part of our diets and our lives.

Children's eating habits are another important consideration. Kids often do not like "adult" food, so care should be taken to serve fun, meaty-like, easily recognizable and hand-held foods. Differences may arise regarding cholesterol and fatty

"Cooking and eating together is an important ritual for me. I want to learn to live with and in a community where members share goals and visions. I am astounded at the creative power inherent in finding like-minded and creative friends."
— *Participant in SLRC consultation session*

"The most rewarding aspect of mealtime has been the opportunity to get to know one another more closely; and it seems to have really anchored a true sense of what community is for us." [17]
— *Member of Nyland CoHousing*

Time Spent on Chores:

Living Alone *vs.* Living in a Group House

These are estimated times comparing how long a person living alone or in a group house would spend on a given task. These figures are based on personal observations and experiences, and informal surveys of people living in each situation. (Figures are in hours/month/person)

Tasks	Single Person	Eight Person Group House	Yourself
Shopping for Food/Misc.	12	3	_____
Preparing 3 Meals a Day	45	20	_____
Paying House & Utility Bills	2	0.25	_____
Recycling/ Composting	6	0.75	_____
House Cleaning	16	3	_____
Yard Work/ Gardening/Plants	8	2	_____
House Maintenance	4	0.75	_____
Totals:	93	29.75	_____

foods, sugar and junk food, and smoking. It is necessary to discuss all this early in the formation of the group. No one should have to eat anything they don't like. In some communities, cooks post the dinner menu in advance and members sign up. If someone doesn't like the selection, they can cook for themselves or in their own unit.

The difference between communes of the 1960s and the new extended family, Village Cluster/ CoHousing, and Intentional Communities of today is the intention of the group to achieve a purposeful, organized, ecological, and socially responsible approach to housing and family. The essence of this new community movement is a participatory and egalitarian decision-making structure wherein the heart of the community revolves around the basic human experience of sharing food-related activities. The kitchen, dining hall, and garden, as well as the private kitchenette, provide all the basic components to bring people together in modern-day, extended family and village communities.

Cost Savings

Cost savings are almost always enjoyed from sharing food. In these times of economic struggle with high unemployment and declining incomes, living in community makes economic sense. The more that is shared, the cheaper it is to live. Buying in bulk, wholesale, or direct from farmers can save a lot of money and significantly reduce the number of shopping-related car trips. The personal time saved by sharing cooking can be spent growing and processing food at home. Also, larger numbers of people are not as likely to let food go to waste. Decomposing produce is a common item in the refrigerators of many single people and small families in which everyone works; not as muchso in a community.

In Ken's own community living experience since 1974, he has consistently spent 20 to 25% less on food when sharing food costs and the responsibilities for shopping, cooking, and gardening with others. Existing communities that grow a substantial amount of their fruits and vegetables enjoy savings of up to 50% or more, although total food self-sufficiency is rare and usually not feasible.

Time for Family and Personal Growth

Many people we talk to say they have been spoiled by the shared households and cooperative communities where they live. They now expect more personal time in exchange for their turn to shop, cook, take out the compost, mop the kitchen floor, or weed the garden. Comparing the time spent on chores by a person living in a community with that spent by a person living alone is proof that living alone wastes time as well as energy, car trips, and money. Living alone or in a small family in a separate house has to be the most unecological, time-consuming and, for many, unhealthy lifestyle there is.

In a well-run community or group house, a person can come home in the evening most of the time and not worry about cooking, cleaning, or shopping, because someone else has already done it. As the testimonials from Muir Commons show, numerous activities can fill the newfound "free time." Some people may explore hobbies, work out in the exercise room, meditate in the greenhouse, or just hang out in the garden or kitchen. There is

more time, as well, for working together to alleviate society's ills, and for the learning and growing that result from meeting people with varying backgrounds and experiences. This enhanced communication creates understanding within the local community which then expands outward into the world.

Pre-conflict resolution

A special benefit of this free time and the common mealtime together is that it automatically serves as a form of "pre-conflict" resolution. Interacting with people on a daily basis — eating, working, and making decisions together — is a direct way to gain an understanding of what is happening in our

"For me, 'free time' is not a reality. I always fill my time with projects. Now my projects often benefit the whole group, not just my family."

"I have more free time, filled with sharing. It is easier to start a movie or a card game."

"I have more time to spend on myself and family after work when eating at the common house. This is a great benefit."

— Members of Muir Commons

Badger's Kitchen
"...at once they found themselves in all the glow and warmth of a large fire-lit kitchen. The floor was well-worn red brick, and on the wide hearth burnt a fire of logs ... a couple of high-backed settles, facing each other on either side of the fire, gave further sitting accommodation for the socially disposed ... Rows of spotless plates winked from the shelves of the dresser at the far end of the room, and from the rafters overhead hung hams, bundles of dried herbs, nets of onions, and baskets of eggs. It seemed a place where ... weary harvesters could line up in scores along the table and keep the Harvest Home with mirth and song, or where two or three friends of simple tastes could sit about as they pleased and eat and smoke and talk in comfort and contentment." [18]

— Kenneth Grahame, The Wind in the Willowss

companions' lives, what motivates them, and how they communicate and express themselves. We tend to have more empathy for people when we understand what they are facing. This is how compromise is learned. Enhanced interaction provides an opportunity for real-life personal and spiritual growth. The common kitchen, dining, and social areas are natural places for this to occur, and for issues to be resolved before they become deeply embedded conflicts. The following sections look at the ways that the community common house and cooking/dining areas can be designed to achieve amiable, interactive, and festive meal-sharing.

The Dream and the Reality

The romantic kitchen of our dreams may resemble an "old fashioned" country kitchen or a sleek,

modern kitchen pictured in Sunset Magazine. It may be large and sunny with plants, pots, and books adorning every corner, or it may be small and streamlined with everything neatly in place. Whatever the image, the kitchen fulfills a longing because it speaks to our own particular needs and desires.

In the 1950s and 1960s, kitchens were touted for their efficiency, ease, and modernity as the savior of the individual housewife. Appliances and gadgets were introduced as if energy and resources were in endless supply. The "work triangle" kitchen layout enabled the solo housewife to prepare food, cook and clean up more efficiently. With the work triangle, the cook usually faces the counter, sink, or stove, often a blank wall or, if she is fortunate, a window. The value of the triangle is its tight arrangement, but it discourages having helpers working side by side. In contrast, a large central counter is almost universally found in the kitchens of Shared

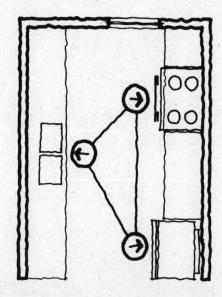

The Old "Mom is Cook" Work Triangle   SLRC

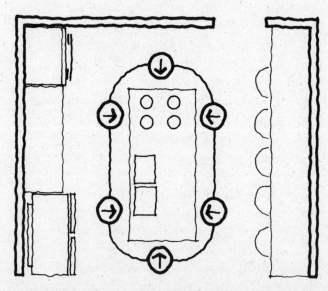

Central Counter Plan in the New Extended Family

Living Communities so that work can be shared with others and be a more sociable experience.

Today's typical tract house kitchen is modern, but it is not efficient. It wastes energy and water, duplicates equipment, materials, and trips to the stove, and tends to isolate the cook, who is usually a woman. This "modern" kitchen was designed by men for the "typical" nuclear family — a working man, his wife whose place was in the kitchen, his 2.4 children, and two cars. It is based on outmoded marketing studies rather than on the real-life feelings and needs of actual families in today's world. Few of us live in a "typical" family anymore. Changing values and demographics have created many different types of families with many different needs. The old adage, "a woman's place is in the kitchen," is no more appropriate than the static pattern of housing it inspired. We must rethink gender roles, cultural standards, and economic systems, and create a rich environment in and out of the home which addresses a diversity of opinions and lifestyles, and offers a multitude of choices.

Whole Community Relationship to Food

The design of the common house of a Shared Living Community acknowledges today's social and environmental concerns and changing lifestyles, and creates an egalitarian setting in which we can fulfill our dreams of a secure and enjoyable home. The key elements of the common house are the common kitchen, dining, and social areas which could be designed by the community core group. But we recommend that an architect who is specially trained in the group design process and sensitive to the greater social, economic, cultural, and environ

The Whole Community Relationship to Food

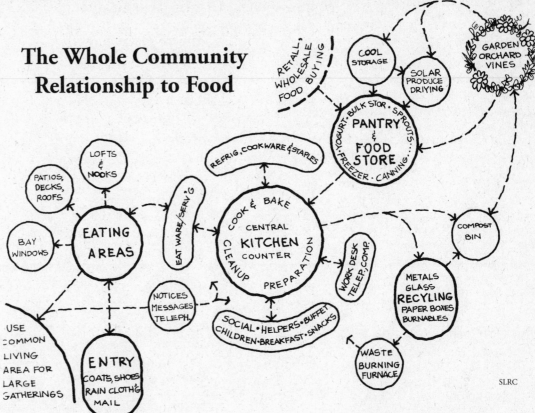

SLRC

mental changes of today be selected to facilitate in design sessions and consultations, and to produce construction drawings and specifications.

Some basic kitchen design precepts are shown in the Whole Community Relationship to Food diagram. They can be designed to work together to create a food supply, processing, cooking, and dining environment which is functional and ecologically sound. Through such an intentionally designed food-related system, the social, ideological, nutritional, and spiritual needs of the community can be more easily supported and sustained.

Ecological Sustainability Starts Here
This is the nurturing center for the community, for nutrition from food to social/emotional support, that provides the basic criteria for a high level of self-reliance and environmental responsibility.

"For us it has been a very good thing to have meals every night together. For us the common dinner is the heart of CoHousing. It helps keep us together…"[20]
— *Member of the Danish CoHousing community, Andedammen*

"The act of food preparation takes place within the larger context of the community gathering. While there is need to create an efficient, functional food preparation and service space, there is the added desire to create a comfortable, homelike atmosphere where conversation flows easily. The common kitchen should be a place where sharing of culinary insights is enhanced and the 'cooks' are not isolated from the rest of the community…"[21]
— *Deborah Holvey & Kathryn Lorenz*

The common kitchen — the heart of the community

In the ideal design for community living the kitchen is centrally located, integrally connecting all the spaces. The key to the kitchen design is the center counter which allows for social activity with others while cooking. The layout must provide for verbal and visual contact with other parts of the common house, while also protecting the kitchen work areas from cross traffic. Circulation paths should go by, but not through, the main cooking area. Bulletin boards for notices and messages could be located near the entrance, while the boards for meal schedules and shopping lists could be in the kitchen itself. Cooking for a group takes time, so the cook(s) should not be isolated and should be able to watch community activities and socialize while they work. The pantry, laundry, play areas, living spaces, mail boxes, and entrances should all be somewhat visible and/or easily accessible from the kitchen. In a community with children, locating outdoor and indoor play areas in clear view of the kitchen means that the cook(s) can also act as guardian(s) while kids are playing.

The adjoining sketch and the diagrams on the next several pages, show designs that demonstrate how a Shared Living Community kitchen differs from conventional kitchens and becomes an important social space for the community. They provide space for food preparation, cooking, baking, refrigeration, and washing, and have a counter for quick snacks, coffee breaks, meals for children, and buffets.

The common kitchen in a larger Village Cluster or Urban Cooperative Block community may be required to meet commercial codes for health and sanitation. The equipment initially costs more, but pays for itself in the long run through its durability, efficiency, and convenience. Good buys can usually be found at used restaurant supply outlets. In smaller group houses, new or remodeled, regular residential kitchen equipment, cabinets, counters, and finish materials will work fine. Local governments vary in their standards, and unless the kitchen work you are doing requires permits, use your own judgment. To avoid strict requirements, avoid being labeled as a public assembly place, restaurant, or an institution such as "Group Home" or "Congregate Living."

• **Appliances, tools, and conveniences** may either be the latest electronic kitchen technology, or selected simple, hands-on equipment. (For environ-

Photo by Ken Norwood

Ananda Village Communty Kitchen
This kitchen contains a large pantry, a walk-in refrigerator, bread baking ovens, and is designed to serve hundreds of people, or even more for special events or special circumstances.

mental health protection, give attention to the toxicity and energy efficiency of manufactured materials. See Chapter Nine for additional information.) The feeling can be warm and homey with natural materials, or sleek and high-tech. This common space can be decorated as desired with photos, plants, and collectibles representing the desires and dreams of the extended family or community members.

• **The central counter** with sinks, cutting boards, and cooking burners is the mainstay of common kitchens, although movable work tables located in the middle of the room are an option. Work counters or tables can be nested together as a single central counter, or placed apart so people can work on separate tasks. The kitchen can then function for one- or two-person cooking teams or for 10 or more on special occasions such as feast celebrations and parties, or for food processing such as canning.

• **Overhead racks for cooking utensils and herbs** save the cost and inconvenience of built-in cabinets, and provide a neat, attractive way to organize things. Also, the sight of fresh herbs and culinary tools used on a daily basis can create a feeling of personal connection and reassurance. Your groups may want to consider cabinets of natural wood over the crisp, clean lines of easy-to-clean plastic laminates that are toxic to the user and the workers who make them. Again, it is the ecological values and ideological priorities of the group that determine which alternatives work best.

• **Movable "walls"** can be made of sectional elements such as refrigerators, vegetable coolers, storage bins, cooking and eating-ware shelves, and planters for flexibility. Solid walls and fixed cabinets can be used for more visual and audio privacy.

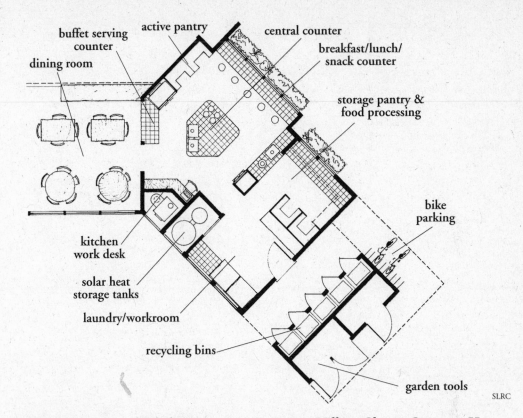

Cooking, Dining, and Food Preparation Areas in a Village Cluster Common House

• **A small work desk** or alcove with a telephone, fax, computer, and modem may be used for ordering supplies, meal planning, cook team scheduling, accounting, and food store distribution.

• **Comfortable places to sit and relax** should be provided in the kitchen and nearby areas. Counters, tables, or window seats can allow one or more persons to read, relax, write, enjoy a snack and converse with the cooks.

• **Bulletin boards** are located in and around the common kitchen and main entry routes. This needs to be a social and management organization, circulation planning, and esthetic consideration.

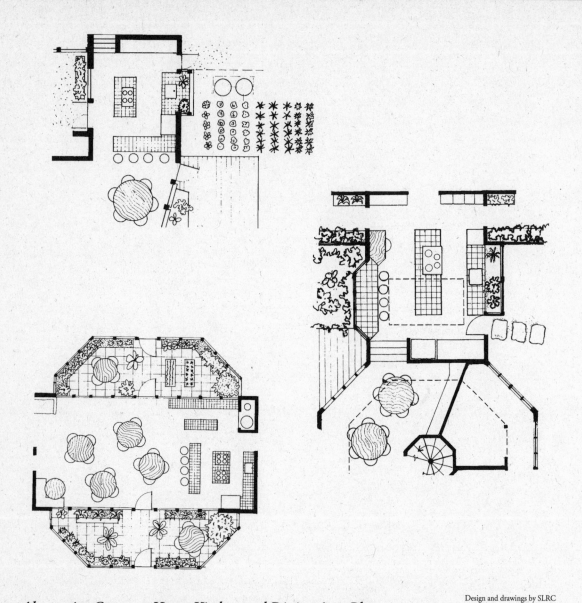

SLRC

The "Solar Earth" House Common Room

In this earth bermed, passive solar social and food sharing center, there is nurturing through shared food preparation and meals, social interchamge, and a physically embracing design of walls and ceiling that become one flowing environment. This is the core, the womb, the heart of the community, conceived intuitively by everyone in the community — for community and sustainable living.

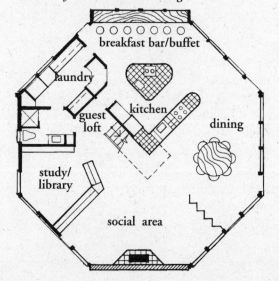

breakfast bar/buffet

laundry

guest loft

kitchen

dining

study/ library

social area

Design and drawings by SLRC

Alternative Common House Kitchen and Dining Area Plans

The various kinds of Shared Living Communities follow the same precepts. This leads to an environment designed for shared food, gender equality, shared responsibilities, social support and nurturing, and social gathering places integrated with the food areas. The above examples show common features designed for making community work, including a central counter, adjacent greenhouse, gardens and decks, breakfast/ lunch counters, and a pantry and circular tables for six to eight people.

Community dining area design

This space should create an intimate and beautiful atmosphere while meeting the diverse needs of the larger group. The dinner area should be big enough for the whole community plus guests to gather in comfortably without being crowded or creating an institutional atmosphere. It should be able to accommodate a variety of functions such as large banquets, dances, children's indoor games, films, and meetings. The transitions from private to public and large to small spaces discussed in Chapter Seven are applicable to dining room design as well. There should be a variety of places to eat, so residents can be more private on some occasions. Nooks, alcoves, lofts, decks, greenhouses, and other edge and transition spaces can be intentionally conceived for small groups or individuals. But resist the tendency to form small cliques that will isolate themselves from the larger group, as this is destructive to the strength and cohesion of the community.

Nooks and alcoves can provide an attached but separate dining area for children, who may get excited and noisy at mealtime with many people around. This may be a problem for adults with or without children who would prefer to have a quieter dining environment. Often the families with "excited" children eat at home, but this excludes some members from the benefits and fun of community. One alternative is to have one or two adults, older children, or teens rotate as moderators. The children can be children and have fun, the adults can eat in peace, and no one is excluded. On certain occasions the whole community would share festivities together. The other option is to establish guidelines for them to sit regularly among the adults This can be a great learning opportunity for

children, but not if stiff regimentation is imposed.

How the common dining area is furnished and decorated is up to the imaginations of the community members. The following dialogue, based upon SLRC workshops, depicts an intergenerational shared housing group designing its dining area with nooks, lofts, and greenhouse patios.

Eloise, a retired 61-year-old, expresses her concern. *"You say we'll need 15 buy-in family members to support the proposed common house, and that means one large dining room with tables to match… and we need space for guests, too. But I don't want the look of an institution."* She looked around the group imploringly. *"You know, like a public housing retirement home. I've been there. Once was enough."*

"I agree," said Marilyn, a 28-year-old part-time secretary and student. *"It'd be a bore to have a big table, too much like a boarding house. Besides, we all know that in a shared household, not everyone will be eating together every night. A big table could be lonely."*

Jerry, a 36-year-old electrician and part-time single parent, spoke up. *"Big tables are obsolete. We can make modular tables, you know, like building blocks… except we won't stack them vertically."*

Marilyn laughed. *"Oh sure, we can move them around and eat in small clusters or by ourselves! But we'll need lots of oddball eating nooks and corners to get away from the institutional look. Let's all describe where we'd really like to eat."* She gestured expansively. *"Heart's desire time!"*

"I want a window seat," said Eloise. *"Maybe a bay window where I can have tea or lunch and be out of the mainstream."*

SLRC

277

"Loft-nooks would be great," offered Claudia, a 35-year-old architect. *"Expanded or widened stair landings, and even balconies off the second floor hallway. I'd like to be able to see into the main kitchen and eating areas and be a people-watcher."*

"I want a table in the greenhouse," said Jerry. *"Imagine picking a strawberry for your oatmeal while you sit snugly warm amongst the greenery, watching the snow fall."*

"Here's another way," said Lou, the recently divorced 45-year-old mother of Sandy and Charles. *"I imagine lots of low tables with cushions and shoji screens for dividers. The tables can be used individually, or arranged in small groupings. We could also push them together whenever we need one really large table."*

Claudia raised her hand as her head bowed slightly. Her long hair momentarily hid her expression, then she looked up abruptly. *"I'm sorry,"* she blurted, *"I see a pattern here that doesn't feel good. We're all Americanizing our community. We have a chance to share meals together, to enjoy a mix of young and old, yet we all want separated space — like staking out our hide-outs, even before we've experienced dining together as a group."* She looked at the others almost apologetically. There was silence.

****

The dining area design process must consider many factors, but table size and arrangement is the foremost, as it can have a huge impact on the sense of togetherness and community. Shared meals, particularly supper, are a time when the cooperative family develops a sense of cohesiveness and members gain strength to meet the responsibilities of living in a community and the world. This careful design of eating areas inreases the groups ability to communicate at mealtimes and still maintain a sense of individuality. At one large table, conversation tends to split into several small groups, at times leaving someone out, and on quiet nights it may seem too empty. A modular table system allows the dining arrangement to change. It is a lot like adding leaves to a table on Thanksgiving, only easier. Each "leaf" is a free standing table, so it is easy to convert from one large table to small arrangements.

Other features can also make group dining more workable and enjoyable. A buffet counter connecting the kitchen and dining areas, for example, will make the serving of meals to separate tables easy and sociable. The common dining area needs to be directly served by its own entrance, being one of the most heavily trafficked areas of the house. Movable dividers, planters, and display boards could allow the dining area to expand into the common social area when there are large gatherings. Cozy sitting areas, nooks, and alcoves in or adjacent to the dining area are recommended, inviting members to arrive early to dinner and stay late to relax and share the day's events with their extended family. The sounds of laughter, vigorous conversation, and children's play should not drive people out, but rather add to the ambiance of a nurturing community. Acoustic treatment is needed, so consider soft and sound-absorbing finishes such as plants, carpets, and wall hangings for floors, walls, and ceilings. Roof/ceiling configurations that are broken up by sloping and undulating surfaces and that have textured and irregular finish materials can also be effective. TV, children's play, and music rooms should also have insulated walls, ceilings, and doors.

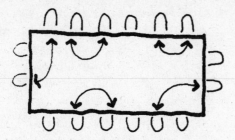

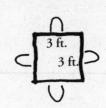

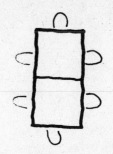

• Large tables have their value at times of major events such as majors feasts, celebrations, and ceremonys. But the daily personal communication desired for regular meals in communities is discouraged by the tendency for sub-converersation groups to isolate themselves and leave others out to form such as shown above and below.

• Modual tables of 3 ft. x 3 ft. offer many options for more intimate sociability while dining, and can be grouped for four, six and eight persons for meals, snacks, conversations, playing board games, or holding meetings.

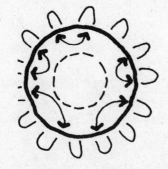

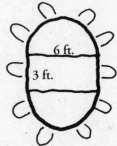

• Circular and oval tables can provide the most amiable dining and conversing arrangement. Here we use a circular module of six feet with two 1/2 circle tables, and in combination with two 3 ft. modular tables to form an oval table for ten people.

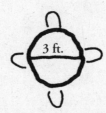

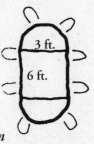

• By using a 3 ft. 1/2 circle module in combination with the above modules, even more social posibililities can be arranged.

• Tables for Four at View Windows

Choices for Table Arrangements in the Common House Dining Area

Private dining in a community

Sometimes it is nice to be all alone or have a private dinner with your partner or friends. That is why there are small kitchens or kitchenettes in each private living unit or suite. Individuals or families are likely to choose to have breakfast and lunch in the privacy of their own place, prepare their own suppers on the weekends, or spend a quiet evening away from the group from time to time.

In a few of the new CoHousing communities in the U.S., residents have opted for large private kitchens and dining rooms. We caution against this. If the community is committed to sharing most if not all evening dinners in the common house, small kitchenettes can still provide the necessary cooking for breakfast, lunch, and occasional private dinners. Each community must decide its priority for sharing meals, and design accordingly. Experience with some CoHousing in Denmark has shown that in successful communities a large private kitchen becomes redundant.

Another option is the group house cluster where a number of private living suites without kitchens share a centrally located common area or solar court containing a kitchenette, tables, and a social lounge area. This arrangement was presented in the Village Acre group house in Chapter One and in several group house prototype designs in Chapter Seven.

Dining Out
— in the Greenhouse

SLRC

Photo by Ken Norwood

A Common House Pass-thru at Ananda Village
This is a classic group house design with a buffet serving counter, a central kitchen counter, and several eating places emmediately adjacent to the fireplace social area. In this common house there are also several outdoor decks nearby.

The objective is to live ecologically and reduce initial construction costs by not duplicating full-size kitchens in each unit. Here again the members will need to re-examine their old habits.

The Pantry, Bulk Buying, and Food Processing

The pantry performs the most ecological, healthful, and cost-saving function in a community. It facilitates buying nutritious and fresh organic foods in bulk from wholesale and farmers' markets and reduces short-and long-run costs. The pantry can also be used for food processing, preserving, and long-term storage. A root cellar can be added, allowing the community to enjoy seasonal produce throughout the year, and to better use farmers' markets, local farms, and community garden sources. The pantry should have its own service entrance so that supplies can be easily delivered.

Photo by Ken Norwood

A Group Living Kitchen Pantry
In the Black Cat kitchen a small pantry, kitchen, and back porch were converted into one large kitchen with a pantry-wall, and a dining table and a social area to one side.

Photo by John Hostetler, *Amish Society*

An Amish Family Pantry
The fruits of the community garden are presented for use throughout the year — this is a picture of self-reliance, a savings account, and great personal empoerment.

The Amish Pantry Way of Providing Food

Bulk buying, combined with a food "store" for residents, reduces the need for shopping trips. When anyone needs supplies for their kitchenettes, they simply walk to the common "store" instead of each driving separately to the nearest grocery store. The operation of a small store could be part of the common kitchen management and cost sharing process, or it could be a separate enterprise operated by a community member.

This is done in some existing Danish CoHousing and American Intentional Communities and group living households. There is usually a "store" manager who orders supplies, and restocks the shelves. There are many ways to organize this. One is to bill each member at the end of the month for purchases recorded on a sign-out sheet in the pantry. Agree in advance concerning these systems, what will be stocked in the store, and how to purchase items for special community feasts and parties, and members' own private dinners.

Another system being introduced is a TV and FAX/phone ordering system which allows viewers to browse through a remote store and select merchandise without leaving their homes. They place orders and have their food delivered. A community that uses this telecommunication amenity can further reduce their own car trips to the store, save time, and reduce the number of delivery trips made by the stores, since more people in one location would be placing one order. These are ways we can be empowered to live ecologically, more abundantly, and joyfully, within community.

How Shared Cooking and Shopping Works

Communities employ different systems for sharing cooking, cleaning, and food buying responsibilities. In some the designated evening cook does everything — buys the food, sets out the dishes, cooks, and cleans up — but can sit back and relax for the rest of the week or month, subject to community size. In others, members rotate responsibilities in teams on a weekly, bi-weekly or monthly schedule. One week your group may buy food, the next it cooks, the next it cleans, the next two it rests. Or the cooking and shopping responsibilities are rotated on separate schedules, but each person is responsible for washing their own dishes. Some large Intentional Communities, cooperatives, and senior communities hire cooks and kitchen managers to organize the shopping and cooking. The options and variations in systems go on and on, adapting to the particular needs and desires of a community. To give an example of how it works, we have provided the following actual arrangements from the Arch Street group house previously mentioned.

An Ecological Shopping List
The entire eight-person Arch Street Group House actively participated in the weekly shopping, but only one car was used. Think of the additional car trips if each of these single people lived alone in a separate unit and shopped as "individuals."

At the Arch Street house, the eight members enjoyed four scheduled evening meals a week, plus two or three spontaneous meals on weekends. The members rotated cooking and shopping responsibilities according to mutual, agreed upon schedules. After move-in, members gathered for weekly meetings where food and other household affairs were discussed and problems resolved. The system that developed actually began with a series of bi-monthly potluck suppers six months before they moved in. Prospective members explored ideas and ultimately agreed upon household operating systems. Here is how the basic system can work for your group.

• **Cooking responsibilities**, including final kitchen cleanup (each person may wash their own dishes or leave for the cooking team), rotate with each member cooking one night every two or so weeks. If members are not going to be home at dinnertime, they can ask or sign up if they want to have their dinner saved. Cooks are responsible for getting a replacement if they cannot cook on their night. (The food was so good at the Arch Street house that by noon the next day there were no leftovers.)

• **Weekly shopping** is done by two people, one of whom has a car. Shoppers check cupboards and refrigerators for what needs replacement, and use the master shopping list on which members check off items they want for their cooking night. The group needs to agree on food choices such as vegetarian, low-fat, low cholesterol, no/low salt food, and the extent of dairy products, snack foods, and special diet foods to be bought with group money. (The Arch Street group ultimately agreed to exclude dairy products, and commercial fish and chicken from the shopping list)

• **The food money jar** system works well. Each person puts in from $16 to $20 a week, subject to decisions made at weekly house meetings . Receipts are saved to verify the amount of unspent food money and to reimburse any shoppers who had to spend more than was in the jar.

• **A bulk organic food** and household supplies list is posted every two to three months. Someone is assigned or volunteers to place the order and collects

A Dialogue in which Community Members Discuss Bulk Food, Appliances, and Saving Money

"What I want is a big kitchen with every kind of food processing gadget and power appliance there is. You know: a juicer, heavy duty blender, cream separator, grain grinder, automatic yogurt racks…"

"Hey, hold on!" said Janie, cutting into bright-eyed Betty Mae's embellished kitchen dream. *"Where's our energy-saving, ecologically sound, labor-intensive, low-cost lifestyle? What kind of electric bill do we want? I prefer just a few appliances, the fewer the better, and to do more by hand. Heck, put the kids to work."* Janie was warming up, enjoying the attention of the others.

Betty Mae appeared to accept Janie's interruption gracefully, but her mind raced to formulate challenges to the words she was hearing. *She's talking like this is a hippie commune where no one has an outside job,* she thought. *She's being unrealistic and hypocritical.* When Janie paused for breath, she pounced. *"We've got 16 adults, and only six of them will be staying at home. Add the eight children, and wow. That's a lot of food to process."*

Janie seemed not to hear. *"We can build a really large pantry and a food storage room,"* she said. *"Naturally, we'll do lots of bulk buying. We can put in a counter for re-packing of bulk foods into kitchen-size containers…"*

"Wait a second, Janie." James, an accountant, spoke calmly. *"You're implying that we'll pool all our money and use central buying for everything. That's way beyond where we've gotten in our earlier meetings."* He looked around at the others. *"I can see some advantages to a group-buying arrangement, but will the savings be enough to pay for the extra space and built-in appliances?"*

John smiled and waved an arm. *"Yeah Jim, why don't you run that problem through your computer mind! I bet we could save 20% of our food costs that way — times five years of food bills for 25 people… WOW!"*

Betty Mae nodded, her own reactions softening. *"Realistically, Janie, with all that bulk food and garden produce to process, we'll never get it all done unless we have the tools. But those will be one-time investments. Calculate all those items in and I bet we'd still make a savings in five years. Remember, all this group sharing is for a better way of life and healthier eating. Let's put a dollar sign on that and see if it's worth it!"*

(see next page)

Quiet and usually docile, Sarah raised her hand aggressively enough to attract attention. *"That's great. A savings in five years if we invest more now. But look — I'm a single parent scrounging off a small income. I'm barely off welfare. I need to have those savings you're talking about right now, each month, or I can't even live here."* She looked around quickly. Tears filled her eyes.

The group members looked at each other. A new level of commitment and mutual caring was edging into view, scaring some and exciting others.

After a long pause Betty Mae spoke pointedly. *"We have to be realistic. Sarah has a point, there is a higher initial cost of setting up a food system that will cost less later. But I want Sarah in this community, and I want a food processing pantry with time-saving equipment, and Janie wants a simple living, low energy consuming approach."*

John responded, *"Yes, we want you, Sarah, and I know there's a way. Looking at our commitment to each other, at the economics and savings from energy and resource conservation, and at the time we can spend on our food processing, we can find a way."*

Jim spoke, *"I like that, John. You're leading us to the bottom line. We'll have to explore an internal economic system and get really innovative with our financial and food planning. I propose that as starters, each of us write a one-page concept of how we could make it all work, and satisfy Sarah's concerns. Let's pass them around for all to read by our next meeting. OK?"*

"We would like to grow all our own food or barter with other organic producers. We are trying to reduce our usage of prepackaged foods — our major source of waste. Our emphasis is on an unhurried, simple lifestyle that allows time to enjoy life. Ecological living will be of the utmost importance in our daily lives."

— A core group responds at an SLRC workshop

additional money for each member, usually $20 to $30. Bulk dry goods or case items that can be bought include wheat, oats, rice, baking flours, olive oil, honey, miso, almonds, raisins, molasses, soap for bathing, dishwashing and laundry supplies, and toilet paper. This system could easily meet the needs of a larger or smaller community. (At the Arch Street house the system worked because the agreements established at the beginning of the group were well maintained during the life of the house, and because the new housemate selection process included an interview of candidates focused on their food and lifestyle orientations.)

Recycling
— the "over and over again" ethic

The kitchen is the prime generator of waste in any household or community. Household garbage and packaging from food is overwhelming landfills. Buying bulk foods in recyclable containers and growing your own produce can significantly reduce the amount of packaging and thus the amount of waste, but some will always be generated. Recycling has been adopted by many Americans, but unfortunately there are still too few who find the time to recycle and compost regularly, and fewer yet who buy bulk food products with less packaging. Ecological living practices can be difficult to maintain for individuals, couples, and small families working long hours and living separately in single-family houses or apartments. However, the design of a Shared Living Community and its self-management and interactive lifestyle offers ways for all members to recycle more materials while using less space and time.

A complete recycling area adjacent to the common kitchen can serve the community and the individual units with bins for paper, glass, tin, and other recyclables. (See the common house plan on page 275) Design a drop hole in the countertop over a stainless steel or tile compost chute to a bucket beneath. Compost bins or piles are located near the garden for kitchen food scraps (no meat or dairy), and landscape and garden cuttings. This waste can be composted by worms and/or microorganisms in an aerobic process that produces little odor. Fertilizers are seldom needed in the garden when compost is turned into the soil, adding the necessary nutrients to grow vegetables and flowers.

The Garden — *Your Own Safe Food Chain*

Solar greenhouses, outdoor gardens and orchards, roof and deck planters, and window boxes are an integral part of the community food system, assuring members, especially in urban settings, that their food is safe and fresh. Many foods are subject to chemical and disease contamination from methods of farming and processing that are exploitative of ourselves, workers, animals, and the environment. Newspaper articles about farmland soil destruction and illness caused by corporate agribusiness and food production and processing have abounded in recent years. The headlines tell the story of cancer, premature physical development in children, and birth defects caused by pesticides and growth hormones in the foods we eat. Food, which is supposed to nurture us, has become yet another thing to fear.

Consumers must carefully read between the lines. When companies are unregulated, government agencies are underfunded, and profits are the only goal, the responsibility for environmental protection and human health is left to us as consumers. We must act in our own best interests and become empowered in community to protect out own health. Individuals and small families living in separate units do not have time or space to grow food and cannot efficiently buy bulk or wholesale natural foods, and therefore are the most vulnerable to uncaring vested interests. Living in a co-owned community, sharing a garden, and cooperatively buying organic food in bulk is the most direct empowerment strategy available. Community members will know where their food comes from and what went into producing it. Home food

growing gives it history and meaning; it becomes more than just a commodity bought in the supermarket. It becomes an integral part of ecological living.

The more that people are in tune with the power of cooperative human enterprise and the processes of nature, the more easily the experience of basic empowerment can arise. "I grew it myself" may be the new cry of triumph for making it in today's world. Even if group members do not want a garden, living in community can provide support and leverage to demand that safe, healthy food be supplied by local food stores.

"She is angry, too, at the food industry 'promoting high fat'. They say there's no cholesterol, but it's full of hydrogenated fats. We know that fats promote this cancer [breast cancer]. The American diet is so miserable, and especially so for poor women. Who has time to cook and who has the money to buy salmon steaks? Poor women can't do that. Working women can't do that." [22]
— *Jan Kirsch*

COOPERATIVE LIVING AND THE NON-TOXIC KITCHEN

Increasingly in the last few years, we have heard more about toxic chemicals being linked to breast cancer, fatigue, reproductive problems, respiratory illnesses, birth defects, and other ailments. These toxic chemicals have become a part of our everyday life — in the air we breath, the soil we walk on and grow our vegetables in, the food we eat, and the homes we live in.

Yes, "the homes we live in." Our greatest exposure to toxic substances is right in our homes. Indoor air is often more polluted than outdoor air, because of poor ventilation and toxic gases that come from synthetic materials and glues. Most people are familiar with the hazards from radon and asbestos, but there are also hazards from formaldehyde, aluminum, nitrogen dioxide and other chemicals in our floors, cabinets, paint, stoves, and cookware. We now know that wood stove emissions are unsafe.

We bring up these issues here in the section on community kitchens and cooking, because it is in our kitchens that we are the most susceptible. In a kitchen, we absorb chemicals not only through the air we breath and through our skin when we touch contaminated surfaces, but also through food. Buying organic and unprocessed foods does not always eliminate this last risk, because chemical contamination of food is not only from pesticides and food preservatives. Food stored in a polluted environment or in polluted containers absorbs the vapors and gases from that environment, and we, in turn, absorb them when we eat the food. So we are ingesting, breathing, and touching chemicals.

But, take heart. There are things you can do to protect yourself and your family and friends from these hazards. Although any individual or family can take steps to protect themselves, working together in a Shared Living Community offers unique opportunities to create a truly healthy and sustainable living environment.

In most new communities, the members themselves design and sometimes build all or some of the community. The core group has personal control over what materials and methods of construction will be used. They can share information and choose alternative techniques and products which may be unknown or too expensive or labor intensive for individuals or single families. In most housing developments, the developer selects materials based on what is standard, least expensive, and most easily available. Most manufacturers and builders are not yet interested in experimenting with non-toxic materials and sustainable building methods. Community core groups can take the time to research alternatives and make informed decisions about what materials and products to use. Your group may even want to select a special person or committee to investigate environmental health hazards and alternative materials, and to work directly with the architect and builder on these issues.

On the opposite page are a few suggestions on how you and your community mates can create a healthy and natural community.

For more information about hazards from household materials and products and safe alternatives, see
The Natural House Book, Healthy House, and *The Nontoxic Home and Office* listed in the resource guide.

Pooling resources makes it easier and cheaper to substitute toxic materials with non-toxic, health-safe alternatives.

• Plywood, chipboard, particle board, and plastic laminates that are used in most kitchen cabinets contain formaldehyde, which continually emits toxic vapors that can contaminate our food and air. Solid wood units with non-toxic paint or varnish surfacing, or stainless steel cabinets provide a safe and attractive alternative, but tend to be more expensive and therefore less financially feasible for a single family.

• PVC tile floors, carpets, and the adhesive used in these products are extremely toxic. Children are especially vulnerable to the effects since they are smaller (i.e. lower to the floor) and spend a lot of time sitting and playing on the floor. Wooden flooring, natural cork or linoleum, earth tiles, and stone are all readily available, safe, and durable materials.

• Natural gas, coal, and wood-burning stoves produce carbon monoxide, nitrogen dioxide, and other pollutants. Adding an extractor fan or range hood and/or installing an electric stove are choices to be made in the planning stages of a community.

Living in a community provides unique opportunities for sharing ideas about safety and healthy products.

These ideas can be shared with the whole community at common meals, meetings, and while cooking and working together in the garden or on other projects. When passed on to friends and family outside the community, the ideas become information with a "we" creditability. The opportunity to positively influence a larger network of people and to "get the word out" is something that today's small families and individuals living alone have few opportunities to do. Information to be shared would include:

• The dangers of certain cookware. Aluminum cookware increases the risk of Alzheimer's disease and other neurological disorders. Copper pans, if not cleaned properly, accumulate toxic verdigris. Teflon and other non-stick coatings may dissolve in foods and cause cancer and other diseases. Use glass, cast iron, porcelain-coated pots, or stainless steel instead.

• The dangers of cleansers. Most dish soaps, bleaches, chlorinated scouring powders, and detergents contain complex toxic chemicals which contaminate food, food preparation surfaces and tools, air, and ultimately the soil, ground water, and sea when they are flushed down the drain. Use biodegradable products instead. Many different kinds are readily available.

• The dangers of some food storage methods. Clingwrap may contain the plasticizer DEHA, which when warm, can be absorbed by foods. Soft plastic containers may also offgas toxic vapors. Use glass, ceramic, and stainless steel containers.

The known and unknown hazards of pesticides can be avoided through the efforts of a community.

• An organically grown garden can be adequately tended with a minimum of individual labor and time when the whole community participates.

• Build a greenhouse in urban settings to avoid airborne pollutants from cars and factories getting into the soil and plants.

• Test the soil, especially in older neighborhoods or those near freeways and railroad tracks, before starting a vegetable or herb garden, since lead or other chemicals present will be absorbed by the vegetables and passed on to you. [23]

The Ecology of Food, Family, and Community

"To garden is to cut the 'middle-man' out of the loop. The person who grows food eats it. No under-paid workers, no pesticide-selling multinationals, no warehouses, no future seller; it is an intimate exercise, between the gardener and the plants and soil she tends." [24]
— *Chris Clarke*

"This work is shared, so it's more fun." [25]
— *Corinne McLaughlin & Gordon Davidson*

Photo by Greenbelt Alliance

Photo by William Porter

The food chain we depend upon may appear to end with us, but it can actually begin with us. Think about the whole social, political, and economic system involving the food we buy. Where did it come from and by whose labor, how was it grown and transported, and where does it go after we are done with it? In this chapter, we have proposed a family-centered, ecological approach to form and design a sustainable community, bringing the user into the cycle. Sustainable community design is centered around the common house where food gathering, growing, processing, cooking, eating, and recycling enable residents to have control over their environment, health, and emotional well-being. We honor the kitchen and eating areas as the heart of the common house and the pulse of the community. Each component of the total living environment works with the others, creating a system that satisfies the criteria for sustainable energy, resource conservation, environmental protection, and the nourishing of the human community.

The Whole Community Relationship to Food diagram on page 273 exemplifies this ecologically conscious food cycle. The consciousness generated within a fully developed Shared Living Community empowers its members to divest themselves of mindless, throw-away consumer habits, and to adopt a way of living that incorporates the "over and over again" ethic of nature. Let us recreate a modern version of our heritage as wild food gatherers and food growers, self-reliant and living in harmony with natural cycles, and seek wisdom from those indigenous peoples today who still live in the village mode, close to the earth. This does not advocate abandonment of contemporary technology, but a selective and appropriate mix of hand, mechanical, intermediate, and high technology. We Americans have been living high on the energy and resource-consumption chain for too long. With our present economic pressures and planetary ecological calamities, we have no choice.

The food-centered activities of ecologically planned communities can unite, focus, and make productive and profitable the endeavors of persons of all incomes, ages, and ethnic backgrounds. The combined person-power enables individuals within a community group to maximize energy and resource conservation, use solar-age technologies, and expand livelihood opportunities in ways not available to the individuals and small families who today cannot afford such benefits.

Living in a Shared Living Community provides an environment that encourages members to commit to and practice caring for each other and all life forms. The many possibilities may seem too good to be true, but amazingly, they are reality for many who have already pooled their resources in CoHousing, Intentional Communities, cooperatives, and group-living households. By extending the family with which you share meals, you too can extend your joy, fulfill your dreams, and gain the experience and empowerment to make positive changes in this changing world.

Notes

Books listed only by name in the endnotes are highlighted in the resource guide at the end of the book, complete with author/publisher information and description.

[1] John Robbins, <u>Diet for a New America</u>, Stillpoint, Walpole, NH, 1987, p. XV.

[2] Peter Farb and George Armelagos, <u>Consuming Passions: The Anthropology of Eating</u>, Houghton Mifflin Company, Boston, 1980, pp. 46-47.

[3] *Ibid.*, pp. 4 & 147.

[4] Jeremy Iggers, "Innocence Lost: Our complicated relationship with food," *Utne Reader*, November/December 1993, p. 60.

[5] Peter Farb, *op. cit.*, pp. 208 & 216

[6] <u>Ancient Futures</u>, p. 185.

[7] David Elkins expanding on the quote by Martin Buber in "Thoughts on Becoming a Person," *AHP Perspective*, Nov. 1991, p. 6.

[8] Victoria Fitch, "The Psychological Tasks of Old Age," *Naropa Institute Journal of Psychology*, vol. 3, 1985, pp. 90-105.

[9] Fitch, *op. cit.*, p. 96.

[10] *Ibid.*, p. 98.

[11] Karie Garnier, <u>Our Elders Speak: A Tribute to Native Elders</u>, K. Garnier, White Rock, BC, 1990, p. 11.

[12] Sandra Scarr, Deborah Phillips, and Kathleen McCartney, "Working Mothers and Their Families," *American Psychologist*, November 1989, p. 140.

[13] Eric Raimy, <u>Shared Houses, Shared Lives</u>, J.P. Tarcher, Inc., Los Angeles, 1979, p. 113.

[14] The Boston Women's Health Book Collective, <u>Ourselves and Our Children: A Book by and for Parents</u>, Random House, New York, 1978, p. 182.

[15] Jeremy Rifkin, <u>Beyond Beef: The Rise and Fall of the Cattle Culture</u>, Penguin Books USA Inc., New York, 1992, pp. 2-3.

[16] *Ibid.*, p. 225.

[17] Nyland Community, "Eating Together at Last," *CoHousing*, Spring 1993, Vol. 6, No. 1, p. 13.

[18] Kenneth Grahame (illustrated by Ernest H. Shepard), <u>The Wind in the Willows</u>, Charles Scribner's Sons, New York, 1933 (copyright renewed 1961 by Ernest H. Shepard), p. 65.

[19] Peter Farb, *op. cit.*, pp. 7-8.

[20] Judy Timmel interviewing members of Andedammen Community in Denmark, "Life in CoHousing: A Report from Denmark," *CoHousing*, Fall 1991, Vol. 4, No. 2, p. 17.

[21] Deborah Holvey and Kathryn Lorenz, "Designing a Common House Kitchen", *CoHousing*, Spring 1993, Vol. 6, No. 1, p. 6.

[22] Kennedy White quoting Jan Kirsch, " Under the Knife: How many will die of breast cancer? Will I?," *Express, The East Bay's Free Weekly*, Jan. 24, 1992, Vol. 14, No. 15, p. 19.

[23] Some of the information used in this section is from <u>The Natural House Book</u> by David Pearson.

[24] Chris Clarke, "Sowing the Seeds of Change," Terrain, *the Ecology Center Newsletter*, Vol. xxii, No. 3, p.1.

[25] <u>Builders of the Dawn</u>, p. 27.

[26] R.K. Prabhu & U.R. Rao (editors), <u>The Mind of Mahatma Gandhi</u>, Navajivan Publishing House, Ahmedabad-14, 1967, pp. 458-9.

"It may seem a distant goal, an impractical Utopia. But it is not in the least unobtainable, since it can be worked for here and now. An individual can adopt the way of the future… And if an individual can do it, cannot whole groups of individuals? Whole Nations?" [26]

—*Mahatma Gandhi*

TOOLS AND TECHNIQUES
— For Living Within the Ecosystem

Can high-density housing cure us of our car-related

Electric-car making could boost economy

Here Comes the Sun — Go for It

Solarization uses the sun's energy to clean garden soil

Development near public transit is answer, says environmentalist

By Bradley Inman
SPECIAL TO THE EXAMINER

BY JANET H. SANCHEZ
Special to The Chronicle

'Green' awareness begins to take root

THE NEW YORK TIMES NEW YORK FRIDAY, MARCH 24, 1989

Green architecture summit

Creative alternatives to urban sprawl: A tale of two cities

Density is answer to cost of housing

Shared housing: Urban plan of young and old

EPA Supports Earth Day

A solar showcase

Sonoma County home shows off the technology's finest features

THE TRIBUNE, Oakland

Court Upsets Zoning Curb on Unrelated People in Family Home

'Practical' environmentalist reshapes American attitudes

Tired and Scared of Living Alone, More Elderly Try Sharing Homes

BY BILL RICHARDS
Staff Reporter of THE WALL STREET JOURNAL

New choice for the elder

By Laura Evenson
The Tribune

20th century village living

Group proposes 'cohousing' concept for Davis

By MIKE FITCH
Enterprise staff writer

TREE PLANT

PUPIL MIKE MURPHY, left, teacher class at Concord Public School out taken on the former landfill site a

The Green Lifestyle: It's Not Too Late — Yet

From Page B4

Converting a Kitchen Into a Recycling Center

BY DEAN JOHNSON AND JOANNE LIEBELER

How 'Green Consumers' Are Changing the Marketplace

Conserving water urged as way to avoid world crisis

America wakes up from its Dream

For many of us, tomorrow,

COST OF THE AMERICAN DREAM
The price of a middle-class lifestyle has risen steadily while most Americans' income has stagnate

Richer, poorer
After-tax income gains and losses between 1977 and 1988.

Americans' weekly incom adjusted for inflation

Seven Arguments for The Elimination of the Automobile

The suburban lifestyle has imprisoned us in a narcissistic world of private property.

CHAPTER NINE

Ecological sustainability of any individual community or the larger system cannot be accomplished by sole dependence upon the conventional tools that are available to us now. We need to discern the best of existing methods and create new ones that advance the various forms of Shared Living Community in this country and the world. In this chapter we will present how to approach and accomplish ecological and sustainable community design and living while recognizing the limitations and flaws in the American social-political-economic system which encourages over-consumption of resources, social and economic injustice, and environmental despoliation. We will propose existing and innovative tools and techniques for rebuilding community in America including construction methods, natural energy systems, self-help and self-reliant community organization, community development processes, alternative ways of co-owning community, and ecological planning and zoning policies. With these ingredients we will be able to bring to reality the Eco Village, Eco City, and Green Belt proposals being presented.

Who is Responsible — *you, me, us, or them?*

The greatest tool for the implementation of ecological communities will be a change of attitude regarding what is acceptable in how we live and relate to each other, what it means to be "responsible" in day-to-day living. We are responsible to ourselves, to our loved ones and family, to other people, and to the planet and all its life forms. To be responsible to yourself is to know your needs, abilities, and aspirations, to be aware of what affects you, and to do what is needed to protect your future and your interests. Responsibility to those close to us, and to others, requires respect for who they are and want to be, and a willingness to understand what they need for their well being as well. We cannot deny to others what we want for ourselves nor can we expect

---

Rochdale Principles for Cooperatives

Today's cooperative movements are based in various ways upon the Rochdale Cooperative Principles. These were first formulated in 1844 by a group of weavers in Rochdale, a suburb of Manchester, England."[4] The Rochdale Cooperative was organized to serve the combined interests of its members as home owners, consumers, workers, and students, and is still operating today.

This is a summary of the seven Rochdale Principles:

1. There is open, voluntary membership, with no religious, political, or other test for joining. Coops are intended to welcome all people, regardless of race, class, sex, age, or political or religious views, who are committed to belonging to and participating in the cooperative and receiving benefits.

2. There is a responsibility to democratic participatory governance involving a system of interactive committees that involves intimate contribution by all members in making decisions.

3. There should be no exploitation of any other person, and there is an emphasis on a limited return on capital and in nonprofit operation.

4. There is a dedication to serve all members and society, and not to generate private profits for an individual investor.

5. There is an intentional cooperative education process to teach all members effective democratic management and to develop leadership capabilities.

6. There is the objective to promote and participate in the cooperation between cooperatives and join a "worldwide cooperative commonwealth."

7. There is a specific policy for the coop to be independent from partisan issues by outside special interest groups. The focus of the coop must be on using the coop resources to serve the members.

"Americans have pushed the logic of exploitation about as far as it can go. It seems to lead not only to failure at the highest levels, where the pressure for short-term payoff in business and government destroys the capacity for thinking ahead, whether in the nation or in the metropolis, but also to personal and familial breakdown in the lives of our citizens." [1]

— Robert N. Bellah,
The Good Society

"The hunger in underdeveloped countries today is equally tragic and absurd [compared to 16th century England]. Their European colonizers understood well that ownership of land gave the owner control over what society produced. The most powerful simply redistributed the valuable land titles to themselves, eradicating millennia-old traditions of common use. Since that custom is a form of ownership, the shared use of land could not be permitted. If ever re-established, this ancient practice would reduce the rights of these new owners. For this reason, much of the land went unused or underused until the new owners could do so profitably. This is the pattern of land use that characterizes most Third World countries today, and it is this that generates hunger in the world." [2]

— J.W. Smith,
The World's Wasted Wealth II

"Investment in people requires far greater lead time than investment in machinery. Countries that fail to invest enough, or in time, will find the costs — sluggish productivity growth, joblessness, and declining real income — very high."[3]
— *The Carnegie Forum on Education and the Economy,*

"In other words, sustainability is not just a characteristic of the 'completed' community; it needs to be part of the thinking and habits of the group from the very beginning."[6]
— *Robert Gilman, In Context*

"...[Third World people] if given access to the land, those unemployed could plant labor intensive — but high-protein and high-calorie — crops and produce more food than the world needs. As all true costs are labor costs, reclaiming their land and utilizing their unemployed would cost their society almost nothing, feed them well, and save that society more money than they now pay for the so-called "cheap" imported foods."[7]
— *J.W. Smith*

them to act responsibly towards us unless we do the same toward them.

Being responsible to all life forms must also include a recognition of our complicity in the mess we have inherited. We are collectively responsible, for dying species, ozone depletion, crime and killing, poverty and wars. You know, I know, Mr. President knows, the man in the next car on the freeway knows, we all know: changes can only be made by all of us saying, Yes! we can stop polluting, mend our broken people, and be responsible for rebuilding community in America. The solution is to act as "we" and not in terms of "us," "they," and "them." Who is "they" when we see a homeless person and say, "they" should do something about "them"?

Responsibility means being able to respond when a situation or need becomes apparent, with the tools and techniques that are appropriate for the moment. That means when you know that there is a danger to a person, a population, or any life form, you do not think, "this is someone else's fault or problem," you act. A homeless person puts out a hand and looks you in the eye and says, "I am hungry," or your roof is leaking, or you learn that an industry is dumping toxic waste in a river, or you are told about ecologically sustainable ways for people to live. Do you respond?

Obviously, no one of us alone can respond immediately or adequately to all situations. The key to solving the dilemmas that we all face lies in doing it together. To try to do all that needs to be done, by ourselves, limits our opportunities for cooperation with others. The ultimate in responsibility is working together, in community, in an interdependent manner. Once on experiences community as a

workable way to solve mutual problems and obtain mutual benefits, then one tends to become a more responsible person with others. This implies that what is fair for me is fair for everyone — no acting unilaterally or looking the other way. When everyone participates in decisions, incentives and rewards can be equitably available to all people. In a responsible community, the poorest are able to meet their expense needs from their own effort, while the more affluent realize that their contribution to the community leads to empowerment for all. This can and does happen in villages, cooperatives, and communities around the world. There is within these cooperative systems a sense of renewal, sustainability, and protection of one's own well-being — a feeling of "I belong."

The Way We Use Energy

With five percent of the world's population, we chalk up approximately 50% of the world's vehicle miles, using about 25% of the world's oil production in the process. The electric car offers no solace, and may create an even greater demand for fossil fuel and nuclear-powered electrical generation plants. The so-called "Dream House" is an energy waster as well — standardized plans, designed for a quick sale, are stamped out without respect for solar orientation or regional climatic conditions. As a result, buildings use 40% of all energy produced in the US.

We have been taught to be "individuals," to demand our own washer and dryer, vacuum cleaner, microwave, lawn mower, leaf blower, snow blower — even individual wind generators and solar collectors. These devices are underused in most households, and take enormous amounts of unrenewable fossil fuels and irreplaceable resources to manufacture, distribute, and operate. The first major step towards reducing energy consumption is the cooperative sharing of resources and products in communities designed and intentionally organized for that purpose.

Breaking fossil fuel dependency must go beyond industrialized conversion of renewable energy sources such as solar, wind, and biomass, since, for these to be used on a large scale, capital is needed for technological development, large and remote plants, and long distribution systems. Energy (i.e. oil) companies are researching these technologies, but because of enormous investments in fossil fuel production, they are maximizing oil profits and deferring development of alternative energy technologies for as long as possible. Corporations are in business to make profits, not progress. The best impetus for a sustainable energy ethic must come from depending on human energy sources. From indigenous village cultures, to Kibbutzim, to Intentional Communities and cooperatives, and to the recent New Communities movement, working in cooperation and relying on commonly owned land has been indispensable to people's survival, and has demonstrated an ecologically sustainable way of living. It is really up to us regular folk to cooperatively conserve resources, grow more of our own food, become renewable resource entrepreneurs, and to put the Green Belt around American cities to use for organic farming cluster communities.

This need for cooperative use of energy is such a radical and, for many, a scary notion, that it is necessary to explain why straight line growth and energy consumption as individuals is not sustainable and becomes too costly to maintain. Sooner or later, the amount of used-up energy increases as available energy diminishes — the entropic process. Jeremy Rifkin, in *Entropy*, describes the entropic process as it pertains to the Second Law of Thermodynamics, which states that in a closed system the

> "The ultimate moral imperative, then, is to waste as little energy as possible. By so doing, we are expressing our love of life and our loving commitment to the continued unfolding of all of life."[8]
> — Jeremy Rifkin
> with Ted Howard,
> *Entropy: A New World View*

> "The second law, the Entropy Law, states that matter and energy can only be changed in one direction, that is, from usable to unusable, or from available to unavailable, or from ordered to unordered."[10]
> — Jeremy Rifkin

> "If humankind is to survive, it is absolutely essential that we start looking at the world through the same lens as Mr. Rifkin. His concepts are very simple and direct. We, and all life, survive through utilizing energy and discarding the waste. We all know that but what we do not realize is that it is a one way street. All resources move in only one direction, from available to unavailable and there are no exceptions. Virtually no scientist has successfully denied this second law of thermodynamics. We can either move to a sustainable society, or we can consume the earth's resources, destroy most species, and possibly destroy ourselves."[11]
> — J.W. Smith

New Idea #1
The Energy Efficiency Ratio — Divide by the Number of People

We propose that an Energy Efficiency Ratio (EER) be applied to houses, appliances, equipment, tools, vehicles, and any other device that uses energy in any phase of its operation. The purpose is to encourage the highest number of users for every energy- using device, be it a car, a house, or a lawn mower. The EER is calculated by taking established data on the total amount of energy consumed by a product from its inception, through to its disposal, and then dividing by the number of people sharing the item or activity. With today's computer and telecommunications capabilities it is quite feasible for such a process to be available for anyone to easily use. You can see that one person per car on the freeway or one person per each housing unit would produce a very high EER, and that a train full of people, or a Village Cluster or group house will have a much lower EER. The EER could be a basis for awarding economic incentives such as energy rebates, tax credits, or lower interest on loans.

energy "flowthrough," or loss of energy, can only increase.[9] In physical terms, the Earth is actually a closed energy storage system. Aside from the influx of energy from the Sun, nothing enters or leaves the system. Solar energy created all plant and animal forms, some of which decayed and become nonrenewable sources of energy, such as fossil fuels, and others have become renewable sources of energy, such as trees. This finite supply of energy and resources can be changed from one form to another, as when we release stored solar energy by burning gasoline in car engines, and other fossil fuels in power plants to generate electricity, and then use even more energy to build freeways and millions of separate cars. Electric cars will demand even more energy, and offer no respite from other social and environmental impacts of undisciplined use of the car. As a result of all of our modern technology and consumption, enormous amounts of unrenewable energy are used and transformed in the process, and most of the energy used is lost forever. Rifkin calls this a "disorder in the system."

New Idea # 2
A Scorecard for Ecological Sustainability

Environmental protection is everyone's responsibility, and it is too important to be left to chance and too complex for effective coordination by millions of lone individuals. We must look to the interaction of all interest groups in the broadest sense of community — locally, regionally, continentally, and globally. For example, importing "energy saving" and "green" products, solar devices, and consumer products from Third World countries that allow manufacturing and transportation processes without sufficient or enforceable environmental standards, and where workers are exploited, cannot be considered an equitable contribution to sustainability.

We suggest an Ecological Sustainability Scorecard (ESS) that would be circulated for anyone to self-evaluate how their lifestyle, daily habits, policies, and practices as individuals, families, enterprises, and institutions add up in terms of ecological sustainability. The ES Scorecard would be similar to the Ecological Badge of Courage presented in Chapter Three, except that special versions could be designed for different interest groups, including cultural sub-groups, organizations, institutions, businesses, and governments. Perhaps the U.S. Environmental Protection Agency or a coalition of environmental, educational, and business groups could be the coordinating sponsor or mentor, to help everyone keep a focus on what kinds of personal and business activities might be most beneficial to the goals of ecological sustainability. As an incentive, businesses and community groups that use ESS techniques could be eligible for tax credits or low interest loans. The ES Scorecard and the EE Ratio (New Idea # 1) would include accompanying educational and training materials that could utilize computerized telecommunications networks and interactive audio and video techniques.

Rifkin points out that the disorder in the Western economic system has to do with the waste of natural resources and energy within the extraction, production, and distribution processes, and of human energy, through exploitation of labor. Much more energy is used, and therefore lost, than would occur with prudent management of human and material resource and energy outflow. The so-called "free market" economic mechanisms of society are rapidly exhausting natural resources. There are predictions that economically feasible and reasonably available energy sources will be depleted in 30 to 50 years. The result of these practices will be recurring recessions, the worsening of worldwide poverty, extensive ecological damage, and eventual economic collapse.

It takes energy to use energy. That tank of gas you just bought doesn't give you nearly as much energy as went into creating it. Oil drilling rigs, refineries, super tankers and even gasoline pumps all consume energy in the process of transforming former solar energy into a usable form. Even using solar energy directly by generating electricity with individual solar panels still consumes nonrenewable resources in the extraction, manufacturing, shipping, and installing of the photo-voltaic collectors on each separate house. Passive solar heating requires a structural design and materials that are more costly for developers of single houses to build; therefore, developers continue to build cheaper energy-consumptive houses. The comparative housing design study in Chapter Two demonstrates that the energy flow-through is higher for one or two persons in separate houses and studio units, than for an extended family group in one large, specially designed group house.

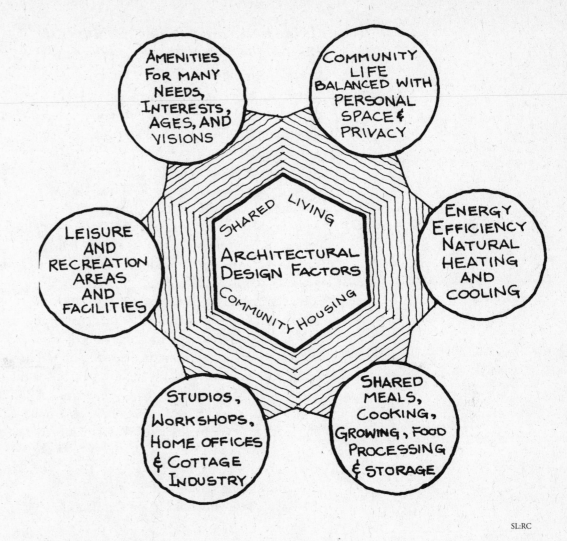

AMENITIES FOR MANY NEEDS, INTERESTS, AGES, AND VISIONS

COMMUNITY LIFE BALANCED WITH PERSONAL SPACE & PRIVACY

LEISURE AND RECREATION AREAS AND FACILITIES

SHARED LIVING ARCHITECTURAL DESIGN FACTORS COMMUNITY HOUSING

ENERGY EFFICIENCY NATURAL HEATING AND COOLING

STUDIOS, WORKSHOPS, HOME OFFICES & COTTAGE INDUSTRY

SHARED MEALS, COOKING, GROWING, FOOD PROCESSING & STORAGE

SL:RC

By extending these cooperatively based community housing precepts to the larger society, it can be very possible to break the cycle of welfare and poverty, workplace exploitation, energy wastage, and car-dependency. We will propose the tools and techniques for how we can include everyone by working with each other to ultimately function as an ecologically sustainable society.

"We are wise with the wisdom of our age only, and ignorant with its ignorance. Observe how the greatest minds yield in some degree to the superstitions of their age."
— *Henry David Thoreau, 1853*

Ecologically Sustainable Architectural Forms and Construction Methods for Communities

American house building methods have not changed for a century. In the 1990's, the entire housing related industry is suffering as the cost of lumber soars due to exploitive mismanagement of forest resources. The industrial revolution influenced milled lumber and "stick-built" ways of building that waste resources, require skilled workers, and are costly to assemble. Many building materials used today contain toxic chemicals, require air and water polluting methods for their manufacture, and are not easily recyclable. The time for inventiveness has arrived. We have the opportunity now to demonstrate that ecological design and development can come directly from the users, cooperating together in Shared Living Communities. Alternatives to the more costly, unhealthy, and energy-intensive "stick-built" conventional wood frame or concrete and masonry house building methods have been known about and used extensively in other cultures. A variety of innovations are now being used in the U.S. These methods are contributing towards affordable, ecological, healthy, and quality housing on a large scale.

The following construction innovations are presented without an attempt to rank them according to cost effectiveness, time to erect, seismic or wind resistance, or code approvals. They all appear to be suitable, in varying degrees, for a cooperative, "hands-on," group building approach, and all of them offer opportunities for building economical non-rectangular and nonconventional forms. Most of them use natural, low-cost, and easily available materials. However, toxicity and health risks should be investigated for all building materials and methods, whether used or new, that will be employed within living spaces. We do not recommend products whose manufacturing requires the use of toxic chemicals that create pollution-causing emissions or non-recyclable toxic residues. Detailed tests regarding chemical pollution and other health dangers should be made mandatory for factory-made and any other building product method. Be aware that residential mortgage lenders shy away from unconventional design forms and construction methods on the often-false presumption of a lack of acceptance in the real estate market.

Earth bermed and/or covered

Earth-covered houses were used by Native Americans, Eskimos, and settlers throughout the world. The work of architect Malcolm Wells and others has elevated this basic form of house construction method to popular use. Curved and angled walls are easy to do. The costs of exterior walls and roof finish materials are greatly reduced and balance to some degree the cost of excavation, water proofing, and drainage. Although requiring some heavier equipment and an experienced earth berm builder/consultant, it can be very cost effective for a supervised group-building crew.

SL:RC

Pole construction

This simple to erect structural system was first popularized for farm buildings, and has proven quite useful for erecting residential structural systems, and is well suited for group construction. The poles are pressure-treated with a non-toxic solution, and are buried a minimum of six feet in auger dug holes as shown. In compressible and expansive soils use a reinforced concrete pad under the poles, or a large rock at the bottom to prevent settling. Soil tests may be necessary to determine the soil resistance to the load on each pole, if the soil type and the pounds-per-square-inch rating are not already known. The local building department may specifically require tests in any case.

We recommend treating the poles with an ACQ preservative [Ammonia Copper Quaternium] instead of the standard CCA and ACA methods, which use an Arsenic compound. These are extremely toxic and leach into the soil when wet, contaminating soil, plants, and the ground water supply, as well as to those constructing the building.

Cross beams for floor and roof supports are bolted onto the poles, then the second floor joists and subfloor, and then roof rafters and sheathing, and then the roof covering is applied. This allows weather protected construction of floors, walls, and interior finish. The example shown was owner-built, and designed for passive solar heating as well as an active solar water heating and radiant coil heated slab. There is also an earth bermed north wall.

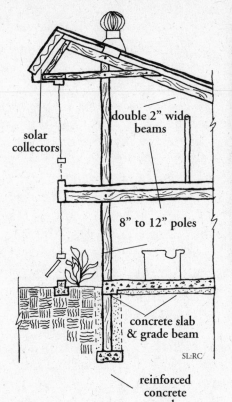

solar collectors

double 2" wide beams

8" to 12" poles

concrete slab & grade beam

SL:RC

reinforced concrete pad

Photo by Ken Norwood

Merle Farrell House Under Construction Showing Poles and Cross Beams

Rammed earth

This system, with a heritage from many lands, has been revived in the U.S. as a popular owner-builder and group-building method. The walls are made from a clay-based soil mixed with a small amount of cement which is then compacted into wall-height forms. Rammed earth techniques vary from simple hand-mixing, loading, and tamping into removable forms with a tamping tool, to the more complex process of power mixers, metal slip forms, loading with a skip-loader, and tamping with electric or compressed-air power tamping tools. Angled walls are easy to do. An extended family group house or Village Cluster could be built inexpensively by the members using the earth on the site. This was done for the ground floor walls of a large, two-story family house in a housing cluster at the Ananda Community using volunteer and hired community members.

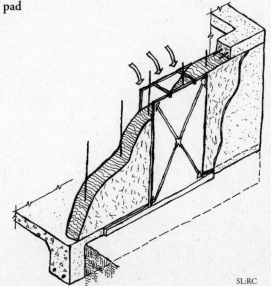

SL:RC

299

Clay-straw walls in timber frame

This is another historically tried and proven method known in Europe and Asia for approximately 1,000 years. It is now being re-introduced in the U.S. by Robert Laporte and George Swanson, designers and builders of non-toxic and all natural houses in Fairfield, Iowa. Clay-straw is used as a non-bearing filler wall between post and beam timber construction, and rests upon a masonry or concrete footing or slab. Straw is mixed with a clay slurry (liquefied clay and water) sufficient to coat the straw thoroughly. This mix is then tamped with great pressure into forms 4, 6, or 12 or more inches wide between the already erected timber frames. The "breathing" feature comes from the minute porous spaces formed by the straw, which allows for three to five complete air changes per hour compared to .2 to 1 change per hour[15] in a typical house. The air passes through in both directions, overcoming the polluted interior air exchange problem of today's well insulated but air-tight houses. Besides allowing for fresh air exchange, walls that are 12 inches thick or more provide good insulation and acoustic control. Mildew and fungus have been a concern, but Robert Laporte's investigations and several years of actual experience have revealed no cause for difficulty.[16]

Adobe brick

This is an old, tried and true hands-on method used throughout the world. A similar earth-cement mix as the rammed earth method is used, or just clayey earth with straw as a binder and steel reinforcing bars. Fiberglass fibers and reinforcing bars are not recommended due to the pollution and toxic residues from their manufacturing process. The walls rest on concrete foundations and have bond beams made of concrete, rot-resistant wood or non-toxic pressure-treated timbers. Adobe brick walls can be built in compliance with building codes. Curved and angled walls are easy to do. Use of on-site materials and local hand labor, and the good insulating value of the thick walls, qualifies this method as ecologically sustainable.

Cob earth building

This is another earthen building method used on all continents for thousands of years and that is now being revived by The Cob Cottage Company in Cottage Grove, Oregon. Cob, coming from the Old English root meaning "a lump or rounded mass," is made of hand-formed lumps or tubular shapes of earth mixed with sand and straw and stacked to form the walls. The hand shaping process allows for complete flexibility in the shape and layout of the building. Cob invites sculptured organic forms, curved walls, and vaults. It requires few tools and can be mixed in mud holes with the feet and shaped by hand, a very sensual

SL:RC

experience that produces an esthetic final appearance, expressing whatever feeling is evoked by the makers. It is being successfully used in cool damp climates and is protected from moisture by an impervious foundation and wide overhangs of the wood construction roof. Walls of one to two feet thick provide good insulation and thermal mass for passive solar deigned buildings. Cob building is most feasible for a community work team where everyone, regardless of age and prior building experience, can be involved. This, and the other earth source methods, is a natural answer to declining wood resources and a declining economy. [17]

Fired ceramic

Architect/builder Nadir Khalili brought the fired ceramic structure system from the Middle East to the U.S. The basic material is clay soil. Curved walls, arches, domes, and vaults are formed using methods similar to those described above. With temporary closure of all wall openings, an intense heat is generated by gas jets or fires from other materials. The objective is to actually fire the clay into a ceramic material — the entire structure becomes one large fired earthen pot. Several groups are exploring, testing, and building prototype models in the U.S. The earthquake resistance of monolithic ceramic vaults and domes needs verification. This is a labor-intensive construction method that would enable a community group to create a building, with cost savings, uniquely shaped to express their community.

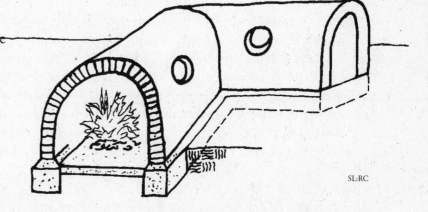

SL:RC

Straw bale construction

This is another revived historic, self-help method that has proven to be durable, strong, energy efficient, economical and easy to build, with easy to obtain materials. Straw bales are merely the recycled remnants of harvested grain, rice, and alfalfa fields. This is a renewable resource and uses materials that are often burned each year, adding carbon monoxide to the atmosphere. The dried bales are stacked like bricks on a concrete foundation, tied together at the top with either a concrete or timber bond beam. For long-term weather and rodent protection they are wrapped with wire mesh, and covered with cement stucco or plaster inside and outside. The layout of

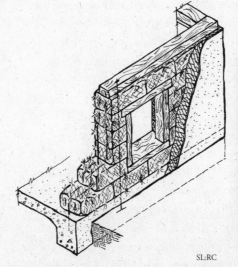

SL:RC

Photo by Catherine Wanek

Straw Bale Building

301

buildings and rooms can take a variety of forms, since the designers are not constrained by the limitations of conventional wood and metal construction techniques. This is a very fast method, and a community group could make short work of the basic assembly of a straw bale house. There is still the need for definitive code recognition and financing programs for builders and self-help groups to develop this kind of housing.

Yurts

From cultures in the high northern hemisphere comes the yurt. Designed for nomadic tribal living, they are relatively easy to assemble, cover, and insulate. In the U.S. today the popular version takes the form of a kit, although people do build them from scratch. They are often used for sleeping cottages at Intentional Communities where common house facilities are shared, for back-to-the-land families and individuals living remotely, and for guest lodging at retreat centers. It is usually classified as movable or non-permanent housing and would not require a concrete foundation. By changing building codes to allow innovative structures in certain locations, yurts could be installed with approved plumbing and electrical wiring. In remote locations yurts could be equipped with electric compost toilets powered by photo-voltaic cell electricity.

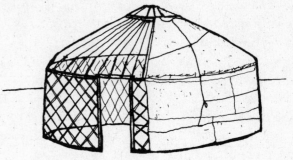

SL:RC

Tipis

This is probably the most successful lightweight nomadic architecture, except perhaps for the tents of the Middle East cultures. The Native Americans who used the tipi as lodging lived an ecologically sensitive lifestyle that allowed them to move around from place to place. Today, tipi kits can be bought, or they are easy to make from scratch. Insulated inner liners are available for winter use. They can be used as supplemental sleeping shelters or clustered around a fully developed common house to form a village.

SL:RC

Geodesic structures

Buckminster Fuller really started something with the geodesic dome. The intricacy of the geometric patterns, the rounded form, the feeling of enclosure on the inside, and the media attention to Fuller's legacy are all part of the compelling attraction to the dome concept. The popular appeal did not create a mass market for its development, even among those who were attracted to it. For example, practical experience has revealed that the geodesic dome skeleton saves materials and can be erected quickly, but finishing the inner and outer surfaces, openings, and interior partitions, and the electrical and plumbing installations, can be labor intensive and expensive due the numerous angles and curves that are encountered. This method has worked for various intentional communities, such as at Ananda

SL:RC

Village in California. Twelve residential domes were built, including a double dome that for a time served several families with a common kitchen and dining area. Several other domes are used very successfully for a chapel and a meeting hall. At Ananda, a dome skeleton could be erected in a day with the aid of inexperienced community work parties, thus making innovative construction feasible. However, the interior finishing of the domes was slower and required skilled carpenters.

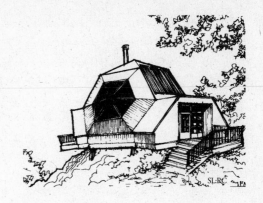

Pre-fab wood, metal, and fiberglass panels

There have been numerous examples of both field-fabricated and factory-built modular residential building parts, including various shapes and forms of panels that are connected together to form a box, dome, or pyramid shaped building. Most often these panels are wood framed with plywood and wallboard covering over insulation, but some have an aluminum or steel outer frame and various kinds of metal or plastic covering. The pre-cut materials are assembled in pre-set forms or jigs, then assembled with staples or screws. Simplified and repetitive systems such as the wood panel systems shown here are especially applicable for a self-help community building project, and can allow untrained people of all ages to work in assembly line fashion and erect the panels as at a barn raising. The field fabrication jigs, templates, and cutting guides can be devised for the members' skill levels, the quantity to be built, and the short-term set up of a self-help project. Be aware of the recent generation of manufactured fiberglass and other pressed plastic panels that can emit an "off-gassing" of toxic chemical vapor. These should not be used for human habitation nor encouraged as a manufactured product.

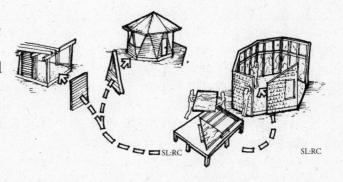

Modular factory-assembled housing

Factory prefabricated panels, modules, components, and entire houses are being produced in the U.S., Europe, Israel, Japan, and elsewhere in the world, mostly in the shape and layout of conventional builders' houses. This factory building system trend continues to increase because of the increased cost of wood construction materials due to serious mismanagement and depletion of forest resources throughout the U.S. and the world. For a short time in the 1950's, George Romney of the Department of Housing and Urban Development inspired "Operation Breakthrough" as an attempt to persuade builders to adopt new, "efficient" methods of factory-produced modular and component housing. Initially his attempts broke down, but since then changes have begun to be made for pre-assembled housing products, alternative materials, and other innovative methods for building. These manufactured building systems must also be examined for health, safety, and other environmental problems.

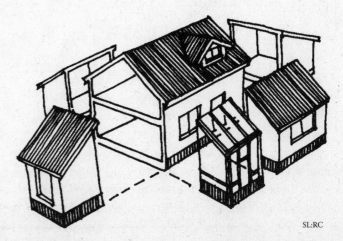

More housing will eventually be factory-fabricated and partially assembled. Although energy and material savings can result from factory production, there are additional transportation costs, often by trucks, which add to the environmental problems. It may be possible that efficient mass production of quality building components in local factories will be available on a large scale and at affordable costs. Local manufacturers could work with a community core group to produce a combination of building components for field assembly of an entire Village Cluster or group house by a contractor and/or a team of community group members. The members could also complete the interiors, landscaping, and recreation amenities themselves. However, such arrangements have not previously been viewed favorably by conventional lending institutions. This problem may be overcome by the amending of regulations, self-help training programs, and/or the sponsorship by for-profit developers, nonprofit developers, Community Land Trusts, Mutual Housing Associations, or Community Development Corporations. This would assure the lender of a quality and timely completion according to plan.

Some "kit," pre-fab, and panel homes can be erected more easily, and have enabled individual owner-builders to create handsome structures with cost savings of varying degrees. But by the time the code requirements, foundations, utilities, wiring, plumbing, and interior finishes are completed the savings may be slim, unless an owner-builder does most of the work him or herself. When built by an individual contractor there may be only a little savings to a buyer. A mutual responsibility approach to building communities can make these systems available and beneficial to the most number of people.

Recycling Building Parts — *an energy re-use option*

Recycled materials and parts from existing and obsolete structures are an ecological source for community-built structures. Timbers, studs, trusses, ceramic tiles, wood windows and doors are great for recycling. Caution is advised in two areas. Avoid the temptation to cannibalize old but useful and historically valuable buildings that could be rehabilitated. Also avoid re-use of industrial products that have toxic properties or whose manufacturing creates toxic waste such as asbestos, lead, petroleum products, formaldehyde, and other toxic materials. Unecological extraction and manufacturing techniques may be encouraged to continue just because recycling of the products are being done. We refer to chemical, aluminum, and petroleum-based products whose energy-intensive manufacturing processes and products can emit toxic atmospheric pollutants. Similarly, using up mountains of old tires to build low-cost housing is another questionable practice, until proof-positive is found that no health dangers exist from emission of toxic gases. Another way of using of old tires is to shred them and compress the fibers into flat pads or mats for use for children's playground surfaces or walking decks. Manufacturer claims that tests show no residual toxicity need to be verified.

Low Energy Design for Shared Living Communities

The greatest possible savings of energy and resources in residential building will come from integrating design and building processes with co-owned and managed communities. It is time we saw ourselves as integral parts of a community building process, which extends from the scale of the new extended family, to the village, to the whole city, to all of America, and beyond to the world community. Unfortunately, advocates of the capital-intensive market economics and the technological approach to energy conservation, efficiency, and sustainability, overlook the powerful role of people cooperating and sharing resources in intentionally designed communities.

The entropic process, the using up of resources and energy, is one of the most basic activities commonly experienced by humankind around the world. But unlike the predictable average norm for each person's consumption of air, food, and water, the inequities in the way all of our energy needs in the U.S. are managed is an ecological disaster. Earlier in this chapter an Ecological Sustainability Scoreboard (ESS) was proposed which would serve as a checklist regarding wasteful use of energy and for encouraging personal conservation techniques and ecological living alternatives. Listed below are ecological living techniques that Shared Living Communities can easily use at the local level to gain ecological sustainability points on their own ES Scoreboard.

• **Build a common house** to share cooking, shopping, meals, and other activities and resources as a new extended family, committed to ecological sustainability.

• **Include a solar greenhouse** for a passive heating/cooling system and for starting beds, a winter garden, and growing food the year around.

• **Install a hot water heat exchanger** in catalytic gas or wood/waste burning furnaces and stoves as a backup to an active or passive solar system.

• **Use centralized community-owned** active solar systems for hot water heating for domestic supply, radiant heating, and hot tubs and pools.

• **Get off the grid** with a community-owned solar electric system.

• **Use wind and/or water generation** of electric power where location allows, but combined with other nearby communities for cost benefits.

• **Compost** organic food scraps, and garden and yard cuttings.

• **Recycle** paper, glass, metal, and other solid wastes.

• **Reuse** discarded materials or products directly, or sell or give away to used goods stores.

• **Design for natural day lighting** and efficient night lighting. Convert incandescent lighting to long-life fluorescent.

• **Use renewable energy** resources directly instead of through manufacturing in remote power or fuels plants and transporting long distances.

• **Co-own cars**, trucks, a van-bus, and bicycles within the community and even with others in the adjoining neighborhood.

• **Organize a Transportation Management Program** that coordinates scheduling for different kinds of vehicles, community members' needs, carpooling , and special events.

• **Share community clotheslines** outdoors, and/or a in dry inside space.

• **Co-own larger parcels** of land (three acres or

"'Northern' consumption is just as great a cause of the crises as is explosive population growth in the poor nations of the 'South.' Energy consumption in the US, for example, is so high that the 250 million Americans consume as much as all four billion people in developing nations." [18]
— *Howard Ris,*
Executive Director,
Union of Concerned Scientists

"Essayist Wendell Berry argues that misplaced values are at the root of our waste problem: Our economy is such that we 'cannot afford' to take care of things: Labor is expensive, time is expensive, money is expensive, but materials — the stuff of creation — are so cheap that we cannot afford to take care of them." [19]
— *John E. Young*

more) with 60% to 80% and more of the land preserved as open space.

• **Create tax credits or other incentives**, for community groups and/or developers, that take into account long-term cost savings from energy-saving design, materials, and equipment, such as passive solar and good insulation, which are initially more expensive to install than conventional designs.

Big Beautiful Planet

Chorus: There is a big beautiful planet in the sky
          It's my home, it's where I live
          You and many others live here too
          The earth is our home. It's where we live.

We can feel the power of the noon day sun
A blazing ball of fire up above
Shining light and warmth enough for everyone
A gift to every nation from a star.

We can feel the spirit of a blowing wind
A mighty source of power in our lives
Offering another way to fill our needs
Nature's gift to help us carry on.

— Raffi

Ecological Reality — *in a community the sun works for you*

The above list of energy-efficient techniques is much too short — there are hundreds of additional existing and emerging new solutions that integrate energy, environmental, and socioeconomic issues. According to the Appropriate Technology Institute in Seattle, Washington,[49] when the scale of building is raised from a single-family residence to even a very small community, it is economically feasible, with state-of-the-art technology, to build solar–collecting roof structures and thermal conversion systems that provide for all the energy needs of the inhabitants, even as far north as southern Canada. Such systems use the sun as the primary activating source, integrated with efficient building design.

Regardless of how affordable they are to operate, the installation costs of well-made passive or active solar hot water heating and other natural energy systems are seldom cost effective for today's individual person and small family households to do by themselves. Similarly, these systems are not installed by housing developers because they need to keep their house prices competitive, and because there is no incentive and requirement to do so. Low and moderate income people are not even considered as a market potential and are left out of energy-saving house design opportunities, unless they own their house and qualify for reduced or no-cost insulation programs by local utility companies. Here again, everyone could benefit by belonging to a cluster community of co-owning and self-managing residents who share the energy and cost savings of these solar heating systems.

Passive solar design

The basic idea in passive solar design, subject to climatic variations, is to let the maximum amount of sun into the building in the winter, and the minimum amount in summer. This is done by taking advantage of the fact that the sun is low in the sky in the winter and high in the summer. Large windows and skylights facing to the south allow sunlight (and thus heat) into the building in the winter, but they can be protected in the summer by either movable sun shades, overhangs, or deciduous vines or trees. To gain the most benefits from passive solar heating, orient the buildings along an east-west axis so that solar gain walls, windows, greenhouses, and collectors face within 20 degrees of south. Once in the house, the sun's heat is captured behind the glass. A heavy concrete slab or rock floor, large containers of water, or other thermal mass is used to absorb the heat during the day and radiate it back at night. Covering all glazed openings at night with insulating draperies, shutters, and movable panels helps the building retain much of the heat gained during the day. Designing for passive solar heating, maximum daylighting, and natural ventilation should be considered early in the group design process.

A more elaborate passive solar design is the "solar greenhouse" (or "Trombe wall", a solid thermal mass wall with glass about six inches away as a heat trap) placed on the south wall of the building, with double glazing glass on the outside wall and roof, and a heat storage mass of rock, concrete, and/or water containers on the floor and back wall. Trapping the sun's heat, the inside of the greenhouse (or Trombe wall) can reach 100 degrees even on a cold day. Vents, ducts, and/or fans are located at the top of the heated air spaces to move the warm air into the house and near the floor to draw cooler return air from the house into the greenhouse. In the summer the glass is shaded, and air circulation induced through vents and operable windows creates a cooling effect. The passive solar greenhouse is the best of ecological sustainability in house design — not only do we have a natural heating source, but a place to grow food all year around.

Active solar house water systems

An active solar heating system involves solar collectors, heat storage in tanks or rock mass, and pipes,

---

New Idea # 3
Incentive Bonds for Natural Energy Design

We propose that bonds to be sold by local and state governments to finance an incentive program that revives the solar tax credit, and includes additional economic incentives such as low-interest loans, utility bill rebates, and grants to encourage Shared Living Community groups, and nonprofit and for-profit developers and businesses, to incorporate passive and/or active solar systems into house designs. Some portion of household savings, from lower utility bills, are used to pay off the energy bonds. This provides capital to encourage constructionof energy-efficient houses with passive solar greenhouses, solar water heating, and solar-electrical power. Otherwise, developers will continue to construct the conventional, less expensive model. As the bonds are paid off the owners of natural energy designed houses get increasingly lower rates and/or tax credits on a sliding scale relative to income and their Environmental Efficiency Ratio (EER). This would mean that the people proposing to build an ecologically designed community such as the Octagonal Cluster House would earn additional incentive points to include the passive solar system when the house was built, and a housing developer could afford solar greenhouses and hot water collectors in the design of the houses. Additional incentive points would be given for cluster housing.

Photo by Ken Norwood

Photovoltaic Panels at Ananda Village

This field of solar panels and a central battery shed serves all of the electrical needs for the five house Almora cluster of the Ananda Community.

motors, pumps, and valves that move the heat around. A solar hot water collector system is basically a shallow box, black on the inside, with a glass cover facing the sun, and tubes of circulating water. The sunlight enters through the glass, which traps the infrared rays and heats the water in the tubes. The heated water circulates up to a storage tank above the collectors by gravity flow when possible, or by pumps to the tank to preheat a small standard domestic or instantaneous water heater. A hot water house-heating system, using radiant tubes in the floor slab or with baseboard or wall radiators, can be provided by adding more collectors, a larger storage tank, and pumps and an electronic control system that circulate the heated water.

Photo-voltaic electric generation systems

The solar-electric or photo-voltaic systems are comprised of solar light sensitive cells that transfer the sun's energy into direct current (DC) electricity, for storage in batteries and for direct operation of appliances, tools, lights, computers, and other electric devices. A cluster of houses sharing central photo-voltaic collectors and batteries can be very cost effective. Solar will become a major source of electrical power, and will be increasingly used as the cost of fossil fuel rises throughout the world.

The Solar Earth house

This group house offers innovative construction techniques, energy self-sufficiency, and a physical form that contributes to the social and emotional support of the community. Sheltered by earth berms on the north side and roof, this group house opens up to the south with large windows and greenhouses facing onto community gardens, social courts, and a pool. Sun scoops on the roof bring more winter sunlight into the interior, and the greenhouses capture solar heat while providing year-round fruits, vegetables, herbs, and flowers. The recycled gray water flows by gravity to the gardens and orchards below the house. The curved, sprayed concrete walls allow the interior spaces to flow comfortably together, and to form unique circular enclosures or rooms where privacy is desired. It can be built in phases through a self-help construction process by the community members.

This earth-sheltered house can be easily extended at the ends to provide more living suites. The construction of this innovative structure is probably more labor and capital intensive than some other alternatives we propose, due to the need

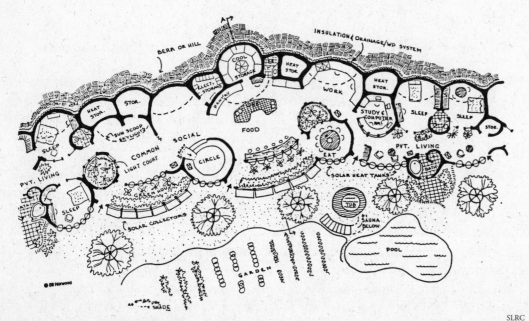

SLRC

Solar Earth House Floor Plan

The term "floor plan," that is actually too mundane to describe this naturally shaped, organic, and spontaneously interconnected flow of spaces, surfaces, enclosures, openings, and curves that allow a balancing of private and common use areas.

for engineering, excavation equipment, reinforcing steel, and the sprayed cement concrete walls and roof systems. To reduce costs, build the long northern walls and the shorter end walls out of concrete block, place an earth berm against the walls, and use wood framing for the roofs, interior partitions, and other exposed walls. This could help reduce the costs of materials and labor, because wood framing is more easily performed by community members or local contractors. This Solar Earth House should earn high Environmental Efficiency Ratio (EER) points.

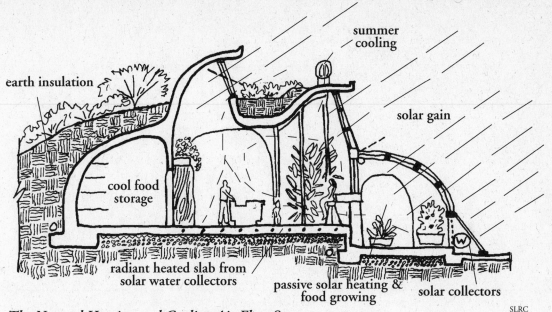

The Natural Heating and Cooling Air Flow System

From summer to winter there is a combination of natural, self-operating manual, mechanical, or electronically operated systems that provide for air circulation and ventilation. The energy source is solar, for passive heat gain and storage in wall and floor mass and water tanks, for hot water collectors for domestic use, and for the radiant heating systems in the floors and walls, and for heating the pools. The electric power is supplied by photo-voltaic cells and a battery storage system.

The Solar Earth House

Snug in the warm folds of Mother Earth, this earth bermed and passive solar group house provides the design possibilities for ecological sustainability. The sun scoop upper windows and the solar gain greenhouses and windows heat and cool the shared living spaces for the 10 to 20 community members. Solar water heating collectors in front of the courtyard preheat domestic water and the hot pools. Solar electric panels on the earth bermed roofs can supply some or all of the electric power needs. Recycled graywater feeds by gravity flow from the house to the gardens and orchards.

309

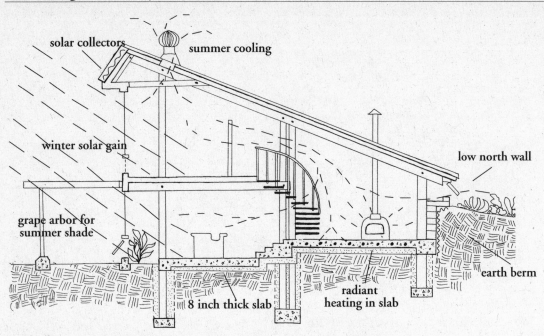

Air flow of Passive Solar Heating and Natural Cooling System

SLRC

The passive solar and natural cooling systems work well, with a very small inside temperature differential from summer to winter.

Photo by Ken Norwood

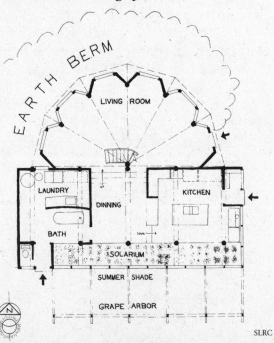

Floor Plan

This house for a family of six plus many guests was designed for simple rural living, low energy use, and food self-reliance through gardens, animals, and fruit trees.

SLRC

Passive/active natural energy rural house

This house on 40 acres in the lower Sierra Nevada Mountains, California, was designed for a large rural extended family and was family/owner-built with the help of the hands-on architect and occasional carpenters. This house was presented earlier in this chapter regarding the innovative pole and beam system and the earth berm method of construction. The complete passive heating and cooling system design was augmented by an active solar system that includes solar collectors on the roof, a 300 gallon storage tank to pre-heat a 30 gallon electric water heater, a wood stove with a hot water converter backup system with gravity feed pipes to the storage tank, radiant-heated coils in a six inch thick concrete slab in the living room floor, and a manual control system to switch between the different systems as needed. The house is well insulated and includes a four foot high earth berm around the low north wall of the living room.

The passive solar and natural cooling systems work well, with a very small inside temperature differential from summer to winter. The eight inch thick concrete slab on the south side is well exposed to the sun during the winter through the 40 feet of solar gain windows. Heated air flows naturally to the higher levels of the living room and the second floor bedrooms, which also have large solar gain windows. The design calls for a small, slow-speed duct fan to force the excess upper level heat back down to the lower level. Cooling works wonderfully in that hot summer climate because of the combination of roof overhangs, a grape arbor over south windows, the cooled mass of concrete slabs and the earth bermed walls, operable windows for cross ventilation on the ground and second floors, and three hot air activated turbine type ventilators mounted on the roof.

The Integral Urban House

This dramatic demonstration of ecologically sustainable living and housing design was on display in Berkeley, California during the late 1970's. The book, *The Integral Urban House: Self-Reliant Living in the City*, was based upon the actual Integral Urban House, a redesigned two-story house on a typical city lot. The house exhibited actual working examples of a wide variety of ecological and sustainable technology. Although the house itself no longer serves the same purposes, the book continues to be a valuable reference for information about several kinds of inexpensively made solar water heating and passive solar space heating methods, composting toilets, graywater recycling systems, rainwater catchment, photo-voltaic cells and battery storage, greenhouse food growing, raised bed intensive gardening, aqua-farming and fish raising, food processing, energy conserving design techniques, windmill generators, and many

The Kachelofen — an answer to wood stoves

— *By David Kibbey, Environmental Building Inspections, Healthy Building and Consultation, Berkeley, CA. 94703*

The kachelofen is a radiant heating stove or oven consisting of a metal nucleus surrounded by ceramic tiles. The first known examples were in China and Rome, as long as 2000 years ago. Masonry heaters are enjoying a renaissance in Europe, and several Master stove-builders have established themselves in America. Initial fabrication costs are high, but running costs are very low.

Open fires have a combustion efficiency rate between 20% and 30%. Kachelofens (tile ovens) commonly reach efficiency levels of 80% to 90%. Wood fuel is added only once or twice a day during cold weather. High firebox temperatures, up to 2000°F, consume pollutants, burning nearly free of creosote, soot, and particles (EPA exempts Kachelofens from no-burn days). Kachelofens are usually centrally located, radiating to the maximum number of rooms. Large houses may require two or more Kachelofens.

Advantages of Kachelofen radiant heating over convection include:
- Surfaces won't burn. Children and cats love to cuddle up to the warm surface.
- Radiant heat gently heats building materials, not air. No cold and hot spots.
- Mechanical air circulation is avoided, reducing dust hazards. Easy to maintain.
- No disturbing odors or noises.
- Can be fueled by wood, electricity, or gas. Energy efficient, clean-burning.
- Safe to leave unattended.
- Makes no electrical, magnetic fields
- Ionized air particles are not formed.

- Humidity levels are maintained at a healthy 40-60% RH.
- Fresh air ventilation and air exchange will not dissipate the radiant heat.
- Often the creative artistry of the Kachelofen enhances building value.
- Often becomes a social gathering place in the form of a bench, stairway, cooking area, etc.
- Virtually permanent.

Photo by Ken Norwood

Kachelofen in the Almora Cluster at Ananda Village
It is located next to the second floor stairs and heats thes entire 3,000 sq. ft. rammed earth house.

THE
INTEGRAL URBAN HOUSE

SELF-RELIANT LIVING IN THE CITY

Sierra Club Books

other ecological design methods. If the Integral Urban House concept is to be successful for mainstream use, a larger extended family community group will be required so that the labor-intensive tasks and the benefits can be distributed among more people. The typical urban or rural nuclear family would not be able to maintain such an array of labor-intensive responsibility — ecological sustainability works when community works.

Community Self-Reliance = Cost Savings = Sustainability

When a group of people come together to share energy and responsibilities in a Shared Living Community, a cooperative spirit is created. In Shared Living Communities, the ecological sustainability processes are made easier by gatherings in the common house, shared meals, and the ability to communicate more easily. People's interests are focused and their energies coordinated. Sustainability in practical terms comes down to the cost of daily living and whether an individuals' energy is used or wasted and resources are shared or duplicated.

It is difficult to fully convey the magical qualities that flow from cooperation. When people use their energy together to harvest the fruits of the earth and replenish their food supply, the immediate satisfaction is profound, and the sense of personal and group empowerment can reach exhilarating heights. We propose the following self-reliant practices and techniques that can be better sustained by a Shared Living Community group; they are neither practical nor economically feasible for individuals and small families to do by themselves.

• **Define the group's vision,** and concepts that will enable each member and the group to participate in an ecologically sustainable community in the most direct and beneficial ways.

• **Research sources** for non-toxic building, agricultural, and household materials and products.

• **Use sustainable agriculture** and Permaculture techniques, and avoid use of chemicals for control of pests and unwanted plant growth.

• **Treat the soil** with natural materials, such as compost, rock dust, and non-toxic additives, that will minimize long-term maintenance and reduce irrigation requirements.

• **Plant edible landscaping**, gardens, and orchards as a major food source.

• **Do much of the community work** with your own labor. Pay yourselves, not outside contractors.

• **Create your own building team,** design cooperatively and spontaneously as a group, and minimize the need for complex technical drawings.

• **Build a community work and craft shop** or barn, and share tools, equipment, and know-how.

• **Build natural energy systems** and other resource-conserving practices into the planning, design, and operating processes.

• **Co-own vehicles**, car-pool, and share the costs of insurance and maintenance.

• **Buy food and supplies** in bulk and case quantities.

• **Contract for health care** and hospitalization services as a group. Apply for tax or fee credits for providing health and preventative care practices within the community.

• **Organize childcare and elder care** services and get tax credits for providing the facilities and services.

• **Install on-site recycling centers** for the separation of organic waste, recyclable materials by types, and non-reusable trash. Research and agree on how to dispose of and how to minimize and eliminate the use of toxic materials.

• **Compost kitchen vegetable** and garden waste materials in order to return nutrients to the soil and support the natural living organisms.

• **Avoid "exporting" excess yard cuttings** and garden and farm wastes to landfill sites, and give it to a neighbor's compost pile. Or join with others in a local bio-mass fuel plant for renewable energy.

Food self-reliance in community

Here are ways that community members can attain some level of food reliance:

• **Grow some of your own food**

Besides raising ordinary vegetables for the dinner table, gardeners can raise herbs for cooking and healing use, and teas, berries, fruits, nuts, and oriental and other exotic produce. A mulberry tree is great for climbing in, and provides delicious berries that are not usually found in a store. Food for snacks can be raised, such as popcorn, peanuts, and sunflowers, as well as foods that are enjoyable to pick and eat while walking in the garden. One person in a group could become the community herbalist and manage the herb growing and storage. In any size community, gardening could be a part- or full-time livelihood, and another opportunity to involve children, teens, and the older people with meaningful responsibilities.

People who live in Urban Cooperative Blocks have their shared backyards for community gardening. Even two or three neighbors could create one shared garden by taking down their backyard fences.

"In keeping with concern for conserving the natural environment, the projects' buildings are designed to go beyond current code requirements to minimize energy use for heating and hot water." [20]
— *A Member of Winslow CoHousing*

"In an age in which the terms 'consumer' and 'person' are used interchangeably, disposing of bagels of garbage each day has become a routine, seemingly inescapable fact of life. But industrial nations were not always so prodigal. Younger people forget that until recently, thrift was a way of life, as it still is in poor countries." [21]

— *John E. Young, World Watch*

But group houses and cooperative apartment buildings without enough yard space can create a community garden together by leasing or buying vacant lots in the cityor by container gardening on the roof. The practice of community gardening is becoming popular all over the country, especially with people from various ethnic cultures who have a recent history of growing their own food.

Passive solar greenhouses can be used for raising vegetables, fruits, and flowers for household use and for sale all year round, as well as for heating living spaces in the winter. Bean and alfalfa sprouts, high in vitamin C and a tasty addition to salads and sandwiches, can be grown in a jar next to the kitchen sink or in projected plant windows in any room. There are modern residential hydroponic units for indoor growing of produce in water containers. Herbs and other plants can be grown in boxes on decks and flat roofed buildings.

• **Animals in the food chain**

Fifty years ago, many households with a small piece of land grew much of their own fruits and vegetables, and kept a few chickens, goats, and/or rabbits to supply fresh eggs and meat. The animals helped sustain the local eco-system by using up kitchen wastes, and providing in return rich manure for garden composting and fertilizing. Beekeeping takes minimal maintenance and can be a rewarding hobby and a good livelihood, and provide a useful service in pollinating the flowers and plants in the community gardens. The honey they produce locally can replace the store-bought cane and beet sugar that is imported from out of state. A full examination of the overall ecological sustainability of a community way of living may open up new ways of thinking about keeping animals as food

sources in city and suburban locations. Many existing Intentional Communities maintain animals as part of the ecological system, while others strictly limit or exclude animal keeping and/or meat eating.

• **Aquaculture**

This method, used for thousands of years in the Far East, applies the principles of agriculture to the cultivation of fish, shellfish, and algae. A writer for the Mother Earth News describes the success of the New Alchemists in Falmouth, Massachusetts:

> What if you could harvest 100 pounds of delectable fish per year, from a tank that is also an efficient solar collector and looks like an oversized living room aquarium? And what if you could drain off about 100 gallons of nutrient-rich waste water from the tank — each week — to irrigate your garden and increase its productivity by as much as 100%? And what if you could then turn around and feed a portion of your fertilized garden's output — a forage crop that's 32% protein and high in B vitamins — back to the fish in the tank? Does it sound too good to be true? If so, consider the fact that such an aquaculture/agriculture symbiosis — a system that enables a one-calorie energy input to yield five calories in tasty fish — is just one of the explorations into the ecological frontier that have occupied the New Alchemists of Falmouth, Massachusetts for the last ten years. [22]

The techniques for doing fish farming, outdoors in larger ponds, or in tanks inside and on roofs, have continued to be well developed for commercial enterprises since New Alchemist's advancements of the process. An enterprising community group could establish aquaculture as their primary food source and as a cottage industry — right in their own backyard.

Water, water everywhere and not a drop to waste
Some of the ecologically sustainable water management techniques listed below are feasible for each individual and family to practice. Some are easier and cheaper to do when a community of people are responsible for conserving and recycling water.

• **Install water conserving toilets**, and composting or electric toilets which use almost no water.
• **Install low-flow showerheads**.
• **Reuse water,** such as household grey water, for watering landscaping, and for toilet flushing. Grey water is piped from bathtubs, showers, and sinks through a filter or treatment system, or directly to the garden.
• **Use natural water treatment** for greywater systems, such as oxidation, circulation, and evaporation and condensation.
• **Use a central water heating** and recirculating system for large group houses and multiple-unit buildings.
• **Use solar cell powered** pumps, control systems, outdoor lighting, and where motors are needed.
• **Use an instantaneous water heater** for small-use situations.
• **Irrigate with a drip pipe** or hose system, and with a solar operated timer.
• **Collect rainwater** in tanks or ponds to serve for a gardening and/or emergency water supply.
• **Plan for an emergency water storage** system in earthquake and fire danger areas, and install necessary distribution systems, pipes, spigots, hoses,

---

buckets, and a water purification process. The emergency water supply can come from pools, irrigation ponds, grey water, and rain catchment.

Self-help construction of community
We all share a rich history of self-help community building, which was the way ancient villages and early American colonies were built, and is the way many villages in the world continue to be sustained today. The "do-it-yourself" movement, owner-builder centers, Habitat for Humanity projects, various government self-help housing financing programs, and the CoHousing and Intentional Communities are testimony that Americans can help each other build their dreams and live sustainably. Group owner-built housing can reduce total construction costs by 30-60%. It has also been well demonstrated that innovative construction and inexpensive local sources of materials can reduce the cost of individual houses. Here are examples of how people's talents and labor can be organized into community design and "barn raising" building teams, to build the private living places and the common spaces and to have more for less.

A community core-group can reduce develop-

Photo by Don Lindemann

Dinner Time for Work Team
Members of the Puget Ridge CoHousing Community, Seattle, WA, work and eat together as they complete their housing. This show of community based self-help building underlies the movement towards self-reliant and ecological living. This intergenerational group self-developed the 23 units and common house. The moderate cost development is located in a low to moderate income Seattle neighborhood.

Photo by Hal Mead

Self-help Builds Harambee Homes in Chicago, Ill.
Community Joint Ventures members working on their
CoHousing project in a North Lawndale existing
neighborhood. Eight homes will house six single parent
families, five headed by women, and two other single persons.

Photo by Hal Mead

Common House at Harambee Homes
One of the women members of the self-help work team that
pre-assembles wall sections in a shop and then erect them.

ment costs by organizing a design committee and having group design workshops. Then they determine how much the skills of an architect, community facilitator, financial consultant, and other experts will be needed, and how to share those costs. CoHousing communities who have used a developer have negotiated to do the landscaping, build their own wood decks, and do other finishing work. Groups who act as their own developer can contract out for the building shell or do their own construction work, and also do their own interior work, insulation, wood trim, sheet rocking, flooring and painting on their own units, and in the common house. This saves money and creates an opportunity for members to personalize their environment

and be taught usable new skills while gaining a sense of belonging to the community. The families of the N Street community, an Urban Cooperative Block, built approximately 550 lineal feet of flagstone walkway that connected their 12 existing houses and the common house on what used to be separately fenced backyards.

Another option is to build the common house as the first phase and include the kitchen, a dining area, and toilets and bathing facilities, and some temporary sleeping rooms so that some self-help workers could live in the common house while they build and complete their own units. This is a perfectly logical and workable brand of "Yankee ingenuity," and needs to be recognized as a valid housing affordability method by the lending and governmental institutions. A strict schedule, inspections, skilled supervision, and a guaranteed completion time by the community workers would be a way of gaining support of the building department, the lender, and the developer if one is involved.

Developing Shared Living Communities
— starting with a core group and getting help along the way

In these changing times there will be found as many diverse ways to develop a Shared Living Community as there are different kinds of people, ideological backgrounds, financial circumstances, and resources. The unique difference between the conventional housing supply process and the types of co-owned communities presented in this book is the involvement, from the very beginning, of the future residents/co-owners. They participate in the planning, organization, and design process, and in the self-management or resident control of the social organization and the physical structures. This then becomes fundemental democracy in action.

In Shared Living Communities, members have the expressed purpose of forming community and will attempt to do so with their own resources to the greatest extent possible. However, most core groups trying to create a Shared Living Community will need varying degrees of development assistance. They must obtain pre-development capital for property acquisition, planning, design, zoning approval, and arranging the financing. The prime objective is to include people of all income levels, requiring an innovative internal financing agreement and/or some kind of affordable housing program. This takes time and expertise. In addition, a jungle of institutional and governmental barriers handicap the acceptance of social, economic, and environmental design innovations in housing and urban development.

We need to understand, however, that in the conventional housing development process the developer makes all the decisions, takes all the risks, obtains the financing, and oversees the architect and

---

New Idea # 4
Proposed Self-help and Alternative Construction Financing Program for Communities

Presently, it is difficult to obtain pre-development or final loans from lenders and government programs in order to co-acquire property or to build a community for self-help. Innovative objectives such as mixed-income, intergenerational composition, ethnic diversity, permanent affordability, resident control and self-management, and innovative and natural energy building techniques are often resisted by lenders. This practice is another form of "redlining," based on a bias and/or lack of understanding concerning deviation from the conventional ownership and design of single-family houses, condos, or apartment complexes. To counteract this deterrent to ecological community development, we propose that a revolving community loan fund or lending pool be established to enable self-help community groups to gain financing. Loans could also be administered through umbrella organizations such as presented later in this chapter. Projects could also gain financing incentive points evaluated through the Environmental Efficiency Ratio and Ecological Sustainability Scoreboard previously proposed.

Dialogue — A Barn Raising Work Day

As of early 1994 at least three CoHousing communities and several intentional communities have recently built their own barn or tool/workshop building. These are moderate to middle income business, professional, and trades-people who ordinarily would have contracted out the work on the premise that staying within their own line of expertise was good business. But America is changing; it is not so much a "back-to-the-land" but a "back-to-the-hands" movement. It is people doing it for each other, on common ground and for a common purpose — like villagers of any era.

This dialogue depicts the Village Acre community in Chapter One and their 32 adults and children, plus 14 volunteer friends. Everyone has a task to do. Several elderly members have the responsibility of keeping the site clean and safe, and another plus, a disabled person is providing "coffee break" refreshments. Children are assigned numerous helpful tasks, being "go-fors," while learning much from observation and participation. Skilled building professionals and trades-persons are being used when their skills are required, and are teaching the others specific jobs.

This is their first day of a marathon work weekend to stack the walls of their 25 ft. x 50 ft. mini-barn/ workshop using the "straw bale" method of construction. The foundation has already been poured, and all of the

SLRC

Straw Bale Construction Party
Building the community workshop at the Village Acre Community

materials and tools have been provided on the job site, ready for the teams to start final assembly.

"Coming through," sang out Melissa, as she balanced some 2 x 8 rafters on her shoulder and wove between a work team stacking straw bales on the walls and a team lifting the ridge beams onto a row of posts.

She was stopped by Libby, a straw bale team worker who asked, *"How can we be sure we're making all the window openings the right size?"*

Melissa replied, *"Ask the window team to make a window template you can use to measure with, and then cut the bales to fit."*

Melissa unloaded the rafters where the roof team was nailing together 3 foot wide panels of roof rafters being pre-assembled before sliding them into place on the roof. *"You're doing great on those panels,"* she said to Osvaldo, the team leader. *"We're right on schedule."* She continued on to the other team leaders, Yoichi and Bob, amidst a calliope of sawing and hammering sounds.

Bob spoke loudly, *"It looks like we're about through building the walls, and the window team is right behind them. Are we ready to shift these gung-ho bale crews to raising the roof panels?"*

Melissa, looking thoughtful, expressed her concern. *"Yes, but, those roof panels look heavy and awkward, even if they are only 3 feet wide by 16 feet long. Maybe we should have stayed with standard construction on the roof."*

Yoichi responded with, *"Yeah, you may be right, but we thought pre-assembling the panels would keep more people busy on the ground doing easy-to-learn tasks, instead of waiting for a few skilled people up on ladders to nail one rafter at a time. Let's review our strategy. I think the next step is to instruct the ridge beam raising team, who are almost finished, to go back up on the scaffolds after our next snack break, and guide the roof panels into those special sockets at the ridge beam — that was your smart idea, Melissa."*

She bowed like a concert conductor and reviewed the rest of the strategy. *"The ground crew will guide the roof panels over the top of the wall while the scaffold crew pulls with ropes until they get their hands on the ends. Then they slip their end into the sockets. Next they let the nailing crew take over while the next panel is being slid into place."*

"There's a problem here," Bob remarked. *"The panel lifting process is going to push the ridge beams around a lot, so let's inspect the post braces to be sure they're all intact first. I saw at least two stakes that were kicked loose."*

A call came from 11-year-old Susan, one of the message runners, *"Hi Melissa — the wall crews are just about through stacking bales. They want to know if the windows go in first or does the wire mesh go on next?"*

Melissa replied, *"Tell them to insert the windows first — and, Susan, ask Libby on the window crew how many windows remain to be assembled, and come back and tell us. OK?"*

"Wow!" said Yoichi. *"Here it is 3:30 on our first day of barn raising. The straw bales are almost all stacked, the windows are ready to go in, and the roof crew has about 10 panels done. It looks good for getting the roof on by tomorrow afternoon."*

Bob spoke up. *"Right! We're doing great. But we'll slow down on the roof plywood phase. We'll need trained people to handle raising and laying out the plywood sheets, and the nailing, without anyone slipping off. That's a five in 12 pitch and the plywood is slick."*

"That's right," said Yoichi. *"Let's select a crew and have a training session. I suggest we rig up some harnesses and ropes as tethers."*

"Hmm!" mused Melissa. *"Let's rehearse this whole process. The plywood crew has three steps: the plywood lifting, placement, and tacking them down with a few nails just to hold them in place. Then the nailers start at the top and lower themselves down on the ropes as they nail the sheets."*

She looked at the other two, and said, *"You'd never guess that most of these folks never built with anything but Legos and Erector sets before this."*

A chorus of celebratory cheers, yahoos, and exclamations punctuated the end of the meeting. *"We're done!" "All the walls are up!" "We've got a wall!" "Where's the roof teams?" "No way! Where's the lemonade and cookie team?"* Forty-six grinning people back-slapped their way to the refreshment table where Rose and Clifford, the two elders of Village Acre, were waiting to serve the goodies.

Photo by Catherine Wanek

Neighbor's Son Helps with Plastering
Out On Bale, (un) Ltd, Tuscon, Arizona

SLRC

The Old Paradigm — a closed loop for developing housing
This closed loop has treated the development of land for housing and commerce as a commodity. Seldom has the "system" involved the end users, the people, in the decision process, nor has the "loop" previously shown consistent attention to the social and environmental values and needs in the design and development processes.

the contractor. The developer's decision about the kind of housing to build is often based more on the risk involved to make a short-term profit and less on a full understanding of user's needs. Housing developers practices are often dictated by the source of their financing and the reality of how much time can be spent between acquisition of a property and when income must be collected from buyers or renters — the users.

Limitations and challenges facing the development of Shared Living Communities

The present day mass housing financing and mortgage methods have only existed a short time, but today are firmly embedded in a closed loop system dominated by speculators, investors, lenders, developers, builders, realtors, secondary mortgage institutions and government-regulated housing finance agencies. The adherents of the old paradigm system do not easily respond to the new community movement, except when market rate clients are available, there is a known market, the design is conventional, the site is acquired, and a substantial down payment, equity collateral, or a subsidy is available. In the past, developer interests have resisted working with and lending to people organized to co-purchase or co-lease existing, remodeled, or new housing for cooperatives and Shared Living Communities. Residents of builder housing normally only become involved as consumers during marketing, perhaps having some choice of interior colors, wallpaper, and floor covering. This practice closes off an increasingly larger segment of the society from seeking alternative and affordable solutions. The difficulties and challenges facing Shared Living Community core groups include:

• Finding a large enough property in a single ownership or putting together several smaller adjacent lots in the existing urban/suburban areas.
• Lack of economic incentives and public policies encouraging new construction in the city, and the relative ease for developers to rezone lower priced rural properties for low-density housing.
• Lack of financing programs to serve "third sector housing" groups forming "permanently affordable" co-owned community housing clusters, group houses, or cooperatives.
• Unnecessarily restrictive and obsolete zoning ordinances in cities, towns, and rural areas which tend to favor single-family lot subdivisions rather than encouraging ecological planning and cluster housing communities.
• Lack of visionary and comprehensive planning at the urban, regional, and state levels to initiate and coordinate ecological land use, transportation, and housing policies and practices, and to influence zoning ordinances and actual programs that will carry them out.
• Resistance by the "closed loop" housing development lenders, such as banking and second- mortgage financing institutions, to deviating from the fixed view that individual single-family house or condo ownership is the best housing "product" to lend for.

The "New Paradigm" open loop development of Shared Living Communities

As more beginning community groups and residents of existing housing complexes become involved in the "open loop" community building process, the role of all the participants will change. In Shared Living Communities the decision-making power is is in the hands of the future residents, who can develop a business agreement with the developer, sponsoring organization, lender, architect, and contractor. These professionals could work with the community core group on the development process from the very beginning, or be brought in at some point along the way. The architect, for example, may serve as the group facilitator, designer, and as a development consultant.

The experience thus far with community core groups working as their own developers ranges widely. In the Muir Commons, Doyle Street, Winslow, Nyland, Southside Park, and other CoHousing communities, the core group involvement from the beginning sets a precedent for creating people-based community housing for the American mainstream. Other non-typical development models come from Intentional Communities, nonprofit low-income housing organizations, various types of cooperatives, group housing, Group Homes, Community Land Trusts, and Community Economic Development Corporations.

Lower income housing groups and existing tenants who lack the in-house organizing skills or the initial capital may require other alternative sources. A team can be formed that may include a nonprofit sponsor, a local city redevelopment agency, and/or a housing agency, for securing property, pre-development services, a construction loan, and assistance with a final loan. Groups can do much of the initial leg-work and design decision process with their own volunteer and out-of-pocket resources and then shop for a nonprofit housing sponsor and/or a developer. Some groups will function more like an intentional community, move onto the land, start living simply, and spread the

work out according to their cash flow and self-help capabilities.

Seed money for starting the core group process might come from the members, and from Foundations, a nonprofit sponsor, local government, and/or an interested developer. Today, skilled community facilitators are available to assist with innovative community housing solutions. The problem up to now is that financing for education, organizing, site acquisition, architectural, legal and other up front costs have not beeneasily available.

How developers can be involved

When a community core group decides that a developer is necessary, there needs to be a clear understanding of how the developer must operate while taking the risk to advance funds. The developer must shift his or her thinking as well, and understand the aspirations of the core group and their strengths and shortcomings. This means that the core group must be well organized, and have their decision-making process well developed in order to avoid the delays that can arise when decisions are made by consensus or other participatory democratic processes. The sequence of steps for the core group process is outlined in Chapter Three.

Showing interest in the array of new community design models is a new younger generation of developers, as well as more established firms that see "community" as a market to tap. Some developers may want to do this without shifting their thinking as mainstream entrepreneurs, and attempt to market a housing product that looks like a Village Cluster with a common house and village street attractions. They may want to build standard size houses with a full kitchen, dining, and living rooms, in order to

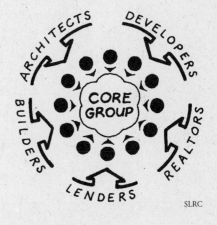

SLRC

The New Paradigm —
building community together
involves everyone
The community and cooperative
movements herald a new "open loop"
process in which core groups will
become involved at the very beginning
of the design and building of their own
community oriented housing. This will
be a transformative process for our
society on its way towards living and
acting in ecologically sustainable ways.

attract a wider market, and to satisfy the conventional criteria of lenders. They may not know how to organize a compatible community core group interested in the on-going community building process and therefore they are more likely to mislead the public as to what Village Cluster, CoHousing, and cooperative housing communities really are. This is where community facilitators can be very valuable to developers, whether profit or nonprofit, in providing staff training and public workshops.

Some developers may wish to promote Shared Living Community developments in advance by attracting core groups through workshops and training classes paid for by the developer. When they have a project ready to build, they will then try to recruit from a larger pool of potential buyers with the financing qualifications. This approach, if sensitively managed, could produce the unity of purpose needed for a committed community. Careful guidance is needed to create a diverse social, cultural, income, and age composition. The key is for the core group to understand the development process, and be in agreement on the group's values and design criteria, and to come to concensus quickly. They must also be aware of possible restraints and the workable alternatives, be clear about what they do and do not know how to do, and know how to obtain professional assistance when needed.

The steps toward community development
For a Shared Living Community core group to follow the precepts advanced in this book and meet the constraints listed above, they will need to follow a careful sequence of planning and development steps. This process applies whether the group is attempting to do it themselves or is working with a nonprofit sponsor or a commercial developer. Here is an overall checklist for a core group acquiring property or for tenants buying their own building (the order may change for different projects):

• **Organize the group**, come to agreements on values and objectives, and select new members — these are ongoing processes.
• **Develop criteria for location,** site needs, and building design.
• **Determine financial resources**, establish bank accounts, explore loan sources, and obtain pre-development loans and/or grants.
• **Determine the legal and ownership** form for your group, and if appropriate, begin the incorporation or nonprofit status process, and develop partnership agreements, by-laws, and operating rules.
• **Find a site and evaluate zoning**, governmental, structural and health safety regulations, workability for shared living, and estimated costs for repair and re-design. This may include soil tests, property surveys, and toxic contamination tests.
• **Enter into escrow contingent** upon building inspections, zoning approval, title search, financing, and other factors.
• **Conduct co-design meetings** to prepare exploratory design, cost projections, operating budgets, and time schedulae.
• **Initiate necessary planning**, zoning and other regulatory approvals.
• **Secure final financing commitments**
• **Make down payments** and close escrow.
• **Finalize preliminary design studies** with the whole core group.
• **Prepare final working drawings**, begin permit process, obtain bids, and select a contractor or

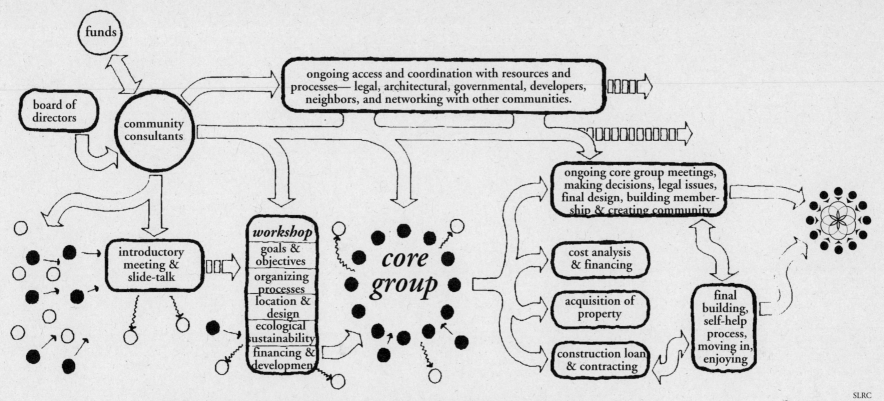

The Overall Process of Community Formation and Development
People hear about the idea of community, start with introductory presentations, and take part in a
workshop by community facilitators. A community core group begins to gain members, losing some and
gaining others, and the community development continues with the planning process and lenders, architects,
and other resource groups. The end of the beginning for forming of a community is the moving in and
beginning to live in the community of their own making.

organize a self-help process for all or some parts of
the work.
• **Obtain construction loans**, and establish a tight
time schedule for yourselves and the contractors.
• **Take out a final mortgage loan**, celebrate, and
continue building your community.

Financing Your Shared Living Community

Nonprofit sponsoring organizations, socially responsible investment groups, nonprofit low-income
developers and housing lenders are among the
sources for property acquisition, pre-development
planning and design, and construction loans. These

323

sources will still be looking for a safe return on their investment, and therefore Community members will usually have to come up with all or some part of the down payment themselves. This may be up to 25% of the total cost of the property. Conventional banks and savings and loans are beginning to fund some innovative housing projects such as CoHousing and Limited Equity Housing Cooperatives, but usually at the market rate of interest. It may be possible to get partial funding from nonprofit housing lenders, local city, county, or state housing trust/revolving loan funds, and grants from charitable foundations when the community is a nonprofit or sponsored by an affordable housing nonprofit provider. There are various federal, state, and local programs offering low-interest loans and grants, for the development of very low, low, and moderate income housing. In the past these housing programs and nonprofit developers have been limited to conventional single-family tracts and apartments. They have had little incentive for bringing together innovative solutions such as ecological design, built-in social services, resident control, community co-ownership, and permanent affordability. Some possibilities of sources for financing and assistance are:

• Private investors who know the group or are interested in its purpose.
• Community members: savings, selling their houses, equity in other properties.
• A community savings account for accumulating core group members' resources.
• Tax credit investors through low-income housing developers.
• Conventional lenders that comply with Community Reinvestment Act lending guidelines for community and socially responsible housing.
• Tax-exempt loans from local or state government bond programs.
• Housing trust/revolving loan funds and other grants and loans from local and state government.
• Community Development Block Grant (CDBG) from local governments.
• U.S. Department of Housing and Urban Development (HUD) housing financing programs, mortgage insurance, and other resources.
• State government financing programs for housing loans and grants.
• Local city and county government housing and redevelopment agencies and programs.
• Employee pension funds and credit unions.
• Private charitable foundation support.
• National Cooperative Bank.
• Community Development Bank (Clinton administration program).
• Community development corporations, community land trusts, mutual housing associations, and other nonprofit sponsors.

Alternative Methods of Ownership for Shared Living Communities

Much of the discussion in the book has been critical of the consumer-based ownership and mortgage methods that divide land into small lots for detached single-family houses. The various models of Shared Living Communities provide alternative approaches for using, designing, owning, and financing land, and development of housing, in ways that encourage land, energy, and resource conservation in a community context. Owning land in common, and permanent affordability, are twin objectives that we and other advocates of socio-economically and environmentally responsible community housing strongly support. Escalation of housing costs drains people's spending power for other goods and services. By increasing the supply of co-owned permanently affordable housing, in context with the establishment of ecologically sustainable ways of living, the overall society is strengthened and the economy is stabilized.

Below is an overview of the methods by which a number of people may cooperatively own and manage a larger piece of property, with clustered buildings used for private and common use. (Refer to the Glossary for concise definitions of the types of ownership presented in this section.)

Condominiums

In this arrangement, each buyer finances and owns his or her own unit, plus an "undivided interest" in common land and amenities. Each condo unit can be sold on the open market by the individual owner without approval of the other members. Owners are required to belong to a homeowners association to which they pay fees for the maintenance of the common spaces and facilities, and which is governed by a set of conditions, covenants and restrictions (CC&R's). Some CoHousing communities attempt to strengthen their cooperative community aspirations with special by-laws and operating agreements, but the CC&R's are still the legal basis for resale of a unit. The problem with condo ownership is that sustainability of the original community objectives and such measures as resale price limits (permanent affordability) can become difficult to enforce when the group cannot select who buys into the community. Some of the

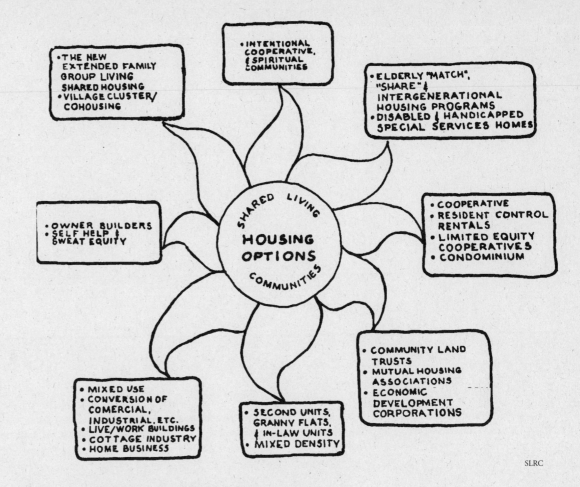

SLRC

CoHousing communities in Denmark have had difficulty maintaining their original cooperative community character due to "gentrification" caused by speculative sales by individual owners. Since condominiums are often priced at the "market rate," they become unaffordable to lower income people who want to be in the community, unless there is a subsidy. In some communities a mix of ownership and rentals for lower income people is accomplished by the inclusion of rental rooms in shared houses and rental living units in the project.

However, the issue of social and economic equity remains inadequately addressed.

Tenancies in common

This is a form of partnership commonly used for co-ownership of small multi-family apartment buildings of two to four units (duplexes to quadplexes or more) or a group house with two or more resident co-owners. Tenancies in common or TIC may also be used for small, cluster housing arrangements. The property is purchased as a "common interest," with all partners owning an interest share in the title and a share in their responsibility for mortgage payments and other obligations for upkeep of the property. The partners are free to enter into almost any kind of agreements and deed restrictions for the operation of the property, such as selection of a new partner, resale price limits, pets, and other rights and responsibilities. Problems can occur when a property escalates in value and an outgoing partner seeks to secure a profit on their share, thus causing a forced sale. An outgoing partner may for any other reason sell their interest to a new person, but because all original parties own a share in the title, selling a share to a new partner may require the entire property to be re-financed. Some lenders have been known to permit the replacement buyer to assume the loan and thus replace the out-going member. More often the remaining partner(s) must themselves finance all of the new buyer's obligation, while the out-going members' name remains on the original mortgage.

Many TIC partnerships have existed successfully, but there have also been considerable problems, often due to the lack of mutual compatibility of the original partners or of well developed operating agreements. This often occurs when a building owner or a real estate person misleads the buyers to believe that they are buying separate property rights as in a condominium. Entering into a TIC should be done in the same ways that any Shared Living Community is formed, with core group meetings and agreeing on a mutual purpose. This can work well for a new extended family of friends seeking

---

New Idea # 5
Education for Ecological Living

We propose nationally sponsored funding to produce educational programs about the reasons, benefits, methods, and options for creating ecologically sustainable communities, Eco Villages, Eco Cities, Green Belts, and the transportation systems to link them all together. The emphasis would be to address the environmental health and well-being of all peoples. This would be in context with local and global ecological healing, and help people learn the personal, economic, and practical advantages for changing to ecologically sustainable lifestyles. Included would be documentary films, videotapes, computer programs, publications, seminars, workshops, classes, counseling sessions, and training classes directed to the general public, the officials and staff of businesses, public bodies, nonprofits, and all levels of the education system. The objective is to increase the opportunity for people of all incomes to learn about the benefits and process for forming some type of Shared Living Community and how they themselves can be empowered as a result.

long-term co-ownership and a lasting community. The TIC method can also be used to initiate the original purchase of a cluster or a building, and then the co-owners can form some other type of cooperative ownership or condominium.

Housing cooperatives

There are many ways the term "cooperative" can be used. For some people it is only a way to secure ownership, while for others, forming a cooperative means following the Rochdale cooperative principles or similar precepts established by today's array of cooperative organizations and Intentional Communities. Cooperatives can be formed as mutual benefit, nonprofit, or for-profit corporations by residents of an existing multi-unit building or by new members of any Shared Living Community. Each resident is entitled to one share in the cooperative corporation that owns the entire property. There are several types of housing cooperatives as determined by various state laws, federal financing programs, and Internal Revenue Service regulations. There are lower income leased cooperatives, market rate and for-profit cooperatives, and housing cooperatives with varying degrees of equity resale limitations. The for-profit, also called a commercial cooperative, can operate like a condominium with an association, by-laws, and operating rules. Regardless of the legal, financial, and ownership structure of the cooperative, the degree of cooperation and commitment to community may vary, depending on the purposes of its formation.

Limited Equity Housing Cooperatives

The LEHC method of ownership of an apartment building or a Village Cluster is an available and

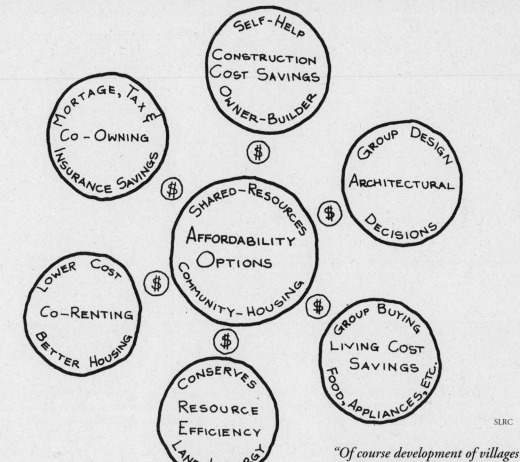

SLRC

proven method of cooperative ownership that assures permanent affordability of the units. LEHC residents co-own the property as a democratically self-managed mutual benefit nonprofit (not tax exempt) corporation. LEHC's effectively remove segments of housing from speculative market pressures. LEHC's can also provide people of lower to moderate incomes the opportunity to co-own decent housing at stable, affordable costs, without

"Of course development of villages based primarily on cooperative principles implies major lifestyle changes, but North America has done it before. After World War II, we built the suburbs, about as massive a societal change as can be imagined. But we drifted in to that change, without thinking it through, without conducting experiments to see how suburbs worked in practice."[24]
— *Joel David Welty, Directory of Intentional Communities*

the need for massive governmental subsidies or expensive new projects. They could be as small as five units.

Laws governing LEHC's vary from state to state, and some states have no specific regulations. In California, when a co-op member wants to sell, their share (representing their unit) is sold back to the co-op. The seller receives their cost-of-investment, usually their down payment, plus an amount for appreciation of value not to exceed 10% each year. The seller also receives an agreed upon amount for the improvements made on the total property, and an adjusted amount for remodeling improvements done on their apartment. Costs to repair damages done to the unit may be deducted from the seller's final settlement. Each member pays a monthly fee, which covers his or her share of the mortgage, as well as operating costs. Should the entire property be sold, profits go to a designated nonprofit organization.

Cooperatives stabilize the members' housing costs, since only operating costs are likely to rise with inflation. Building and land costs are stabilized because there is no speculative profit to be gained in an LEHC. If owning the building is initially impossible, similar functions and benefits of an LEHC can be implemented by the cooperative group obtaining a master lease from a nonprofit developer, city housing agency, or a nonprofit housing organization. This method, called a leasing cooperative, could include the option to purchase the property at a later time as a fully incorporated LEHC.

LEHC's have usually been established in existing rental apartment buildings, and can be as small as five units, but we propose an expanded nationwide LEHC development program. New or redesigned LEHC communities using the Village Cluster, CoHousing, and Urban Cooperative Block models could be formed and developed, each with a common house, central kitchen and dining room, and other shared amenities. Group houses, and especially designed ones like the Octagonal Cluster House, with it's eight private living suites and common areas, could qualify to become an LEHC. A cooperative may begin as a condominium, a for-profit cooperative, a tenancies-in-common, or a partnership, and then convert to an LEHC after getting established, building its membership, completing major improvements, and obtaining final financing. Some adjustments in state or local laws may make cooperative ownership easier, but the extent to which LEHC's become truly ecologically sustainable communities is primarily up to the group to make a commitment to cooperative social structure and environmental design precepts.

New Idea # 6
A model law for Limited Equity Housing Cooperatives

We propose the establishment of a national model LEHC law that would be recognized by HUD, which in turn would establish various kinds of incentives to encourage States to enact their own laws. A LEHC network could be established, enabling coop members to transfer their shares to LEHC's in other parts of the country when they need to move. Regardless of the location, such expanded model cooperative housing programs should embrace the precepts of permanent affordability, mixed income, participatory management, energy conserving design, and other ecologically sustainable community features. Through the expansion of umbrella support groups such as Community Land Trusts, Mutual Housing Associations, and Community Development Corporations, a nationwide federation of LEHC's can be developed.

Mutual Housing Associations

A Mutual Housing Association is a public benefit nonprofit organization that may have a range of "umbrella" functions, including development, ownership, and management of cooperative and resident-controlled housing. They can assist with the financing, management, member education, and continuing technical support of cooperative housing groups and LEHC's that become members of a MHA. As a membership organization, MHA's can represent many housing units and assist the founding of new groups. By holding the title of cooperative buildings, an MHA is likely to have the resources to start new communities, a financial leverage that is usually not available to tenants and individual founding groups.

A MHA can help residents of HUD assisted multi-unit buildings who are organizing for the purchase and control of their properties. An MHA could assist the residents of existing absentee-owned single-family houses to form an Urban Cooperative Block and convert to an LEHC, and an MHA can master lease buildings from private owner(s), and either to or from a Community Land Trust or a Community Development Corporation. With these capabilities, MHA's are empowered to provide a wider range of affordable housing and social services. They can sponsor livelihood development, childcare, and food self-reliance programs, and be a resource for creating ecologically and socially responsible Shared Living Communities.

Community Land Trust

The land trust movement has grown out of the simple act of small groups of people co-buying woods and wetlands to prevent their being ruined by development. This practice has evolved into the conservation land trust model, a permanent trust to preserve and care for land in its natural state in perpetuity. This effectively removes the land from the speculative market — it is no longer a commodity. This movement is in direct response to the tragic attitude in America that any unprotected and so called "unused" land is fair game for profit-driven development. Many people are now embracing the ideal that preservation of land for public benefit purposes should be linked to ecologically sustainable community purposes. The CLT is an umbrella model appropriate for the development of co-owned and mixed-income Shared Living Communities, such as Urban Cooperative Blocks in existing neighborhoods and new Eco Villages covering large areas. The CLTs are becoming recognized at state and federal levels and being incorporated into housing programs as stated in Resources Newsletter:

> Community Land Trusts received their first formal recognition by the federal government in the Housing and Community Development Act of 1992. The housing bill included a variety of changes to the new HOME program, and one of these changes was to define community land trusts and establish them as a special category of Community Housing Development Organizations. An additional change … amends the Section 502 program at Farmer's Home [Finance Agency] to allow loans to purchasers of limited equity homes on land held by a community land trust.[25]

The Institute for Community Economics (ICE) in Massachusetts has pioneered the approach that CLT's can preserve natural resources, protect open

"Over the past two or three years, 'sustainability' has entered the political, economic and environmental lexicon. A concept that means many things to many interests, it is essentially a linking of the economic, and environmental in a more organic way than does current, primarily regulatory, environmental policy…. But, sustainability can mean much more: the opportunity to connect economic, social and environmental concerns, to create new measurements of development of progress that weigh justice and equity as well as environmental quality."[26]
— Catherine Lerza,
"Race, Poverty and Sustainable Communities"

New Idea # 7

A Continual Series of White House Conferences on Rebuilding Community in America — Living the Visions for the 21st Century Now

All organizations and groups that would be benefited by and that would affect ecological community development need to coalesce their efforts to make a positive contribution to the "Rebuilding America" movement. The conference series would be a platform for how to rebuild America's communities in an ecologically sustainable way. The emphasis would be on stimulating the local economy, employing local people, strengthening the family, stabilizing and rebuilding pedestrian/transit node neighborhoods, and reducing auto dependency through the introduction of comprehensive networks of rail transit systems. This could be a national exercise in interconnective thinking, creating integrated action programs to achieve ecologically sustainable urban revitalization goals. It would provide an arena for sharing the process, monitoring progress, and celebrating the achievements of each year.

Powerful New Tools for Ecologically Sustainable Development

The individual tools and techniques covered in this chapter all contribute to carrying out some facet of designing communities that are ecologically sustainable. We have also equated social and economic justice objectives as being integral with the values of ecologically sustainable community, with the reasoning that all things are interconnected. Now there is the challenge to find the tools and techniques that will fulfill those ideals. The following programs and processes speak of the encouraging trend toward integration of social, economic, and environmental factors in our daily lives.

The community development corporation (CDC)

Another umbrella organization model that holds great potential for supporting the community movement, rebuilding our cities, and protecting the Green Belt is the Community Development Corporation. The CDC approach is to assist local people in urban neighborhoods and rural towns to create local businesses and cooperatives, jobs, affordable housing, community service programs, self-help and training programs, and to stimulate investment, grants, and loans for use in the local community.

"Oregon CDC Program Leads to Dramatic Increase in CDC's … As of 1992, there were 35 CDC's in Oregon… In addition to the increase in number, the geographic location of CDC's has become more varied. Originally, Portland was the sole location of CDC's, but now CDC's can be found in rural areas across the state." [27]

— Resources, National Congress for Community Ecological Development

space, and provide permanently affordable housing and ecological ways of living, by not treating property as a speculative product. The CLT organizational and legal structure is similar to the MHA, and can include the basic precepts of the cooperative and ecological community movements, such as:
• **Open membership**, affordable dues, and local salient enterprise..
• **Democratically elected board** with 1/3 from the CLT-owned land and 2/3 from a broad range of people and interests in the larger community (the proportions may vary).
• **Commitment to the community** and the environment, to providing homes to those in need, and to perpetuate stewardship of the land.
• **Limited-equity resale limits** are attached to all property that the CLT leases. Residents own their lease, similar to a coop share in an LEHC .[28]

The CDC can also be an umbrella for MHA's, CLT's, and LEHC's, and a support resource for the creation of Shared Living Communities. A CDC can serve as a coordinating body, community organizer, financing guarantor, and conduit for private and public sources of funds. One example is the Institute for Community Economics in Springfield, Massachusetts, which sponsors Limited Equity

Housing Cooperatives, Community Land Trusts, and small businesses. The Sabin CDC in the Sabin Neighborhood of Portland, Oregon, is assisting several Urban Cooperative Block communities, Group Homes, and the general economic and social recovery of the Sabin area. The rising number of CDC's demonstrates that localized community - based economics can be an appropriate balancing process in this time of global economics. However, some CDC's have limited their scope to only housing or business development, and lack the vision and capabilities for a comprehensive approach to neighborhood revitalization. An exciting potential exists however for the use of CDC's as another tool for the formation of Shared Living Communities, in combination with the Clinton Administration's Empowerment Zone and Enterprise Community proposals. This is an opportunity to empower the local community and build towards a sustainable larger community, while not adding to governement at the top.

Local Empowerment Zones and Enterprise Communities

The potential for Shared Living Communities to make a significant contribution toward the ecological sustainability of American society can best be realized by utilizing every people-empowering and community-building tool that is available. This would include voluntary community building efforts initiated by the people, enlightened business interests, dedicated nonprofit organizations, educational institutions, and responsible government at all levels. One new tool that may be exactly right for that job is the Economic Development Act of 1993, which includes the Empowerment Zone and

the Enterprise Community proposals. The Clinton Administration is making this a new approach, as quoted in "Resources,"

> President Clinton has announced a proposal to create 10 Empowerment Zones and 100 Enterprise Communities around the country to stimulate the revitalization of low-income communities. [29]

The Clinton Administration's variation of the Reagan-Bush Administration's Enterprise Zone (EZ) goes beyond the singular focus on economic investment through tax credits. The original EZ program has had little effect on the broader needs of impoverished areas in terms of housing, education, health, and community building, and had dubious value in raising the poverty level. The EZ introduced manufacturing and commercial investment into rural areas without regard to the long-term environmental, agricultural, and socio-economic future of rural areas. To implement these programs the Clinton Administration has created the Community Enterprise Board (CEB), which has the responsibility of insuring that the overall quality of life in a urban or rural Empowerment Zone area is enhanced by these measures.

> The CEB is chaired by Vice President Al Gore and is composed of representatives of all federal agencies .... such as Labor, Housing and Urban Development, Commerce, Transportation, Health and Human Services, Agriculture, and the Small Business Administration. [30]

While the great battles of the decade ahead are likely to be economic, the greatest challenge to our economic strength is certainly not competition from the Pacific Rim or Europe. No; the greatest challenge to our economic strength is here at home — where the decaying cores of too many inner-cities and the poverty-stricken heartlands of rural America threaten to erode our dynamic regional economies from within. That is what we intend to change. I believe we can do it." [31]
> *—Al Gore*
> *December 6, 1993*
> *Boston, Massachusetts*

"*Our challenge is to provide opportunity to all Americans. We believe the best strategy for community empowerment is a community-driven comprehensive approach which coordinates economic, physical, environmental, community and human needs.*" [32]
> *— Henry Cisneros, Secretary, Department of Housing and Urban Development*

"...the Economic Empowerment Act of 1993, would serve as the first piece of a larger community empowerment agenda, along with the soon-to-be announced proposal for community development banks, and other legislation at a later date. The Empowerment Zone proposal would combine new tax credits with redirected funds from other programs."[33]
— *Resources Newsletter*

"A sustainable economic system will not of itself change conditions of inequity and poverty, nor will it automatically improve the conditions under which increasing numbers of Americans (and the majority of the world's population) live. In fact, it could exacerbate current inequities unless we demand a definition of sustainability that gives equal value to issues of distributive justice, access to opportunity, and objective measures of quality of life (health care, housing, education, employment) along with measures of environmental quality."[34]
— *Catherine Lerza*

Rebuilding Community in America – *prototype programs*

The innovative tools and techniques offered in this chapter, and the comprehensive problem solving and ecologically sustainable development proposals offered throughout this book are represented in the three prototype programs listed below. The accomplishment of these key objectives would represent a major breakthrough for "Rebuilding Community in America " because they represent the integration of the social, economic, and environmental elements that form the basis for a sustainable system.

• **Recycling abandoned or ailing shopping centers** and business strips into higher density multi-purpose, mixed-use community service centers, served by light rail networks, can transform urban sprawl suburbs. This is where the Clinton Administration's Community Empowerment Board's (CEB) powerful array of coordinated resources could effectively empower local enterprises and solve social, economic, and environmental problems at a neighborhood participation level.

• **The Urban Cooperative Block (UCB)** as a means for revitalizing suburban and inner-city areas could be very appropriate for CEB support, acting through the various local umbrella nonprofits presented earlier. In a UCB of redesigned older houses, the extended family groups have the maximum opportunity for live-work and community enterprises, given the same tax credit incentives as larger businesses. This will broaden community empowerment but keep the capital flowing locally.

• **The Green Belt is a key counterpart to the Eco City** revitalization proposals. The permanent agricultural Green Belt needs to be recognized by the CEB, government at all levels, and the people,

as a strategically critical component for the revitalization of both urban and rural areas and as a tool for halting urban sprawl. The CEB's umbrella of resources and programs, coordinated with local nonprofit organizations such as MHA's, CLT's, and LEHC's, will hopefully assist rural community core groups to form the Organic Farm Village Clusters and New Rural Towns presented in this book. However, the real impetus for the new rural society to become socially and economically vital must come directly from those who will benefit the most by forming community — the new breed of organic farmers who will populate the Green Belts.

Additional Innovations for Creating Community Type Housing

There is an urgent need for better financing sources for ecologically designed, co-owned, mixed-income, intergenerational, and permanently affordable Shared Living Communities. Some changes and techniques for implementation of social and environmental innovations for housing and community development are:

• **Make changes in the Low Income Housing Tax Credit program,** which is expensive to operate, and provide direct grants, subsidies, and deferred, low, and no interest loans to user groups for permanently affordable, self-reliant, community based housing.

• **Make pre-development loans or grants** readily available to community core groups and existing building residents to prepare a resident control or co-ownership proposal, such as with a LEHC or CLT.

• **Provide incentives for nonprofit housing organizations** to acquire ownership of housing to prevent speculative market rate resale, assure permanent affordability, and provide the social and organizational structure for ecological community design and lifestyle.

• **Increase acceptance of innovative community housing** by the mainstream populations and institutions through education conducted by community advocacy organizations, educational institutions, and community facilitators.

• **Authorize Fannie Mae and Freddy Mac** (secondary mortgage purchasers for single-family and rental projects) to purchase mortgages for group houses, housing cooperatives, and other types of Shared Living Communities.

• **Include incentives and bonuses** in all planning, housing, and redevelopment ordinances and programs to encourage sustainable community housing.

• **Reform or eliminate the homeowner tax deduction** and other subsidies for single-family housing, and equalize the present discrepancy by offering tax deduction incentives for co-owned or co-leased Shared Living Community housing.

• **Establish a special loan/grant program for self-help** projects where the co-owners contribute sweat equity instead of down payments, and can live in semi-completed community buildings while finishing individual units and common facilities.

• **Provide incentive bonuses,** such as a "write-down" of land cost, grants, low-interest loans, and self-help construction financing, to self-organized and nonprofit-sponsored community core groups who include mixed-use, mixed age, mixed-income, and other social and environmental amenities in a cooperative community environment.

• **Do not penalize social service and subsidized rent recipients** for rent savings from shared housing and other common amenities.

• **Provide a direct grant or other financial resources** for the acquisition of properties by nonprofit sponsors at very low to no interest rates that will enable the property to operate from current income. This interest subsidy is then repaid into the housing trust fund through refinancing when much of the principal has been paid off.

• **Encourage equity sharing/joint ownership** among family members, nonprofits, pension funds, churches, or other local entities with no/low-interest loans or direct grants available to the community project. Lenders would keep a specified share of ownership in a property and claim their share of the deferred interest when the principal is reduced.

• **Provide pre-development grants and loans** to buy surplus and foreclosed properties for various types of Shared Living Community demonstration projects and for planning and design work.

• **Enable transit system programs to include tax increment financing** that capitalizes on the increased land value and tax revenues created around rail transit stations. Provide planning and development funds for pedestrian and bike ways and other amenities in Eco Villages and for the reservation of sites for ecologically sustainable Shared Living Communities including affordable housing for moderate and lower income people who would otherwise be displaced due to land value increases in the vicinity of transit stations. Tax increment financing would enable transportation planning programs to take into account housing, local businesses and jobs, and alternatives to the car from the beginning of the project. Local government would gain some percentage of tax revenues plus sales tax increases.

"The Low Income Housing Tax Credit is still with us ... What's wrong with it? For one, it is unseemly and redistributively unjust to help the poor by helping the rich — those upper-income investors and big corporations that avoid paying parts of their income taxes by offsetting these obligations via investment in low-income housing. ...Second, there's an unbelievable amount of waste in paying all those middlemen: the lawyers, syndicators, accountants and other $200+/hour types to structure these fantastically complicated deals." [35]

— Chester Hartman, "Feeding the Sparrows by Feeding the Horses"

Land Use Planning and Zoning Issues

Our recommended change towards co-ownership of larger one-piece sites for Shared Living Communities is a major shift from the practice of individual ownership of small, subdivided lots by many different people. This change portends a fundamental change from some aspects of the early "property rights" rationale for zoning and subdivision ordinances, and a move back toward the practice of "common" lands. Community core groups may find it helpful in their zoning investigation to understand more about historic precedents in America for land use controls, and how that affects the acceptance of innovations such as Shared Living Communities. Zoning dates from early colonial times with the establishment of local "nuisance" ordinances, and later expansion of that approach with "protective" laws and lower court decisions through the late 1800's. By the beginning of this century, a rash of zoning ordinances and state enabling acts had been passed. In 1926 the precedent-setting U.S. Supreme Court case of *Village of Euclid, Ohio, vs. Ambler Realty Co.,* dealt for the first time with the constitutionality of zoning and established the precedent that:

> ...represented a significant extension of the police power in that it enabled a municipality to prohibit uses which were not 'nuisances' in the strict sense of the term. In particular, shops, industry, and apartments were excluded from single family zones. [37]

The basic underlying reasoning behind planning and zoning laws traces back to the Latin maxim

"sic utere tuo ut alienum non laedas" (use your own property in such a manner as not to injure that of another) which was quoted in the *Euclid* case.[38] From that early precept for civil conduct in the use of property, we can see how to transcend the zoning practices born out of the narrow concern for the economic impact (the "nuisance" factor) upon individual pieces of residential property created by certain non-residential uses. Although the *Euclid* case opened the door to more comprehensive planning policies to protect the public health, safety, and general welfare, the actual application has resulted in hierarchical zoning (from most restrictive to least restrictive) of almost all the land in this country. As a result, zoning tends to be conducted in a manner that can be considered bureaucratically mechanical, economically exploitative, and socially fragmenting.

The consumer-based system of individual ownership has been so codified by the zoning process that it has more to do with real estate economics than with creating well-planned sustainable communities. This is a distinction that we, as people using the land, need to understand as we pursue higher aspirations for rebuilding communities in America. The dichotomy of there being differences between "zoning" and "planning" has been recognized by the courts. As the New Jersey Court said in *Angermier v. Borough of Sea Girt:*

> Zoning is not devoid of planning, but it does not include the whole of planning. ...Planning has a much broader connotation. It has in view...the physical development of the community and its environs in relation to its social and economic well-being for the fulfill-

" No country subsidizes private home ownership with more negative economic or environmental results than the U.S. ... the federal tax subsidy for private housing — mostly tax deductions for interest paid on mortgages — total more than $70 billion a year. Some make out like bandits under this arrangement, especially upper-income taxpayers with the biggest homes and hence, the biggest deductions. But others don't, particularly first-time home owners who must pay inflated prices and go deeply into debt. Since the private housing market in this country is overwhelmingly geared to single family suburban homes, apartment dwellers also suffer, while low-income renters wind up hurting the most." [36]

— *Daniel Lazare
"Economics for a Small Planet"*

ment of the rightful common destiny, according to a "master plan" based on careful and comprehensive surveys and studies of present conditions and the prospects of future growth of the municipality, and embodying scientific teaching and creative experience. [39]

Zoning, which has had little relationship to comprehensive planning, has generally reached a point of irrelevance in regard to the changing socioeconomic and environmental realities of today. Single-family residential zoning has been married to the single-occupancy vehicle, the car, and to the business of conventional single family house development. In addition, local jurisdictions allow zoning for industrial and corporate parks, regional shopping centers, "urban flight" rural subdivisions, and so-called "new towns" on farm and open space lands for tax base reasons and political favoritism. This practice continues without regard for the cumulative impact on the environment, infrastructure demands, and the need for a comprehensive planning process for the region.

We would be naive to think that zoning approval for a 25- unit Village Cluster community on 40 acres in a rural wooded and farmland area would not result in a rash of similar rezoning applications in the surrounding area. The potential environmental consequences are measurable, since most Village Cluster groups consist of middle income people with livelihoods and lifestyles that involve city type jobs, interests in cultural and education amenities, sophisticated shopping needs, and usually one car per employed person. There is then the inevitability that local county roads are widened, land costs, demand for services, and taxes go up, wildlife and plant ecosystems are interrupted, and

the amount of farmland for food growing is reduced. All of this occurs not on the basis of planning, but on the ability to obtain zoning from local officials.

Zoning with an ecological sustainability credo

Many urban planners and environmentalists support the opinion that old style zoning seriously impedes comprehensive land-use planning policies that recognize ecologically sustainable precepts. The direct access by car to individual lots or units has became the basis for zoning, thereby molding the urban sprawl form of our cities, and the alienated social ambiance we live with. There is no simple remedy. Even the electric car is not an adequate answer, but rather could encourage further car dependency and more sprawl.

Visions, policies, and regulatory tools are needed that allow people to create participative and ecologically sustainable communities as the underlying premise for a way of living. Today, faced with mounting socioeconomic inequities and the need for environmental protection, the Shared Living Community housing forms are appearing based on mutual responsibility — people working together.

The best urban model for sustainable development is the compact rail transit node or Eco Village. In this model, Shared Living Communities, such as the new extended family group house and Village Cluster, are clustered around the transit station to form an Eco Village. The most critical precept that we advance is that for these higher density transit-node neighborhoods to be socially stable and economically equitable, there must be a large supply of permanently affordable housing, with an emphasis upon social cooperation and participative man-

"Much if not most of the land use planning in the United States is not planning but zoning. The former implies comprehensive policies for the use, development, and conservation of land. Zoning — which can be one instrument of this — is the division of a local government area into districts which are subject to different regulations regarding the use of land and the height and bulk of buildings which are allowable." [40]
— *Fred Collingsworth*

"Zoning ordinances, deed restrictions, and other land-use mechanisms have been widely used as a 'NIMBY' (not in my backyard) tool, operating through exclusionary practices. Exclusionary zoning has been used to zone against something rather than for something. Exclusionary zoning, a form of government authority and power, has been used to foster and perpetuate discriminatory practices. With or without zoning, deed restrictions or other 'protectionist' devices, various racial and ethnic groups are unequally able to protect their environmental interests. More often than not, communities of color have a history of getting shortchanged in the urban neighborhood protection game." [41]
— Robert D. Bullard,
"Residential Apartheid in Urban America"

"Incentive zoning programs are more relevant now than ever before as Californians look at rebuilding urban areas and the economy. Incentive zoning programs are an attempt to provide affordable and senior housing and childcare facilities, and promote open space, environmental preservation, mixed use development, and efficient use of transportation." [42]
— Ellen Rambo & Joel B. Miller,
"California Incentive Zoning Practices"

agement. The healing of our cities and society will happen when people share responsibility in close proximity with each other on common land.

The "carrots on a stick" way to ecological sustainability

Recently a development guideline technique has emerged which offers incentives or bonuses such as an increase of housing density or commercial floor area, reduction or waiver of parking requirements, assessment and permit fee reductions, and other provisions, in exchange for a variety of social and environmental improvements. This incentive zoning technique has been used to encourage inclusion of low-income units in market rate housing, and the addition of pedestrian plazas, parks, walking and bike paths, and other public benefit amenities. Underlying the use of this municipal "police power" are court precedents allowing local discretion in zoning practices for the overall public benefit. This discretionary power is more legally supportable when there are approved comprehensive planning policies that justify special incentive zoning techniques. Properly sought after, these incentive techniques can be used equitably by all, and help to bring together the social, economic, and environmental elements for community.

One of the most successful and most copied examples is the City of New York's incentive zoning policy, which allows additional office floor area for provision of public plaza open space according to stipulated ratios and guidelines for types of pedestrian and urban design amenities. [43] The precedents set in New York and elsewhere have opened the door for other innovative uses of the incentive and bonus zoning practice throughout the planning

process in this country. Although mis-applications and excesses have been associated with this technique, there appears to be a growing precedent for some negotiation of incentives based on detailed guidelines. This is proving to be quite workable for applicants, planning agencies, and the general public. [44]

The objective of ecologically sustainable community living and urban development can be readily implemented through selective use of incentives and bonuses as a fundamental planning policy and zoning practice. We are returning to the use of land ethic quoted in the *Euclid* case. We expand upon that reference to mean that the use of a property must be judged on the degree to which that use positively influences and affects the health, safety, and general well being of the adjacent properties and people, all living beings, natural habitat, and wildlife, at the moment and into the future, and at any distance away. Given this level of responsibility as a basic guideline for the establishment of human behavior in the use of property, we propose the following zoning model as a basis for guiding ecologically sustainable community development in the future.

Ecological Incentive Planning Districts (EIPD)

In the real world, all things are interconnected and the law of cause and effect is immutable. If we agree that the governmental dictum "to protect the public health, safety, and welfare" applies to all people, we cannot go on using land and building housing without attention to social and environmental responsibility. The objective is to identify the techniques to serve all people with the full range of affordability and livability opportunities.

The "Ecological Incentive Planning District" (EIPD) represents an integrated planning and zoning process. Its purpose is to give preferential treatment to housing and land use that fulfill the criteria for ecologically sustainable development, especially when located near a transit station. The EIPD planning and zoning process would in effect create a disincentive for land use, social, and economic practices that generate wasted energy and resources, excess car trips, social instability, alienation, and discrimination. This is not an environmental pricing scheme, but a way of offering direct rewards for creating ecologically responsible developments in a rail transit node.

The following incentive implementation criteria and processes to be included in an EIPD apply equally to revitalization of older cities, suburban areas, smaller cities, and to new developments:

• **The EIPD** must be part of a comprehensive regional jobs, housing, and transit planning program that provides for an ecologically designed, moderate and mixed density, mixed-use pedestrian neighborhood within a transportation corridor or node as part of a comprehensive rail-linked system.

• **The transit node area** is overlaid by the EIPD designation, which provides incentives for increased density according to a point system or a plan review process with specific performance criteria described.

• **A base density** is established for conventional car-dependent, single-family owner/renter housing neighborhoods, with restrictions and limits imposed for unecological features. Higher densities are based on points earned by ecologically and socially reponsible features.

The Widespread Use of Incentive and Bonus Zoning
There is hope for implementation of sustainable communities through the precedents being set by planners using the zoning incentive and bonus requirements as conditions for approval. The applicant obtains final approval and may gain special exceptions by responding to special needs of the neighborhood, and specific socioeconomic and environmental considerations that serve the "public health, safety, and general welfare." Some of the amenities and improvements that have been used in incentive and bonus ordinances are well described by T.J. Lassar quoted in *"The Political Culture of Planning:"*

a) building amenities: urban spaces, ground-floor retail, retail arcades, artwork, sculptured rooftops, atriums, and day care;

b) pedestrian amenities: sidewalk canopies and other overhead weather protection devices, landscaping, multiple building entrances;

c) pedestrian movement: sidewalk widening and through-block connections;

d) housing and human services: employment and job training;

low-income health clinics; low-income, affordable, and market-rate housing;

e) transportation improvements: transient parking, below-grade parking, and transportation access and upgrading;

f) cultural amenities: cinemas, performing arts centers, art galleries, and live theaters; and

g) preservation: historic structures, theaters, and low-rent housing stock. [45]

Another precedent is the inclusionary and density bonus laws in California and some other states which provide for increased density, height, floor area, and ground coverage when various percentages of the units (a range of 15% to 40%) are made permanently available for moderate, low, and very low-income people. Several CoHousing developments have gained approval and favorable financing because they complied with the local inclusionary requirement for affordable housing.

• **Density increases and other bonuses** are allowed as incentives according to a sliding scale point system for providing all or some of the following social-environmental amenities (point values need to be determined). The larger the site area of a Shared Living Community and/or the transit node Eco Village project, the greater the number of incentive points that could be included, and therefore the higher the density and other special considerations. The possibilities include:

— Innovative community housing such as Village Clusters, Urban Cooperative Blocks, new or redesigned group houses, and cooperatives.

— At least 20% of all units assured for mixed-income affordable financing or rents, from very low to moderate income people. Density bonus varies relative to percentages of population included in each income category within the region.

— Co-ownership/resident control opportunities for all housing types.

— Permanent affordability through equity caps and resale limits, whether for nonprofit sponsors, or public-assisted or for-profit housing.

— Mixed-use residential units over commercial developments, including live-work units.

— Open space preservation, public plazas, play lots, athletic courts, street furniture, walking and bicycling paths, and conversion of streets to such uses.

— Opening up of backyards for cooperative use by neighborhood residents.

— Intergenerational composition of residents, with an additional bonus for elder care units and services, and childcare services.

— On-site social services such as health clinics, job training, adult education, family counseling, drug counseling, and other programs.

— Group homes for special-need population groups distributed in the area.

— Indoor and outdoor common recreation facilities for people of all ages.

— Handicapped access for ground floors, and an additional bonus for upper floor ramps or a wheelchair lift or elevator.

— Central solar collectors, passive solar design, and other natural energy and resource-conserving building design methods.

— Self-help construction, a phased completion schedule, and use of job training apprentices.

— Common kitchen and dining room with shared meals on a regular schedule, with additional bonus for bulk food buying and food processing facilities.

• **Additional incentive points** could be earned for various elements of a Transportation Management Program (TMP) in which voluntary and enforceable agreements are made to reduce car trip generation and the numbers of cars needing to be parked, such as:

— Restricted use of on-street parking with permits required for extra cars.

— Reduction of parking standards based on the ratio of permanent residents who are non-drivers, handicapped, or elderly.

— Leased and co-owned vehicle agreements within community clusters, cooperative buildings, or group living households in lieu of ownership of individual cars.

— Cooperative building or household-owned bicycles and mopeds with ample enclosed and secure parking.

— Transit pass books discounted to building residents and workplace employees.
— Streets closed to traffic and redesigned into green strips for plazas, gardens, play areas, landscaping, local resident parking, and to enhance walking and biking to shops and transit.
— Car and van pooling agreements for both residential communities and places of employment.
— Time share use of parking facilities among residents, employees, and patrons in mixed-use buildings.
— Installation of bus stop shelters, bus loading turnout lanes, and pedestrian pass-throughs.
— Mini-bus shuttles and subsidies provided for local bus service to adequately serve all users.

• **There are many bonuses** that could be granted besides density increases. Various of the above incentive possibilities may be put together to provide an ecologically sustainable package that results in extra bonuses, such as:
— Reduce, postpone, pro-rate, or waive fees for property transfer, development, planning and zoning, building permit, and special districts.
— Give tax credits to investors and also to community core groups, building residents, local businesses, and other user groups.
— Pay for passive or active solar systems at the project start, to be charged against future lower utility bills.
— Provide low interest loans, grants, and deferred payment loans.
— Modify maximum density, building height, and floor area limits.
— Provide fast tracking of permits, and administrative approval in lieu of public hearings when ecologically sustainable criteria are met.

• **Allow community based cluster housing** as a permitted use in multi-family zoning (apartments), and rural residential zones. Allow group houses and group homes as a permitted use in single-family zoning. Allow all types of Shared Living Community housing in an EIPD around transit nodes.
• **Allow cottage industry and home businesses** and live-work spaces within a cluster development by administrative permit using criteria such as the Ecological Sustainability Scorecard and the Energy Efficiency Ratio processes.
• **Reduce building permit fees** for low to moderate income self-help housing by the proportion of value accredited to self-help labor, or defer the fees until the final loan is issued.
• **Make a phased-completion agreement** with a local building department, owner-builders, and cooperatively owned self-help housing groups that would stipulate items to be completed by agreed-upon dates. Permit living in the common house while individual units are still being completed.

Getting Communities Developed Within the System

To accomplish the rebuilding of community in America as proposed in this book will require visionary leadership from the White House on down and from our own backyards on up. It will require participation and support from the very people who are hurting the most at the local levels. We as a society have the know-how to create social, economic, and environmental change that could alleviate wasteful and exploitative development and production methods. Dependence upon continual

"… it is also true that others will struggle to deny the coming of the new age, preferring decaying familiarity to uncharted opportunities. Trapped within the framework of a philosophy they barely comprehend, these people will turn their attention to finding some mechanism that will provide them an out. We have been trained to think that there is always an out, that no force is beyond the human's ability to manipulate. We have been taught that there are no limits, that only narrow minds that have lost their nerve will give in to limits. But twist and turn as we might, there is no out."[48]
—*Jeremy Rifkin*

Older cultures have from ancient times correctly understood that the relationship between humankind and nature must be one of harmony, in which humanity is at one with the natural order. The rest of us are only now, and only partially, coming to appreciate the wisdom of that point of view as science leads us, step by step, and often unwillingly, to conclusions that have been waiting for us since antiquity.[47]
— Al Gore,
"Politics of Environment"

economic growth, immigration, and military spending, and other practices contributing to the national and global dilemma will also be reduced. We will need to face the reality that to rebuild community in America, we cannot continue the blatantly unecological and unsustainable practices of the old economic paradigm. Deriving centralized capital profits from costly labor sources, and marketing to a mass of uninvolved people, is not a sustainable system. These practices have moved the profits from the local area to centralized coffers, thus destabilizing and disinvesting the local population and contributing to the breakdown of communities. We see the creation of Shared Living Communities within an Eco Village composition as the new paradigm.

The environmental and community movement is often criticized for being reactionary, a regression from modern times into economically less productive and therefore undesirable ways of living. We are not proposing to go back to the stone ages or any other time in the past, but we recognize that tribal and village societies of the ancient times, in the recent past, and even in today's world, have been, and are, sustainable to a remarkable degree. They did not deplete resources faster than they could be renewed, and everyone had food, a place to live, a role, and a responsibility in the group. They had ecologically sustainable social, economic, and political systems that worked and evolved with them, unlike our society where we must adapt to a relatively fixed system. Their needs were met and rituals performed as social creatures that sustained themselves by working together.

We cannot deny or ignore that we have built unsustainable cities, inefficient transportation

systems, and urban sprawl — these are our legacies. Not everything in urban society is evil and not everything in rural farm or village life is desirable. By combining high technology with hand craftsmanship and simple living, we can make a truly sustainable society. The new view of sustainability is that it pertains to our ability to progress within the availability and continuity of replenishable energy. That cannot be done just with technology and market economics, but it can be done by people cooperating together in their own behalf — this is the enlightened American Dream.

Notes
Books listed only by name in the endnotes are highlighted in the resource guide at the end of the book, complete with author/publisher information and description.

1 Robert N. Bellah, et. al., <u>The Good Society</u>, Vintage Books, a Division of Random House Inc., New York, 1991, p. 271.
2 J.W. Smith, <u>World's Wasted Wealth II</u>, book manuscript, June 1993, p. 106.
3 The Report of the Task Force on Teaching as a Profession, "A Nation Prepared: Teachers for the 21st Century," The Carnegie Forum on Education and the Economy, May, 1986, p. 13.
6 Robert Gilman, "The Eco Village Challenge," *In Context: A Quarterly of Humane Sustainable Culture,* No. 29, p.14. (In Context Subscriptions $24/yr; Single Issues $6; PO Box 11470, Bainbridge Island, WA 98110)
7 <u>World's Wasted Wealth 2,</u> p. 111.
8 <u>Entropy,</u> p. 255.
9 Ibid, pp. 33-59.
10 <u>Entropy,</u>.pg. 6.
11 <u>World's Wasted Wealth 2,</u>, p. 2.

12 Entropy,.p. 250.
13 "Comment," The Progressive, July 1993, vol. 57, no. 7, p. 10
14 World's Wasted Wealth 2, p. 107.
15 The Natural House Book, p. 97.
16 "Architecture for Community: Natural Home Building, Part 1," *Growing Community,* No. 4, October 1993, pp. 6-7.
17 "Building with Earth," Brochure by The Cob Cottage Company, April 30, 1994.
18 Letter, Union of Concerned Scientists, June 1992, p. 2.
19 John E. Young, World Watch.
20 "Winslow Community Well Underway," CoHousing, Fall, 1991, p. 6.
21 John E. Young, World Watch.
22 "The New Alchemy Institute Starts its Second Decade," *The Mother Earth News,* January/February 1980, p. 118.
23 Tom Bender, Environmental Design Primer, Schoken Books, New York, 1973, p.140.
24 Joel David Welty, "The Rochdale Principles of 1844 in Today's Cooperatives," Directory of Intentional Communities, p. 97.
25 "Community Land Trusts Model Recognized by Federal Government," *Resources,* National Congress for Community Economic Development, Washington, D.C., Summer 1993, p. 5.
26 Catherine Lerza,"Race, Poverty and Sustainable Communities," *Poverty and Race,* March/April 1994, Vol. 3: No. 2, pp. 1-2.
27 "Oregon CDC Program Leads to Dramatic Increase in CDCs," *Resources,* National Congress for Community Economic Development, Washington, D.C., Summer 1993, p. 5.
28 Cooperative Housing Compendium, p. 106.
29 "President Clinton Announces Enhancement Zone Proposal," *Resources,* National Congress for Community Economic Development, Washington, D.C., Summer 1993, p. 6.
30 Richard Cowden, "Low-Income Communities and Enterprise Zones," *Targeting Times,* Fall 1993, Vol. 4, No. 4, p. 4.
31 Albert Gore, *Building Communities: Together, The President's Community Enterprise Board, Empowerment Zones & Enterprise Communities Application Guide,* U.S. Department of Housing and Uban Development and U.S. Department of Agriculture, January 1994, HUD-1445-CPD, p. 2.
32 Henry Cisneros,Ibid., p.3.
33 "President Clinton Announces Enhancement Zone Proposal," *Resources,* National Congress for Community Economic Development, Washington, D.C., Summer 1993, p. 6.
34 Catherine Lerza,"Race, Poverty and Sustainable Communities," *Poverty and Race,* p. 4.
35 Chester Hartman, "Feeding the Sparrows by Feeding the Horses," *SHELTORFORCE,* Jan./Feb. 1992, p. 12.
36 Daniel Lazare, "Economics for a Small Planet," *E Magazine,* Sept/Oct 1991, pp. 52-53.
37 The Political Culture of Planning, p. 29.
38 Ibid., p. 29.
39 Ibid., p. 11.
40 Ibid., p. 11.
41 Robert D. Bullard, "Residential Apartheid in Urban America," *Earth Island Journal,* Fall 1993, p. 36.
42 Ellen Rambo & Joel B. Miller, "California Incentive Zoning Practices," *California Planner,* California Chapter of the American Planning Association, September 1992, Vol. IV, Issue 8, p. 1.
43 The Political Culture of Planning, p. 87.
44 Ibid., pp. 88-89.
45 Ibid., p. 92.
46 Matt Fisher, "Community Controlled Development, what does it mean?," The Catalyst — Newsletter of The Halifax Project, April 1993, Issue no.1, p. 3.
47 Albert Gore, "Politics of Environment," *Resurgence,* May/June 1993, p. 25.
48 Entropy, p. 239.
49 Carl Andrews, "Energy Independence is Feasible." Newsletter of the Appropriate Technology Institute.

Rebuilding Community in America
— from extended families to Eco Villages and Eco Cities

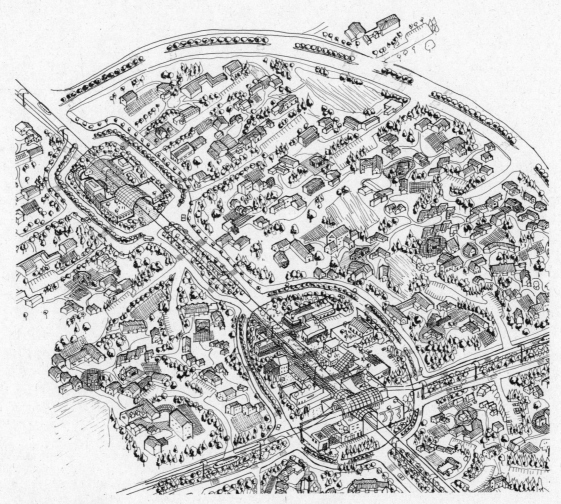

Eco Village

CHAPTER TEN

We Present a Condensation of the Story
"The Man Who Planted Trees"
by Jean Giono
Recited at Kathleen and Chris' wedding, September 18,1993

In the year of 1910 I was taking a long trip on foot over mountain heights quite unknown to tourists. After three days walking I found myself in the midst of unparalleled desolation, a barren and colorless land where nothing grew there but wild lavender.

I thought I glimpsed in the distance a small black silhouette and took it for the trunk of a solitary tree. It was a shepherd, and I went to him.

He was thrusting his iron rod into the earth, making a hole in which he planted an acorn; then he refilled the hole. He was planting oak trees. I asked him if the land belonged to him. He answered no. Did he know whose it was? He did not, and he was not interested in finding out whose it was.

For three years he had been planting trees in this desolate wilderness. He had planted one hundred thousand. Of the hundred thousand, twenty thousand had sprouted. Of the twenty thousand, he still expected to lose half, to rodents or the unpredictable designs of Providence. There remained ten thousand oak trees to grow where nothing had grown before.

Several years later I again took the road to the barren lands. The oaks of 1910 were then ten years old and taller than either of us. It was an impressive spectacle. I was literally speechless. We spent the whole day walking in silence through his forest. He had pursued his plan to plant beech and birch trees, and both were now as high as my shoulder, spread out as far as the eye could reach.

Creation seemed to come about in a sort of chain reaction. He did not worry about it; he was determinedly pursuing his task in all its simplicity. But as we went back, I saw water flowing in brooks that had been dry since the memory of man. As the water reappeared, so there reappeared willows, rushes, meadows, gardens, flowers, and a certain purpose in being alive. The transformation took place so gradually that it became part of the pattern without causing any astonishment.

I saw Elzéard Bouffier [the shepherd] for the last time in June of 1945. He was then eighty-seven. [As we walked together], I no longer recognized the scenes of my earlier journeys. Everything was changed. Even the air. Instead of harsh dry winds that used to attack me, a gentle breeze was blowing, laden with scents. A sound like water came from the mountains: it was the wind in the forest. Most amazing of all, I heard the actual sound of water falling into a pool. I saw that a fountain had been built, that it flowed freely and — what touched me most — that someone had planted a linden tree beside it. A linden that must have been four years old, already in full leaf — the incontestable symbol of resurrection.

Hope, then, had returned. Ruins had been cleared away, and houses restored. Old streams, fed by the rains and snows that the forest conserves, are flowing again. The villages abandoned since ancient times have been rebuilt.

When I reflect that all this had sprung from the hands and the soul of this one man, without technical resources, I am convinced that in spite of everything, humanity is admirable. [1]

Community in America
— growing and spreading

Starting new communities is like the growing of trees in a desolate land. The more seeds that are planted, the more saplings will survive to grow into maturity. In the beginning the work may seem inconsequential, even futile, but as one tree and community grows, so will others. They will give nurturing support to each other, creating more trees and communities. But today, the time is too short for one lone shepherd to rebuild community in America. We must become many Elzéard Bouffiers, planting many seeds of change — a multiplying effect in which a new spirit of community in America spreads and grows — a ground swell of planting for a sustainable future.

The rising numbers of CoHousing communities, Intentional Communities, group living houses, and cooperatives are powerful evidence that this process has already begun. Throughout this book we have examined how the community movement is challenging the old paradigms. In this chapter we look more closely at the transformational processes by which more people will form new extended families and a sustainable community way of living, and how this can be instrumental in the creation of Eco Villages, Eco Cities, and rural Green Belts.

Rebuilding community in America can and must include people of all income levels, ethnicities, ages, and family sizes, living in a variety of housing types, densities, and sizes. These need to be closely integrated with a mix of services, and planned for low car dependency and high pedestrian movement. The fundamental criteria for forming Eco Villages and Eco Cities is compact, ecologically designed development located around transit stations (transit nodes) served by high speed trains, local light rail, feeder bus lines, and walking and bicycling paths.

This transformation could come about by the realization that there are undeniable truths and responsibilities about living sanely on this planet, as aptly expressed in Ernest Callenbach's poem "The Earth's Ten Commandments." From such inspiration, more of us will be able to agree: Yes, the ecosystem is being ruined by uncontrolled pollutants and the negative impact of the car; Yes, Eco Villages connected by rail lines to each other and to the Eco City are critically needed to revitalize our cities; Yes, we all need supportive social, family, and community oriented housing; and Yes, we can make these social, economic, and environmental transformations without loss of livelihood and income by the simple admission that we will work together to establish an ecologically sustainable society.

"We the people" must take personal responsibility to democratically initiate the process of working together, face to face, on a daily basis, in an environment created for sharing. We can then forget labels and divisions and see government and community as one and the same. Government can become, as it should be, an extension of the community at large, delegating responsibility for the management and coordination of local and broader affairs to members of the community. When community breaks down, government becomes a self-serving, indifferent, and heavy-handed power, alienated from the people and accountable to the ruling elite. It is our responsibility as advocates of

"My hunch is that we will not achieve sustainability or even decent habitability unless we accomplish a couple of very difficult things. One is to displace the car which is our 19th. century technology for getting around — a kind of ersatz horse. This has to be displaced for it's central position so that we can turn our land use patterns to traditional city mixed use form. We have to reduce both consumption and population in the rich north. We are the population problem in the world, not the poor but numerous south."[2]

— Ernest Callenbach
"Our Sustainable Future,"

The Equation: Government = Community

To govern = to democratically self-govern with participative management, open communication, cooperative enterprise, and service to all = to participate, communicate, cooperate, serve, and take responsibility = to be in community.

"When a public government becomes identified with a public economy, a public culture, and public fashions of thought, it can become the tool of a public process of nationalism or 'globalization' that is oblivious of local differences and therefore destructive of communities.

'Public' and 'community,' then, are different — perhaps radically different — concepts that under certain circumstances are compatible but that, in the present economic and technological monoculture, tend to be at odds. A community, when it is alive and well, is centered on the household — the family place and economy — and the household is centered on marriage." [3]

— *Wendell Berry*

ecologically sustainable communities to secure representation in the governing framework on all levels. To do so, we must act in concert as members of cohesive social structures, such as an extended family, a neighborhood, a community group, business, or governmental body. When groups of people are acting with a unanimity of spirit and purpose, it becomes obvious when someone shrugs off group responsibility for selfish reasons; their actions are quickly noticed or learned of by other community members. Therefore, in a close interactive community, stringent laws and bureaucratic regulations are replaced by mutual agreements, clear communication, and consensus.

In a local community, created and operated by the people themselves, we have the best opportunity for a sustainable system of democratic governance. The people themselves are responsible for the use of their own resources and therefore less dependent on centralized economic power and "government" as conventionally defined. Tom Atlee, writing in <u>Think Peace</u>, addresses this prospect:

> The best government is that government which enables communities ... to nurture and utilize their wisdom and resources ... especially their diversity — in such a way that they require less and less government. ... As individuals, we are inherently more limited than a community.

Although we can consult books and friends and critics, in the end we are limited to our own single perspective. We are, alas, only one person, looking at the world from one place, one history, one pattern of knowing. A community, on the other hand, can see things through many eyes, many histories, many ways of knowing. The question is whether it dismisses or creatively utilizes and integrates that diversity. [4]

In a community, people "govern" by being responsible for each other and the community as a whole. Here is a small scale example of how community and government can be one process. Imagine eighty people who are preparing land for a community farming enterprise. A number of steps are required: financing, scheduling, gathering material resources, assigning tasks, etc. It would not work for compost materials to be mulched in before the planting beds were laid out or after the starter plants were set out, or for some members to buy chemical fertilizer while others were applying for organic farming certification, or for some to plow the ground for one specific crop while others were buying seeds and setting up marketing agreements for diversified crops. This community project will likely require internal coordination through a manager or group council, and possibly outside expertise, to achieve efficiency in use of labor, materials, and energy, and for cost savings, and a more successful and harmonious enterprise.

This whole process works more naturally within extended family living groups and Shared Living Communities because frequent interaction and established channels of communication already exist in a commonly owned physical place. They may need fewer outside resources or not need to hire an executive manager because they have learned to use and trust the resources, skills, and experience found within their own diversity. When this "community" scale of governing is well practiced by many people and integrated with other local communities, it becomes feasible to extend democratic community governance to the Eco Village and Eco City, and ultimately to the national scale.

The ecological sustainability of the whole body can work when its institutions, at all levels of governing, are accountable for and contributing to the *social, economic,* and *environmental* health of the system. When these three elements are integrated into the daily lives of people in many communities their combined actions will profoundly influence the larger society. But, again, the same social structure and environmental design precepts that work at the scale of Shared Living Community must be consistently carried out at the Eco Village and Eco City levels.

Human gregariousness bonds together the essential elements for community

Transformational new directions involving ecological community lifestyles are an expression of the gregarious instinct of humans to coalesce around three fundamental interconnected elements that underlie our lives: Social, Economic, and Environmental (SEE). This triad represents the essential foundation for reshaping the governing forces of our time to create an ecologically sustainable society. When these elements are functioning together in an ecologically balanced way, the whole community can be sustained.

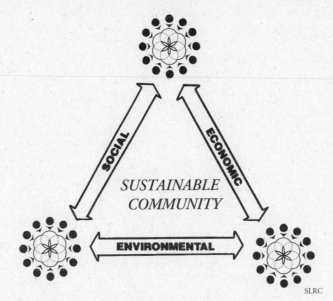

SLRC

Social, Economic, & Environmental (SEE)
These three elements touch every aspect of our lives and represent what is needed for ecologically sustainable community. The sub-parts that make up each side of the SEE triangle are well represented in the Objectives and Benefits diagram presented in Chapter Three.

"For us, hope lies in the possibility of moving beyond our authoritarian past in order to build together a future that values keeping this planet habitable for its interwoven and interdependent forms of life. If the challenge is met, the world will have to be a better place for those living in it, because for the first time since the early small bands of humanity's infancy, everyone's well-being is once again linked with survival."[5]
— *Diana Alstad & Joel Kramer,*
The Guru Papers

Photo by William A. Porter

But when any side is not fully integrated with the other two, the system or community will suffer from social and economic injustice, friction, discord, and alienation, never reaching its highest potential, as is the case with society today.

The gregariousness of humankind, as a manifestation of the instinct for perpetuation of the species, can be a powerful influence for uniting the SEE elements inherent within us. The new extended family in a community setting is the fundamental socioeconomic unit within which these elements can positively interact to strengthen community and thereby the larger community. In order to more

Suburban Sprawl, Anywhere USA
Here lies the potential social, economic, and environmental resources for creating many hundreds of eco-village neighborhoods. As it is, urban sprawl is a nameless accumulation of streets and parking lots (30-40%) and repetitive patterns of small lots and scattered services. By adding a network of transit lines, people will again be able to focus their energies and rebuild neighborhoods. The above desolation will blossom with identifiable small and larger centers, defined by open spaces, transit lines, and residential clusters.

Photo by Greenbelt Alliance

clearly show how to transform the social, economic, and environmental disorder within this society, we will examine more closely the uneco-logical growth of American cities, the challenges they pose, and the solutions rising from them.

Understanding Unecological and Non-sustainable City Growth

Cities of the past grew in a more organic and socially and economically integrated way than they do today. This occurred because of the high degree of human interaction and participation, the short travel distances and pedestrian scale, the accessibility of local resources, and the sustainability of the extended family and village socioeconomic system. Today's urban patterns work against human interaction, tending to become simplistic economic mechanisms whose form is dictated by the business of selling cars and land, not for building sustainable communities. But as we presented in Chapter Six, our cities can be the strength of a stable society and potentially the most ecologically sustainable system for human habitat. We cannot let this valuable resource wither further by condoning urban flight.

The adjacent drawing portrays how the pre-car original core of American cities of the 1800's was destroyed. Then, cities were centered on a compact mixed-use downtown business district surrounded by moderate to higher density housing areas. The proliferation of rail transit lines induced some spreading out of growth, but housing remained clustered in relatively compact "transit neighborhoods."[6] After WW II, the wanton removal of transit lines and increased dependence on the car drastically altered the city form. Urban sprawl

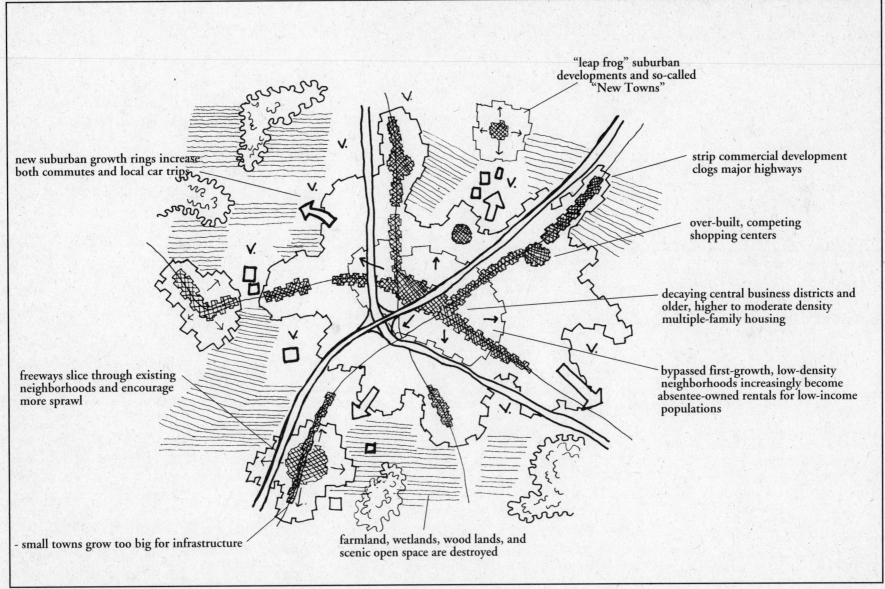

"leap frog" suburban developments and so-called "New Towns"

new suburban growth rings increase both commutes and local car trips

strip commercial development clogs major highways

over-built, competing shopping centers

decaying central business districts and older, higher to moderate density multiple-family housing

freeways slice through existing neighborhoods and encourage more sprawl

bypassed first-growth, low-density neighborhoods increasingly become absentee-owned rentals for low-income populations

- small towns grow too big for infrastructure

farmland, wetlands, wood lands, and scenic open space are destroyed

SLRC

America's Greatest Social and Environmental Disaster

Post-WW II urban growth sprawls into open space and farmlands. The central city and first-growth low-density neighborhoods wither due to red-lining, poorly maintained absentee-owned rentals, and abandonment of buildings n o longer deemed profitable. Suburban development, glittery malls, and corporate office parks sponge the economic vitality away from established businesses in the city. As the outer perimeter becomes increasingly wider the scattered access to services and jobs adds greatly to the number of daily car trips.

Photo by Greenbelt Alliance

The Roots of Inner-city Injustices and Community Breakdown

The breakdown of community and family structure discussed in other chapters has occurred in direct correlation with the breakdown of the physical structure of our cities. Simultaneous with a lack of comprehensive planning and coordination regarding economic development, land use, housing, transportation systems, and the environment, we have an increase of negative images of urban living and a growing mistrust of people. It is axiomatic that as our live and work places become scattered, connections between family, friends, and neighbors become strained and difficult to maintain, and fear and prejudice increase. The media feeds into this process of separation by reinforcing cultural and racial stereotypes, deadening people's sensitivity to violence, glamorizing brutality, and emphasizing the values of appearance and instant gratification. This in turn increases the urban flight reaction, which is then exploited by urban fringe land speculators and "new town" advocates. In such an atmosphere, the prospect of ecological living in the city is not an objective with which many people can identify with. But, it is within this present reality that we must gather support for the rebuilding of community in America.

We must look beyond the labels and stereotypes parroted in the media as we seek workable solutions; We must look to see the person who is there. Homelessness, poverty, gangs, poor education, crime, and using prisons as a solution are symptoms of huge structural flaws in this society, signs of greater social breakdown and cultural conflicts to come, and a warning that democracy and freedom

"But it can be argued that community disintegration typically is begun by an aggression of some sort from the outside and that in modern times the typical aggression has been economic. The destruction of the community begins when its economy is made — not dependent (for no community has ever been entirely independent) — but subject to a larger external economy." [7]

— Wendell Berry

moved outward from the core city, abetted by highway widening, freeway construction, the relative availability of low-cost farmland, and the eagerness of city officials to annex raw land for the mythical tax base. Today, farmers are still persuaded to sell to investors who, in turn, obtain zoning approval for low-density "rural-estate" acreage lots, housing tracts, shopping centers, and office parks. There is a critical need to cease the real estate boom cycles that induce low-density growth on the periphery, resulting in economic abandonment and decay of the central city, a pattern which continues in many American cities. To add to the grievous harm caused to open space and farmlands by previous generations of "planned subdivisions," there is now the attempt to capitalize on urban flight by a new breed of suburban development.

could easily be lost. Band-aid solutions like housing the homeless in small hotel rooms or plywood huts so they can experience "independent living" is telling people who have lost touch with or never had a sharing family that now you can permanently live in places that are not designed to support family. Whether without a home or housed in prisons, these people are already isolated and forgotten, lonely and in immense emotional pain. Building more prisons in response to joblessness, poverty, gangs, drugs, and crime and the "throw the key away" mentality is creating a medieval-like "fortress America" syndrome.

The need for intimate community is being cried out for in a very fundamental ways at all levels. Gangs, for example, are an attempt to create community in racial minority and low-income neighborhoods, just as country clubs do in upscale developments. Members of both seek self-esteem and personal empowerment through group involvement, interaction, and empowerment. They have surrendered themselves to the gang mentality with its loyalty to those who are "in" and disregard for those who are "out." The country club gang wields its power through surrogates — the police, the politicians, and business interests. They fare much better because of their income and social status, and for this they are respected, envied, and copied. Youth are taught about power and violence by the dominant system through the "power" role models they see in the entertainment and news media, and through their bitter experiences with exploitative employers, racism, law enforcement, and the criminal justice and prison systems. Today's street gang bonds together through desperation, machismo, guns, "turf" control, and drugs. Defiant of the broader society and alienated from other generations and groups within their own people, gang members become isolated and have few alternative role models, surrounded instead by hopelessness, personal powerlessness, and a perceived lack of opportunity among their parents, other adults, and their own peer group. The above examples represent aspects of the socioeconomic breakdown of the larger urban society that directly mirrors the scattering of the urban physical structure.

How this breakdown is manifested in social costs is expressed by Walter Dickey, Professor of Law at the University of Wisconsin, and a former director of the Wisconsin Department of Corrections, writes about his observations of offenders in *In Context*:

> ... they characterize 75 percent of the offender population. They live isolated and lonely lives with few, if any, dependable friends or family. They believe they have few choices of opportunities they tend to have little education. Some have mental or learning deficiencies. Many of the offenders are in poor health with no access to health care. Drug and alcohol abuse are a problem for virtually all of these offenders. Many offenders have repeatedly been the victims of crime. Their own crimes were usually unsophisticated and impulsive and brought small monetary reward. [8]

If we can instead learn to share with the less advantaged, a well-being and real solutions can be cultivated from the experience of belonging and from mutual responsibilities and support in common physical places. It is within the intentionally created community environment in which all are

"The violence in movies is powerful and terrifying; we've become addicted to it.... Violence sells. And the movie industry is, to my mind, taking it far less seriously than television.... All there is is lip service in the movie business on this issue. Are they taking this issue seriously? Of course not."[9]
— Dr. Carole Lieberman, psychiatrist
"Hollywood Drags Its Feet on Film and TV Violence,"

"Nor is community interest or community need going to receive much help from television and the other public media."[10]
—Wendell Barry

"Slavery, circa 1980. Crack— ol'massas' whip still sounds the same."
— Author Unknown

"For people of color, crack addiction has become part of the new urban slavery, a method of disrupting lives and regulating masses of young people who would otherwise be demanding jobs, adequate health care, better schools and control of their own communities.... This is the new manifestation of racism in which we see a form of social control existing in our communities, the destruction of social institutions, and the erosion of people's ability to fight against the forms of domination that continuously try to oppress them." [11]
— *Manning Marable,*
"Racism and Multi-Cultural Democracy"

"In modern America, the village, the neighborhood, the hamlet, or the city, often has become but an economic aggregation or only an incidental grouping, without the acquaintance, the personal relationships, and the common interests and activities, which are the essential characteristics of a community. Such aggregations do not fully satisfy the emotional cravings for fellowship, common interests, and unified planning and action." [12]
— *Arthur E. Morgan*
"Homo Sapiens:
The Community Animal"

co-owners that the healing of our sick society will occur. In Chapter Seven we presented examples of the growing trend to move away from institutional-like shelters to "extended-family" shared living transition houses and Group Homes. Simultaneously, we are seeing increasing numbers of moderate, middle, and upper income people voluntarily adopting group living and community lifestyles as a permanent housing solution. Shared Living Communities hold the promise of improving the quality of living for the low income people and providing less consumptive lifestyles for the middle and upper income people as everyone tries to adjust to the declining economy. True equity can be found in community.

We see the possibility that through Eco Village community building we will avoid creating future offenses and violence by providing the physical and social atmosphere for children to grow up in stable families and for people harmed by dysfunctional backgrounds to have a supportive place for recovery. This is possible by consciously integrating the social, economic, and environmental elements into all aspects of our lives and in the process of building sustainable communities. However, this will mean major changes and adaptations within the existing socioeconomic structure and in our attitudes about the root causes of poverty and crime and the idea that prison detention is a crime deterrent.

In rebuilding community in America, we envision transforming prisons into community rebuilding centers where new life directions are inspired through finding self-esteem, livelihood, and fulfillment in community enterprises, as an alternative to dependency on vanishing corporate and industrial jobs. By shifting resources from prison

building to community rebuilding, we can reclaim wasted lives and be a vital component in creating social and economic equity for all people. Such a program would begin with non-violent inmates. Some offenders of course are determined to be beyond rehabilitation, yet even for them community assistance projects can be introduced within the remaining prisons. We have precedents in the earlier Civilian Conservation Corps (CCC) and the Works Progress Administration (WPA) that were created to put the large numbers of unemployed to purposeful work while also providing education and job training. More recently, youth rehabilitation camps and community service as alternatives to sentencing have been actively used in place of detention. The specific objective of the community retraining centers is to bring back people who were once unable to contribute to the community well being, as active participates in the rebuilding of both urban and rural communities. The overall goal is to solve social and economic injustices by revitalization of urban areas through stimulation of local community enterprises, abundant local livelihood, the inclusion of rail networks, and the creation of economically viable, agriculture–based Green Belts around our cities.

It does not take much savvy in economics to also see how the corporations and the global economic system have turned their backs on the American people by creating circumstances where there are no longer enough jobs for "full employment," in the old industrial-America definition. Why continue to offer job training to welfare recipients and the unemployed? Where do the urban gang members, addicts, or ex-prison inmates go for a job when the jobless working and middle class are taking lower-paid jobs in order to survive?. These exploitative economic practices are contributing to the breakdown of social order in America and fueling reactionary and punitive "anti-crime bills" and policies that cause the prison population to grow as fast as unemployment— a huge waste of lives and public funds. We must address these serious structural flaws in the entire American political-economic system with bold, courageous, and enlightened leadership that recognizes the importance of rebuilding community and the culture of cities for all of society, from the most disadvantaged to the most privileged. We cannot allow our higher aspirations to dissolve in an avalanche of fear, social discord, economic decline, and continued environmental spoliation. Otherwise we shall never see safety on our streets.

Who Becomes Eligible and Responsible for Ecological Community ?

The underlying message of the "Earth's Ten Commandments," is that ecological community living is everyone's responsibility, implying as well that everyone benefits. In this book we emphasize that the opportunities, benefits, and responsibilities of Shared Living Community are meant to apply equally to people of all ethnicities, incomes, and ages, in all locations, rural, suburban, and urban locations. People everywhere have the same human instincts and similar wants and needs. Therefore, everyone should have an opportunity for co-ownership and self-management of land and housing, personal and community empowerment, environmental protection, economic security, secure neighborhoods, and adequate and safe food sources.

We all must let go of our double standards concerning ecologically sustainable living. All people, regardless of background and characteristics, must have the opportunity and responsibility to live a more self–reliant, energy–efficient, and resource conserving lifestyle. No group can be excused for living in ways that contribute to waste, environmental degradation, human exploitation, racism, or any other form of violence. A higher income and quality of living must not be seen as justification for generating more car-trips, using more energy, destroying open space and agricultural lands for country living, or depriving anyone else of the enjoyment of an improved quality of living.

Paradoxically, there are many minorities, low–income people, and others as well, who do not see themselves as being environmentalists. However, they are the ones who often live near environmentally hazardous and unhealthy areas, toxic dumps, waste fills, industrial pollution, and heavy traffic, freeways, and railroads, and in older housing with lead, asbestos, and other contaminants. These are among the many good reasons why all people should be sustainable community advocates and not yield to the urban flight temptation. Low-income and minorities in particular are increasingly making long commutes to work from housing in the suburbs, contributing further to the breakdown of community in the city. If city residents co-own land in Shared Living Communities, whole Eco Villages can be created and a new breed of environmentalists empowered. It is also true that people of moderate and middle income and the wealthy breathe the same polluted air as everyone, and are also subject to long commutes, chemically tainted food, and toxic waste. All people have a major

"With the exception of limited collaboration between environmentalists and Native American groups, and anti-toxic campaigns, there has been little communication between environmentalists and non-European minority groups within the US. Critical issues such as population control, limiting human intervention in the ecosystem, or rebuilding our cities in balance with nature have been discussed almost entirely from a European and often elitist perspective." [13]
— *Carl Anthony,*
"Why Blacks Should Be Environmentalists"

Photo by David Goldberg

Young Gardeners at Potrero del Col Garden, San Francisco, League of Urban Gardeners

"An environmental perspective could provide much needed focus for a new generation of Black Americans. Indeed, Blacks may have a great deal to gain by forging closer bonds with existing environmental organizations working to save the planet…. These new environmentalists could provide guidance to hundreds of thousands of people in society at large and in their own communities, making the difficult transition from industrial to more sustainable patterns of urban life."[14]

— Carl Anthony

reason for promoting ecological communities and creating coalitions to improve our environment.

Americans, especially those generations of middle income people who lived so high on the consumption scale in the post-WWII boom years, now must live up to a new sense of responsibility as we change to an ecologically sustainable way of living while confronting a declining economy. The recent success of CoHousing communities demonstrates how increasing numbers of people can live better for less by learning to share meals in a common house, reduce car trips, and save costs, energy, time, and resources. Thus far, these substantial benefits have been enjoyed mostly by the middle class. The challenge now is to expand the advantages of living better for less to the lower income population groups who are increasingly being abandoned to declining income and fewer options, yet are being sent the double standard message that they cannot impose an adverse environmental impact as they try to improve their standard of living.

The challenge for us all is to work together to transform absentee-owner housing and businesses in aging neighborhoods into Eco Villages, in which upper, middle, moderate, and low income tenants and resident home owners, local business people, and ex-gang members, ex-jobless, ex-inmates, and ex-homeless, all become community builders. We believe that people's gregarious nature and propensity to ascend to a higher quality of living will draw more people into forming Shared Living Communities instead of gangs, walled neighborhoods, or country club hideaways. With the tools that are now becoming available to create ecologically designed community housing, everyone has a

wonderful chance to heal and recover from pseudo-individuality, consumerism, alienation, poverty, homelessness, environmental degradation, and addiction to the car.

We observe today a significant trend toward forming self-help coalitions in urban neighborhoods with youth support groups, resident control of housing projects, rehabilitation of abandoned houses, community gardens, recycling businesses, and conversion of vacant lots to playlots. Inner-city neighbors and youth are joining together on community projects, creating local jobs, obtaining better education, and fighting for, rather than against each other. These grassroots community empowerment efforts must be expanded to confront and reverse the greatest tragedy of community breakdown, the high percentage of people being sent to prison.

Ann Whiston Spirn in a talk at the 1993 American Planning Association conference, in describing her students work in the West Philadelphia community gardens said:

…. the phenomenon of the community garden contains lessons for the design of larger neighborhoods…. The gardeners soon get the idea that the patterns that they are creating in their garden are very much like the patterns of their block, their neighborhood, and their city…. And with this understanding they can communicate with others about what they want for their community. [15]

Regardless of income level, there are those who may not have the skills to self-organize into effective community. Many people do not know of the benefits of living in Shared Living Communities or working within a local Community Development Corporation or Community Land Trust to produce jobs, housing, and stable neighborhoods. Many Americans, regardless of income, education, or ethnicity, will need assistance with group living skills, and training in community formation processes in order to fully benefit from community-oriented housing. Such training programs can be a part of comprehensive urban and rural sustainable community planning and development programs as proposed in earlier chapters. They would be offered to everyone, by schools, universities, businesses, non-profit organizations, and community consultants. Community rebuilding courses would include learning about co-ownership, management, ecological design and living, new extended family and Village Cluster housing options, personal empowerment building, alternative livelihood, cooperative/employee–owned businesses, self-reliant living, and self-help construction. It has taken decades for community to breakdown; we deserve to invest intraining to become a sustainable society.

Photo by David Goldberg

San Francisco League of Urban Gardeners (SLUG)
Below: here are the future farmers of America learning food growing as a new livelihood. SLUG, directed by Mohammed Nuru, has expanded from a gardening group of four people in 1991 to a full time staff of ten in 1994 involving urban gardeners in over 100 gardens around the city, amounting to over 1000 plots. This includes 35 gardens on public land, plus 38 gardens in schools, 30 gardens at homeless shelters, and others at senior centers and housing complexes. The SLUG programs includes youth job training and the "Green Team," an alternative sentencing community service program for youths. This model for urban self reliance and revitalization is enthusiastically being adopted in many other American cities.

"The Fruits of the Earth Belong to Us All"
From *A Discourse on the origins of Inequality,* by Jean Jacques Rousseau, quoted in *The Worlds Wasted Wealth 2* by J.W. Smith.

The first man who. having enclosed a piece of ground bethought himself as saying 'this is mine,' and found people simple enough to believe him, was the real founder of civil society. From how many crimes, wars, and murders, from how many horrors and misfortunes might not any one have saved mankind, by pulling up the stakes, or filling up the ditch, and crying to his fellows: 'Beware of listening to this imposter; you are undone if you once forget that the fruits of the earth belong to us all, and the earth itself to nobody.' [16]

Sustainability Comes Down to Basics

— our ability to procreate healthy babies

We are all so vulnerable and yet we ourselves are the most essential link in our survival. We are a symbol of life, the nurturing force, and the cause for sustainability of our species. Women and men, the female and the male of the human species, have together the responsibility for the reproduction of human life and the sustainability of human society. By accomplishing that we will have also contributed to the sustainability of the eco-system — one cannot survive without the other. But, to procreate healthy babies, we must protect our bodies from environmentally and socially caused damage. This opens up a multitude of preventive and health maintenance responsibilities that are intricately linked and are presently being neglected. To do what is necessary for our survival we must have a completely healthy, ecologically sustainable community system whose interior workings are so arranged to support women and men in the care of each other and their children. Sustainability means having the ability to sustain or to continue to be, which implies that our existence should not be weakened from one generation to the next in ways that present a threat to reproduction and continuity of the species, family, and culture. This means we must be capable of permanently protecting women's and men's bodies by creating an ecologically sustainable living environment.

However, we are learning the hard way that the chemical-laden environment is a major cause for women at younger ages to have increasingly higher rates of cancer in their breasts, ovaries and uterus, and is suspected to be a factor in the increase of cancer in children and men. To maintain the mutual health of all women, men, and children, the healthy functioning of the entire ecosystem is imperative. Therefore, we must look at how every influence in our daily lives affects us and how we affect each other, through emotional stress from social alienation and economic exploitation, to unhealthy physical environments in the home and at work, and the outer environmental influences.

To have healthy minds and bodies, we must have healthy sources of emotional and physical nourishment from people, air, water, food, and the land. An unhealthy physical or mental condition of any human or other being, be it male domination of women and children, environmental exploitation by corporations, filling in creeks and building over farm lands, the wanton killing of whales, dolphins, and sea turtles, and the spewing of toxic residue from factories and cars, can cause harm to any part of the whole. The seeing of the interconnectedness of these practices with our health is essential.

Through the design and creation of ecologically sustainable communities lies the path to a harmonious and healthy future for all on the planet, and the assurance that all life forms are born healthy throughout the ecosystem.

The Emergence of Ecologically Sustainable Cities

The Eco City, Eco Village, and Green Belt concepts previously introduced will now be presented as one unified approach for rebuilding community in America. The catalysts for this transformation are the rail transit networks, which herald a new socio-economic prosperity. The intention is to stimulate the local economy and provide new sources of livelihood through self–reliant community enterprises, and provide more livable residential neighborhoods free of the influence of the car.

However, the "Eco" prefix should be used only when the land uses and the population of a city are served by a system of rail transit and feeder shuttle buses that are integrated with ecologically designed housing and intentional neighborhoods that favor walking and bicycling. Primarily, Eco Villages and Eco Cities will meet the following performance criteria: They are low in consumption of energy and resources. They generate few car trips because of the rail transit networks. They are high in commonly owned properties and amenities, high in democratic and participatory local government, and high in live-work and employee-owned offices. An Eco Village forms around a rail station or "transit node" and is made up of a rich diversity of housing types and densities. The center is a mixed-use composition that serves a wide range of social, economic, and community service needs — it is a whole-community approach, not just a real estate development. These criteria will provide the greatest opportunity to create ecologically sustainable Shared Living Communities.

Eco Cities do not yet exist, but they can be formed out of the old cities to become an interconnected composition of many Eco Villages as defined above. A well-functioning Eco City would represent a smoothly working integration of the *social, economic, and environmental* (SEE) elements presented earlier, and of people who, because they live in Shared Living Communities in an Eco Village, have a sense of belonging to the larger Eco City.

"The only sustainable city — and this, to me , is the indispensable ideal and goal — is a city in balance with its countryside: a city, that is, that would live off the net ecological income of its supporting region, paying as it goes all its ecological and human debts." [19]
— Wendell Berry,
"Out of Your Car, Off Your Horse"

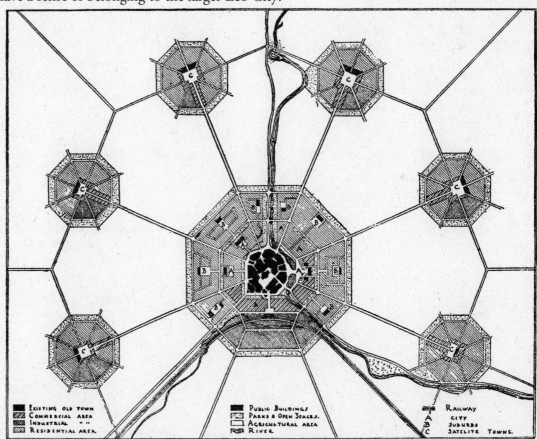

Existing Old Town
Commercial Area
Industrial " "
Residential Area
Public Buildings
Parks & Open Spaces.
Agricultural Area
River
Railway
A   City
B   Suburbs
C   Satellite Towns.

Avery Architectural and Fine Arts Library, Columbia University, in the City of New York

Garden Cities and Satellite Communities, as Conceived by Sir Raymond Unwin [20]
Visionary planners and indigenous peoples throughout time have expressed organic, circular and radial patterns for human habitat, from villages to whole cities.

357

A Vision

Eco City (revitalized old city center) with mixed use residential, commercial, cultural, and live-work spaces — a car free zone served by the SLRT network, feeder bus lines, and high speed interurban trains

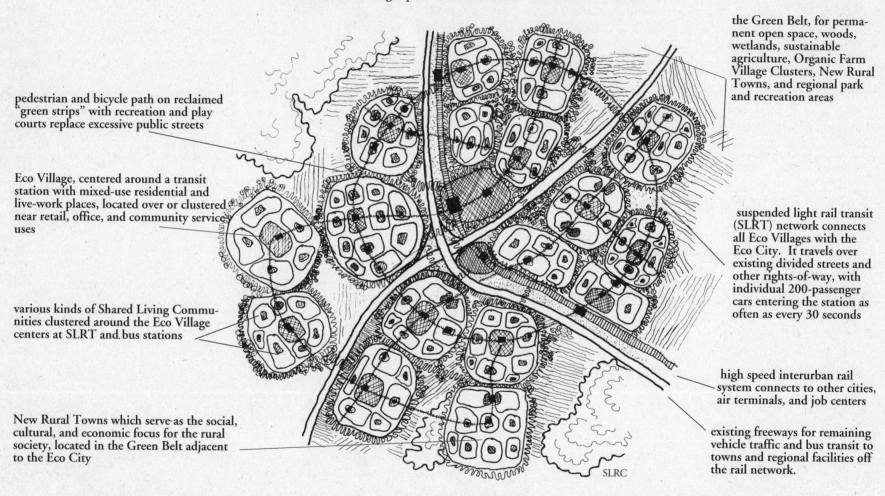

the Green Belt, for permanent open space, woods, wetlands, sustainable agriculture, Organic Farm Village Clusters, New Rural Towns, and regional park and recreation areas

pedestrian and bicycle path on reclaimed "green strips" with recreation and play courts replace excessive public streets

Eco Village, centered around a transit station with mixed-use residential and live-work places, located over or clustered near retail, office, and community service uses

various kinds of Shared Living Communities clustered around the Eco Village centers at SLRT and bus stations

New Rural Towns which serve as the social, cultural, and economic focus for the rural society, located in the Green Belt adjacent to the Eco City

suspended light rail transit (SLRT) network connects all Eco Villages with the Eco City. It travels over existing divided streets and other rights-of-way, with individual 200-passenger cars entering the station as often as every 30 seconds

high speed interurban rail system connects to other cities, air terminals, and job centers

existing freeways for remaining vehicle traffic and bus transit to towns and regional facilities off the rail network.

SLRC

The Eco City = Communities of Eco Villages = Shared Living Communities = New Extended Families and Village Clusters
This drawing is a redesign of the socially and environmentally unworkable city example shown in "Dangerous Growth Patterns." The Eco City becomes ecologically sustainable when numerous existing neighborhoods become transformed into Eco Villages connected by a network of rail transit. Eco Villages composed of variations of Shared Living Communities, either new design clusters and group houses or redesigned existing housing like in the Urban Cooperative Block. A network of pedestrian and bicycle path green strips lead to the Eco Village center and the transit stations.

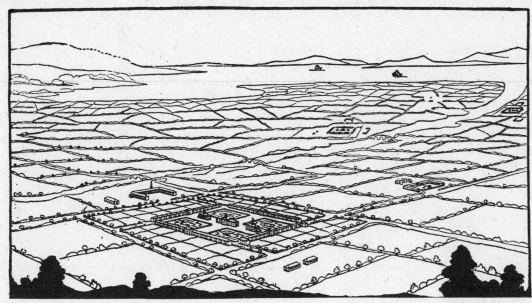

*Robert Owen's Scheme
for a Utopian Community;
A bird's eye view.* [21]
*A view and plan of agricultural
and manufacturing villages of Unity
and Mutual Cooperation.*

Avery Architectural and Fine Arts Library, Columbia University, in the City of New York. (From a broadside of 1817, courtesy of the Saligman Library, Columbia University)

*The Green Belts
Around San Francisco*
*The San Francisco Bay Area is blessed
with several permanent open space areas
which include the Pacific Ocean, the San
Francisco Bay, and various coastal hills
that are preserved as Green Belts by either
regional park systems or zoning policies
that have limited urban expansion
in several direction. In this picture
is a portion of San Bruno Mountain
County Park, 2064 acres of protected
open space to the south of San Francisco.
However, much of the open space areas
around the bay are still at risk of being
overrun by low density development.*

Photo by Greenbelt Alliance

The Green Belt is the Food Source for Eco Cities

None of this discussion about containment of urban sprawl, revitalization of inner cities, transit systems, and Eco Cities is meaningful without addressing the Green Belt as an integral part of a comprehensive regional planning process. The Green Belt is proposed as a social, economic, and physical entity that skirts the edges of cities and towns and establishes a permanent urban limit line. The feeding of population centers from immediately adjacent farming areas has much precedent historically, and is still the prevailing relationship throughout Europe and many parts of the world. Eighteenth-century idealist planners such as Sir Raymond Unwin and Robert Owen visualized an integrated social, economic, and environmental design relationship in their community concepts. The New Rural Towns, as described in Chapter Five, are sustainable, agriculture–based, and intended to become the focus of a stable and vital rural society — the small family farmer returns. The revitalized local agricultural economy provides direct marketing of organic food to urban farmers' markets, food stores, and restaurants, as well as local food packing and processing plants and related cottage industries.

Rail transit lines for transport of farm products and local passenger service to the cities would be extended to rural Eco Villages and small towns only when there are deliberate regional planning policies not to induce real estate speculation that attracts urban commuters. A policy for establishing intentional and comprehensively planned Green Belts would provide enabling processes for assisting the formation of Organic Farm Village Cluster commu

Photo by Greenbelt Alliance

The Ever Present Green Belt Around Münster, Germany
This timeless scene— agricultural resources surrounding a compact pedestrian city— is the basic model for ecologically sustainable Eco Villages and Eco Cities.

The Garden is the paradise of nature,
and the City is the paradise of culture.
Or at least it could be…
Today, both are out of balance.

If we build the ecocity we will regain
the Garden and finally aspire to the full
ideal of the City — the City built with,
not against, nature.

Then, when we hold in reverence that which
we cannot build, which is given to us by
the Earth herself, we will create not just
a home for ourselves but a future
for all who follow.[22]

— Richard Register
Ecocity Berkeley: Building Cities
for a Healthy Future

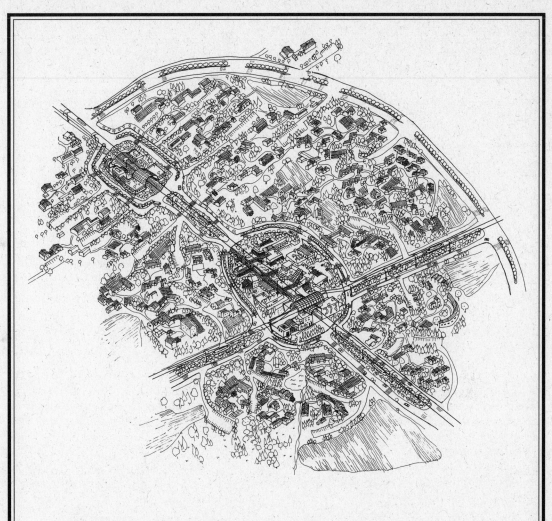

SLRC

The Eco Village Grows Naturally with Village Cluster Housing
The informal and organic pattern of residential clusters and group houses reflects the extended family and participatory nature of the community. A network of pathways meander past gardens, orchards of fruit trees, recreation courts, play lots, and schools, linking them with the common houses of each residential cluster, and to the Eco Village core. The private driveways designed as "slow streets" lead to parking courts, and are the only sign of the car, which is of much less importance in the Eco Village.

Photo by William Porter

Farmers Market in London
Wherever they are in the world, farmers' markets tell of direct marketing of small farmers produce and wares from the surrounding countryside. This timeles, universal trait of humankind is a direct expression of the Green Belt as a vital role in the transformation to ecologically sustainable cities.

" *In fact, much of the land you fly over on a trip across the country isn't prime farmland at all. Although suitable for corn, wheat, and other grains, it's not ideal for growing much of the fresh produce — tomatoes, peaches, apples, oranges — that we're beginning to import. You'll find the land which is best sited for growing these desirable crops — and most any other crop you can think of — in and around our metropolitan areas. It's only logical really. Our ancestors originally settled on the very best farmland the nation had to offer. And now, what remains is on the out skirts of population centers — threatened by development.* " [23]

— *Ralph Grossi,*

nities such as Dear Valley, and New Rural Towns. We are definitely prescribing full–scale adoption of a community pluralism for America, a rural society and an urban society, unified by common precepts and lifestyles of ecologically sustainable community and served by efficient passenger and freight rail systems.

The Integration of People, Community, and Rail Transit

During the rapid growth of America's higher density cities, from the 1850s through the 1920s, we actually had "transit neighborhoods" in this country.[2] The transit lines in those days were often owned and operated by investment partnerships that also bought up the farmlands and open space green belts that surrounded the core cities. They built rail lines to outlying public recreation centers and small towns, sold small lot subdivisions around transit stops, and created "transit neighborhoods" where people could walk to the train.[24]

It was the business development logic in those days to cater to the pedestrian needs of the transit riders by locating retail and convenience shops and small businesses around the station, with apartments over them for the shop owners' families or for rentals to local workers. Two and three story buildings with apartment flats, row houses, and "family" hotels were often intermixed. Schools and churches followed, and an early version of the Eco Village transit node was formed. With that precedent to guide us, we have the challenge of transforming our 20th century auto-sprawl cities into new kinds of transit neighborhoods.

Photo by Richard Tomalch, *"Moving Peopl;e"*

Light-rail Cars at a Neighborhood Station
The train or transit station becomes a familiar and reliable institution in a community setting just as the school, church, and town hall have been symbols of continuity and strength in past times.

The Eco Village sketch shows how various types of Shared Living Communities can be nestled together to form an Eco Village. The planning guidelines for such a village would place an emphasis on ecological design, co-ownership, local self-reliance, mixed-uses, moderate to higher densities, pedestrian circulation, low car dependency, and rail and bus service. The village transit station can be located in a redesigned shopping center, a cluster of existing strip retail stores, or in a new mixed-use Eco Village core. Various residential communities can also include small convenience food and service shops to serve the immediate neighborhood — the "mom and pop store" tradition.

The Eco Village would be a vital socio–economic and cultural core because of the participatory management by the Eco Village council composed of resident co-owners of the housing and small businesses. Eco Villages may be entirely owned and locally managed by a Community Development Corporation (CDC) or a Community Land Trust (CLT). The basic precept for Eco Village planning is creating large co-owned parcels using the Ecological Incentive Planning District (EIPD) process introduced in Chapter Nine, and the Village Cluster land planning techniques described in Chapters Four and Five.

"Eco-plots," an ecologically sustainable way to subdivide land

Development of Eco Village intentional neighborhoods, whether using new designs or existing neighborhoods, will be planned as co-owned parcels of three to five acres or larger, for various types of Shared Living Communities. This is recommended as the minimum development standard. The density for Eco-plots may range from 10 to 20 units per acre or higher, subject to the Eco Village transit node location and the comprehensive planning policies for the broader Eco City. The Ecological Incentive Planning District process could provide incentives for development of Eco Villages on even larger size parcels composed of groupings of Eco-plots for building Shared Living type housing. Incentives can include higher density bonuses, and other social, economic, and environmental benefits.

Development of individual Eco-plots or groups of Eco-plots can be done by community core groups, local nonprofit sponsors such as an MHA,

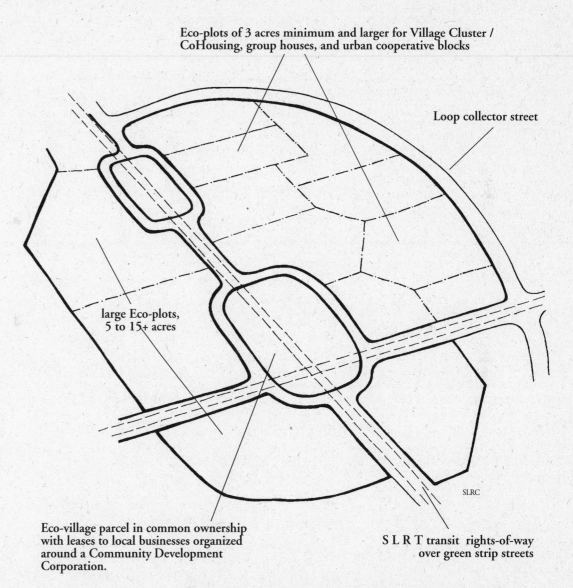

Eco-plots of 3 acres minimum and larger for Village Cluster / CoHousing, group houses, and urban cooperative blocks

Loop collector street

large Eco-plots, 5 to 15+ acres

SLRC

Eco-village parcel in common ownership with leases to local businesses organized around a Community Development Corporation.

S L R T transit rights-of-way over green strip streets

Subdivision Plan for an Eco Village
Gone are the typical postage-stamp lots and dedicated paved streets for detached single-family houses. Here is the "common ground" where the modern day village builders can co-design and co-own a sustainable new American Dream way of living.

*"... 'community' must mean a
people locally placed and a people,
moreover, not too numerous to have
a common knowledge of themselves
and of their place. Because places
differ from one another and
because people will differ somewhat
according to the characters of their
places, if we think of a nation as an
assemblage of many communities,
we are necessarily thinking of some
sort of pluralism."* [25]

— *Wendell Berry*

CDC, or CLT, a for-profit developer, a Redevelopment Agency, a Housing Authority, or a joint venture by combinations of the above. In all situations, the participation of the future co-owner residents should be provided for in the manner of community organization, co-design, and mutual responsibility as we have previously presented. The coordination of development planning and core group organizing for the different clusters by the Eco Village sponsoring organization or developer is crucial for the creation of an integrated, total community.

The Bondebjerget community, built in 1981-82, near Odense, Denmark, provides a good example of how an originating core group can develop the Eco Village concept on large parcels of twenty to forty acres or more without subdividing into small separate lots. Bondebjerget is a member-originated cooperative of four 20– unit clusters, each with their own common house. The clusters were occupied over a period of eight months by groups with varying degrees of participation in the initial planning process, and with some of the people having had little prior connection with each other before moving in. This affected the cohesiveness of the later–to–be–completed clusters. However, the "positive example and support" of the founding core group and other clusters ameliorated the internal differences. [26]

The Bondebjerget example serves as a perfect working model for the Eco Village prototype design we have presented. Multiple Village Clusters of 15 to 30 units each, grouped together on various sizes of Eco-plots, will enable each cluster to be more sociable and manageable and than large complexes with a huge kitchen and common dining room.

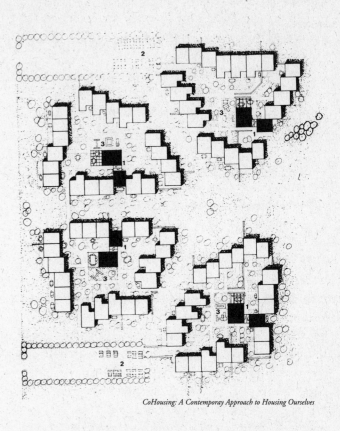

CoHousing: A Contemporay Approach to Housing Ourselves

"Bondebjerget" in Denmark: An Eco Village Example of CoHousing Clusters

Ecologically sustainable transit node planning guidelines

Here are some basic guidelines for planning and managing an Eco City transit node :

 • **Incentives to encourage higher density ecologically designed community housing** around transit stations in existing urban areas should be included in transit funding programs. This is needed to offset the tendency for developers to call existing cities "built-up" when they appear at zoning hearings to justify rezoning more open space and farm lands for low density housing. Cities are often considered to be "built-up" if there is no vacant land remaining within their borders to be developed. But it cannot be said that a city is built-up when the density is only six to eight single-family houses per acre, and when 40% to 60% of the land is being used for auto related purposes. Our low density cities can be appropriately densified with infill housing and other uses and abundant open space by use of the social and environmental incentive zoning and financing techniques previously proposed.

 • **The "jobs, transportation, and housing balance"** is a regional planning and environmental policy that has often been recommended by planning and environmental protection agencies as a way to reduce workplace generated car trips by providing housing near employment. This objective is not being well implemented because of weak laws and inadequate enforcement, and by lack of vision and a deep understanding of the problem of urban sprawl. We must go beyond the reasoning that the car problem can be solved by agencies measuring exhaust emissions and setting maximum levels, and see the multiple ills associated with

SLRC

The Renaissance of the Railroads
This portends the rebuilding of community in America. The irony is that rail transportation is being modernized everywhere in the world except in the U.S.

British Rail terminals and lesser stations on the Underground had never been exploited as sites for major developments. Then BR had three office tower projects in quick succession at Fendchurch Street, Charing Cross, and Liverpool Street stations. Now the concept has arrived, with copycat developments happening even at secondary London Transport stops like Gloucester Rd. The plans may be more neighborhood-oriented, but the same design concepts are present."[27]

— Richard Tolmach,
"British Discover Stations
as Magnets for Development"

"In a now famous study, Appleyard and Lintell (1971) graphically illustrated the impact of traffic on communities…. People in low traffic streets have far more friends and acquaintances than those in high traffic streets."[28]

— Peter Newman &
Jeff Kenworthy,
Winning Back the Cities

dependency on the car as a transportation system.

Comprehensive policies are needed for increased funding of expanded rail systems that directly coordinate workplace, land use, and housing development in compact rail transit nodes throughout existing urbanized regions. This is the framework from which Eco Villages and Eco Cities will emerge. There is finally the opportunity for the short range electric vehicles to augment walking, bicycles, shuttle busses, and rail transit.

• **Turn existing streets into a network of green strips** that surround Eco Village residential clusters. These reclaimed rights-of-way can be used for tree belts and landscaped open space, pedestrian and bicycle paths, sitting courts, play areas, recreation courts, and community gardens. There are practical advantages to reusing the surplus rights-of-way of existing streets that are excessively wide and too numerous in conventional developments. They represent a major investment in utility line infrastructure and public rights-of-way, over which green strips and transit systems can be built. Some secondary and even major highways could be reduced in the number of lanes to local collector streets and some converted into "slow streets." Most of the car circulation routes within the Eco Village housing clusters would be limited to driveway-like roads. Due to a variety of incentives and the attractiveness of transportation alternatives, car traffic will tend to be low, and walking, biking, and bus and transit use correspondingly high. Green strips would also be planned into designs of new Eco Villages using the same design criteria and rationale. But it there is a huge urban land opportunity for reducing the oversupply of streets and reclaiming them for playing and growing on..

• **Transit station nodes are good for rebuilding community** because, if properly planned for, they can stimulate economic growth and generate employment for residents of the surrounding higher density, mixed-use residential buildings. The crossing points of caravan routes and seaports were the very earliest transit nodes and from there grew the major cities of the world. Inter-city train terminals in European cities are increasingly the major points of public interest and sources of economic vitality in the surrounding areas, with apartments, offices, retail spaces, farmers' markets, and a variety of cultural and entertainment attractions within walking distance of the stations. The September-October 1993 issue of *Moving People* described the development of business establishments within and around several British and French rail station sites, with the revelation that:

> Retail developers recognize the high speed rail passenger base as being an affluent market, like air travelers. A station like Waterloo with as many as 50,000 daily international travelers, has as much draw just from passengers as a large shopping center, and French [investment] capital has planned an even more aggressive rail-based center at the new TGV-Nord station at Lille, which will be the only intermediate stop for Paris-London expresses.[27]

Rail systems can efficiently bring large numbers of passengers into the heart of every American city and along with them economic opportunities, cultural resources, and social interaction. Therefore, in cities, we have a tremendous opportunity for this country's economic recovery and social healing. The successful U.S. experience with train stations located in the middle of vital downtown commercial areas is well known historically. Good examples are the BART and MUNI lines whose stations open directly into retail and office buildings under San Francisco's Market Street and New York's Grand Central Station which is integrated with the intensive commercial and pedestrian activities at the World Trade Center. The stimulation of commerce around transit stations can be repeated again in this country with new, rapid rail and light rail systems, and an intentional policy for building full functioning transit nodes.

• **Gentrification of the housing supply,** caused by free market land speculation, is often the direct result of the success of a transit node as a people and trade generator. Because of the inevitable displacement of lower income people from successful transit node de-velopments, we recommended, in Chapter Nine, the Ecological Incentive Planning District as an incentive process for Shared Living Community type housing, planned and managed to include affordable housing for people of all income levels in proportion to their numbers in the urban area. Strong social, economic, and environmental ethics will be necessary to serve all population sub-groups when building thousands of Eco Village/Eco City transit nodes in the U.S. This will require a broadening of Commuity Reinvestment Act criteria for lending to end redlining and to provide more local innovative community development. At the heart of ecologically sustainable Eco Cities will be a diversified population who are empowered as co-owners to share responsibilities and resources as active participants in community based housing.

Photo from *"Moving Society,"* by Richard Tomalch

Shops at Victoria Station, London
Retail shops in train stations follows the highest rule for successful commerce, and that is to locate where the highest possible pedestrian count can be found, and the lowest numbers of cars to get in the way. Victoria station is also a hub for three underground lines, major inter-city bus stations, busses and trains to Gatwick Airport, and has three theaters, offices, and other commerce.[29]

"The potential success of more energy-efficient, ecologically and economically sound urban transportation networks that reinvest in the urban core raises issues about shifting community demographics or "creeping gentrification." The result has often been that poor people are driven out by increasing property values and costs of living resulting from the "success" of economic revitalization. Another displacement of certain communities from one area to some other less desirable area, perpetuating the same dynamic of racial and class stratification."[30]
— Henry Holmes, "Social Justice"

Big Plans to Meet Big Problems

We think and act on too small a scale compared to what we are capable of, because of our American preoccupation with individualism. We need to think of our unified power as members of our local community, the national community, and the world community. We need to see ourselves on a larger scale as a gathering of people empowering each other beyond the limits of our own individual experiences and resources. We need to think on the scale of large Eco Cities made up of Eco Villages connected by rail systems and surrounded by Green Belts. The empowerment of each person to contribute to this grand scale of community endeavor will arise naturally from the economic security and shared resources of extended family groups living in Shared Living Communities. Building local community empowerment will, in turn, lead to rebuilding America.

An example of courageous urban planning and design and civic leadership is found in the "City Beautiful" movement accredited to Daniel Burnham. This late 19th Century architect and planner for the 1893 Chicago Worlds Fair and for monumental urban designs in Chicago, said:

Make no little plans; they have no magic to stir men's blood and probably themselves will not be realized. Make big plans; aim high in hope and work, remembering that a noble, logical diagram once recorded will never die, but long after we are gone will be a living thing, asserting itself with ever growing insistence. Remember that our sons and grandsons [children and grandchildren] are to do things that would stagger us. Let your watchword be order and your beacon beauty. [32]

This was spoken over 100 years ago at a time of wealth for a few, immense urban squalor and human misery, as well as courageous social reforms, and a rising of hope and expectations. The challenge was directed to architectural students hoping to emulate the Master Architect's grand boulevards, bridges, plazas, libraries, civic buildings, and parks. They believed that City Beautiful projects would correct the social and economic ills of that day. Perhaps the massive urban beautification and public works projects of that time did stimulate the business economy, create jobs, and trickle down to help the working poor. But what is significant is how the great visions, leadership, and commitment, and pride in the urban landscape, was translated into self-esteem — people remembered their city. Those kinds of public works were replicated in many other

> "We can be grateful for what one person can create, but when we see what abundance we can create together, it will baffle the intellect and arouse our spirits to celebrate the oneness of humanity and the need for cooperating in sustainable community."
> — Ken Norwood

Faith is following what my heart knows and my mind can't prove.
— Mountain Man Insight

Stumbling Block or Stepping Stonmes

Isn't it strange that princes and king
And clowns that caper in sawdust rings
And common folks like you and me
Are builders of eternity?

To each is given a bag of tools
A shapeless mass and a book of rules
And each must make, ere life is flown
A stumbling-block or a stepping-stone. [31]

— R.L. Sharpe

cities. The grandiose City Beautiful movement occurred at a time when American cities were at their height of growth and maturation, rail service went everywhere, and people walked and talked to each other.

Now, a century later, our society is marked by similar sounds of socioeconomic conflict, a centralized economic system controlled by a few elite, and great reform movements being born. We also endure much urban decay, environmental degradation, and inattentiveness to social needs. Worse yet, there has been a dearth of bold socially and environmentally responsible leadership in government, business, and the planning and architectural professions. There are no big plans, just big office buildings and even bigger shopping centers, and too few comprehensive plans for balancing jobs, housing, and transportation in central areas of cities. Too little effort is being made to protect natural open space and farmlands from single-family tracts and so-called New Towns. We desperately need a new breed of "big plans," such as expanded rail networks that link Eco Villages and Eco Cities across America. It is a remarkable coincidence that, at this turn of the century, the attention to sustainable communities comes when we need massive social change and job–making programs, when our cities are decaying, and the infrastructure is dangerously obsolete. This *is* the time for the Clinton and Gore's "Rebuild America" vision to be carried out — but it is not for just "them" or big government or big business to do it. This time "we the people" must be deeply involved as the community builders. We can start at the family dinner table, expand to a larger extended family and community, take down fences, and demand a major rail transit system.

A Rail Tour of Eco Villages and Eco Cities

This story takes place in the very near future, when the rebuilding of America has begun in earnest. In this dialogue, we revisit some of the Shared Living Communities that were presented in other dialogues in this book. Doris is a member of an international coalition of environmental, nonprofit housing, and sustainable community advocacy groups. She is leading a group of 16 environmental educators from 12 countries around the world, on a joint U.S. and UN tour of Shared Living Communities, Eco Villages, Eco Cities, and new transportation systems in the U.S.

This story begins in Dear Valley, the Organic Farm Village Cluster we visited in Chapter Five. The group has spent the last two days doing extensive walking tours around the farm and the preserved creeks and wildlife habitat within and around the farmed areas. They attended seminars about Permaculture, sustainable agriculture, organic farming, and marketing directly to the farmers' markets, food stores, and restaurants. They examined the "off-the-grid" solar energy power system, the earth-bermed private living suites, and the centrally located common house with its many activity rooms, including the childcare center and the school which also serves children from surrounding farms. In the separate food processing kitchen, they watched a demonstration of how Dear Valley grown food is dried, canned, or frozen for later use. They spoke with several members who have a part-time business of making and marketing jams and herbal seasonings, as well as various other members about their personal experiences living in the Dear Valley community.

The group is now in the common house enjoying a breakfast feast hosted by the community before they embark on the rest of their journey. The feast is to celebrate their visit and the beginning of their intensive tour of other ecologically designed communities in the San Francisco Bay area. The food is shared with a lively discussion, and question and answer session. Susan, from France, asked, *"You say you have an educational grant to teach inner-city people about ecological farming in a village community. How do you pick the students?"*

Nicole answered, *"We don't pick them; the inner-city Community Development Corporations and Land Trusts tell their members about our program, people apply, and they self-select who is next. You know, ours is only one of hundreds of ecological farming and community rebuildingtraining programs around the U.S. This live-in program is open to everyone: school children, college students, recovering drug users, disabled people, ex-gang members, school teachers, ex-prison inmates, and ex-corporate managers."*

Doris concluded by thanking the Dear Valley community and then each of the visitors in turn gave their thanks in their native languages. As the visitors were getting into the van-bus and the two Dear Valley cars, Rosalinda and Jonathan appeared with several small baskets filled with peach cobbler. The entire community lined the entry road, waving and singing out good-byes and happy landings.

While waiting at the Vacaville train station for the next Amtrak Capitol Express from Sacramento to the San Francisco Bay area, Doris explained, *"This is a newly built Eco Village transit node that is part of the Rebuild America program, which offers incentives for building mixed-use transit nodes with residential units over commercial space. See that new*

construction? The developer was given tax credits, reductions in parking requirements, fee waivers, and approval to build more units in exchange for building a pedestrian-only complex near this station. This provided for 40% of the units to be low and moderate income intergenerational housing, and reserved space for several nonprofit developers to build Shared Living Community clusters for extended family living groups."

The tour group settled into their seats for a fast ride to the Berkeley station as they passed out peach cobbler on souvenir ceramic plates made by one of Dear Valley's cottage industries. Maria from Brazil added, *" They made so much of their income right there in Dear Valley. They said that now no one is unemployed or has to commute to work. In Brazil, we need to relearn village living before more cars take over."*

At the Berkeley station they took an escalator up to catch a Suspended Light Rail Transit (SLRT) car that would take them to the next community on their list, the Bay Street Group House. On board, Doris described the SLRTsystem. *"This Suspended Light Rail Transit or SLRT — you've probably seen them in other parts of the world — is being tried out here in the Bay Area, as a connector system between the Amtrak stations, existing Bay Area Rapid Transit Stations, called BART, and city centers. They are not trains but single cars that come along very frequently. This is new, and the Eco Village station stop neighborhoods are just beginning to make the transition from low-density single-family neighborhoods to mixed-use moderate-density pedestrian areas with co-op apartments and condominiums over shops. See, here comes another car now."*

They glided over the landscaped center strips of streets, some of which had become more like

Postcard by courtesy of Lyman Richardson

*The Original Suspended Light Rail System
in Wupertal, Germany*
*Because it can glide over existing streets, parking lots,
waterways, and open space areas, it can be less costly and
obtrusive than surface light rail systems.*

driveways, with walking paths and bikeways instead of typical suburban streets. When they arrived, all the members of the Bay Street House, as well as some city officials, were waiting at the SLRT station.

James from the Bay Street house stepped forward to greet Doris and the others, and said, *"Wecome to all of you. We of the Bay Street House are thrilled to host you."*

Doris introduced the visitors and then James introduced the Sustainable Community Coordinator for the city, and several City Council members. They all merged in a noisy talkative procession for the six block walk to the Bay Street House.

They did a quick tour of the Bay Street House which at the time had 17 residents; 12 adults and five children, with Stephanie being the oldest. Paul and Barbara showed a video of their four-year process to remodel the two original houses into one large group house of eight living suites. They had done all the work themselves and the video showed their many work parties, meetings, celebrations, and their pride in their community.

Brennan and Alice introduced the rest of their household and asked Doris and the UN group to share with them what they were learning from the trip. Some of the teachers gave a summary of their social and environmental observations, and shared questions and concerns about ecological and economic issues in their countries.

Keita from Burkino Faso summed up what they all were saying. *"For many years you, Westerners,"* he gestured to the tour group, *"and some of our own group, we admit, have exported chemicals, cars, and consumer goods in an attempt to industrialize the world, even after centuries of industrialization were destroying the atmosphere, many species of animals, and people. Our countries, and I speak for the so-called 'developing countries' now, tried to copy your lifestyles, and we found it didn't work. We were losing our extended family heritage and sense of community just as you did. Now, we have come to learn how high technology, which you export to us, and simple self-reliant village living, which we are rapidly losing, can be combined into an ecologically sustainable way of life that we can all enjoy. You have progressed with your Eco Village and Green Belt work, but we too have been reviving and modernizing our village ways, so we share that with you also. Now, we are all building railroads again just like 100 years ago. We can export environmental knowledge to each other, instead of poisons, bullets, and cars."* He smiled broadly as he bowed, *"Let us all thank each other."*

The music began while the food and beverages brought by neighbors and friends were set out for another feast. When Paul and Barbara finally got to bed at 2:30 a.m., they both exclaimed how exhilarated they were about the magic of community gatherings. They agreed that next year they would like to do a reciprocal tour to visit communities in other countries and to be royally hosted.

When the visitors departed in the morning, some of the Bay Street Group members joined the tour group for a bicycle procession through Berkeley's "slow-streets" to the Eco City Berkeley pedestrian center around the BART station. When they were on the train, Doris reminded them that their next community visit would be City Gardens in Eco City San Francisco, and they would have two hours of free time to tour the city on their own. When they arrived, some walked along the pedestrian-only streets that led to the convention center,

Illustration by Jim Leritz

Ferry Plaza Harvest Market
This farmers' market at the end of Market Street in San Francisco serves downtown workers, central area residents, and tourists. Much of the produce is marketed dirtectly by local farmers in the surrounding agricultural regions.

the Ferry Plaza Harvest Market, the financial district, and the live-work districts south of Market Street. Ohers went on a sight-seeing tour via cable car, or rented bicycles for a ride along the Embarcadero to Fisherman's Wharf. One group rode the new SLRT line out Geary Boulevard, over to Golden Gate Park, and out to the Pacific Ocean.

Back together again, they caught the Municipal Railway under Market Street to the City Garden Urban Cooperative Block Community. Many of the 125 members of City Garden, along with some local city planners and architects, and several San Francisco environmental teachers, were there to greet the international visitors with a festive and musical welcome. They assembled in the central court of City Garden's block of old Victorian houses converted to group houses. Matt, the coordinator of the housing cooperative, welcomed the visitors and conducted a tour of several group houses, the common house, childcare center, work/craft/tool building, the fruit tree grove, gardens, chicken pens, and recreation courts. In the central court, lavish food-laden tables awaited them. Ingrid from Norway shook a finger at the food and said, *"Ah, more of your good food to tempt me."*

Cornelia who was nearby, saw a chance to say hello. *"I'm Cornelia — yes, we do eat well here. I moved here seven years ago. I was nearly homeless, and was eating the wrong food."* She waved to the array of dishes, breads, and desserts, *"This is the healthiest food in the world, all vegetarian, all organic, and grown in our own backyard. It is low in salt, sugar, fat, and cholesterol, so eat your heart out."* Ingrid and Cornelia talked steadily about food, gardening, nutrition, and the benefits of community.

After lunch, they all talked about community living, Eco Cities, and environmental education techniques. Several City Garden members escorted the tour group on the historic streetcars down Market Street back to the San Francisco regional train terminal to board a commuter train toward San Jose and catch another SLRT to their next visit: a newly built Octagonal Cluster House located on the edge of the Green Belt.

Doris briefed them on what they would see at the Octagonal House. *"Here is the ultimate in ecological group house design for an intergenerational extended family group. They have babies and octogenarians, and they use solar power for water heating and to generate their own electricity. The people who work outside the community all commute to their jobs by SLRT, Cal-Train, shuttle bus, or bicycle. Twenty people live in this compact village-like group house, but they live as ecologically as the Dear Valley and the other communities we visited. This will be your best chance to photograph this type of community group house. You will all get an Octagonal Cluster Ecological Design information packet, which goes into detail about their way of living and their natural energy systems."*

This time the elders of the house and several children were the welcoming entourage, because all the others were at work. The Octagonal House tour was conducted by the eldest elder, 84-year-old Hannah. When the other community members returned from work, Doris announced that dinner would be at a new Eco Village redesigned from an old shopping mall just two SLRT stops away.

The group got off at the SLRT stop located over a comfortable looking pedestrian street that used to be a glitzy shopping mall. Doris described how many regional shopping centers had gone out of business because of post WW II overbuilding, scandalous investments, decline of the US economy, and the closing of department stores due to fierce competition from warehouse stores. Fernando spoke up. *"I have lived in Mexico, Columbia, and Brazil, and I can tell you the gringo shopping center developers did not disappear from the face of the earth — they reappeared south of your border — trying to make consumers out of our people. It's a dirty trick to dangle fancy clothes and designer gadgets in front of village youth and low-paid working people. The profits go back up to northern banks and international corporations, not to the local people. I want to talk to people who work here about how this center is different."*

Anticipating that request, Doris had already contacted the community council manager. She introduced Heather who operated her own live-work clothes-making business. Heather told how the Community Development Bank financed a local Community Development Corporation to rebuild the center. She explained, *"In this redesigned shopping center, we have the same participatory involvement and dedication to social and environmental responsibilities as the smaller cluster communities you visited. The success of the community enterprises here comes from their trusting in the democratic self-management process. We try to operate as one whole social-economic enterprise community. Eco Villages are cutting unemployment and helping to stabilize the regional and local economy as well as providing a livelihood for more people, less strain on us as individuals, more free time, and stronger family ties. There has been a huge drop in gangs and violence, because this multi-service center offers jobs, youth activities, and personal empowerment. This is all a*

new experience for a lot of us Americans, and we're only beginning to learn how to do it."

She was interrupted by a question from Antoine from France. *"Please, what in your opinion is the one overall most influential policy to create this Eco Village and community system?"* Heather pondered for a few moments and responded. *"It has been people forming community, and it has been the building of the rail networks — throughout the USA as well as the local transit lines. The transit systems have become the blood veins that feed strong communities. When we were all driving our own car, the whole system came apart. Now we talk to each other — the trains really did it. But you from Europe and elsewhere must already know this."*

The group soon became immersed in the tour of the Eco Village community center. Of special interest during the tour were the rooftop gardens, live-work studios built on top of what used to be discount stores, and the permanent farmers' market set up in the old mall. The tour became extremely sociable because the many local live-work trades and crafts people, professionals, artists, and performers appeared along the converted arcades and shopping mall shaking hands, hugging, talking, and enticing the overwhelmed visitors to see their particular business or craft studio. The teachers tried to refuse the deluge of gifts, but when one of the local business people gave them two of the locally manufactured combination tote-cart/bicycle trailers to help carry their belongings, they could not refuse.

Doris thanked Heather, the center manager, and announced, *"We are now headed for our last ecological community in the Bay Area, Village Acre. You will stay there overnight before streaking to Los Angeles tomorrow afternoon on the Amtrak 'Golden*

Zephyr' to see how transit networks and Eco Villages have begun to weave that fragmented city together."

At the last SLRT stop on the urban fringe, and at the beginning of the permanent Green Belt along the California coast, they were met again by a bicycle fleet of enthusiastic residents to escort them to the Village Acre Community. Doris explained that the rural area they would be passing through was zoned as a permanent GreenBelt transition zone, which allowed one-acre to five-acre cluster communities, but only if certain ecologically sustainable criteria were met.

The bicycle procession rode into Village Acre and there in the parking lot was a noisy welcoming committee of children playing instruments and noisemakers. Susan, Gabriella, and Ronald showed their guests to sleeping nooks arranged in the common house and in the central social areas of the two group houses at Village Acre. In the morning, after a hilarious breakfast praising Village Acre's peach cobbler, they broke into small study groups with various Village Acre members to discuss the community solar energy design, elder care, conflict resolution, the grey water recycling system, home businesses, the straw-bale workshop building, gardens and orchards, parenting, and the childcare and teen activities.

Kieta asked a burning question. *"I am confused. You and all the other community people talk about ecological living and low consumption of resources and consumer products, but I see much luxury here in all your common houses', so much excellent kitchen equipment, beautiful furnishings, and telecommunication devices. How do …"*

Susan quickly spoke up to answer Kieta's obvious question. *"Well yes, we have good things —*

but divide what you see by the number of members at Village Acre, and you'll see we come out very low on the Energy Efficiency Ratio scale. I share with the rest of the community the top information highway technology; it serves us with valuable information we use in our daily work. But remember that most of our private living suites are really simple. Much of what you see is hand-made right here, and we share most of our possessions with each other. The common house is where we live our ecological beliefs — the more we share, the more we all have."

On the high-speed train trip to Los Angeles that afternoon, various people in the tour group engaged in vigorous discussions about how the various communities compared with ones in their countries, which ones they would like to live in and transport to their own countries. Rodriguez from Mexico reminded them that he was the official photographer on the trip, and that each would receive a VCR cassette later on so that they could show what they have seen about sustainable communities in America to their students. He added, *"You and the Americans performed beautifully. It is like a wonderful kaleidoscope of people, beautiful communities, Eco Villages, rich cultural diversity, and gardens, all well mixed with clean air, solar energy, peach cobbler, and efficient transit systems. We can be grateful. The time has come for us all to enjoy the future we once only dreamed about."*

* * * * * * *

Illustration by Chuck Trapkus; "In Context"

Life in the Eco Village Around the Transit Station

This is an intentional neighborhood designed and organized for social-environmental interaction. Balconies, porches, walkways, courtyards, outdoor eating tables, sitting areas, and lots of plants and trees help make it happen. Cars are no longer the predominate design influence on housing and land use patterns. People walk and bicycle to home and work. Eco Villages and Eco Cities are the place where people can communicate face to face, where there is family, and where children, youth, and elders belong.

There is a Time for Everything
— a marriage is under way

All that we have previously presented in this book carries the message that a marriage is a coming together — a worldly communion of positive forces. The last dialogue tells that this is the time to bring into union our blessings under the sun. We have had a time for tearing apart, and now we have a time for bringing us all together and rebuilding community in America.

In the previous chapters we presented how rebuilding community in America starts with the new extended family composed of adults, parents, children, elders, and friends as equals. The time has decidedly come to build many extended family Shared Living Communities. By increasing the nurturing goodness that can come from these new community groups, there can be a blossoming that extends to whole neighborhoods, Eco Villages and Eco Cities, and outward to the world.

We have had a time for building technology, spacecraft, industry, and weapons of destruction. Now it is time for us to build community. See this as an affirmation, a marriage ceremony that joins all peoples together in a joyous bond with the wonder and beauty of the natural forces that drive all living forms, porpoises, salamanders, flowers, oak trees, sparrows, lions, women, men, and children. Instinctively, we now turn to forgiveness of the past, ready to allow love to replace vengeance as we rise to new possibilities for social and environmental harmony.

Let us now create many common gathering places for nurturing each other. Just as the gathering place for Intentional Communities, Village

Wedding at N Street CoHousing

Photo by Kathryn Syroboyrasky

Clusters, and CoHousing is the dining table in the common house, there must be a gathering place for all in the neighborhood. Let us hold aloft the joy of places where people join in work, play, food, learning, giving and sharing, and in places for sitting, talking, walking, bicycling, and traveling in trains — as a community. Let our transportation devices take less space and less prominence. Let our gardens and orchards take more space and overflow with shared abundance. Let our human communion be further sanctified by joyful gatherings in protected natural places, where healthy connections with earth, sky, and water can be enjoyed by all.

"If you depreciate the sanctity and solemnity of marriage, not just as a bond between two people but as a bond between those two people and their forebears, their children, and their neighbors, then you have prepared the way for an epidemic of divorce, child neglect, community ruin, and loneliness. If you destroy the economies of household and community, then you destroy the bonds of mutual usefulness and practical dependence without which the other bonds will not hold." [33]
— Wendell Berry

"Acts of creation are ordinarily reserved for gods and poets, but humbler folks may circumvent this restriction if they know how. To plant a tree for example, one need be neither god nor poet; one needs only a shovel. By virtue of this curious loophole in the rules, any clodhopper may say: "Let there be a tree," and there will be one. If his back be strong and his shovel sharp, there may eventually be ten thousand. And in the seventh year he may lean upon his shovel, and look upon his trees, and find them good."[34]

— *Sand County Alamac,*
Aldo Leopold

Photo by Ken Norwood

Oak Tree Planted by Chris and Kathleen
during their Marriage Ceremony

Planting a Tree of Life

(Chris)
A tree is a special being,
A spirit with which we feel an intimate
connection.
Each lives its life to the fullest, opening wide
in a loving embrace with sun and sky.
Each bending in the winds of fate, joyful,
tenacious, and forever optimistic.

(Kathleen)
We place this tree in its home, in the nurturing soil, into the body of the earth,
A home which we all share.
We place it as a symbol of our love of life
and our faith in the future,
And to commemorate this moment of our
union of love and life together.

(Chris and Kathleen)
As the wind rustles its leaves,
May it whisper the story of this day,
Of two people in love,
And carry it in eternity across the lands and
seas for all to hear.

— Read by Christopher Gutsche & Kathleen
Smith as their marriage affirmation,
September 18, 1993

Photo by Greenbelt Alliance

Peach Cobbler and Friends
— a way to find community

This recipe is dedicated to the nurturing warmth, camaraderie, sense of belonging, and mouth-watering stimulation that occurs in a kitchen full of steamy aromas, talkative adults working together, and children bubbling with curiosity and eagerness to help. Making peach cobbler together is a fun way to bring human energy, the feeling of family, and community together. This occasion is at its greatest when the full ripe peaches are picked at a family outing to a local farmer's orchard, from trees in your own neighborhood, and especially from your own community orchard. There are many jobs to share for people of all ages — from two-year-olds helping older children wash the peaches, to the sage advice and tutoring of the 80 year-olds. The halving, pitting, and slicing of ripe peaches is a sensuous tactile, visual, olfactory, and audio experience — the smell of fresh peaches that permeates the air seems even more personal when it runs between the fingers and saturates the skin. Heating up of the sliced peaches really gets the juices flowing. The kitchen fills with a sugary, syrupy smell that mesmerizes all those present into silent contemplation of hot peach cobbler. At the same time, others have been mixing the dough, blending flour and spices and cracker crumbs. Preparing the dough is a pleasantly tactile experience whether the dough is rolled out with the rolling pin or kneaded with fingers and hands. Children want to do it because the pliable dough looks so touchable . After all, why should adults have all the fun?

Here is our peach cobbler recipe

- Ingredients for one pan, 8 x 12 x 1-1/2 inches deep.
  - 5 to 6 ripe, organic peaches
  - honey or brown sugar as needed for taste
  - season with cloves and/or cinnamon
  - 1 cup whole-wheat flour
  - 1 cup unbleached white flour
  - 1/2 cup moderate-fine graham cracker crumbs
  - 1/3 cup oil
  - 1/4 cup water
  - 2 tbsp sorghum molasses
- Preheat oven to 375 degrees F.
- Thinly slice peaches or cut into chunks and put into a cooking pot at low heat, but do not boil. Collect the juices that flow off your knives and fingers in a saucer and add to the pot.
- Add water and seasonings to the pot of peaches, and heat slowly until the liquid starts to simmer, then remove from the heat. Watch closely to determine the amount of juiciness. You do not want a thin juice, nor to cook out the flavors.
- Add sweeteners only if needed, subject to the sweetness of the peach.
- This no-yeast, no-shortening dough makes a chewy and tasty crust: Mix flours with graham cracker crumbs into a large bowl. Bring together the liquids, and add slowly, mixing well into the dry mix, blending until a doughy consistency is reached.
- Roll out or hand knead the dough into a flat, thin sheet (1/8th to 3/16th inch thick).
- Spread butter or vegetable oil on the sides and bottom of the pan. Place the dough sheets into the pan and shape to the sides.
- Spoon peaches into pans with some juice but not too liquidy, and cover the top with a sheet of dough or strips of dough.
- Bake for approximately 40 minutes.

•••• *Serve and celebrate your community* ••••

Notes

Books listed only by name in the endnotes are highlighted in the resource guide at the end of the book, complete with author/publisher information and description.

1 Condensed version, Jean Giono, <u>The Man Who Planted Trees</u>, Chelsea Green Publishing Co, Post Mills, VT. 05058, (800) 639-4099, 1985.

2 Ernest Callenbach, "Our Sustainable Future," Northern California ADPSR Bulletin, Vol. 2, No. 1. Jan./Feb. 1994, p. 2.

3 Wendell Berry, <u>Sex, Economy, Freedom, and Community</u>, Pantheon Books, New York, 1993, p. 148.

4 Tom Atlee, writing in *Think Peace*, Whole Earth Study Group, Oakland, CA.

5 Diana Alstad & Joel Kramer, <u>The Guru Papers</u>, North Atlantic Books/Frog, Ltd., 19??, p. 374.

6 Professor Sherman Lewis, *Neighborhood Systems: A Quarterly Journal,* May 1987, Vol. 1, No. 4, pp 3-52.

7 Wendell Berry, <u>Sex, Economy, Freedom, and Community</u>, Pantheon Books, New York, 1993, p. 126.

8 Walter Dickey, *In Context,* 1994, No. 38, p. 15.

9 *"Hollywood Drags Its Feet on Film and TV Violence,"* by Bernard Weinraub/NY Times, San Francisco Chronicle, December 29, 1993, p. E1.

10 Wendell Berry, <u>Sex, Economy, Freedom & Community,</u> Pantheon Books, 1993, pp. 123-124.

11 Manning Marable, "Racism and Multi-Cultural Democracy," *Poverty and Race,* Poverty and Race Research Action Council, Sept/Oct 1993, Vol. 2, p. 2.

12 Authur E. Morgan, *"Homo sapiens: The Community Animal,"* Claude Whitmyer, Editor, <u>In the Company of Others</u>, Jeremy P. Tarcher/Perigee, 1993, p.17.

13 Carl Anthony, *"Why Blacks Should Be Environmentalists,"* <u>Call to Action,</u> Edited by Brad Erickson, Sierra Club Books, 1990, p.144.

14 Ibid, p.149.

15 Anne Whiston Spirn, professor of landscape architecture and regional planning, University of Pennsylvania, in an article by Ruth Eckdish Knack, "Dig These Gardens," *Planning,* American Planning Association, Vol. 60, No. 7, July 1994, p. 21.

16 J.W.Smith, *Worlds Wasted Wealth 2,* Institute for Economic Democracy, Cambria, CA, 1994, p. 339

17 "Breast Cancer: What You Should Know," San Francisco Chronicle, October. 10, 1993.

18 Diana Alstad & Joel Kramer, <u>The Guru Papers</u>, p. 373.

19 Wendell Berry, <u>Sex, Economy, Freedom and Community,</u> Pantheon Books, New York, 1993.

20 Illustration no.116, Sir Raymond Unwin,.Talbot Hamlin, <u>Architecture Through th Ages,</u> GP Putmans Sons, New York, 1940, p. 620.

21 *Ibid,* Illustration no.115, Robert Owen, p.618.

22 Poem by Richard Register, <u>Ecocity Berkeley: Building Cities for a Healthy Future,</u> North Atlantic Books, Berkeley, CA, title page.

23 Ralph Grossi, President, American Farmland Trust, letter, January, 1994, p, 2.

24 Professor Sherman Lewis, *Neighborhood Systems: A Quarterly Journal,* Vol. 1, No. 4, May 1987, pp. 26-33.

25 Wendell Berry, p.168.

26 McCamant & Durrett, Bondebjerget: Four in One, <u>CoHousing,</u> Ten Speed Press, Berkeley, 1994, pp. 123-31.

27 Richard Tomalch, "British Discover Stations as Magnets for Development," *Moving People,* Modern Transit Society, Vol. XVI No. 4, Sept/ Oct 1993.

28 Peter Newman & Jeff Kenworthy with Les Robinson, <u>Winning Back the Cities,</u> Australian Consumers Association, 1992,p.7.

29 Professor Sherman Lewis, *Neighborhood Systems: A Quarterly Journal ,* Vol.2, No. 3, September, 1988, p.5.

30 Henry Holmes,"Social Justice," *The Urban Ecologist,* Summer 1993, p.6.

31 *"Stumbling Block or Stepping Stone,"* R. L. Sharpe,

32 Danial Burnham, Edited by Mary McLean, <u>Local Planning Administration,</u> Third edition, The International City Managers Association, Chicago< Ill., 1959, pp. 5-6.

33 Wendell Berry, <u>Sex, Economy, Freedom and Community,</u> Pantheon Books, New York, 1993, p. 125.

34 From the <u>Sand County Almanac,: Sketches Here and There</u> by Aldo Leopold, Oxford University Press, 1987

THE AUTHORS

Ken Norwood

Ken is an architect, planner, and member of the American Institute of Certified Planners (AICP), with over 40 years of experience. After receiving a B.A. in Architecture from the University of Southern California in 1952, Ken worked in the architectural and planning professions in Los Angeles until 1970, including five years with his own planning consulting and architectural practice. In the early 1970's, disillusioned due to the environmental degradation and social alienation he associated with the way conventional housing and commercial development practices used land and resources, he began his search for socially and environmentally responsible alternatives. He traveled in Europe and the U.S., working as a carpenter-architect, and visiting and living in various communities. In 1975-79, he served as master planner and architect for the Ananda Village Community in Nevada City, California, designing their main community building and helping finalize their master plan. He has designed numerous new and remodeled group houses. He has co-written for or been quoted in *Utne Reader, Open Exchange,* the <u>Directory of Intentional Communities</u>, <u>Macrocosm USA</u>, the <u>Cooperative Housing Compendium,</u> <u>Creating Community Anywhere</u>, and in newsletters and newspapers. He has lectured at the University of California at Berkeley, Stanford, the University of Southern California, and the New Jersey Institute of Technology. He has given over 150 presentations in the United States and Canada to groups exploring community alternatives, and has counseled hundreds of people interested in ecologically responsible Shared Living Communities. In the early 1980s he perceived the need for a book addressed to all people and which would support the widespread implementation of socially and environmentally responsible community design. In 1987 he founded the Shared Living Resource Center, and now serves as Executive Director.

Kathleen Smith

Kathleen is a designer, writer, and craftsperson who graduated from the University of California at Berkeley in 1991 with a B.A. in Architecture. She has done extensive research into ecological community design, non-toxic and sustainable building materials, and alternative building systems. In 1990, she co-founded the Berkeley Ecological Design Group to explore varying visions of ecology, social justice, community, and sustainability. With this group, she coordinated and facilitated a six-day conference at the College of Environmental Design at UC Berkeley. She has also been active with Architects/Designers/Planners for Social Responsibility (ADPSR), with whom she has volunteered as a writer, organizer, and consultant to research, experiment with, and educate about community and alternative building materials, systems, and practices. She has co-organized and given tours, workshops, and lectures on these topics, including the Healthy Building Conference in 1992. She has worked as a designer and carpenter on several projects, and as a cabinet maker/woodworker. From 1991 to 1994 she served as the Associate Director of SLRC. She has co-written articles for *Open Exchange,* <u>Macrocosm USA</u>, and the *ADPSR Bulletin,* and co-wrote and researched "Creating a Healthy Habitat," a healthy materials resource guide. Her own community experience includes four years of living in group houses and cooperatives. She now lives in Berkeley with her husband where she is working on her graduate degree in architecture. She plans to continue to pursue her interests in family, community, participatory design, and ecology in the hopes of helping to create environments that are healthy, sustainable, and enriching to the soul.

The co-authors would like to hear your comments about the book and Shared Living Communities.
Write to them c/o the Shared Living Resource Center, 2375 Shattuck Avenue, Berkeley, CA 94704.

THE SHARED LIVING RESOURCE CENTER

2375 Shattuck Avenue Berkeley, CA 94704
(510) 548-6608

The Shared Living Resource Center (SLRC) in Berkeley, California was founded in 1987 by Ken Norwood, an architect and planner. The primary mission of SLRC is to study, promote, and develop Shared Living Communities that are affordable, socially supportive, and ecologically sustainable. SLRC has created several prototypes of such communities including the Village Cluster, Urban Cooperative Block, Octagonal Cluster House, and Solar Earth House to demonstrate how a community can be intentionally designed and organized to provide the opportunity for co-ownership, co-management, gender and racial equality, energy and resource conservation, reduced use of the automobile, a supportive intergenerational extended family, and a balance between privacy and community. These communities are envisioned to ultimately form the basis for Eco Village and Eco City development.

Since 1990, SLRC has operated as a nonprofit [501(c)(3)] corporation, providing educational, promotional, and design development services to people of all incomes, ages, and ethnic backgrounds who are interested in learning about and forming ecologically sustainable communities. Current services include lectures, slide presentations, workshops, profile/consultation sessions, and ecological planning, design, and development for urban and rural communities. SLRC also provides group facilitation, planning, and design services for extended family group houses, Limited Equity Housing Cooperatives, and Village Cluster type communities with an emphasis on passive solar and natural energy design, and alternative structural systems. Future plans include computer-based networking to support all of the above. SLRC will also be releasing other publications, guidelines, articles, and informational brochures that expand upon the topics included in Rebuilding Community in America. Articles and features about the work of SLRC have appeared in numerous newsletters, newspapers and on cable TV and radio shows. This book is the center's most comprehensive education endeavor. Please contact us for more information.

---

copy this form and send it in

If you would like to purchase more copies of Rebuilding Community in America, or to become a member of Shared Living Resource Center, or make a contribution to SLRC, please send us this form. Call for discount rates on orders of five or more books. For qauntity dicount and Visa and Master Card ordering, call: (1-800) 475-7572

Name _____

Address _____

City _____ State _____ ZIP _____

Phone _____

Number of books: _____ @ $24.50 (up to five) $_____
$3 shipping/handling for 1st, $1.50 each additional $_____
(sales tax included in California)
Membership fee (includes publication mailings) $_____
($15 Simple living & Seniors; $25 Professionals & Groups)

Tax-deductible contribution to SLRC of $_____

TOTAL ENCLOSED $_____

RESOURCE GUIDE

We have created a representative list of key organizations and communities around the country, and newsletters, periodicals, and books to aid you in your search for ecologically sustainable and socially supportive community. We have not tried to create a completely comprehensive list, because other literature, such as the *Directory of Intentional Communities, Macrocosm USA,* and the *Cooperative Housing Compendium* have already done an excellent job at creating such lists. Good Luck!

COMMUNITIES

The following is a list of all the communities we highlight in the book, plus a few key others that you may want to explore.

Alpha Farm
Deadwood, OR 97430
(503) 964-5102

Ananda Village
14618 Tyler Foote Rd.
Nevada City, CA 95959
(916) 292-4100

Ananda Community of Palo Alto
240 Monroe Dr.
Mountain View, CA 94040
(415) 941-9507

Covenant House
346 West 17th St.
New York, NY 10011
(212) 727-4000
1-800-999-9999 (Hotline for children)

Doyle Street CoHousing Community
5514 Doyle St.
Emeryville, CA 94608
(510) 655-7399
Contact: Joani Blank

Dwight Way Shelter and Transistional House
(510) 841-2789

EcoVillage at Ithaca
c/o Center for Religion, Ethics, and Social Policy
Anabel Taylor Hall
Cornell University
Ithaca, NY 14853
(607) 255-8276

Elizabeth House
PO Box 1175
Berkeley, CA 94701
(510) 237-9973
Contact: Martha McCarthy

Fairfax Vest Pocket Community
c/o Innovative Housing
2169 E. Francisco Blvd., Suite E
San Rafael, CA 94901
(415) 457-4593
Contact: Debbie Greiff

Ganas Community
135 Corson Ave.
Staten Island, NY 10301
(718) 720-5378
Contact: Susan Grossman

Muir Commons CoHousing
2236 Muirwoods Place
Davis, CA 95616
(916) 753-4638
Contact: Cathy DuVair

N Street CoHousing
724 N Street
Davis, CA 95616
(916) 758-4211
Contact: Kevin Wolf or Linda Cloud

Nyland CoHousing Community
3501 Nyland Way South
Lafayette, CO 80026
(303) 499-8915
Contact: Sumati Fernie

OnGoing Concerns
1905 NE Going
Portland, OR 97211
(503) 284-8870
Contact: Diane Meisenhelter

Raphael House
1065 Sutter
San Francisco, CA 94109
(415) 474-4621

Sandhill Farm
Route 1, Box 155-D
Rutledge, MO 63563
(816) 883-5543

Shannon Farm
Route 2, Box 343
Afton, VA 22920
(804) 361-1180

Sirius Community
Baker Rd.
Shutesbury, MA 01072
(413) 259-1251

Southside Park CoHousing
438 T Street
Sacramento, CA 95814
(916) 444-2712
Contact: Bob O'Brien

Twin Oaks
Route 4, Box 169-D
Louisa, VA 23093
(703) 894-5126

Village Homes
2655 Portage Bay Ave. E
Davis, CA 95616
(916) 753-6345
Contact: Sheila Kenward

Winslow CoHousing Group
353 Wallace Way NE
Bainbridge Island, WA 98110
(206) 780-1323

PERIODICALS, & NEWSLETTERS

The organizations, periodicals, and newsletters listed below provide a myriad of services and information about topics covered in this book. (Newsletters and periodicals are in italics.)

AFM Enterprises Inc.
1140 Stacy Ct.
Riverside, CA 92507
(714) 781-6860
(Supplier of non-toxic products for the chemically senitive and environmentally aware: paints, stains, and sealants.)

The Alternatives Center
1740 Walnut St.
Berkeley, CA, 94709
(510) 540-5387
publishes: *Converting Multi-Unit Buildings into Limited Equity Cooperatives* and *Buying a House as an Investment: A Cautionary Tale*

American Farmland Trust
1920 N Street, NW, Suite 400
Washington D.C. 20036
(202) 659-5170
publishes: *Farmland Update*

Appropriate Technology Institute
P O Box 70601
Seattle, WA 98107
(Designs hybrid energy systems and roof
structures for buildings)

**Architects/Designers/Planners
for Social Responsibility**
Northern California Chapter
PO Box 9126
Berkeley, CA 94709-0126
(510) 273-2428
publishes: *ADPSR Bulletin* and *The Guide to
Creating a Healthy Habitat*

Building with Nature Newsletter
PO Box 369
Gualala, CA 95445
(707) 884-4513
Contact: Carol Venolia

California Action Network
PO Box 464
Davis, CA 95617
(916) 756-8518
publishes: *Agrarian Advocate*
and *Organic Wholesalers Directory*

**California Association of Cooperatives/
California Association of Member Owned
Organizations**
3561 Woodley Dr.
San Jose, CA 95148
(408) 274-0753 or (916) 753-8857
publishes: *Newsletter*

California Association of Family Farmers
PO Box 363
Davis, CA 95617
(916) 756-8518
publishes: *Farm Link*

California Certified Organic Farmers
PO Box 8136
Santa Cruz, CA 95061-8136
(408) 423-2263
publishes: *California Organic Farmer's
Statewide Newsletter*

California Mutual Housing Association
Northern California Office
1678 Shattuck Ave. #72
Berkeley, CA 94709
(510) 548-4087
Contact: Dave Kirkpatrick

California Mutual Housing Association
Southern California Office
2500 Wilshire Blvd.
Los Angeles, CA 90057
(213) 385-5365
Contact: David Etezadi

Center for Communal Studies
8600 University Blvd.
University of Southern Indiana
Evansville, IN 47712
(812) 464-1727

Center for Cooperative Housing
1614 King St.
Alexandria, VA 22314-2719
(703) 684-3185
Contact: R. Ted Stewart

Center for Cooperatives
University of California
Davis, CA 95616
(916) 752-2408
publishes: *The Co-op Quarterly*

The Cob Cottage Company
P O Box 123
Cottage Grove, OR 97424
(503) 942-3021
Researxches and teaches natural building
techniques, includes hand-molded earth

Cohousing Center, Inc.
103 Morse St.
Watertown, MA 02172
(617) 923-1300
Contact: Mino Sullivan
publishes: *The Cohousing Center News* and
Neighborhoods of Tomorrow

The CoHousing Company
1250 Addison St., #113
Berkeley, CA 94702
(510) 549-9980

CoHousing Journal
The CoHousing Network
PO Box 2584
Berkeley, CA 94702
(510) 526-6124 (business)
(303) 494-8458 (editorial)

**Committee for Sustainable
Agriculture**
PO Box 1300
Colfax, CA 95713
(916) 346-2777
publishes: *Organic Food Matters* and
organizes Ecological Farming Conference

***Communities: Journal of Cooperative
Living***
1118 Round Butte Drive
Fort Collins, CO 80524
(303) 490-1550
(A quarterly dedicated to exploring issues
affecting communities)

Community Service, Inc.
PO Box 243
Yellow Springs, OH 45387
(513) 767-2161 or 767-1461
publishes: *Community Service Newsletter*

Co-op America Quarterly
Co-op America
1850 M. St. NW, Suite 700
Wahington DC 20063
1-800-58-GREEN

**Cooperative Resources and
Services Project (CRSP)/
LA EcoVillage**
PO Box 27731
Los Angeles, CA 90027
(213) 738-1254
Contact: Lois Arkin
publishes: *Networker*

Earth Island Institute
300 Broadway, Suite 28
San Francisco, CA 94133
(415) 788-3666
publishes: *Earth Island Journal*

EarthSave Foundation
706 Frederick St.
Santa Cruz, CA 95062
(408) 423-4069
publishes: *EarthSave Newsletter*
and *Our Food Our World*
(Dedicated to create a healthy world by
encouraging a plant-based diet.)

Earthword: The Journal for Environmental and Social Responsibility
Eos Institute
580 Broadway, Suite 200
Laguna Beach, CA 92651
(714) 497-1896
Contact: Lynn Bayless:

Ecology Center
2530 San Pablo Ave.
Berkeley, CA 94702
(510) 548-2220
publishes: *The Terrain*

Environmental Building News
RR 1, Box 161
Brattleboro, VT 05301
(802) 257-7300

Family Farm Series
Small Farm Center
University of California
Davis, CA 95616
(916) 757-8910

Fellowship for Intentional Community
PO Box 814
Langley, WA 98260
(206) 221-3064
Contact: Betty Didcoct

Greenbelt Alliance
116 New Montgomery St., Suite 640
San Francisco, CA 94105
(415) 543-4291
publishes: *Greenbelt Action*

Growing Community Associates
PO Box 5415
Berkeley, CA 94705
(510) 869-4878
Contact: Carolyn Shaffer or Sandra Lewis

Growing Community Newsletter
1118 Round Butte Dr.
Fort Collins, CO 80524
(303) 490-1550

Habitat International
121 Habitat St.
Americus, GA 31709-3498
1-800-HABITAT

Heartwood Timber Structures
RR 1, Box 115F
Fairfield, IA 52556
(515) 472-7775
Contact: Robert LaPorte
(Offers design, construction, and consultation services, as well as workshops on natural
building systems with a special interest in
workshops for Intentional Communities.)

Human Investment Project
364 South Railroad
San Mateo, CA 94401
(415) 348-0284
publishes: *HIP Happenings*

Innovative Housing
2169 E. Francisco Blvd., Ste. E
San Rafael, CA 94901
(415) 457-4593

In Context: A Quarterly of Humane
Sustainable Culture
PO Box 11470
Bainbridge Island, WA 98110
(206) 842-0216

Informed Consent:
The Magazine of Health, Prevention,
& Environmental News
International Institute of Research for
Chemical Hypersensitivity
PO Box 1984
Williston, ND 58802-1984
(701) 774-7760

Institute for Community
Economics (ICE)
57 School St.
Springfield, MA 01105-1331
(413) 746-8660
publishes: *Community Economics*

Interior Concerns
PO Box 2386
Mill Valley, CA 94942
(415) 389-8049
publishes: *Interior Concerns Resource Guide*
and *Interior Concerns Newsletter*
(Provides information and design and
consulting services to people interested in
non-toxic building materials and design.)

International Institute for
Bau-Biologie and Ecology, Inc.
Box 387
Clearwater, FL 34615
(813) 461-4371
Contact: Helmut Ziehe
publishes: *IBE Newsletter*
(Helps people resolve environmental dangers
in their home and work environment.)

Land Utilization Alliance
PO Box 1259
Stockton, CA 95201
(209) 467-7554
publishes: *Land Utilization Alliance News*

Modern Transit Society
PO Box 161362
Sacramento, CA 95816
(916) 443-1529
publishes: *Moving People*

National Association
of Housing Cooperatives
1614 King St.
Alexandria, VA 22316-2719
(703) 549-5201
publishes: *Cooperative Housing Bulletin*
(bimonthly) and *Cooperative Housing*
Journal (annually)

National Shared Housing
Resource Center
321 E. 25th. St.
Baltimore, MD 21218
(410) 235-4454
publishes: *Shared Housing News* and *Shared*
Housing for Older People

The Natural Building Network
PO Box 1110
Sebastopol, CA 95473
(707) 823-2569 or (510) 841-1039
publishes: *Building Naturally: A Guide to*
Professionals and a Compendium of Articles

Natural Environments
1618 Parker St.
Berkeley, CA 94703
(510) 841-1039
Contact: David Kibbey
(Conducts environmental home and
workplace inspections and consults on
healthy building materials and design).

North American Students
of Cooperation
(NASCO)
PO Box 7715
Ann Arbor, MI 48107
(313) 663-0889

Northwest CoHousing Quarterly
711 W. 11th
Eugene, OR 97402
(503) 343-5739

Northwest Intentional Communities
Association
22020 East Lost Lake Rd.
Snohomish, WA 98290
(206) 936-7157
Contact: Rob Sandelin
publishes: *Northwest Intentional Communi-*
ties Association Newsletter

Out On Bale (un)Ltd.
1037 East Linden St.
Tucson, AZ 85719
(602) 624-1673
publishes: *The Last Straw*
(A clearinghouse for Straw-Bale construction
information. Offers seminars, workshops,
designing, and supervised wall raisings.)

The Permaculture Activist
Rte 1, Box 38
Primm Springs, TN 38476
(615) 583-2294

The Planet Drum Foundation
PO Box 31251
San Francisco,
Shasta Bioregion, CA 94131
(415) 285-6556
publishes: *Raise the Stakes*
(Advocates bioregionalism.)

Planners Network
1601 Connecticut Ave. NW, 5th Flr.
Washington D.C. 20009
(202) 234-9382
publishes: *Planners Network*

Poverty & Race Research Action Council
1711 Connecticut Ave. NW, Suite 207
Washington, DC 20009
(202) 387-9887
publishes: *Poverty & Race*

Puget Sound Cohousing Network
22020 East Lost Lake Rd.
Snohomish, WA 98290
(206) 936-7157
Contact: Rob Sandelin

RAIN
PO Box 30097
Eugene, OR 97403-1097
(Magazine dedicated to economically self-reliant, ecological communities & regions).

Real Goods
966 Mazzoni St.
Ukiah, CA 95482-3471
(800) 762-7325
publishes: *Alternative Energy Sourcebook* and a catalog of alternative energy products.

Resurgence
US Office: Rodale Press
33 East Minor St.
Emmaus, PA 18049
(215) 967-5171
(Provides world-wide news on pressing political, ecological, and social issues.)

Rocky Mountain CoHousing Association
1705 14th St. #317
Boulder, CO 80302
(303) 494-8458

San Francisco League of Urban Gardeners, (SLUG),
2088 Oakdale Avenue,
San Francisco, CA 94124,
(415) 285-7586
Sponsors Community Gardens and organic gardening training; The Director is Mohammed Nuru.

School of Living
Route 1, Box 185-A
Cochranville, PA 19330
publishes: *Green Revolution*)
(Explores decentralization, cooperative living, and land reform, and administers Community Land Trust alliance.)

Shared Living Resource Center
2375 Shattuck Ave.
Berkeley, CA 94704
(510) 548-6608
Contact: Ken Norwood
(Provides educational publications, counseling, slide-talks, workshops, and planning and design services for Shared Living Communities.

Sun Frost - Lo Energy Refrigerators
PO Box 1101
Arcata, CA 95521
(707) 822-9095
Contact: Larry Schlussler

Sustainable Agriculture Research and Education Center
University of California, Davis
Davis, CA 95616
(916) 752-755
publishes: *Sustainable Agriculture News*

Sustainable Urban Neighborhoods
3116 N. Williams
Portland, OR 97227
(503) 284-7868
publishes: *The SUN*

Targeting Times
Coalition for Low-Income Community Development
513 N. Chapel Gate Lane
Baltimore, MD 21229
(410) 945-2835

Thinkpeace
Whole Earth Study Group
6622 Tremont St.
Oakland, CA 94609
(510) 654-0349
(Forums for ways to build peaceful, life-affirming, sustainable, and wise cultures.)

Timeweave
PO Box 348
Boulder, CO 80306
(303) 939-8463
publishes: *Strands of the Weave*
(Seeks to influence cultural evolution through cooperative and sustainable living.)

Trust for Public Land
116 New Montgomery St., 3rd Floor
San Francisco, CA 94105
(415) 495-5660
publishes: *Trust for Public Land: Conserving Land for People*

Urban Ecology
PO Box 10144
Berkeley, CA 94709
(510) 549-1724
publishes: *The Urban Ecologist*

Worldwatch Institute
1776 Massachusetts Ave., NW
Washington, DC 20036-1904
(202) 452-1999
publishes: *WorldWatch Magazine,*

Worldwatch Papers, State of the World, and *Vital Signs.*

BOOKS

There are many aspects of community, Eco City planning and design, environmental issues, and sustainable building materials and techniques that this book has only touched upon. If you are interested in finding out more about any of these topics, some of these titles may be of interest. (We used many of these books in our own research.)

Alternative House Building, Mike McClintock, Sterling Publishing Co., New York, 1989. (Guide to building techniques for self-construction, energy efficiency, and use of local and ecological materials. Includes rammed earth, earth shelter, pole construction and others. Excellent resource)

Ancient Futures: Learning from Ladakh, Helena Norberg-Hodge, Sierra Club Books, San Francisco, 1991. (Through the story of the native people of Ladakh, a region in the Himalayan highlands, this book explores the causes of the malaise of industrial society and how gentler ways of living are possible.)

Architecture without Architects: A Short Introduction to Non-Pedigreed Architecture, Bernard Rudolfsky, Doubleday, Garden City, New York, 1964. (A fresh look at communal architecture — architecture produced not by specialists but by the spontaneous and continuing activity of a people with a common heritage and common experience.)

Builders of the Dawn: Community Lifestyles in a Changing World, Corinne McLaughlin and Gordon Davidson, Stillpoint Publishing, Walpole, NH, 1985. (An overview of community lifestyles, interviews with founders, and extensive guidelines for building communities.)

Call To Action: Handbook for Ecology, Peace, and Justice, edited by Brad Erickson, Sierra Club Books, San Francisco, 1990. (Explains the connection between environmental and social concerns, and proposes solutions. Great resource lists.)

Ceramic Houses: How to Build Your Own, Nader Khalili, Harper and Row, Publishers, San Francisco, 1986. (Shows how to glaze, and fire adobe and rammed earth buildings that resist sun, rain, and earthquakes.)

Cohousing: A Contemporary Approach to Housing Ourselves, Second Edition, Kathryn McCamant and Charles Durrett with Ellen Hertzman, Ten Speed Press, Berkeley, CA, 1994. (Case studies of CoHousing communities in Europe and the United States with illustrations, photographs, and personal experiences.)

Collaborative Communities: Cohousing, Central Living and New Forms of Housing with Shared Facilities, Dorit Fromm, Van Nostrand Reinhold, New York, 1991. (Addresses the issues in and obstacles to creating cooperative ownership, congregate housing, and community.)

Commitment and Community: Communes and Utopias in Sociological Perspective, Rosabeth Moss Kanter, Harvard Univ. Press, Cambridge, MA, 1972. (A classic sociological study of communities of the 1800s and 1960s - somewhat dated, but still of interest.)

Communes, Law, and Commonsense: A Legal Manual for Communities, Lee Goldstein, New Community Projects, Boston, 1974. (Basic know-how related to municipal ordinances, real estate transactions, and partnership agreements.)

Communities Directory: A Guide to Cooperative Living, Fellowship for Intentional Community, PO Box 814, Langley, WA 98260, (206) 221-3064, 1994. (Articles on different aspects of community living and a directory of Intentional Communities around the world with descriptions and contact information.)

Community Group Homes: An Environmental Approach, Architecture, Research, Construction, Inc., Van Nostrand Reinhold Company, New York, 1985. (A survey of 35 group homes evaluating how various design options meet the special needs of the residents, and guidelines for interior and exterior designis with emphasis on making them more communal and supportive.)

Community Land Trust Handbook, E.F. Schumacher Society, Box 76, RD 3, Great Barrington, MA 02130, (413) 528-1737. (Carefully complied legal documents and lease agreements required for do-it-yourself community land trusts.)

The Consumer's Guide to Earth Sheltered Housing, Mary Rollwagon, Susan Taylor, and T. Lance, Van Nostrand Reinhold Publishers, New York, 1983. (A consumers guide in non-technical terms, that addresses zoning, construction, and underground house models, and how to find assistance.)

Consuming Passions: The Anthropology of Eating, Peter Farb and George Armelagos, Houghton Mifflin, Boston, 1980. (Explores the pivotal role of food in every society.)

Cooperative Housing Compendium: Resources for Collaborative Living, Lottie Cohen and Lois Arkin, Center for Cooperatives, University of California, Davis, 1993. (Descriptions of types of cooperative living arrangements and methods for establishing them. Great resource guide and glossary.)

Creating Community Anywhere: Finding Support and Connection in a Fragmented World, Carolyn R. Shaffer and Kristin Anundsen, Jeremy P. Tarcher/Perigee, Los Angeles, 1993. (Explores opportunities for creating community in our daily lives. Includes guidelines for effective communication, conducting meetings, making group decisions, and resolving conflicts.)

The Different Drum: Community Making and Peace, M. Scott Peck, Simon and Schuster, New York, 1987. (Shows how to make the leap from individual growth to small community groups, and ultimately to global community.)

Directory of Shared Housing Programs and Resources, National Shared Housing Resource Center, 431 Pine St., Burlington, VT 05401, 1993. (Lists programs and resources throughout the United States. Listings relate to senior shared housing.)

Discrimination by Design: A Feminist Critique of the Man Made Environment, Leslie Kanes Weisman, Univ. of Illinois Press, Urbana, 1991. (Presents feminist themes from a spatial perspective and documents how a variety of settings transmit privileges and penalties of social caste.)

Dewlling on Earth, David Easton, Blue Mountain Press, Wilseyville, CA. (Methods and technology for building rammed earth houses. Also by this author: *The Rammed Earth Experience.*)

Earth in the Balance: Ecology and Human Spirit, Al Gore, Houghton Mifflin Co., New York, 1992. (Demonstrates that the origins of our environmental problems transcend every aspect of society and urges a radical change in our relationship with nature.)

Ecocity Berkeley: Building Cities for a Healthy Future, Richard Register, North Atlantic Books, Berkeley, CA, 1987. (Presents the concept of ecologically healthy cities and suggests ways for people to transform existing cities and towns.)

Ecotopia, Ernest Callenbach, Bantam Books, New York, 1975. (A novel that explores the possibility of an environmentally and socially conscious society which secedes from the United States.)

End of the Road: The World Car Crisis and How We Can Solve It, Wolfgang Zuckerman, Chelsea Green Publishing Company, Rte 113, PO Box 130, Post Mills, Vermont 05058, 1991. (A systematically laid out case against the automobile, listing steps to solve the "car crisis.")

Entropy, A New World View, Jeremy Rifkin, with Ted Howard, Bantam Books, New York, 1980. (Explains the breakdown of the industrial society world order and urges us to rethink our social system.)

Envirnmental by Design: A Sourcebook of Environmentally Aware Material Choices, Kim LeClair and David Rousseau, Hartley and Marks, Inc., Pt.Roberts, WA, 1992. (Comprehensive list of environmentally safe materials with a system for evaluating and comparing materials. A professional version in a 3 ring binder is also available.)

The Essential Whole Earth Catalogue: Access to Tools and Ideas, Doubleday & Co., New York, 1986. (Brief reviews of just about everything you need for cooperative living aligned with ecological ideals.)

Gendered Spaces, Daphne Spain, University of North Carolina Press, Chapel Hill, 1992. (Shows how the physical and symbolic barriers that separate men and women in the office, at home, and at school block women's access to the socially valued knowledge that enhances status.)

Habits of the Heart: Individualism and Commitment in American Life, Robert N. Bellah, Harper and Row, Publishers, New York, 1985. (Presents the conflict between Americans' fierce individualism and their urgent need for community and commitment.)

The Healthy House: How to Buy One, How to Cure a Sick One, and How to Build One, John Bower, Carol Communications, Secaucus, NJ, 1989. (Avoiding toxic construction materials and ensuring healthy air and water quality in your home.)

Housing As if People Mattered: Site Design Guidelines for Medium Density Housing, Clare Cooper Marcus and Wendy Sarkissan, University of California Press, Berkeley, CA, 1986. (Guidelines for designing between and around clustered units to address the values and needs of the users and create a sense of community.)

How Buildings Learn: What Happens After They're Built, Stewart Brand, Viking Press, New York, 1994. (Explores buildings through time — how they adapt and change to the life within them. It asks the questions "what makes some buildings come to be loved and how can we work with time to preserve and enhance buildings.")

How the Other Half Builds, Vol. 1: Space, Centre for Minimum Cost Housing, McGill University, 3550 University St., Montreal, P.Q., Canada H3A 2B1, 1984. (Results of a study based in India to examine the success of the housing created by the poor given)

In Praise of Single Parents: Mothers and Fathers Embracing the Challenge, Shoshana Alexander, Houghton Mifflin Company, New York, 1994. (A powerful account of the struggles and joys of raising a child alone.)

In the Absence of the Sacred: The Failure of Technology and the Survival of the Indian Nations, Jerry Mander, Sierra Club Books, San Francisco, 1991. (Mander urges that our increasingly technological society must develop an appreciation for the sacredness of nature and the limits to human endeavor, values long respected by native peoples.)

In the Company of Others: Making Community in the Modern World, edited by Claude Whitmyer, Jeremy P. Tarcher/Perigee, Los Angeles, 1993. (Brings together various writers to offer guidance in starting community. Includes ways to deal with economic and emotional difficulties that arise when we live and work closely with others.)

The Integral Urban House: Self Reliant Living in the City, Farallones Institute, Sierra Club Books, San Francisco, CA, 1979. (Manual for the design of self-sufficient, resource-efficient urban housing.)

Intentional Communities: How to Start Them and Why, J. Donald Waters, Crystal Clarity, Nevada City, CA, 1968. (Offers both a historical view of the successes and failures of communities worldwide, and a number of practical suggestions for starting and maintaining communities with a spiritual base.)

Living by Design: Ecology and the Making of Sustainable Places, Sim Van Der Ryn and Stuart Cowan, Island Press, Covelo, CA, 1995. (Explores the complex relationship of ecology and design, offering an understandable five step process for creating a place that is sustainable and enriching.)

Macrocosm USA: Possibilities for a New Progressive Era, edited by Sandi Brockway, Macrocosm USA, Inc, Cambria, CA, 1992. (Handbook with more than 200 articles and 5000 listings of progressive organizations, periodicals, media outlets, businesses, and reference sources. Identifies today's problems and offers comprehensive and holistic solutions.)

More Other Homes and Garbage: Designs for Self-Sufficient Living, Jim Leckie, Gil Masters, Harry Whitehouse, and Lily Young, Sierra Club Books, San Francisco, 1981. (The theory behind and practical application of self-sufficient living methods including: alternative architecture, generation of electricity, waste-handling, water supply, and agriculture.)

The Natural House Book: Creating a Healthy, Harmonious, and Ecologically Sustainable Home, David Pearson, Simon & Schuster Inc., New York, 1989. (A comprehensive hand-book on how to turn any home into a sanctuary for enhancing your well-being. Includes suggestions for using non-toxic materials, improving air and water quality, and saving energy.)

New Households, New Housing, edited by Karen Franck and Sherry Ahrentzen, Van Nostrand Reinhold, New York, 1989. (Detailed information on the design, planning, and management of alternative housing for the non-traditional household.)

The New Solar Home Book, Bruce Anderson with Michael Riordan, Brick House Publishing, Inc., Andover, MA, 1987. (Information on passive solar heating and solar powered electricity in simple, non-technical terms with many diagrams and sketches.)

The Nontoxic Home and Office: Protecting Yourself and Your Family from Everyday Toxics and Health Hazards, Debra Lynn Dadd, Jeremy P. Tarcher, Inc., Los Angeles, 1992. (How to eliminate toxic products and create a healthy home environment.)

The One Straw Revolution: An Introduction to Natural Farming, Masanobu Fukuoka, Rodale Press, Emmaus, PA, 1978. (Proposes that healing of the land and purification of the human spirit are one process achieved through natural farming.)

Ourselves and Our Children: A Book by and for Parents, Boston Women's Health Book Collective, Random House, New York, 1978. (Explores issues related to parenthood and the different forms that families take. Excellent resource lists.)

Partnering: A Guide to Co-owning Anything From Homes to Home Computers, Lois Rosenthal, Writers Digest Books, Cincinnati, OH, 1983. (Advice on co-ownership. Includes sample agreements and tests to determine the partnering aptitude of you and your potential co-owner.)

A Pattern Language: Towns, Buildings, Construction, Christopher Alexander, et.al., Oxford University Press, New York, 1977. (2nd in a series. An archetypal language and working document which allows lay persons to design for themselves.)

Permaculture: A Designer's Manual, Bill Mollison, Tagari Publishers, Tyalgum, Australia, 1988. (Manual for designing sustainable human settlements which preserve and extend natural systems.)

Pole Building Construction, Doug Merilees and Evelyn Loveday, Garden Way Publishing, Charlotte, VT, 1975. (Information for every step of building a low-cost pole constructed home: plans, materials, etc.)

Policy Before Planning: Solving California's Growth Problems, Judith Kunofsky, et. al. Sierra Club California's 1991 Green State of the State Report. (Policies to address the growth-management issues facing California's communities.)

The Political Culture of Planning: American Land Use Planning in Comparative Perspective, J. Berry Cullingworth, Routledge, Inc., New York, 1993. (Compares the methods of land use planning used in Canada, England, and the United States by local, state, and federal government.)

Prolonging the Good Years, Doris Berdahl, Innovative Housing, Inc., San Rafael. (Guidelines for planning and implementing nonprofit sponsored shared housing programs for seniors.)

Putting Democracy to Work: A Practical Guide for Starting Worker-Owned Businesses, Gary Hansen and Frank Adams, Hulogosi's Communications, Eugene, OR, 1987. (Important information for forming a worker-owned business as an economic base for a cooperative community.)

Redesigning the American Dream: The Future of Housing, Work, and Family Life, Dolores Hayden, W.W. Norton, New York, 1984. (Alternatives to our current housing patterns which don't meet the 20th Century concerns of transportation, marriage, divorce, aging, and women's employment. Another pertinent book by Hayden is *Seven American Utopias*.)

Shared Housing for Older People: A Planning Manual for Group Residences, Dennis Day-Lower, Shared Housing Resource Center, Burlington, VT, 1983. (Explores the steady emergence of shared housing alternatives for seniors. Also: *Designing Shared Housing For the Elderly, Social and Architectural Considerations*.)

Site Planning for Cluster Housing, Richard Unterman and Robert Small, Van Nostrand Reinhold, New York, 1977. (It provides, in layman's terms, information on site planning, design and scale, and open space planning for cluster housing.)

The Small Community: Foundation of Democratic Life, Arther E. Morgan, Community Service Books, Yellow Springs, OH, 1984. (Definitive work on the significance and potentials of the small community.)

Small Places: In Search of a Vanishing America, Thomas H. Rawls, Little, Brown, Boston, 1990. (Explores the traditions and sense of community and the isolation and lack of opportunity that have alternately plagued the small towns of America.)

Solar Home Book: Heating, Cooling, and Designing with the Sun, Bruce Anderson and Michael Riordan, Cheshire Books, Harrisville, NH, 1976. (Reference and guide book for architects, solar enthusiasts and homeowners with ideas and detailed information on how to capture the sun's energy. Includes the design, technology, and history of solar heating and cooling.)

Space and Place: The Perspective of Experience, Yi-Fu Tuan, University of Minnesota Press, 1977. (Considers the ways in which people feel and think about spaces and places.)

State of the World: A Worldwatch Institute Report on Progress Toward a Sustainable Society, Lester Brown, W. W. Norton and Co., New York. (A new edition is published every year to provide in-depth analysis of global environmental trends and problems. Other Worldwatch books: *Saving the Planet, How Much is Enough,* and *Last Oasis*.)

Sustainable Communities: A New Design Synthesis for Cities, Suburbs, and Towns, Sim Van Der Ryn and Peter Calthorpe, Sierra Club Books, San Francisco, 1986. (A vision of how different types af American communities can make the transition to a sustainable, resource conserving, socially and economically healthy way of life.)

Sustainable Cities: Concepts and Strategies for Eco-City Development, edited by Bob Walter, Lois Arkin, and Richard Crenshaw, Eco-Home Media, Los Angeles, 1992. (A collection of writings from experts in many disciplines discussing how urban development and the environment can coexist in a healthy and sustainable way.)

The Timeless Way of Building, Christopher Alexander, Oxford University Press, New York, 1979. (A new theory of architecture, building, and planning for a new traditional post-industrial architecture created by the people.)

Toxic Struggles: The Theory and Practice of Environmental Justice, ed. Richard Hofricher, New Society Publishers, 4527 Springfield Ave., Philadelphia, PA 19143, 1993. (Documents the environmental movement led by people of color, women, and low-income and working -class population.)

The Unsettling of America: Culture and Agriculture, Wendell Berry, Sierra Club Books, San Francisco, 1977. (In this and his many other books, Berry uses his talents as a teacher, poet, and farmer to look into our relationships with nature and the land.)

Woman on the Edge of Time, Marge Piercy, Ballantine Books, New York, 1976. (A novel about a woman who lives part in our time and part in an ecologically sustainable world 250 years in the future. This future world combines simple living with high technology in community.)

The World's Wasted Wealth II: Save Our Wealth, Save Our Environment, J.W. Smith, Institute for Economic Democracy and Macrocosm USA, 1994. (The causes and cures for poverty in today's world are explained in this controversial book, which supplies a new economic and political vision for the fractionalized left and progressives.)

GLOSSARY

The terms in this glossary are derived from a number of sources. Wherever possible, we have chosen to use the definitions of other organizations instead of inventing our own in the hopes of creating a common language and understanding of what these terms mean. In some cases, however, we have slightly modified them. The numbers at the end of each definition correspond to the following list of resources:

[1] *Cooperative Housing Compendium,* edited by Lottie Cohen & Lois Arkin
[2] *Sustainable Agriculture News,* UC Davis Sustainable Agricultural Research and Education Center
[3] Shared Living Resource Center
[4] *Websters New Collegiate Dictionary*
[5] *Entropy: A New World View,* by Jeremy Rifkin with Ted Howard
[6] *Permaculture: A Designer's Manual,* by Bill Mollison
[7] American Society of Agronomy

Acre. A land area of 43,560 square feet (about 209 feet by 209 feet). Equivalent to 0.40 hectares.[2]

Active Solar System. An electro-mechanical system designed to gather the radiant energy from the sun and convert it into thermal energy for use in heating water or a building, or in making electricity. There are many different types of systems, depending on the intended use, but most consist of four basic elements: energy collectors to absorb solar radiation to convert into thermal energy; a storage system for the energy such as water, rocks, concrete, and certain chemical salts; a circulation or distribution system to transfer the energy from the collectors and storage system to its intended destination (such as a house interior); and a control mechanism to control the transfer of energy and the function and interaction of the other elements.[3]

Affordable Housing. Used by housing activists and developers to describe housing for very low to moderate income people that rents for no more than one-third of the residents' gross monthly household income.[1] Unfortunately, in most rural and urban areas, there is an insufficient amount of this kind of housing to meet the growing need.[3]

Agribusiness. Farming done by corporations that control large areas of land, water rights and services, and agricultural production. It is usually characterized by large mono-crop fields and orchards, employment of seasonal workers at low pay, and use of chemical pesticides, fertilizers, and soil enhancers. (See Conventional Agriculture.)[3]

At Risk Housing. Affordable housing, previously developed under various federal housing programs, at risk of being sold at market rates, thereby displacing many low income persons.[1]

Bioregion. A specific geographic area that has developed plant, animal, and human cultures that are deeply inter-twined and interdependent with each other, and distinctly independent from relationships being practiced in surrounding regions. Also, an ecosystem in which the land, economic, and resource development is integrated within the region in an ecological sustainable way. A bioregion may also be defined by a biotic shift such as a boundary between distinct plant communities, a watershed area, land and water forms, personal perception, and/or topography.[3]

CoHousing. A term coined by Kathryn McCamant and Charles Durrett to describe resident-developed, -owned, and -managed cooperative communities in which individual households are clustered around village-like courts and streets and a large common house with shared facilities for group cooking and dining, work, play, social activities, and childcare. Shared gardens, orchards, workshops, and outside recreation areas are also common features. A variety of ownership and financing methods can be used, and the social composition is often a multi-generational mix of singles, families, and elderly persons.[3]

Collective. A member owned and/or controlled organization or enterprise of three or more persons in which the workers function as peers fully sharing in decision making and surplus revenues or profits.[1] Also refers to group houses and cooperatives in which decision making and financial responsibilities are shared equally.[3]

Common. 1) Belonging to the community at large; public. 2) Shared simultaneously by two or more individuals or by all members of a group. 3) The people; community. 4) Land held in common by a community.[4]

Common Areas. The shared spaces in a Shared Living Community or broader neighborhood that everyone in the community or neighborhood may use.[3]

Common House. The central structure in a Shared Living Community serving as the primary location for group activities. The specific features in a common house depend on the interests and needs of the residents, but most include a large kitchen and dining room, a laundry room, a sitting room, and childcare facilities.[3]

Commune. An intentional group or community in which common land, buildings, businesses, and other primary assets are owned or leased by the group as a whole, with all or most group and personal income pooled in a communal treasury. All group and personal expenses are paid by the communal treasury; personal discretionary expenses may be limited. No communal assets accrue to individual members.[1] Communes are often based on a set ideological, spiritual, or political belief system and specific lifestyle practices, similar to an Intentional Community. In mainstream culture, the term and concept are often (negatively) associated with the "hippie" communes of the 1960's (most of which are virtually extinct), and therefore quickly dismissed. Communes, however, are viable and are, in many places, popular forms of community that have survived for hundreds of years. Some Israeli kibbutzim fit this description.[3]

Communicate. To share, impart, or partake of, and to participate in the process of passing ideas, services, or goods on to others in words, writing, and other modes of conveyance, including a variety of art forms. In a community context, the process implies the presence of a speaker and a listener, a sender and a receiver, and that these exchanges would regularly take place on a face-to-face personal level in a common physical place.[3]

Community. There are numerous definitions for community. The dictionary says it is a group having common organization, or interests, or living in the same place under the same laws; an assemblage of animals or plants living in a common home under similar conditions.[4] *The Cooperative Housing Compendium* says it's a group of people who have a common interest and/or geographical boundary; also a socially and/or economically integrated residential group.[1] We add to these definitions the criterion that a community forms only when there is a physical domain that is shared by the members and under the control and democratic management of a secure social structure to which the members belong.[3]

Community Land Trust. A legally established and democratically managed nonprofit organization that acquires control of land and buildings in order to preserve open space and natural resources for ecologically sustainable development and to provide permanently affordable housing and commercial space through long-term leases.[3]

Comprehensive Planning. A thorough planning process used by various state and local planning agencies to develop integrated policies for urban and rural regions. This process seeks to consider the physical, social, and economic issues as interrelated elements of the whole system, not individual entities. The elements of a comprehensive plan may include residential, commercial, and industrial land use, housing, transportation, agriculture, open space, public safety, disaster/emergency services, etc.[3]

Condominium. A form of ownership which combines separate ownership of one's unit with shared ownership of common areas. Each owner has a separate mortgage and is individually responsible for making the payments on it. An elected board of directors is legally responsible for operations and management. A monthly association fee is paid for upkeep of common areas. Each owner has the right to sell their unit on the open market. An agreement, called covenants, conditions, and restrictions (CCR), specifically regulates use of common areas and other matters of interest to owners.[1]

Consensus. A decision-making process in which group decisions are based on consent by all members, and which all members agree to uphold. Common agreement is reached by discussion and persuasion rather than voting, so as to avoid the deep divisions which sometimes result from a slim majority voting action. In consensus, it is often agreed beforehand that no action will be taken until all are in agreement. There are many techniques for modified consensus which involve some voting in certain situations.[1]

Conventional. Any process or method that is accepted or has been adopted by the dominant socioeconomic system as general custom or the "right way" or customary way of doing something.[3]

Conventional Agriculture. Although the majority of farming operations fall into this category, the term is difficult to define because its scope is so broad and varied. In general, it is characterized by the use of mono-cropping, mechanized planting and harvesting machinery, and inorganic/chemical fertilizers and pesticides to control weeds, insects, and plant diseases, and may include overtilling, overgrazing, and nonrotational cropping. (See Organic Agriculture and Sustainable Agriculture.)[3]

Cooperative. Any type of organization that is owned and controlled by its residents, member-users, or workers who wish to equally share the benefits, services, and/or profits (in the case of a worker cooperative). Members own shares of the common assets which may be sold at the end of their membership. There are distinguishing differences between consumer, housing, and worker/producer co-ops, but all are based on cooperative precepts like the Rochdale principles.[3]

Cooperative Housing. A type of housing ownership in which residents set up, own shares in, and control a corporation which owns their housing.[3] In market rate co-ops, there are no restrictions on the resale price of shares. In limited equity co-ops, the resale value is tied to a pre-agreed formula and limited by legal agreements and sometimes by state law. In structured equity co-ops, resale is tied to the book value of the share with limited appreciation. In all cases, members elect a board that is legally responsible for the co-op. Members pay monthly assessments which include each unit's proportional share of all of the expenses of ownership. Members agree to any type of management that suits their needs, ranging from full service professional property management to hands-on self-management. The cooperative form of ownership is most effective when participants have a healthy relationship with one another, exercise broad participation in decision making, and have ongoing training and education.[1]

Core Group. The people who voluntarily initiate a Shared Living Community project, create the vision, goals, and objectives, establish an organizational structure, select new members, handle the financing, and implement the design and building phases of the project.[3]

Democratic Control. The second Principle of Cooperation, as adopted by the International Cooperative Alliance in 1966, which states: "Cooperatives are democratic organizations. Their affairs should be administered by persons selected or appointed in a manner agreed by the members and accountable to them. Members of…cooperatives should enjoy equal rights of voting (one member, one vote) and participation in decisions affecting their organization."[1]

Densification. A planning term meaning to increase the existing density of an area by allowing mixed use and increasing the allowable ground coverage and height of residential, retail, office, and community service buildings.[3]

Density Bonus. A land use incentive strategy that offers an increase in the number of housing units allowed per acre or an increase in the floor area to land area ratio for residential or commercial projects, in exchange for provision of lower income units and/or social and environmental amenities and improvements.[3]

Eco City. A network of Eco Villages interconnected by transit systems within a town- or city-sized area. [3]

Eco Village. A human-scale neighborhood in which most basic human needs can be met in healthy ways without jeopardizing the ability of future generations to similarly meet their needs. "Sustainable" neighborhoods or Eco Villages are pedestrian friendly, have nonprofit forms of land and housing ownership, organic community gardens and orchards, participation from the residents on issues affecting the neighborhood, and employment, shopping, and recreational opportunities in the core neighborhood. In Eco Villages, social, economic, and physical systems are integrated and planned to be in balance with available natural resources. Eco Villages have mixed land use patterns and are designed to relieve the need for auto dependence.[1] A critical element in developing successful Eco Villages is the inclusion of high levels of rail and bus services.[3]

Ecological Living. A way of living, using energy and resources, and interacting with other people, other species, and the land which is balanced, nurturing of relationships, and socially and environmentally responsible.[3]

Ecologically Sustainable. Used to describe a community, material, method of conducting government or business, or way of living that does not harm, exploit, or compromise any living thing or any ecosystem in its creation, maintenance, and renewal, and that is instead sensitively integrated and functions within its environment in a healthy, vital, and regenerative way. It also implies that the ability of other ecosystems or future generations to sustain themselves and thrive is in no way compromised.[3]

Ecosystem. A system in nature in which all living things and their environment function in an integrated, balanced, and holistic way as an interdependent entity and thereby provide for the harmony, well-being, and perpetuity of each other and the system.[3]

Entropy. The Entropy Law is the second law of thermodynamics which states that matter and energy can only be changed in one direction, that is, from usable to unusable, or from available to unavailable, or from ordered to disordered. Entropy is the measure of the unavailable, unusable, or disordered energy or matter in a system.[5]

Environmental. That which is concerned with the quality and health of the physical environment including the land, water, and air.[3]

EPA. The Environmental Protection Agency. The federal agency responsible for enforcing and overseeing the implementation of U.S. environmental laws and policies.[3]

Extended Family. Conventionally, a multi-generational group of people who are related to each other through blood lines and who have strong connections to one another. Often includes parents, grandparents, children, aunts, uncles, and cousins. As used in this book, the people forming the group do not need to be blood relatives, although they must still have the close personal connections and commitments to one another as may be found in conventional extended families.[3]

Feasibility Study. A process in which information is efficiently organized to help people make informed decisions. The process includes planning of physical structures, financing, and operations necessary to insure the financial, physical, and social success of a proposed project; for cooperatives and communities, it also takes account of probable member and public reaction. The process might take a few weeks to several months and is often performed by a consultant or team of consultants. Grass roots groups or core groups with a strong commitment to their projects are often able to provide much of the research for the study.[1]

FHA. The Federal Housing Administration. The agency that has insured most housing loans, and was organized in the late 1930's as part of President Franklin D. Roosevelt's New Deal Plan.[3]

Gaia. Mother Earth. The planet perceived as a single living organism and a self-sustaining, ecological system.[3]

Green Belt. The intentionally established and permanently maintained land area surrounding and between towns, cities, or other urbanized areas, that includes open space, hills, mountains, forests, wetlands, and meadow lands, within which grazing, agriculture and certain related industries, recreation areas, and rural Eco Villages may be allowed. [3]

Group Home. A home that serves residents with special needs who live with one or several professional care-givers. Typical groups sharing services include teenage mothers, recovering substance abusers, the elderly and disabled, or young people who are wards of the court. The group home program provides necessary practical services, such as meals and childcare, along with support systems like tutoring, job training, and counseling. Transitional housing for the homeless may be handled in a group home environment. Operation of a group home often requires some special combination of special zoning permit and/or agency licensing. Group homes fall into several size categories, from small group homes with six or fewer residents to large institutional complexes. In certain cases, funding for the residents comes through state programs or county social services.[1]

Group House. A residential group, usually of unrelated persons but sometimes of blood relations, living together voluntarily in a single, commonly owned or leased dwelling, sharing dining and other facilities, as well as the common expenses.[1]

Hectare. A metric unit of land area equivalent to 10,000 square meters and 2.47 acres. [4]

HUD. The U.S. Department of Housing and Urban Development, The agency responsible for establishing and implementing certain federal housing and related urban affairs policies.[3]

Implementation. The activities and strategies causing an idea, plan, or project to be accomplished. This may be a system of techniques, processes, policies, legal enactments, and laws, or simply the actions of an individual or group carrying out their goals.[3]

Inclusionary Zoning. A legal requirement applied to housing developments that requires a minimum percentage of lower income units in any residential project consisting of more than a certain number of units. The requirement may also include standards for the number of bedrooms per unit, and may require a certain percentage of units for elderly and handicapped persons, or a mix of family groups.[3]

Infill. Residential, commercial, or community service buildings built on vacant or reused urban lots or in other available spaces, often between or above existing structures or in abandoned right of ways.[3]

Intentional Community. A group of people who have chosen to live together with a common purpose (religious, ideological, spiritual, political, or economic) and work cooperatively to create a community lifestyle that reflects their shared basic values. Many of these communities practice a high level of group process, gender equality, and democratic self-management, and often make use of consensus, conflict resolution, and personal growth techniques. Intentional communities may be located in a rural area or an urban or suburban neighborhood. The people may share a single residence, a large house, an apartment building, or a cluster of dwellings. They may own and/or lease their housing and land, and have varying degrees of economic interdependence and entrepreneurial involvement.[3]

Intentional Neighborhood. An existing or newly constructed area of housing and support services such as shops, parks, recreation facilities, schools, and transit that is intentionally planned and organized to encourage and support communication, social interaction, conservation of energy and resources, cooperation, and a sense of place and belonging.[3]

Intergenerational Community. A cooperative living situation in which people of all ages come together to share resources, expenses, and amenities. Also called mixed-age, mixed-generational, and age-mix community.[3]

Kibbutz. A type of Intentional Community in Israel that is collectively and communally organized. Kibbutzim usually have an agricultural/light industrial economic base with collective ownership of assets and communal labor from individual members sharing common food sources and common kitchen and dining facilities.[1]

Limited Equity Housing Cooperative. A legal form for owning a multi-unit dwelling in which the selling price of the unit or share of a departing member is limited by law and/or the co-op's bylaws. In general, this amount includes the original cost of the share plus a percentage based on increases in the cost of living plus the value of any improvements authorized by the board of directors. Overall ownership is in the hands of a nonprofit corporation owned and managed by the residents through a democratically elected board. Public subsidies for low and moderate income rental housing may be available to Limited Equity Housing Cooperatives. On-going member training and education and a healthy spirit of cooperation create the best foundation for a limited equity co-op.[1]

Limited Partnership. A legal entity consisting of a general partner or partners and limited partners, in which the general partner(s) manage and control the business affairs of the partnership, while limited partners are essentially investors, taking no part in the management of the partnership and having no liability for the debts of the partnership in excess of their invested capital. Limited partnerships are called syndications, and are sometimes utilized to provide financing for the development of cooperative housing.[1]

Live-Work Space. A dual-purpose residential/work building, oftentimes industrial buildings, where artists or other professionals both live and work. Living and working spaces may be shared, accommodating self-employed individuals or those living and working together as a group. Those sharing live-work spaces — individuals or groups — can choose to share work space and/or equipment related to their activities. Members can also choose to have individually owned equipment inside their private living quarters. Live-work sharing can be for renters and/or owners. A number of properties for this purpose have been devoted to artists and craftspersons, self-employed consultants, or those engaged in small cottage industries.[1]

Livelihood. Means of life-sustaining support and subsistence obtained by working for or with someone else or for one's self and receiving compensation in money, goods, and/or services.[3]

Market Rate Cooperative. A legal form of housing ownership in which a specially established corporation owns the housing. Individual members of the corporation own a share of stock which entitles them to occupy a unit of housing owned by the corporation. Members are entitled to elect a board of directors, get homeowner tax benefits, and sell their share for whatever they can get to anyone approved by the board or duly authorized membership committee. Ethically and legally, co-ops are bound by the same fair housing laws as other forms of ownership and rentals.[1]

Member Participation. The activities of members in the various aspects of their community. Some of these activities may be part of programs and projects, while other forms of participation are as informal as a conversation about community business while picking up one's mail. The important point is the act of meaningful involvement; the direct participation of all members in important cooperative activities and decisions.[1]

Mortgage Loan. Loan made to finance real estate.[1]

Mutual Housing Association. A nonprofit corporation that develops, owns, and/or manages or assists cooperatives and other forms of nonprofit resident-controlled housing. It is democratically structured for participation by its organizational members, its resident members, those waiting to become residents, and other public-spirited persons who support its purposes.[1]

Natural Energy Systems. Methods of generating energy which rely on naturally occurring phenomena and are generally less polluting and less damaging to the environment and personal health than conventional methods. Systems can be either passive or active depending on whether or not they employ mechanical devices. Such systems include windmills, waterwheels, solar greenhouses, and photovoltaic cells.[3]

Nonprofit Housing Developer. A public benefit tax-exempt corporation whose purpose is to create affordable housing for very low to moderate income households. Many groups focus on the provision of housing for a variety of groups with special needs. Limited Equity Housing Cooperatives are one type of community usually developed by nonprofits.[1]

Nuclear Family. A family consisting of two parents in a committed relationship and their children.[3]

Organic Farming. A system of farming in which strong emphasis is placed on the use of organic materials such as plant and animal manure and composts to maintain the fertility and productivity of the soil. The use of chemical fertilizers, insecticides, fungicides, etc. is avoided or at least significantly minimized.[2]

Partnership. A business arrangement in which two or more persons jointly carry on an unincorporated business, each fully responsible for the debts, commitments, and obligations of the other(s). In housing, where the owner-occupants are the partners, the partnership makes the mortgage payments. The partners pay a "rental equivalent" to the partnership according to their percentage interests. Other costs including maintenance, taxes, and insurance are handled in similar ways.[1]

Passive Solar System. A system in which the sun warms or lights the interior of a building by entering directly through windows, a solar greenhouse, or a sunspace. In regard to heating, the building structure is designed to store the heat in "thermal mass" such as ceramic tiles, water walls, or other building elements and release it at night or on cloudy days. Shade structures or other devices (often simply trees) are often incorporated into these systems in order to moderate the heat and light entering the building in the summer. The system is also designed to gather and circulate the sun's energy with no mechanical or electrical devices — natural thermal movement (convection, conduction, and radiation) is all that is used.[3]

Permaculture. The conscious design and maintenance of productive ecosystems that have the ability, stability, and resilience of natural ecosystems. The harmonious integration of landscape and people that provide food, energy, shelter, and other material and non-material needs in a sustainable way.[6] Permaculture design principles are becoming increasingly popular in CoHousing and Intentional Communities.[3]

Permanently Affordable. Refers to housing that is owned and managed under bylaws and/or state laws that prevent escalation of resale prices through speculation by setting a resale limit or cap on the equity or appreciation that the seller can earn. The limit is established through bylaws and mutual agreement of the co-owners in Limited Equity Housing Cooperatives and by nonprofit sponsors of Community Land Trusts, Mutual Housing Associations, and Community Development Corporations.[3]

Photovoltaic Cell. A device that converts sunlight directly into energy. The cells, which may be flat or disc shaped, are often used in series and have no moving parts as it is a chemical process that makes the electricity. The current generated is DC, which is stored in batteries and converted to an AC current at the time of use.[3]

Polyfidelitous Community. A group of adults that mutually and voluntarily agree to live together as primary partners committed to sexual fidelity within the group and a life-long partnership. Also known as a closed group marriage.[3]

Private Living Suite. The rooms within a Shared Living Community that an individual, couple, or family occupies privately. Typically from one to five rooms with private bathroom(s); a small kitchenette and dining/sitting nook is sometimes substituted for a full kitchen, living room, and dining room.[3]

Quality of Life. The relationship that people have to one another and to the environment as distinct from their relationship to things and their level of material comfort.[1] In community the quality is defined and enhanced by the level of cost and time savings, emotional support, security, social interests, and communication. An improved quality of life often fosters personal empowerment and social and ecological responsibility.[3]

Rochdale Principles. The basic principles of cooperation accepted by most cooperatives and communities. The principles were developed from the practices of the Rochdale Society of Equitable Pioneers, which established a popular co-op association in 1844 in England. The principles include: open membership, democratic control, limited return on investment, distribution of economic savings, on-going education and training, and cooperation among cooperatives. In recent times, some co-ops have added

honest business practices and the ultimate goal of advancing the common good.[1]

Self-Help. The use of resident owners' own labor and that of friends outside the community to construct or remodel a structure and provide food, clothing, energy, childcare and/or a means of livelihood for themselves and the community. The result is a more personalized and empowering way of life at a lower cost.[3]

Shared Housing. Covers any type of housing where unrelated people live under one roof and share common living, dining, and kitchen facilities as a voluntary family group. The ownership can rest with one, some, or all of the housemates, or the housemates can rent from an absentee landlord or a nonprofit organization that owns or leases the property. This type of housing, often referred to as co-op living, (shared living, or group living,[3]) and once popular primarily with college students, is gaining popularity among the general population, especially among intergenerational and environmentally oriented groups seeking an extended family-like environment along with more sharing of resources. Shared housing is usually the least expensive housing option available in any community.[1]

Shared Living Community. An umbrella term that includes all forms of cooperative living situations in which people share ownership and/or management control, meals, responsibilities and expenses, energy and resources, gardens, and other amenities. Various forms include, but are not limited to, Village Cluster/CoHousing, the Urban Cooperative Block, group houses, and Intentional Communities.[3]

Simple Living. Ethos of personal restraint in the ownership and consumption of goods and services. Often practiced as an act of social and environmental responsibility and to manifest sustainable practices.[3]

Single Occupancy Vehicle (SOV). A vehicle on the road which contains only one passenger, the driver.[3]

Single Room Occupancy (SRO) Buildings. Dormitories, boarding houses, and residential hotels with private rooms and shared and/or private baths (or wash basins in the private rooms), often with some type of common eating arrangement. Common meals or meal service is sometimes provided by the landlord for a fee, or organized by the residents themselves. Usually each room is modestly furnished with just the basics. In many cases, these rentals accommodate a specific sub-population (e.g., students, seniors, disabled, very low income, homeless) and may or may not provide support services. Some buildings are very transient; others develop loyal long-term residents. A group could acquire an SRO property to live in and own cooperatively, although most are rentals.[1]

Spiritual Community. A group of people who voluntarily join together as followers, believers, or practitioners of a shared religious/spiritual belief or teaching to live together in an Intentional Community setting.[3]

Standard of Living. The relationship that humans have to their level of material comfort, as distinct from quality of life which refers to the relationship that people have to others and to the environment.[1]

Strategic Planning. Mutually supportive set of long-term activities designed to move a group toward a set goal, based on a systematic assessment of resources and constraints, and methods to use resources to overcome restraints.[1]

Student Cooperative. Located near colleges and universities across the country, these co-ops provide a variety of group living arrangements to meet student needs for low-cost, highly social living arrangements. Many co-ops are federated through the North American Students of Cooperation in Ann Arbor, Michigan, along with student-owned bookstores and other student-owned cooperative businesses.[1]

Sustainable Agriculture. Agriculture that, over the long term, enhances environmental quality and the resource base on which agriculture depends, provides for basic human food and fiber needs, is economically viable, and enhances the quality of life for farmers and society as a whole.[7]

Sweat Equity. The act of a resident-owner providing personal labor in building or rehabilitating a property in order to reduce the price and/or as part of a purchase agreement, especially as used in subsidized or self-help housing.[1]

Tenancy-in-Common (TIC). The most common form of ownership in which members of a "share purchase group" can own their property. Tenants-in-common can pass on their ownership rights to heirs. Usually there is agreement giving each owner an exclusive right to use of a particular unit. Sometimes participants in a share purchase arrangement will use a short tenancy-in-common agreement in the interim between the time they purchase and the time they convert to a co-op, condominium, or other form of common ownership.[1]

Transit or Transportation Node. The area around a mass transit station with a higher density of mixed residential and business uses, and a strong emphasis on pedestrian access.[3]

Transportation Management Program (TMP). An organized plan, often required by local planning agencies, for residential and commercial/industrial developments where access by car, transit (rail or bus), walking or bicycle is subject to standards, incentives, and/or bonuses to reduce the number of car trips by residents, employees, or customers.[3]

Twin Pines Emblem. Symbol of the cooperative movement in the U.S., originally registered by the Cooperative League of the USA (CLUSA, now the National Cooperative Business Association). Originated in 1922 by Dr. James Peter Warbasse, then President of CLUSA, the pine tree is a symbol of endurance and of life, representing the enduring nature of cooperation. Two pine tree roots form the circle symbolizing that which has no end, and also the planet and the universe, which depend for their existence on cooperation. The trees and the circle are dark green, which is the color of chlorophyll, the life principle in nature; and the background within the circle is golden or orange, "typifying the sun, the giver of light and life."[1]

Urban Cooperative Block. Cooperative communities intentionally created by assembling a portion or all of a block of existing properties including single-family houses and/or multiple-unit buildings and possibly commercial buildings. The fences are removed and the yards and buildings are redesigned to provide common amenities and private living spaces including shared group houses and individual houses or units, as in Village Cluster/CoHousing.[3]

Urban Fringe. The area immediately surrounding developed urban areas that is conventionally used for scattered low-density development, which creeps uncontained into the surrounding rural and natural areas. We propose a new definition as a designated and permanent belt between dense urban areas and the Green Belt (rural and natural land) within which housing, specifically Shared Living Communities, can be located on larger parcels of land, with preservation of open space as a major site criterion.

Utopian. Any idealistic goal or concept for social and political reform that implies perfection.[1]

Village Cluster. A resident developed and owned cooperative community of new or existing buildings designed as a modern day village, with private living spaces clustered around a common courtyard, pedestrian paths, and a common house with a central kitchen, dining room, and other amenities. Similar to CoHousing in design, ownership, and management method. (See CoHousing.)[3]

Worker Cooperatives. Businesses owned and operated by the workers themselves. This model of ownership has roots in the late 1770's, when various groups of artisans joined to produce and market their own wares. Worker co-ops flowered in the 1800's in England and France, and were common in the early 20th century in the U.S., flourishing again in the 1960's and 70's in the U.S., Canada and England. The success of the worker-owned enterprises in Mondragon in the Basque region of Spain has stirred new interest in this form of business, which is advanced by many as a practical way to meet problems of layoffs, plant closings, and shrinking economic opportunities. More than six states have worker co-op laws based on the Mondragon model.[1]

ILLUSTRATION CREDITS

Front Cover; Color photo of children working on walkway at N Street Community, Davis, CA; Photo by Philip Thompson

Back Cover; Color photo of dining at On Going Concerns Community, Portland, OR; Photo by Bryan F. Peterson Photography

xxiv-xxv "The Earth's Ten Commandments," © 1990 Earnest Callenbach. A four-color poster by David Lance Goines incorporating the Earth's Ten Commandments is available from Celestial Arts Publishing, P.O. Box 7327, Berkeley CA 94710

19. "Why Can't I Cope ?" Cartoon, Reprinted with permission from the Child Care Resource Center, Inc., Cambridge, MA

26. Cars on freeway; Photo by Greenbelt Alliance, San Francisco, CA

27. Single family house subdivision; Photo by Greenbelt Alliance

28. "Chug, Chug, Plop!" Cartoon, © Bradley Inman, Oakland, CA

30. Tenth annual illustrated catalog of S.E. Gross famous city subdivisions and suburban towns, 1891; Chicago Historical Society

32. "Bad Habits" cartoon; © 1991, Norman Dog, East Bay Express, December 6, 1991

33. Environmental disasters; photo by Greenbelt Alliance

40. Taos Pueblo; Photo by John K. Hillers, Courtesy Museum of New Mexico, Neg. No. 16096

41. Wadsworth Map of 1748, New Haven, CT.from American Architecture and Urbanism, by Vincent Scully; Permission by Beinecke Rare Books and Manuscript Library,Yale University

41. Amish Barn Raising; Photo by Hostetler, John A, Amish Society, 4th Edition, p. 269, The Johns Hopkins University Press, Baltimore/London 1993

42-43. Jane Adams Photo and Hull-House floor plan; Jane Adams Memorial Collection, Special Collections, The University Library, The University of Illinois at Chicago

44. Circle Dancing, Fjordvang Ecovillage Community, Skumvej, Denmark; Photo by Albert Bates, The Farm,Tennessee

44. Front Porch at Ananda Community; Photo by Ken Norwood

51. Copy of a map poster; LE RAGIONI DELL' ARBITARE, Mostra Itinerate, Prato-19 Dicembre 1987-14 Febbraio 1988

72. Father and Son; Photo by William A. Porter, San Francisco, CA

73. HIP Shared House residents; Photo by Tim Hinz

92. Closing Ceremony at Celebration of Community Conference, August, 1993, Olmpia, WA; Photo by Albert Bates, The Farm

103. Santorini, Greece; Painting by Sally Bookman, Aptos, CA

104. Ziuma's Compound; Drawing by Jean Paul Bourdier from African Spaces, 1985

106. Adono's Compound; ibid

107. Pueblo Bonito; Photo courtesy of National Anthropological Archives, Smithsonian Institution, No. 168-B

109. Woodstock, New York; Photo by Mark Antman, The Image Works, Contemporary and Historical Stock Photography

110. Nevada City, CA.; Photo by Dave Carter, Writer/Photographer

112. Children at Muir Commons; Photos by Don Lindemann

113. Muir Commons central walkway; ibid

114. Winslow CoHousing site plan; Edward Weinstein & Associates

115. Winslow CoHousing pathway; Photo by Therese Kunzi-Clark

117. Nyland CoHousing site plan, Nyland, CO; by Wonderland Development Co., Boulder, CO

122. Sun/Tree Relationship; Drawing by Christopher Gutsche

125. Muir Commons sitting court; Photo by Kathleen Smith

126. Muir Commons work party; Photo by Don Lindemann

128. Neighbors visiting at Winslow; Photo by Therese Kunzi-Clark

130. Amish Farm; Photo by Hostetler, John A, Amish Society, p. 87

140. Farm Workers; Photo by Greenbelt Alliance

143. Rural Estates/County Sprawl; ibid

145. Housing tracts in farm valleys; ibid

152. Tassajara hills; Photo by Greenbelt Alliance

158. From Ananda Village brochure; Art by Carol Padget, Ananda Village, Nevada City, CA

165. What open space is all about; Photo by Greenbelt Alliance

167. Photo Collage; San Francisco plaza, Cable Car, Downtown, and London by William A. Porter; Santa Cruz Mall, by Bill Mastin

168. "El Greco's Toledo;" © 1992 Gerdsa S. Mathan, Berkeley, CA

169. Berkeley downtown farmers' market; Photo by Ken Norwood

170. Feeding the pigeons, London; ibid

171. City parking lot; ibid

175. Children in community; Photo by Susan Gravely, Twin Oaks

176. "Eco-City Los Angeles;" David Spellman, Glendale, CA

178. N Street backyards; Photo by Philip Thompson

179. N Street walkway work party; Photo by Steve Evans

179. N Street patio gathering; Photo by Kathleen Smith

180. Southside Park CoHousing; Site Plan by Mogovera Notestine Associates, overlay drawing by SLRC

182. Southside Park work party; Photo by Don Lindemann

188. N Street chicken pen; Photo by Ken Norwood

189. Childrens story time; Photo by Kathleen Smith

192. Parking lot into garden, Berkeley, CA; Tom Levy, Photographer

195. Parkng lot into garden, Mountain View, CA; Photo by Mariel Hernandez, Ananda Community

197, 198, 199. Doyle Street Cohousing, Emeryville, CA; Drawings and photos by CoHousing Company

215. Igbo Village Group; Based on drawing from African Spaces, 1985, by Jean Paul Bourdier

216. Bakos Compound; Drawing by Jean Paul Bourdier

226. Muir Commons common house; Plan drawing by Dean Unger, Architect, Sacramento, CA

227. Winslow Common House; Plan by Edward Weinstein & Assoc.

228. Meeting at Muir Commons; Photo by Don Lindemann

239. Sun-Mar composting toilet; From Sun-Mar Corp. brochure

242. Ananda Village common house sitting nook; Photo by SLRC

251. Seniors in shared house; Three photos by Harvest Houses, Emmaus House Foundation, Inc., Syosset, NY

253. Fairfax "Vest Pocket" Community, by Soloman Architecture and Planning, Daniel Soloman: Design Principal. Philip C. Rossington: Project Architect (floor plans). Gary Strang: Landscape Architect (site plan)

254. Picnic on Raphael House roof; Photo by Raphael House

255. Thanksgiving dinner, Rapheal House; Photo by Rapheal House

259. Chapt. 8 Photo Collage; Serving at Ananda Village, & Farmers Market, by Ken Norwood; Doyle Street Dining, by CoHousing Co.; Vegetables, by Green Belt Alliance; Group House Kitchen, by Ken Norwood; Seniors Dining, by Harvest House

265. Drawing from Parents Magazine, January 1945, reproduced from p.88 of Dolores Hayden book, Redesigning the American Dream:The Future of Housing, Work, and Family Life., Henry Holt, Publisher, New York, NY

266. Muir Commons kitchen scene; Photo by Kathleen Smith

271. "Badgers Kitchen;" Reprinted with permission of Charles Scribner's Sons, an imprint of Macmillan Publishing Company from THE WIND IN THE WILLOWS by Kenneth Grahame, illustrated by Ernest H. Shepard. Copyright 1933 Charles Scribner's Sons; copyright renewed © 1961 Ernest H. Shepard.

281. Amish Pantry; Photo by Hostetler, John A, Amish Society, p. 87

288. Tomatoes; Photo by William A. Porter

288. Corn; Photo by Greenbelt Alliance

301. Straw bale building; Photo by Catharine Wanek

312. Copy of cover of book, Integral Urban House; Sierra Club Books, San Francisco,1979

315. Work team at dinner, Puget Ridge; Photo by Don Lindemann

316. Harambee Homes common house; Photo by Hal Mead

316. Harambee Homes work party on roof; Photo by Hal Mead

319. Neighbors son helping to stucco; Photo by Catherine Wanek

347. San Francisco plaza people scene; Photo by William A. Porter

348. Urban Sprawl; Photo by Greenbelt Alliance

350. Real estate signs in country; ibid

354. Young urban gardeners; Photo by San Francisco League of Urban Gardeners (SLUG), Mohammed Nuru, Director

355. SLUG organic gardening crew; ibid

357. Garden Cities and Satellite Communities, by Sir Raymond Unwin; from Architecture Through the Ages, by Talbot Hamlin, p. 620, Avery Librarian Columbia University, GP Putmans Sons, New York, 1940

359. Robert Owen's scheme for a utopian community; ibid, p. 618

359. Green Belt around San Francisco; Photo by Greenbelt Alliance

360. Green Belt, Munster, Germany; ibid

362. Farmers' Market in London; Photo by William A. Porter

362. Light rail station: Photo by Richard Talmach, "Moving People"

364. "Bondebjerget" site plan" excerpted from Cohousing: A Contemporary Approach to Housing Ourselves, by Kathryn McCamant and Charles Durrett. Used by permission of Ten Speed Press, P.O. Box 7123, Berkeley, CA 94707

367. Victoria Station; Photo by Richard Talmach, "Moving People"

371. SLRT system in Wupertal, Germany; Courtesy of Lyman Richardson, Transyt Canada, from old postcard

372. "Ferry Plaza Harvest Market;" Illustration by Jim Leritz, courtesy of the San Francisco Public Market Collaborative

376. Life in Eco Village; Illustration by Chuck Trapkus, first published in "In Context" No. 35

377. Wedding at N Street; Photo by Kathryn Syroboyrasky

378. Young oak tree; Photo by Ken Norwood

379. Mature oak tree; Photo by Greenbelt Alliance

SLRC Illustration and Photo Credits

All illustrations and photographs not listed above have an "SLRC" credit line which designates work done by the following SLRC principals, staff, volunteers, or apprentices. They include the following (italics indicate major contributors):

Brett Clavio
Michael Caruzo
Jill Cruz
Ken Norwood
Fernando Marti
Maria Moscato
Adriana Sarramea
Andrew Schmidt
Vincent Segal
Kathleen Smith
Tanya Sparnicht
Felipe Romero

INDEX